THE ROUTLEDGE HISTORY OF LATIN AMERICAN CULTURE

The Routledge History of Latin American Culture delves into the cultural history of Latin America from the end of the colonial period to the twentieth century, focusing on the formation of national, racial, and ethnic identity, the culture of resistance, the effects of Eurocentrism, and the process of cultural hybridity to show how the people of Latin America have participated in the making of their own history.

The selections from an interdisciplinary group of scholars range widely across the geographic spectrum of the Latin American world and forms of cultural production. Exploring the means and meanings of cultural production, the essays illustrate the myriad ways in which cultural output illuminates political and social themes in Latin American history.

From religion to food, from political resistance to artistic representation, this handbook showcases the work of scholars from the forefront of Latin American cultural history, creating an essential reference volume for any scholar of modern Latin America.

Carlos Manuel Salomon is Professor of Ethnic Studies at California State University East Bay. He is the author of *Pio Pico: The Last Governor of Mexican California*.

THE ROUTLEDGE HISTORIES

The Routledge Histories is a series of landmark books surveying some of the most important topics and themes in history today. Edited and written by an international team of world-renowned experts, they are the works against which all future books on their subjects will be judged.

THE ROUTLEDGE HISTORY OF DISEASE
Edited by Mark Jackson

THE ROUTLEDGE HISTORY OF AMERICAN SPORT
Edited by Linda J. Borish, David K. Wiggins, and Gerald R. Gems

THE ROUTLEDGE HISTORY OF EAST CENTRAL EUROPE SINCE 1700
Edited by Irina Livezeanu and Árpád von Klimó

THE ROUTLEDGE HISTORY OF THE RENAISSANCE
Edited by William Caferro

THE ROUTLEDGE HISTORY OF MADNESS AND MENTAL HEALTH
Edited by Greg Eghigian

THE ROUTLEDGE HISTORY OF DISABILITY
Edited by Roy Hanes, Ivan Brown and Nancy E. Hansen

THE ROUTLEDGE HISTORY OF NINETEENTH-CENTURY AMERICA
Edited by Jonathan Daniel Wells

THE ROUTLEDGE HISTORY OF GENDER, WAR, AND THE U.S. MILITARY
Edited by Kara Dixon Vuic

THE ROUTLEDGE HISTORY OF THE AMERICAN SOUTH
Edited by Maggi M. Morehouse

THE ROUTLEDGE HISTORY OF ITALIAN AMERICANS
Edited by William J. Connell & Stanislao Pugliese

THE ROUTLEDGE HISTORY OF LATIN AMERICAN CULTURE
Edited by Carlos Manuel Salomon

THE ROUTLEDGE HISTORY OF LATIN AMERICAN CULTURE

Edited by Carlos Manuel Salomon

Routledge
Taylor & Francis Group
LONDON AND NEW YORK

First published 2018 by Routledge

2 Park Square, Milton Park, Abingdon, Oxfordshire OX14 4RN
52 Vanderbilt Avenue, New York, NY 10017

Routledge is an imprint of the Taylor & Francis Group, an informa business

First issued in paperback 2018

Library of Congress Cataloging-in-Publication Data
Names: Salomon, Carlos Manuel, 1967– editor.
Title: The Routledge history of Latin American culture / edited by Carlos Manuel Salomon.
Description: New York : Routledge, 2017. | Series: The Routledge Histories | Includes bibliographical references and index.
Identifiers: LCCN 2017031013 (print) | LCCN 2017032938 (ebook) | ISBN 9781315697253 (ebook) | ISBN 9781138902565 (alk. paper)
Subjects: LCSH: Latin America–Civilization–1948-
Classification: LCC F1414.2 (ebook) | LCC F1414.2 .R68 2017 (print) | DDC 980–dc23
LC record available at https://lccn.loc.gov/2017031013

ISBN: 978-1-138-90256-5 (hbk)
ISBN: 978-0-367-21783-9 (pbk)

Typeset in New Baskarville
by Apex CoVantage, LLC

FOR MY WIFE DOMINICA RICE CISNEROS WHO HAS HELPED OUR FAMILY AND COMMUNITY GROW WITH HER UNBRIDLED LOVE AND PASSION.

CONTENTS

ACKNOWLEDGMENTS

The Routledge History of Latin American Culture was one of the most challenging tasks of my career. Not only did I solicit work that touched on the question of "how does colonialism affect culture" but nearly half of the essays had to be translated into English. For that task I sought the help of friends and colleagues. While Spanish is spoken throughout Latin America, the regional differences create challenges for the translator. I was constantly second guessing myself and sought advice from Eduardo Escobar, a Chilean PhD candidate at UC Berkeley who studies the ancient world in the Department of Near Eastern Studies. I also sought advice from one of my star former students, Eduardo Valadez Arenas, an Oakland-based artist by way of Mexico City.

But it was Paulina M. González, a PhD student in literature at UC San Diego, who took on the most critical role as my assistant. She helped translate and give advice on many of the essays. I am grateful for their help and am pleased that they will take the helm of teachers and artists of the future. I would also like to thank my family. My wife Dominica Rice Cisneros and my daughter Xiomara gave constant support and love.

CONTRIBUTORS

Silvia Alvarez Olarra is Assistant Professor of Spanish at CUNY's Borough of Manhattan Community College. Her research on Latin American literature and film has appeared in collective volumes and journals such as Revista Canadiense de Estudios Hispánicos, Letras Peninsulares, and Mexican Transnational Cinema and Literature. She is currently working on a book manuscript tentatively entitled *A Transfigurative Violence: Sacrifice in Contemporary Mexican Film* (2000–2014).

Xóchitl Bada is Associate Professor in the Latin American and Latino Studies Program at the University of Illinois at Chicago (UIC). Her research interests include immigrant access to political and social rights, Black-Latino relations, immigrant organizing strategies, and transnational labor advocacy mobilization in Mexico and the United States. Her research has appeared in the journals *Population, Space, and Place, Revista de la Asociación Latinoamericana de Sociología Rural, Migraciones Internacionales, Latino Studies,* and *The Latinamericanist.* She is the author of *Mexican Hometown Associations in Chicagoacán: From Local to Transnational Civic Engagement* (Rutgers University Press, 2014).

Nielson Rosa Bezerra received his PhD from the Universidade Federal Fluminense, he is a former Banting Fellow (2012–2014), at The Harriet Tubman Institute for Research on Africa and its Diasporas, York University, Canada. He is the author of a number of articles and seven books on slavery and the African Diaspora in Brazil, including *Escravidão Comércio e Farinha no Recôncavo do Rio de Janeiro, século XIX* (2011). He is also the Director of Museu Vivo do São Bento of Duque de Caxias, Rio de Janeiro and Professor at Universidade do Estado do Rio de Janeiro (UERJ).

Gabriela Cano received her doctorate in History from UNAM in Mexico City. She is Professor of History at El Colegio de México where she is the coordinator of the graduate program Gender Studies. She is the author of many books and articles of women in twentieth century Mexico including with Amalia de Castillo Ledón, *Mujer de letras, mujer de poder. Antología,* (2011), *Se llamaba Elena Arizmendi,* (2010), and co-author with Mary Kay Vaughan and Jocelyn Olcott, *Género, poder y política en el México posrevolucionario,* (2009), and Jocelyn Olcott and Mary Kay Vaughan, *Sex in Revolution: Gender, Politics, and Power in Modern Mexico,* (2006).

Laura Inés Catelli earned her PhD in Hispanic Studies at the University of Pennsylvania and is full professor of Problematics del arte latinoamericano del siglo XX, Escuela de Bellas Artes, Universidad Nacional de Rosario, Argentina. She is a researcher and director of the Centro de Investigaciones y Estudios en Teoría Poscolonial in the Instituto de

Estudios Críticos en Humanidades, Consejo Nacional de Investigaciones Científicas y Técnicas (CONICET). Her work focuses on Latin American racial discourses, imaginaries, and legacies from a postcolonial perspective, which she has traced comparatively throughout diverse critical and disciplinary areas of interest, including Latin American Colonial and Postcolonial Studies, the Decolonial Turn, Subaltern Studies, Anthropology and Cultural Studies, and Latin American Art and Literature. She has published numerous book chapters and articles in academic journals in Latin America, Europe and the United States.

Gloria E. Chacón is Assistant Professor in the Literature department at UCSD. She earned her Ph.D. in Literature from the University of California Santa Cruz. Postdoctoral work in the Native American Studies department at the University of California Davis as well as a postdoctoral CLIR Fellowship at UCLA's Charles Young Research Library has shaped her unique interdisciplinary and transnational approach to indigenous literatures. Chacón's work has appeared in *Cuadernos de Literatura* (Colombia), in *Diversidad y diálogo intercultural a través de las literaturas en lenguas mexicanas* (Mexico), *Poéticas y Políticas* (Germany), and *Revista de Estudios Hispánicos* (Canada). She co-edited a special issue focused on indigenous literature for DePaul's University academic journal, *Diálogo* (USA). Her book, *Cosmolectics and the Rise of Contemporary Maya and Zapotec Literatures* (tentative title) is under contract with UNC Press.

Ana Clarissa Rojas Durazo has a PhD in Medical Sociology from UC San Francisco and degrees in Ethnic Studies from San Francisco State University and in Women's Studies and Chicano Studies from UC Santa Cruz. Rojas co-founded *INCITE! Women of Color Against Violence* and co-edited the ground-breaking *The Color of Violence: The INCITE! Anthology*, which asks critical questions that emerge when we center the lives of women of color in our understanding and attempts to end violence. She is currently Assistant Professor of Chicano/a Studies at UC Davis in California.

G. Antonio Espinoza is an Associate Professor of Latin American History at Virginia Commonwealth University. Born and raised in Lima, Professor Espinoza majored in history at the Catholic University of Peru. Granted a Fulbright Fellowship to pursue graduate studies in the United States, Espinoza obtained his Ph.D. in Latin American History at Columbia University in 2007. A member of the editorial board of *History of Education Quarterly*, Professor Espinoza is the author of *Education and the State in Modern Peru: Primary Schooling in Lima, 1821 – c. 1921* (New York: Palgrave-Macmillan, 2013), as well as several articles on the intellectual and educational history of Peru and Modern Latin America.

Tatiana Flores is an associate professor of art history, with a joint appointment in the Department of Latino and Caribbean Studies at Rutgers, The State University of New Jersey, New Brunswick. A specialist in Latin American as well as contemporary art, she is the author of *Mexico's Revolutionary Avant-Gardes: From Estridentismo to ¡30-30!* (New Haven: Yale University Press, 2013), winner of the 2014 Latin America Studies Association, Mexico Section, Humanities Book Prize.

Miranda Lida is Professor of History at the Argentine Catholic University and also at Universidad Torcuato Di Tella in Argentina. She is the author of many books and articles on the history of the Catholic Church in Argentina including *Histora del catolicismo argentino. Entre el siglo XIX y el XX* (editorial Siglo XXI, 2015) and *Monseñor Miguel de Andrea. Obispo y hombre de mundo* (Edhasa, 2013).

María del Socorro Gutiérrez Magallanes holds a PhD in Political and Social Sciences (Sociology) with an emphasis in Feminist Cultural Critique and Gender Studies from UNAM (2015). She has a Master's Degree in Latin American Studies with an orientation in Literature and Culture also from UNAM (2006). She studied her basic education in Los Angeles as an undocumented immigrant student and did her undergraduate years on a full scholarship as a James Irvine Scholar at Occidental College in Los Angeles, California where she got her BA in Sociology and Spanish Literary and Cultural Studies (1998). As an undergraduate she held internships in Los Angeles and Washington, DC, and studied abroad in Madrid and Mexico City. As a graduate student she did research stays in Santa Cruz and Berkeley, California, USA as well as Buenos Aires, Argentina. She is a binational migrant-activist-scholar with a critical academic formation and an internationalist cultural perspective. Currently she is a postdoctoral fellow at the Benemérita Universidad Autónoma de Puebla, BUAP (Institute of Social Sciences and Humanities "Alfonso Vélez Pliego") with a research project on *Latin American and Chicana Political Autobiography. Conflict, Memory and Subjects* (in process).

Jorge Majfud, a child of Uruguayan military dictatorship (1973–1985), is a Uruguayan American writer and professor at Jacksonville University. An architect from the University of the Republic of Uruguay and a PhD in Latin American Literature from the University of Georgia, before settling in the USA he lived and worked in South and Central America, Africa and Europe. He is the author of many essays books such as *The Eternal Return of Quetzalcoatl, A Theory of Semantic Fields,* and novels like *The Queen of America* (2001), *The City of the Moon* (2009), and Crisis (2012). He worked and published many other books in collaboration with other authors like Eduardo Galeano and Noam Chomsky and regularly contributes to different media like Huffington Post, El Pais, Pagina/12, etc. He has been translated into many languages. He currently teaches Latin American Literature and International Studies at Jacksonville University.

Andrae Marak is the Interim Dean of the College of Arts and Sciences and a Professor of History and Political Science at Governors State University. He received his B.A. in Political Science at Marquette University, his M.A. in Political Science at Syracuse University, and an interdisciplinary Ph.D. in Latin American Studies at the University of New Mexico. He is a contributing editor for *The Middle Ground Journal* and is the author, co-author, or co-editor of four books, including *From Many, One: Indians, Peasants, Borders, and Education in Callista Mexico, 1924–1935* (Calgary: University of Calgary Press, 2009), and has contributed articles to the *World History Bulletin,* the *Harvard International Review,* the *Review of International Political Economy, Paedagogica Historica,* the *New Mexico Historical Review,* the *Journal of the West, Criminal Justice and Law Enforcement Annual: Global Perspectives, The Homeland Security Review,* and the *Journal of the Southwest.*

Javier F. Marion is Associate Professor of History at Emmanuel College in Boston. Originally from Sucre, Bolivia, Marion received a B.A. in Anthropology and a PhD in Latin American History at the University of New Mexico. He received a Fulbright in 2001 to complete his doctoral research on patronage, rural politics, and identity during the wars of independence in Bolivia. Marion has since published articles and book chapters in *Colonial Latin American Historical Review* and *Gender and Race, Empire and a Nation: A Documentary History on the Making of Latin America.* He current research interests explore the blurring of ethnic, class, and gender lines during periods of social conflict in the Andes.

Paloma Martínez-Cruz, Ph.D. works in the area of contemporary hemispheric cultural production, women of color feminism, performance, and alternative epistemologies. Martinez-Cruz' book entitled *Women and Knowledge in Mesoamerica: From East L.A. to Anahuac* (2011) argues that healing traditions among Mesoamerican women constitute a hemispheric intellectual lineage that thrives despite the legacy of colonization. She is the translator of *Ponciá Vicencio,* the debut novel by Afro-Brazilian author Conceição Evaristo, about a young Afro-Brazilian woman's journey from the land of her enslaved ancestors to the multiple dislocations produced by urban life. She is the editor of *Rebeldes: A Proyecto Latina Anthology,* a collection of stories and art from 26 Latina women from the Midwest and beyond.

Yolanda Martínez-San Miguel is the Marta Weeks Chair in Latin American Studies at the University of Miami and Professor at Rutgers-New Brunswick. She is the author *of Saberes americanos: subalternidad y epistemología en los escritos de Sor Juana* (Iberoamericana, 1999), *Caribe Two Ways: cultura de la migración en el Caribe insular hispánico* (Callejón, 2003); *From Lack to Excess: 'Minor' Readings of Colonial Latin American Literature* (Bucknell UP, 2008); *and Coloniality of Diasporas: Rethinking Intra-Colonial Migrations in a Pan-Caribbean Context* (Palgrave 2014). She recently finished two co-edited anthologies: *Critical Terms in Caribbean and Latin American Thought* (with Ben. Sifuentes Jáuregui and Marisa Belausteguigoitia, Palgrave 2016) and *Trans Studies: The Challenge to Hetero/Homo Normativities* (with Sarah Tobias, Rutgers University Press, 2016).

Rosamel Millaman is an associate professor of anthropology at the Catholic University of Temuco, Chile. Between 1978–1986, he was a national and international Mapuche leader. He publishes regularly on the Mapuche movement, indigenous rights and racism. In 2001 he participated as director of *Comision de Trabajo Autonomo Mapuche* (COTAM) dependent on the National Commission of Historical Truth and New Treatment. Currently, he directs an international research on the impact of the forest plantations on the Mapuche people.

Claudia Montero holds a PhD in Latin American Studies from the University of Chile. Dr. Montero is the author of numerous articles of the history of feminism in the Southern Cone. She is an investigator at the Center of Interdisciplinary Studies on Political Culture, Memory and Human Rights of the Universidad de Valparaiso, Chile.

Stefan Pohl-Valero is Associate Professor of History of Science at the Univiersidad del Rosario in Bogotá, Colombia. He received his PhD in 2007 from the Universidad Autónoma de Barcelona. He has spent two terms as visiting researcher in the Department of History and Philosophy of Science at the University of Cambridge (England, 2004 and 2005). Between 2008 and 2010 he was Assistant Professor in the Department of History at the Universidad Javeriana (Bogotá, Colombia) and editor-in-chief of the Journal on Latin American history *Memoria y Sociedad.* In 2010 he was visiting professor in the Center of History of Science at the Universidad Autónoma de Barcelona. In 2009 he received a two year Colombian national research grant (Colciencias) for the project "La

conformación de saberes científicos sobre lo social en Colombia, 1870-1930." Currently, his research interests focus on the relation between knowledge, power and culture in nineteenth and twentieth-centuries Colombia.

Magalí Rabasa is Assistant Professor at Lewis & Clark College. She received her PhD from the University of California, Davis in Cultural Studies with an emphasis in Feminist Theory and Research in 2014. Her teaching focuses on social movements and popular media, as well as feminist and postcolonial studies in the Americas, with a particular focus on the US, Mexico, Bolivia, and Argentina. Her current research examines popular media markets in Mexico, Bolivia, and Argentina. Over the last decade, she has worked extensively with alternative media and popular education projects across the Americas. She is a founding member of the Colectivo Radio Autonomía (Oakland) and Changing Suns Press (Saskatchewan). She has published articles and commentary in the Journal of Latin American Cultural Studies, Anthropology Today, Tabula Rasa, La Jornada, Rebelión, and Herramienta, and her translations include the "Subalternisms" entry by Ileana Rodríguez in the Dictionary of Latin American Cultural Studies (University Press of Florida, 2012).

Enrique Salmón is author of, "*Eating The Landscape*," a book focused on small-scale Native farmers of the Greater Southwest and their role in maintaining biocultural diversity. Enrique holds a PhD. in anthropology from Arizona State University. His dissertation was a study of how the bio-region of the Rarámuri people of the Sierra Madres of Chihuahua, Mexico influences their language and thought. Enrique has been a Scholar in Residence at the Heard Museum, on the Board of Directors of the Society of Ethnobiology, and has published several articles and chapters on Indigenous Ethnobotany, agriculture, nutrition, and traditional ecological knowledge. He teaches American Indian Studies in the Department of Ethnic Studies at Cal State University East Bay.

Carlos Manuel Salomon received his Ph. D. at the University of New Mexico in Borderlands and Latin American History. He is an interdisciplinary scholar and activist who works in the area of borderlands, oral history, and migration. Dr. Salomon is the author of *Pio Pico: The Last Governor of Mexican California* (2010). He is currently Professor of Ethnic Studies at California State University East Bay.

Astrid Ulloa received her doctorate in Anthropology from University of California, Irvive. She is full professor in the Department of Geography at the Universidad Nacional de Colombia and head of the investigation group *Cultura y Ambiente.* Her main research interests include indigenous movements, indigenous autonomy, gender, climate change, territoriality, extractivism, and anthropology of the environment. She is author of *The Ecological Native: Indigenous Peoples' Movements and Eco-Governmentality in Colombia (2013)* and *La construcción del nativo ecológico: Complejidades, paradojas y dilemas de la relación entre los movimientos indígenas y el ambientalismo en Colombia* (2004). Her recent articles and essays include: "Geopolitics of carbonaized nature and the zero carbon citizen" (2017), "Feminismos territoriales en América Latina: defensas de la vida frente a los extractivismos" (2016), "Justicia climática y mujeres indígenas en América Latina" (2016), "Environment and Development: Reflections from Latin America" (2015), "Territorialer Widerstand in Lateinamerika" (2015), and "Controlando la naturaleza: Ambientalismo transnacional y negociaciones locales en torno al cambio climático en territorios

indígenas, Colombia" (2013). She is currently writing about gender and mining and territorial feminisms in Latin America.

Umi Vaughan, Ph.D. is Associate Professor of Africana Studies, CSU Monterey Bay. He is the author of *Carlos Aldama's Life in Batá: Cuba, Diaspora, and the Drum* (Indiana University Press) and *Rebel Dance, Renegade Stance: Timba Music and Black Identity in Cuba* (University of Michigan Press)

INTRODUCTION

Cultura en Llamas

Carlos Manuel Salomon

While editing this book and translating many of its chapters, I was reminded of the radical difference between how Latin Americans and U.S. Latinxs[1] have traditionally viewed race, and in many regards, culture. Fortunately, that difference is beginning to erode. The United States has become a temporary and permanent destination for Latin Americans. Ideas, trends, expressions, and knowledge travel back and forth at a dizzying pace. It has also been at the crossroads of a changing identity among Latin Americans and a source of inspiration for new ways of viewing race. In the United States there is more cultural intersection and understanding between mestizos and American Indian groups. In fact, because of the debilitating effects of anti-immigrant racism in the United States, it becomes clear to us that we are, in fact, Black or indigenous, or more simply put, not white. There is no more pretense of fitting into a racial category when you are clearly rejected. This has facilitated the process of decolonization during the Chicano/a Movement by proclaiming the outright acceptance of our indigenous selves. The Chicano/a Movement partly came about as a defense mechanism: *somos ni de aqui ni de alla*. We were rejected for being too *gringo* and not *gringo* enough. Instead of suffering the effects of rejection because of our skin color, and therefore being traumatized, we rejected shame. We made peace with the idea of not being white. Culturally, we invested in our indigenous ancestry. And as César E. Chávez reminded the world: "Once social change begins, it cannot be reversed. You cannot un-educate the person who has learned to read. You cannot humiliate the person who feels pride. You cannot oppress the people who are not afraid anymore."[2] Chicanismo represented a cultural shift; it lifted a demoralized people out of the dregs; it healed our trauma and made us confident enough to pursue our dreams. It also created a path for future generations of *migrantes* to follow.

It is with this combative passion of change that I position the concept of Latin American culture and chose the essays included in this volume. There are many perspectives on culture and many opinions on what it should or should not represent. Culture in Latin America, and among the Latinx population in the United States, has often been produced out of struggle. In many ways, this is a book that explores how colonialism has affected culture. The quest for identity and autonomy, the defiance of borders and homogeneity, the fight for equal rights and the rise of social movements, and the evolution of feminism and sexuality may seem politically driven but they have also contributed profoundly to culture in Latin America and among Latinxs in the United States. Even if we speak of the great works of art and literature in Latin America, they are often inspired by conflict.

However, in this increasingly globalized world, Latinxs are learning from one another. We have more shared experiences now and it is possible for Latinxs from all parts of the Americas to sit down and map out commonalities, analyze differences, and reveal to one another how the voices of the past, once enunciated by the brute force of colonialism, have shaped local subjectivities and the production of culture. The arrival of so many brilliant Latin American students to the United States has helped to invigorate the field of Latin American studies. Along the way those same students and others have begun to utilize theories put forth by marginalized voices. The result has been explosive.

In universities and high schools across the nation, civil rights spawned the creation of ethnic studies programs. Although ethnic studies began as a method to diversify the curriculum in the humanities and social sciences, it quickly moved to define new theoretical spaces. In the process, ethnic studies had a major impact on traditional fields such as history, sociology, and anthropology. In 1969 Lakota scholar Vine Deloria Jr. turned the field of anthropology on its head with the publication of *Custer Died for your Sins: An Indian Manifesto.*[3] Deloria questioned adademic practice within indigenous communities as a means not to help the people, but to enhance the career of the researcher. "Their concern is not the ultimate policy that will affect the Indian people, but merely the creation of new slogans and doctrines by which they can climb the university totem pole."[4] Because there is little or no reciprocity in the research process, the audience remains outside of tribal communities and the perspective is often one-sided. Although there is still a lack of accountability, non-Indian historians who write about American Indians clearly understand that they are being watched and must tread lightly. After Deloria's book came out, it sparked a wave of intense resentment against the academy[5] within indigenous communities. Scholars could no longer expect to come, observe, and take. There were new protocols that had to be followed. They had to be responsive and respectful to those communities, otherwise shunned. In some cases, new, non-indigenous scholars had to evolve into an entirely different type: a student. He was no longer the master of indigenous knowledge in a sea of ignorant Indians. He was there to learn and listen. Any form of disrespect was taken as an insult from a privileged interloper.

The incorporation of civil rights action into academic disciplines was a slow process that is still evolving. But the impact it has had is undeniable. The scholar/activist of color fought for the inclusion of multiethnic histories, literatures, identities, and subjectivities. Moreover, it sought to influence the research agenda of mainstream disciplines to include more studies of race, class, gender, and ethnicity. Ethnic studies scholars were determined to show the link between imperialism and racism, and in the process, reveal its devastating effects on racialized minorities. Decolonization was one of the primary goals of ethnic studies and led to high school and college students across the nation no longer seeing themselves through a debilitating, Eurocentric prism. The impact of a new urban ethnic culture brought about a renewed cultural understanding in the United States. Ethnic studies scholars wrote about this new identity and, in the process, influenced traditional disciplines. The intellectual shift brought about by the theoretical approach of ethnic studies was widespread. Traditional departments began to hire, for example, experts in subjects such as African American literature, Latinx politics, and scholars who focused on issues pertaining to women of color. As time passed, this view was embedded within mainstream departments and ethnic studies was not necessarily credited as the origin of this change—it was seen as simple evolution. Scholars in general began to focus on the intersectionality of race, class, and gender. Many began to look at Third World countries through the lens of U.S. imperialism. After the dust settled, there was hardly a scholar in the nation who would defend the pejorative, racist Eurocentrism that earlier scholars used to portray people of color in the United States and around the world.

One wonders to what extent this theoretical development impacted Latin American scholars. Writing from Duke University, the Argentine scholar Walter Mignolo rearticulated Vine Deloria's idea some forty years later when he wrote: "modern epistemology . . . created the figure of the detached observer, a neutral seeker of truth and objectivity who at the same time controls the disciplinary rules and puts himself or herself in a privileged position to evaluate and dictate."[6] Mignolo's theories have had major influence on Latin American studies and are a result of his training, life experiences, and of his rebirth as a student of marginalized voices in the United States, one of them the Chicana feminist Gloria Anzaldúa.[7] Mignolo celebrates the liberation of Latin American epistemology from the vices of having to rely on European theories:

> Anzaldúa uncouples the "homogeneous mestizaje" prototype of Latin/Ibero America by revealing the masculine heterosexual perspective operating beneath it, and by opening a hole through which to escape from that asphyxiating opposition between Latin and Anglo America upon which the very "idea of Latin" America was founded and maintained.[8]

The recent changes in Latin American studies are certainly a result of transcultural, particularly diasporic, logic. Even so, the changes are slow to come, and many scholars who are at the height of their research potential were trained in an entirely different way in the United States and continue to pass on traditions that result in U.S. students writing about Latin America from a privileged position.

For U.S. students in the 1980s and 1990s it became far less problematic to study the indigenous and mixed-race populations of Latin America than it was to study the indigenous population of their own country. The same can still be said today. In the United States, Black and indigenous communities (and their allies) are critical of outsiders writing about them, unless they are responsive to their communities. The field was wide-open in Latin America and had many of the unique issues that were in vogue after the cultural shift in social science research in the United States. Non-indigenous anthropologists, historians and others could write entire manuscripts about indigenous or Afro-Latin America by visiting archives, without consulting, contacting, or visiting the indigenous people who they wrote about.

Nevertheless, Latin Americanists in the United States, for the most part, side with the anti-colonialist struggles of the communities they are studying. While at graduate school at the University of New Mexico, and at all of the conferences I attended, I was constantly reminded that the most current theoretical position I could pursue in the field of Latin American history was to bring out the true voice of those who were silenced; it was my task to give these historical subjects "agency." I was told that I had to make them come alive in my prose and to bring back to life a sea of voices, silenced by the brutality of Spanish colonial rule. Much of what my professors and their colleagues were talking about had merit. They borrowed some of the vigor for oppressed communities that ethnic studies scholars had used for over two decades prior. They had found hope in postcolonial theory as a way to respond to the subjugation of the marginalized. They understood the importance of feminist theory and Latin American testimonial literature. Some found commonality with a group of Indian scholars, who, in 1980, formed the Subaltern Studies Group and, in turn, proposed their own "subaltern studies" group for Latin American scholars. They noted that the movement of millions of marginalized, "subaltern" individuals was an historic "action" giving agency to immigrants. Along these lines the group proposed a reconceptualization of the concept of the nation. They blamed political leaders and scholars alike for formulating a nationalist concept of the nation based on dichotomies such as colonial/modern, elite/peasant, mestizo/Indian, etc. What they proposed was a more dynamic view of Latin America, which extended beyond borders and simplistic dualities. They took into account language, gender, ancestral territory, and political action. They termed these cultural realities "de-nationalization."[9]

Their approach is not without criticism, however, and has led many to new interpretations. Subaltern studies often relies on the theories of Jacques Derrida and other European scholars that may not adequately represent the true motives of Latin American subjectivities. Even Florencia Mallon admits that Latin Americanists are "often Eurocentric in our borrowing from other historical or theoretical traditions."[10] The perspective or place of the writer is key in the equation of this volume. Ideas are embedded within the perspective of the writer, a point that has been argued from many circles of struggle to remind us that all individuals speak from a unique position within structures of power. Western scholarship, on the other hand, has always sought to "conceal" the position of the writer, crediting itself with objectivity, and so, the apparent ability to write about any culture or subject with complete objectivity and authority.[11] Walter Mignolo's idea of the *Locus of Enunciation* can help to explain the approach in the essays that follow in this volume. In our globalized world, the voice of the scholar often relies on transborder perspectives. Diasporic voices and experiences change what it means to be Argentinian, Mexican, Black, white, or even *gringo*.[12] True reciprocity means that all students approach the study of Latinx culture from a position of acceptance, adaptation and with the understanding that Latin American culture has emerged from under the sway of multiple colonialisms.

The convergence of multiple subjectivities, diasporic voices, and the dethroning of Occidental epistemic privilege have influenced many of the essays in this volume. Many Latin American origin writers, who would traditionally not venture out of the context of their native land, find comfort in writing about diverse issues situated far beyond the lands of their birth. For example, Uruguayan writer Jorge Majfud examines Mesoamerican and Andean cosmology before and after the Spanish Conquest. Rarámuri ethnobotanist Enrique Salmon, whose people live in the remote Sierra Tarahumara in Chihuahua, Mexico, clearly has more commonality with Southwestern Native American culture than he does with Mexican or "Latin American" culture. María del Socorro Gutiérrez Magallanes explores the promise and pitfalls of advancing Chicano/a studies in an elite Mexican university, while Chilean scholar Claudia Montero explores the trajectory of an insurgent feminist journalism in the Southern Cone. These are but a few of the essays in this volume that explore resistance as a form of cultural production.

The essays included here are not meant to be an exhaustive exploration of Latin American culture, but a snapshot of how scholars from different regions are interpreting a particular strand of culture. The diverse range of scholars are not only historians. They show how different scholars utilize history and how they conceptualize it. Along the way many subjectivities emerge as the scholars tend to be deeply committed to the sectors of history, culture, and society they explore. For example, African American scholar and musician Umi Vaughan has for years played with, visited, and lived among master drummers in his quest to find ancestral roots among the African diasporic population of the Americas. The essays come from scholars trained in a variety of disciplines. Some of the essays are geographically comparative in nature and some look at issues of particular nations. There is a notable lack of regional balance in the volume as a whole due to the thematic choices. For example Brazil, Central America, and to some extent the Caribbean receive less attention than other areas. This collection offers a unique series of essays, however, written by committed scholar/activists. The unique perspectives found in this volume represent the work of both seasoned and emerging voices in the field. The essays help the reader to understand how Latin American culture is produced and under what circumstances. They challenge the student to imagine culture not only as aesthetic beauty but also as an expression of resistance.

Notes

1 The terms Latinx and plural Latinxs are relatively new terms used by some in the Americas as a way to eliminate the problem with gender binaries.
2 Cesar Chavez, *Address to the Commonwealth Club in San Francisco*, November 9, 1984.
3 Vine Deloria Jr., *Custer Died for your Sins: An Indian Manifesto* (New York, NY: Palgrave Macmillan, 1969).
4 Ibid., 94.
5 The academy is a term used to encompass a university and its body of teaching and learning.
6 Walter Mignolo, "Epistemic Disobedience, Independent Thought and Decolonial Freedom," *Theory, Culture & Society*, Vol 26 (December 2009): 159–181.
7 Walter Mignolo, *The Idea of Latin America* (Oxford: Blackwell Publishing), 135–141.
8 Ibid., 138.
9 "Founding Statement: Latin American Subaltern Studies Group," *Boundary* 2, Vol 20, No. 3 (1993): 110–121.
10 Florencia E. Mallon, "The Promise and Dilemma of Subaltern Studies: Perspectives From Latin American History," *The American Historical Review*, Vol 99, No. 5 (December 1994): 1491–1515. Mallon offers a critique of certain aspects of the Latin American Subaltern Studies Group and a way to expand the scope of Subaltern Studies in Latin American history.
11 Ramón Grosfoguel, "Decolonizing Post-Colonial Studies and Paradigms of Political-Economy: Transmodernity, Decolonial Thinking, and Global Coloniality", *TRANSMODERNITY: Journal of Peripheral Cultural Production of the Luso-Hispanic World*, Vol. 1, No. 1 (2011): 3–4.
12 See Walter D. Mignolo, "Editor's Introduction," *Poetics Today*, Vol 15, No. 4, Loci of Enunciation and Imaginary Constructions: The Case of (Latin) America, I (Winter 1994): 505–521.

1

INDIGENOUS COSMOLOGY AND SPANISH CONQUEST

Jorge Majfud

Shortly after the U.S. annexation of half of Mexico's territory in 1848, not only was slavery re-instituted, but Mexicans viewed the process as one of dispossession and humiliation. As a result many rebels, some real and some imagined, rose in defiance during the second half of the nineteenth century. The uprisings produced figures that emulated a Robin Hood of the Southwest, who were eventually stylized as the character Zorro.[1] These anti-*gringo* masked avengers, who led secret lives, were appropriated and quickly transformed into symbols of Anglo-Saxon culture.[2] The Lone Ranger, Batman, and all of the superheroes that followed them are nihilistic myths that exposed the dualities, day/night, exposed the dualities, day/night, discourse/reality, of a new U.S. culture. Actors such as John Wayne, Gary Cooper, and Clint Eastwood helped to elevate the cowboy as a prototypic symbol of the "authentic American," which had little or no connection to the Quakers, Puritans, Pilgrims of the Mayflower, or the intellectualism of the Founding Fathers. The cowboy is another mutation of the Mexican *vaquero* who, in turn, is rooted in the Hispano-Arab culture. It is no coincidence, then, that current conservative groups who resist the nonexistent "Mexican invasion" were and are from Texas and other Southwestern states. The more distant states, such as in New England, were more removed, and thus, less critical.

History—at least popular history—is basically a construction of social myths composed of masks and hermetic symbols, shaped by select memories and well-timed amnesia. Perhaps its most powerful components are those which, for good reason, have been repressed, although not exterminated.

A similar process, but on a more grand and profound scale, took place during the centuries of conquest and colonization in what we know today as Latin America. In the same way that Christmas takes place on a date that has nothing to do with Jesus, in Mexico, pilgrimages to the Virgin of Guadalupe are made at the same place where the Aztecs worshiped the goddess Tonantzin, "our mother," the goddess of fertility. According to Octavio Paz, the fact that the Conquest coincides with the defeat of Quetzalcoatl, the god of self-sacrifice and the creator of the world within the flames of Teotihuacan, and the defeat of Huitzilopochtli, the young god of war, represents the return to female divinities.[3] Although the Conquest had nearly destroyed the indigenous world and on its ruins had raised another, "between the old society and the new Hispanic order an invisible thread of continuity exists: the thread of domination. That thread is not broken: the Spanish viceroys and Mexican presidents are the successors of the Aztec chieftains."[4]

The process of repression and conversion, which is traditionally called syncretism—a psychological parallel of *mestizaje*—was widespread and inevitable. It would be difficult to limit this phenomenon to a few religious rituals. Unlike the Anglo-Saxon settlers, the

Spanish Conquest did not proceed by displacing the indigenous population. For practical reasons, most of this colonization was carried out in regions where the native population counted in millions and had, in the eyes of the Spaniards, developed sophisticated civilizations. The Spanish abandoned the more uninhabited lands such as North Carolina, since its interest was mineral wealth, converting souls to Catholicism, and finding bodies for cheap labor when slavery was not an option.[5]

For this reason, the cultural repression imposed by Iberian colonization should be seen as more severe with less absolute achievement. Colonization was achieved by force, although at times, there was a more devastating and absolute approach. The moral repression originated in the shame of the colonized indigenous people because of what they were, which was anything except white or European. After the wars of independence, and in the absence of a powerful Catholic Church, which was perceived as a source of backwardness and ignorance, this task was taken up by the *criollos* in the name of liberalism and scientific positivism. Until the late nineteenth century, for example, the educator and eventual Argentine President Domingo Sarmiento, in an attempt to promote the successful model of the United States, wrote passionately against the races who resisted Western progress.[6]

Time and again we face the issue of separation and the repression of one group over the other. For example that of the "lettered city"—high society and enlightened culture—over that of spoken society, the mass of popular culture that, far from being dead, is ignored and depreciated domestically and abroad. With access to books, newspapers, and universities, the lettered European culture was the only visible and legitimate media at the time. Well into the twentieth century, many in Bolivia were unaware or unwilling to see that the vast majority of its population was indigenous; they considered their homeland a country of whites because they were white *criollos* or "whitened" who wrote in newspapers and held posts in government and administration.

Ángel Rama defines four appearances of the Indian theme in Latin American literature: (1) in the missionary literature of the Conquest; (2) in the critical literature of the mercantile bourgeoisie during the revolutionary period; (3) in romanticism as a mourning for their destruction; and (4) "in the twentieth century, in the form of a demand, which presented a new social sector from the lower strata of the middle, white or mestizo class. Needless to say, in none of these themes did the Indian speak; it was the authors who spoke for him."[7]

It was not until the middle of the twentieth century that this trend was reversed. Despised races and cultures became the center of vindication, particularly among the committed writers on the left including rebels and revolutionaries. Yet this was not a simple infatuation of *indigenismo* but the expression of a thought:[8] the restoration of lost origin, not of the industrial future paradoxically voiced by those who were defined as Marxists. The *sentipensante*, defined by Eduardo Galeano, is incarnated in the social critic and in the Latin American rebel.[9] The Peruvian historian Manuel Burga observed in *Nacimiento de una utopía* that "all peoples without writing turn to rituals to remember their mythical ancestors."[10] Colonial societies were ritualistic societies: "The past was more important than the future for them. The Conquest produced anguish and then colonial violence, and threw them into the past."[11] Huamán Poma de Ayala sketched several of these rituals and dances where you can see Spaniards reproducing indigenous rituals in a Catholic ceremony. To Burga, they were Indians disguised as Spaniards representing a ritual submerged in Catholic symbols. The cursed memory survives despite the eradication of idolatry in a manner that is even more profound than formal ceremony.

It is repressed memory recorded with fire by the conquerors. Even today, as Burga demonstrates, the silent narration persists in the local celebrations of what once was the Inca Empire. On the other hand, as we shall see later in this chapter, the veneration of the past as a superior time, which is experienced in the future, is a concept inherent in languages like Quechua and in the mythic-ideological aspirations of pre-Columbian cultures. This concept is opposite to modern progressive time, where the past is inferior, backward, and located behind us.

But the need to suppress and merge according to both the forces of colonial power and by colonized resistance occurred in an opposite way but with the same goal. Unlike the chroniclers of the Conquest, in the *Comentarios Reales*, the Inca Garcilaso de la Vega (in some ways a *converso* in Spain) tried to assimilate a Spanish Catholic mentality, but could not forget his origin. To resolve this conflict or apparent contradiction, he integrated them into a common destiny: According to de la Vega, the Inca culture, its theological conception, and its religious destination, were previously in a state of a natural evolution towards Christianity. Garcilaso solves the zeal of Christian monotheism by identifying Pachacámac as Yahweh and Zúpay as Lucifer.[12] For de la Vega, the Inca had one god, the sun; and on the other hand, the universal Spirit of Pachacámac, who is the Father and the Holy Spirit. The third element of the Trinity, the Son, is actually Christ, the hallmark of the Conquest.[13] Prior to the Incas, according to de la Vega, nature was revealed as a false adoration and inferior: "there was no animal, however vile or filthy, that they didn't consider a god."[14]

In each of its possibilities, the discussion of continuity and survival of the pre-Hispanic world has been avoided over and over. From *Ariel* (1900) by J. E. Rodó, *La raza cósmica* (1925) by José Vasconcelos, and *Siete ensayos de interpretación* (1928) by José C. Mariátegui to *El espejo enterrado* (1992) by Carlos Fuentes or *Las raíces torcidas de América Latina* (2000) by Carlos Alberto Montaner, the writers of the continent have scarcely recognized pre-Columbian roots as a vivid sign of the present. Leopoldo Zea and other Latin American specialists have observed that in no other continent but Latin America did European colonization replace the original cultures. *El laberinto de la soledad* (1950) by Octavio Paz—a refined version of a similar work by Samuel Ramos, also in reference to Mexico—is an exception, in addition to a few less significant works. In all others, the indigenous heritage survives only when it coincides with the defects of Spain: hierarchical societies of Mesoamerica were replaced by the hierarchical society of Spain, which explains why Latin America has always found it difficult to create a democratic culture.[15] Similarly, Mariátegui argued that the only thing that survived from Tawantinsuyu (the four regions of Inca Empire) was the Indian as a biological organism, since its civilization had perished.[16] Carlos Fuentes, in *El espejo enterrado* (1992), observes that:

> when Moctezuma and his empire sank in the bloody waters of the lake, the old indigenous world disappeared forever; its broken gods and forgotten treasures were all buried in the end under baroque Christian churches and viceregal palaces.[17]

The very idea that the multitudes of indigenous people, from Mexico to the Tierra del Fuego, could have a non-European thought continued to be denied, even by some contemporary researchers.

However, through many centuries, the illiterate masses, who, because of colonialism, had learned to feel ashamed of their own culture and their braided hair, had no other choice but to continue speaking their vernacular languages, practicing their own habits away from the centers of Spanish civilization and their own ways of thinking and feeling. In countries like Peru, natives still did not speak Spanish, the language of the conquerors, by the nineteenth century. "For tribes like the Huichol, who live in the northwest of Mexico, the Nahuatl religion has survived in many beliefs and ceremonies."[18] Perhaps in a more anecdotal tone, Eduardo Galeano recalls when passing through Quito in 1976 that "the Indians still wear black for the crime of Atahualpa."[19] The historian and anthropologist Manuel Burga interprets the festivals, dances and performances in Bolivia and Peru as proof of the permanence of indigenous identity and the existence of "an Andean utopia."[20] Moreover, "studies on the same performance in Central America and Mexico are abundant; all seem to agree on presenting them as different variations of a single dance."[21] Thus, the pre-Hispanic cosmos survives, despite the colonial repression, as well as the common origin, nature, and understanding of it among different native cultures. For centuries, European authorities made a meticulous task of cultural extermination. The indigenous responded by using memory in order to adapt for survival. Catholic priests have been aware of this fact since the sixteenth century, which is why they came to change the religious calendar, "even if this meant changing the patron saints for all."[22]

Today the survival of myth, or even a repressed cosmology, is not a simple narrative or a revindication of the past, but is strongly associated with the ideas of the present and future. One of the foundational books of modern utopias was, without a doubt, *Utopia* (1516), by Thomas More. Latin America played a decisive role in this new tradition as More was inspired by the letters that Amerigo Vespucci wrote earlier during the era of discovery. Vespucci reported that in this land the natives were very healthy people with strange habits, who did not hold material wealth in high esteem, were unaware of private property and bathed every day. Furthermore, machismo, as an institution, was mostly imported from Europe, where it was much stronger than in the Americas. Machismo was not as influential among the indigenous as the people had far less preoccupation over female virginity and paid much less attention to keeping women away from public affairs.[23]

Beyond the argument that the Vespucci letters (similar to those of Hernán Cortés and Bartolomé de las Casas) are exaggerated or not, the truth is that they bring the past to life: Both America and *Utopia* expressed the dreams and aspirations of a Europe left to individualistic passion, money, and conquest. Greed and cupidity ceased to be a sin and became a virtue. Renaissance Christianity desacralized the world and sacralized individual salvation: If the world was no longer sacred, only material, it was fine to exploit without condemning humanity to destruction. In other words, utopia was, from multiple perspectives, a collective dream, the symbolic expression of the desire for what you cannot be or cannot not possess, the blame for what you have done or what you have done wrong, a dream that in many cases ended in a nightmare. The new European concept of time, which, thanks to the first modern humanists of the fourteenth century, was no longer conceived of as it had been during the Age of Metals. Existence was no longer an inevitable process of degradation and corruption, and, in the later centuries, ascended up a linear scale along with progress. Life in the past was worse. The best was ahead, towards the future: Man progressed and overcame all maladies thanks to his knowledge of the world.

Conversely, the Amerindian world did not separate blood from the spirit, nor men and women from the natural universe, nor were they governed by the Judeo-Christian conception of linear time. As in many other cultures, time was circular. Progress, virtue, and the sense of justice was and continues to be a restoration of their origins. And this is how utopia ended for the Spanish, with committed intellectuals and revolutionaries, just as it had begun in the sixteenth century. Inspired by indigenous America, the questioning of the irrationality of consumerism, greed and individualism, from an ecological vision, is also an indigenous and *indigenista* revindication.

Another particular aspect related to the Amerindian cosmos was its conception of time. In our Western world, it is common to consider that the past goes back and the future forward. This is a concept, though universal, that is entirely arbitrary. Just as north doesn't move toward the top, the future doesn't move forward. Language has entangled the idea that our bodies walk forward, which reflects our concept of time. Particularly in English, where actions are more common than contemplations, where there is no distinction between *ser* and *estar* [to be] but between *to do* and *to make*, for which in Spanish there is only one word, *hacer*. In English, the distinctions of the past tenses are less sophisticated than in Romance languages such as Spanish, not to mention a vast colloquial vocabulary.

In mindsets and civilizations such as ours, action predominates over the contemplation of existence, and therefore the future moves forward. In more contemplative cultures such as ancient Greece or the Andean world, time was a river flowing from our back to what lays ahead. In other words, the past was forward and the future backward. This concept, which may seem absurd in principle, is even more logical than the Western conception of time: If we can see the past in the form of our memories and we cannot see the uncertain future, then what we have before us is not what is to come, but what has been; that is, memory. In the Andean world, this view of time is the *ñaupa-q*, a word that, like many others, survives even in most Hispanic regions such as the Southern Cone.[24]

Amerindian influence is everywhere, often surviving in an underground, unnoticed form, which brings up the question: How far does the colonial mentality go back for the people of Latin America today? Is it possible to revert this process from within culture itself? According to Eduardo Subirats, the colonial process exists today even in the contemporary university system. For example, the colonization of Latin American poetics consisted of "the kidnapping of intellectual intent, the domestication and neutralization of the historical and political commitment to theory."[25] Subirats focuses on the mythical and oral importance of Latin America's poetics of resistance to oppose academic neutralization.[26] Subirats understands that "cultures and memories of Iberians and Latin Americans must be reviewed and redefined from its spiritual centers, not its borders."[27] One of these centers should be the spaces and sacred symbols shared by a strategically forgotten tradition: the Jewish-Christian-Muslim in Spain and the ancient cosmological ideas of the Americas. "These traditions and forms of knowledge range from manuscripts and works of art to the ancient, millennial oral and artistic traditions surviving to the present day."[28]

Quetzalcoatl-Viracocha

The discovery of America exacerbated European fantasies. On the same day that the Jews were required to abandon Spain, Christopher Columbus sailed into the unknown. That same year the Christians had expelled the last Muslim rulers and continued *la Reconquista* with the Conquest of America.The first explorers like Hernán Cortés, with a mind so full of Spanish literary fantasy, that he became another Quixote, Don Alonso de la Mancha, and confused Mayan and Aztec temples with mosques. Hernán Cortés was also a bestseller of his time, though the stories of his own barbarity were far from the idealism of Don Quixote. Before the conquerors transformed America into a living hell, it was seen as Eden, as described by Amerigo Vespucci, when he found healthy people and strange customs, such as daily bathing or giving little importance to virginity and freedom to women.[29] Europe's machismo was exported to America, but not the custom of daily baths. The natives, which for ages to come carried Vespucci's name, with the exotic habits of ignoring private property and despising greed, represented the opposite of Renaissance Europe, thirsty for conquest and riches. Christian Europe, which had separated the spiritual world from the material, had also failed to condemn wealth; On the contrary, from day to night it came to value greed as the engine of material progress—and as a symbol of belonging to God's elect.

Amerigo Vespucci's letters inspired the politics of Thomas More in his famous *Utopia* (1516). Vespucci complains, "they slander me because I said that those people do not esteem gold or other riches."[30] Perhaps these stories should not be taken as strictly true; they are apparently not without exaggeration, but as fiction they reveal much about the time. In fact, few chronicles were written without a good dose of magical realism. But fantasies are often more real than reality. The fanaticism of the conquistadors made possible the submission of millions of Aztecs and Incas to a few Spaniards. The fantasies of the conquered, such as the idea that the Spaniards were Viracocha or Quetzalcoatl returning to claim their thrones, did great damage; the new imported diseases, for which native people had no immunity, did the rest.

According to Amerindian ontology, humans are responsible for maintaining the cosmos in motion. The worst for them was not a crisis and a cyclical collapse, but inertia and immobility. Justice, morality, and the behavior of men and demigods were the engines of movement, sometimes harmonious and sometimes violent, brought about a healthy world. The fall of the spirit into matter, the desecration of blood and spirit, the exploitation and commercialism of nature, were worse than hell.

One of the most paradigmatic gods of Aztec cosmology is the Feathered Serpent or Quetzalcoatl (Figure 1.1), including his many variations. As in any mythological hero, his birth is invested with tragic or unusual signs. Quetzalcoatl was born in a world of conflicts and in many versions, from parents who faced struggle. With strong psychoanalytic overtones, some legends refer to this birth as a result of the eroticism of opponents in a fight. The mother, a Chichimeca descendant of the warrior-god Tezcatlipoca, provoked or challenged the father, the warrior Mixcoatl, leaving their weapons on the ground and disrobing. Mixcoatl also pierces the naked warrior with arrows but all of his attempts failed to hurt her. This symbolism directly translates into a sexual action. After a short flight through the forest, the warrior takes her to a cave and impregnates her.

Quetzalcoatl was born into a world of battles, human sacrifices, and permanent conflicts.[31] He killed his predecessors and revolutionized society, abolishing temporarily a recurring element of Mesoamerican culture: human sacrifice. A period of great creativity follows this Tolteca revolution. The enlightened people, unlike the more warrior-like Aztecs who came after, created a sophisticated culture where the arts thrived.[32]

The change and the flourishing of this new orientation was guided by a human god, as seen in many accounts of Mesoamerican culture. Quetzalcoatl warned about the threat of collapse from the East. But this is not just a psychological condition or the fate of a god with many faces but the very nature of Mesoamerican cosmology. The other gods were also aware of the instability in which they existed, so that they increasingly demanded more action to keep the sun and moon moving. Quetzalcoatl was chosen to execute this redeeming sacrifice of the gods. But his radical action did not produce the desired effect and the sun became motionless. Because of this Quetzalcoatl decides to self-sacrifice. Because of his self-sacrifice, the sun resumes its path and thus the birth of the Age of the Fifth Sun occurs, solidifying Quetzalcoatl's importance. The story of

Figure 1.1 Head of Quetzalcoatl in the national Museum of Archaeology, Mexico City. Courtesy of PRISMA ARCHIVO/Alamy Stock Photo.

Quetzalcoatl reminds us that within Mesoamerican myths, the creation of the world is always incomplete, forever in motion. There is a permanent "divine doubt." The result is not a vision of the cosmos governed by rhythm and order, which prevails over chaos, but a revolutionary model where one part fiercely confronts the other. Each period of harmony is followed by a period of revolution, which keeps the universe in motion.[33]

The idea that Quetzalcoatl is the creator of the *new humanity* is important. In the legend of the Fifth Sun, humanity is created after four failed attempts of the gods, who refused to try for the fifth time. The *new human* of Quetzalcoatl, as a result, is also imperfect. According to the *Legend of the Suns*, the feathered serpent restores human life through a hero-journey—an archetypal element—to the land of the dead. Quetzalcoatl demands from the god of the dead, Mictlantecuhtli, the bones of ancestors in order to create a "new humanity." In exchange for the remains, he gives Quetzalcoatl an impossible task: to sound a conch shell that has no opening. Faced with this obstacle, Quetzalcoatl turns to the natural world, worms and bees, to pierce the shell. The lord of the underworld recognizes the achievement of Quetzalcoatl and willingly gives him the bones but then orders his servants to detain him. Quetzalcoatl challenges Mictlantecuhtli verbally and tries to escape the underworld. But demons create an abyss where Quetzalcoatl fell and died, breaking his bones. His twin (the duality of Quetzalcoatl) regenerates and escapes the abyss. But his ancestor's bones were broken and so Quetzalcoatl gave them to his friend, Cihuacoatl-Quilaztli, the goddess of human creation, who puts them into her stone mortar and grinds them up. Quetzalcoatl pierced his penis, which bled over the bone powder, from which a male child is born, and four days later, a female child. From these children humanity descends. This event conforms to the Toltec idea that the human soul descends from heaven to the womb.

Davíd Carrasco summarizes the different variations in the persistence of a duality in struggle from which every age is created by combat or the sacrifice of a pair of opposites; or creation occurs with *a cosmic descent*, where the creator descends to an inferior world. The idea of descending makes Quetzalcoatl the most human of all gods. The creation was imperfect; the achievement had not been completed. The existence of unfortunate outcomes is common in Mesoamerican religious culture. But the idea that the final destruction of the world must be deferred through lifelong sacrifice is reversed by Quetzalcoatl of Tollan (or Tula), who replaced the anxiety of instability and chaos of the cosmos and ritual sacrifices with harmony and creativity. For this reason, Quetzalcoatl is a symbol of legitimate authority who is capable of creating sacred order in an unstable world. Even at the time of Chololan (Cholula), Quetzalcoatl is known as the god of the masses, who was able to integrate a great social structure. Later in Aztec Tenochtitlán, it is possible that Quetzalcoatl had become the god of the upper class. The promised return of Quetzalcoatl was met with an atmosphere of cosmic instability that marked the Aztec capital, Tenochtitlán. It was this promise that caused Aztec rulers to suffer from the anxiety of illegitimate authority.[34]

The repeated idea of an empire boasting an illegitimate power arises in a very particular way, through power itself. To reverse this, the Aztecs resort to psychological shock. They invited representatives of neighboring villages to witness ritual massacres as a way to sustain their power through terror force. This policy contained but also enhanced the rise of rebellion that was later exploited by the Spaniards. Moctezuma, aware of the imminent arrival of Quetzalcoatl, deserted the grand palace and occupied a smaller one, pending the arrival of true authority. Moctezuma's case is incomprehensible to Western history but it reveals an interior feature of Mesoamerican culture: A ruler can hold absolute power and then reject it because of his moral conscience. This gives us an idea of the significance of sacred terror that joined the Mesoamerican with the cosmos. A similar view of *the illegitimacy of authority* is taken up by various authors, who refer to the historical perception of Latin American people toward power and rulers.[35]

Quetzalcoatl is not the creator god of the universe, but a donor of humanity, like Prometheus, who gives men and women the arts, knowledge, and food. He is one who repairs chaos or is a server to the needs of the natural world. Quetzalcoatl is not a god who punishes his creation, but a limited and fragile god struggling against adversity for the benefit of humanity, which has been punished in advance by superior forces. But he is also the ideal of legitimate and supreme authority able to order, regulate, and bring prosperity to a town permanently threatened by the cosmos and the imperial violence of warring gods.

A feature of the pre-Hispanic world seems to be the conscience of destruction, abandonment, or resignation. As in many parts of the ancient and modern world, each new culture or civilization was bound to develop with the nearby memory of another great civilization, the creators of monumental buildings, cities, and myths of golden days. The vision of the past had to be radically different from the complacent view that comes from our proud modernity. The cosmogonic myths of Mesoamerica relapse into a cyclical idea of creation and destruction, which is common in older civilizations such as in Asia, but are dramatized, sometimes subtly, by a particularity: the violent destruction by earthquakes and hurricanes, by the fury of nature, or—for the Mesoamerican world—by the fury of the gods. Both gods and nature were directly connected with sacrifice, with human blood. With violent penance, men communicated with the gods hoping to change the unpredictability of nature, humanizing it. The aim was not the eternal life of the Christians or the liberation of the Hindus but to prevent the end of the universe or its movement toward destruction. Not only is the enigmatic abandonment of these great cities a distinguishing feature, but also the similar monumentality of its artistic expression: from Tula and Teotihuacan to Machu Picchu through a celebrated collection of abandoned sites. This memory must have been, at the same time, the teleology of the cycles of grandeur and destruction. A culture or a civilization did not replace another like it did in the Middle East, Asia, or Europe. A space was abandoned and new wanderers settled somewhere else to start again, conscious of the catastrophe to come.

If the myth or the will of Prometheus is a legacy of the enlightened culture of Europe, which opposed and criticized the organization of European conquest and colonization, then the myth or will of Quetzalcoatl-Viracocha is the inheritance of the people—which resisted, imposed, and shaped the mentality of a continent that shares more than a language—they also opposed the invader. According to Carlos Fuentes, Quetzalcoatl became a moral hero, like Prometheus; both were sacrificed for humanity, and they gave mortals the arts and education. Both represented liberation, even when it came at the cost of the hero's sacrifice.[36] Fuentes points this out in two paintings by the Mexican muralist José Clemente Orozco, one at Pomona College in Claremont, California and the other in Baker Library at Dartmouth College in Hanover, N.H. In the first Prometheus symbolizes the tragic fate of humanity and the second Quetzalcoatl, the inventor of humanity who is exiled to discover his face and infer from it their human destiny; that is to say, of joy and pain. At the Cabañas Hospital in Guadalajara, Orozco synthesizes the two figures into one man perishing in the fire of his own creation.

Both Prometheus and Quetzalcoatl are defeated gods because their human trait imparts a degree of imperfection and injustice by the higher gods (Zeus, Mictlantecuhtli, Tezcatlipoca).[37]

Figure 1.2 Cuban women walking past graffiti of heroes of the revolution including Julio Mella, Camilo Cienfuegos, and Che Guevara; Havana, Cuba, Caribbean. Courtesy of Kumar Sriskandan/Alamy Stock Photo, 2013.

In both, like Jesus, the symbolism of blood is central because it is the most human and most sacred element among the elements of the universe against which they must constantly struggle to survive, to ascend (Prometheus) or to avoid chaos, the final destruction (Quetzalcoatl). But if the "divine humanism" of Prometheus and Quetzalcoatl have elements in common, they also have opposing elements, reproducing the Mesoamerican cosmology of opposites in battle that create and destroy: Prometheus defies the ultimate authority to benefit humanity. The history of European humanism from the thirteenth century integrates a historical consciousness of progression, equality, and freedom in the individual and society that radically opposes the traditional paradigm based on religious authority. The humanism of Quetzalcoatl, although it signals a challenge to the upper and lower gods for the benefit of humanity, is also marked by the fatality of the cycles and his own duality. Destructive authorities are replaced by the demigod who is regularly defeated by superior forces.

The god Viracocha in Peru also encompassed multiple representations and probably multiple ways of being. Like the Mesoamerican god, duality is common and can be summarized as a higher god, creator of the Cosmos, and as a human god, overseer of the world's chaos. Like Quetzalcoatl, Viracocha abandoned his people going off into the ocean, not to the East but the West, with a promise to return. Viracocha is not only god and the creator but "he who put everything in its place and who told the people when to occupy it"—that is, a kind of great architect and at the same time, the rightful ruler.[38]

Viracocha possesses the same duality as Quetzalcoatl, while being the creator of the world (emerging from Lake Titicaca) and a "cultural hero." As in Mesoamerican cosmology, creation is not unique but is preceded by failed attempts. After Viracocha created the world and "certain people" in a second appearance, he turns these people into stones. Viracocha created the sun, the moon, and an archetype of human beings in different places on Earth. Then he departs west for the ocean and disappears. Like in Mexico, the ancient Peruvian world was built and destroyed by the opposition of two forces in battle. In the capital of the Inca Empire the ritual combat consisted of youth confrontation. It was, "the ritual opposition of two halves, Hanan and Hurin, who formed the city of Cuzco. These battles were part of the ceremony of Kamay, linked to the cultivation of maize and the legitimacy of indigenous nobility."[39]

The tragedies of Moctezuma and Atahualpa are also parallel, although separated by ten years and thousands of miles. They unite a similar cosmology, the sense of the illegitimacy of power and, therefore, the same story of defeat. When the Emperor Huayna Capac died, the Inca empire was split between two brothers: in the north, Quito was in the hands of Atahualpa, and in the south, Cuzco was ruled by Huascar. Soon Atahualpa waged war on his own brother and defeated him.

Like the Aztecs in Mexico, the Inca Empire was composed of different Andean peoples. When Pizarro reached Peru the empire was divided. The idea of power, challenged by the oppressed and also by those who held it, is accented with the dispute Atahualpa had with his brother, before him and the people of the great capital, Cuzco. Atahualpa, after three years of civil strife, was about to celebrate his victory by going to Cuzco to receive the royal insignia, but he received news of the Spanish arrival in Huamachuco, and so, decided to march to Cajamarca in order to question the newcomers.

It was shortly after Atahualpa had become the highest authority when distress signs began to arrive. Every sign, like the passing of a comet, were reminders to Atahualpa of a coming disaster. Coincidentally, the messengers of the empire began to arrive with news of Viracocha, who had returned from the sea.

> Huamán Poma indicates, which had been a consensual idea among peasant beliefs of his time, that at the death of Huayna Capac and during his funeral in Cusco, the prophecy that had been kept secret for many generations was deciphered: men would come from the sea (cocha) to conquer the Empire.[40]

According to the *quipucamayos* Vaca de Castro said, "the natives believe that the arrival of the Spaniards signaled the return of the gods."[41] Eduardo Galeano in *Open Veins of Latin America* (1971) recalls—and somehow confirms—this popular prophecy, which states that the Incas themselves, who wanted to take advantage of the Potosi silver, were met with a Quechua warning: "It is not for you; God reserves those riches for those who come from beyond."[42] The messengers of the Inca empire said "that people had come to his realm with habits and clothing very different from our own who seemed to be Viracochas, which is the name formerly given in antiquity for the creator of all things."[43] It was then that Viracocha made his march against the sun and in the direction of civilization, "it was a march of punishment."[44]

On January 5, 1533 Hernando Pizarro, a cousin of Hernan Cortes, arrived at the "mosque" of Pachacamac and managed to "publicly desecrate the sanctuary in order to destroy its spiritual significance."[45] The illiterate soldier, "thinking more of his military duties and the collection of precious metal, was not interested in the rituals, but rather, was a good soldier of the sixteenth century dedicated to creating ties of allegiance with ethnic leaders of the Central Coast."[46] Noting the return of Viracocha, Atahualpa awaited the god-men in Cajamarca and soon welcomed them. The Spaniards found no armed resistance. "On the contrary, the Inca reverted to their ritual behavior, singing and dancing to celebrate the arrival of foreign visitors."[47] At sunset, in a confusion that lasted half an hour, Pizarro and his men attacked the central square and captured Atahualpa. Shortly after they decided to execute him using a *garrote* on July 26, 1533, under the pretext of punishing the murderer of Huascar, the legitimate emperor, and promised to return power to the old nobility.[48] According to Burga, there was an "open satisfaction of the Cuzco nobility about the execution of Atahualpa."[49] Soon after Pizarro named Tupac Huallpa as successor, and later Manco Inca, the descendant of Huayna Capac.

The Spanish spread the rumor that the body of Atahualpa was cremated after his death. Thus, they sought to end the messianic hopes among the natives, which seemed to wake them up. Interestingly, these hopes "appeared as a popular feeling, rather than the attitude of the indigenous nobility."[50] According to the version of Huamán Poma de Ayala—who collected the oral tradition, not chronicles, that he knew about—they cut off Atahualpa's head by order of Pizarro. "This completes a cycle of indigenous distortions on the death of the Inca in Cajamarca and leaves open the possibility of the birth of a new cycle of messianic hopes."[51]

At the same time, the Andean gods "become fallible and as a consequence, liars."[52] In captivity, Atahualpa accused Pachacámac of failing when he announced that his father, Huayna Capac, would heal, although he later died. The gods lost credibility and the indigenous resorted to apocalyptic readings of the facts. Huamán Poma de Ayala declared himself Christian but he insisted on making a moral distinction based on greed as its main defect, which would lead to the destruction of the world. Addressing Spanish readers, he writes:

> see here, in all of Christian law I have not found the Indians to be so greedy for gold and silver, nor have I found one who owes a hundred pesos, or a liar, or gambler, or lazy, or a whore . . . and you have idols in your hacienda, and silver everywhere.[53]

Both Incas and Aztecs adapted their mythology for political purposes. In both cases it was the cosmic illegitimacy of their reign and guilty consciousness that brought them to resignation, defeat, and martyrdom. For men and women of the pre-Hispanic world, the power was not merely a question of strength but had a moral nature. Atahualpa and Moctezuma both suffered from their perceived illegitimate power, which aided in their defeat.

The Spaniards, however, did not have a guilty conscience. According to Américo Castro, the belief of being "the chosen people"[54] helped inspire Spanish and Portuguese companies in the sixteenth century and later brought them to ruin.[55] However, the idea that equates gold with the favoritism of God was more typical of the Calvinist ethic, not of Catholic Spain. But the motivation of quick riches in the New World never ceased to be a priority in the actions of the conquerors. Repeated invocations for the evangelization of Indians took second place to the lust for wealth, which can be read as moral justifications of their objectives understood as deadly sins by Christian tradition. Both Cortez and Pizarro solved their moral dilemma—based on greed and the need for fame, both Renaissance features of medieval Spain—by adapting religion to their actions, not their actions to religion or conscience, as Cortés did in his mature years.[56] That is to say, although motivated by religion, perhaps as moral justification, their faith wasn't as profound as that of the Amerindians.

Soon the Inca and other conquered peoples began to understand that the Spaniards could not be gods because they lacked the moral virtues of a legitimate ruler. Their biggest flaw was the pursuit of riches. According to Inca Garcilaso de la Vega, the Indians realized that the Spaniards "were not gods, but simply men and, even more, they were the very embodiment of *Zupay*, a demon."[57] Gold became the symbol of death, the antithesis of blood. Eduardo Galeano remembers an anecdote by Humboldt, that, in 1802 shows the persistence of the gold-sin among the indigenous population. Astorpilco, a descendant of Incas,

> while walking spoke of the fabulous treasures hidden beneath the dust and ashes. "Do you not feel the craving sometimes to dig for treasures to satisfy your needs?" asked Humboldt. And the young man said, "The craving does not come. My father says it would be sinful. If we had the golden branches with all the golden fruits the white neighbors would hate us and would do us harm.[58]

Another popular story, according to Carlos Fuentes, was that Jose Gabriel Condorcanqui (Túpac Amaru) in 1780 rebelled against Spanish rule, captured the governor and "since the Spaniards had shown such a thirst for gold, Túpac Amaru . . . executed him, forcing him to drink molten gold."[59] Using the same symbolism, in 1781 the Spanish designed an exemplary death for the rebel, cutting off the tongue first—ridding him of the spoken word, then trying in vain to tear him apart pulling his ends by four horses, until they eventually decided to behead him. Then they cut off hands and feet. Juan Gelman, in *Exile*, believes that "Europe is the cradle of capitalism, and that the child in the crib was fed gold and silver from Peru, Mexico, Bolivia, and millions of American Indians had to die to fatten the child."[60] Literary references like these are endless. All summarize the idea that sin comes from the deconsecration of blood and grows, like the Spanish gods arriving from the sea, consuming gold and silver.

In this cosmology, the martyr's death becomes a moral victory and, therefore, becomes a memory and example against illegitimate power by greed. Even a questionable emperor like Atahualpa became an example of resistance, for once the ambitious Spanish empire was defeated in a global context, "the Latin American" would resurface as a force in opposition to U.S. materialism. Gold, again, once desacrilized, becomes an agent of desacrilization, in the ultimate sin. The blood of Latin America, which runs through its "open veins" becomes a commodity and, therefore, the greatest sacrilege, the moral defect of oppressed and oppressors. To resist this sin is a moral mandate measured by a sacrifice that sometimes leads to the offering of blood. Francisco Urondo, a poet whose militancy led him to death, had revealed this feeling in his poetry; "Nothing/will set us back: we have more fear of success than of/failure."[61]

Quetzalcoatl, Huitzilopochtli, Coatlique/Guadalupe

What is often identified as the head of the feathered serpent Quetzalcoatl, incredibly coincides with representations of Korean dragons in some Mayan ruins. For example, the heads of dragons emerging from the walls of Naksan Temple on the east coast of South Korea, whose origins are not so old (676 AD) but suggest a strong connection with the representations of Kukulcan (600–900 AD), which is the Mayan origin version of the more known Aztec Quetzalcoatl. The head of the Korean dragon, apart from scales, has feathers, teeth, and jaws of a dragon, all represented in the same style of Mexican deities. It is also likely that the original colors are the same since green was a sacred color in the Mesoamerican world.

This leads to other problems. Recall that one of the central allegories of Aztec mythology, which appears today on the Mexican flag, represents the struggle of a snake with an eagle. Aztec culture is much younger than the Mayan and many others that have spread across the continent. In many cases, different versions of Quetzalcoatl appear, either as Kukulcan or the more distant Viracocha in Peru. Quetzalcoatl contains both the serpent or dragon and the quetzal or bird of paradise. From this period, most likely, comes one of the most unique rituals in the world, which originated before the classical period and still lives today in Mexico: the flying men [*los hombres voladores*]. Originally the participants wore green quetzal feathers, and symbolized the four previous worlds (suns), including the 5th sun in the center.

The myth of Huitzilopochtli seems to reinforce this change of ages. His sister, Coyolxauhqui (face painted with *cascabeles*), tried to kill her mother Coatlicue because she became impregnated in a dishonorable way when a feather fell between her breasts (or when a feather entered her womb) while sweeping the Mountain of Serpents. Not coincidentally Coatlicue in Nahuatl means "Skirt of Snakes," and not by chance she was impregnated by a feather, a powerful symbolic representation of a betrayal or adultery, and a change of era, that of the snake (earth/fertility/female) and that of the bird (heaven/abstraction/male). Before Coatlicue gave birth to Huitzilopochtli, Coyolxauhqui tried to kill her mother. But the newborn Huitzilopochtli, draped in feathers, killed his sister and her followers, and threw them to the sky, turning them to stars.

It is very difficult to know how such an important deity like Huitzilopochtli was represented since there are probably fewer representations of him than minor deities. However, in some códices, he usually appears with large green feathers, such as those of the quetzal. Moreover, the name means *hummingbird*, which is also a bird with green feathers. We know he was the chief god of war and we can speculate that he belonged to the celestial sphere because of the origin of his birth (a feather) and for his opposition to his sister, represented by snakes as a representative of the Earth.

Nor is it a coincidence that Coatlicue gave birth to Huitzilopochtli in an asexual way, fertilized by a feather, which is a clear parallel with the birth of a celestial and masculine era over a terrestrial and female past. Huitzilopochtli was also the representation of the sun or was the sun itself. Traditionally, the heavenly gods have belonged to patriarchal religions. Moreover, the importance of the absence of sex in the mother of god is a symbolic substitute of virginity; to Coyolxauhqui this was a sin, but is typically a virtue for patriarchal cultures.

It is no coincidence that the pre-Columbian inhabitants of the valley of Mexico worshiped Coatlicue on Tepeyac hill, the same site where the cult of the Virgin de Guadalupe (Figure 1.3) emerges in the fourth decade of the sixteenth century. At that time, she was known as Coatlicue, goddess of the skirt of snakes, but also as Tonantzin or Teteoinan, "mother of the gods." If we consider that Huitzilopochtli was the only survivor of the war between his siblings, then indeed Coatlicue was the "Mother of God," who conceived him without having sex. The skirt or dress in the actual image of the Virgin of Guadalupe (Ave Maria) is decorated with unnecessary figures that are only explained by its indigenous aesthetics. This could well be a stylized snake-skirt and its green layer is the substitute for the figure of the quetzal (bird of paradise). Green was a divine and royal color in the Amerindian cosmos and perhaps also represented freedom because the quetzal cannot reproduce in captivity. Also green was the brilliant color of the hummingbird (Huitzilopochtli, the "left Hummingbird") and the agave (maguey), which blooms after five years only to die and reproduce.

Although the angel who appears to uphold Guadalupe might have come from the pictorial tradition of Europe, from the perspective of the indigenous the European association is impossible. For them, the angel could not be other than Huitzilopochtli, the hummingbird, the newborn child dressed in feathers to protect his mother.[62] Some theories have suggested that in fact the Arabic word "Guadalupe," which gives its name to the Black virgin of Spain, originally had to be Coatlalopeuh, meaning "she who dominates the serpents."[63] The black horns that we see at the foot of the famous Mexican virgin image (often associated with the moon) would be this hidden snake. While this reading is consistent with an interpretation of the Judeo-Christian origins, it would also be similar to what we previously proposed: Through her son, Coatlicue is victorious against her daughter Coyolxauhqui, representing the world of snakes that began to give way to Huitzilopochtli, the masculine world of the birds.

If Huitzilopochtli is the ultimate triumph of the Age of the Bird over the Age of the Serpent, another hypothesis we might consider is Quetzalcoatl as the representation not of a consolidated world but as the myth and character of an ambiguous and transitional world; from the reptile world (the world of land), to the bird world (the world of heaven).

Obviously, the American continent is characterized by its population of birds. But we can not say that Asia has adopted the dragon for its abundance of dragons or reptiles. The reason comes from a period when a culture and a civilization matures or receives its historical imprint, which is consolidated and perpetuated. We can see this in cultures

Figure 1.3 Virgin Mary Guadalupe painting shrine in Mexico City. Courtesy of bpperry/iStock by Getty Images.

derived from the imprint of the Old Testament, from Moses, or Christian cultures from Christ and Greco-Roman cultures in the first centuries of this era.

The symbol of the foundation of Tenochtitlan, Mexico, made relatively recent by one of the last of the Mesoamerican cultures, represents the end of ambiguity, the final contest, and the final victory over the feathered serpent. From what has been discussed, it is no coincidence that it was precisely the god Huitzilopochtli who instructed the Aztecs to found their city, Tenochtitlan, in the place where an eagle on a cactus was devouring a snake.

The feeling of guilt or illegitimacy that the last Aztec emperor had (and the last Inca emperor) for having displaced the legitimate creators of an earlier culture, Tula, was explicit, especially during the time when both Hernán Cortés and Francisco Pizarro conquered both empires in the early decades of the sixteenth century.[64] Tula had flourished with the culture of Quetzalcoatl, a culture less warlike and more artistic, more educated and creative. Mexican sensitivity adapts and easily adopted to the Virgin Mary, not only because it is a form of replacement, of the conversion of Huitzilopochtli (or directly from a syncretism between European culture and American), but because it represents a female figure who gave birth to a sky god. One can understand the idea of Ave Maria not only for being an *Ave* [bird], which is *Eva* [or Eve] backwards, as has been explained in a somewhat forced way, but because the sky is the kingdom of birds and the birds (the quetzal, the eagle devouring the serpent, symbol of the earth) are the symbols of the new era.[65]

However, the existential and spiritual sensitivity of the Amerindian world is primarily visual. It is characteristic of a living world where the Earth and the body are not part of a kingdom cursed by a celestial abstraction but part of the cosmos, of the union and communion between the Earth and heaven. Within this religious experience, a remarkable reminder is the sightings of the Virgin. While there are known apparitions of virgins in other parts of the world, in Latin America the importance of these appearances is much larger and different in nature. The phenomenon is not about the appearance of the virgin but a physical image of the Virgin and at times of Jesus. The miracle is always material and symbolic, as a footprint is to a foot.

In fact, the apparitions of a virgin are minimal and usually result in a story that justifies the venerated image. The representation is venerated on behalf of the represented. This is how the miracle occurs: It mixes water with oil, making Amerindian sensuality compatible with the Judeo-Christian abstraction. The optical mysteries are of such a degree of importance that those who believe them discover that they are not worried about the message or what the interpretation of the miracle can mean but about the miracle itself and of the image that is often attributed shamanic healing powers. This is resolved with the same repeated message, which is always trivial, like the claim that an apparition signifies terrible times are ahead.

The process of conquest and colonization was, of course, a process of acculturation and repression. Due to cultural reasons, but mainly because of the massive native population, and that Spanish colonial wealth was superior to British North America, miscegenation and cultural repression were higher and more persistent.[66] For these same reasons, the survival of myths, practices, rituals, languages and ways of seeing, feeling and thinking about the world and the pre-Columbian period survived in various forms. An academic feature of colonial violence, however, was to systematically deny the relevance of this inheritance.

Notes

1 Johnston McCulley, *The Mark of Zorro* (New York, NY: Grosset & Dunlap, 1924).
2 Felipe Fernández-Armesto, *Our America: A Hispanic History of the United States* (New York, NY: W.W. Norton & Company, 2014).
3 Octavio Paz, *El laberinto de la soledad* (Barcelona: Penguin, 1993), 108.
4 Ibid., 282.

5 Guamán Poma de Ayala, *Nueva crónica y buen gobierno,* Transcripción, prólogo, Notas y Cronología de Franklin Pease (Caracas: Biblioteca Ayacucho, 1980), 266.
6 Faustino Domingo Sarmiento, "El sistema colonial," [1844] *Conciencia intelectual de América,* Antología de Carlos Ripoll (New York, NY: Las Ameritas Publishing Company, 1966), 72.
7 Ángel Rama, *Transculturación narrativa en América Latina* (México: Siglo XXI, 1982), 139.
8 *Indigenismo* was a state-sponsored effort in Mexico and other parts of Latin America that sought to incorporate indigenous communities into the life of the nation.
9 *Sentipensante* is a neologism that combines two words: *sentir* (to feel) and *pensante* (thinker); that is, the thinker who also feels. The *sentipensante* thinks because he feels and feels because he thinks.
10 Manuel Burga, *Nacimiento de una utopía: Muerte y resurrección de los incas* (Lima: Instituto de apoyo agrario, 1988), 390.
11 Ibid., 390.
12 Inca Garcilaso de la Vega, *Comentarios Reales,* Prólogo, edición y cronología de Aurelio Miró Quesada (Venezuela, Sucre: Biblioteca Ayacucho, 1976), 63.
13 Ibid., 67.
14 Ibid., 27–28.
15 Carlos Fuentes, *El espejo enterrado* (México: Fondo de Cultura Económica, 1992), 138.
16 Ángel Rama, *Transculturación narrativa en América Latina* (México: Siglo XXI, 1982), 149.
17 Carlos Fuentes, *El espejo enterrado* (México: Fondo de Cultura Económica, 1992), 124.
18 Laurete Séroujé, *Pensamiento y Religión en el México antiguo* (México: Fondo de la Cultura Económica, 1957), 168.
19 Eduardo Galeano, *Días y noches de amor y de guerra* (Barcelona: Laia, 1978), 107.
20 Manuel Burga, *Nacimiento de una utopía: Muerte y resurrección de los incas* (Lima: Instituto de apoyo agrario, 1988), 26.
21 Ibid., 27.
22 Ibid., 45.
23 Luis Vitale, *La mitad invisible de la historia: El protagonismo social de la mujer iberoamericana* (Buenos Aires: Sudamericana-Planeta, 1987).
24 William Hurtado, de Mendoza, *Pragmática De La Cultura Y La Lengua Quechua* (Lima: Universidad Nacional Agraria La Molina, 2001), 77.
25 Eduardo Subirats, *Las poéticas colonizadas de América Latina* (Guanajuato: Universidad de Guanajuato, Campus Guanajuato, División de Ciencias Sociales y Humanidades, Departamento de Filosofía, 2009), 25.
26 Ibid., 35.
27 Ibid., 51.
28 Ibid., 53.
29 Américo Vespucio, *El nuevo mundo: Cartas relativas a sus viajes y descubrimientos,* Textos en italiano, español e inglés. Estudio preliminar de Roberto Levillier (Buenos Aires: Nova, 1951), 211.
30 Ibid., 165.
31 Davíd Carrasco, *Quetzalcóatl and the Irony of Empire: Myths and Prophecies in the Aztec Tradition* (Chicago: University of Chicago press, 1982), 80–81.
32 *Codex Vaticanus A: Il Manoscritto Messicano Vaticano 3738, ditto Il Docice Rios,* ed. Franz Ehrle (Rome, 1900).
33 Davíd Carrasco, *Quetzalcóatl and the Irony of Empire: Myths and Prophecies in the Aztec Tradition* (Chicago: University of Chicago Press, 1982), 80, 98.
34 Ibid., 150, 184.
35 Carlos Alberto Montaner, *Las raíces torcidas de América Latina* (Barcelona: Plaza & Janés Editores, 2001).
36 Carlos Fuentes, *El espejo enterrado* (México: Fondo de Cultura Económica, 1992), 107.
37 The same fate will follow the so-called Latin American liberators. You could say that, for the collective memory, if the founding fathers of the United States died as successful men, Latin American fathers of the nineteenth century died as defeated gods, as did the emperors and rebel chieftains of past centuries and as Ernesto Che Guevara became in the twentieth century, the "new man."
38 Manuel Burga, *Nacimiento de una utopía: Muerte y resurrección de los incas* (Lima: Instituto de apoyo agrario, 1988), 126.

39 Ibid., 44.
40 Ibid., 58.
41 Ibid., 59. The *quipucamayos* were government officials responsible for accounts and records. Cristóbal Vaca de Castro was a sixteenth century Peruvian administrator.
42 Eduardo Galeano, *Días y noches de amor y de guerra* (Barcelona: Laia, 1978), 31.
43 Manuel Burga, *Nacimiento de una utopía: Muerte y resurrección de los incas* (Lima: Instituto de apoyo agrario, 1988), 59.
44 Ibid., 132.
45 Ibid., 70.
46 Ibid.
47 Ibid., 71.
48 Execution by garrote was a common practice of the time when the condemned were placed in a chair and strangled with a metal collar.
49 Manuel Burga, *Nacimiento de una utopía: Muerte y resurrección de los incas* (Lima: Instituto de apoyo agrario, 1988), 72.
50 Ibid., 79.
51 Ibid., 81.
52 Ibid., 58.
53 Ibid., 265.
54 Américo Castro. *Los españoles: cómo llegaron a serlo.* [1959] (Madrid: Taurus, 1965), 115.
55 Ibid., 79, 103, 105.
56 "[L]a manera y orden que yo he dado en el servicio de estos indios a los españoles es tal, que por ella no se espera que vendrán en disminución ni consumimiento [consumación / realización], como han hecho los de las islas [Cuba, etc.] que hasta ahora se han poblado en estas partes; porque como ha [hace] veinte y tantos años que yo en ellas resido, y tengo experiencia de los daños que se han hecho y de las causas de ellos, tengo mucha vigilancia [cuidado] en guardarme de aquel camino, y guiar las cosas por otro muy contrario, porque se me figura que me sería aún de mayor culpa, conociendo aquellos yerros [errores], seguirlos, que no ha los primeros los usaron; y por esto yo no permito que saqueen oro con ellos, aunque muchas veces se me ha requerido [. . .] Ni tampoco permito que los saquen [a los indios] fuera de sus casas a hacer labranzas [trabajo esclavo], como lo hacían en otras islas." Hernán Cortés, *Cartas de relación* [*Tercera Carta-Relación*: 1522] (México: Ed. Porrua, 1963), 177.
57 Inca Garcilaso de la Vega, *Comentarios Reales*, Prólogo, edición y cronología de Aurelio Miró Quesada (Sucre, Venezuela: Biblioteca Ayacucho, 1976), 82.
58 Eduardo Galeano, *Días y noches de amor y de guerra* (Barcelona: Laia, 1978), 70.
59 Carlos Fuentes, *El espejo enterrado* (México: Fondo de Cultura Económica, 1992), 223.
60 Osvaldo Bayer and Juan Gelman, *Exilio* (Buenos Aires: Legasa, 1984), 39.
61 Francisco Urondo, *Obra poética*, Prólogo de Susana Cella (Buenos Aires: Adriana Hidalgo, 2006), 262.
62 Inga Clendinnen, *Aztecs* (Cambridge: Cambridge University Press, 2014).
63 Gloria Anzaldúa, *Borderlands: The New mestiza. La frontera* (San Francisco: Spinsters/Aunt Lute, 1987), 49.
64 Enrique Florescano, *The Myth of Quetzalcoatl* (Baltimore, MD: The Johns Hopkins University Press, 1999).
65 Fr. Pedro Gual, *Discurso teológico sobre la definibilidad dogmática del augusto misterio de la Concepción Immaculada* (Barcelona: Pons y Cia., 1851), 19.
66 A paradigmatic example was Haiti. In the eighteenth century, 40 percent of all foreign trade of France, the largest European power of the time, occurred in Haiti. In fact, the island was exporting more wealth than all of North America. A similar situation was Britain in regard to its tropical Caribbean islands.

2

ANDEAN IDENTITY AND HISTORICAL AGENCY

Javier F. Marion

On the third Sunday each March, the Bolivian town of Tarabuco hosts the annual Pujllay festival to close out the carnival season and mark the beginning of Lent. During Pujllay, a period of playful release and pageantry, the population of this highland community swells with ethnic Yampara celebrants from Tarabuco and neighboring communities. The size and reach of the celebration has grown in recent decades along with the number of tourists and street vendors selling hats, trinkets, and textiles.[1] Tarabuco is also renowned for the earth tones, order, and symmetry of its textiles. Almost iconic in style, the production and sale of these textiles represents important economic and cultural links to the outside world. Tourists arrive in vans and busses and empty out into the streets to haggle with vendors along the main streets and central plaza before eventually making their way to the dance grounds.

The celebrants dance around a *pukara*, a makeshift altar over 12 feet in height and adorned with bread, fruits, and flowers and other items which represent abundance, fertility, and thanksgiving. The offerings are meant for *Pachamama*, an Andean expression of femininity and the earth and with whom Andeans enter into *ayni* or reciprocal relations along an intricate cosmological-agricultural set of calendrical relations. The dancers, donned in ceremonial garments and accoutrements and playing traditional wind instruments, make a distinctive auditory and visual impact. They project the deity, Tata Pujllay, a playful being associated with the harvest, the carnival season, and boundless energy. The dancers animate Tata Pujllay with their deliberate and aggressive movements. The music itself forms a ritual and gendered language that places the Pujllay in perspective along the ritual cycle: bellicose-masculine, bountiful-feminine, and historical-celebratory. The Pujllay, a raucous event celebrated in the rainy season, has its calendrical and complementary "pair" in the Ayarichi, a more Catholic-temperate festival held in the dry season.

At first glance, the Yampara community of Tarabuco appears relatively intact as an endogamous example of indigenous culture in the southern Andes. The Pujllay may also resemble an indigenized version of the Catholic and agricultural festive found elsewhere in the southern Andes. But the Tarabuco celebration belies a much more complex history of exposure to external forces—as *mitimaes* [colonists] of the Inca empire, as mercantilist laborers in the Spanish empire, and as globalized citizens of the plurinational Bolivian state. All of these regimes and their respective economic systems left their mark on the Yampara community in indelible ways. Indeed, much of the Tarabuqueño identity now associated with its textiles, the Pujllay, and its musical expressions did not take form until relatively recently. Quechua, the lingua franca of Tawantinsuyu [the Inca empire], for example, replaced original languages such as Pukina, believed to be the original Yampara language by some scholars.[2] Pukina is long extinct. The headgear worn by the Pujllay dancers bears a striking resemblance to the *monteras* [helmets] used by Spanish conquistadors in the sixteenth century when they first entered the southern Andes. In the Tarabuco version, the montera is made of leather and adorned with colorful fringes around the perimeter.[3] The dancers also use an adaptation of *espuelas* [spurs] originally worn by Spanish horsemen but again, the design is meant for a different purpose. The *espuelas* here are intended to be noise-makers and mounted on elevated shoes that thump and rattle in the act of dancing to animate Tata Pujllay. Last, and along with its ceremonial underpinnings, the Pujllay coincides with the anniversary of the Jumbate, a famous battle against royalist troops during Bolivia's wars of independence (1809–1825), in which the Yamparas, and the Tarabuco community specifically, played a pivotal role. The dancers commemorate the heroes of the Jumbate and align themselves to the process of nation building that contributed to the founding of the Bolivian state in 1825.

The Yamparas have an extensive history of negotiating political frontiers. Like many ethnic communities that once dotted the southern Andes, the Yamparas experienced centuries of political confrontations, land loss, and challenges to their cultural integrity. The pressures associated with these challenges reduced many communities into liminal laborers living on the edges of increasingly globalized and exploitative societies. Despite long and elaborate traditions of ritualized resistance, adaptation, and accommodation, none of the original corporate Andean communities survived unscathed; some disappeared altogether while others suffered varying degrees of culture loss. The Yamparas likewise experienced profound transformations but they somehow reached a historical-cultural coherence that eluded many of their neighbors. The degree of cultural survival and communal agency evident in Tarabuco is particularly surprising given its proximity to the political and economic hubs in the region: Chuquisaca (Sucre) and the mining center of Potosi.

This study explores the trajectory of social transformations experienced by the ethnic Yampara community of Tarabuco with a focus on the strategies it cultivated in dealing with external polities. To this end, we consider the Jumbate and its insertion into the Pujllay celebration as a case study to uncover the relationships that link local identity with an imagined past. Last, we will also explore their ability to employ the past as an act of resistance to validate traditional hierarchies and cosmologies.

The Yampara town of Tarabuco sits at over 11,000 feet in elevation along a high fertile plain. During the pre-Inca period, the region denoted as Charcas was occupied by communities from a bewildering multiethnic range. Some of the earliest recorded groups produced ceramic remains referred to as Mojocoya (7–11 AD) and Yampara (9–14 AD). These styles ranged from the region of the present day community of Mojocoya east to Valle Grande. Both of these styles point to a relatively stable degree of social complexity compared to the subsequent period and the Inca expansion into the region. The Incas under the ruler Topa Inca absorbed Charcas into the Kollasuyo quadrant of Tawantinsuyu in the fifteenth century. Tarabuco was located along the eastern edge of Kollasuyo that bordered lands occupied by marginal groups—known as the Chiriguanos—that were hostile to the Incas and their allies. The Chiriguanos were a semi-nomadic confederation of Guarani who referred to themselves as the *Ava* which translates as "men" in the Chiriguano vernacular of Guarani.

The Incas relocated ethnic communities from distant parts of the empire to form resettlement towns as part of a buffer zone to keep the lowland groups at bay. The relocated colonists were known as *mitimaes*. Some of them may have come from as far north as Ecuador or Colombia while others such as the Chilki, Kana, Kanchi, Qullawa and Yanawara emigrated to Charcas from Arequipa and Cuzco regions. The Karanka, Killaka, Lupaqa, and Pakasa were Aymara (Kolla) speakers from the nearby *altiplano* [highland plateau] while others, such as the Churumata and Muyu, came from the lower valley regions. All of these groups—either forcibly as *mitimaes* or voluntarily as *llacta runa* [original inhabitants to the region]—merged with the existing Yampara population to form a defensive vanguard centered in the agricultural communities of Tarabuco, Pajcha, and Presto.[4] Besides their strategic placement within Kollasuyu, the Yamparas and their collective provided the empire with lowland and subtropical commodities such as coca, medicinal plants, and exotic bird feathers. Before the arrival of the Incas, Tarabuco and the other frontier towns aligned themselves along a trajectory of reciprocal exchange with highland Aymara communities. The Incas restructured these outlying communities into a political and ethnic unit called Jatun Yampara which was divided along two moieties or sectors—one centered around the Tarabuco region and the other in Quila Quila.[5] Thus, the Inca restructuring added yet another layer of affiliations to the Yampara's aggregate identity. The phenomenon of variegated ethnic groups living alongside one another and negotiating hierarchies and reciprocal obligations along ecological niches and corporate (*ayllu*) arrangements is not unique to the Charcas region of Kollasuyo. It can be found elsewhere in the Andes.[6]

Spatial and political restructuring notwithstanding, the Yamparas, as among the *llacta runa*, appear as one of the dominant groups within the hierarchy of ethnicities. The *kurakas* [political lords] who ruled these communities were in fact ethnic Yamparas, a position they did not relinquish with the arrival of the Spanish. When Gonzalo Pizarro first entered the region in 1538, for example, it was the Yampara leader, Francisco Aymoro, who set aside lands for the founding of the Spanish city of Chuquisca (Sucre).[7]

The Yamparas likely entered into reciprocal relations with the Spaniards after learning from the Inca troops accompanying the Spanish expedition that resistance against the Europeans would be folly.[8] Instead, the regional *kurakas* resorted to a segmentated form of alliance building similar to other expressions of political alliances seen in the southern Andes. Segmentation was a political mechanism that sought *ayni*, or a reciprocal understanding of relationships, between members and entities within a given territorial and cosmological range. In describing segmented relationships in the nearby region of Chayanta, Tristan Platt observed that the Chayantakas viewed *ayllus*, *llactas* [provinces], and nations as "the ascending levels of a segmentary system whose smallest units were found within the kinship and residential group. This segmentary system was accompanied by a corresponding hierarchy of administrative authorities," which in the case of the Yamparas in Tarabuco would eventually reach and include the colonial capital of Chuquisaca.[9] Segmentation established a degree of autonomy for the *ayllus*,their satellite communities and corresponding networks of exchange.[10] But it inevitably established a hierarchical arrangement wherein the Yamparas assumed a subservient position. They provided the Spanish with laborers and paid tribute, an Indian head tax that was originally paid in kind.

The Spanish had much to gain from an alliance for, despite the dissolution of Tawantinsuyu, the Spaniards had co-opted Inca networks of tribute and exchange. The colonial system was particularly interested in preserving the mita or labor tribute that conquered communities provided the empire as part of their ritualized set of relations with Cuzco. The Spanish placed the Yamparas and adjoining native communities under the tutelage of Martín de Almendra who was granted an *encomienda* [Indian labor grant] called the Mayorazgo de Tarabuco. The *encomienda* provided agricultural with a steady supply of laborers—denoted in the records as *yanaconas*—to work on private estates for the benefit of the Almendra family. The terms of these arrangements were originally seasonal but many of the *yanaconas* devolved into the status of demesne laborers and full-time hacienda residents. Private Spanish estates also absorbed lands previously controlled by Yampara *ayllus* which, together with the demesne labor requirements and a reorientation of economic networks away from traditional ayllu networks, resulted in a steady decline in the number of *originarios*, a landed class within the corporate communities.

The colonial economy centered in the nearby mining districts of Potosi and Chayanta also proved devastating for the corporate communities in the southern Andes, and the Yamparas were not immune from its influence. The demand for laborers and agricultural products to supply the mines and the burgeoning population in nearby Potosi reoriented energies away from the *ayllus* and toward commerce generated in the mining areas and the cities of Potosi and Chuquisaca. In 1573, Peruvian viceroy Francisco Toledo reconstituted the heterogeneous inhabitants of Tarabuco into a "reduction town" as part of an effort to centralize the extraction of tribute from these communities. The Indian tribute served as a sort of "head tax" that sustained the administrative expenses of colonial government. The amount of tribute owed depended on an individual's status, longevity in the community, and access to arable lands. But Toledo's reforms signified important cultural changes for Tarabuco and the Yamparas generally. In an effort to Christianize and Hispanicize these composite communities, Tarabuco was renamed San Pedro de Montalbán and made a *curato* [parish] and *cabecera* [a principal town] within the archdiocese of Chuquisaca and province of Tomina. The reforms accelerated the process of cultural negotiation. Tribute lists from the seventeenth century, for example, denote multiple ethnic enclaves within the reduction town but legal records indicate that Quechua was the common idiom with an increased number of Spanish speakers and mestizos in their midst.

Reduction, land loss, population reduction, and the colonial tribute mechanism challenged traditional orientations among the Yamparas, but they were spared the most destructive of colonial extractions: the Potosi mita. The mita had been responsible for massive cultural and economic disruptions. Many mitayos destined for the mines never returned to their communities. Others outmigrated to communities in the eastern Andes attempting to hide from the census and mita obligations. Colonial officials determined to exempt the Tarabuco and Presto communities from the mita largely due to their proximity to the Chiriguano frontier. The early colonial records mention frequent and violent encounters between the frontier Andean towns and the Chiriguanos.

Keeping with a defensive pattern adopted by the Incas, the Spanish established garrisons and auxiliary communities to stage campaigns against the Chiriguanos along the eastern flank of the cordillera. Tarabuco and Presto served as the two principal garrisons in the region. They protected roads—important conduits for subtropical trade items. Thus, the major thoroughfare connecting Chuquisaca to Santa Cruz passed through these two communities. For Tarabuco, its strategic location as an important stop between these two cities ensured that it would always play an important role in political events. To the residents of Tarabuco, the arrangement with colonial authorities was reciprocal insofar as both shared a common adversary. The Tarabuqueños agreed to serve as sentries and auxiliaries and pay tribute in return for a degree of autonomy. It similarly benefitted the Spanish to ensure that the Tarabuco population along with the other garrison towns flourished along this frontier region.

If colonial records serve as any indication, relations between Tarabuco and colonial authorities in Chuquisaca remained remarkably stable throughout the colonial period.

Disputes over labor allotments and agricultural boundaries between the corporate community and private estates frequently ended up in the courts but rarely did they result in bloodshed or prolonged standoffs. This also holds true for the tumultuous eighteenth century, when submission to Spanish authority was steadily diminished, particularly among native Andeans. The decline coincided with an increase in levels of colonial exploitation of Andean resources and labor, and thus a shift in reciprocal relations. The changes sparked a variety of protests and revolts. The most prominent, the Tupac Amaru and Katari rebellions (1780–1783), nearly succeeded in dismantling the colonial mechanism. The Katari movement was predominantly an Indian protest against exploitation that evolved into an anticolonial project with racial and millenarian overtones. The conflict took form in nearby Macha (Chayanta), an Andean community which was connected to Tarabuco's trade networks. The rebellion quickly swept south and sparked confrontations in the neighboring communities of Quilaquila and Yamparaez, but stopped short of Tarabuco.[11] A handful of residents used the opportunity to lobby for the removal of the Tarabuco cacique, Yisidro Calli, but they were more concerned about an impending Chiriguano invasion.[12] The Chiriguanos took advantage of the disruptions created by the Katari rebellion to raid frontier towns, take captives and hold them for ransom. As had occurred in previous occasions, members of the Tarabuco community were dispatched in pursuit of the Chiriguanos and stood guard against potential encroachments to highland towns and roadways. Thus, in the wake of the Katari rebellion and nearing the end of the colonial period, the Yamparas of Tarabuco had solidified relations with the Spanish administration and used that standing to establish a degree of political and cultural stability. Census records, for example, indicate that relative to the surrounding corporate communities the *ayllus* in Tarabuco were larger and populated by the largest number of *originarios* with the most expansive *ayllus* in Tomina province.[13]

Why then, did the Tarabuqueños side against colonial authority thirty years after the Katari rebellion during the wars of independence? This is a difficult question in light of the political disruptions that affected many corporate communities in the southern Andes between 1809 and 1825.[14] The political climate surrounding the independence period created deep divisions in the corporate Andean communities, oftentimes pitting the landed [*originarios*] against the landless [*forasteros*] and traditional Andean hierarchies against town [*cabildo*] administrative authority. The political fallout associated with the wars likely created discord in Tarabuco, but precious little of it fell across partisan lines. Instead, the Tarabuqueños trended toward the rebel factions and played a decidedly proactive role in dismantling colonial authority in the southern Andes. It should be noted, however, that the period referred to as the wars of independence was a complex, violent, and protracted struggle. Political categories such as royalists against patriots were rarely formal categories and participants did not always place their participation into these static terms.

In the end, the key determining factor that pushed the Tarabuqueños into taking an anticolonial stance was their location along the Chiriguano frontier. The Chiriguanos had again been waging an intermittent war against Spanish settlements and garrison towns since the 1780s. Despite brief periods of peace between the Spanish and an influential Chiriguano cacique named Cumbay from the Valley of Ingres, the conflict between the two sides had intensified in the decades preceding 1809 and the start of the independence struggle in Alto Peru.[15] Cumbay viewed the independence schism as an opportunity to gain an advantage against his adversaries and perhaps halt the flow of settlers into the Ingre Valley. He reached out to Martín Güemes, the insurgent leader of Salta, in May of 1810 asking for an agreement of peace.[16] Conditions seemed favorable in 1813 when a rebel army from the Rio de La Plata region (present day Argentina and Uruguay) led by Manuel Belgrano won key victories over the royalists and took Potosi and Chuquisaca. Cumbay arranged a meeting with Belgrano in Chuquisaca in May of 1813. The two quickly reached an accord. Cumbay allied with the rebel army along with two thousand warriors under his command. Apart from gifts, including uniforms for his men, it is unclear what favorable terms the Chiriguanos received in return. Belgrano probably allowed them the spoils associated with waging war against frontier towns loyal to the crown. Raiding and the taking of hostages was an essential rite for young men who sought to distinguish themselves as Ava warriors.[17]

The Chiriguano peace is indicative of a marked shift in the political landscape. In the absence of Spanish authority, new actors emerged to represent the political center and establish new lines of patronage. The Tarabuqueños, with their proximity to Chuquisaca and at the crossroads of marauding armies, were keenly aware of the changing landscape. To them, the demise of colonial authority and the pacification of the Chiriguanos pointed to an annulment of the old segmented arrangement they held with the crown and its administrative network. The new colonial agents were military men who directed royalist campaigns; they conscripted men and resources and waged a war of attrition against rural communities suspected of collaborating with rebels. By November of 1811, royalist demands (called contributions) on Tarabuco and the surrounding towns created a severe shortage of grains. The shortage spawned outrage as well as rumors of an armed Indian assault on Chuquisaca.[18]

The hardened political lines represented a quandary for Tarabuco and many rural *vecinos* (townspeople) who, despite whatever personal convictions they may have held, could not avoid contact with kinsmen—within their *ayllus* or via *compadrazgo* [Catholic kinship relations] obligations in their parishes—who held anticolonial sentiments. The hardened lines similarly challenged the network of trade contacts between communities from varying elevations and micro-niches that depended on each other for access to range of agricultural products. Relations between these communities were often bound by kinship and ritualized expressions of reciprocity. Kinship relations in the form of *compadrazgo*, for example, extended well beyond the Indian sphere and included clerics, *españoles* [class and ethnic designation denoting someone of predominantly European descent], and mestizos. In sum, political identities in these highland communities were dictated by personal and kin relations to the land, the ayllu, and an array of economic and religiously based affiliations.

Tarabuco's sizable originario population also played a determining role in the political alignments made during this period. The 1806 Padron (Indian tribute census) records 209 *originarios* in Tarabuco, the highest number of landed heads of household in Tomina province by a wide margin. The garrison town of Presto came closest with twelve *originarios.*[19] *Originarios* like other landed classes such as *kurakas* (referred to as caciques by the eighteenth century) were more likely to transcend the Indian sphere and enter into wider range of contacts in the mestizo-Spanish spheres. By the turn of the nineteenth century, caciques and other high-ranking members of the corporate towns were oftentimes considered mestizos—at least culturally in their dress and ability to speak Spanish. Taking advantage of Tarabuco's location along an established trade route, *originarios* and other affluent vecinos made business deals with an extensive network of contacts. They served as brokers between the Tarabuco Andean community and the outside.

Two of the prominent rebel combatants—Ildefonso Carrillo and Pedro Calisaya—hailed from Tarabuco's originario ranks.[20] Identifying the specific motives that led these individuals to take an anticolonial position and side with the rebel factions is nearly impossible to discern. It is clear, however, that they played a crucial role in politicizing and mobilizing their communities in the unfolding conflict. Both of these men were in their late forties at the start of the war (1809) which, as members of the landed class, signifies that they held positions of influence and prestige. Statues of both Carrillo and Calisaya respectively blowing a *pututu* [a cornet used to signal maneuvers] and wielding a sling sit in Tarabuco's main plaza.[21]

Carrillo and Calisaya and Tarabuco's rank and file combatants did not fight alone against royalist forces. They allied or "segmented" their efforts with an emergent rebel enclave led by Manuel Asencio Padilla and his intrepid wife, Juana Azurduy. Padilla came from the community of Moromoro which also lay along Tarabuco's trade networks. He was among the earliest to declare his position against the colonial government during the May 1809 Chuquisaca revolt while serving as Moromoro's junior magistrate.[22] As the independence conflict grew, it took hold in rural communities surrounding Chuquisaca. The rebel enclaves that sprouted in these communities were based on regional affiliations and personal relations. When Argentine forces entered the region under the rebel leadership of José Castelli in 1811 and Manuel Belgrano in 1813, Padilla aligned himself with their campaigns. Both of these campaigns featured reform elements that aimed to attract the support of the indigenous Andean populations. Castelli, for example, issued a series of decrees promising to abolish the Indian tribute and the dissolution of all social and legal categories separating the region's Indians from the rest of colonial society.[23] Belgrano envisioned similar reforms, as well as the establishment of an American empire with an 'Inca Monarch' at its head. He even designed a flag invoking *Inti*, the Inca sun deity, as the official banner of the new liberal government.[24] Very few of the proposed reforms were brought to fruition but they were successful in garnering the support of the Andean communities.

Belgrano's progressive reforms also sought to empower women in the classroom as well as the field of battle as combatants for the independence cause. Juana Azurduy eventually reached the rank of lieutenant colonel under his command. Her reputation as a combatant and guerrilla strategist in the independence struggle reached near mythical proportions in the pantheon of Argentine and Bolivian liberator classes. Her work politicizing and mobilizing the native Andean combatants into a guerrilla unit known as *Los Leales* [the loyal ones] is well documented.[25] She recruited people from the highland towns of Chayanta and Quilaquila to the corporate communities found along the Chiriguano frontier, including Tarabuco, the largest town in Tomina province.[26]

The Padillas drew a large number of followers from Tarabuco. Apart from serving as guerrilla auxiliaries, they provided the guerrilla resistance with smuggled supplies and intelligence reports. Early accounts describe Azurduy as having a Virgin Mary-like hold over her Andean followers which led subsequent authors to suggest that they venerated her as *Pachamama*, an Andean expression of the sacred feminine and earth mother.[27] Some of these interpretations are bound in paternalist and mythical narratives that attempted to rationalize her *varonil* [masculine] abilities as a mestiza leading men in a patriarchal and classist society. Azurduy was doubtless a convincing and charismatic leader but her appeal for Tarabuqueños lay in the fact that she was baptized in Tarabuco and her *madrina* [godmother]—Rosa Zarate—was a resident of the town. Azurduy's baptismal entry describes her as a mestiza and Zarate probably came from a similar background.[28] Thus, Azurduy was linked to a Tarabuco kinship network that reached beyond

Hispanicize residents and into the Andean *ayllus*. This in part explains why Tarabuqueños today consider the Padillas as their own. They refer to Manuel Asencio Padilla, for example, as "Tata Padilla," a term of endearment for a male ancestor and elder member of the community.[29]

Tactical reasons also explain an alliance with the Padillas. His rebel network had reached an agreement with Cumbay, which further solidified the Chiriguano peace for those who sided with the rebels.[30] But it is perhaps Padilla's approach to warfare that played a larger role in securing Tarabuco's support. Padilla waged an irregular and guerrilla form of warfare that suited native Andeans. The tactics and collective consciousness associated with guerrilla warfare was well established in Andean, historical expressions of *auqankuy* [Quechua for combat or warfare]. Andean warfare took advantage of the mountainous geography and rural character of the towns located in the southern Andes. It included tactics that are mainstays in the canon of guerrilla warfare: establish defensive positions in higher elevations, decoys and false movements, drawing the enemy into vulnerable terrain; hit and run tactics, knowledge of the terrain and *chakanchanas* [escape routes], etc. The Katari rebellion thirty years previous had demonstrated the devastating efficacy of *auqankuy*, and rural leaders such as Padilla who were at military disadvantage in the face of royalist armaments were quick to incorporate these strategies.[31] Padilla also kept low numbers of regular combatants so as not to overburden local food supplies.

One of the earliest rebels to be positioned in Tarabuco was an individual named Apolinar Zarate who had been there since 1811. It is unclear if he was related to Rosa Zarate, Azurduy's godmother, but given his refusal to abandon his position due to his large number of children, it's likely that he was from Tarabuco if not from one of the surrounding towns. By his own telling, Zarate defended the community "solely with indigenous *honderos* [slingers]."[32] Zarate played an important role along with Carrillo and Calisaya in bridging the relationship that bound the local Yampara community to Padilla and the broader array of political actors.

Andean expressions of guerrilla tactics would play a critical role in the years 1814–1817; a period of heightened violence in the Andean countryside as royalists waged devastating purging campaigns to rid themselves of persistent guerrilla activities found there. These expeditions were in reality attrition campaigns that scourged the region, burned entire towns, and razed fields. Correspondence between royalist officers reflect a perceived correlation between the largely indigenous combatants of the Katari rebellion with rural resistance in the independence period.[33] Thus, in pacifying the countryside, royalist troops murdered many innocent people.

According to Yampara oral tradition, the Jumbate (a Quechua derivation of *combate*, or combat in English) began when a royalist battalion entered Tarabuco on March 12, 1816 during the annual Pujllay celebration.[34] Royalists frequently targeted rural towns during holiday and religious festivals; they presumed that local rebel factions would let down their guard and come out of hiding to participate in the celebrations.[35] On this occasion the *Batallón del General*, known simply by the green color of their uniforms as *Los Verdes*, found the town relatively vacant. They moved north toward the city of Chuquisaca but not before sacking the town and humiliating some of the elderly women. As they entered a narrow stretch of road surrounded by high peaks they encountered thousands of Yampara combatants led by Carrillo, Calisaya, and two other rebel leaders under Padilla's command: José Serna and Prudencio Miranda.[36] In keeping with Andean guerrilla tactics, the Tarabuqueños had abandoned the town and set up new, militarized encampments in difficult and inaccessible areas. They had intercepted the royalist correspondence days before and knew that the battalion, led by Pedro Herrera, would be passing through. Women, children, and livestock hid in caves and makeshift corrals while the men kept watch. As the road passed an area known as *Carretas* [literally, wagons], the Yampara combatants overwhelmed the battalion, forcing them to retreat back toward Tarabuco. As they retraced their steps along a steep valley named Wanu Wanu lined with large boulders, they spotted large stacks of succulents called *achupallas* donned in traditional Tarabuco clothing and headwear on the high slopes. From a distance, they resembled Yamparas. Already low on ammunition, the battalion fired upon the decoys before retreating yet further to a relatively open area named Misana Pampa and site of an old chapel. It was here that the Yamparas finished off the last of the unfortunate royalist soldiers. None of the 150 soldiers survived, except for a drummer boy who had somehow managed to escape.

Here we see aspects of *awqu'a*, or total warfare. It was a ritualized state of mind more than an event, denoting a complete inversion of *ayni*, reciprocal relations when differences become irreconcilable.[37] Oftentimes induced by dance-fighting and ritualized drinking, combatants engaged their enemies with the knowledge that they will kill or be killed.[38] There was no room for compromise or the taking of prisoners when combatants arrived at this point. The fiercest warriors shapeshift themselves into predators such as pumas and owls. According to Tristan Platt's observations on the practice of *ch'ajwa*, or Aymara warfare, victims could be dismembered and their body parts designated as offerings to the earth.[39] It represents a complete and utter annihilation of the adversary. With some variations, tradition holds that after vanquishing the royalist soldiers the Yampara combatants removed their hearts and ritually devoured them. Although none of the extant written sources—rebel or royalist—make mention of the event, the memory of it appears to have been handed down through oral tradition. Neighboring communities, for example, continue to refer to the residents of Tarabuco by their nickname, *sunku mikhus* [those who consume hearts].[40] The macabre scene is also memorialized with an oddly informed statue in Tarabuco's main plaza.

It is curious that while Tarabuqueños and ethnic Yamparas generally refer to past events in mythic time—that is, they are more apt to project their own (personal and communal) relationship to past events rather than emphasize a linear chronology of them—their accounts of the Jumbate (Figure 2.1) adheres to a historical and sequential delivery of events. It was clearly a formative event in the development of their political identity which explains why it remains prominent in the Pujllay. Still, it is unclear when exactly and in what form Tarabuco incorporated Jumbate elements into the Pujllay festival. It was most likely inserted in the years immediately following the 1816 battle. The festival underwent layers of alterations in the years since, but the deep structure of the dance and its symbolic meaning appear intact for, as ethnologist Xavier Albo observed, the elaborate and bellicose nature of the Tarabuco Pujllay "does not appear to be a last-minute innovation."[41]

Leaders of the new Republic of Bolivia did not reciprocate in the way that Tarabuco's oral and ceremonial narratives would lead us to believe following independence from Spain in 1825. For, despite promises to the contrary, native Andeans were not incorporated with the full privileges of citizenship; they continued as an exploited fiscal category and paid the Indian tribute. The town of Tarabuco would remain in ruins for decades following the war and private estates would usurp large tracts of arable lands, eventually surrounding the once intact and powerful *ayllus*.[42] Large numbers of people from these corporate communities were pressed into *pongeage* [indentured servanthood] as hacienda laborers. This pattern was particularly common in the years 1880–1930 with

Figure 2.1 Batalla de Cumbati (Jumbate) March 12, 1816. By José Ponce de León (1926).

the recovery of Bolivia's silver and tin mining economies and a diminished dependence on the Indian tribute as a tax base. More than half of Tarabuco's communal lands were in the hands of private estates by 1930. These dispossessions did not go unopposed. Yamparas from all over the region rebelled and waged counter land invasions of their own which culminated in brutal reprisals at the hands of the Bolivia army in the 1930s.[43]

Given the tenuous historical backdrop, it is hard to imagine how the memory of the Jumbate survived as part of a ceremonial performance of segmentation. Why would these beleaguered communities continue to commemorate a historically bound relationship in the absence of state reciprocity? The answer partly lies in their ability to employ the past and affirm their place in it as a mechanism to confront an uncertain future. In projecting the Jumbate narrative, they are situating themselves in the unfolding of national events that contributed to the founding of the state. By incorporating it into the annual Pujllay, they are ensuring not only the survival and transmission of Jumbate narrative; they also retain *control* of the narrative and its relational significance to the *community*.[44] As owners of the Jumbate narrative, they not only align themselves to a national past; they also accentuate their own sense of separateness from national versions of the past that depict Indians as ignorant, unadaptive victims of historical forces. It is important to remember also that the Jumbate and its symbolic projections represent but one of many themes that are synthesized and performed in the Pujllay. And, in their telling, all of these themes are interrelated.

The past—along with the delineation of sacred cosmologies—are invoked in an effort to strengthen the community and its sense of cultural authenticity. In the act of dancing, singing, and dressing in ceremonial garb, the participants commemorate the connections as well as the frontiers that inform to their personal and collective identities. With subtle inflections, the instruments, melodic scales, lyrics, cadences, and dance movements form a ritual language that denotes important boundaries: the calendrical-agricultural station; Catholic from Andean representations of the sacred world; the female realm from the male realm; the living from the ancestors; and Yampara from external contingencies. To this end, the ritual language inherent to the Tarabuco Pujllay accentuates degrees of difference in relation to neighboring Jalq'a communities that share many cultural features with the Yamparas. The Jalq'as also speak Quechua and adhere to similar ritual festivals with similar musical forms. Yet both Yamparas and Jalq'as engage in a complementarity-oppositional relationship insofar as they emphasize their cultural and historical differences in music, dress, and textile design.[45] Their historical juxtaposition in relation to the Jalq'a may also shed light on the central place that the Jumbate plays in the Tarabuco version of the Pujllay. Some of these elements are inherently oppositional and counterhegemonic, but when blended with *ayni*-reciprocal sentiments they together form a coherent and ever evolving cultural framework.

By the turn of the twenty-first century, the Tarabuco community had redefined its relationship to the centers of political power. Besides gaining greater political and cultural autonomy, it received financial assistance to build basic infrastructure and the authority to allocate those resources at a local level. In truth, the path to greater autonomy had begun in the wake of the 1953 Agrarian Reform with the creation of a *sindicato campesino* [agricultural labor unions] and picked up steam in the 1990s with the Popular Participation Act, which decentralized power of federal government located in La Paz and empowered municipal governments. The same period witnessed the resurgence of the ayllu, although in altered form, with seven of Tarabuco's satellite communities filing for Originario Communal Territory (TCO) status with federal agencies.[46] In 2009, and after the formation of the Plurinational State of Bolivia, the move toward legal recognition of autonomy for rural municipalities such as Tarabuco received overwhelming support in the referendums and elections of that year. The Tarabuco municipality and surrounding satellite communities were reconstituted as the *Nación Indigena Yampara* [Indigenous Yampara Nation].[47]

But progress and change came with a price, a concept that the Yamparas understood firsthand. Tarabuco's success in safeguarding its cultural authenticity would create a powerful market demand for the tourist industry in the southern Andes. The Pujllay in particular emerged as a keystone attraction for ethnotourism. Profits associated with the event have attracted a large number of external vendors—providing transport, food services, and souvenirs—who siphon off revenues that would otherwise remain in the community.[48] More worrisome to some is the manner in which the event has been publicized. Many longtime participants fear that the Pujllay and the Yampara-Tarabuco culture generally have been packaged as a folkloric brand that misrepresents the original meaning of the event and its originators. The debates surrounding the benefits and liabilities associated with the "folklorization" of the Pujllay reach back to the 1970s, when municipal authorities reordered the schedule and presentation of the festival in an attempt to broaden its appeal.[49] These debates reveal a divide between the indigenous Yamparas and the more mestizo-Hispanicized members of the community. The latter are more likely to make commercial concessions. But given that many ethnic Yamparas live in extreme poverty, tourism is viewed as an important opportunity to augment their incomes. The weavers of the famous Tarabuco textile style, for example, are largely women from the surrounding area who predominantly work as agricultural laborers. The Pujllay allows them to boost their earnings in a relatively short period of time.[50]

The power and pageantry of the Pujllay have not gone unnoticed by the international community. In November of 2014 the United Nations Educational, Scientific, and Cultural Organization (UNESCO) inscribed the Pujllay and its complementary festival, the Ayarichi, in the Representative List of the Intangible Cultural Heritage of Humanity. Bolivian president Evo Morales has since showcased the Pujllay as an example of

Bolivia's deep indigenous legacy when negotiating bilateral agreements with neighboring nations. A version of the Pujllay, for example, was performed in 2015 to commemorate the unveiling of the Juana Azurduy statue in Buenos Aires. Azurduy's statue replaced an existing statue of Columbus near Argentina's *Casa Rosada* presidential palace and the Yampara dancers took the opportunity to accentuate their role in the independence process via the Jumbate as well as their own relation to the heroine.[51] The widened exposure has resulted in larger numbers of tourists who travel to Tarabuco each March and new markets for traditional textiles.

It is difficult to understate the ironies associated with the international celebrity of a festival passed down against great odds by an indigenous community that has historically used the festival to retain its identity in the face of external forces. The ironies were not lost on many Yamparas who, despite the economic advantages, sense that the meaning and power of the event have been compromised. To this end—and in keeping with historical avenues of adaptation—ethnic Yamparas have taken steps to protect the ritual meaning of the Pujllay (and the Jumate narrative within it) by holding smaller celebrations on alternate dates, usually the Saturday before the more popular event. Since at least 2003, the Tarabuco Yampara and surrounding communities hold an alternate Pujllay at Misana Pampa, the very grounds of the original Jumate. As in the larger celebration, the participants begin by attending a Mass in Quechua. They also don traditional regalia and dance around a *pukara*. But unlike the more publicized event, the alternate Pujllay does not have any official sponsor. All of the participating communities contribute to the items fashioned to the *pukara* and share in the associated costs. The discourse following the mass—speeches and commentaries made by local Yampara authorities—are more political and decidedly more *indigenista* in tone.[52] In some ways these modest celebrations more closely resemble the Aymara *anata* [carnival] celebrations held in villages along the *altiplano*.

The alternate Pujllay represents yet another negotiated frontier that separates local from external contingencies. These are not mere examples of passive acquiescence to a subaltern status. Far from the primordial versions of themselves, the Yamparas of Tarabuco experienced profound transformations—spanning over five centuries—but their real adaptation involves a legacy of active resistance, direct action, and a historical agency that allowed them to continually reorder the terms of their relationships. Above all, the Pujllay emphasizes transformative frontiers that align personal and communal experience to historical and cosmic events within contemporary sociopolitical contexts. Each animate and provide meaning to the other in an endless stream of survival, celebration, and reinvention.[53]

Notes

1 The Chamber of Culture and Tourism in Tarabuco reports that the 2016 Pujllay witnessed the participation of thirty groups comprised of over six hundred dancers. See "Hoy vuelve la majestuosidad del Pujllay," *Correo del Sur*, 20 marzo 2016.

2 Historian Rosanna Barragán refers to the original Yamparas as Indians of the "bow and arrow" which denotes them as a transitional culture group, between highlands and lowlands. Despite other cultural affiliations with highland cultures which primarily used slings in warfare, they used the bow and arrow which are associated with lowland cultures. Barragán, *Indios de arco y flecha? Entre la historia y la archeologia de las poblaciones del norte de Chuquisaca (siglos XV–VI)*, Ediciones ASUR 3 (Imprenta "Tupac Amaru": Sucre, 1994), 161–163.

3 It is unclear when (during what century) the Yamaparas first starting wearing their version of the montera. They may have adopted it, along with other European-inspired accoutrements, during the colonial period when Indians, as an inferior class and legal category, were

forbidden from wearing European clothes. They may have adopted the montera as a way of differentiating themselves from the Indian categories and its associated social disadvantages. Although the ubiquitous ball cap has gained widespread use among young men in surrounding rural communities, the montera continues to be the headgear of choice among Tarabuqueños.

4 For an excellent discussion on the multiethnic range of Tarabuco and other communities along this eastern frontier, see Mercedes del Rio and Ana Maria Presta, "Un estudio etnohistorico en los corregimientos de Tomina Yamparaez: casos de multietnicidad," In *Espacio, Etnías, Frontera. Atenuaciones Politicas en el Sur del Tawantinsuyu, SIglos XV-XVII*, edited by Ana Maria Presta Ediciones ASUR 4, 189–218 (Imprenta "Tupac Amaru": Sucre, 1995).

5 Barragán, 57–59.

6 Nathan Wachtel described similar processes in the Cochabamba valleys. For a discussion on mitimaes in the Cochabamba region, see Nathan Wachtel, "The Mitimaes of the Cochabamba Valley: The Colonization Policy of Huayna Capac," In *Inca and Aztec States, 1400–1800: Anthropology and History*, edited by George A. Collier, Renato I. Rosaldo, and John D. Wirth, 199–235 (New York, NY: Academic Press, 1982). See also Nicolás Sánchez-Albornoz, *Indios y tributos en el Alto Perú* (Lima: Instituto de Estudios Peruanos, 1978).

7 The city was actually founded by Pedro de Anzures in the valley of Chuqui Chaka, hence the name Chuquisaca. The city was also referred to alternately as Charcas, Chuquisaca—and presently as Sucre.

8 Tristan Platt, "Imagined Frontiers: Recent Advances in the Ethnohistory of the Southern Andes," *Bulletin of Latin American Research*, Vol 18, No. 1 (1999): 102.

9 Tristan Platt, "Simon Bolívar, the Sun of Justice and the Amerindian Virgin: Andean Conceptions of the *Patria* in Nineteenth-Century Potosí," *Journal of Latin American Studies*, (February 1993): 169.

10 Andean kin groups known as ayllus often stretched across ecological niches as part of a segmented network that exchanged and distributed agricultural produces form one ecological satellite community to the next. See John Murra, *Formaciones Políticas y Económicas Del Mundo Andino* (Lima: Instituto de Estudios Peruanos, 1975). See also John Murra, "Did Tribute and Markets Prevail in the Andes before the European Invasion?" In *Ethnicity, Markets, and Migration in the Andes: At the Crossroads of History and Anthropology*, edited by Olivia Harris, Brooke Larson, and Enrique Tandeter. (Durham, NC: Duke University Press, 1995).

11 "Expediente promovido por Andrés Tinajero De La Escadera, Corregidór de la provincia de Yamparaéz," 1784, Archivo Naciónál de Bolivia (ANB), Sublevación General de Indios (SGI), no. 306.

12 "Expediante formado en virtud del informe del capitán Luis Ortis," Tarabuco, 30 de diciembre 1780, ANB, SGI, no. 30, fs 1–2. The reference to the Chiriguano invasion is found in "Expediente promovido por Juan Martierena de Barranco, Marqués del Valle de Tojo," Jujuy, 7 de mayo 1781, ANB, SGI no. 253.

13 "Padrón y Revisitas de Indios, Provincia de Tomina, 1806," Tribunal Naciónál de Cuentas ANB, Revisitadas (RV) no. 24.

14 For examples of political disruptions in the independence period for Ayopaya and Sicasica provinces, see Javier F. Marion, "Indios Blancos: Nascent Polities and Social Convergence in Bolivia's Ayopaya Rebellion, 1814–1821," *Colonial Latin American Historical Review*, Vol 15, No. 4 (Fall/Otoño 2006): 1–31.

15 "Carta del Intendente Francisco de Viedma," La Plata, 15 de marzo de 18008, Biblioteca Naciónál de Bolivia (BNB), Colección Rück no. 257, f. 2.

16 Luis Güemes, *Güemes Documentado vol 1* (Buenos Aires: Editoriá; Plus Ultra, 1979), p 156.

17 Thierry Saignes, "Historia de Cumbay: Derrotero de un líder chiriguano," A/BNB, Colección Rück no. 257, 125–129.

18 "Testimonio de Vicente Palacios sobre sospecha de sublevación de los Indios de Tarabuco e Yamparaez," Chuquisaca, 1811, ANB, Eman 65, f. 1–1v.

19 "Padrón y Revisitas de Indios, Provincia de Tomina, 1806," Tribunal Naciónál de Cuentas ANB, Revisitadas (RV) no. 24.

20 Ibid. Calisaya is listed as an originario from the Ayllu Puno, Paucarrollo y Guaca on f 35v. He was age 36 in 1806 and married to Manuela Sisa. Ildefonso Carillo appears in Bautismos, San Pedro de Montalban, 1754–1795, Chuquisaca, Bolivia, Latter Day Saints Film number: 1224473.

21 Bartolomé Mitre, *Historia de Belgrano en la independencia argentina* Tomo 2 (Buenos Aires: Biblioteca de la Nación, 1902 [1850]), 136.

22 "Autobiografia del Teniente Coronel don Manuel Asencio Padilla," In *Documentos ineditos*, edited by Miguel de los Santos Taborga, 33–38 (Sucre: Sociedad Geografica Sucre, 1902).

23 "El Exmo. Señor Representante de la Junta Provicional Gubernativa del Rio de Chuquisaca a los Indios del Virreinato del Perú," April 28, 1811, BNB, Colección Rück, no. 327.

24 Bartolomé Mitre, *Historia de Belgrano en la independencia argentina* Tomo 2 (Buenos Aires: Biblioteca de la Nación, 1902 [1850]), 56. The flag was initially rejected by the governing junta in Buenos Aires, but vestiges of it were eventually adopted as the official flag of Argentina.

25 Some of the more recent and reliable sources for Juana Azurduy include Berta Wexler, *Las heroías altoperuanas como expression de un colectivo, 1809–1825* (Rosario, Argentina: Centro de Estudios Interdisciplinarios Sobre las Mujeres, UNR, 2013); William Lofstrom, Norberto Benjamín Torres, and Mario Castro Torres, *Juana Azurduy de Padilla. Perspectivas y Documentos, Tomo1* (Ciencia Editores: Sucre, Bolivia, 2014); Benjamín Torres, *Juana Asurdui de Padilla: Perspectivas y Documentos Tomo 2* (Ciencia Editores: Sucre, Bolivia, 2015).

26 See "Informe del Ayuntamiento de Chuquisaca," Chuquisaca, 3 de setiembre 1825, Archivo Casa de La Libertad (CDLL), 12–07–980, ff. 1–4.

27 Bartolomé Mitre, *Historia de Belgrano y de la independencia argentina* Tomo 2 (Buenos Aires: Biblioteca de la Nación, 1902 [1850]), 141.

28 Zarate was probably Azurduy's maternal aunt, "San Pedro de Montalban, Chuquisaca, Bolivia, 1754–1795," LDS film no. 1224473.

29 Much of the Yampara oral history of the Jumbate is expressed in a documentary named: *Jumbate: Homenaje al 12 de Marzo de 1816*, produced by Dario Arcienega Medrano, Directór del Programa "Municipio en Desarrollo," Gobierno Autónomo Municipál de Tarabuco, Dirección de Turísmo (2015).

30 Bartolomé Mitre, *Historia de Belgrano y de la independencia argentina* Tomo 2 (Buenos Aires: Biblioteca de la Nación, 1902 [1850]), 136.

31 This sentiment was made clear in a letter between the conspirators of the 1809 La Paz Rebellion, Julián Plaza and Antonio Medina. See "Carta de Julian Plaza a José Antonio Medina, 15 de setiembre de 1809, Chuquisaca, transcibed in Humberto Vasquez Machicado," in "La Efervescencia libertaria en el Alto Peru de 1809 y la insurección de esclavos en Santa Cruz," Humberto y Jose Vasquez Machicado, *Obras Completas* vol. III (La Paz: Don Bosca, 1988), 339–341.

32 "Oficio del comandante Zarate al gobernador Guemes," Colpa, December 4, 1816, In *Partes Oficiales y Documentos Relativos a la Guerra de Independencia Tomo 2*, Archivo General de la Nación Argentina (AGNA) (Taller Tipográfico de La Penitenciaría Nacional: Buenos Aires, 1901).

33 "Informe de Dn. Antonio de Allende, Capitán provisional del Regimiento de Caballería . . . respecto al avance de indios rebeldes, al pueblo de Tapacarí . . .", Cochabamba, October 15, 1811, CDEQ, (IV-1–1–22), f. 2.; Eman., no. 1812.10, ANB, fs. 5–8.; "Decreto de Peuyrredón," Salta, October 12, 1811," In *Gazeta de Buenos Ayres*, no. 3, 1811.xi. 17, Archivo Familiar Gunnar Mendoza (AFGM), fichero no. 2.

34 "*Cumbati*," another Quechua derived word for combate, also appears in historical accounts and sometimes alternates with "Jumbate." In written records, the 1816 battle was known simply as the battle of Tarabuco or the battle of Las Carretas. Versions of the battle can be found in the following sources: "Oficio de Manuel Asencio Padilla al General José Rondeau, Tomina, April 24 1816," in *Partes Oficiales vol. 2*. See also *Jumbate: Homenaje al 12 de Marzo de 1816* (2015).

35 The scribe and rebel combatant José Santos Vargas made mention of royalists targeting feast days. See José Santos Vargas, *Diario de un comandante de la independencia americana, 1814–1825*, transcripción, introducción e índices de Gunnar Mendoza Loza (Mexico: Siglo Veintiuno Editores, S.A., 1982).

36 Bartolomé Mitre, *Historia de Belgrano n la independencia argentina* Tomo 2 (Buenos Aires: Biblioteca de la Nación, 1902 [1850]), 136.

37 Marie—Danielle Demélas, *L' Invention Politique: Bolivie, Équateur, Pérou au XIX Siècle* (Paris: Éditions Recherche sur le Civilisations, 1992), 222. See also Tristan Platt, "Desde la perspectiva de la isla: Guerra y transformación en un archipielago vertical andino: Macha (norte de Potosi, Bolivia)," *Chungara: Revista de Antropología Chilena*, Vol 42, No. 1 (Enero–Junio, 2010): 302–303. For an analysis of Andean ritualized warfare during the Tupac Amaru Rebellion see Jan Szeminski, "Why Kill the Spaniard? New Perspectives in Andean Insurrectionary Ideology in the 18th Century," In *Resistance, Rebellion, and Consciousness in the Andean Peasant World, 18th*

to 19th Centuries, edited by Steve J. Stern, 166–192 (Madison: University of Wisconsin Press, 1987).

38 Padilla mentions the total disregard for their own safety as Yampara combatants attacked the royalist battalion. See "Carta de Manuel Asencio Padiilla a José Rondeau," Tomina, 24 de abril 1816, in *Partes Oficiales Vol 2*, 200.

39 Tristan Platt, "Desde la perspectiva de la isla: Guerra y transformación en un archipielago vertical andino: Macha (norte de Potosi, Bolivia), *Chungara: Revista de Antropología Chilena*, Vol 42, No. 1 (Enero–Junio 2010): 303. Abercromie describes ch'ajwa as a form of land war, the most serious and violent confrontation between two opposing sets of interests. In patriline societies, the men claim title to agricultural lands and transform into combatant defenders of the land when threatened with encroachment. See Thomas Abercrombie, *Pathways to Memory and Power: Ethnography and History Among an Andean People* (Madison: University of Wisconsin Press, 1998), 102.

40 Jhonny Davalos, Veronica Cereceda and Gabriel Martinez, *Textiles Tarabuco* 2nd ed. Ediciones ASUR (Imprenta "Tupac Katari," 1992), 10.

41 Xavier Albo, Tres municipios andinos camino a la autonomía indígena: Jesús de Machaca, Chayanta, Tarabuco. Cuadernos de investigación N°78, (La Paz: Editorial CIPCA, 2012), 221–222.

42 The French chronicler Alcides D'Orbigy passed through the town in the 1840s and reported its devastation. See Erick D. Langer, *Economic Change and Rural Resistance in Southern Bolivia, 1880–1930* (Stanford, CA: Stanford University Press, 1989), 53.

43 Ibid., 188–207.

44 Abercrombie makes a similar argument for the K'ulta community near Lake Poopo. He writes that the K'ulta "have found themselves engaged in not only in a political struggle but also a struggle to gain control and retain control over the definition, transmission, and interpretation of the past." See Thomas Abercrombie, *Pathways to Memory and Power: Ethnography and History Among an Andean People* (Madison: University of Wisconsin Press, 1998), 10.

45 Differences in themes and color gradations in the woven art produced by Jalq'as and Yamparas are particularly indicative of the relational juxtaposition between the two ethnic communities. The Yampara Axsu, an elaborate decorative article worn by women, for example, underscores the world "above ground" with recognizable images of people and animals in bright colors. The Jalq'a version highlights the underworld and associated disorder with strange creatures woven in red and black. See Veronica Cereceda, *Una diferencia. Un sentido: los diseños textiles tarabuco y jalq'a* (Sucre: ASUR, 1993).

46 Xavier Albo explains that unlike in previous eras, the lands within these communal holdings are not distributed or managed by a traditional, centralized authority. They are each managed autonomously, and many of the residents in these communities are not *originarios* to these lands. The resurgence of the ayllu model grew popular in the 1990s with many different corporate landholding models referring to themselves as ayllus. See Xavier Albo, *Tres Municipios Andinos*, 235–238.

47 Xavier Albo, *Tres Municipios Andinos*, 242. Two residents from Tarabuco also served in the Constitutional Assembly of 2006, which produced the document which resulted in a refounding of the Bolivian state under the guidance of Evo Morales: Esteban Urquizo Cuéllar and Savina Cuéllar Leaños. The latter also served as Prefect of the Department of Chuquisaca.

48 Shan Kai Thè, *Following Financial Tourism Flows: Linking Leakages to Multipliers in Tarabuco, Bolivia* (Utrecht: University of Utrecht, 2010), 12.

49 José Fernández, *Los tarabuqueños y su relación con el turismo: Turismo sostenible basado en las comunifdades andinas, realidad o utopia?* (Sucre, 2009, unpublished manuscript), 70–71. See also José Fernández, *Comunidades indígenas, textiles y turismo: Un estudio de caso del programa textil de ASUR y las comunidades Tarabuco* (Sucre: Universidad Mayor de San Francisco Xavier de Chuquisaca, 2014).

50 Shan Kai Thé, *Following Financial Tourism Flows: Linking Leakages to Multipliers in Tarabuco, Bolivia* (Utrecht: University of Utrecht, 2010), 13.

51 See "Argentina Replaces Columbus Statue With Indigenous Heroine," *Telesur*, July 15, 2015. www.telesurtv.net/english/news/Evo-Morales-Unveils-Independence-Heroine-Statue-in-Argentina-20150715-0004.html accessed August 6, 2015.

52 Jose Fernández, *Los tarabuqueños y su relación con el turismo: Turismo sostenible basado en las comunifdades andinas, realidad o utopia?* (Sucre, 2009, unpublished manuscript), 83.

53 The notion of ethnogenesis is often cited when referring to the indigenous populations of the central Andes and their transformative abilities. Ethnogenesis can be defined as a pattern of cultural reproduction in which ethnic communities merge and negotiate with distinct external entities without compromising their core cultural values. It was initially introduced into the field of Andean studies in 1978 by Nicolás Sánchez-Albornoz in his landmark study on tribute, migrations, and cultural reproduction in sixteenth century Peru. See Sánchez-Albornoz, *Indios y tributos en el Alto Perú* (Lima: Instituto de Estudios Peruanos, 1978). While the concept of ethnogenesis is not unique to the study of native Andeans, it has since been used extensively by archeologists, ethnologists, and ethnohistorians to explain their ability to survive the Inca, colonial, and republican periods. The concept, while useful, needs to be properly contextualized for it to be applied to the present study. In fact, the idea of "cultural refusal" may also need to be considered. See Rachel Corr and Karen Vieira Powers, "Ethnogenesis, Ethnicity, and Cultural Refusal: The Case of the Salasacas in Highland Ecuador," In *Latin American Research Review*, Vol 47 (Special Issue 2012): 5–30.

3

THE TRAJECTORY OF THE AFRICAN MICHELINA

Identities, Slavery, and Post-Abolition at the Parish of Nossa Senhora do Pilar, Rio de Janeiro, Brazil

Nielson Rosa Bezerra

In late 1872, as slavery took new directions in Brazil, vicar João Antônio da Silva Barriga baptized the innocent Crescência, a creole registered as a freeborn because of the *Lei do Ventre Livre* [Law of the Free Womb], which had been enacted the previous September 28. The little girl was the natural daughter to an African named Michelina and goddaughter to Bento and Thereza, who, like her mother, were the slaves of Donna Ignácia Antônia do Amaral Mattos.[1] Such a baptism entry exemplifies the different dimensions of the life of Africans and creoles during the last days of slavery in Brazil.

Crescência's mother, Michelina, descended from Africans who used to constitute the greater part of the enslaved population in Brazil. With the end of the Atlantic slave trade,[2] Africans began to arrive in smaller quantity, but they were still considerably abundant due to the persistence of the illegal trade. In the parish of Pilar, the African presence suffered a disaggregation within the enslaved population—at least with regard to baptism data. Such fluctuations in the number of Africans promotes the idea of a constant connection between the Atlantic world and the Recôncavo[3] da Guanabara's economy and society.[4] That not only happened during the apogee of the slave trade, but also throughout its disintegration process. Of the 201 mothers who gave birth to freeborn children, only Michelina was identified as an "African." Besides Michelina, only one slave was identified with the label "of a nation," pointing out the minority rates of Africans among slave women between 1871 and 1888.

The absence of African women who baptized their children after the Law of the Free Womb does not mean that they were nonexistent in that parish. The 1872 census counted 1129 slaves in the parish of Pilar.[5] A brief comparison with the figures from the baptismal book allows us to identify a difference of almost a thousand people. There is a difference of over seven hundred people between the parents registered by the baptismal book and the people registered by the census. Therefore, the baptismal book offers an interesting perspective on society and slave families, but its data may be questionable when it comes to the demography of the parish of Pilar.

The absence of Africans among the women who had their freeborn children baptized in Pilar could be explained by a biological factor. By then, twenty-two years had passed since the end of the trade. The slave labor force in Pilar had not been renewed with Africans for a long time. The remaining African women, among those 1,129 slaves verified by the census, could possibly be "grandmothers," considering their advanced age for reproduction. The fact that the Atlantic trade privileged male adults creates even more doubt, and explains the absence of African women in the entries. When studying the slave families in Vale do Paraíba, in the inland of Rio de Janeiro, Ana Rios and Hebe Mattos have found different references to "African grandparents" in the recollections concerning the period after 1871. Those references make an interesting allusion to the baptism of children, which gathered many people apart from their mothers and godparents. At the time, baptisms were seen as an important social space where grandparents, and even fathers attended—despite not being registered in the entries. One may presume, according to Mattos and Rios, that the baptism gathered families into celebration. Even so, the connection among those people, who lived together for decades, who raised their children and grandchildren together, who were united by marriages and baptisms, existed well before this formal celebration.[6]

This chapter focuses on the enslaved people of Brazil during last official year of African slavery, which was abolished in 1888 with the *Lei Aurea* [Gold Law]. Almost two decades before, the Brazilian Government passed *Lei do Ventre Livre* [Law of Free Womb] which proclaimed that every child who was born after that day would be free. Furthermore, this chapter details the condition of Black lives at the Parish Nossa Senhora do Pillar, Rio de Janeiro, during a specific period of Brazilian history. I want to show how African people lived during the last years of slavery in Brazil in order to contribute to the understanding of how much the post-Abolition period impacted the lives of Brazilians of African descent.

We cannot dismiss the fact that the majority of the Africans around the Recôncavo Fluminense (the stretch of land between the city of Rio de Janeiro and Serra do Mar) were from West and Central Africa, a place where the Bantu culture predominated. According to Robert Slenes, "talking of hopes and recollections of enslaved people from that part of Brazil necessarily means turning our attention to the cultural heritage that those exiled from Africa brought along with them."[7] Considering that it was a common characteristic to almost all African societies to be structured around the family lineage organization—that is, a group of relatives that delineates their origin from ancestors in common—it is likely that "African old people" attended the social meetings of slave communities by the end of the nineteenth century.

Like little Crescência, 97 percent of the freeborn children baptized in the parish of Nossa Senhora do Pilar did not have an identified father, so they were considered "natural children" instead of "legitimate children" (when father and mother are identified), which account for only 3 percent.[8] Many hypotheses were created to explain the high frequency of natural children among slave women. Because the Atlantic trade prioritized male adults, it is likely that there were not enough women available to the "matrimonial market" within the slaves' quarters, leading to conflict between Africans from different nations interested in a partner for a stable relationship.[9] Robert Slenes, for instance, pays to attention to a greater number of legitimate marriages in larger estates. There was also a probable existence of "fictitious marriages," having only the master's consent, that were not always formalized by a clerical representative.[10]

However, Table 3.1 shows six fathers identified along the 201 entries. Legitimate children, those born to couples who had married under the rules of the Catholic Church, were an exception. Nevertheless, if those entries have little quantitative importance, an intense analysis on their details may contribute to the understanding of the relationships the enslaved forged among themselves and with people from other social spheres, such as freed slaves.

Table 3.1 Slave family, Pilar (1871–1888)

	Father	%	*Mother*	%	*Baptized*	%
African	–	–	1	0.5	–	–
Creole	–	–	141	70.1	112	55.7
Of a nation	–	–	1	0.5	–	–
Slave	6	3.0	17	8.6	–	–
Not identified	195	97.0	6	2.9	4	2.0
Mulatto	–	–	32	15.9	81	40.3
Black	–	–	3	1.5	4	2.0
Total	201	100	201	100	201	100

Source: Arquivo da Diocese de Duque de Caxias. Livro de Registro de Batismo de Escravos da Freguesia de Nossa Senhora do Pilar (1871–1888)

All the slaves who had legitimate children baptized belonged to José Pereira Bulhões de Carvalho, owner of the farm Santa Cruz, where the chapel of Nossa Senhora do Rosário, a filial church in Pilar, was located. The parish baptismal book contains entries from 1873–1875, registered by the entrusted priest, who signed as José Antônio da Silva Barriga. Among the slaves who stand out were Zeferino and Apolinária, a couple from the parish of Santo Antônio da Jacutinga. They took active part in the registration of their two legitimate children, Anacleta and Veríssimo. They were also the godparents of Marcelina, legitimate daughter of Joaquim and Cândida, who were also slaves who belonged to the same owner. Besides this, Zeferino also appears as the godfather of Marcelino, son of the same slave couple from the previous entry. However, in this case, the godmother was Angela, another slave.[11]

The few couples who had legitimate, baptized children suggests that the slaves had autonomy in relation to the plantation, and as a family with spatial mobility. Such a perspective offers a broader view on the life conditions of those people throughout the last moments of slavery. The formation of a family was the first step in the long process of the social establishment that those people experienced during the transition to freedom. These few entries of legitimate, baptized children in Pilar offer an important glimpse of the close social relations the enslaved weaved throughout that period.

In many cases, the lack of a formal marriage prevented couples from registering their children as legitimate, producing a great number of natural children—as in the case of the parish of Pilar. With or without ecclesiastical consent, the formation of a family was a stabilizing factor initiated by the masters, who saw the slave family as an interesting way of assuring their authority—which by then was questionable due to the legal transformations that Brazil was slowly absorbing. Forming a family was advantageous to the enslaved since it could represent an important manorial permission, such as a small plot of land, a house apart from the slave quarters and some other little, yet significant, privileges. We should not forget that the parish of Pilar, as well as the entire Recôncavo, was dotted by small and medium estates, which were inhabited by no more than thirty slaves.

Of the mothers, 70.1 percent were identified as creoles, which means they had a closer African ancestry. This meant that the children's grandparents were most likely Africans, even though they are not registered in the accounted entries. Mulatto women accounted for 15.9 percent, demonstrating that the society in that parish, in the one generation was rapidly transforming. On the other hand, slightly more than 55 percent of the children were identified as creoles and 40.3 percent as mulattoes. Such apparent plurality may hide a common ancestry, which could reveal a cultural pattern based on African traditions and family lineage. Although many inhabitants from São José, in Valença, were considered distant relatives, a genealogical study in that community based on baptism records revealed a common ancestry: All of them had some kind of kinship, even though their collective lineage had been forgotten. Nevertheless, the jongo dance became a common cultural practice that, incidentally, is likely of Bantu origin.[12]

It may be argued that as the number of Africans decreased in the parish of Pilar, the number of creoles and mulattoes would increase. However, we cannot disregard the fact that lighter skin designated social prominence. Many people of color who integrated into Brazilian society used the information about their skin color as a method for gaining social mobility.[13] The small number of Africans in the entries changed the picture of social designations among the slaves of Pilar and demonstrates the collective strategies of freedom and social mobility that were undertaken in the bosom of the slave family. The absence of fathers in most baptism entries does not that they were absent. Still, after 1871, the figure of the slave mother became significant again within the relations established by slavery because of the *Lei do Ventre Livre*. The same womb that provided the reproduction of the slave condition would now secure freedom for children like little Crescência. So once freedom came, it was necessary to articulate a collective strategy of social mobilization, even though it was possible only through a generational perspective. The skin color designated in the baptism entry could represent the first and major step towards such a goal. Thus, the increase in the number of "mulattoes" throughout generations of slave families is no surprise. Another way of contributing to such a goal was through the strategic choice of godparents.

According to Silvia Brügger, godparenting tended to connect the children's family to people of equivalent or higher status in the social hierarchy. Godparents were essential elements for family ties in the slavery environment.[14] As can be seen in Table 3.2, all the baptism entries evidenced godparents, whatever their social condition was. When cross-matching data related to (free or slave) godfathers and godmothers, the numbers are equivalent. Regarding the godfathers, the slaves (52.3 percent) show a slight advantage; the free or freed godfathers (46.2 percent) are close to an equivalence. Though reversed, the percentage of free or freed godmothers (28.4 percent) was not so different from the slave godmothers (25.4 percent). Especially in the case of the godmothers, we can highlight the various devotions to Our Lady, who was registered as godmother in 44.2 percent of the entries.

Table 3.2 Social condition of godfathers and godmothers in Pilar (1871–1888)

	Godfather	*%*	*Godmother*	*%*
Freed creole	–	–	1	0.5
Devotions*	1	0.5	89	44.2
Slave	105	52.3	51	25.4
Freed	1	0.5	1	0.5
Free	93	46.2	57	28.4
Not identified	1	0.5	2	1.0
Total	201	100	201	100

Source: Arquivo da Diocese de Duque de Caxias; Livro de Registro de Batismo de Escravos da Freguesia de Nossa Senhora do Pilar (1871–1888)

* *Devotion*: A saint or representation of Mary in absence of a human godparent.

It is interesting to notice that although fathers are disproportionately absent, accounting for the great number of natural children, the same is not true among godparents. The majority of the godfathers were slaves. Free godfathers are likely the ones who had a surname and no mention of captivity. Given the minimal amount of freed godparents, we can assume that many of them did not mention their skin color in order to acquire social distinction. Another hypothesis, though less likely, is the possibility of the biological father attending the baptism as the godfather. This may have been a chance for the fathers to be with their children, since godparenting was a space of stabilization and creation of social ties. Although not necessarily a rule, baptism and godparenting—as well as the formation of families—were also forms of reassuring manorial authority.

Godparents have always compensated for the absence of one member of the family, usually the father. Godparenting was an important strategy to access the family's resources. The family was the main space of slave autonomy, which godparenting ensured, leading to greater social mobility. It is obvious, therefore, that godparents were carefully chosen and, regardless of manorial intervention, slaves had ways to monitor and discuss such intervention. However, there was a balance between godfathers and godmothers in the parish of Pilar. While there was a majority of slave godfathers, there was also a majority of free and freed women serving as godmothers for those innocent children.

In Brazil, more women were manumitted than men, making it likely that there were more free and freed women available to serve as godmothers for those children. Nonetheless, it seems to me that the kind of the estates and the characteristics of the slavery in Pilar—which can be seen as a representation of the Recôncavo Fluminense—also interfered in the pattern of choosing godparents.

Godparenting as a social mobilization strategy within different generations of a slave family is a factor that can be strongly identified in the parish of Pilar. There was an equivalence of godfathers and godmothers who held the same condition or were at a higher level in the social hierarchy.

According to the 1872 Census, there were 1,129 slaves in the parish of Pilar, of which 1.2 percent were seamstresses or bricklayers; 36 percent had household occupations; 37 percent were ploughmen; and 26 percent did not have their occupation registered.[15] Considering this data, we can see that most slaves were somehow involved in farming, particularly food goods such as cassava flour. As it is known, many household slaves were employed in different activities of the house and the plantation, as the percentage of slaves in the region was low—an average of thirty slaves per estate. In general, slaves who had no "specialty" that deserved to be registered were employed in agriculture. So we can see that the Parish of Pilar was basically an agricultural area where the family ties

Table 3.3 Slave population in the parish of Pilar by gender (1871–1888)

Sex	*Number*	*%*
Men	306	40.4
Women	252	33.3
Boy	90	11.8
Girl	110	14.5
Total	758	100

Source: Livro de Registro de Batismo de filhos de mulheres escravas da Freguesia de Nossa Senhora do Pilar (1871–1888)

of the slaves, the lease of small allotments, and ladinization were all aspects of this late nineteenth century slave society.

Table 3.2 also reveals that in Pilar there was a blend of slave godfathers and free (or freed) godmothers. This factor is likely to be the same in other parishes of the area as well. Many women who appear with surnames and without mention of manumission or freedom in Table 3.2 were possibly free. Most of the men were employed as ploughmen on small estates located on the outskirts of the city of Rio de Janeiro. The closeness to the capital and the daily flow of goods induced a strong confluence of the Recôncavo and the urban world, causing the social inequalities characteristic to that society.

When comparing the total number of slaves registered in the 1872 census (1,129 slaves) and those 758 people involved in the baptism, such as parents, children to be baptized and godparents, it is possible to establish that a large proportion of people who lived in Pilar somehow took part in that Catholic ritual. In addition, Table 3.3 shows that the adult males had a small advantage (40.4 percent) over adult females (33.3 percent). Even after the end of the slave trade, the small landowners in the Recôncavo do Rio de Janeiro continued to prefer men to women as plantation workers. Interestingly, the birth of freeborns shows an inversion in the figures as the girls represented 14.5 percent and only 11.8 percent were boys. Apparently, there is a contraction in the data, since the freeborns should not be included in the figures of the slave population. However, these children remained in the bosom of the slave family because they were cared for by their parents. In addition, the Law of 1871 established a series of conditions that guaranteed freedom for these children.

At the Parish of Pilar, as well as throughout the region now known as the Baixada Fluminense, slavery was marked by constant influence from many social actors, causing dents and asymmetry in the idealized imperial society. Everyday slave life preserved interactions among people who did not belong to the same society, as it can be seen through the analysis of the baptismal book. It was also possible to identify the strong connection between the histories of the Parish and the debate about the end of slavery. The life of those people proceeded. Many already had a prospect of freedom on the horizon, either by negotiating manumission letters or even through expectation, since children born after 1871 were granted freedom, regardless of slave-owner resistance. Regardless, slave resistance was also present as well as the rebellious actions characteristic to the spreading of maroon communities of fugitive slaves and their descendants throughout the nineteenth century.

Peasantry and Social Rooting

Recôncavo da Guanabara was a place of food production, an economic activity that presupposes the existence of peasantry. In this case, the peasantry was more than a form of work organization. In the surroundings of the plantations, there was an economic and social conjuncture that marked the limits and levels of autonomy of the workers—either free men, freedmen, or slaves. With the advent of the Golden Law and the general freedom of all enslaved workers, the coffee sector suffered a direct impact. However, other sectors of agricultural production remained as an important foundation of the economy in Rio de Janeiro.[16] The transformations of late nineteenth century Brazil led to a reorganization of national interests—whose main impulses were the end of slavery and the Proclamation of the Republic.

The society changed; the national wealth and the power relations that directed the course of the nation were significantly displaced. Nevertheless, the lives of ordinary people proceeded. In this case, the Black population also underwent a major transformation since slavery, freedom, and citizenship were issues that directly involved them. Although the debate about the course of the nation was restricted to the elite, the impoverished population, formed mostly by former slaves, was also involved in the process. According to José Murilo de Carvalho, though an ideological construction had been carried out, which aimed for a social detachment during the Proclamation of the Republic, ordinary people got involved in the process, revealing a sense of citizenship.[17]

The Golden Law had multiple impacts on national life. The masses of people who had descended from slaves were not indifferent to these changes. At least they would cease being a slave to become a wage earner. An analysis of the impact of the Golden Law in the lives of the Black people is an interesting step toward increasing knowledge about that region during the early twentieth century. According to the *Jornal do Comércio* in 1890, cassava flour, corn, and bean were still the goods that came from places like Magé, Suruí, and São Matheus, places located in the Recôncavo, close to Pilar.[18] This information is repeated in an issue of early January 1900. At that time, the railways had already mingled the transportation of goods and passengers, causing a reaction from the National Service of Public Health.[19]

Some studies have explored the demographic explosion in Baixada from 1930 on.[20] However, it is necessary to leave the statistical data behind and analyze the documents, such as the ecclesiastical books, that have greater opportunity to demonstrate the local reality. Here I chose to quantify the data from the slave baptismal book of Pilar, which, despite the Golden Law, kept being used. Note that the book begins in 1871, with a beautiful opening and recommendations made by the bishop, on behalf of the Law of the Free Womb. However, in the case of the Golden Law, there is only an interval of blank pages, but the records continued to be written in the same book without any recommendation. By censoring skin color, it is impossible to be sure that all entries made after 1888 were of children of former slaves. It is hard to imagine that a freeman under the previous system would have agreed to register his children in the same book of the former slaves—even if the Republic, in theory, would make them fully equal.

For some reason, no entry was registered for about ten years. The book fails to register children in the year of 1888 and only returns to be used in the year of 1897. However, it was possible to identify fathers, mothers, and godparents who "were born and lived" in the parish of Pilar, which shows the rooting of the people in that region even after the transformations in Brazil. Specifically in 1897, only ten entries were recorded. The meager amount limits the analysis, although table 3.4 reveals their location.

Aside from Isabel da Conceição, in the entry of her daughter Etelvina, everyone else, besides being residents, were also born in the parish of Pilar. Surely, this would be the case of people who had settled in that parish before the end of slavery due to the regional trade. But the fact that all the other mothers appear as "born" in the parish of Pilar nine years after the Golden Law demonstrates the fact that the Black population was roote in the Recôncavo during the post-Abolition period. People were born into slavery in that place, but remained there after receiving freedom because they had ties to the land, with other people, within their social spaces and, of course, because they had minimal economic means to maintain themselves and their families.

The box of entries registered in 1897 shows the adoption of surnames in place of color designations such as "creole," "African," "of a nation," and "mulatto," among others so common during the slavery period. Despite the concentration of natural children, which refers, at least on the records, to the absence of fathers, mothers, godfathers, and godmothers, they turned out to be identified by surnames. The reason for these choices

Table 3.4 Baptism entries, Parish of Pilar, 1897

Year	*Child*	*Status*	*Place*	*Father*	*Mother*	*Godfather*	*Godmother*
1897	Joaquim	Legitimate	Pilar	Carlos Manoel Assunção	Carolina Rosa dos Santos	Joaquim Maria dos Reis	Maria Joaquina dos Santos
1897	Victalina	Natural	Pilar	XXX	Antonia Soares da Silva	Francisco Soares da Silva	Elvira Correa de Mattos
1897	Francisco	Natural	Pilar	XXX	Rita Luiza da Conceição	Francisco Vieira Netto	Rita da Conceição Netto
1897	Severiano	Natural	Pilar	XXX	Eufrásia Joaquina Botelho	Luiz Antonio d'Araujo	Felizarda Pereira da Silva
1897	Manoel	Natural	Pilar	XXX	Lucrécia Alves da Conceição	José Teixeira da Conceição	Antônia Drotheia da Conceição
1897	Felix	Natural	Pilar	XXX	Eulídia Maria das Neves	Bonifácio da Conceição	Genoveva da Conceição
1897	Ambrósio	Natural	Pilar	XXX	Maria Ritta da Assunção	Alfredo da Silva	Genoveva Isabel da Conceição
1897	Carina	Natural	Pilar	XXX	Maria Rosa dos Passos	Francisco Borges de Carvalho	Laurinda Justina da Conceição
1897	Joaquim	Natural	Pilar	XXX	Maria Rosa dos Passos	Paulino Ribeiro	Geraldina Ribeiro
1897	Etelvina	Natural	Pilar (resident)	XXX	Isabel da Conceição	Guilherme Maia	Ana Alexandrina de Araujo

Source: Arquivo da Diocese de Duque de Caxias; Livro de Batismo de escravos. Freguesia de Nossa Senhora do Pilar (1871–1888)

is not clear, but considering how often it happened, it seems that family names of former slave owners—particularly of Nossa Senhora da Conceição—were the preferred identification of the Black population in those days. Similarly, Ana Rios and Hebe Mattos found that the surname of the former masters was perpetuated by the Black population of the Vale do Paraíba, even after the end of slavery.[21] In the first decades of the twentieth century, the surname of slave owners became the only tie that connected those people to slavery.

I would like to draw attention to the entry of Severiano, natural son of Eufrásia Joaquina Botelho, whose godparents were Luís Antônio de Araújo and Felizarda Pereira da Silva. The archives also revealed the identity of the creole Eufrásia, slave of Joaquim da Silva Botelho, who had her daughter Hortência baptized in 1874.[22] In both cases, the children were natural; they did not have their father's name registered. However, in the case of Hortência, the godmother was described only as "Devotion," while the godfather was the slave Luis, who belonged to Pedro José Botelho. We cannot say for sure that the slave Luis was her father who served as her godfather. Before 1888, few Black children were legitimate; most had just the name of mother and godparents in the entries. That did not mean the father was absent. In any case, even if the slave Luis was not the father of Hortência, a bond was certainly created between those two people. Besides her mother, Luis and "Devotion" were responsible for Hortência, a minor, according to the Law of the Free Womb.

It was impossible to know if the creole Eufrásia received her manumission before 1888, which would easily explain the adoption of the surname Botelho. It is interesting to note that she became Eufrásia Joaquina Botelho, as registered in the entry of her son Severiano in 1897. Her former master was Joaquim da Silva Botelho. It is interesting to note how former slaves chose their names in the post-Abolition period despite the cruelty of slavery. In previous research, I found the case of an entire family that was manumitted and kept the name of their masters, even baptizing their younger children with the same names of their former masters. However, this was a case from 1857, in full legality of slavery.[23] The recognition of freedom was urgent since the dangerous possibility of being unduly enslaved was always at hand. But the case of Eufrásia was different because slavery already come to an end. It was the time of freedom. Still, Eufrásia kept ties with her former master. We may imagine that she kept on working in Mr. Botelho's plantation, but now as a wage-earning peasant or even a sharecropper. That is only a possibility, since the source does not offer more information about Eufrásia, who was listed at the time as a Creole and named Joaquina Botelho.

After listing the first ten baptism entries in Pilar after the abolition of slavery and having found Eufrásia, who could be the same person found in the entries from the slavery period, I decided to search a little more for her in entries done after 1897. I wondered if she kept on living in Pilar or had moved to another place after the turn of the century. In 1900, Eufrásia Botelho (no Joaquina listed as middle name) had her natural son Benedicto baptized at the parish church in Pilar. His godparents were José Maria do Espírito Santo and Joana Francisca. However, in this case, the entry indicates that Benedicto was born in Iguaçu, although it also states that Eufrásia still lived in Pilar.

The Pilar River is a tributary of the Iguaçu River. Thus, the traffic among parishes of Pilar, Piedade do Iguaçu, and Santo Antônio da Jacutinga happened daily. It is possible that Eufrásia had sought some help for the birth of Benedicto among friends or relatives in the neighboring parish. After all, after 1874 (when she had her first child), twenty-six years had passed. Considering the minimum age for a woman to have children, one can tell that Eufrásia was in her middle ages—probably more than 40 years old. It is needless to say that adequate health care did not exist for her at that time, especially for the Black population of the Baixada Fluminense.

The trajectory of Eufrásia's family, after she had more children and baptisms, would not end yet. In 1905, a woman named Hortência da Silva Botelho had her natural son Paulino baptized; his godparents were the couple Manoel Antonio Sampaio and Rita Rufina de Jesus. It is important to notice that some years later Hortência also assumes the surname of the former master of her mother, with whom she had contact, since he would have been responsible for raising her until the age of eight and had rights on her work until she was twenty-one, as determined by the Law of 1871. In this case, the freeborn Hortência was past the age of thirty and was still living in Pilar, living her life, looking after her children, surely working and attending the same social events.

Following the model of the trajectory of Eufrásia, I sought to identify others who had been slaves and who are in some way identified in the entries registered after the advent of the Golden Law. By then, it was no longer a surprise to find dozens of people who had something to do with those entries. As a method, I have listed the names of all the masters who appeared in the entries between 1871 and 1888. The almost complete absence of them is symptomatic, because it shows that godparenting was a manorial prerogative. Even if the slaves were consulted or occasionally chose who would be their childrens' godparents, the masters were the ones who made the final decisions. The presence of masters as godparents of slaves usually depended on their relation with the owner of the slave. With the end of slavery, former slaves began to choose the godparents of their children, making the godparenting relationship a more effective space for sociability among them. Nevertheless, with the "tip" of Eufrásia, I searched the main surnames from the list of masters and found many former slaves who kept on living in Pilar. Sometimes they had moved to nearby places such as Jacutinga, Iguaçu, or Meriti.

Mr. José Manoel da Câmara appears as the owner of three slaves who had their children baptized in the chapel of Santa Rita da Posse. Their names were Agostinha, Efigênia, and Eufrásia. Besides them, the same master owned Juliana, a slave who was registered as the godmother of the natural daughter of the Creole Eva, a slave of Mrs. Clara Maria de Jesus.[24] Following the surname analysis, it was impossible to find any of those people in the entries registered after 1888. However, different people were found using the surname Câmara. For example, in 1898, Thereza was the legitimate daughter of Alfredo Moreira Coelho and Antonina Proencia Câmara. Her baptism, held at the parish church in Pilar, had as godparents the couple Isak Manuel da Câmara and Euphânia Proencia da Câmara.[25] Similarly, the legitimate son of Amélia Menezes Câmara and Afonso Soares Pereira had as godparents the couple Carlos Menezes Câmara and Sophia Rosa da Câmara in 1903.[26]

Even though I have not found the same people registered as slaves and then as free people using the surname of their former masters, it is possible that entire families who kept the surname of former slave owners were not registering their legitimate children in the same book that had once been used to register the children of slaves. Certainly, those people had some relation to slavery. The presence of families of free people using the surname of former slave owners also offers a dimension of the social rooting process linked to the practice of the peasantry during that period.

Continuing my research, I found the Mattos family. One of the most prominent women in the slave entries was Mrs. Ignácia Antônia de Amaral Mattos, owning eight slave women who were registered as residents of the Santa Cruz farm. The baptisms had been held in the parish church, the chapel of the farm, and the chapel of Santa Rita da Posse. Six different people in eight different entries had the surname Mattos. Again, none of her former slaves reappeared in the entries of the period after slavery. However, what draws attention is the couple Tito Lívio Mattos and Elvira Correira de Mattos, who, besides having a legitimate son baptized in 1899, served as godparents at different times, sometimes together, sometimes separately. Elvira even appears as the godmother of Victalina, baptized in 1897, as seen in the baptism box.

In the search for those people, almost by chance, the African Michelina appeared in the records. Michelina appears as the only slave mother identified as African over all 201 entries registered between 1871 and 1888. At a time of skin color censorship and transformations involving the end of the African slave system in Brazil, the permanence of the African identity is symptomatic. Besides her, some seven or eight men were still identified with the label "of a nation." Gradually, the records made African ancestry invisible for those who contributed so much to the economy and the national culture of Brazil. The registration of Michelina's children contributes to the threads of African memory in the vicinity of Rio de Janeiro.

As we have seen, in 1872 Michelina was a slave of Mrs. Ignácia Antônia do Amaral Mattos, mother of her natural daughter Crescência, whose godparents were Thereza and Bento, slaves of the same woman. According to the entry, this baptism was held at the parish church in Pilar, although, as stated earlier, Mrs. Ignácia owned the Santa Cruz farm, which had a chapel. Mrs. Ignácia Mattos died in 1873 and her slaves became the property of her heirs. Gradually the names of the heirs begin to appear and the name of the matriarch disappears completely. In 1876, Michelina had another natural son, named Manoel, baptized. His godfather was Américo, slave of Captain Luís Ignácio da Costa Vale. Although the entry states that she still lived at the Santa Cruz farm, now she appears as the slave of José Pedro Martins, possibly one of the heirs of Mrs. Ignácia. Despite having a chapel at Santa Cruz, Manoel was baptized at the chapel of Santa Rita da Posse.[27]

It is impossible to know the real age of Michelina or how she ended up at the Santa Cruz farm. However, considering that the slave trade had ended nearly thirty years before and that she already had two children baptized by 1876, we can imagine that she was not a young woman. At least in Pilar, she was the last enslaved African woman. We do not know about her African identity, but, if we consider that more than 78 percent of Africans were from West and Central Africa, it is possible to think that Michelina could have come from any Bantu cultural area.

After the end of slavery, I wondered about Michelina. Searching the surnames of her masters, I found no records of her. However, when I was about to give up on finding the "last of the African women," almost by chance I found a Michelina Ignácia as the godmother of Antônio, natural son of Benevides Maria da Conceição, whose baptism occurred in late 1898 in the parish church in Pilar.[28]

After twenty-six years, Michelina returned to the same church, now as a free woman, to be the godmother of her friend's son. Michelina was no longer registered as an African, although she had never ceased to be one. The invisibility imposed by the change in the post-slavery records and documents was somehow circumvented by her insistence on being recognized as an African. It may not have been the insistence, but the excessive zeal of the priest who registered the entry.

My interest here is the little information available about Michelina's African roots, which help us to understand the lives of people who were taken from Africa to work in Brazil during the nineteenth century. On different occasions, the Brazilian legislation stated the possibility of returning former slaves to Africa. We know, however, that it rarely happened. Besides, Michelina rooted herself in Pilar. Her permanence in the region, even after the final release of all slaves, is proof. In 1898, Michelina may have been a grandmother; her daughter Crescência was almost 30 years old. I do not mean to say that the African references were lost, as it happened in the records, but that Michelina transformed them, turning herself into a ladino African woman. Michelina was an old woman, mother, grandmother, and godmother. She is an example of the collective Black experience that formed the Brazilian population during the early twentieth century.

The African collective experience involved not only themselves, but also all those who were around them. There are countless studies on Africans seeking traces of their identities through their names, either African or adopted, during the slavery period. Perhaps the most famous one is Mahommah Gardo Baquaqua, who adopted an African name when he was a free man in the United States and Canada. Before that, in Brazil, the same person was José Mina in Pernambuco, and José da Costa in Rio de Janeiro, after being bought by Captain Clemente José da Costa.[29] I have researched the meanings of the freed African names in the parish of Nossa Senhora da Piedade do Iguaçu during the eighteenth and nineteenth centuries. It was common to use the surnames of the former masters, but it was also common to use the name of the most appreciated devotion to the Virgin Mary. Apparently, Nossa Senhora da Conceição was very popular among Africans and creoles from the Recôncavo of Rio de Janeiro.[30]

In the case of Michelina, there is an insistence on being identified as "African" in the baptism entries of her children. However, in the only record we have about her after the Golden Law, her name appears as Michelina Ignácia. Unlike most of the people who appear in the period after 1888, she has not adopted the surname of her former masters nor the name of any Catholic devotion. It has been argued that slavery was only a moment, however violent, in the lives of the people who were born in Africa. Slavery was just one of the transformations experienced by those people throughout their personal trajectory.[31] In the case of Michelina, she was not born a slave and she did not die as a slave. Slavery was only a part—a significant part, in fact—but only a part of her trajectory, which began in Africa and went through the painful experience of crossing the Atlantic to arrive at the port of Rio de Janeiro and then reach the cassava plantations at the farm in Santa Cruz. We cannot say if she still had habits and cultural references of her childhood in Africa, let alone what levels of ladinization she had after the Golden Law. However, at least in the early years after slavery, Michelina remained in the same region.

I do not know how the process of adopting the former owner's surname worked. I do not know if only those who remained working for their masters acquired the right to bear their surname or each one made a random choice. Michelina reappears using the first name of her deceased master, a mark that enables her identification, though completely different from the recurring pattern seen in the records. Therefore, I prefer to recall her as Michelina the African. Certainly, much of the cultural diversity of the Baixada was formed through the cultural heritage left by African women such as Michelina.

Notes

1 Arquivo da Diocese de Duque de Caxias and São João de Meriti. Livro de Batismo de Escravos da Freguesia de Nossa Senhora do Pilar (1871–1934).

2 In Brazil, the Eusébio de Queiróz Act was enacted in 1850, determining the end of the slave trade.

3 The word "*recôncavo*" refers to the hollow of the Guanabara Bay. Recôncavo do Rio de Janeiro, Recôncavo Fluminense or Recôncavo da Guanabara were common names used to designate the stretch of land between the city of Rio de Janeiro and Serra do Mar. It was divided into many parishes.

4 See Nielson Rosa Bezerra, *Escravidão, Farinha e Comércio no Recôncavo do Rio de Janeiro, século XIX* (Duque de Caxias: Clio, 2011).
5 Biblioteca Nacional do Rio de Janeiro. OR-095. Freguesia do Pilar, 1872.
6 Ana Lugão Rios and Hebe Mattos, *Memórias do cativeiro: família, trabalho e cidadania no Pós Abolição* (Rio de Janeiro: Civilização Brasileira, 2005).
7 Robert Slenes, *Na senzala, uma flor: esperanças e recordações na formação da família escrava, século XIX* (Rio de Janeiro: Nova Fronteira, 1999), 142.
8 It is important to remember that natural children were those born from a union not recognized by the Church. Sometimes the father was known, but the child was considered natural if not recognized by him.
9 Manolo Florentino and José Roberto Góes, *A paz das senzalas: famílias escravas e tráfico atlântico, Rio de Janeiro, 1790–1830* (Rio de Janeiro: Civilização Brasileira, 1997).
10 Robert Slenes, *Na senzala, uma flor: esperanças e recordações na formação da família escrava, século XIX* (Rio de Janeiro: Nova Fronteira, 1999), 96.
11 Arquivo da Diocese de Duque de Caxias and São João de Meriti. Livro de Batismo de Escravos da Freguesia de Nossa Senhora do Pilar (1871–1934).
12 Ana Lugão Rios and Hebe Mattos, *Memórias do cativeiro: família, trabalho e cidadania no Pós Abolição* (Rio de Janeiro: Civilização Brasileira, 2005).
13 For better understanding of this debate, see Hebe Maria Mattos, *Das cores do silêncio: os significados da liberdade no sudeste escravista: Brasil, século XIX* (Rio de Janeiro: Nova Fronteira, 1998). Roberto Guedes, *Egressos do cativeiro: trabalho, família, aliança e mobilidade social. Porto Feliz, São Paulo, 1780–1850* (Rio de Janeiro: Mauad-Faperj, 2008).
14 Silvia Maria Jardim Brügger, *Minas Patriarcal: Família e Sociedade. São João Del Rei, séculos XVIII e XIX* (São Paulo: Annablume, 2007).
15 See Nielson Rosa Bezerra, *As chaves da liberdade: confluências da escravidão no Recôncavo do Rio de Janeiro, 1833–1888* (Niterói: EdUFF, 2008), 39.
16 Sônia Regina de Mendonça, *O ruralismo brasileiro (1888–1931)* (São Paulo: UCITEC, 1997).
17 José Murilo de Carvalho, *Os bestializados: o Rio de Janeiro e a República que não foi* (São Paulo: Companhia das Letras, 1987).
18 Biblioteca Nacional, *Jornal do Comércio* (Rio de Janeiro, 06 de janeiro de, 1890).
19 Biblioteca Nacional, *Jornal do Comércio* (Rio de Janeiro, 10 de janeiro de, 1900).
20 Marlúcia dos Santos de Souza, "Escavando o passado da cidade: Duque de Caxias e os projetos de poder local, 1900–1964," Dissertação de Mestrado em História, Universidade Federal Fluminense, 2002.
21 Ana Lugão Rios and Hebe Mattos, *Memórias do cativeiro: família, trabalho e cidadania no Pós Abolição* (Rio de Janeiro: Civilização Brasileira, 2005).
22 Arquivo da Diocese de Duque de Caxias, "Livro de Batismo de Escravos," *Assento*, 56 (1874), Pilar, 1871–1934.
23 Ver: Nielson Rosa Bezerra, *As chaves da liberdade: confluências da escravidão no Recôncavo do Rio de Janeiro, 1833–1888* (Niterói: EdUFF, 2008). (Especialmente o capítulo 2).
24 Arquivo da Diocese de Duque de Caxias. Livro de Batismo de Escravos. Assentos 24, 73, 74, 98, 137, 177, 178 (Todos anteriores a 1888). Pilar, 1871–1934.
25 Arquivo da Diocese de Duque de Caxias, "Livro de Batismo de Escravos," *Assento*, 249 (1898). Pilar, 1871–1934.
26 Arquivo da Diocese de Duque de Caxias, "Livro de Batismo de Escravos," *Assento*, 300 (1898). Pilar, 1871–1934.
27 Arquivo da Diocese de Duque de Caxias, "Livro de Batismo de Escravos," *Assento*, 109 (1876). Pilar, 1871–1934.
28 Arquivo da Diocese de Duque de Caxias, "Livro de Batismo de Escravos," *Assento*, 234 (1898). Pilar, 1871–1934.
29 Robin Law and Paul Lovejoy, *The Biography of Mahommah Gardo Baquaqua: His Passage from Slavery to Freedom in Africa and America* (Princeton, NJ: Markus Wiener Publishers, 2007).
30 See Nielson Rosa Bezerra, *Escravidão, farinha e comércio no Recôncavo do Rio de Janeiro, 1833–1888* (Duque de Caxias: APPH-CLIO, 2011). Especially, see the topic: Gracia Maria da Conceição Magalhães: africana, forra, ladina e produtora de farinha, 42–50.
31 Paul Lovejoy. *A escravidão na África: uma história de suas transformações* (Rio de Janeiro: Civilização Brasileira, 2002). Paul Lovejoy, *Identity in the Shadow of Slavery* (London: Continuum, 2000).

4

CASTE, RACE, AND THE FORMATION OF LATIN AMERICAN CULTURAL IMAGINARIES

Laura Inés Catelli

Introduction

In many Latin American countries, various racial terms circulated and became linked to cultural identity during the first four decades of the twentieth century, such as *mestizaje* (José Vasconcelos, Mexico), *mulataje* and transculturation (Fernando Ortiz, Cuba), and hybridity and racial democracy (Gilberto Freyre, Brazil).[1] The circulation of these enduring concepts signaled a time in which many Latin American nations celebrated a century of independence from Spain and Portugal, a drawn-out process that began taking place in the nineteenth century. The construction of national cultural identities during this time entailed engaging with the different local histories of Iberian colonialism. These were vastly celebrated by a *criollo* sector [European-descended ruling classes] that identified strongly with European roots. As a system of domination, though, Iberian colonialism had produced lasting social and racial inequalities, triggered by the exploitation of indigenous peoples and the trade and enslavement of Africans since at least 1492. The reality of a large, impoverished, and socially discriminated indigenous and Black population at the turn of the nineteenth century inevitably collided with *criollo* ideas of integrated, harmonious, multiracial societies that circulated in nineteenth century art and literature, as well as other cultural expressions. Narratives and images of racial and cultural *mestizaje* were used to construct original and attractive images of Latin America, *América Latina*, for a world in which progress and novelty were becoming values in themselves. In this context, the concepts mentioned previously appear controversial, because while they represented Latin American societies as original and homogeneously hybrid (both racially and culturally), the reality of social inequality created by colonial racial dynamics remained largely unresolved. Given that racial inequality still exists, these ideas were not influential and conflictive just in their own time, but continue to crisscross conceptions of national identity and culture today. Cultural imaginaries in Latin America have been tied up with socioracial power dynamics ever since colonial times.

Socioracial dynamics appear as a theme in major Latin American cultural artifacts, like artworks and literary works, almost as an organizing axis. Though race appears as a problematic or a theme in cultural expressions of other imperial/colonial contexts, it does so in a situated, locally specific way. In Latin America, race, *mestizaje* [race mixture], and racial conflicts were deployed and explored from different fields in different local, historical and discursive contexts, spanning from the Conquest and colonial times to early twentieth century modernization. Sociological and anthropological essays like

La raza cósmica: misión de la raza americana (José Vasconcelos, Mexico, 1925), *Eurindia* (Ricardo Rojas, Argentina, 1925), *Casa grande e senzala* (Gilberto Freyre, Brazil, 1933), *Contrapunteo cubano del tabaco y el azúcar* (Fernando Ortiz, Cuba, 1940), to name just some of the most prominent works, take Latin American and Caribbean racial dynamics as a crucial factor in the construction of national culture. At the same time, these crucial essays cannot be said to articulate meaningful critiques of colonialism, racial inequality, racism, and discrimination.

Other works seem to take a more critical stance toward colonial and postcolonial power relations by commenting on racial dynamics. Diego Rivera's *El arribo de Cortés* (1951) (Figure 4.1), depicts the central role that mestizo subjects, and *mestizaje* overall, played in colonial power relations.[2] In the fresco in Mexico's *Palacio de Gobierno*, three European male figures stand facing one another, as in an exchange. One of the men holds a bag of gold, another holds a sword, and another holds a pen. These three objects, held in the hands of the men and in the circle created by their interaction, symbolize main elements in the exercise of colonial power: the obtention and movilization of material resources through the dehumanizing exploitation of Indians and Blacks, achieved through the weight of the conquerors' swords, and legitimized by men of letters [*letrados*]. Outside the circle but in its immediate area, a fourth element appears:

Figure 4.1 El arribo de Cortés 1519 (The Arrival of Cortes 1519). By Diego Rivera. Palacio Nacional de México, 1951. Fresco.

The figure of an indigenous woman behind Cortés carries a blue-eyed infant on her back, a mestizo, son of the conqueror and the woman. The infant gazes directly into the eyes of the observers from the center of a violent scene of conquest. The mestizo gaze destabilizes the closed circle of Spanish power relations.[3] The mural's placement in *Palacio de Gobierno*, a monumental building erected by Hernán Cortés, only meters from the *Templo Mayor* of the Aztecs, underlines the foundational nature of race, gender, and sexual relations and colonialism in the construction of power in Mexico.[4] Furthermore, it shows that *mestizaje* is not simply a metaphor that can be used to describe the historical process of Spanish colonization—it was a power strategy that was used as part of the colonizing project itself.

El hombre controlador del universo (1934) (Figure 4.2), a later mural also by Rivera, takes us to another historic moment of race. The artist works on themes like domestication and the control of life and bodies, linking them with discourses on social evolution, progress, and white supremacy in postcolonial contexts. Rivera painted a second version of this mural in Mexico's Palacio Nacional de Bellas Artes after Nelson D. Rockefeller, who had commissioned Rivera to paint it in New York, ordered it to be destroyed because it featured the communist leader Vladimir Lenin.[5] It is interesting to see the mural convey an explicit linkage between race and capitalism, a relationship that lies at the heart of colonialism.[6] This controversial pictorial work is organized around a central figure: a white, blond, blue-eyed, strong, and able male operator. He controls a great machine that penetrates and organizes the different scenes of the pictorial space with four helixes that contain cells, microorganisms, stars, planets, and galaxies. The mural is a powerful visual synthesis of the deployment of scientific discourses and imagery in the exercise of social order and control in the nineteenth and twentieth centuries. The control of life and thought through politics and scientific discourses,

Figure 4.2 El hombre controlador del universo (Man Controller of the Universe). By Diego Rivera. Palacio Nacional de Bellas Artes de México, 1934. Fresco.

Figure 4.3 *Operarios* [Factory Workers]. By Tarsila do Amaral, 1933. Oil on canvas.

especially biology, is highlighted by Charles Darwin's notorious presence in the mural's lower left quadrant.

The Brazilian avant-garde painter Tarsila do Amaral's *Operarios* (1933), "Factory Workers" (Figure 4.3) also comments on postcolonial socioracial dynamics in her country. This work is seen as marking a change of direction in her *ouevre*, steering it away from the stages known as *Pau Brasil* and *Antropofagia*, which were concerned with the indigenous world of the Tupi, Blackness, and colonization (as well as formal, aesthetic experimentation) to a more more social, class-oriented reflection that also touched on race.[7] Tarsila's large format painting depicts a multiracial, multireligious, and mixed-gender yet enduringly hierarchical industrial working class. In spite of the end of colonialism, the abolition of slavery,[8] and the advance of modernization, a pyramidal structure reminiscent of colonial times persisted in Brazilian society, even in the context of what the sociologist Gilberto Freyre would call a "racial democracy."

Following these examples, race and race mixture in Latin American cultural imaginaries should be understood in relation with imperial/colonial dynamics. The two most well known and researched moments of racial thinking in Latin America are the arrival of positivism and eugenics in the nineteenth century[9] and the culturalist turn in racial thinking during the twentieth century under the direct and indirect influence of Franz Boas, not the Conquest or the colonial period.[10] Yet, race, race mixture, and colonialism still remain intimately entangled in Latin American cultural imaginaries and social dynamics, including the ones in our own time.

Colonialism, Coloniality, Racial Formation, and Cultural Imaginaries

Colonialism is a complex system of relations of domination.[11] As such, it can adopt different forms. Spanish colonialism in the New World had specific characteristics. Intermarriage among different groups, for example, prevailed in Spanish and Portuguese

America much more so than in British America. Also, the *requerimiento* or requisition was a legal tool that the Spaniards began using as early as 1510 to subjugate indigenous peoples, conferring on them the status of vassals to the Crown. The conquerors would read the document out loud to indigenous men and women, forcing them to submit peacefully to Catholic and Spanish rule; that is, to accept conversion to Christianity. Becoming vassals entailed an obligation to pay tribute to the Crown. Any resistance would be interpreted as failure to submit peacefully and, in consequence, as a declaration of war. The latter would warrant the use of force on the part of the Spaniards. In an impeccable performative manner, the act of reading the royal decree automatically put people in categories. When read, it turned indigenous people into vassals or enemies of the Crown, into Christians or heretics. The *requerimiento,* as Rivera's *El arribo de Cortés* could also suggest, shows that Spanish colonialism depended very early on the creation of socioracial and legal categories, like *indio,* in order to function as a system of domination and exploitation.

Many scholars have explored the links between race and colonialism in the Americas through a postcolonial lens. In the context of Latin America specifically, the Peruvian sociologist Aníbal Quijano proposed the concept of *coloniality,* claiming that power relations based on race are intrinsic to the development of colonialism and capitalism. According to Quijano, race as social classification is a *sine qua non* condition for the exercise of capitalist power.[12] In their study of racial formations in the United States, sociologists Michael Omi and Howard Winant also see the Spanish Conquest as the "first" and "greatest" racial formation project.[13] These authors relate race directly to social classification and subjugation. Omi and Winant use the concept of *racial formation* to refer to, "the sociohistorical process by which racial categories are created, inhabited, transformed, and destroyed."[14] This process is accomplished by "historically situated projects in which human bodies and social structures are represented and organized."[15] Furthermore, they affirm that, "From a racial formation perspective, race is a matter of *both social structure and cultural representation.*"[16]

When compared, both Quijano's idea of coloniality and Omi and Winant's concept of racial formation approach the race-power connection through the lens of colonialism. Nonetheless, Quijano's analysis focuses on race on a sociopolitical level, while Omi and Winant, who understand racial categories in social structures as bound to culture, insist on analyzing the construction of race in both social *and* cultural terms. In this regard, Cornelius Castoriadis's work on the interconnections between "institutional symbolism" and "social life" in *The Imaginary Institution of Society* (1975), adds another angle from which to approach the multifaceted mechanisms of race. Following Castoriadis, classificatory practices should be understood as being malleable and specific to context.[17] Furthermore, for Castoriadis classificatory practices need to be understood in terms of their interactions with cultural and social modulations. He claims that the imaginary, defined as a relation between institutional symbolism (classificatory practices of race and caste in our case) and social life (the practices and spaces of colonial life) can arch over a wide array of interrelated meanings, practices, and spaces. Most importantly, what is emphasized is the fluidity of the dynamics between social life and the imaginary.[18]

From a postcolonial perspective, Walter Mignolo has proposed the expression "colonial legacies" in order to identify links between the Iberian colonies of the fifteenth and sixteenth centuries and "the present."[19] Following Mignolo, Latin American racial formations in cultural imaginaries, as in the examples cited previously, can be seen as colonial legacies. Gustavo Verdesio has insisted with nuance that what is interesting about thinking in terms of colonial legacies is not the analogies one may find between the colonial past and the present, but the possibility of prying into sociocultural processes that occurred in the long duration. According to Verdesio, a colonial legacy is not just an "analogy between colonial and present-day situations—something like a stable structural homology between past and present—but rather entails a notion of change and historical process."[20] A postcolonial approach shows that conquest, colonization, nation building, and modern democracies are all phases of a single process in which colonial power relations, sociocultural hierarchies, and other modalities of the power dynamics of colonialism persist beyond this system's formal end, always and necessarily weaving in with cultural dynamics. Thus, questioning racial formations through the lens of coloniality and cultural imaginaries can reveal some of the ways in which colonial cultural processes have produced lasting legacies through effects of their own, multifaceted power dynamics. These effects have taken root to such a point that today social, scientific, cultural, and political discourses in Latin America continue to be imbricated with recognizable, yet fluid, colonial racial dynamics.

With these observations in mind, in the next section I would like to bring to the fore part of the process of colonialism in Spanish America that deals with the formation of a racial *criollo* imaginary,[21] a crucial stage in which specific ideas about race and race mixture were weaved into the cultural and social life of the past to become colonial legacies that still flow through the imaginaries and lived experiences of the present.

Limpieza de Sangre, Caste, and *Casta* Painting

This section focuses on caste [*casta*] as a central and sometimes ignored aspect of the construction of race in Latin America. Because caste, caste society, caste culture, caste logic, and caste power relations need to be understood in their own complexity and specificity, the focus here will be on colonial caste society and one of its cultural expressions, the genre known as *casta* painting [*pintura de castas*]. My intention is to underscore a constitutive aspect of racial formation in Latin America that, in spite of some enlightening contributions, has not received sufficient critical attention outside the extended field of Colonial Studies, neither quantitatively nor qualitatively speaking. Approaching colonial caste society through one of its cultural productions is one way to unearth poorly known aspects of the process through which persistent and recurring social and racial inequalities were bred in Latin America. What happened in colonial times regarding race is relevant and continues to play out in social relations and cultural imaginaries in the present, while postcolonial forms of racism persist.

Historians have explored the topics of racial mixture and caste society in order to understand the specific dynamics underlying the political and social processes that gave way to modern Latin American societies. Many agree that the colonial American caste system had its origins in Iberian ideology of *limpieza de sangre*, or blood purity.

In the Iberian Peninsula of the fifteenth century, having pure blood meant proving to be free from Jewish or Muslim ancestry through the formal presentation of witness accounts and birth documents. A distinction was made between Old Christians and *conversos*, Muslims and Jews who converted to Christianity. Interestingly, this is also a theme in some of the work of Rivera, who was born in a *converso* family. Even though notions of purity and impurity were already in circulation in the Late Middle Ages (roughly the second half of the fifteenth century), the founding of the Inquisition in 1480 made blood purity requirements become more widespread, institutionalized, and linked to stable categories of caste and race.[22] One could say that the Inquisition first institutionalized race categorizing "pure blood" Christians and "impure blood" ones. In general terms, this distinction regulated an individual's access to certain social spaces and occupations, the selection of a spouse, and a general sense of social legitimacy and belonging according to religion *and* lineage. At the same time, anyone under suspicion of impurity could be more easily charged with heresy, and be chastised privately or publicly in *autos de fe*, persecuted by Inquisition officials, and stigmatized physically through visual markers placed or done onto impure bodies.[23] Religious purity was not just a thing of the soul, but of the body as well.

Since Christopher Columbus's arrival in the New World in 1492, these ideas about blood and purity persisted, taking a turn of their own. Interestingly, the first colonizers of Brazil were *conversos* and heretics who had been banned [*degredados*] from the kingdom of Portugal to the New World. These religiously "impure" men married Tupi (one of the numerous indigenous groups that inhabited Brazil) women not just to survive, but as a way of building immense power networks through alliances with their brides' next of kin and through their own mestizo offspring.[24] The Iberian practice of taking indigenous women as wives or concubines was widespread, though, and can also be traced back to the instructions the Spanish Crown gave to the first conquerors in Hispaniola, urging them to "take" indigenous women in order to facilitate colonization and conversion.[25] In the early seventeenth century Peru, the Yarovilca author Guaman Poma de Ayala denounced the domestic and sexual exploitation of indigenous women at the hands of Spanish soldiers, administrators, and priests, in his *Nueva corónica y buen gobierno*.[26] These and other examples alert us to a close relation between colonial control, the governing of bodies, gender, sexualities, and the construction of race, as well as to the presence of "other" views on caste and mixture, and the socioracial dynamics of this period.

As Quijano and other critics have indicated, the resulting diverse and mixed population of the Spanish and Portuguese colonies began being classified, in some cases meticulously, in order to maintain governability and economic productivity. Categories like *indio* and *negro* were deployed twofold. On one level, they worked through religious discourses of evangelization and conversion to Catholicism. The Church exercised control over Indian and Black bodies, minds, imaginaries, and sexualities in a way that was functional to Christian European interests and dominance. On another level, the colonial legal system deployed these classifications in order to guarantee Spanish and, later, creole socioeconomic privilege and superiority over the Black and Indian population, by restricting their rights and determining their place in society. From a philosophical perspective, Sylvia Wynter, in dialogue with Quijano, Mignolo, Omi and Winant, and Fanon among others, sees a process of dehumanization of Indians and Blacks in modern/colonial cultural imaginaries.[27] She connects this process with the classification of Indians as vassals to the Crown, to be exploited as tributaries, and of Blacks as slaves, to be exploited as slaves. Seen in this light, classification according to race and gender created legal categories of subjects that served to produce the conditions to legitimize the brutal exploitation of Blacks and Indians.

Colonial social racialization would gradually beget the formation of *casta* society. This formation has been analyzed partially by historians[28] and sociologists through the study of a diversity of sources, from Church birth and marriage records, documents of Inquisition procedures, testaments, among others.[29] In many of these studies, there is a certain emphasis on tracing the origins and/or the classification dynamics of the caste system.

In *Genealogical Fictions: Limpieza de Sangre, Religion, and Gender in Colonial Mexico*, the historian María Elena Martínez traces the formations of caste [*casta*] and race [*raza*] from the religious ideology of blood purity, along with their imbrication with gender discourses and practices.[30] Following a passage from the Iberian Peninsula to the New

World, she notes that in the Iberian Peninsula, the terms *raza* and *casta*[31] had religious connotations, and worked to construct differentiations on multiple levels while deploying the inculcation of moralistic behavior (Roman Catholic values), predominantly through the control and subjugation of women's bodies.[32] Martínez then moves chronologically and transatlantically, analyzing Iberian racial formations and their deployment in the early stages and areas of conquest and colonization in the Americas. Specifically, she follows the utilization of *raza* and *casta* in the colonies and underscores the changes that the term *casta* underwent in its transatlantic voyage.[33]

The New World use of the term *casta* to refer to the mixed population and the deployment of terms like *mestizo* and *mulato* denote Spanish and *criollo* anxieties over an increasingly "impure" and uncategorizable *casta* population, in spite of the Church's and the Crown's efforts to keep these groups apart.[34] Martínez's work, like other studies mentioned here, links racial classification to colonialism.[35] It also brings to the fore the religious institutional context of the Inquisition where these classifications originated, and situates the specific institutional contexts, categories, and cultural expressions linked to the *criollo* imaginary of the seventeenth century.

Casta painting surfaces in this context, in New Spain (today Mexico), as a *criollo* cultural expression. The art historian Ilona Katzew suggests the genre emerged in part because of creole anxieties over the increasingly difficult task of categorizing (and controlling) the racially mixed population, the *castas*.[36] The large corpus of paintings does show a specific system and mode of representation of racial mixture and social classification. It was mostly *criollo* painters who worked throughout the eighteenth century on the genre, which is articulated completely around the specific modes of social organization and classification of the *casta* system.[37] With a high level of synthesis, the *casta* genre represents creole visions of eighteenth century colonial, caste society. It deploys an extensive range of names and images that revolve around Iberian ideas of purity and mixture, conveyed and recontextualized through multiple versions of one central motif, colonial family groups.[38]

Casta sets are usually made up of sixteen scenes that appear together, on one (Figure 4.4) or separate panels. In each one of these scenes, a man and a woman of different races are shown together with a child that represents the result of their mixture. The groups are portrayed in varying scenes that become more detailed and complex over the course of the eighteenth century.[39] The sets produce a taxonomic effect by using multiple panels with verbal descriptions that include racial legends like "*Español e india, produce mestizo,*" "*De español y negra, mulato,*" "*Indio y negra produce lobo,*" and so on. These racial, sometimes "witty" nomenclatures are one of the genre's characteristics. In all these series, hierarchization is concurrent with racial classification, while occupation, gender, social status, family values, and poverty or wealth, are weaved in with race mixture. Furthermore, the genre deploys colonial and *criollo* symbolism in great complexity, because the paintings were mostly commissioned by European patrons interested in the customs of the diverse population of the New World.[40] As a result, the genre helped to construe an interest in all things American, while becoming illustrative of numerous aspects of colonial social and cultural life that interacted with racial classification, like domestic life, occupations, family life, child rearing, and gender relations.

These increasingly more detailed and complex renditions of colonial society and life reveal certain social dynamics and behaviors produced in consonance with social classification by caste and race. They do so from a specific perspective, the creole one. In this sense, in the first book-length study on *casta* painting, which includes the most complete account of *casta* artists and the genre's development, Katzew offers a succinct overview

Figure 4.4 Las castas mexicanas (The Mexican Castes). By Ignacio María Barreda, 1777. Oil on canvas.

of relevant historical works on the "spread of racial ideologies and the allocation of power and prestige in accordance with perceived racial identities."[41] In relation with this corpus of works, she observes, "precisely how the sistema de *castas* was interpreted ideologically has remained largely unexplored by historians."[42] This is a provoking argument to consider because it points toward an absence of questions linked not to what race is or how it is reified and transmitted through its world of categories, but on race as a situated problem linked to ideology, social dynamics, and cultural imaginaries in the Latin American colonial and postcolonial space.

Casta painting is a cultural expression of the racial project of a colonial, *criollo* elite. In that capacity, it reveals some of the foundational and defining aspects of the racial logic of the dominant colonial caste. We need to understand how *criollos*—the

European-descended, white members of colonial society—interpreted, performed, and manipulated the racial and gender ideology of the Iberian Peninsula in order to uphold their privilege locally. The reason for this is that while the *criollo casta* project may have changed over time, many of its effects remain, especially the centrality of caste and race as organizers of extremely complex and enduring social and cultural dynamics. While *casta* painting as a cultural artifact reproduced a specific racial ideology linked to caste society in the context of eighteenth century colonial Mexico, elements like classificatory racial terminology, or the association of caste with certain behaviors and "belonging" to specific social spaces, continue resurfacing as colonial legacies in Latin American cultural imaginaries and in different facets of everyday life.

Conclusion

From the perspective of coloniality and cultural imaginaries, *casta* painting marks a point of inflection in how race weaves in with cultural imaginaries and power relations. In this sense, while one could analyze the genre as creating, circulating, and reifying racial categories, one could also inquire into commonplaces and themes it set off in the formation of the dominant *criollo* colonial cultural imaginary, especially those where *raza*, *casta*, gender, and sexuality intersect and give way to social power dynamics. Thus, *casta* representations, in paintings, literature, songs, performances, and so on, can be seen as actual cultural devices that aid in modulating Latin American racial formation projects.

Clearly, "race" is not taken here as an object of study (like in physical anthropology, for example) but as the exercise of power by different subjects and groups, as well as the totality of the effects of the exercise of that power. In this general sense, *casta* painting is a paradigmatic example of a foundational deployment of race in *criollo* cultural imaginaries and a crucial piece in the labyrinth of Latin American intersubjective, power dynamics.[43] I approached here a fragment of this labyrinth, one that allows us to obtain a partial view of some ways in which "race" was deployed in the construction of identities and subjectivities in Latin America as well as construed in its social and cultural imaginaries.

The popular concept *mestizaje* is one telling example of the resilience that colonial ideas of race have in our cultural imaginaries. While an idea of *mestizaje* was crystalizing symbolically in *casta* painting in the seventeenth and eigteenth centuries, the neologism itself only appeared in the last decade of the nineteenth century, in the context of the field of physical anthropology. Thus, this concept is charged with colonial and racist significations that circulate mostly unquestioned in Latin American cultural imaginaries. If the latter are predominantly tied up with socioracial dynamics as a result of what we could call a *casta* project (following Omi and Winant's racial formations concept), then much of our questioning can be taken to the realm of the imaginary, where some heavily charged notions remain hidden in a "blind spot," recalling the literary critic Jean Franco's expression for the place of race in Latin American critical thought.[44]

In *Black Skin White Masks* (1962), the Martinican Frantz Fanon questioned these imaginary constructions and their impact in lived experience, situating his reflection in his own transits through France and its Caribbean and African colonies.[45] Taking an anticolonial stance, he referred to a process of racialization that, in the extended Latin American context, appears as a moving mesh of an insurmountable set of practices, images, ways of seeing, relations, contacts, borders, bodies, and words that is constantly being reorganized and is always in movement. Fanon concludes his book with a cry and an invocation to his own, racialized body, to be a constant site from which to question experience and the world of constructions and domination in which we strive to live. Fanon teaches us that the way one understands race will always be inexorably tied to one's body and experiences. As the heterogeneous corpus of works explored here shows, Latin American cultural imaginaries articulate an endless chain of subject positions, a dissonant chorus of voices that tell the complex story of our racial formation. Any one particular version will always be partial and subjective, and in conflict with *other* registers of racial experience.

Finally, thinking about race in terms of racial formation, coloniality, racial formation projects, and imaginaries allows one to envision that race is not something one *is*, but a social, cultural, political, and imaginary construction that takes place in the long duration. As such, it continues to be enacted and negotiated, sometimes violently, in the realm of the cultural imaginaries we inherit collectively, as legacies of the exercise of power by dominant class groups or, more precisely, *castas*.

Notes

1 José Vasconcelos, *La raza cósmica: misión de la raza iberoamericana,* 2nd ed (Buenos Aires: Espasa Calpe, 1948); Fernando Ortiz, *Contrapunteo cubano del tabaco y el azúcar: advertencia de sus contrastes agrarios, económicos, históricos y sociales, su etnografía y su transculturación* (La Habana: J. Montero, 1940); Gilberto Freyre, *Casa Grande e Senzala: Formação da familia brasileira sob o regimen da economia patriarcal* (Rio de Janeiro: Maia e Schmidt, 1933).

2 Laura Catelli, "Arqueología del mestizaje: colonialismo y racialización en Iberoamérica," PhD Dissertation, University of Pennsylvania, 2010.

3 Ibid., 137–139.

4 The subject of the mural is the conquest of Mexico, but it also articulates a commentary on race relations in colonial situations that can be applied to Latin America in general.

5 Robert Linsley, 1994. "Utopia Will Not Be Televised: Rivera at Rockefeller Center," *Oxford Art Journal,* Vol 17, No. 2 (1994): 48–62.

6 Aníbal Quijano, "Colonialidad del poder y Clasificación Social," *Journal of World Systems Research,* Vol VI, No. 2 (2000): 342–386.

7 Tarsila is most famous for her abstract painting *Abaporu* (1928), which broke with traditional, realist painting and experimented with Cubism and abstraction to represent this "man that eats" (the translation from the work's title in Tupi). Abaporu was the anthropofagous figure that inspired the famous *Manifesto Antropofago* (1928) by her husband, the poet and writer Oswald de Andrade. This document gave way to the avant-garde movement known as *antropofagia.* See Jorge Schwartz, *Las vanguardias latinoamericanas: Textos programáticos y críticos* (Madrid: Cátedra, 1991).

8 Brazil was the last Latin American country to abolish slavery, as late as 1888.

9 Nancy Leys Stepan, *'The Hour of Eugenics': Race, Gender and Nation in Latin America* (Ithaca, NY: Cornell University Press, 1991); Lilia Moritz Schwarcz, *O Espetáculo das Raças: Cientistas, Instituições e Questão Racial no Brasil, 1870–1930* (Rio de Janeiro: Companhia das Letras, 1993).

10 Laura Catelli, "The Persistence of Racism in Critical Imaginaries on Latin America," In *Critical Terms in Caribbean and Latin American Thought,* edited by Martínez-San Miguel, Yolanda, et al. (New York, NY: Palgrave Macmillan, 2015), 145–151.

11 Jürgen Osterhammel, *Colonialism: A Theoretical Overview* (Princeton, NJ: Markus Wiener Publishers, 1995), 16.

12 As Quijano argues,

> Two historical processes associated in the production of that space/time converged and established the two fundamental axes of the new model of power. One was the codification of the differences between conquerors and conquered in the idea of 'race,' a supposedly different biological structure that placed some in a natural situation of inferiority to the others. The conquistadors assumed this idea as the constitutive, founding element of the relations of domination that the conquest imposed. On

this basis, the population of America, and later the world, was classified within the new model of power. The other process was the constitution of a new structure of control of labor and its resources and products. This new structure was an articulation of all historically known previous structures of control of labor, slavery, serfdom, small independent commodity production and reciprocity, together around and upon the basis of capital and the world market.

(Aníbal Quijano, "Colonialidad del poder y Clasificación Social," Journal of World Systems Research, Vol VI, No. 2 (2000), 533–534)

13 Michael Omi and Howard Winant, *Racial Formation in the United States: From the 1960s to the 1990s* (New York, NY: Routledge, 1995), 62.

14 Ibid., 56.

15 Ibid.

16 Ibid. (Emphasis mine).

17 Cornelius Castoriadis, *The Imaginary Institution of Society* (Cambridge: Polity Press, 1987), 125. In Castoriadis's own words, "As for the relation between the institution and the social life that unfolds there, it cannot be seen as relation between matter and form in the Kantian sense, and in any case not as one implying the 'anteriority' of one with respect to the other. It is a question of moments in a structure—which is never rigid and never identical from one society to another."

18 Ibid. In fact, for Castoriadis this relation is absolutely fluid, almost impossible to be fixed structurally: "It cannot be said that the institutional symbolism 'determines' the content of social life. What is involved here is a specific, *sui generis* relation, which is misunderstood and distorted when it is apprehended as pure causation or as a pure interconnection of meanings, as absolute freedom or as complete determination, as transparent rationality or as a sequence of raw facts."

19 Walter Mignolo, *The Darker Side of the Renaissance: Literacy, Territoriality and Colonization* (Ann Arbor: University of Michigan Press, 1995), viii.

20 Gustavo Verdesio, "Colonialism Now and Then: Colonial Latin American Studies in Light of the Predicament of Latin Americanism," In *Colonialism Past and Present: Reading and Writing About Colonial Latin America Today*, edited by Alvaro Felix Bolaños and Gustavo Verdesio, 2 (Albany, NY: State University of New York Press, 2002).

21 The term *criollo* comes from the Portuguese crioulo, which is still used in Brazil with its original sixteenth century meaning: the offspring of African slaves born in the New World. It was adopted in the Spanish colonies to refer to American born sons and daughters (criolla) of Spaniards. See Herman L. Bennett, *Africans in Colonial Mexico: Absolutism, Christianity, and Afro-Creole Consciousness, 1570–1640* (Bloomington, IN: Indiana University Press, 2003), 86; Yolanda Martínez-San Miguel, *Saberes Americanos: Subalternidad y epistemología en los escritos de Sor Juana* (Pittsburgh: Nuevo Siglo, 1999) 209; José Antonio Mazzotti, "Creole Agencies and the (Post) Colonial Debate in Spanish America," In *Coloniality at Large: Latin America and the Postcolonial Debate*, edited by Enrique Dussel, Mabel Moraña y Carlos Jáuregui (Durham, NC: Duke University Press, 2008), 3. Antony Higgins has claimed that one of the distinctive traits of eighteenth century *criollo* ideology is the development of a discourse of authority and legitimacy in the secular spheres of literature, culture, and science:

> In New Spain and the other viceroyalties, the structure of an imperial and, at least nominally, theocratic regime remains largely in place, albeit marked by a potentially destabilizing contingency and heterogeneity vis-à-vis subsisting indigenous and African belief systems. Instead, the salient features of a conjunctural tension and located in the domains of authority and knowledge: first, in the spheres of literature and culture; and second, in the modes of scientific knowledge that can be articulated within the traditional regime, so long as they do not threaten its own authority and order.

Antony Higgins, *Constructing the Criollo Archive* (West Lafayette, IN: Purdue University Press, 2000), 5. See also Santiago Castro-Gómez, *La hybris del punto cero: Ciencia, Raza e Ilustración en la Nueva Granada, 1750–1816* (Bogotá: Editorial Pontificia Universidad Javeriana, 2005).

22 María Elena Martínez, *Genealogical Fictions: Limpieza de Sangre, Religion, and Gender in Colonial Mexico* (Stanford, CA: Stanford University Press, 2008), 43.

23 Georgina Dopico Black, *Perfect Wives, Other Women. Adultery and Inquisition in Early Modern Spain* (Durham, NC: Duke University Press, 2001), 1–47.

24 Darcy Ribeiro, *O povo brasileiro: A formação e o sentido do Brasil* (São Paulo: Companhia das Letras, 1995); Ronaldo Vainfas, *A Heresia dos Indios: Catolicismo e rebeldia no Brasil colonial* (Rio de Janeiro: Companhia das Letras, 1995).

25 Laura Catelli, "'Y de esta manera quedaron todos los hombres sin mujeres.' El mestizaje como estrategia de colonización en La Española," *Revista de Crítica Literaria Latinoamericana* 74 (2011): 217-238; Richard Konetzke, comp. and ed. *Documentos para la historia de la formación social de Hispanoamérica, 1493–1810.* 4 vols. (Madrid: Consejo Superior de Investigaciones Científicas, 1953), 5.

26 Felipe Guaman Poma de Ayala, *Nueva corónica y buen gobierno* [1615]. Vol 2, ed. Franklin Pease G.Y (Lima: Fondo de Cultura Económica, 2008), 463, 472, 420.

27 Sylvia Wynter, "Unsettling the Coloniality of Being/Power/Truth/Freedom Towards the Human, After Man, Its Overrepresentation—An Argument," *CR: The New Centennial Review*, Vol 3, No. 3 (2003): 257–337.

28 Katzew offers a succinct overview of the most relevant historical works on caste society. Ilona Katzew, *Casta Painting: Images of Race in Eighteenth-Century Mexico* (New Haven: Yale University Press, 2004), 42.

29 Michel Bertrand, "Las redes de sociabilidad en la Nueva España: fundamentos de un modelo familiar en México (siglos XVII–XVIII)," In *Poder y desviaciones: génesis de una sociedad mestiza en Mesoamérica*, edited by Georges Baudot, Charlotte Arnauld, Michel Bertrand, 103–133 (México: Siglo XXI, 1998); John K. Chance, y William B Taylor, "Estate and Class in Colonial Oaxaca: Oaxaca in 1792," *Comparative Studies in Society and History*, Vol 19, No. 3 (1977): 454–487; Susan Kellogg, "Depicting Mestizaje: Gendered Images of Ethnorace in Colonial Mexican Texts," *Journal of Women's History*, Vol 12, No. 3 (2000): 69–92; Richard Konetzke, comp. y ed, *Documentos para la historia de la formación social de Hispanoamérica, 1493–1810.* 4 vols (Madrid: Consejo Superior de Investigaciones Científicas, 1953); Martínez 2006; Magnus Mörner, "Presentación del tema," *El mestizaje en la historia de Ibero-America* (México: Instituto Panamericano de Geografía e Historia, 1961); Verena Stolcke, *Racismo y sexualidad en la Cuba colonial* (Madrid: Alianza, 1992); Ann Twinam, *Public Lives, Private Secrets: Gender, Honor, Sexuality, and Illegitimacy in Colonial Spanish America* (Stanford, CA: Stanford University Press, 1999).

30 María Elena Martínez, *Genealogical Fictions: Limpieza de Sangre, Religion, and Gender in Colonial Mexico* (Stanford, CA: Stanford University Press, 2008).

31 As Martínez details,

> Raza and casta, terms central to early modern Spain's lexicon of blood, referred to breed, species, and lineage, and thus could be used interchangeably to describe groupings of animals, plants, or humans. Their uses and connotations were not identical, however. Whereas the first became strongly identified with descent from Jews and Mulsims and acquired negative connotations, the second remained more neutral and was hence more frequently applied to Old Christians. But casta also had multiple meanings. If as a noun it was usually linked to a lineage, as an adjective it could allude to chastity, nobility ('good breeding'), and legitimacy, and more generally to an uncorrupted sexual and genealogical history. Casta was thereby able to give way to the term castizo, which referred to notable ancestry. By implication, the mother of a castizo would have been a casta, a woman who had remained faithful to her husband. When applied to humans, then, the sixteenth century Spanish word for casta and its various connotations were alluding to a system of social order centered around procreation and biological parenthood, one in which reproducing the pure and noble 'caste' was mainly predicated on maintaining the chastity of its women. Whethether in Spain or Spanish America, notions of genealogical purity and their privileging of endogamic marriage and legitimate birth were never divorced from discourses of gender and female sexuality, from a sexual economy constituted by gendered notions of familial honor.
>
> *(María Elena Martínez, Genealogical Fictions: Limpieza de Sangre, Religion, and Gender in Colonial Mexico [Stanford, CA: Stanford University Press, 2008], 162–163)*

32 Also studied and analyzed in other contexts by Dopico Black in *Perfect Wives*; Laura de Mello e Souza, "O padre e as feiticeiras. Notas sobre a Sexualidade no Brasil Colonial," In *História e sexualidade no Brasil*, edited by Ronaldo Vainfas (Rio de Janeiro: Edições Graal, 1986), 9–18;

Irene Silverblatt, *Moon, Sun, and Witches: Gender Ideologies and Class in Inca and Colonial Peru* (Princeton, NJ: Princeton University Press, 1987); Verena Stolcke, *Racismo y sexualidad en la Cuba colonial* (Madrid: Alianza, 1992); Lisa Vollendorf, *Reclaiming the Body. Maria de Zayas's Early Modern Feminism* (Chapel Hill, NC: UNC Press Books. 2001).

33

> In the colonial context, Spaniards came up with even more uses for the word casta, for by the mid-sixteenth century it was functioning in the plural, as an umbrella term for the children of the 'mixed' unions. In Mexico, this application of the term began around the mid-sixteenth century, almost simultaneous with the rise of the nomenclature distinguishing people of different lineages, its first and most enduring terms being mestizo and mulato.
>
> *(María Elena Martínez, Genealogical Fictions: Limpieza de Sangre, Religion, and Gender in Colonial Mexico [Stanford, CA: Stanford University Press, 2008], 162–163)*

34 Richard Konetzke, *Documentos para la historia de la formación social de Hispanoamérica, 1493–1810.* 4 vols (Madrid: Consejo Superior de Investigaciones Científicas, 1953); Magnus Mörner, "Presentación del tema," *El mestizaje en la historia de Ibero-America* (México: Instituto Panamericano de Geografía e Historia, 1961).

35 Aníbal Quijano, "Colonialidad del poder y Clasificación Social," *Journal of World Systems Research*, Vol VI, No. 2 (2000)"; Michael Omi and Howard Winant, *Racial Formation in the United States: From the 1960s to the 1990s* (New York, NY: Routledge, 1995); Sylvia Wynter, "Unsettling the Coloniality of Being/Power/Truth/Freedom Towards the Human, After Man, Its Overrepresentation—An Argument," *CR: The New Centennial Review*, Vol 3, No. 3 (2003).

36 Ilona Katzew, *Casta Painting: Images of Race in Eighteenth-Century Mexico* (New Haven, CT: Yale University Press, 2004), 39.

37 Laura Catelli, "Pintores criollos, pintura de castas y colonialismo interno: los discursos raciales de las agencias criollas en la Nueva España del periodo virreinal tardío," *Cuadernos del CILHA*, Vol 13, No. 17 (2012): 146–174.

38 Ilona Katzew, *Casta Painting: Images of Race in Eighteenth-Century Mexico* (New Haven, CT: Yale University Press, 2004), 93.

39 Ibid.

40 María Concepción García Sáiz, *Las castas americanas: un género pictórico americano* (Milan: Olivetti, 1989); *Ilona Katzew, Casta Painting: Images of Race in Eighteenth-Century Mexico* (New Haven, CT: Yale University Press, 2004), 7–9.

41 Ilona Katzew, *Casta Painting: Images of Race in Eighteenth-Century Mexico* (New Haven, CT: Yale University Press, 2004), 42–43.

42 Ibid.

43 Pablo González Casanova, "El colonialismo interno: una redefinición," In *La teoría marxista hoy: problemas y perspectivas*, compiled by Atilio A. Boron, Javier Amadeo and Sabrina González (Buenos Aires: Consejo Latinoamericano de Ciencias Sociales, 2006), 409–434; Leopoldo Zea, (1943) *El positivismo en México: nacimiento, apogeo y decadencia* (México: Fondo de Cultura Económica, 1968).

44 Jean Franco, *The Decline and Fall of the Lettered City. Latin America in the Cold War* (Boston, MA: Harvard University Press, 2002).

45 Frantz Franon, *Black Skin, White Masks* (New York, NY: Grove Press, 1967).

5

AFRICAN FLAVOR IN LATIN AMERICAN MUSIC

Umi Vaughan

The roots of Afro-Latin music lie in West and West Central Africa. Our ancestors who were transported to the Americas as slave laborers brought with them profound musical traditions with a heavy emphasis on polyrhythm and the drum in combination with dance and antiphonal (call and response) singing. Between the early sixteenth and late nineteenth centuries, more than 10 million Africans came to the New World predominately from the region stretching south from the Senegal River through the vicinity of present-day nations such as Sierra Leone, Liberia, Ghana, Togo, Benin, Nigeria, and down through Angola—the majority of them arriving in the Caribbean and Latin America.[1] In all of their homelands, music was organized and performed as an important part of every day life. As such the Black music traditions they initiated in Latin America incorporate the drum and related musical concepts. This chapter focuses on Afro-Cuban batá drumming, *currulao* from Colombia, the *cajón* (box drum) tradition from Peru, and *bloco afro*-style samba from Salvador da Bahia, Brazil. I chose these styles because I am personally familiar with them and because they represent key points along a continuum of African-influenced music/dance styles in the Americas. Each in its own way exemplifies the resilience, ingenuity, and soulfulness of Black music that some refer to in Spanish as *duende*.[2]

At intervals throughout the chapter I have included: (1) short sections taken from field notes I created while conducting *participant observation* research in each setting; and (2) original photographs I have taken during my time conducting said research and in one case by Peruvian photographer Milena Carranza. The field notes move between English, Spanish, and Portuguese, using various text strategies: narrative, poetry, quotations from news and conversation, personal reflections, and anthropological theory. The photographs included in this chapter help convey the *feeling* of the music/dance events by capturing the embrace of the eyes, the expressiveness of drumming hands, and the swinging release of dance—images thus speak along with the text.

There are a wide variety of Afro-Latin music styles. Some of them seem transplanted almost entirely from Africa, such as Afro-Cuban batá, Brazilian Candomblé, or Haitian Vodun drumming. They do involve New World innovations including an evolution of the instruments used, shifts in the language of singing (sometimes incorporating European languages or creole mixtures of European, West African, and indigenous languages), but they maintain a clear relationship to specific, earlier drum traditions in West and Central Africa. These styles usually have religious associations. Additionally, there are styles that are more completely products of New World innovation and mixture, even as they continue to employ African performance principles, such as improvisation, polyrhythm, marathoning, call and response, and so on. Cuban rumba, Brazilian *samba de roda*, or bomba from Puerto Rico are examples. They are totally *criollo*, homegrown in the Americas. Furthermore, there are modern, contemporary styles that go even further combining elements from the former two categories—including specific rhythms and instruments, but also musical concepts—with European instruments and approaches as the foundation for many styles of Afro-Latin dance music from the late nineteenth century to the current day and into the future. Examples include Cuban *danzón* and *timba*, Brazilian samba and *baile funk*, Dominican bachata and merengue, *música criolla* from Peru, and reggaeton.

Drums have come to symbolize African-descended spiritual practices in the Caribbean and Latin America. Drummers play a key role by supporting ceremonial events with music, synchronizing their art with singers and dancers to make these spiritual events *happen*. Whenever a state has attempted to eradicate African religion in the Americas, they have begun by forbidding the use of the drum.[3] The drum was attacked as a dangerous representation of Black identity and agency. The religious communities in question are largely African in character, and participants often sing in African languages. Harassed by Iberian-American authorities, Afro-Latin people maintained evolving music traditions that combine drum, dance, and song in ways that fomented wellbeing in the community. The maintenance of these traditions, against all odds, is a testament to the resilience of African peoples in the New World. Afro-Cuban batá drumming is one great example among many.[4]

The batá are two-headed, hourglass-shaped talking drums originally developed among the Yoruba people of Nigeria. The earliest batá tradition dates back to the fifteenth century reign of Changó—*alafin* [owner of the palace] of Oyo, seat of the Yoruba Empire. In the nineteenth century, as the Yoruba Empire crumbled with the effects of civil war, and simultaneously the agricultural industries of the Americas called for more labor, the batá were transplanted to Cuba and adapted there by related enslaved African ethnic groups that came to be known collectively as Yoruba. The largest and lead drum is called the *iyá* [mother]. The middle-size drum is called the *itótele* [the one that follows]. The smallest drum is called the *okónkolo* [the stutterer]. All together the tones of the drums recreate language to praise and tease or "call down" the spirits, known as *oricha* or *santos* in the Yoruba-derived Afro-Cuban religion called Santería. Whereas in the Oyo area of Yorubaland the batá had saluted only ancestor spirits and Changó himself, king of the drum and dance, in Cuba they were reoriented to address an entire pantheon of *oricha*. The batá tradition was established in Cuba in the early 1800s. Although the drum tradition did evolve and transform as its earliest practitioners reinvented and reestablished it in Cuba, it still lies at the African end of a spectrum of musical fusion sparked by Black people in the New World.[5]

The batá exemplify the kind of precarious history shared by many Afro-Latin music styles from the colonial era. Colonial laws and European racism pushed to eradicate the tradition by proscribing the times and contexts in which Blacks could gather and by outlawing the fabrication of drums. Simultaneously, the influx of large numbers of enslaved Yoruba in the early decades of the nineteenth century and their organization by colonial authorities into *cabildos* [Catholic Church-affiliated mutual aid societies, based on African ethnic origin] inadvertently helped keep the practices alive. Within the *cabildos*, Cuban Blacks had some freedom to practice their old traditions and adapt them to their new circumstances.[6] This situation contrasts with the British North American colonies where protestant evangelism did a lot more to erode and eradicate African musical practices.[7]

Figure 5.1 is from a batá ceremony or *toque* in Holguín, Cuba. The drummers are dressed uniformly in white as a symbol of purity and unity. They wear special hats that

Figure 5.1 Spirit of the Drum. Holguín, Cuba, 2002. Photo by Umi Vaughan.

mark the fact that they are in ceremony and protect their heads from the spiritual power activated by the drumming. The young man whose eyes hold us exudes calm authority and serene intensity. The drums themselves are wrapped with aprons of fabric called *banté* encrusted with beads and mirrors. This adornment is a sign of honor signaling that these drums have been specially crafted, ritually prepared, and devoted to the Spirit of Sound called *Añá* for use in sacred ceremony. The posture of the three men shows fluidity, composure, and power. They stand together and move as one in the performance.

At batá ceremonies like this many African Diaspora performance principles come into play. Drumming, singing, and dancing happen in a circular or semi-circular formation and there are *multiple points of focus* as various or all participants contribute to the event, often through *improvisation.* This communal action or interplay allows energy to flow, be redirected, and redouble to carry the ceremony forward. Thus the performance can last seemingly beyond normal human capacity, beyond "clock time" in a phenomenon called *marathoning* (Think Carnival in Rio de Janeiro, Haitian Rara marches, or conga processions in Cuba). *Polyrhythm* is strong. Each of the three drums in the batá ensemble plays interlocking patterns that form composite rhythms that support song, dance, and other elements of ritual. There is a definite connection between the mundane and spiritual worlds as drummers, singers, and dancers endeavor together to "bring down" the deities to give advice and heal people in the ceremony.[8]

Today I played batá for the first time in a ceremonial setting, which was exciting. I played okónkolo *on four different oricha rhythms (Eleguá to Inle) as a substitute for another drummer who was late. I messed up at the start of the Eleguá rhythm called Latopa and again on rhythm called Ibaloke, because I got nervous, but even still I was proud to have stepped up and not been afraid to play. I was paid 40 pesos (about $1.50 USD) as my*

> derecho *(literally, my right) for sitting down to the drum. Later I sang for a man possessed by Eleguá and got paid 35 pesos for it. The drummers split in half with the singer all the money dropped into the* jícara, *or kitty, as people salute the drums. The lead singer, or akpwon, guides the proceedings with song selection and energy manipulation, seeking the spirit. The derecho for the owner of the drums, who stayed at home in Centro Habana, was about 100 pesos. The sweeter the drums sound, the better organized and punctual the musicians, and the more effective they are in bringing down the oricha, the greater the demand and the higher their price. Drummers for the most part are not rich. On this occasion and others we came and went with the drums by bus.*[9]

Spirit-based drums brought to life African music, song, and dance on American soil, and in time changed much of the music and dance of the world. It brought European music and dance in direct contact with those of the African, and produced a mulato hybrid of rumbas, jazz, cha-chas, sambas, plenas, merengues, spirituals, Charleston, gospel songs, congas, sones, pachangas, and many other rhythms, songs, and dances.[10] These new rhythms were largely secular. But they had overtones/echoes of the older styles. They drew on rhythmic patterns and performance practices from the older sacred music/dance traditions. The new rhythms still conjured "the spirit," activating inspired singing and dancing, creating *comunitas*—the feeling of unity and collective action—but now in gatherings that were not necessarily religious. The rhythm *currulao* from the Pacific region of Colombia is another beautiful fusion of African and European influences in the Americas. It is an important ingredient in the potent contemporary dance music created by Colombian bands like Grupo Niche and Herencia de Timbiquí.[11]

After Brazil, Colombia has the highest population of African-descended people in Latin America. There in the Pacific coast region, the earliest roots of *currulao* music sprung from social gatherings and religious/funerary rites among enslaved Africans in the 1600s. By the 1820s, at the close of the colonial era, a range of variations and sub-rhythms developed that fall under the umbrella of *currulao*. Although this music/dance style is commonly known as *currulao*, the original name of the rhythm is *bambuco*. *Currulao* comes from the name given to the gatherings where the *bambuco* rhythm and related variants would be played. This is community music, performed at street parties, in the backyard of family homes, or at patron saint celebrations in the town plaza. It is poor people's music. Community members of all ages would attend a *currulao* to socialize, eat, drink, dance, quarrel, or fall in love. As in the case of Cuban rumba, Brazilian samba, and other styles from throughout Afro-Latin America the rhythm and the event are one. An old saying goes: "*Se sabe cuando (un currulao) comienza, pero no cuándo termina*" ["It is known when (a currulao) begins, but not when it ends"].[12]

The instruments include two wooden, staved drums called *cununu* (usually with one tuned higher than the other) played with open hands; horns borrowed from military bands; two bass drums known as *bombo* (also tuned to different pitches); and several shaker instruments called *guasá*, made with wooden tubes filled with seeds or pebbles. A wooden xylophone known as *marimba de chonta* replaces horns in some ensembles and has become closely identified with the *currulao* sound.[13] All the instruments are free to improvise, sometimes subtly speeding up, slowing down, or playing seemingly "out of time." Antiphonal singing in classic African Diaspora style is an important element. The rhythm is usually in 6/8 time, with an emphasis on the fifth eighth note. The overall effect of the richly textured musical flow is intoxicating.

Throughout the African Diaspora and within Afro-Latin communities, music and dance are tightly linked.[14] Dance is a central element in the *currulao*. At times a male/

Figure 5.2 Currulao. Valle del Cauca, Colombia, 2013. Photo by Umi Vaughan.

female couple dances, clearly communicating with each other, but without touching. They enact a ritual of *enamoramiento* [romantic pursuit] in which the male dancer flaunts his vitality with staccato rhythmic foot stomping [*zapateo*] adorned with flourishes of a large handkerchief. The lead *cununu* drummer, who emphasizes and encourages the dancer's movements with percussive phrases, closely accompanies these exuberant improvisations from the male dancer. Figure 5.2 shows the grace in the young man's hands and his mischievous smile. The female dancer displays elegance, sensuality, and flirtatiousness as the dance builds to a climax. She wields her dress to entice the suitor and ward off his bold advances. The words to most *currulao* songs are in Spanish and the dancing is secular, referring to no specific deity, although movements are highly stylized and spirited.

> *A lean, ebony-skinned young man enters a circle of dancers, stepping side to side, twirling his bandana up with one loping step and down with the next, approaching a chocolate woman dancer with intricate braids in her hair. He starts to roll his shoulders and hips, circling the woman. His movements remind me of Congolese dances I have seen before. Then he begins to spring back and forth from one leg to the other, rhythmically throwing his arms in the air, while rocking his neck side to side. He brings his solo to a climax when he begins to tap/stomp staccato rhythmic patterns with one foot, then the other—always in communication with the woman dancer and the other folks who make up the circle. This is the third day of the nearly weeklong* Festival de Música del Pacífico Petronio Álvarez *in Cali, Colombia. There are whole families, old folks, groups of teen cousins and school friends, and some crews of foreign tourists assembled on a large sports field, with a huge stage, sound system, and multiple gigantic video screens. Vendors are set up on the sidelines and move throughout the crowd selling bandanas, water, and local drinks like*

viche. *Everyone is here to enjoy currulao and other styles of music performed by amateur and professional groups from throughout the Pacific coastal region and Valle del Cauca.*[15]

Africans were first brought to Peru starting in 1529. In the beginning, they were intended to work the mines of the Andes region; however, soon they were rerouted to the coast. They came from a variety of regions and ethnic groups in West and Central Africa. Over time, their common experiences as slave laborers—as well as their treatment by Spanish authorities and their living conditions on plantations in the countryside or in urban *callejones* [tenement houses]—created a group consciousness that transcended specific ethnic groups. The interactions within music-filled recreational spaces—*tabernas*, bars, brothels, gambling houses, etc.—also helped to develop an entire set of social relations based on African traditions reshaped by the slave experience.[16] The Afro-Peruvian cajón is an emblem of the African presence in Peru. It has influenced much Peruvian popular music and become a symbol of Peruvian national identity. The cajón developed during the colonial era when drums with animal skins were outlawed. Since Lima, Peru was a center of Spanish power in the New World, direct manifestations of African culture including music and dance were more effectively suppressed, stamped out.[17] Even still, the use of percussion and African performance principles survived. Many throughout Latin America use the phrase *duende* to mean a certain musical soulfulness richly influenced by African culture in the Americas.[18]

Africans and their descendants in Peru used boxes intended for shipping merchandise or for use as furniture to accompany guitar, song, and dance whenever the occasion demanded. The first documented mention of cajón as a musical instrument comes from the mid-1800s, though the playing of boxes likely began long before (Figure 5.3). The cajón was considered a "household instrument" rather than a drum, and so largely ignored or missed entirely by authorities, historians, and casual observers.[19] Prohibition and sanctions against African people and their music/dance expressions did a lot to erode specific African musical traditions and eliminate many African instruments. In response, Afro-Peruvians invented new instruments and ways of playing that fit the social environment. Afro-Peruvian musical expressions are often called *música criolla* [creole or homegrown, autochthonous music]. Principle instruments associated with the style are the cajón; the *cajita*, a small box hung around the neck, played percussively by opening and closing the top and striking the side with a stick. It was improvised and adapted from the Catholic offerings box. The *quijada* [donkey jaw bone] is struck with a fist, as well as tapped and scraped with a stick. Cowbell and Afro-Cuban conga drums have also been incorporated as standard instrumentation. These percussion instruments combine with guitar played in a uniquely Peruvian style. Despite being denigrated and criminalized during much of Peru's history, the cajón still managed to mark Peruvian cultural identity.[20]

Since the 17th century there has been an important religious procession in honor of the Cristo Negro de los Milagros (The Miraculous Black Christ) in Lima, Peru. The image of a brown Jesus painted by an enslaved man from Angola survived several devastating earthquakes and was attributed with healing powers. Catholic devotees follow the image in procession or meet it at various points throughout the city on October 18, 19, and 28 each year. Devotees carry the saint along with candles, flowers, and incense, stopping at key points like churches, courthouses, and hospitals. Sometimes Catholic prayers are recited to honor the saint. At other times small ensembles play música criolla *with guitar and cajón* pa' que baile el santo—*for the devotees and the saint itself to dance. Peruvians of*

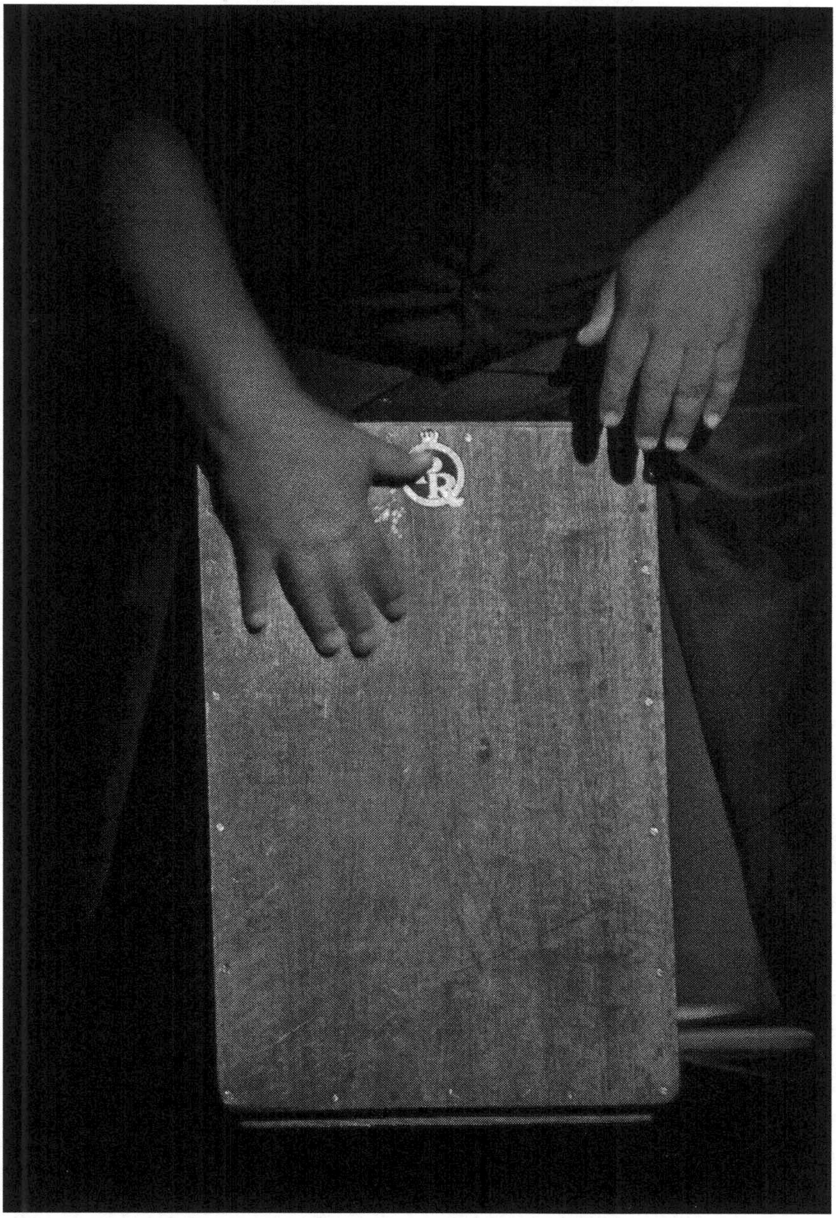

Figure 5.3 Afro-Peruvian Cajón. Cajoneador Papeo Abán performs at the 5th Annual Festival Internacional de Cajón Peruano. Lima, Peru, 2012. Photo by Milena Carranza.

all skin tones and social classes venerate this saint and hold it as an important national symbol, seemingly without much thought about its origin. El Cristo Negro in Lima is a beautiful example of African influence on the dominant Catholic tradition, and the African imprint on Peru's mixed cultural identity. Like so much of Latin America's African heritage, it is visible and incredibly important, but not always seen for what it is.[21]

The earliest Brazilian samba emerged during the seventeenth century in the northeastern state of Bahia, heavily influenced by the religious and musical practices of Africans brought from the Congo or Bantu region of Central Africa. (The area includes modern-day nations such as Democratic Republic of Congo, Congo, Gabon, and Angola). Over time, throughout the eighteenth, nineteenth, and twentieth centuries, samba has evolved into many distinct variations. African musical concepts, rhythmic patterns, and playing techniques were applied to percussion instruments such as snare and bass drum from European military bands. The *batucada* rhythm played by the samba schools [*escolas de samba*] in Rio de Janeiro starting in the 1930s has become the most famous style of samba worldwide.

Samba afro and *samba reggae* developed in the 1970s in Salvador da Bahia, Brazil, a combination of Rio de Janeiro style *samba batucada*, Bahian *samba duro*, and a sacred rhythm called *ijexá* associated with the Candomblé cult houses or *terreiros*. Samba afro and samba reggae have close connections to notions of Black pride and protest, inspired in part by the African American Civil Rights Movement, Bob Marley's Jamaican reggae, and armed liberation struggles in Africa. Within the city of Salvador, the organizations [*blocos afros*] that perform and promote this music constitute important spaces/voices for Afro-Brazilian cultural expression.[22] A family of three bass drums (*surdo 1, surdo 2*, and the slightly higher pitched *dobra*) played with mallets; snare drum; *repique* (a tight, high-pitched drum played with two plastic sticks or alternately with one wooden stick and one open hand); and *timbão* (played with open hands, similar in sound to the West African djembe) are common instruments used to play this style.[23]

Ilê Aiyê was the first bloco afro, founded in 1974. It embodies the link between sacred and secular music, as it was literally born out of the Candomblé terreiro Jitolú, in the neighborhood of Liberdade in Salvador da Bahia. Only Black folks can belong to the group and participate as official members of the annual Carnival procession. Group organizers maintain that their intention is not to exclude whites out of hate, but rather to emphasize the beauty within Black culture through the symbolism of Black bodies unified in performance. They explain that when anti-Black racism no longer exists, this policy will change. Ilê Aiyê represents Black pride, celebrates African aesthetics, and teaches about African Diaspora history/culture in their songs. Every year the Ilê Aiyê Carnival procession is based on a different theme extolling Black culture worldwide (Ancient Egypt, the Congo Empire, Senegal, Esmeraldas Black Pearl of Ecuador, and so on). Songwriters compose a repertoire of songs that develop the theme and compete to have their work chosen. These new songs are performed during Carnival processions along with classics from throughout the group's history of now forty-plus years. The boy and the drum in Figure 5.4 symbolize Ilê Aiyê's standing and function in the Afro-Brazilian community of Liberdade. He stands right outside the Ilê Aiyê headquarters. As he grows up he will receive academic tutoring, attend cultural events, and so forth provided by the organization. He represents the intergenerational transmission of samba in which young people are socialized with music (the drum) as a central element of their identity and way of being.

There are many blocos. Each represents and serves a particular neighborhood and cultivates its own unique style including instrumentation, tempo, and themes. Ara Ketu from Peri Peri, Male de Bale from Itapoan, Timbalada from Candeal, are other longstanding groups. Olodum from Pelourinho may be the most internationally known of the blocos, but many consider Ilê Aiyê to be the best. *O mais belo dos belos*, the most beautiful of all.

It's Saturday night and Ilê Aiyê is about to take to the streets for the first time in this year's Carnival. Before the procession begins, the directors of the bloco and the head functionaries

Figure 5.4 Drum Child. Salvador da Bahia, Brazil, 2008. Photo by Umi Vaughan. A boy raises a repique drum near Ilê Aiyê headquarters.

of the neighboring religious temple (terreiro) conduct a ceremony called Padé, *to bless the group and pray for peace throughout the march. In the ritual they sing in honor of the Yoruba deity Oxalá, the Spirit of Peace and Wisdom and release white doves into the air. After that, a strong woman's voice rises in slow, acapella song, now in Portuguese.*

The atmosphere on the street beyond the ceremony is festive; people eat, laugh, talk, dance enjoying the Carnival. For a long while the singer stirs the energy, calmly, intently calling the procession to order. Later one drummer starts to accompany her song with his timbão. Gradually the entire battery of percussionists—hundreds of men and women strong—begins to play. As we move along the avenue, we open and "cleanse" the way, with spiritual energy, spreading knowledge, healing social wounds. We are a whirlwind of colors rocking and spinning. Channeling ancestral voices. Old and new messages aimed at the future. We are carried away chanting, drumming, and dancing. A thunderous, sweet sound. Singing:

Que bloco é esse? (Ilê Aiyê!)
Quero saber (Ilê Aiyê!)
É o Mundo Negro que viemos mostrar pra voce . . .

[What bloco is this? (Ilê Aiyê!)
I want to know (Ilê Aiyê!)
It's the Black World that we have come to display. . .][24, 25]

Afrodescendientes have influenced musical production throughout Latin America, even in places like Argentina and Mexico where their historical legacy and/or modern-day presence are often overlooked.[26] Today evidence of the African musical legacy in Latin America can be seen in a range of manifestations from sacred and secular drumming traditions, creolized music/dance styles, modern commercial dance music like hip-hop and reggaeton, as well as symphonic compositions. There is *duende* present in styles from across this vast spectrum. This is the African flavor in Latin American music. It has to do with keeping the cultural past alive, maintaining the dynamism and ever-changing nature of the music in the present, moving toward the realization and extension of a vitally beautiful African Diaspora culture in the future.

Notes

1 Joseph Curtin, *The Atlantic Slave Trade: A Census* (Madison, WI: University of Wisconsin Press, 1972), 5–13.
2 Literally, "duende" is a mythical gnome-like creature. But the term has been extended in Spain and Latin America to describe the magic of music and dance. Take for example the phrase "*La Habana tiene un duende que enciende,*" about Cuba's very musical capital, which translates loosely as "Havana's got soul."
3 Joseph Howard, *Drums in the Americas* (New York, NY: Oak Publications, 1967), 105.
4 Ibid., 160–214.
5 For more information about batá drumming see Fernando Ortiz, *Africanía de la música folklórica de Cuba* (Havana: Editorial Letras Cubanas, 1993 [1951]); Umi Vaughan and Carlos Aldama, *Carlos Aldama's Life in Batá: Cuba, Diaspora, and the Drum* (Bloomington, IN: Indiana University Press, 2012); Vélez, María Teresa, *Drumming for the Gods: The Life and Times of Felipe García Villamil, Palero, Santero, and Abakuá* (Philadelphia, PA: Temple University Press, 2000); and Kenneth Schweitzer, *The Artistry of Afro-Cuban Batá Drumming: Aesthetics, Transmission, Bonding, and Creativity* (Jackson, MS: University of Mississippi Press, 2013).
6 Fernando Ortiz, *Los cabildos y la fiesta de Día de Reyes* (Havana: Editorial Ciencias Sociales, 1992).
7 Dana Epstein, *Sinful Tunes and Spirituals: Black Folk Music to the Civil War* (Urbana: University of Illinois Press, 2003).
8 On African Diaspora performance principles see Brenda Dixon Gottschild, "Crossroads, Continuities, and Contradictions," Susanna Sloat, *Caribbean Dance From Abakuá to Zouk: How*

Movement Shapes Identity (Gainesville, FL: University Press of Florida, 2002). On trance possession specifically see Yvonne Daniel, *Dancing Wisdom: Embodied Knowledge in Haitian Vodou, Cuban Yoruba, and Bahian Candomblé* (Chicago, IL: University of Illinois Press, 2005) and Maya Deren, *Divine Horsemen: The Living Gods of Haiti* (New York, NY: McPhereson & Company, 2004 [1953]).

9 From author's field notes, Havana, Cuba, 2001.

10 Joseph Howard, *Drums in the Americas* (New York, NY: Oak Publications, 1967), 110.

11 For more on how regional Black music styles informed commercial popular music traditions that achieved national fame, see Peter Wade, *Music, Race, and Nation: Música Tropical in Colombia* (Chicago, IL: University of Chicago Press, 2000).

12 Germán Patiño, *Con vose de caramela: aproximaciones a la música del Pacífico colombiano* (Cali, Colombia: Alcaldía de Santiago de Cali, Secretaría de Cultura y Turismo, 2013), 15–17, 39.

13 Marimba were adopted from the native (Indian) population in Esmeraldas, Ecuador and taken from there to Cauca (Colombia) in the 1600s by enslaved Blacks who would move back and forth between plantations and mines throughout the region carrying their music/dance with them (Ibid., 24).

14 For more on the connection between music and dance see George H. Béhague, ed., *Music and Black Ethnicity: The Caribbean and South America* (Miami, FL: North-South Center, University of Miami, 1994); Yvonne Daniel, *Rumba: Dance and Social Change in Contemporary Cuba* (Bloomington, IN: Indiana University Press, 1995) and Yvonne Daniel, *Dancing Wisdom: Embodied Knowledge in Haitian Vodou, Cuban Yoruba, and Bahian Candomblé* (Chicago, IL: University of Illinois Press, 2005); Katherine Dunham, *Dances of Haiti* (Los Angeles, CA: UCLA Press, 1983); Susanna Sloat, *Caribbean Dance From Abakuá to Zouk: How Movement Shapes Identity* (Gainesville, FL: University Press of Florida, 2002); and Umi Vaughan, *Rebel Dance, Renegade Stance: Timba Music and Black Identity in Cuba* (Ann Arbor, MI: University of Michigan Press, 2013).

15 From author's field notes, Cali, Colombia, 2014.

16 Rosa Elena Vázquez Rodríguez, *La Práctica Musical de la Población Negra en el Perú* (Havana: Casa de las Américas, 1982), 17.

17 See Luis Rocca Torres, *Herencia de Esclavos en el Norte del Perú* (Lima: Centro del Desarrollo Étnico—CEDET, 2010).

18 Caitro Soto, *Del Cajón, Caitro Soto: El duende en la música afroperuana* (Lima, Peru: Servicios Especiales de Edición S.A. del Grupo Editora El Comercio, 1995), 9–11.

19 Rafael Santa Cruz, *El Cajón Afroperuano* (Lima, Peru: Cocodrilo Verde Ediciones, 2004), 19.

20 For more on how black instruments and styles moved from rejection to acceptance in the mainstream, see Robin Moore, *Nationalizing Blackness: Afrocubanismo and Artistic Revolution in Havana, 1920–1940* (Pittsburgh, PA: University of Pittsburgh Press, 1997); Alma Guillermoprieto, *Samba* (New York, NY: Vintage Press, 1991); and Peter Wade, *Music, Race, and Nation: Música Tropical in Colombia* (Chicago, IL: University of Chicago Press, 2000).

21 From author's field notes, Lima, Peru, 2015.

22 Goli Guerreiro, *A trama dos tambores: a música afro-pop de Salvador* (São Paolo: Editora 34, 2000).

23 Usually no harmonic instruments are included, but some groups will incorporate them at times to achieve a more pop sound. Olodum, Muzenza, Ara Ketu, and Timbalada (under the direction of Carlinhos Brown) have iterations of their bands that use horns, synthesizers, and so on.

24 The lyrics to this song "Que Bloco é esse?" were written by famous Brazilian singer Gilberto Gil and appear on Ilê Aiyê's 1992 album *Canto Negro.*

25 From author's field notes, Salvador de Bahia, Brazil, 2009.

26 See George Reid Andrews, *Afro-Latin America, 1800–2000* (Oxford, UK: Oxford University Press, 2004); George Reid Andrews, *The Afro-Argentines of Buenos Aires, 1800–1900* (Madison, WI: University of Wisconsin Press, 1980); Robert Farris Thompson, *Tango: The Art History of Love* (New York, NY: Vintage Books, 2006) and Marta E. Savigliano, *Tango and the Political Economy of Passion* (Boulder, CO: Westview Press, 1995); on Panama see Victoriano Arturo Gavidia, *Diablitos de Espejo: Una Tradición Portobeleña* (Colón, Panamá: Emprenta Árticas, 2011); Gonzalo Aguirre Beltrán, *La población negra de México* (Veracruz, Mexico: Universidad Veracruzana. 1989 [1946]).

6

THE POLITICS OF ENUNCIATION

Indigenista and Contemporary Indigenous Literatures

Gloria E. Chacón

During my undergraduate years, I resided in the Pioneer Valley of Massachusetts. The Five College Consortium offered students a wide range of courses.[1] One of the first Latin American literature courses I took was in the sister institution next to my alma mater. I had never been exposed to Latin American literature in my high school, and was eager to immerse myself in the experience. The faculty member methodically discussed the different thematic and chronological components of the syllabus. We followed along, then, suddenly, he came to an abrupt halt for the section organized under Pre-Columbian Literature. "We'll skip this segment," he stated. Everything that is considered indigenous literature, he continued, was written under Christianity and in Latin letters. Although our immigrant experience played out in Los Angeles, my family never severed its ties to its Maya Ch'ort'i origins. The Ch'ort'i communities have historically shared the territories intersecting the geopolitical boundaries of Guatemala, El Salvador and Honduras, referred to as el Trifinio.[2] The professor's position ran counter to my understanding of literature because of all the stories I had learned growing up, including the various stories of Uncle Rabbit and Uncle Coyote, cadejos, and those of people who transform, the nahuales, which are also prevalent among other indigenous communities on the continent.

A couple of years later as I explored further into the field of Latin American literature, in a more advanced course, a different professor challenged my critique of José Saer's *The Witness* as a European perspective. Cannibalism and orgies were documented, she said, therefore Saer's perspective about the practices he described was not exclusively a European interpretation of history, but rather on factual and documented events.[3] My attempts to point out that readers were never offered access to the indigenous view were unsuccessful, and I resigned myself to her assessment of my paper. Of course, these frustrating and isolated anecdotes were not the norm as I also met many more professors throughout the colleges who vehemently defended and valued my views. Coincidentally, in the course of my early college years, indigenous peoples throughout the continent began to loudly protest Columbus Day during the 1990s. The Quincentennary celebration, a spectacle organized by Spain and Italy that tacitly assumed everyone in the world would celebrate Columbus's so-called discovery of America, spurred a continental protest movement. Colleges throughout the Pioneer Valley in Massachusetts (as I am sure happened in other states) opened up spaces for indigenous intellectuals and other activists from various parts of the Americas to share their histories of resistance and the problems they continued to face from the ongoing reality of colonization.[4] Swept in this fervor of change, other sister institutions programmed various events to offer indigenous intellectuals a forum to express themselves. After one of those events, I ran into my former professor. She approached me and expressed regret for not understanding my critique of Saer's *The Witness.* Native American and indigenous activism made her aware of the existence of alternative historicity and changed not only her rethinking of historical facts, but made her aware that indigenous peoples continued to resist colonialism and that the academy was not neutral but complicit. Since then, many things have changed in the world and my life, but twenty-five years later the absence of indigenous literature still resonates in Latin American Literary Studies.

Although I recognize personal anecdotes are subjective, in the context of this essay, I raise them to illustrate a continuous absence of indigenous works of fiction in Latin American literary studies taught in higher education institutions. Most of our curriculum continues to ignore up-and-coming indigenous authors; instead, courses focus on more cosmopolitan and *indigenista* writers, or in the more progressive cases, the testimonio—a genre that has occupied center stage in the North American academy until now.[5] Textbooks that offer an account of indigenous literature tend to focus on colonial indigenous literature emphasizing that these are accessible due to the adoption and adaptation of a European writing system. Others advance a more folkloric stance, focusing on oral literature, prayers, and song. In trying to offer a different way of thinking about indigenous literatures in Mesoamerica, this essay addresses three fallacies that continue to dominate discussions around indigenous literary production.[6] The first one has to do with the widely accepted premise that indigenous peoples did not have writing until Europeans introduced the alphabet; second, that indigenous literature can be compartmentalized through a traditional orality/literacy divide; and third, that authenticity should be associated to a pre-Columbian way of being in the world. In this essay, I offer a short historiography of contemporary indigenous literature produced in the late twentieth century and twenty-first century and emphasize how they depart from these three assumptions to carve out a new intellectual, political, and artistic space that challenges nation-state lines. More important, by offering this short historiography, I delineate how it differs from the *indigenista* literary trend and the more canonical Latin American tradition as it establishes its own tradition—one that precedes nation-state formations.

Indigenista literature represents but one strand in an array of *indigenismo*-inspired political and aesthetic projects in Latin America.[7] Giraudo and Lewis argue that a pan-American *indigenismo* emerges in the 1940s with the creation of the Inter-American Indian Institute, ironically funded by the United States. That decade also marks the formation of different entities throughout the Americas, following the initial meeting of nation-state heads that sought to address the "Indian problem."[8] While the first *indigenista* novel dates back to the nineteenth century, the core corpus was written in the first half of the twentieth century. Many of the novelists espoused politically progressive ideas and expressed sympathy to the indigenous communities they wrote about in their ouvres.[9] The intellectuals and writers who defended *indigenismo* believed that indigenous peoples represented an exploited class, and needed to come to consciousness to articulate a class struggle.

The struggle for representation manifests through fundamental distinctions between indigenous and *indigenista* literature, where the latter represents those texts written about indigenous peoples by non-indigenous writers. I argue that contemporary indigenous literatures depart from the *indigenista* tradition because they offer new ways of thinking about bilingual writing, orality, and history. Of course, it is important to acknowledge that reading the work of a writer like Peruvian José Maria Arguedas who grew up speaking Quechua and with close ties to this community makes one question this division.

But, my focus here is on those *indigenista* writers who constructed an image of the Indian in stereotypical ways. Furthermore, indigenous literature aims to gain equal terrain in the way knowledge travels and is received locally and globally. These texts make clear that who speaks, writes, paints, or acts is critical to forging an indigenous literary tradition in Mesoamerica.

Marxist critic José Maríategui first proposed the difference between indigenous and *indigenista* literatures in the 1920s. Maríategui explains that readers cannot expect *indigenista* literature to be indigenous as an indigenous literature had yet to come.[10] Antonio Cornejo Polar, of course, interrogates this intervention by asserting that Maríategui does not take into account oral literature or other forms like performance and songs. In the Guatemalan context, Miguel Angel Asturias, considered one of the most foundational Guatemalan writers, utilized Maya texts and culture to create his novels. The critic Luis Cardoza y Aragón argues that Asturias's work moves beyond the *indigenista* novel because he "universalized the Indian." Cardoza y Aragón characterizes the *indigenista* novel as incapable of fully penetrating the Indian's reality, because it represented only an exotic, superficial image. He writes:

> *Todo eso de indios mágicos y otras puerilidades suele ser ocultamiento impensado de lo recóndito y esencial. Cuando se muestra a los indios, burlados como muñecos, los visten de piñatas, los visten de tarjeta postal* [All that stuff about magical Indians and other childishness conceals thoughtless ideas about the unknown and essentialism. When Indians are exhibited, ridiculed as toy dolls, they dress them like piñatas, they dress them like post cards].[11]

Cardoza y Aragón rightfully dismisses the *indigenista* narrative as a gaze from above and as a tradition of paternalism. However, when referring to indigenous literature and specifically the novel, Cardoza y Aragón asserts that "*cuando los indios acierten a escribirlas [las novelas] intuyo que tendrán coloración mestiza*" ["When the Indians actually get to write them [novels] I suspect that these will have a mestizo sensibility"].[12] Both Latin American thinkers assume historical truths. The first one, as literary critic Cornejo Polar identifies, has to do with the conception of literature as strictly alphabetic. Cardoza y Aragón's use of *acierten* assumes the genre may be more of a challenge and thus indigenous writers will produce them, but with a mestizo sensibility, meaning that somehow the act of writing and intellectual work is not indigenous. In counterpoint, the Maya linguist and anthropologist Fidencio Briceño Chel, explains that there is a point where *indigenista* traditional and indigenous literature *"se entrecruzan, se entretejen y sale esa mezcla de historia, fantasía, realidad."* [they intersect, intertwine and produce that mixture of history, fantasy, reality.][13] The Zapotec intellectual Victor de la Cruz adds to the debate by arguing that the main difference between *indigenista* and indigenous literature lies in the movement of indigenous intellectuals from the oral to the written.[14] This said, Cruz is highly critical of the notion of "oral literature" and terms it "a monstrous concept" because for him the term reveals a prejudicial limitation attributed to indigenous people and tied to the written even if (according to him, the oral tradition) has nothing to do with writing.[15]

In my analysis, I assert that the most radical difference between *indigenista* and contemporary indigenous literature lies in the politics of enunciation.[16] While the relationship between *indigenista* and indigenous literature may be seen as diametrically opposed, the discursive and symbolic connection may be far more complex as noted by Briceño Chel previously. In *The Inner Life of Mestizo Nationalism*, Estelle Tarica sees *indigenismo* as a connecting "individual aspirations to the mystique of nationalist thought and enables them to coalesce."[17] The relationship between these two literary traditions may be through Edward Said's contrapuntal reading as described in *Culture and Imperialism.* Said advances his idea of a contrapuntal reading as a way of reading back and realizing what was subjugated.[18] To return to the title of my essay, what is at stake is history, who gets to narrate the story, and the power relations involved. A contrapuntal reading of *indigenista* and indigenous texts exemplifies to a great degree the epistemic and ontological investments in a decolonial process through writing.[19] Of course, this decolonization process is not exempt from contradictions. In 2013, a celebration of indigenous peoples day took place in Chiapas, showcasing indigenous poets, musicians, and other artists. However, the most arresting event had to be the presentation of Rosario Castellanos' poetry, *El rescate del mundo,* which debuted in a multilingual compact disc.[20] Castellanos, considered a foundational writer in Mexico, did not have an indigenous family background, but she successfully and beautifully dramatizes the Indian/ladino conflict in her novels.[21] Contemporary writers in Chiapas see her work as sharing their plight against racism in Chiapas. Castellanos wrote memorably about her Indian nanny and other characters whose representations oftentimes relied on racist stereotypes. Mayan nannies doted on Castellanos; indeed, as a child the writer had a girl servant to play and care for her until her death.[22] Indigenous writers Roselia Jiménez (Tojolabal), Mikeas Sánchez (Zoque), Adriana López (Tseltal) and Enriqueta Lunez Pérez (Tsotsil) translated the poems for this project into the main indigenous languages of Chiapas. To return to Said's contrapuntal reading, what does this multilingual collaborative project represent? In a way, this type of cultural production speaks to the complex ways indigenous writers relate to *indigenista* writers and their work. We can hear indigenous poets ventriloquizing Castellanos, in that sense they invert her gaze, if you will. Nonetheless, we cannot forget that Rosario Castellanos worked for the INI (National Indigenist Institute). This fact is important because the INI opened its first offices in Chiapas as a kind of testing ground or pilot to be implemented in the rest of Mexico. Needless to say, the agency had as its main mission the assimilation of indigenous peoples, but Castellanos' novels and short stories candidly illustrate the racism, sexism, and classism embedded in the elite families of Chiapas. In addition to representing the racism in her novels, Castellanos' work for the INI offers another complex dimension to the *indigenista* and indigenous relationship. Castellanos's work through the INI led her to write the scripts for the plays performed by Petul theater. This performance troupe sought to instruct the indigenous community in hygiene, gender relations, and health. In other words, a contrapuntal analysis requires an analysis of Castellanos as a feminist writer who tried to distance herself from the racism that plagued her class, but who benefited from indigenous servants and nannies throughout her life.[23] In an ironic twist, the legacy of this theater in the highlands inspired the work done by Tzotsil and Tzeltal actors in the 1980s.[24] Accordingly, one of the members of a now rather famous indigenous theater troupe recalled how part of the impetus for organizing a puppet theater was his father's role in Petul Theater. His father had conserved the puppets. In Said's methodological contribution, we can read both *indigenista* literature and indigenous literature to understand the foundational contributions of indigenous writers.

Indigenismo and Literary Forms

Despite the relational complexities that may be drawn between *indigenista* and indigenous literary production, or in the different manifestations of literary *indigenismo,* my interest is in how certain *indigenista* authors exploited the image of indigenous characters as abject, uneducated, and inarticulate. Some of these texts clearly exhibit a historical denial of "other ways of knowing," the subjugation of indigenous languages, and demonstrate the pervasive racism of Latin American societies. Noteworthy is that the *indigenista* literary tradition in Latin America reaches its most mature expression in the genre of the novel. The Peruvian literary critic Antonio Cornejo Polar incisively notes that *indigenista* intellectuals utilized the genre of the novel in particular to announce the demise of indigenous peoples.[25] Prominent writers in Latin America used indigenous material to write their novels. Miguel Angel Asturias and Francisco González Rojas were paradigmatic in this regard. Q'anjobal writer Gaspar Pedro González, in an interview by Robert Sitler conducted in the 1990s, charges that Miguel Angel Asturias obtained the Nobel Literature Prize precisely because he wrote about Mayas.[26] González asserts that a day will come when more Maya writers will have emerged so as "to expand our own concepts that differ from Asturias."[27] He concludes that Mayas were simply another resource Asturias utilized. In this context, Gaspar Pedro González offers a severe critique of the *indigenista* literary tradition. The Maya writer concludes that Miguel Angel Asturias was opportunistic at best. He accuses that Asturias:

> *ve en la situación del indio una oportunidad para poder sobresalir él. Pero de ninguna manera valora aquella persona humana. Cuando viaja Miguel Ángel Asturias a Europa, especialmente Francia, comienza a madurar y aprende a sentir la importancia de la civilización maya ante sus anfitriones. Su visión es una visión ladina sobre los mayas* [sees in the situation of the Indian an opportunity to self-profit. But does not in anyway value the person. When Miguel Angel Asturias travels to Europe, especially France, he begins to mature and learns to perceive just how important the Mayan civilization is to his hosts. His vision is a vision of a ladino].[28]

Gaspar Pedro Gonzáles illustrates the way that writers appropriate indigenous culture for their own means to an end, and in this case, for national identity.

In Mexico, where the institutionalization of *indigenismo* acquired greater force, indigenous writers have consistently differentiated their work from the *indigenista* tradition. Zapotec novelist Javier Castellanos Martínez, in his essay, "Los que hablamos Dila Xhon" takes to task the work of an important *indigenista* writer Francisco Rojas González. Castellanos Martínez discusses Rojas González's "La Tona," a short story included in his collection, *El diosero.* Castellanos Martinez accuses the *indigenista* writer of representing indigenous people from the sierra in an animalistic and uneducated way.[29] Castellanos Martinez condemns the racist way Francisco Rojas González represents the young indigenous woman. He specifically focuses on this description:

> *sus pies-garra a ratos, pezuñas por momentos-resbalan sobre las lajas, se hundían en los líquenes o se asentaban como extremidades de plantígrado en las planadas del serillo* [her feet—claws at times, hooves at other times—slipped on the flagstones, sunk in lichens or settled like the extremities of plantigrade in the plains of the hill].[30]

In Castellanos Martinez's critique, what is dangerous here is not only that the *indigenista* author does not actually know the topography of the region, but that he also personifies the character as an animal. The Zapotec novelist asserts that:

> Para el que se siente y es parte de la gente como la que menciona Francisco Rojas González, la comparación con animales es burlesca, denigrante e innecesaria

> For he who feels part and is part of the people like those mentioned by Francisco Rojas González, the comparison to animals is mocking, humiliating and unnecessary.[31]

Castellanos Martínez underscores that the description of this *indigenista* writer contrasts with how the Zapotec know the region. Similar to the critique of other indigenous writers, the Zapotec author identifies two of the most notable characteristics of *indigenista* literature in the continent—mainly, the animalistic comparisons and the linguistic disfiguration of the Indian characters' speech. The novelist concludes that when an indigenous subject reads this type of narrative, he or she is doubly humiliated.

The *indigenista* narrative tradition—in its very definition—functions in opposition to the concerted effort by indigenous writers who make indigenous literature possible. The decade spanning between the 1980s and 1990s marked the consolidation of a group of indigenous writers and intellectuals who articulated the importance of producing literature as part of cultural (re)vindication movements in Mexico and Guatemala. Their entrance into the literary world challenged the monolingual and mestizo paradigm entrenched in official discourse thereby reenergizing the power of literature and the humanities. Ironically, the palpability of their work surfaces at a time when the humanities in general are devalued around the world. Of course, the irruption of indigenous writers in the literary terrain does not necessarily put an end to *indigenista* literature.[32]

The Formation of an Indigenous Literary Tradition

In stark contrast to the *indigenista* literary tradition, the protagonists of the indigenous literary movement, particularly in the 1980s, insisted on a unique *cosmovisión* manifested through their works in what I refer to as a millenarian literary tradition. Q'anjob'al novelist and critic Gaspar Pedro González in *Kotz'ib', nuestra literatura maya* (1997) writes that *cosmovisión* can be found in numerous community-making sites such as in the oral tradition, the discourse in textile signs, and in the written tradition (both in glyphs and alphabetic systems). In its most recent iteration, the critic Arturo Arias synthesizes *cosmovisión* in English to refer to the Mayas in the Guatemalan context as the "will to become constituted as subjects through an agency process permeated by the community's cultural values, regardless of whether these are liminal to Western values or a hybrid of both Western and ladino values."[33] This strategic posture enables writers to conjure literary legacies that date to pre-Columbian contact, allowing them to claim a two thousand years-old literary tradition. The writers involved in proclaiming a millenarian literary tradition affirmed the continuity of oral traditions and the memory of hieroglyphic writing. While it is important to note that not all contemporary indigenous writers continue or adhere to this millenarian discourse, all of the first generation of bilingual writers expressed this epistemological difference vis-à-vis other literatures in the 1980s. In that sense, the first generation of writers advanced an alternative way of periodizing the work of contemporary indigenous writers whose stake in knowledge and literature production aims to dismantle vestiges of colonialism. My work does not discount the newer generation of writers who think of their creative efforts differently, but rather engages with the strategies that the first generation of writers deployed at a time when they could not dialogue with or distinguish themselves from any living predecessors. Thus, these writers took on the task of thinking about their work in relationship and in difference to the literary frameworks established in Latin America.

Writers identify three contemporary literary practices that are not characterized in a linear or evolutionary fashion.[34] Many theorize this literature as having not only political but aesthetic aims. In that sense, the writers conform to conventional ideas about literature as having an aesthetic component by definition. The most widely recognized manifestation of indigenous literatures is the oral tradition, including stories, anecdotes, performance, and spiritual beliefs passed down from generation to generation. The second component—described as *recopilación* or the writing down of stories, anecdotes, fables and songs by members of the different Maya communities—aims to preserve and perpetuate these stories to larger audiences. These literary modalities serve as a point of departure for the third discursive practice carried out by the *creadores* or creators. These individuals consciously frolic with language to generate their own literary enterprises inspired by both oral and written traditions. All three discursive modes are also seen as co-existing simultaneously and all continue to be seen as important in the articulation of an indigenous identity and its preservation.

At the onset of the indigenous literary movement, writers and intellectuals remained steadfast in privileging the oral tradition to preserve the elders' stories of their respective communities. The oral tradition, rhetorically or otherwise deployed, served an important role in maintaining a different literary genealogy locally while at the same time, reinforced the idea of orality as the origins of all literature (i.e., the *Odyssey*, *Iliad*, and the *Bible*) as well as the idea of transmission. The Maya-K'iche' poet Humberto Ak'abal, for instance, incisively notes, "*la oralidad es el pilar de la literatura universal no solamente de la indígena*" ["orality is the pillar of universal literature not just of indigenous literature"].[35] As writers and other intellectuals gained audiences and more publishing territory, they also affirmed intertextuality with pre-Columbian references in the *Popol Wuj, the Chilam Balam, Los Cantares de Dzitbalché* and *Los anales de los Kaqchikeles*—texts that also referenced a glyphic tradition. This initial millenarian literary discourse contested and reconfigured the traditional Latin American literary and cultural model that positioned them outside the production of literature.

Implicit in the making of this millenarian literary tradition is a *cosmovisión*, a lens that enables writers to carve out a new conceptual, literary, cultural, political, and social space. In this strategic move, writers defy temporality and the conventional dating of Maya literature and reclaim hieroglyphs and the oral tradition. Although literary publications do not proliferate until the 1990s, key writers like Jorge Cocom Pech (from the Yuacatán Peninsula), Feliciano Sánchez Chan (from the Yuacatán Peninsula), Briceida Cuevas Cob (from the Yuacatán Peninsula), Humberto Ak'abal (Maya K'iche' from Guatemala), Gaspar Pedro González (Maya Q'anjobal from Guatemala), and Victor Montejo (Maya Pop ti' from Guatemala), among many others, publicly asserted that contemporary literature is a continuance of the millenarian traditions of indigenous peoples. Writers take their cues from the existing references to hieroglyphic writing in Maya colonial texts as well as physical evidence such as lintels and stelae. Victor Montejo, for example, sustains that "the Maya writer has been present since 3114 BC"[36] and Enrique Sam Colop affirms that an "invisible thread of continuity" through language persists.[37]

Gaspar Pedro González consciously builds this millenarian trope in his novels and poetry. In his book *Kotz'ib'*, which translates into "our writing," González includes the poem "Stz'ib'" where he gracefully foregrounds this millennarian continuity. Gaspar Pedro González theorizes "*Kotz'ib'* as denoting the flowered word and encompassing non-traditional writing expressions such as textiles and lintels. In the poem, a young Maya writer gradually becomes intoxicated by the omnipresence of Maya glyphs surrounding him. The first line creates an ambiguity between the speaker and the subject of the poem: "Y sobre la piedra, aparecen las huellas de sus manos" ["And over the stone, his hand imprints appear"].[38] The speaker's unexpected findings on the rocks of an ancient city allude to a Maya glorious past, coming full circle to face his contemporary identity. In fact, one may argue that it is the speaker's immediate presence making the prints visible to the reader. The reference to "his hands" functions as a literal discovery of his own identity, a reconciliation of his contemporary identity with the past, and serves as a synecdoche for the whole of Maya culture. The rest of the lines employ strong verbs that reflect the perseverance and persistence of Maya writing:

> *Un enjambre de signos/Brotaron entre los glífos/Incrustrados en los amplios frontispicios,/Enraizados en los silenciosos monumentos/Rodaron sobre las escalenatas, Cayeron de las bóvedas/Surgieron de los altos y bajos relieves,/Estallaron como ruge de jaguares/ Entre la espesura de tambores y atabales/enrollados, entre pentagramas de amate [A throng of signs/Sprung amid the glyphs/Engraved in the ample facades/Rooted in silent monuments/Rolled over the steps/Fell from the vaults/Surged from the high and low reliefs/Exploded like the jaguars' roar/Between the thickness of drums and tambours/ Rolled between pentagrams of amate].*[39]

The metaphors gradually move from the image of "sprouting signs amidst glyphs" to their explosive jaguar-like roar near the end. Gaspar Pedro González's poem ends with the image of the códices, the sacred books. His poem documents the underpinnings in this millenarian literary tradition based on the palpability of the ancient Maya cities and codices. Gaspar Pedro González's work reconciles past and present in this literary continuum.

In a similar move, but from a different geopolitical location, is Briceida Cuevas Cob. Born in Campeche, she became known for imbuing Mayan cultural symbols and stories from oral tradition to create her poems. Almost all of her poetry (re)signifies traditional symbols and allusions to fashion the contemporary. Her critique of gender double standards gains full force in her collection, *Je'Bix K'in/Como el sol.*[40] The title of her poetry collection, *Je'Bix K'in/Like the Sun*, suggests gender equality since in Maya cosmology the sun has male attributes while the moon has female ones.

"Tu primer arete/Your First Earring," the first of three interrelated poems, depicts a mother's joy in learning of her child's sex, as the mother's subjectivity will continue through the daughter.[41] In this poem, women are the biological reproducers of culture through the teachings they pass down to the daughters. Marked neither by defiance or irony, a sense of continuity and transmission through reproduction permeates its tone. The title alludes to the Maya practice of piercing girls' ears with a red thread to prevent the evil eye. The thread emanating from the mother's womb to the girl's ear acquires both a symbolic and symbiotic aura. It establishes a profound relationship between mother and daughter as one. The second poem, "Tu primer arete" (number II), contrasts with the idea of women as reproducers of culture.[42] Instead, it foretells the future of the third-generation woman. The female speaker addresses an unborn daughter and conveys the expectation that she (the third-generation woman) must attend school so as not to be a *cabeza hueca* [empty head]. One may interpret this position as an assimilationist or integrationist one. It is not. The contradiction of a tradition that maintains women as the biological reproducers of culture reaches other dimensions through formal schooling. The speaker insists that education should not come at the cost of surrendering identity, and that formal learning must be complemented by spirituality—represented by the element of fire in the poem. This poem is clearly not a teleology about education and modernization. It is about using education in the twentieth century as a means to decolonize indigenous people's history and literature.

The first stanza celebrates the potential liberating role of scholarly training in the formation of the third generation. In the second stanza, the tone shifts where the mother counsels the daughter and cautions her that the gaining a Western education will not lead to a complete acquisition of knowledge, as knowledge is wisdom and spiritual stasis. The daughter must also understand the history of women in her culture. Cuevas Cob's choice of language is significant; she describes an old Maya woman with tired breasts after having *desparramar* [spilled] life on this earth. The poet's use of the word implies squander, waste, or a spilling of life. In another unexpected turn, the speaker sets hieroglyphic writing beyond the monuments of ancient ruins or pre-Columbian texts, which male poets invoke. In contrast, the poet perceives ancient glyphs on the heels of women. Women personify time, knowledge, and writing. The speaker of the poem imagines a young woman who acquires a Western education and returns to her culture after navigating the mestizo world. She returns not as a biological reproducer of culture but as a creator of stories who invigorates culture. The speaker evokes the fire, a euphemism for storytelling. She writes:

> *Irás a la escuela pero volverás a tu casa,*
> *A tu cocina,*
> *A pintar con achiote el vientre del metate,*
> *A inflar con tus pulmones el globo-flama,*
> *A que juzguen tus ojos los delgados dedos*
> *Del humo,*
>
> *A leer el chisporroteo en el revés del comal,*
> *A leer el crepitar del fuego.*
> *Volveras a tu cocina*
> *Porque tu banco te espera.*
> *Porque el fogón guarda en sus entrañas un espejo.*
> *Un espejo en el que estampada se halla tu alma.*
> *Un espejo que te invoca con la voz de su resplandor.*
>
> [You will go to school but will return to your house
> To your kitchen,
> To paint with achiote the womb of the metate,
> So that the tongue of the soot licks your underskirt,
> To inflate with your lungs the globe-flame,
> So that your eyes judge the thin fingers of smoke
> To read the sparks beneath the comal
> To read the crackle of fire.
> You will return to your kitchen
> Because your bench awaits you.
> Because the fire guards in its entrails a mirror.
> A mirror in which stamped is your soul
> A mirror that invokes you with the
> voice of its splendor.][43]

This third-generation Maya woman has a different historic responsibility. She is the source and disseminator of knowledge. She is the priestess who reads the fire and paints the *metate* with *achiote*. Her potential as a writer and spiritual leader unburdens the load of history and tradition. The ubiquitous mirror trope associated with Western femininity as well as with the emergence of a critical self acquires new meaning. The mirror does not function as a confirmation of a physical self. Rather, it bears the presence of her soul. The (re)signification creates a contradiction between the mirror, which offers a fleeting image, and the speaker's use of the word "stamped," which reflects a solid identity. Cuevas Cob claims cultural symbols associated with women and imbues them with new meanings to empower Maya women.

The memory of hieroglyphic texts plays an important role in the revision of dominant literary and cultural histories. Contemporary indigenous writers have not attempted to write in hieroglyphics, yet the cultural referent provides an alternative genealogy to the idea of knowledge/power. Glyphs are prominent in recent publications and they represent a significant link to heritage and a pre-Columbian literary tradition. The collective memory of hieroglyphic writing serves to contest the social stigmas attached to the colonial binaries of literacy/orality, progress/backwardness, and modernity/pre-modernity. While glyphic writing may have been in a state of decline by the time the Spanish arrived, writers sustain colonialism severed the practice even if this may not be historically accurate. Contemporary Maya writers and intellectuals participate in efforts to understand and reconnect to them while they assert its role in the production of literature.[44]

A distinct invocation of this millenarian literary tradition relies on the idea that books had to be committed to memory. Books disappeared, as they were no longer necessary. Writing, memory, and orality are interrelated concepts that do not have a linear order in contemporary indigenous worldviews. In 2005, Ámbar Past, in her translation and transcription of Maya-Tsotsil incantations, underscores the presence of books, memory, and orality.[45] While a project like Ámbar Past's differs from the formation of an author in the Foucauldian sense that many contemporary indigenous writers fall under and assume, it does offer a glimpse to a different logic. Put differently, the idea that one cannot have orality without writing and vice versa resonates with what Jacque Derrida theorizes in his work.[46] In her introduction to *Incantations*, Past explains: "The Tzotzil authors of this anthology claim their spells and songs were given to them by the ancestors, the First Fathermothers, who keep the Great Book in which all words were written."[47] She cites Pasakwala Kómes as having "learned her conjurations by dreaming the Book."[48] Past concludes:

> It is clear the First Fathermothers were writers, and it is rumored that some of their books—that no one can read anymore—lie hidden in old chests in Chamula. Each year they are taken out with great reverence, perfumed with incense and wrapped up again in embroidered cloths. Some say the books inside the chests have begun to talk. Women who learn the words are said to have writing in their hearts.[49]

Today's contemporary Maya writer animates a memory of hieroglyphic writing into the present by making it a central cultural referent in the poetry and novels. Jacinto Arias, in *Cuentos y relatos indígenas*, boldly asserts that:

> *Nuestros padres y madres de la antigüedad sabían leer y escribir. Se olvidaron cuando les quitaron sus escritos los españoles. Por eso solo sabemos escribir nuestra lengua como si nuestros ojos estuvieran cerrados* [Our fathers and mothers of antiquity knew how to read and write. They forgot when the Spanish confiscated their writings. That is why we write our language as if our eyes were closed].[50]

The idea of reenergizing the oral tradition through the written advances an additional millenarian literary position by writers. The "rescuing of the oral tradition" projects financed in the 1990s by the Instituto de Cultura de Yucatan; Miatzil Maayáa, A.C.; and Indemaya maintain their written efforts will lead to the reinvigoration of the oral tradition through the written word. Feliciano Sánchez Chan, a prolific playwright, poet, novelist, and a strong advocate for "rescuing projects" reverses the premise that the transcription of the oral tradition is for written dissemination. In our interview, Sánchez Chan argues the book is conceived as a tool to return the oral tradition to its social function.[51] Writers also subvert the notion that literature remained in the oral realm because an ontological determination between "Indians" and orality exists. Rather, the reason for this orality is because indigenous peoples have been denied literacy in their own languages. Underlining this position is that "illiteracy" in Native languages or Spanish serves a political purpose. Ak'abal eloquently captures this idea in his essay, "Literatura Maya contemporánea." He passionately writes that:

> *Mantener analfabeta al indio ha sido la política para marginarlo y a la vez explotarlo, así como enajenarlo y a la vez explotarlo, así como enajenarlo por medio de la radio y la televisión que no cumplen con una función educativa sino todo lo contrario : son el medio para llevarlo a la alienación y de allí a la perdida de su identidad.* [Keeping the Indian "illiterate" has been the policy to marginalize and at the same time exploit him, as well as to . . . alienate him via radio and television, which don't serve an educational purpose but all the contrary: they are the means used to take him to alienation and from there to lose his identity.][52]

The sense of being denied access to literacy while lamenting the discontinuity of pre-Columbian systems of writing due to colonization saturates the poetry and literary production of the 1990s.

Indigenous Languages and Translation

Insistence on being an indigenous writer entails an intricate involvement in Spanish as well as in the Maya languages. The production, publication, and distribution of this literature expose vexed issues of literacy, language, and translation. Maya languages, perceived as the repositories of culture and worldviews of indigenous communities, acquire an aura of resistance and a triumph against colonialism. When the colonizers imposed the Spanish language, they did not foresee the continuance of indigenous languages. Yasnaya Aguilar, the Mixe linguist, avers that to speak an indigenous language is to escape to an uncolonized space, at least partially, as the state cannot access it, even though it fiercely combats indigenous languages. Aguilar explains:

> Cada vez que hablas una lengua indígenas, resistes. Hablar una lengua indígena, en las circunstancias presentes, es habitar un territorio cognitivo que todavía no ha sido conquistador, al menos no del todo [Every time you speak an indigenous language, you resist. In the present circumstances, to speak an indigenous language is to live in a cognitive territory that has not yet been conquered, at least not entirely].[53]

The appropriation of the Western alphabet, standardization of native languages, the demands for bilingual education, and the efforts to create a literary tradition generate fissures in the homogenous national imaginary in Guatemala and Mexico.

Indigenous writers' organizations are conscious of the need to generate readers and sustain readership. Indigenous writers face a serious audience problem. Given the lack of audience, to whom do they write? How does one publish in indigenous languages and create readers in Spanish as well as Maya languages? The response varies from writer to writer. Some are cynical about the future of indigenous languages; thus, they claim to write for posterity. Others are far more hopeful and point out that readers in indigenous languages are increasing. Considering this problematic, many indigenous writers are committed to teaching in their communities, holding workshops for people interested in learning how to read and write Native languages. Other indigenous writers are educators who are producing a literature that caters to children, thereby, forming readers (See the Maya-Roselia Jimenez or the Zapotec Francisco de la Cruz).

One of the most significant differences between indigenous and non-indigenous writers lies in that indigenous writers must translate their work in order to be published. The fact remains that being an indigenous writer means to function as a translator. There are few readers in indigenous languages, making translation necessary not only for those who do not speak an indigenous language, but also for those who have been denied literacy in native languages. During our interview sessions, most writers expressed their frustration with translation because they felt it changed the meaning of the original. But not all writers perceived this as a difficulty. Poets such as Ruperta Bautista Vásquez (Maya Tsotsil from Chiapas) and Nicolás Huet (Maya Tsotsil from Chiapas), among others, regard the translation process as an exercise that allowed them to see the ways in which their craft could improve.[54] A few commented that they started writing their poems in two languages simultaneously, while others claimed that they began in a native language and altered the original only after translating their work. Other writers seek the assistance of colleagues who specialize in linguistics when translating. Despite pressures for poets and writers to write originally in their native language, the younger ones admitted beginning their work in Spanish. Humberto Ak'abal, the most renown Maya K'iche' poet, recalls that he began writing in Spanish because he was "illiterate" in his own mother tongue.[55] Writing in a native language and ensuring its translation remains a commitment that most indigenous writers take very seriously and are prepared to continue despite the intense labor involved.

Knowledge of the indigenous language in which a poem, a short story, or a novel is originally written would be most optimal. This said not all indigenous authors publish in indigenous languages and some do so explicitly in Spanish. When reading the self-translated versions of a poem, I treat the verses as equally authentic in their meaning. Nonetheless, when they are published bilingually, a general understanding of indigenous languages can illuminate the meaning of the Spanish version. When I first read "dxu'udziko'ob/Las beso" ["I kiss them"], a poem by Maya writer Gerardo Can Pat (from the Yucatán Peninsula), I puzzled over the logic of one of the lines. The speaker of the poem playfully recalls how kissing changes throughout his life, from a mother's kiss to a lover's.[56] Then he writes in the third line of the fourth stanza that in his old age, he only kisses cigarettes. I didn't understand it at first—until I broke down the Maya version with the help of my dictionary and another writer. In Spanish, the line's meaning is lost to an audience which does not know that Can Pat plays with the verb *dzu'udz* for kiss and smoke in Maya, which does not translate in the Spanish so the play on words is lost. Can Pat writes "*in chaamal kin t'abkin dzu'udz/prendo mi cigarro para fumar*" ["I light my cigarrette to kiss"].[57] Hence, the pun in the Maya version is lost in the Spanish translation of the verbs *besar* [to kiss] and *fumar* [to smoke]. Not only that, but to understand the last stanza even with the Spanish translation, the reader must understand the significance of eclipses for the Mayas.

Continuity and Agendas

Literature becomes an important and transformative act for indigenous peoples and an open-ended site for articulating and expressing the changing discourse over indigenous experience. Indigenous writers and other intellectuals offer (an)other genealogy for thinking about literacy, orality, and power in Mesoamerica vis-à-vis Latin American cultural and literary studies. Writers insist on the value of the oral tradition and ancient glyph writing, the production of literature in indigenous languages in standardized alphabets and the use of Spanish. Indigenous intellectuals have produced terms to reflect their insistence on the reliance of both orality and literacy. These terms include *oralitura, letrado-orales,* or a return to ancient terms that connote more than one medium such as the new *tlacuilios* or *aj'tzii'b,* both terms reference writing and painting. Indigenous writers and other intellectuals now are driven by a similar mandate that the ancestors initiated: to preserve a *cosmovisión,* a way of understanding the world. Contemporary indigenous intellectuals, then, are (re)constructing a millenarian literary tradition.

The production of literature becomes a site of ideological struggle over the means of representation, one that necessarily alters the traditional role of the *letrado* (usually a non-indigenous intellectual) as the spokesperson, if not main interlocutor, for indigenous communities. It impels us to recognize the limitations of institutionalized knowledge and learn from indigenous epistemologies as indigenous writers come from traditionally unacknowledged spaces devalued by dominant societies. The construction of a millenarian literary tradition redirects our understanding of how indigenous identity and everyday practices are affirmed and contested across temporal, spatial, and linguistic grounds. The power of this periodization lies in its ability to allow cultural producers to disembody binaries commonly associated with indigeneity: present/past, tradition/modernity, and writing/orality. This disembodiment leads indigenous writers and other intellectuals to theorize their own subjectivities and activate a set of epistemologies that have been neglected within the field of Latin American Literary Studies. It allows writers to claim to a pre-Columbian heritage that confronts the suppressed condition of Latin America as a *plurilingual* and *pluricultural* site. The proliferation of indigenous writings in Mesoamerica destabilizes the unitary conception of Latin America as well as challenges the subordinated status of indigenous languages and cultural practices. Contemporary indigenous literature demands that readers and critics engage with linguistic and cultural difference, but not in the way that *indigenista* writers engaged indigenous subjects. This cultural difference does not equate a universal subalternity. As Humberto Ak'abal's verses read, "speak to anyone, or they'll think you are mute, grandfather said, but be careful that they don't turn you into an other."[58] Contemporary indigenous literature profoundly impacts knowledge/power genealogies in the academy, departing from the *indigenista* literary tradition that strove to what seems for non-indigenous peoples an eternal "Indian problem."

Notes

1 The Five College Consortium includes the University of Massachusetts, Amherst College, Hampshire College, Smith College, and Mount Holyoke College.

2 I use the term Maya to identify multiple linguistic nations living in Southern and Southeast Mexico, Guatemala, and other parts of Central America. Although Mayas live in Belize and in Eastern Salvador and Western Honduras, there is a marked absence of writers in these three countries. While I recognize cultural and political differences in the ways Mayas relate to nation-states, I focus on the writers and poets that articulate a Maya literature that transcends

national borders. My family is from an area called *el Trifinio*, where Honduras, El Salvador, and Guatemala meet. In terms of nation-state citizenship my father had roots in the aldea, Pie del Cerro, a border area shared by Guatemala and Honduras, whereas my mother has roots in La Palma, a border area between El Salvador and Honduras. I point out the border status because it is an area of both confluence and conflict, guided by nationalisms on all sides. Many people maintain double citizenship. Historically and culturally, this area is Maya Ch'ort'i, and their descendants recognized by both the nation-states of Honduras and Guatemala. However, in the Trifinio part of El Salvador, indigenous peoples are not recognized as Ch'ort'i because they do not have external cultural markers or speak Ch'ort'i, nor is there a collective identity. The other issue is that the indigenous peoples movement in El Salvador has been criticized for assuming Maya identity when in fact the overwhelming majority is Nahuat (see Tilley, Virginia. *Seeing Indians.* [Albuquerque, NM: University of New Mexico Press, 2005]). Not to mention that the nation-state in El Salvador officially acknowledged three indigenous nations in its constitution in 2014. Brent E. Metz (in The Ch'orti' Maya Area: Past and Present, edited by Metz, Cameron L. McNeil, and Kerry M. Hull [Gainesville, FL: University Press of Florida, 2009]) has conducted important contemporary work on the Maya Ch'ort'i in the Trifinio area.

3 Indeed, Saer's *The Witness* (Saer, Juan Jose. *The Witness.* Translated by Margaret Jull Costa. London: Serpent's Tail, 2009) took as a point of departure a real shipwreck that took place in the sixteenth century and retold in a chronicle.

4 The beginning of the 1990s marked the first time I met Adrián Esquino Lizco from ANIS (Asociación Nacional Indígena Salvadoreña). "Don't let them say we don't exist," he pleaded. During these years in the early 1990s, I also met the poet Crystos (Menominee), Donna Good Leaf (Mohawk) and many others.

5 In the Latin American Studies Association's journal *Forum*, in their article, "Literaturas de Abya-Yala," Arias et al. (Arias, Arturo, Luis Cárcamo-Huechante y Emilio del Valle Escalante. "Literaturas de Abya Yala". Lasaforum XLIII.1 [2012]: 7–10) write that "*En este contexto, la irrupción autoral indígena en el sistema literario canónico—sea poesía escrita, novela o cuento—posee hitos tempraneros en dicha contemporaneidad, los que paulatinamente se hacen visibles con la autoridad alcanzada por el testimonio*" ["In this context, the indigenous authorial irruption in the canonical literary system—possesses early milestones in the contemporary world, which gradually become visible with authority reached by the testimonio"]. Although I recognize the importance of the testimonio, I don't see the slow emergence of contemporary indigenous literature as visible due to the testimonio.

6 I use the term Mesoamerica to refer to parts of Mexico and Central America because it offers me a way of thinking outside the modern nation-state and it also makes explicit reference to the main indigenous civilizations that continue to resist assimilation.

7 *Indigenismo* as a discourse antecedes nation-state policy and is traceable to Fray Bartolomé de Las Casas and his defense of indigenous peoples. See an account of *indigenismo* in Luis Villoro, *Los grandes momentos del indigenismo* (Mexico City: COLMEX, 1950). Critics differentiate between *indianismo* and *indigenismo* in their overall aesthetic and political goals. *Indianismo* idealized a pre-Hispanic past, focusing on Indians as noble savages. While *indigenista* literature shares some of this idealization, the main political goal was to illustrate the oppressive conditions indigenous peoples endure. For more information on the genealogy of *indigenista* literature see Julio Rodriguez Luis, "El indigenismo como proyecto literario: Revaloración y nuevas perspectivas," in *Hispamérica*, Año 19, No. 55 (April 1990), pp. 41–50; and Julio Rodriguez Luis, *Hermenéutica y praxis del indigenismo: La novela indigenista, de Clorinda Matto a José María Arguedas* (Mexico: Fondo de Cultura Económica, 1980).

8 A recent special issue revisits *indigenismo*: Laura Giraudo and Stephen E. Lewis eds, "Re-Thinking Indigenismo on the American Continent," *Latin American Perspectives*, Issue 186, Vol 39, No.5 (September 2012): 100–110. See also Also see the foundational works by Angel Rama, *Transculturación narrativa en América Latina. Critical Literara* (Mexico: Siglo veintiuno, 1982) and Antonio Cornejo Polar's, "La novela indigenista: un género contradictorio," *Texto Crítico*, 14 (1979): 58–70.

9 See for example, *El Indio, El callado dolor de los tzotziles, Huasipungo, Balún Canan, Hombres de Maíz.* After the heralding of the end of *indigenista* literature by Julio Rodriguez, some critics characterized similar novels focusing on the Indian as neo-*indigenista* novels—see Natalio Ohanna, "Redoble por Rancas" y la conceptualización del (neo) indigenismo: una tendencia

a la homogeneidad. Alicante: Biblioteca Virtual Miguel de Cervantes, 2009. www.cervantes virtual.com/nd/ark:/59851/bmc223c1 accessed August 11, 2006.

10 José Carlos Maríategui, *Siete ensayos de interpretación de la realidad* peruana (Mexico: Ediciones Era, 1993), originally published in 1928.

11 Luis Cardoza y Aragón, *Miguel Ángel Asturias: casi novela* (Mexico: Ediciones Era, 1991), 88.

12 Ibid.

13 See Fidencio Briceño Chel, "¿Literatura indigenista o Literatura?" In *Arguedas Entre la antropología y la literatura*, edited by Francisco Amezcua Pérez, 26 (Mexico: Ediciones Taller Abierto: Mexico: 2000).

14 See Victor de la Cruz, "Reflexiones sobre la escritura y el futuro de la literature indígena," In *Escritura zapoteca: 2500 años de historia*, edited by Maria de Los Angeles Romero Frizzi, 487–501 (Mexico: Porrúa: CONACULTA, Instituto Nacional de Antropologioa e Historia, 2003).

15 Ibid., 331.

16 I have also argued this issue in "Poetizas Mayas: subjetividades contra la corriente," *Cuadernos de Literatura*, Vol 11, No. 22 (January–June 2007): 94–106.

17 See Estelle Tarica's introduction in *The Inner Life of Mestizo Nationalism* (Minneapolis: University of Minnesota Press, 2008), xxi.

18 Edward W. Said. *Culture and Imperialism* (London: Vintage, 1993), 66.

19 I am relying here on Walter Mignolo's definition of the decolonization process as "epistemological reconstitution" (see Mignolo's introduction to the *Cultural Studies*, Vol 21, Nos. 2–3 (March/May 2007): 164.

20 *El rescate del mundo. Poemario de Rosario Castellanos.* Puertavor, 2013, CD ROM.

21 The term ladino is used to describe the non-indigenous subject in Guatemala and Chiapas.

22 For a discussion of Castellanos and her relationship to her indigenous servants see Carter Wilson's "Serving Two Mistresses: María Escandón's life with Rosario Castellanos and with Trudi Blom," *Southwest Review* Vol 96, No. 3 (2011): 414–431.

23 The INI, founded in the early 1940s, had as its agenda the full integration of indigenous peoples as citizens of Mexico, which meant acculturation and the imposition of Spanish, mainly through education. Castellanos was employed by the INI.

24 See Donald Frischmann, "A Question of Balance: Indigenous Theatre at the Conjunction of Millenia," In *Words of the True Peoples*, vol. 3, edited by Carlos Montemayor and Donald Frischmann, 19–47 (Austin, TX: University of Texas Press, 2007).

25 See Antonio Cornejo Polar's "La novela indigenista: un género contradictorio," *Texto Crítico*, Vol 14 (1979): 58–70.

26 Robert Sitler, "Entrevista con Gaspar Pedro González," *Abya Yala*, Vol 10, No. 2 (Summer 1996): 22–24.

27 In the original interview, González says, "El día en que haya más escritores Maya vamos a ampliar nuestros conceptos diferentes que Asturias," See Robert Sitler, "Entrevista con Gaspar Pedro González," *Abya Yala*, Vol 10, No. 2 (Summer 1996): 22–24.

28 Quoted in Sitler, "Entrevista con Gaspar Pedro González," 22–24. The category ladino has changed over time and can be used to name individuals who do not want to be identified as indigenous.

29 Francisco González Rojas, *El Diosero* (Mexico: Fondo de Cultura Económica, 1952).

30 Ibid. Also published in "La narrativa de los que hablamos el Dilla Xhon," In *Los escritores indígenas actuales, Vol II* edited by Carlos Montemayor, 45 (Mexico: Fondo Editorial Tierra Adentro, 1992).

31 Castellanos Martinez, "La narrativa de los que hablamos el Dilla Xhon," In *Los escritores indígenas actuales, Vol II*, edited by Carlos Montemayor, 45 (Mexico: Fondo Editorial Tierra Adentro, 1992).

32 See Cynthia Steele, "Indigenismo y posmodernidad: narrativa indigenista, testimonio, teatro campesino y video en el Chiapas finisecular," *Revista de crítica literaria latinoamericana*, Vol 19, No. 38 (1993): 249–260. Also refer to Brian Goldnick. "El ciclón de Chiapas," *Revista de crítica literaria latinoamericana*, Vol 25, No. 49 (1999): 199–216.

33 See the work of Arturo Arias, *Taking Their Word: Literature and the Signs of Central America* (Minneapolis, MN: University of Minnesota, 2007), 75.

34 See for example the short essay by Antonio López Hernández, "Generos Literarios Indígenas en el estado de Chiapas," www.laneta.apc.org/menriquez/12oct2001.html accessed October 12, 2001.

35 Telephone conversation with Humberto Ak'abal, August 2006.
36 Victor Montejo. "The Power of Language: The Mayan Writer (Ahtz'ib')," *Review*, Vol 67 (Fall 2003): 7–50.
37 See Enrique Sam Colop's dissertation. "Maya Poetics," PhD Dissertation, State University of New York at Buffalo, 1994.
38 Gaspar Pedro González, *Kotz'ib', Nuestra Literature Maya* (Rancho Palos Verdes, CA: Fundación Yax Te', 1997), 7.
39 Ibid., 141.
40 Briceda Cuevas Cob, *Je' Bix K'in/Como el sol* (Mexico: Instituto Nacional Indigenista, 1998).
41 Ibid., 39.
42 Ibid., 41.
43 Ibid., 42.
44 Kay B. Warren, *Indigenous Movements and Their Critics* (Princeton, NJ: Princeton University Press, 1998).
45 Ámbar Past, Xun Okotz and Xpetra Ernándes, *Incantations by Mayan Women* (Chiapas, Mexico: Taller leñateros, 2005).
46 See Derrida's *Of Grammatology*, translated by Gayatri Chakravorty Spivak (Baltimore, MD and London: The Johns Hopkins University Press, 1976), especially 120–121.
47 Ámbar Past, Xun Okotz and Xpetra Ernándes, *Incantations by Mayan Women* (Chiapas, Mexico: Taller leñateros, 2005), 17.
48 Ibid.
49 Ibid., 19.
50 Quoted in Micaela López Morales, *Raíces de la ceiba: Literatura Indígena de Chiapas* (Mexico: Miguel Angel Porrúa, 2004), 66.
51 Feliciano Sánchez Chan, interview with writer, Mérida, Yucatán, 2004.
52 Humberto Ak'abal, "Literatura Maya contemporánea," In *Revista Blanco Móvil* (Mexico, 1996), 70, 8–9.
53 Yasnaya Aguilar, "Hablar como acto de resistencia," *Este Pais*, July 2015.
54 Ruperta Bautista Vásquez and Nicolás Huet, personal communication, Chiapas, 2004.
55 His admission speaks to the historical exclusion of indigenous peoples from learning how to write in their own languages and forced to learn in Spanish. Interview conducted by Gerardo Guinea for Humberto Ak'abal and Carlos Montemayor. *Tejedor De Palabras: Ajkem Tzij*. Guatemala: Organización de las Naciones Unidas para la Educación, la Ciencia y la Cultura, 1998. Print. Not paginated.
56 Gerardo Can Pat, "Dxu'udziko'ob/Las beso," *Navegaciones Zur*, Número. 20 (1998): 16. At the time, I was trying to learn Maya and read the original, but the change in the verb did not make sense to me so I looked it up and also asked for the help of my friend Ana Patricia Martínez Huchim who is a Maya writer.
57 Ibid., 16.
58 The poem, "concejo/no'j" in K'iche' reads: "*Chattzijon ruj' japachinoq/man kachomaj taj che at mem/xub'ij ri numam chuwe/Xa kachajij awib':/rech man kak'ex taj awech,*" In *Aqajtzij/Palabramiel*, edited by Humberto Ak'abal, 46 (Guatemala: Nawal Wuj, 2001).

7

RESISTANCES IN CARIBBEAN LITERATURE (1930S TO THE PRESENT)

Yolanda Martínez-San Miguel

A New Roadmap for the Many Threads of Resistance in Caribbean Literature since 1930

The association of Caribbean literature with notions like identity and resistance has had a long intellectual trajectory.[1] A central theme in the literary and artistic representation of Caribbean resistance has been a meditation about the legacies of colonialism and the alternative master narratives that have been provided by postcolonial and decolonial frameworks. I therefore propose, as a theoretical experiment, a review of the some iconic works of Caribbean literature written between 1930 and the 2000s by establishing a dialogue with three distinct intellectual traditions in which the notion of colonialism and cultural representation have been key: Latin American colonial studies, postcolonial theory, and the decolonial turn. This experiment presents some advantages, as well as some limitations and challenges. On the one hand, it allows us to think about the *long durée* of resistance and colonialism as a central topic informing aesthetic and poetic projects in the Caribbean. On the other hand, since the essay proposes a survey of some of the authors and texts from the Caribbean region, my exposition could create an illusion of chronological progression or teleology of theoretical approaches and particular topics. This is not my contention here, but I take this risk as a hopefully productive exercise to reimagine artistic and political resistance in the Caribbean.

This essay also provides an overview of the literary production of the Spanish Caribbean in conversation with the French and Anglo Caribbean, paying particular attention to three specific threads of literature of resistance. My main contention is that although it is important to acknowledge and analyze the specificities of the different linguistic regions in the Caribbean, the history of political and cultural resistance in the region cannot be understood fully unless the connections and relationality between these different Caribbeans is also explored. In the following section, I focus on texts that engage racial and ethnic debates in the definition of a Caribbean subject and relate with colonial conceptualizations of the Caribbean. I then focus on the postcolonial and neocolonial definitions of Caribbeanness through the articulation of a Caribbean geopolitical imaginary. Finally, I review a series of texts in which gender and sexuality are used to index a new Caribbeanness that does not necessarily depend on sovereignty to define its own uniqueness or specificity. In the conclusion, I will briefly discuss how the use of a comparative framework to study the Anglo, Spanish, and French Caribbean is crucial to identify the specific discourses about colonialism and resistance that have been developed in the region from the 1930s to the present.

Colonialism, Blackness and Insularity (1930s–1940s)

> *Ay ay ay, que mi negra raza huye*
> *y con la blanca corre a ser trigueña;*
> *¡a ser la del futuro,*
> *fraternidad de América!*
> [Oh my, oh my, oh my, my black race flees
> and merges with the white, becoming bronze,
> to be the race of future,
> of America's fraternity!]
>
> —Julia de Burgos, "Ay ay ay de la grifa negra"[2]

In the Caribbean the discourse of resistance has traditionally been imagined in dialogue with the colonial past and present of the different countries included in the region. One of the central legacies of colonialism is linked to the massive voluntary and coerced displacements of populations to the archipelago that were linked to the European imperial/colonial enterprise. I would therefore like to frame this discussion of race, ethnicity and insularity in the Caribbean with central debates in Latin American colonial studies. Latin American colonial studies have traditionally focused on the interdisciplinary study of texts and discourses produced in the Americas between 1492 and 1800. The corpus analyzed in this field includes *relaciones*, chronicles, travel diaries, and narratives produced by European, *criollo*/creole, mestizo, and indigenous writers. Foundational works like those of Miguel León Portilla and Nathan Watchtel—in their study of indigenous oral cultures and performances that they denominate "the vision of the vanquished"—served as precursors to more recent studies on khipus, textiles, codices, and pictorial documents, and oral traditions, indigenous textualities and performances.[3] In the late 1980s, the field experienced one of its main epistemic crisis, and as a result notions like "colonial discourse"[4] and "colonial semiosis"[5] were proposed as alternatives to the predominantly literary analytical methodology to question the privileging of written accounts that followed the model of the modern book and alphabetical writing. Colonial semiosis made it easier for cultural critics to incorporate new and existing studies on oral, visual and performatic modes of representation into the corpus of colonial discourses in Latin America. Josaphat Kubayanda, José Rabasa and others have also questioned the Eurocentric perspective in the canon used to theorize colonization in the Americas and the rest of the Global South.[6]

Although Latin American colonial studies include the Caribbean, certain tensions have complicated the conversation among historians and cultural critics focusing on the colonial period in the Caribbean. First, the periodization for colonialism is different in the continental Americas and the Caribbean. Second, several countries in the Caribbean were or are still colonies in the late nineteenth century, the early twentieth century, and even today. Third, the process of decolonization in the Caribbean includes a whole array of alternative political structures that transcend the national or sovereign state, the predominant model in the continental Americas. As a result, although we have several historians who study the colonial period in the Caribbean, we have fewer literary and cultural critics who focus on the colonial period as a specific field of specialization that is comparable to Latin American colonial studies.

The 1930s are an important point of departure to understand the constitution of a contemporary literary discourse in the Caribbean since it is then that several authors begin to explore the uniqueness of Caribbean sociopolitical history, as well as its ethnic and racial differences when compared to the rest of Latin America. This decade is also particularly important due to the emergence of the *negrista* and *négritude* movements in the Spanish and French Caribbean as aesthetic projects that conversed with a Black International Movement that was consolidating in collaboration with several early decolonial struggles in the Caribbean, Asia, and Africa.

Debates about racial identity in the Caribbean are interesting, since it is precisely in this region where the Americas had their first Black republic with the independence of Haiti in 1804. However, racial discourse is complicated by the division produced by European colonialism in the region that translates into different genealogies for *criollos* and creoles in the Spanish, French, and Anglo Caribbean.[7] Josaphat Kubayanda links *negrismo* and *négritude* in their exploration of Afrocentric aesthetic projects grounded in the historical and social reality of the Caribbean.[8] Although *negrismo* and *négritude* have different genealogies that implicate Europe and the Caribbean in distinct ways,[9] I would like to conceive these two movements through their common interest in visibilizing the racist experiences of Afro-Caribbean people in the context of nation formation or the articulation of national formation discourses.

Linked to several *modernista* and *vanguardista* poetic movements in the Spanish Caribbean, as well as the Harlem Renaissance aesthetics,[10] *negrismo* questioned the white *criollo* imaginary prevalent in Spanish America. In Puerto Rico, Luis Palés Matos (1898–1959) was the most important poet of the negrista movement. His poetry experimented with onomatopeia and rhythm to uncover the rich Afro-Puerto Rican culture in the island. Although his poetry often does not escape to the hegemonic gesture of the exotization of Blackness, his *Tuntún de pasa y grifería* (written in the late 1920s and published in 1937), has become a canonical text in Puerto Rican literature. Palés Matos's poetics represent an important response to *Insularismo* (1934), an essay by Antonio S. Pedreira that privileged a white *criollo* identity for Puerto Ricans and that depicted miscegenation as the source of the confusion of identities produced by racial mixing.[11] In 1935, Tomás Blanco wrote his essay "Elogio de la plena," validating Afro-Puerto Rican music and questioning the privileging of the *danza* as a musical genre closer to European music.[12] A few years later, Blanco wrote *El prejuicio racial en Puerto Rico* (1940), a meditation about racial relations published just after the Masacre de Ponce in 1937.[13] Although Blanco's intent was to promote racial harmony, it is clear from his essay that racial tensions were central in the political nationalist movement in the island. Finally, in her poetry Julia de Burgos explored a redefinition of Puerto Rican identity that included links with gender and race. "*Ay ay ay de la grifa negra*" included in *Poema en veinte surcos* (1938), for example, reclaims the body of the *mulata* as a place of vindication of the former enslaved people, and as the origin of *mulataje* (invoked through "*ser trigueña*") in the Americas.[14]

Nicolás Guillén (1902–1989) from Cuba would devote several of his poetic collections—like *Motivos de Son* (1930), *Sóngoro cosongo* (1931) and *West Indies Ltd.* (1934), among others—to the representation of Blacks and mulattoes as important social actors and voices in the Spanish Caribbean.[15] One of his most famous poems, "Balada de los dos abuelos" (1934), depicts the assymetrical relationships of power, as well as the unequal visibility of Africans and Europeans in the myths of *mestizaje* that inform Cuban nationalism:

> *Sombras que sólo yo veo,/me escoltan mis dos abuelos./Lanza con punta de hueso,/ tambor de cuero y madera:/mi abuelo negro./Gorguera en el cuello ancho,/gris armadura guerrera:/mi abuelo blanco* [Shadows that only I can see,/ guarded by my two grandfathers./ A bone-point spear,/ wood and hide drum:/ my black

> grandfather./ A ruff round his broad neck,/ a warrior's grey armour:/ my white grandfather].[16]

Guillén's poetry focused very closely on the emergence of a public voice for Afro-Cubans, a poetic initiative that was crucial in his recognition as a national poet after the trimph of the Cuban Revolution. After writing several opera librettos and ballet pieces focusing on Afro-Cuban themes, Alejo Carpentier (1904–1980) published *¡Ecué-Yamba-O!* (1933), a short experimental novel in which Afro-Cuban cultures are presented as the backbone of Cuban identity.[17] Carpentier actually took advantage of Fernando Ortiz's (1881–1969) important sociological studies of Afro-Cuban cultures included in his books *Los negros brujos* (1906), *Los negros esclavos* (1916) and the *Glosario de afronegrismos* (1924).[18] This theme continued to be a central focus of Carpentier's narrative work that explores Afro-Caribbean religions and cultures and proposes them as the diasporic origin of Caribbean identities in his famous short story "Viaje a la semilla" (1944).[19]

The Dominican Republic's major *negrista* poet is Manuel del Cabral (1907–1999). His *Doce poemas negros* (1935), *Compadre Mon* (1942) and *Trópico negro* (1941) link Afro-Dominicanness with issues of class.[20] In the case of the Dominican Republic, the discourse on Blackness is closely linked to the tense and complex relationship with Haiti, the other country in the same island and the first Afro-creole republic in the Caribbean that dominated Hispaniola between 1822 and 1844. The result of this intimate but tense relationship between the two countries was the basis for a literary and cultural discouse that interrogates the white ideology behind Spanish *criollismo*.[21] In order to bypass the opposition between *criollismo* and Blackness, *indio* occupied the racial place of mulatto and *mulataje* in the rest of the Spanish Caribbean. 1937 marks an important moment in Dominican history as well, since in an attempt to "Dominicanize the border," Trujillo ordered a massacre in which many Haitians residing in the Dominican Republic were killed.[22]

The anti-Haitian and anti-Black sentiment in the Dominican Republic find their most official expression in Joaquín Balaguer's *La isla al revés: Haiti y el destino dominicano* (1983), a monographic essay that attempts to explain the fundamental differences between the Dominican Republic and Haiti using the binary opposition between civilization and barbarism.[23] Milagros Ricourt has recently questioned the white identification of *criollismo* in the Spanish Caribbean by complicating the relationship between indigeneity and Blackness for the case of the Hispaniola (Dominican Republic and Haiti).[24] Her work resonates with several Dominican artistic interventions that explore a more nuanced discourse about Blackness and Dominicanness. For example. Juan Bosch (1909–2001) explored the many dimensions of the Dominican identity in his narrative, including the anti-Haitian sentiment in "Luis Pie" (1943), a short story that was awarded the Hernández Catá Prize in Cuba.[25] Josefina Báez uses her diasporic experience in the United States as a point of departure to define a new Caribbeanness constituted by the contacts with all the other diasporic cultures in New York City. Her performance *Dominicanish* (1999) combines Caribbean, Black, Indian, U.S., and American ethnic and racial elements in the articulation of a diasporic *dominicanidad* that is conceived as a new language.[26] Blas Jiménez (1949–2009) is perhaps one of the Dominican writers that discussed Afro-Dominicannes in most detail in his narrative poetry and essays: *Caribe africano en despertar* (1980), *El nativo (versos en cuentos para espantar zombies)* (1996) and *Afrodominicano por elección, negro por nacimiento: pseudoensayos* (2008).[27]

In the case of the French Caribbean, *négritude* would be linked to surrealism as well as avant-garde poetry. It was originally a political movement conceived in the context of French colonialism and Blackness in an international setting and included the collaboration of Léopold Sédar Senghor (1906–2001) from Senegal, Léon Gontran Damas (1912–1978) from Guiana and Aimé Césaire (1913–2008) from Martinique. The main literary exponent of this genre in the French Caribbean is Aimé Césaire. His *Cahier d'un retour au pays natal* (1939) is a narrative poem that represents the decolonization of the Caribbean imaginary through the realization and acceptance of the central role that Blackness and slavery had in the constitution of the global capitalist modernities that link the Caribbean with Europe, Africa, Asia, and the United States. By reclaiming the centrality of the Black subject in the history of the world, Césaire resignifies the centrality of Caribbean colonialism in the constitution of an European and First World modernity:

> *J'accepte . . . J'accepte . . . entièrement, sans réserve/ma race qu'aucune ablution d'hysope et de/ lys mêlés ne pourrait purifier/ ma race rongée de macules/ ma race raisin mûr pour pieds ivres/ ma reine des crachats et des lèpres/ma reine des fouets et des scrofules/ ma reine des squasmes et des chloasmes* [I accept . . . I accept . . . totally, without reservation. . ./ my race that no ablution of hyssop mixed with lilies could purify/my race pitted with blemishes/ my race ripe grapes for drunken feet/ my queen of spittle and leprosy/ my queen of whips and scrofula/ my queen of squamae and chloasma].[28]

The 1940s are then characterized by the dissemination of important work redefining the role of Blackness in Caribbean and global history. That is the case of the foundational work done by Fernando Ortiz in the *Contrapunteo cubano del tabaco y del azúcar* (1940), the text in which he coins the notion of transculturation to study the cultural exchanges taking place between Europeans, Africans, and Asians in the assymetrical matrix of power of colonialism and postcolonialism.[29] Lydia Cabrera, anthropologist and poet, collected and recreated manifestations of *santería* and Afro-Cuban religiosity in *Cuentos negros de Cuba* (published first in French in 1936 and in Spanish in 1940), that were followed by *El Monte* (1954), *Refranes de negros viejos* (1955), among many others.[30] Finally, in 1949 Alejo Carpentier published *El reino de este mundo*, a short novel that takes the Haitian revolution as the point of departure to imagine the Black and mulatto Caribbean.[31] It is in this novel that Carpentier included his first version of "De lo real maravilloso americano," an essay that proposes Latin American and Caribbean history and temporality as a distinct cultural sensitivity that defies Western notions of modernity and rationality.

In the 1940s and 1950s, a group of poets in the Hispanic Caribbean focused on the relationship between Caribbeanness, insularity and the aquatic to propose different poetic imaginaries. For example, Virgilio Piñera (1912–1979) published his long poem *La isla en peso* (1943) in which Cuba is conceived in a dialectic relationship between land and sea, community and isolation, modernity and stagnation.[32] In *El mar y tú* (finished in 1940, but published in 1954), Julia de Burgos proposed the relationship with the fluidity and limitless space of the sea as an alternative space to conceptualize Caribbean insular and archipelagic identities, not as an index of isolation, but of connectivity.[33] Finally in the Dominican Republic, in *Mi mundo el mar* (1953) and *Una mujer está sola* (1953) Aída Cartagena Portalatín, a member of the Poesía Sorprendida group,[34] develops a poetic project in which gender becomes a central prism to imagine an alternative and fluid Dominican collectivity that exists beyond the confines of Rafael Leonidas Trujillo's dictatorship.

Foundational as well is the work of the economic and cultural historian Eric Williams (1911–1981). One of his major contributions is *Capitalism and Slavery* (1944), a political and economic history of the Caribbean that locates the region at the heart of the development of global modernity by arguing that slavery and the slave trade financed the Industrial Revolution.[35] Another central example is C. L. R. James's foundational historical analysis of the Haitian revolution and its significance as the first Afro-Creole revolution in the Caribbean in *The Black Jacobins* (published in 1938 and revised in 1963).[36] These two texts documented historically and philosophically what Césaire imagined in his *Cahier* when he invited his readers to celebrate the centrality of Caribbean Black subjects in the constitution of a global history.

The 1950s and 1960s will question the political sovereignty of the Caribbean archipelago, and the postcolonial framework allows for a productive analysis of the cultural and literary works produced in the region. In the next section, I propose a reconceptualization of the literature produced from the 1950s to the 1980s using a postcolonial lens.

Postcolonialism, Neocolonialism, and Caribbean Geopolitical Imaginaries

> *¿No había adoptado y abandonado con increíble facilidad y rapidez patrias, religiones, cultura, actitudes, ideas? Ahora iba a adoptar su cultura, su patria, la suya, que quizás, quizás le necesitara.* [Hadn't he adopted with incredible ease and promptness mother countries, religions, culture, ideas? Now he was going to adopt his culture, his motherland, his own, that perhaps, perhaps needed him.]
>
> —Calvert Casey, "El regreso"[37]

To think about the literature of resistance in the Caribbean from a postcolonial framework is to ponder about the complex development of political structures and state formations in the region. Not only does the Caribbean achieve its political independence earlier and later than other countries in Latin America, but the particular status of many of the countries in this region includes a whole series of states that became independent between 1804 and 1983, colonies, incorporated territories, a few British and American "commonwealths," associated states, departments of France, and other overseas territories.[38] This explains why colonialism, postcolonialism, and nationalism are tricky terms for studying the Caribbean. As a result, several scholars have proposed alternative political frameworks to study this archipelago, such as "extended statehood," "fragmented nationalism," and "cultural anomaly" to refer to discourses of cultural nationalism that are not necessarily manifested in conditions of political sovereignty and the consolidation of modern nation-states.[39] One of the theoretical frameworks used to think about the Caribbean is postcolonial theory.

Postcolonial theory emerged in the late 1970s, specifically after Edward Said's crucial interrogation in *Orientalism* (1978) of the Eurocentric assumptions informing Area Studies programs in the United States and Asian Studies more specifically.[40] Using the decolonization of former English and French colonies taking place in the twentieth century as its point of departure, Gayatri Spivak, Homi Bhabha, Paul Gilroy, and Stuart Hall meditate on the ways in which the colonial subject constitutes her or his own identity under and after the end of colonialism.[41] Postcolonial theory resonated profoundly in the Caribbean region, where many of the countries of the Anglo Caribbean became independent at the same time in which the decolonization of Africa was taking place (1960s to 1980s). Postcolonialism has been particularly productive for the study of nationalism, multilingual literary and cultural productions, and migratory and exilic experiences from the Global South to the First World.[42]

In the case of Latin America, however, postcolonial theory became a problematic framework since it did not distinguish colonialism between 1492 and 1800 and the colonization and decolonization process taking place primordially in the nineteenth and twentieth centuries.[43] Jorge Klor de Alva has interrogated the use of postcolonialism to study the Latin American context since the *criollo* sectors that benefited from the independence movements did not advocate for the creation of national cultures that were fundamentally different from the Eurocentric oppressive structures of the colonial period.[44] Klor de Alva's argument coincides in many respects with central arguments on coloniality and decoloniality that I will discuss later, but his work does not contemplate the articulation of a decolonial turn. One particular framework that proved to be very useful in the Latin American context was the Subaltern Studies group (founded by John Beverley, Robert Carr, José Rabasa, Ileana Rodríguez, and Javier Sanjinés) that focused on the analysis and representation of marginal colonial and postcolonial voices.[45] Caribbean studies scholars like Shalini Puri and Stuart Hall take advantage of notions like mimicry and hybridity to think about the creolized, transcultural, and translocal cultural productions of the Caribbean as a point of encounter of American, European, African, and Asian subjects.[46]

Given the problematic condition of some countries that have not attained national independence or political sovereignty (as is the case of almost half of the countries comprised by the Caribbean), in their foundational study *The Empire Writes Back*, Ashcroft, Griffith, and Tiffin proposed an alternative definition of postcolonialism that neutralizes the temporal echoes of the term:

> "Post-colonial" as we define it does not mean "post-independence," or "after colonialism," for this would be to falsely ascribe an end to the colonial process. Post-colonialism, rather, begins from the very first moment of colonial contact. It is the discourse of oppositionality which colonialism brings into being.[47]

This alternative definition did not solve the tensions within Caribbean studies, since as Silvio Torres-Saillant would note:

> The new marketing of the Third World knowledge under the globalizing label of "post-colonial theory" came to the academic industry precisely at the moment when the prominence of Caribbean ideas, championed by such figures as Sylvia Winter, Lamming, Césaire, Carpentier, and Fanon, had begun to command international attention.[48]

The 1940s and the1950s are a crucial period in the political history of the Caribbean, since postcolonialism during this time coexists with new forms of colonialism. Some of the countries that had not become nation-states end up in alternative political statuses. That is the case of Guadeloupe and Martinique, which become departments of France in 1946. In the case of Puerto Rico, in 1952 the island will attain its current status of Estado Libre Asociado [Commonwealth of Puerto Rico], while in the Anglo Caribbean the West Indies Federation (1958–1962) will attempt to unify the area beyond the confines of the colonial insular territories. Although the ultimate result of the revival of the Caribbean confederation was indeed the independence of many Anglo Caribbean countries between 1960 and 1983, the West Indies Federation activated a collective and archipelagic imaginary that served as an alternative political model for the region. One of the most important meditations against colonialism as an indictement to European and Western modernity is Aimé Césaire's *Discours sur le colonialisme* (1950).[49]

These two decades of intense political change were depicted in a series of texts that explored the vulnerable sovereignties of a colonial, neocolonial, and postcolonial Caribbean. In the Dominican Republic, the national poet Pedro Mir explored the configuration of a Dominican collective identities in books like *Hay un país en el mundo* (1949), *Contracanto a Walt Whitman* (1952), and *Viaje a la muchedumbre* (1971).[50] In Puerto Rico, René Marqués's short stories, dramatic pieces and novels focus on the crisis of masculinity in the paternalistic context of the island's transition from Spanish to U.S. American colonialism. Texts like *La víspera del hombre* (1959), *Los soles truncos* (1958), and "En la popa hay un cuerpo reclinado" (1959) address the complex gender relations that inform modern life in *la gran familia puertorriqueña* [the big Puerto Rican family].[51] Marqués laments the loss of the Hispanic values under Spanish colonialism and longs with nostalgia for the return of a society lead by a patriarchal Catholic white *criollo* elite. His famous essay, "*El puertoriqueño dócil*" (1960) explores further what Marqués conceives as the feminization of Puerto Rican culture, a byproduct of U.S. American colonialism facilitated by the adoption of U.S. feminist ideologies that displaced the role and place of the Spanish *pater familiae*.[52] "La carreta" (1953) is a dramatic piece that represents the failure of Puerto Rican migration to the United States and ends by advocating for the return to the island to defend national identity.[53] Pedro Juan Soto and José Luis González explored with more success the complications produced by Puerto Rican migration to the United States in texts like *Spiks* (1959) and "La carta" (1948).[54] They shared Marques's resistance to U.S. American colonialism in the island, but they did not embrace a nostalgic desire to return to the life and traditions under Spanish colonialism.

A key figure to think about Caribbean postcolonialism in the 1950s and 1960s is the Martinican psychyatrist and thinker Frantz Fanon (1925–1961). Fanon's *Black Skin, White Masks* (1952) proposes a psychoanalytical and material analysis of colonialism that focuses on racism and the dehumanization of the Black colonized subjects.[55] Although the focus of *The Wretched of the Earth* (1962) transcends the Caribbean to focus on the decolonization process in Africa, in this second book Fanon continued his meditation about the dehumanizing and racializing effects of colonization, and set the basis for the establishment of a decolonization movement through a critique of nationalism and imperialism.[56] Another key figure from the Anglo Caribbean is George Lamming, who depicts colonial migrations to London to propose a literary meditation about the legacies of colonialism in the Caribbean in *The Emigrants* (1954) and *The Pleasures of Exile* (1960).[57] Both Lamming and Fanon use the experiences of Antilleans in the metropolis to reflect about the very concrete limits and challenges experienced by people of Caribbean descent in their journeys to the imperial "motherland." The result of this rite of passage is the loss and recovery of a Caribbean identity through the colonial and postcolonial lense of intracolonial migration.[58]

The 1960s are also an important time in the history of the Caribbean, since this is the period for the independence of several countries in the Anglo Caribbean and this decade also marks the triumph of the Cuban Revolution. In the Dominican Republic,

Rafael Leonidas Trujillo is assasinated in 1961 after thirty years in power, and in 1965 the United States invades this country for the second time. This decade is also considered as the period during which massive transnational migration from the Caribbean to the United States and Europe consistently takes place. Postcolonial narratives that interrogate and complicate the Eurocentric definitions of Caribbean identities are quite visible in this time period. Blackness, Asian migration to the Caribbean, feminine and queer desires, and marronage are central counternarratives in Sylvia Wynter's *Hills of Hebron* (1962), *Wide Sargasso Sea* by Jean Ryss (1966), *Paradiso* (1966) by Lezama Lima, and Severo Sarduy's *De dónde son los cantantes* (1967).[59] The year 1966 also marks the emergence of the *testimonio*, and the first example of this genre is Miguel Barnet's *Biografía de un cimarrón*, a narrative account of Esteban Montejo's journey from slavery to *cubanía* [Cubanness].[60] Nancy Morejón became the most visible poet of the 1960s and 1970s, and her poetry represents the perspective of slaves—with a special focus on women—in the coerced displacement of the African Diaspora, and how the Cuban Revolution, with its promise to erradicate racism, allows for the emergence of an Afro-Cuban nationalist and revolutionary perpective.[61] The exploration of the legacies of colonialism from a decolonial perpective is central in *Discourse on Colonialism* (1950) and *The Tempest* (1969) by Aimé Césaire.[62] Finally, intracolonial diasporas and transnational migrations function as a central subtext in Calvert Casey's "El regreso" (1962) and *The Mimic Men* (1967) by V.S. Naipaul.[63]

In the 1970s, Caribbean literature takes advantage of the consistent massive migration to and from the region to reflect on the connections between the archipelago with Latin America and the rest of the world. In a sense, the project of the Caribbean confederation is revisited one more time, but in this occasion the motive would be the archipelago as a central node in a global network. It is therefore no coincidence that in the early 1970s both Eric Williams and Juan Bosch would each publish a book with the same title—*From Cristopher Columbus to Fidel Castro*—in which the history of the region is considered from an archipelagic and global perspective, using a framework that begins with Spanish colonialism and closes with ideals of decolonization and liberation of the Cuban Revolution.[64] According to Bosch:

> *El Caribe está entre los lugares de la tierra que han sido destinados por su posición geográfica y su naturaleza privilegiada para ser fronteras de dos o más imperios* [The Caribbean is among the places of the earth that have been destined due to its geographic position and its privileged nature to be a frontier of two or more empires].[65]

In this context, Blackness continues to be a central topic in the articulation of a postcolonial Caribbean imaginary. Roberto Fernández Retamar's (1930–) essay "Calibán" (1970) adopts Shakespeare iconic rebellious character from *The Tempest* to propose a mulatto identity for the Caribbean and Latin America.[66] By locating Blackness at the center of Caribbean identity, and by interrogating savagery and lack of civilization as accurate representations, Fernández Retamar is echoing the new outlook of a Caribbean that has experienced the first decade after the triumph of the Cuban Revolution along with the continued decolonization and independence process taking place in the Anglo Caribbean. Likewise, Lourdes Casal (1938–1981) engages in a fictional project that explores the symbiotic relationship between colonial histories—and its incomplete archives—and the articulation of a Caribbean identity that goes beyond *mulataje* to include Chinese migration to Cuba in her short story collection *Los fundadores: Alfonso y otros relatos* (1973).[67]

In Puerto Rico, Isabelo Zenón's foundational study *Narciso descubre su trasero* (published in two volumes in 1971 and 1974) changes definitively the cultural debate when he documents the racist legacies informing the representation of Black Puerto Ricans in literature.[68] A few years later, José Luis González will publish his book *El país de cuatro pisos y otros ensayos* (1980) in which he proposes descendants of Black slaves as the first ones to identify Puerto Rico as their native land after the demographic crisis of the indigenous populations in the Caribbean.[69] González's essay is actually an example of what Sylvia Wynter would describe as the indigenization of the Black populations in the Caribbean.[70] In many of these literary imaginaries, one of the central strategies to define a postcolonial Caribbean is to propose the formation of another notion of the indigenous and the autochtonous through the diverse discourses on *créolité* and creolization that will emerge at the end of the 1980s. The projects of this next decade proposed and explored two new dimensions. First, Caribbean writers and artists assumed the uniqueness of Caribbean history and its ethnic identities to propose a decolonial imaginary. Second, in that decolonial imaginary, sexuality and desire were used as metaphors to advance a new notion of Caribbeanness.

Decoloniality, Diaspora, Creolization, and Queerness (1980s to the 2000s)

> Is it possible to overcome the horrible legacy of slavery and find decolonial love? Is it possible to love one's broken-by-the-coloniality-of-power self in another broken-by-the-coloniality-of-power person?
>
> —Junot Díaz[71]

In the early 1990s, sociologist Aníbal Quijano consolidated a series of theorizations around the notion of the "coloniality of power."[72] Quijano's work focuses on the continuity and legacies of colonialism after the independence in Latin America and uses the case of Peru as his point of departure. He studies the structural and cultural legacies of colonialism by focusing on a racial paradigm that defines white Europeans as the center, and that locates African and indigenous subjects at the margins of the colonial and national orders. In this regard, Quijano's work converses with previous studies focusing on dependency, internal colonialism, and the currency of colonialism in Latin America.[73] For the specific case of the Caribbean, in my work I have suggested "coloniality of diasporas" as a friendly ammendment to the term that includes coercive migrations as central in the articulation of a series of creolized societies that were ultimately constituted by translocal populations from Europe, Africa, and Asia, and where the native populations were displaced or annihilated very early on.[74]

Coloniality had a tremendous resonance in Latin America, especially through the configuration of the Modernity/Coloniality/Decoloniality network that included scholars and public intellectuals from Latin America, the Caribbean, and the United States. The decolonial turn takes as the point of departure 1492 and colonialism in Latin America to think about the global dissemination of modernity in conjunction with the centrality that colonialism had in the articulation of a capitalist world order.[75] Taking the work of thinkers from the Third World, as well as Chicana theorizing[76] closely linked to women of color feminism from the 1980s and the 1990s,[77] Decolonial theory focuses on the legacies of colonialism in knowledge production and in the definition of the human.[78] Decolonial theory includes a significant contingent of Caribbean writers, scholars and thinkers, like Aimé Césaire, Frantz Fanon, and Sylvia Wynter, among others. The term has gained an important reputation in the French and Hispanic Caribbean.[79] In the Caribbean more specifically, decolonial theory is particularly productive when thinking about new frameworks for cultural and identity formulations that go against the grain of mainstream articulations of Americanness, such as creolesnness, translocality, and queerness. It also focuses on the locus of enunciation of the thinker, writer, or cultural producer, and as such on the articulation of non-Eurocentric or First World imperial epistemologies and more expansive definitions of the human that are forged as a result of coerced or voluntary diasporas and migrations taking place in modern/colonial world systems.[80]

In the late 1970s and the 1980s, the Anglo and French Caribbean engaged in a vindication of regional cultural practices closely linked to creole languages and creolization. The Grenada Revolution and the U.S. invasion (1979–1983) also sparked a whole series of meditations about the problematic and vulnerable postcolonial condition of many of the countries in the region.[81] Some of the literary meditations about the impossibility of the Grenada Revolution include essays, poems, and narrative by Dionne Brand and Merle Collins's essays and poems. Several scholars have recently proposed the Grenada Revolution as an important counterpoint to the Haitian and Cuban revolutions to conceive political resistance, memory and trauma in the Caribbean.[82] Brathwaite's *The Development of Creole Society in Jamaica, 1770–1820,* (1971) and *History of the Voice* (1979) reconstruct a Caribbean archive that includes oral and folkloric traditions in creole to recognize the richness and heteroegeneity of Caribbean cultures and that claims the need for the invention of a poetics for the region.[83] Stuart Hall also advanced a creolized paradigm in his critical reapropriation of a postcolonial framework to understand the relationship between the archipelago and the metropolitan centers.[84] In the French Caribbean, Bernabé, Chamoiseau, and Confiant made a similar claim in the *Éloge de la créolité* (1989), a manifesto that proposes the need of a literature that is written in the native languages of the Caribbean.[85] Edouard Glissant coined concepts like *antillanité,* poetics of relation, and *tout-monde* to showcase how Caribbean histories and temporalities have informed and transformed a world history.[86] Important as well was René Depestre's meditation about the contributions and limits of the *négritude* movement as proposed in his book *Buenos días y adiós a la negritud* (1985).[87]

Many authors cultivate a literature that has focused on the multiple translocal postcolonial and decolonial identities in the Caribbean from the 1980s until the present. Some of the best examples are Chamoiseau's *Texaco* (1992), *Slave Song* (1984) by David Dabydeen, *Abeng* (1984) and *No Telephone to Heaven* (1987) by Michelle Cliff, and Derek Walcott's *Omeros* (1990) and *The Bounty* (1997).[88] An important dimension of this new Caribbean literature dwells on the dilemma between writing from a colonial and small place and/or writing from smaller islands in the Caribbean to promote a decolonial framework to think about the entire region.[89]

Gender and sexuality also occupy a central role in the articulation of new Caribbean identities in the Caribbean from the late 1970s until the present. Race, gender and sexuality are central in Luis Rafael Sánchez's *La guaracha del Macho Camacho* (1976) *Maldito amor* (1985) by Rosario Ferré, *Vírgenes y mártires* (1981) by Ana Lydia Vega and Carmen Lugo Filippi and *Página en blanco y staccato* (1988) by Manuel Ramos Otero.[90] In the Spanish Caribbean more broadly, the work of Magali García Ramis, Ángela Hernández, and Ena Lucía Portela are good examples of how the experiences of Caribbean women inform a different version of national, regional and archipelagic histories. In many of these narratives a female protagonist, often a *mulata*, embodies the internal contradictions that are constitutitve of contemporary Caribbean identities. Through the prism of gender, Blackness returns to interrogate the white supremacist ideology of *criollismo* in the Spanish Caribbean.

In the French Caribbean, Maryse Condé and Gisèle Pineau have written important narratives that explore a *womanist* conceptualization of Caribbean history in the archipelago and in the context of several intracolonial diasporas. On the one hand, Condé's narrative projects meditate about the limitations of the *négritude* imaginary by exploring the impossibility of escaping coloniality and racialization in the Caribbean, Europe or even Africa. Pineau, on the other hand, explores the nuances of creolization among diasporic characters who travel between Europe and the Caribbean and find themselves redefined between the native and the transnational. In both cases, intergenerational memories of colonialism, slavery and exploitation produce short-circuits that explain the difficulty of imagining the contemporary nations that emerged from the many translocal communities that collided in the Caribbean.

Sexuality and queer desire are one of the most recent iterations of contemporary Caribbean literature of resistance. In many cases, queerness is presented as an alternative to the patriarchal, white, and heteronormative imaginary of the nation, as well as an alternative to First World metropolitan mainstream identities. Reinaldo Arenas and Manuel Ramos Otero each cultivated an open queerness to propose a new Caribbean identity, by questioning the hetero-virility of the Cuban Revolution in Arenas's case and the white *criollo* imaginary of the Commonwealth of Puerto Rico in Ramos Otero's case. In 2008, Thomas Glave published *Our Caribbean*, the first anthology of gay and lesbian writers to include the Anglo, French and Spanish Caribbeans.[91] This anthology was soon followed by gay and queer anthologies in other countries, as well as by a special issues by *Centro Journal* and *Sargasso*.[92] More recently, work on queer marronage in narratives by Michelle Cliff, Dionne Brand, Patricia Powell, and Shani Mootoo explore the intersections between colonialism, sexual, and gender regulation and writing in the Anglo Caribbean.[93]

Lesbianism has also been an important component in the reimagination of contemporary Caribbean identities. Interestingly, there is an important contingent of writers who explore feminine queerness in poetry, a genre that has traditionally been excluded from research on nationalist literary imaginaries, but that has been crucial in the articulation of Caribbean literarure of resistance. Therefore, poets like Lourdes Casal, Audre Lorde, Nemir Matos Cintrón, Michelle Cliff, Liliana Ramos Collado, Aixa Ardín Pauneto, and Magaly Alabau combine in their works a long tradition of Caribbean identities that are imagined through the prisms of womanist and queer perspectives. Lesbian narratives have also been important to question the patriarchal representation of national discourse by delving into the woman-centric experiences common in many Caribbean societies. That is the case of narratives by Sonia Rivera Valdés, Ena Lucía Portela, and Rita Indiana Hernández, among others. Natasha Omise'eke Tinsley, Gloria Wekker, Kamala Kempadoo, Yuderkys Espinosa, and Mimi Sheller have all conducted important studies focusing on women's erotic agency in contexts of colonialism and racialization in slavery and post-slavery societies.[94]

Bisexuality and pansexuality have also become important dimensions in the exploration of the ambivalent condition of Caribbean identities in the national and postcolonial contexts that are still prevalent in the conceptualization of contemporary Caribbean literature. Rey Emanuel Andújar explores urban life, bisexuality and/or queerness in his short narratives *El hombre triángulo* (2005), *Amoricidio* (2008) and *Candela* (2007).[95] In all of his narratives, the boundaries between masculinity and Dominicannes are in crisis, and the characters' race, gender identity and expression, as well as their sexual orientation, become extremely fluid. Rita Indiana Hernández has produced a series of narratives that focus on the urban experiences of Dominicans. *La estrategia de Chochueca* (2000) and *Papi* (2005) problematize gender, race, and nationality in the definition of Dominican identity.[96] Her narrative questions traditional definitions of Caribbeanness to unseat the patriarchal and racist assumptions behind the official discourse that supports the constitution of a white *criollo* national identity in the Dominican Republic. More recently, in the short story collection *Mundo cruel* (2010), Luis Negrón has explored the end of homophobia as a new frontier in the articulation of a Puerto Rican identity conceived as an act of imagination that requires a reinvention of the self beyond the framework of anti-normativity and marginality.[97]

In the Anglo Caribbean, trans characters have become the new embodiment of the unreadable postcolonial Caribbean identities in Michelle Cliff's *No Telephone to Heaven*, Shani Mootoo's *Cereus Blooms at Night* (1996), and *The Pagoda* (1998) by Patricia Powell, among other texts.[98] In these narratives, the unreadablity and marginality of the trans body becomes the point of departure to present a critical view of the possibilities and challenges of contemporary Caribbean identities.[99] Cliff plays a central role in the inclusion of trans characters in Caribbean narratives when she proposes a dialogue between the fluidity of gender expression in the Jamaican nationalist character Harry/Harriet, and the bisexual *mulata* Clare. Both Mootoo and Powell connect the queerness of the non-binary gendered body with the unreadability of Indo and Chinese Caribbean identities, a topic that has been explored by Sam Selvon, V.S. Naipaul, David Dabydeen, Calvert Casey, Lourdes Casal, and Severo Sarduy.[100] The extreme exotization of the Asian and the queer and trans bodies in the context of an Afro-creolized Caribbean, serves in many of these narratives as the source of an internal critique against the adoption of *mulataje* as another normative identity script. Finally, in *Sirena Silena vestida de pena* (2000) Mayra Santos Febres combines race, gender expression and pan Caribeannism in the creation of a protagonist that symbolizes a new voice and perspective for the Caribbean.[101]

Some authors have explored intra-Caribbean connections as part of their decolonial imaginaries of resistance. In Puerto Rico, Ana Lydia Vega published *Encancaranublado* (1983), a short story collection dedicated to the Caribbean confederation of the future, that includes stories connecting Puerto Rico, Cuba, Martinique, the Dominican Republic, Jamaica, and Haiti.[102] Manuel Ramos Otero reimagines the Caribbean and diasporic dimensions of Puerto Ricanness through a series of queer characters that imbricate the Afro and Asian Caribbeans, as well as the Caribbean and Latino diasporas in the United States.[103] His narrative and poems make visible the perspective and experiences of Black queer Puerto Rican who are also linked to the Anglo and French Caribbean through their African and Asian roots, or make references to Puerto Rican migration to Hawai'i. Pedro Cabiya and Mayra Montero question the traditional definition of Caribbean writers who use nationality as a defining category by producing narratives that explore intra-Caribbean connections, as well as texts in which Afro-Caribbean religiosity, *espiritismo* and sci-fi redefine the coexistence of modern and traditional customs and beliefs in contemporary Caribbean cultures. Finally, Tiphanie Yanique, invokes and explores an archipelagic imaginary in her book *How to Escape from a Leper Colony* (2010) that includes not only the major islands of the Caribbean, but also smaller islands or less visible parts of the archipelago, like the U.S. Virgin Islands.[104] Although this constant invocation of the Caribbean confederation and the archipelagic does not go beyond the realm of the imaginary, all of these recent works interrogate the currency of the national and the postcolonial as the prevalent modes to imagine resistance in the region.

Conclusion: Comparative Colonialities in the Caribbean

In this essay, I have discussed the development of a Caribbean literature of resistance taking into account three parallel discourses: the definition of Afro-Caribbean and Asian Caribbean identities, the exploration of alternative political imaginaries for the region, and the depiction of gender and sexuality as other ways of conceiving the uniqueness of the archipelago. In the overview proposed in this essay, I am making several implicit claims that I would like to discuss briefly here.

First, although the usual conceptualization of the Caribbean from a Latin American Studies perspective tends to focus on the Spanish Caribbean, in this essay I have attempted to address the Spanish, Anglo, and French Caribbeans. The main rationale for this approach is that it would be difficult to understand the historical and cultural development of a literature of resistance that does not take into account the contacts of the Spanish Caribbean with Latin America as well as with the other Caribbeans. Resistance to colonialism and imperialism in the Caribbean emerges and takes place in a constant dialogical exchange between the structures and legacies of Spanish, French, English, and Dutch colonialisms in the region, as well as the postcolonial and decolonial relationships with Spain, France, England, Holland, and the United States. Decolonizing the Caribbean implies questioning the nationalist framework that reiterates colonial fragmentations in the way in which we study and conceive the cultural and geopolitical organization of the region.

Second, to understand the density and complexity of the many layers of colonialism, extended colonialism and resistances in the region, it is crucial to maintain a comparative approach that recognizes the points of political and historical contact, as well as the internal tensions and differences that have informed the constitution of a Caribbean imaginary. This comparative paradigm invokes colonialism, postcolonialism and decoloniality as important theoretical paradigms that illuminate the different aspects of the cultural, literary, and discursive strategies invoked by Caribbean writers and thinkers from the 1930s to the present. I have proposed as an experiment to use each one of these theoretical frameworks to rethink different time periods in the Caribbean, but I am also arguing that the three frameworks could illuminate different aspects in all the diverse statges of the cultural representations of resistance in the region.

Finally, in this essay I am redefining resistance beyond the political, to focus on the many embodiments of alterity in which alternative definitions of Caribbean identities are predicated. Therefore, this essay traces the development of a discourse of resistance that is linked to political sovereignty, autonomy, and colonialism, but it also includes debates on race and creolization, as well as issues of gender, sexuality and gender expression that have all been used as referents for the many states of exception that are common in the articulation of unique Caribbean identities. By redefining the Caribbean as that region where Latin America meets the broken imperial frontier of modernity, this essay serves as a pretext to question the imperial/colonial paradigms informing area studies, and invites the readers to reconceptualize literary and cultural studies from a decolonial perspective. In this context, resistance is transformed from a strictly political and ideological category that inflects cultural productions and historical processes into a disconcerting motive that interrogates the notion of identity to privilege the incommensurate possibilities of archipelagic *diversality*.[105]

Notes

1 Selwyn R. Cudjoe, *Resistance and Caribbean Literature* (Athens, OH: Ohio University Press, 1980).

2 Julia de Burgos, "Ay, ay ay de la grifa negra." www.elboricua.com/Poems_Burgos_AyAyAyGrifaNegra.html accessed October 15, 2015. "My, oh my, oh my of the Nappy haired Negress," In *Puerto Rican Poetry: A Selection of Aboriginal to Contemporary Times*, edited and translated by Roberto Márquez (Amherst, MA: University of Massachusetts Press, 2007), 223–224.

3 For the vision of the vanquished, see Miguel León Portilla, *Visión de los vencidos: crónicas indígenas* (México: UNAM, 1959) *and* Nathan Watchtel, *La Vision des Vaincus—Les Indiens du Pérou devant la Conquête Espagnole (1530–1570)* (Paris: Gallimard, 1971). Recent studies on khipus include Frank Salomon, *The Cord Keepers: Khipus and Cultural Life in a Peruvian Village* (Durham, NC: Duke University Press, 2004) and Galen Brokaw, *A History of the Khipu* (Cambridge: Cambridge University Press, 2010); textiles, codices and pictorial documents are analyzed by Justo Cáceres Macedo, *Tejidos del Perú prehispánico* (Lima, Peru: Justo Cáceres Macedo, 2005), Elizabeth Boone, "Pictorial Documents and Visual Thinking in Postconquest Mexico," In *Native Traditions in the Postconquest World*, edited by Elizabeth Boone and Tom Cummins, 149–199 (Washington, DC: Dumbarton Oaks, 1998); and oral traditions, indigenous textualities and performances have been studied by Martín Lienhard, *La voz y su huella* (México: Ediciones Casa Juan Pablos /Universidad de Ciencias y Artes, 2003); Laura León Llerena, "Historia, lenguaje y narración en el Manuscrito de Huarochirí," *Diálogo andino*, Vol 30 (2007): 33–42; *and* Diana Taylor, *The Archive and the Repertoire: Performing Cultural Memory in the Americas* (Durham, NC: Duke University Press, 2003).

4 Rolena Adorno, "Nuevas perspectivas en los estudios literarios coloniales hispanoamericanos," *Revista de crítica literaria latinoamericana*, Vol 14, No. 28 (1988): 11–28 and "Reconsidering Colonial Discourse for Sixteenth- and Seventeenth-Century Spanish America," *Latin American Research Review*, Vol 28, No. 3 (1993): 135–145.

5 Walter Mignolo, "Afterword: From Colonial Discourse to Colonial Semiosis," *Dispositio*, Vol 14, No. 36–38 (1989): 333–337.

6 Josaphat Kubayanda, "On Colonial/Imperial Discourse and Contemporary Critical Theory," *1992 Lecture Series* (College Park, MD: University of Maryland, 1990) and José Rabasa, "Reading Cabeza de Vaca, or How We Perpetuate the Culture of Conquest," In *Writing Violence on the Northern Frontier: The Historiography of Sixteenth Century New Mexico and Florida and the Legacy of Conquest* (Durham, NC: Duke University Press, 2000), 31–83.

7 *Criollo* in the Spanish Caribbean usually refers to a white Spaniard born and raised in the Americas. Creole in the Anglo and French Caribbean usually includes populations of black descent, that through adaptation and intermixing produced the unique cultures existing in the Caribbean today. For more information on the difference between these two terms in the Caribbean, see Yolanda Martínez-San Miguel, "Poéticas caribeñas de lo criollo: creole/criollo/créolité," In *Poéticas de lo criollo: la transformación del concepto "criollo" en las letras hispanoamericanas (siglo XVI al XIX)*, edited by Juan M. Vitulli and David Solodkow, 411–412 (Buenos Aires: Editorial Corregidor, 2009); José Antonio Mazzotti, "*Criollismo*, Creole, *Créolité*," In *Critical Terms in Caribbean and Latin American Thought*, edited by Yolanda Martínez-San Miguel, Ben, Sifuentes-Jáuregui and Marisa Belausteguigoitia, 87–100 (New York, NY: Palgrave Macmillan, 2016); H. Adlai Murdoch, "II. Creole. Criollismo, and Créolité," In *Critical Terms in Caribbean and Latin American Thought*, edited by Yolanda Martínez-San Miguel, Ben, Sifuentes-Jáuregui and Marisa Belausteguigoitia, 101–107 (New York: Palgrave Macmillan, 2016); and Magaly Roy Fequière, *Women, Creole Identity, and Intellectual Life in Early Twentieth-Century Puerto Rico* (Philadelphia, PA: Temple University Press, 2004).

8 Josaphat Kubayanda, *The Poet's Africa: Africanness in the Poetry of Nicolás Guillén and Aimé Césaire* (New York, NY: Greenwood Press, 1990).

9 See Josaphat Kubayanda, "On Colonial/Imperial Discourse and Contemporary Critical Theory," In *1992 Lecture Series* (College Park, MD: University of Maryland 1990); Jerome Branche, *Colonialism and Race in Luso-Hispanic Literature* (Columbia, MO: University of Missouri Press, 2006); and Mamadou Badiane, *The Changing Face of Afro-Caribbean Cultural Identity: Negrismo and Négritude* (Lanham, MD: Lexington Books 2010).

10 James A. Arnold, *Modernism and Négritude: The Poetry and Poetics of Aimé Césaire* (Cambridge, MA: Harvard University Press, 1981); Frank Guridy, "From Solidarity to Cross-Fertilization: Afro-Cuban/African American Interaction During the 1930s and 1940s," *Radical History Review*, Vol

87 (2003): 19–48; and Víctor Figueroa, *Not at Home in One's Home : Caribbean Self-fashioning in the Poetry of Luis Palés Matos, Aimé Césaire, and Derek Walcott* (Madison, NJ: Fairleigh Dickinson University Press, 2009).

11 Antonio S. Pedreira, *Insularismo* (Madrid: Tipografía artística, 1934).

12 Tomás Blanco, "Elogio de la plena," In Literature puertorriqueña del siglo XX, antología, edited by Mercedes López Baralt, 50–58 (Río Piedras, Puerto Rico: Universidad de Puerto Rico, 2004).

13 Tomás Blanco, *El prejuicio racial en Puerto Rico* (Río Piedras, Puerto Rico: Huracán, 1985). The Ponce Massacre took place on March 21, 1937 (Palm Sunday) in Puerto Rico, when a pacific march organized by the Nationalist Party turned into a police shooting. Nineteen persons were dead and hundreds were wounded. For more information, see Juan Manuel Garcia-Passalacqua, "*Remembering Puerto Rico's Ponce Massacre.*" Interview with Juan Gonzalez; Amy Goodman. *Democracy Now*, March 22, 2007. www.democracynow.org/2007/3/22/remembering_puerto_ricos_ponce_massacre accessed Oct. 20, 2015.

14 Julia de Burgos, *Poema en veinte surcos* (San Juan, Puerto Rico: Impresora Venezuela, 1938).

15 Nicolás Guillén, *Motivos de son* (Habana: Imprenta y Papeleria de Rambla, Bouze y Ca., 1930); *Sóngoro cosongo* (México: Presencia Latinoamericana, 1981); and *West Indies Ltd.* (La Habana: Imp. Ucar, García y Cía., 1934).

16 Nicolás Guillén, "Balada de los dos abuelos," In *Sóngoro cosongo y otros poemas* (Madrid: Alianza Editorial, 1980), 27–28; "Ballad of the Two Grandfathers," In *Nicolás Guillén: Yoruba from Cuba. Selected Poems*, translated by Salvador Ortiz-Carboneres (Leeds, UK: Peepal Tree Press, 2005), 27–29.

17 Alejo Carpentier, *¡Ecué-Yamba-O!* (Madrid: España, 1933).

18 Fernando Ortiz, *Los negros brujos* (Madrid: Librería de Fernando Fe, 1906); *Los negros esclavos* (Habana: Revista bimestre cubana, 1916); and *Glosario de afronegrismos* (Habana: Imprenta "El Siglo XX", 1924).

19 Alejo Carpentier, *Viaje a la semilla* (La Habana: Ucar y García, 1944).

20 Manuel del Cabral, *12 poemas negros* (Santo Domingo, RD: Tip. Femina, 1935); *Compadre Mon* (Buenos Aires: Los Editores del Autor, 1942); and *Trópico negro* (Buenos Aires: Editorial Sopena Argentina, 1941).

21 *Criollismo* refers to the Spanish discourse on *criollos*, conceived as white people of European descent born and raised in the Americas. In this essay, I use *criollo* and *criollismo* to refer to the specific inflections of creole discourse in the Spanish Caribbean.

22 For more information on the 1937 massacre at the border between the Dominican Republic and Haiti, see Richard Turits, "A World Destroyed, A Nation Imposed: The 1937 Haitian Massacre on the Dominican Republic," *Hispanic American Historical Review*, Vol 92, No. 3 (2002): 589–635; and Lorgia García Peña, "Speaking in Silences: Literary Interruptions and the Massacre of 1937," *The Borders of Dominicanidad: Race, Nation, and Archives of Contradiction* (Durham, NC: Duke University Press, 2016).

23 Joaquín Balaguer, *La isla al revés: Haiti y el destino dominicano* (Santo Domingo, República Dominicana: Fundación José Antonio Caro, 1983). The tensions between Dominicans and Haitians continue until today. On September 23, 2013, a new law was approved in the Dominican Republic revoking the citizenship of any descendant of Haitian immigrants born in the Dominican Republic after 1929. This law potentially affected up to two hundred thousand persons residing in the Dominican Republic.

24 Milagros Ricourt, *The Dominican Racial Imaginary: Surveying the Landscape of Race and Nation in Hispaniola* (New Brunswick, NJ: Rutgers University Press, 2016).

25 Juan Bosch, "Luis Pié," in *Cuentos escritos en el exilio* (Santo Domingo: Alfa y Omega, 1979).

26 Josefina Báez, *Dominicanish* (New York, NY: Josefina Báez, 2000).

27 Blas Jiménez, *Caribe africano en despertar* (Santo Domingo: Editora Nuevas Rutas, 1984); *El nativo. (versos en cuentos para espantar zombies)* (Santo Domingo: Editora Búho, 1996); and *Afrodominicano por elección, negro por nacimiento: pseudoensayos* (Santa Domingo: Editora Manatí, 2008).

28 Aimé Césaire, *Cahier d'un retour au pays natal* (Paris: Editions Presence Africaine, 1971), 129; *Notebook of a Return to the Native Land.* Trad. Clayton Eshleman (Connecticut: Wesleyan University Press, 2001), 39–40.

29 Fernando Ortiz, *Contrapunteo cubano del tabaco y del azúcar* (La Habana: J. Montero, 1940).

30 Lydia Cabrera, *Cuentos negros de Cuba* (La Habana: La Verónica, 1940); *El Monte.* (La Habana: Ediciones C.R., 1954); and *Refranes de negros viejos* (Habana: Ediciones C.R., 1955).

31 Alejo Carpentier, *El reino de este mundo* (México: Edición y Distribución Ibero Americana de Publicaciones, 1949).
32 Virgilio Piñera, *La isla en peso* (La Habana: Tipografía García, 1998).
33 Julia de Burgos, *El mar y tú, y otros poemas* (San Juan, Puerto Rico: P. R. Printing and Publishing Company, 1954).
34 Aida Cartagena Portalatín, *Mi mundo el mar* (Santo Domingo: Colección La Isla Necesaria, 1953) and *Una mujer está sola* (Santo Domingo: Colección La Isla Necesaria, 1955). La Poesía Sorprendida was a group of poets organized around a literary journal of the same name that was founded in 1943. Their poetry was characterized by surrealist and avant-garde motifs and is linked to the resistance against colonialism and neocolonialism in the Caribbean, and the Trujillato in the Dominican Rrepublic. For more information see Anthony Dawahare, "'La Poesía Sorprendida'; or the Surrealist Poetic Imagination Against Neocolonial Dictatorship in the Dominican Republic, 1943–1947," *South Central Review*, Vol 32, No. 1 (2015): 96–115.
35 Eric Williams, *Capitalism and Slavery* (Chapel Hill, NC: University of North Carolina Press, 1944).
36 Cyril Lionel Robert James, *The Black Jacobins* (New York, NY: Vintage Books [1963]).
37 Calvert Casey, "El regreso," In *El regreso, cuentos* (La Habana: Ediciones Revolución, 1962), 120. The English translation provided here is mine.
38 Yarimar Bonilla researches the issue of the sovereignty in the Caribbean in her book *Non-Sovereign Futures: French Caribbean Politics in the Wake of Disenchantment* (Chicago: University of Chicago Press, 2015). She notes, for example, that of the forty-five countries that constitute the insular and continental Caribbean, only twelve are sovereign and independent states, while twelve are independent states within the British Commonwealth of Nations, six are overseas territories of the United Kingdom, three are overseas departments of France, four are unincorporated territories of the United States, three are "constituent countries within the Kingdom of the Netherlands," three are special municipalities of the Kingdom of the Netherlands and two are overseas collectivities of France. For more informtion, see Yarimar Bonilla, "Non-Sovereign Futures: French Caribbean Politics in the Wake of Disenchantment," In *Caribbean Sovereignty, Democracy and Development in an Age of Globalization*, edited by Linden Lewis, 209–212 (New York, NY: Routledge, 2013).
39 See Lammert De Jong and Dirk Krujit, eds. *Extended Statehood in the Caribbean: Paradoxes of Quasi Colonialism, Local Autonomy, and Extended Statehood in the USA, French, Dutch, & British Caribbean* (Amsterdam: Rozenberg Publishers, 2006.); Franklin W. Knight, *The Caribbean: The Genesis of a Fragmented Nationalism* 2nd ed (New York: Oxford University Press, 1990); and Ramón Soto-Crespo, *Mainland Passage: The Cultural Anomaly of Puerto Rico* (Minneapolis: University of Minnesota Press, 2009).
40 Edward Said, *Orientalism* (New York, NY: Vintage Books, 1978).
41 See Gayatri Chakravorty Spivak, *In Other Worlds: Essays in Cultural Politics* (York, UK: Methuen, 1987); Homi Bhabha, *The Location of Culture* (London and New York, NY: Routledge, 1994); Paul Gilroy, *The Black Atlantic: Modernity and Double Consciousness* (Cambridge, MA: Harvard University Press, 1995); and Stuart Hall, "When Was 'the Postcolonial': Thinking at the Limit," In *The Postcolonial Question*, edited by Iain Chambers and Lidia Curti, 242–260 (London and New York, NY: Routledge, 1996).
42 See Yomaira Figueroa, "Duelo de Teorías/Theory Duel?: Post(De)Colonial Theories in Relation," (Paper presented at the annual Latin American Studies Association Conference, New York, May 27–30, 2016); and Anjali Nerlekar, "Beyond National Bounds, the Indo Caribbean," (Paper presented at the annual Latin American Studies Association Conference, New York, May 27–30, 2016).
43 See Fernando Coronil, "Beyond Occidentalism: Toward Nonimperial Geohistorical Categories," *Cultural Anthropology*, Vol 11, No. 1 (1996): 52–87, and "Elephants in the Americas? Latin American Postcolonial Studies and Global Decolonization," In *Coloniality at Large: Latin America and the Postcolonial Debate*, edited by Mabel Moraña, Enrique Dussel and Carlos Jáuregui, 396–416 (Durham, NC: Duke University Press, 2008).
44 Jorge Klor de Alva, "The Postcolonization of the (Latin) American Experience: A Reconsideration of 'Colonialism,' 'Postcolonialsim,' and 'Mestizaje,'" In *After Colonialism: Imperial Histories and Postcolonial Displacements*, edited by Gyan Prakash, 245 (Princeton, NJ: Princeton University Press).

45 Latin American Subaltern Studies Group. 1993. "Founding Statement," *Boundary 2*, Vol 20, No. 3: 110–121.
46 Shalini Puri, *The Caribbean Postcolonial* (New York, NY: Palgrave Macmillan, 2004), and Stuart Hall, "When Was 'the Postcolonial': Thinking at the Limit," In *The Postcolonial Question*, edited by Iain Chambers and Lidia Curti (London and New York, NY: Routledge, 1996).
47 Bill Ashcroft, Gareth Griffiths, and Helen Tiffin, *The Empire Writes Back: Theory and Practice in Postcolonial Literature* (London and New York: Routledge, 1989) and "Introduction," to Postmodernism and Postcolonialism, In *The Postcolonial Studies Reader*, edited by Bill Ashcroft, Gareth Griffiths, and Helen Tiffin, 17 (London and New York, NY: Routledge, 1995).
48 Silvio Torres-Saillant, *An Intellectual History of the Caribbean* (New York, NY: Palgrave Macmillan, 2006), 43.
49 Aimé Césaire, *Discours sur le colonialisme* (Paris: Présence Africaine, 2004).
50 Pedro Mir, *Contracanto a Walt Whitman* (Guatemala: Ediciones Saker-Ti, 1952); *Hay un país en el mundo* (Santo Domingo: Educarte 2009); and *Viaje a la muchedumbre* (Santo Domingo, RD: Lucerna, 1971).
51 René Marqués, *La víspera del hombre* (San Juan: Club del Libro de Puerto Rico; *Los soles truncos* (Río Piedras: Editorial Cultural, 1958); and "En la popa hay un cuerpo reclinado," In *Cuentos puertorriqueños de hoy*, edited by Abelardo Milton Díaz Alfaro and René Marquès, 129–146 (México, DF: Club del Libro de Puerto Rico, 1959).
52 René Marqués, *El puertorriqueño dócil: literatura y realidad psicológica* (Buenos Aires: Cuadernos Americanos, 1962).
53 René Marqués, *La carreta* (Río Piedras: Cultural, 1983).
54 Pedro Juan Soto, *Spiks* (Río Piedras, PR: Editorial Cultural, 1973) and José Luis González, "La carta," In *El hombre en la calle* (Puerto Rico: Editorial Bohique, 1948), 9–22.
55 Frantz Fanon, *Peau Noir, Masques Blancs* (Paris: Seuil, 1952).
56 Frantz Fanon, *Les damnés de la terre* (Paris: Gallimard, 1991).
57 George Lamming, *The Emigrants* (London: Michael Joseph; New York: McGraw Hill, 1954) and *The Pleasures of Exile* (London: Michael Joseph, 1960).
58 Yolanda Martínez-San Miguel, *Coloniality of Diasporas: Rethinking Intra-Colonial Migrations in a Pan Caribbeann Context* (New York, NY: Palgrave Macmillan, 2014).
59 Sylvia Wynter's, *Hills of Hebron* (New York, NY: Simon and Schuster, 1962); Jean Ryss, *Wide Sargasso Sea* by Jean Ryss (New York, NY: Norton, [1992]); José Lezama Lima, *Paradiso* (Madrid: Cátedra, 1980); and Severo Sarduy, *De dónde son los cantantes* (México: J. Mortiz, 1970).
60 Miguel Barnet, *Biografía de un cimarrón.* (La Habana: Instituto de Ethnología y Folklore, 1966).
61 Nancy Morejón, *Poemas* (México: Universidad Nacional Autónoma de México, Difusión Cultural, Departamento de Humanidades, 1980); and *Cuerda veloz: Antología poética, 1962–1992* (La Habana: Editorial Letras Cubanas, 2002).
62 Aimé Césaire, *Discours sur le colonialisme* (Paris: Présence Africaine, 2004) and *Une tempête; d'après "La tempête de Shakespeare. Adaptation pour un théâthre nègre"* (Paris: Éditions du Seuil, 1969).
63 Calvert Casey's "El regreso" *El regreso, cuentos* (La Habana: Ediciones Revolución, 1962), 107–124 and Vidiadhar Surajprasad Naipaul, *The Mimic Men* (New York, NY: Palgrave Macmillan, 1967).
64 Eric Williams, *From Columbus to Castro: The History of the Caribbean, 1492–1969* (New York, NY: Harper & Row, 1971) and Juan Bosch, *De Cristóbal Colón a Fidel Castro* (Madrid: Alfaguara, 1970).
65 Juan Bosch, *De Cristóbal Colón a Fidel Castro* (Madrid: Alfaguara, 1970), 11. The translation into English is mine.
66 Roberto Fernández Retamar, "Calibán," *Casa de las Américas*, Vol 68 (1971): 124–151.
67 Lourdes Casal, *Los fundadores: Alfonso y otros relatos* (Miami, FL: Ediciones Universal, 1973).
68 Isabelo Zenón, *Narciso descubre su trasero*, 2 vols (Humacao, Puerto Rico: Editorial Furidi, 1974–1975).
69 José Luis González, *El país de cuatro pisos y otros ensayos* (Río Piedras, Puerto Rico: Ediciones Huracán, 1980).
70 Sylvia Wynter, "Jonkonnu in Jamaica: Towards an Interpretation of Folk Dance as a Cultural Process," *Jamaica Journal*, Vol 4, No. 2 (1970): 34–48.
71 Paula Moya, "The Search for Decolonial Love: A Conversation between Junot Díaz and Paula M. L. Moya," *Boston Review* (2012). www.bostonreview.net/books-ideas/paula-ml-moya-decolonial-love-interview-junot-d%C3%ADaz accessed July 13, 2016.

72 Although the concept of coloniality of power was coined in the early 1990s, its best formulation can be found in Aníbal Quijano, "Coloniality of Power, Ethnocentrism, and Latin America," *NEPLANTA*, Vol 1, No. 3 (2000): 533–580.

73 See Fermando H. Cardoso and Faletto Enzo, *Dependency and Development in Latin America* (Berkeley, CA: University of California Press, 1979); Rodolfo Stavenhagen, "Classes, Colonialism and Acculturation," *Studies in Comparative International Development*, Vol 1, No. 6 (1965): 53–77; Pablo González Casanova, "Internal Colonialism and National Development," *Studies in Comparative International Development*, Vol 1, No. 4 (1965): 27–37; Álvaro Félix Bolaños and Gustavo Verdesio, *Colonialism Past and Present* (Albany, NY: State University of New York Press, 2002).

74 Yolanda Martínez-San Miguel, *Coloniality of Diasporas: Rethinking Intra-Colonial Migrations in a Pan Caribbeann Context* (New York, NY: Palgrave Macmillan, 2014).

75 Walter Mignolo, "Coloniality: The Darker Side of Modernity," In *Modernologies: Contemporary Artists Researching Modernity and Modernism*, edited by Sabine Breitwisser, 39–49 (catalogue of the Exhibit at the Museum of Modern Art, Barcelona, Spain). (Fall, 2009).

76 Emma Pérez, *The Decolonial Imaginary: Writing Chicanas into History* (Indianapolis, IN: Indiana University Press, 1999); and Chela Sandova, *Methodology of the Oppressed* (Minneapolis, MN: Minnesota University Press 2000).

77 Gloria Anzaldúa, *Borderlands/La frontera* (San Francisco, CA: Spinsters/Aunt Lute, 1987); Chandra Talpade Mohanty, Ann Russo and Lourdes Torres. *Third World Women and the Politics of Feminism* (Bloomington, IN: Indiana University Press, 1991); and Cherríe Moraga and Gloria Anzaldúa, *This Bridge Called my Back: Writings By Radical Women of Color* (New York, NY: Kitchen Table, Women of Color Press, 1983).

78 Nelson Maldonado-Torres, Colonialism, Necolonialism, Internal Colonialims, The Postcolonial, Coloniality and Decoloniality," In *Critical Terms in Caribbean and Latin American Thought*, edited by Yolanda Martínez-San Miguel, Ben Sifuentes-Jáuregui, and Marisa Belausteguigoitia, 67–78 (New York, NY: Palgrave Macmillan, 2016).

79 Aimé Césaire, *Discours sur le colonialisme* (Paris: Présence Africaine, 2004. [1950]); Frantz Fanon, *Peau Noir, Masques Blancs* (Paris: Seuil, 1952) and Sylvia Wynter, "Jonkonnu in Jamaica: Towards an Interpretation of Folk Dance as a Cultural Process," *Jamaica Journal*, Vol 4, No. 2 (1970): 34–48.

80 Yomaira Figueroa, "Duelo de Teorías/Theory Duel?: Post(De)Colonial Theories in Relation," (Paper presented at the annual Latin American Studies Association Conference, New York, May 27–30, 2016); and Anjali Nerlekar, "Beyond National Bounds, the Indo Caribbean," (Paper presented at the annual Latin American Studies Association Conference, New York, May 27–30, 2016).

81 Shalini Puri, *The Grenada Revolution in the Caribbean Present: Operation Urgent Memory* (New York, NY: Palgrave Macmillan, 2014); David Scott, *Omens of Adversity: Tragedy, Memory, Justice* (Durham, NC: Duke University Press, 2014) and Brian Meeks, *Caribbean Revolutions and Revolutionary Theory* (London: Macmillan Caribbean, 1993).

82 Shalini Puri, *The Grenada Revolution in the Caribbean Present: Operation Urgent Memory* (New York, NY: Palgrave Macmillan, 2014); David Scott, *Omens of Adversity: Tragedy, Memory, Justice* (Durham, NC: Duke University Press, 2014); Laurie Lambert, "The Revolution and Its Discontents: Grenadian Newspapers and Attempts to Shape Public Opinion During Political Transition," *The Round Table: The Commonwealth Journal of International Affairs*, Vol 102, No. 2 (2013):143–153; and Laurie Lambert, "The Sovereignty of the Imagination: Poetic Authority and the Fiction of North Atlantic Universals in Dionne Brand's Chronicles of the Hostile Sun," *Cultural Dynamics*, Vol 26, No. 2 (2014): 173–194.

83 Edward Kamau Brathwaite, *History of the Voice* (Westport, CT: Praeger Publishers, 2004) and *The Development of Creole Society in Jamaica, 1770–1820* (Oxford: Clarendon Press, 1971).

84 Stuart Hall, "When Was 'the Postcolonial': Thinking at the Limit," In *The Postcolonial Question*, edited by Iain Chambers and Lidia Curti (London and New York, NY: Routledge, 1996).

85 Jean Bernabé, Patrick Chamoiseau, and Raphaël Confiant, *Éloge de la Créolité/ In Praise of Creoleness*, translated by Mohamed B. Taleb Khyar (Baltimore, MD: Johns Hopkins University, 1990).

86 Edouard Glissant, *Poétique de la rélacion* (Paris: Gallimard, 1990) and *Traité du tout-monde* (Paris: Gallimard, 1997).

87 René Depestre, *Buenos días y adiós a la negritud* (La Habana: Casa de las Américas, 1985).

88 Patrick Chamoiseau, *Texaco* (Paris: Gallimard, 1992); David Dabydeen, *Slave Song* (Mundelstrup, Denmark: Dangaroo Press, 1984); Michelle Cliff, *Abeng* (New York, NY: Plume Books, 1995) and *No Telephone to Heaven* (New York, NY: Plume, 1996); and Derek Walcott, *Omeros* (New York, NY: Farrar, Straus, Giroux, 1990) and *The Bounty* (New York, NY: Farrar, Straus, Giroux, 1997).

89 Jamaica Kincaid, *A Small Place* (New York, NY: Farrar, Straus, Giroux, 1988); Don E. Walicek, "Pathways of Language and Memory: The Origins of Anguillian in Sociohistorical Context," PhD thesis, University of Puerto Rico, 2009; Jessica Swanston Baker, "Too Fast: Coloniality and Time in Wylers of St. Kitts and Nevis," PhD Dissertation, University of Pennsylvania, 2015.

90 Luis Rafael Sánchez, *La guaracha del Macho Camacho* (Buenos Aires: Ediciones de la Flor, 1976); Rosario Ferré, *Maldito amor* (Río Piedras: Ediciones Huracán, 1994); Ana Lydia Vega and Carmen Lugo Filippi, *Vírgenes y mártires* (Rio Piedras: Antillana, 1981); and Manuel Ramos Otero, *Página en blanco y staccato* (Madrid: Playor, 1987).

91 Thomas Glave, *Our Caribbean: A Gathering of Lesbian and Gay Writing From the Antilles* (Durham, NC: Duke University Press, 2008).

92 Examples of other anthologies are David Caleb Acevedo, Moisés Agosto and Luis Negrón, eds. *Los otros cuerpos: Antología de temática gay, lésbica y queer desde Puerto Rico y su diáspora* (San Juan, Puerto Rico: Editorial Tiempo Nuevo, 2007); Jacqueline Polanco, *Divagaciones de la luna: voces e imágenes de lesbianas dominicanas* (Santo Domingo: Idegraf Editora, 2006); and Mélida García and Miguel de Camps Jimeenez, *Antología de la literatura gay en la República Dominicana* (Santo Domingo: Editora Manatí, 2004). The special issues are Luis Aponte-Parés, Jossianna Arroyo, Elizabeth Crespo-Kebler, Lawrence La Fountain-Stokes, and Frances Negrón-Muntaner, eds. "Puerto Rican Queer Sexualities," *CENTRO: Journal of the Center for Puerto Rican Studies*, Vol 19, No. 1 (Spring 2007); Don E. Walicek and Susan Muhleisen, eds. "Constructions of gender, desire and sexuality" *Sargasso* (2008–2009); and "Love, Hope, Community: Sexualities and Social Justice," *Sargasso*, Vol 1–2 (2014–2015).

93 Ronald Cummings, "Queer Marronage and Caribbean Writing," PhD Dissertation, University of Leeds, 2012 and Ronald Cummings, "(Trans)Nationalisms, Marronage and Queer Caribbean Subjectivities," *Transforming Anthropology*, Vol 18, No. 2 (2010): 169–180.

94 See Natasha Omise'eke Tinsley, *Thiefing Sugar* (Durham, NC: Duke University Press Books 2010); Gloria Wekker, *The Politics of Passion: Women's Sexual Culture in the Afro-Surinamese Diaspora* (New York, NY: Columbia University Press, 2006); Kamala Kempadoo, ed. *Sun, Sex, and Gold: Tourism and Sex Work in the Caribbean* (Lanham, MD: Rowman and Littlefield, 1999); Yuderkys Espinosa, *Escritos de una lesbiana oscura: reflexiones críticas sobre feminismo, política e identidad en América Latina* (Buenos Aires: En la Frontera, 2007) and Mimi Sheller, *Citizenship from Below: Erotic Agency and Caribbean Freedom* (Durham, NC: Duke University Press, 2012).

95 Rey Emanuel Andújar, *El hombre triángulo* (San Juan, Puerto Rico: Editorial Isla Negra, 2005); *Candela* (Santo Domingo: República Dominicana: Alfaguara, 2007); and *Amoricidio* (Santo Domingo, República Dominicana: Dirección General de la Feria del Libro, 2008).

96 Rita Indiana Hernández, *La estrategia de Chochueca* (República Dominicana: Riann Editorial, 2000) and *Papi* (San Juan, Puerto Rico: Ediciones Vértigo, 2005).

97 Luis Negrón, *Mundo cruel* (Río Piedras, Puerto Rico: La Secta de los Perros, 2010).

98 Rosamond King, *Island Bodies: Transgressive Sexualities in the Caribbean Imagination* (Gainesville, FL: University Press of Florida, 2014) and Yolanda Martínez-San Miguel, "Trans-Caribe: fluidez genérica en tres novelas del Caribe inglés," *80 grados:Prensa sin prisa*, February 28, 2014. www.80grados.net/trans-caribe-fluidez-generica-en-tres-novelas-del-caribe-ingles/ accessed July 14, 2016.

99 Michelle Cliff, *No Telephone to Heaven* (New York, NY: Plume, 1996); Shani Mootoo, *Cereus Blooms at Night* (New York, NY: Grove Press, 1996) and Patricia Powell, *The Pagoda* (Orlando: Harcourt Books, 1998).

100 Scholarship on Indo Caribbean literature includes Samuel Selvon, "Three Into One Can't Go—East Indian, Trinidadian, Westindian," In *India in the Caribbean*, edited by David Dabydeen and Brinsley Samaroo, 13–24 (London: Hansib Publishing, 1987); Marina Carter Marina and Khal Torabully, eds. *Coolitude: An Anthology of the Indian Diaspora* (London: Anthem Press, 2002); Gaiutra Bahadur, *Coolie Woman: The Odyssey of Indenture* (Chicago, IL: University of Chicago Press, 2014); Shalini Puri, *The Caribbean Postcolonial*; *Critical Perspectives on Indo-Caribbean Women's Literature*, edited by Joy Mahabir and Mariam Pirbhai (New York, NY: Routledge, 2012); Frank Birbalsingh, "The Indo-Caribbean Short Story," *Journal of West*

Indian Literature, Vol 12, No. 1–2 (2004): 118–134. For the study of Chinese migration to the Hispanic Caribbean see Kathleen Lopez, *Chineses Cubans: A Transnational History* (Chapell Hill, NC: The University of North Carolina Press, 2013) and José Lee Borges, *Los chinos en Puerto Rico* (San Juan, Puerto Rico: Ediciones Callejón, 2015).

101 Mayra Santos Febres, *Sirena Selena vestida de pena* (Barcelona: Mondadori, 2000).

102 Ana Lydia Vega, *Encancaranublado* (Río Piedras, Puerto Rico: Editorial Antillana, 1983).

103 Manuel Ramos Otero, *Página en blanco y staccato* (Madrid: Playor, 1987).

104 Tiphanie Yanique, *How to Escape From a Leper Colony* (Minneapolis, MN: Graywolf Press, 2010).

105 I use the term to refer to universal diversity as used by Jean Bernabé, Patrick Chamoiseau, and Raphaël Confiant, *Éloge de la Créolité/ In Praise of Creoleness*," translated by Mohamed B. Taleb Khyar (Baltimore, MD: Johns Hopkins University, 1990), 114.

8

ART, REVOLUTION, AND INDIGENOUS SUBJECTS

Tatiana Flores

The Mexican Revolution (1910–1920) propelled a cultural renaissance at home and sparked the imagination of leftist intellectuals throughout Latin America, who dreamed of a future in which a commitment to social justice would replace centuries of oppression and inequality. The conflict, which began as liberal opposition to the re-election of Porfirio Díaz, president since 1876, became an unequivocal expression of discontent from Mexico's disenfranchised communities.[1] United in the south under Emiliano Zapata and under Pancho Villa in the north, revolutionaries demanded land reform, improved working conditions, and betterments to social welfare from the state—calls answered by the Constitution of 1917. The post-revolutionary moment became a time of spirited optimism during which different public actors worked together to construct a new society.

The Mexican Revolution offered to intellectuals a hopeful new direction for humanity following the carnage that Europe experienced during World War I (1914–1918), which left in its wake a great deal of soul-searching and cast doubt on the commonplace perception of the Old Continent as the paragon of civilization, provoking instead a "crisis of modernity."[2] According to Jean Franco, "The spectacle of the great powers dedicating the resources of science and industry to the task of exterminating one another seemed a mockery to those Latin Americans for whom Europe had been equated with the highest human values."[3] Post-revolutionary Mexico provided a model for breaking free from European cultural hegemony. To shed its colonial character, intellectuals began rethinking the place of the indigenous native in the national imaginary. Whereas during the Díaz presidency—known as the Porfiriato (1876–1911)—Mexico shaped itself according to European standards, and the dominant view was that Indians were an impediment to modernization and progress,[4] the cultural architects of the post-revolutionary period placed native Mexicans front and center in the construction of a national identity. As a result, Mexico became a paradigm for promoting an autochthonous culture across Latin America, and its artistic and literary achievements were both celebrated and debated throughout the region.

In Peru especially, home to a similarly large indigenous population, Mexico's example resonated strongly. A group of Peruvian intellectuals spearheaded by the Marxist critic José Carlos Mariátegui promoted *indigenismo* as the way forward for their own culture and society at large, imbuing it with revolutionary values of their own—in their case, of a revolution to come. According to Mariátegui, "The vindication of the Indian and by extension his history is embedded in the program of a revolution."[5] He predicted that this social movement would result in an endogenous model of communism based on ancient Inca social structures, a dreamed-for egalitarian state that recalled the Inca empire of Tawantisuyu. These ideas and those of like-minded thinkers were expounded in the influential journal *Amauta*, which he edited from 1926–1930. This essay offers a comparative approach to early twentieth century Mexican and Peruvian art and thought around the theme of indigenous representation.

The views of Mariátegui and his allies were a minority position in Peru, whereas in Mexico indigenist "concerns slowly generated the public interest and bureaucratic authority to emerge as a hegemonic perspective."[6] As opposed to Mexico's climate of intellectual debate and artistic innovation fostered by the revolution, the American journalist Carleton Beals, whose books on Mexico and Peru published in the 1920s and 30s are valuable primary sources, observed that Peruvian artists "must work in a void."[7] He noted that though local painters offered a "faithful portrayal of the Indian," they were "painting for an unborn society."[8] José Sabogal, as Beals remarked, was the most prominent artist—"revolutionary in technique, social in purpose."[9] His oil painting of an indigenous mother and child (Figure 8.1) conveys a deep respect for his subjects. Though the genre of portraiture typically depicted wealthy sitters, who could afford to commission their painted likenesses, in this case, the subject is from a humble background, yet stoic and dignified. Around her shoulders is a striped textile, which calls attention to native crafts and serves to juxtapose indigenous practices of abstraction with Renaissance conventions of perspective that allow the artist to create a remarkably lifelike image. Both forms of representation are treated as having equal merit. The work, regardless, is a fiction—a sign of "the new Peru to arise,"[10] where the Indian may sustain the gaze of an elite as an equal. No such reciprocal communication was possible in the Peru of the 1920s, and in Mexico, despite the promises of the Revolution, artists struggled with how best to represent (and ideally address) native subjects.

A complex term suggesting various attitudes towards the indigenous peoples of the Americas, *indigenismo* in relation to progressive thinkers may be defined as a "critical response to the conquest and colonization of indigenous peoples and the unjust societies that developed in their wake . . . [which] denounces the injustice to which Indians have been submitted and promotes some forms of Indians' resistance."[11] To avoid assigning a fixed meaning to this term and to appreciate its contingent nature, the words of Marisol de la Cadena and Orin Starn bear emphasizing: "Indigenism has never been a singular ideology, program, or movement, and its politics resist closure. To assume that it possesses a unified much less predetermined trajectory is historically inaccurate, conceptually flawed, and simplistic."[12] In Peru, *indigenismo* was a complex and disputed project. On the one hand, it was adopted as a populist measure by the dictator Augusto B. Leguía, who recognized the legal rights of indigenous communities in the Constitution of 1920 but whose underlying agenda was one of capitalist expansion; on the other, it was the reigning ideology of his most ardent critics, Mariátegui chief among them. His brand of *indigenismo* had both a political and aesthetic component. It is identified primarily as a literary movement and related especially to his critical thought and to writers of his and subsequent generations, including Gamaliel Churata, Ciro Alegría, and José María Arguedas. Though it had a significant visual counterpart, the corresponding artistic production of Mexico is much better known. Muralism became the revolutionary art form par excellence, but other visual modes addressing the indigenous inhabitants of Mexico proliferated, from prints, paintings, and sculptures to photography and even activism.

Indigenismo typically implies the representation of indigenous subjects by those who are not indigenous themselves, taking "representation" in its broadest sense so as to encompass the political and rhetorical as well as the aesthetic. The Mexican painter Diego Rivera built his mature career on representing Indians in murals and easel paintings,

Figure 8.1 José Sabogal, *Maternidad indígena*, ca. 1931. Oil on canvas, 89 x 73 cm. Private collection. Photo by Daniel Giannoni. Courtesy of ARCHI, Archivo Digital de Arte Peruano.

profiting—financially and otherwise—from a community to which he did not belong. Aware of the ethical dilemma of speaking for others, Mariátegui made a preemptive defense of *indigenismo* in his landmark 1928 study *Seven Interpretive Essays on Peruvian Reality*, writing, "A critic could commit no greater injustice than to condemn indigenist literature for its lack of autochthonous integrity or its use of artificial elements in interpretation and expression. Indigenist literature cannot give us a strictly authentic version of the Indian, for it must idealize and stylize him. Nor can it give us his soul. It is still a mestizo literature and as such is called indigenist rather than indigenous."[13] Mestizo in Mexico and the Andes normally describes the offspring of a Spaniard and an indigenous native, while in other Latin American countries, the term may also refer more broadly to mixed-race peoples. Despite their large concentrations of indigenous populations, the differences between Mexico and Peru are striking, as Florencia Mallón points out in the following analysis:

> In contrast to Mexico, the Peruvian state has been unable to centralise its power through a unifying process of mestizaje, and has not relegated the Indian to the country's periphery. Instead, the political construction of "Indianness" has been a bipolar one: Indian highlands, white and mestizo coast; white and mestizo cities, Indian countryside. In this context, mestizaje separates rather than unites the population: the *misti*, or highland mestizo, is a figure signifying domination. *Mistis* mediate between the city and the Indian communities by accepting privileges from the whites in order to dominate the Indians. Historically, during the twentieth century, becoming a mestizo in urban areas often meant cutting ties with the countryside and the community of origin.[14]

The passage makes clear the pejorative connotations associated with the mestizo in Peru. In this light, Mariátegui's acknowledgement that *indigenista* literature is mestizo literature reads like an apologia. Later in the text, he enters into debate with the Mexican philosopher José Vasconcelos, a public intellectual known throughout the Americas, who became the first minister of education after the Revolution. Mexico's leading promoter of *mestizaje*, Vasconcelos posited that the mix of ethnicities in the Americas would yield the most elevated race, the *raza cósmica* or "cosmic race."[15] Mariátegui is critical of the fact that Vasconcelos' theory describes a race to come, not one grounded in present day realities. For Mariátegui, "mestizaje is a phenomenon that has produced a complex variety instead of solving a duality, of the Spaniard and the Indian."[16]

The attitude in Mexico was indeed different because the conception of *mestizaje* was explicitly tied to post-revolutionary social policy and in particular the project of nation building. Mexican statesmen and intellectuals regarded the country's diverse indigenous population as "presenting a major challenge to the nationalist project,"[17] and it was thought that a lack of national unity had contributed to the outbreak of the revolution and continued to threaten the country's stability. In the words of Alan Knight, "according to the emerging orthodoxy of the Revolution, the old Indian/European thesis/antithesis had now given rise to a higher synthesis, the mestizo, who was neither Indian nor European, but quintessentially Mexican."[18] Knight posits that "the mestizo . . . became the ideological symbol of the regime," and argues that "*Indigenismo* fitted well within this vision, since the very aim of the *indigenistas* was, as we have seen, to integrate the Indians, in other words to 'mestizo-ize' them."[19] In Peru, the project of integration of indigenous peoples into national life was, by contrast, not a mainstream position but rather a leftist project calling for "economic and political rights, [and] the eradication of feudalism," in addition to having an artistic dimension with utopic overtones, manifested in "the interest for the autochthonous, the cultural past, and Incaic greatness."[20] Like his Mexican counterparts, Mariátegui promoted national identity. His recurring column in the Lima-based weekly *Mundial* during the second half of the 1920s was titled "Let Us Peruvianize Peru" ["Peruanicemos al Perú"], and he believed that a socialist revolution would institute "a new Peruvian nationality capable of integrating the Indian, with his traditions and spirituality."[21] *Mestizaje* was for him a necessary evil in the process of the redemption of the Indian. According to Natalia Majluf, for such *indigenista* thinkers as Mariátegui and Luis Valcárcel, "mestizaje was a strictly negative term, a hybridism in which the best of each race became lost in 'imprecision.' "[22]

Post-revolutionary discourse notwithstanding, *mestizaje* in Mexico also had pejorative associations. Writing about colonial-era mestizos in his influential 1909 treatise "*Los grandes problemas nacionales*" ["The Great National Problems"], Andrés Molina Enríquez remarked:

> All the mestizo groups had the same goal: to shed themselves of the remaining racial elements and overcome them. Overall, the mestizos, like all hybrid products, reflected the defects and vices of the primitive races, which is why they were rejected by them, and they, in turn, for the same reason, felt an aversion for the dominant characteristics of the primitive races. It had to be that way: the creoles at that time representatives of Spanish blood, saw in the mestizos the vices and defects of the indigenous race: the indigenous, the vices and defects of the Spanish race.[23]

Later in the text, however, Molina Enríquez argued that Indians and mestizos were the best adapted to the geographic conditions of the country and that the mestizo, as the most patriotic, represented the future of Mexico.[24] The author concludes, "The fundamental and unavoidable base of all future-oriented work for the good of the country has to be the continuation of the mestizos as the principal ethnic element and as the governing class of the population."[25] Carleton Beals, likely reflecting contemporary perceptions, also offered simultaneous disdain and admiration for the mestizo:

> The mestizo, though more Indian than Spanish, has less moral integrity than the former. He is skilled in treachery, cunning, and self-seeking . . . Yet he is probably the Mexican of to-morrow, the only Mexican that can withstand the pressure of the rising industrial system; and with all his weakness he is a type that promises ultimately to be more tenacious, progressive, and peaceful than the purely Latin races, and more adaptable to modern civilization than the pure Indian.[26]

In a country that had long associated the Indian with backwardness, only the mestizo—for better or worse—could be a legitimate agent of modernity.

Visual imagery around the mestizo yields similarly conflicting narratives. Diego Rivera's first mural *Creation* (1922) depicts an allegory of race based on Vasconcelos' notion of the "cosmic race." In this multifigural composition set on the backdrop of the amphitheater stage of the Escuela Nacional Preparatoria (National Preparatory School) in Mexico City, an indigenous man and woman, both nude, sit on the ground on opposite sides of an arched frame. They are surrounded by allegorical figures of women that hover over them in hierarchical fashion, including the nine muses, the seven virtues, and two angels. In a recessed niche in the middle arises a man with arms outstretched: He represents the mestizo, emerging triumphant. The composition is heavily Eurocentric, not only through its subject matter celebrating and idealizing Western culture, but also in the pictorial forms, which were inspired by Rivera's study of Byzantine art and travels through Italy. The middle section was painted last, after Rivera visited Tehuantepec with the purpose of drawing inspiration from his own land and its people, but even here, though the man is pictured in dense jungle foliage, he is surrounded by symbols of the Evangelists: a lion, angel, eagle, and ox, representing Mark, Matthew, John, and Luke, respectively. Most problematic, the indigenous subjects, especially the woman, are depicted as primitive and uncouth in relation to the refined group above them. They stand out for being fully nude (the mestizo is bare-chested, with only his top half visible). The woman's facial features are exaggerated to emphasize her thick lips and crooked nose, while the man, positioned with his back to the spectator, has a head that is disproportionately small in relation to the rest of his body. The mestizo, however, is so well formed that his open-armed gesture recalls Leonardo da Vinci's *Vitruvian Man* (ca. 1490), an iconic drawing representing the ideal proportions of man. Rivera idealized the mestizo in a manner that corresponded to his role in post-revolutionary cultural discourse, giving visual form to Vasconcelos' utopic ideals for the redemption of indigenous peoples through racial mixing. The eugenecist implications of this philosophy are clearly visualized in the mural, and Rivera positions himself as a staunch ally of the minister, an attitude that he would later reject.

Ignacio Sánchez Prado summarizes the critiques leveled at Vasconcelos' concept of the "cosmic race," noting Peruvian critic Antonio Cornejo Polar's opinion that *mestizaje* "falsifies in the most drastic manner the condition of our culture and literature . . . as what it does is to offer harmonic imagery of what is obviously sundered and belligerent."[27] The idea of *mestizaje* as the product of rape is forcefully articulated in the mural *Cortés and Malinche* (1926) by José Clemente Orozco (Figure 8.2), located in the vault of a stairwell in the Escuela Nacional Preparatoria, in close proximity to the main courtyard which was entirely decorated by the artist. The image depicts the Spanish conquistador alongside his concubine, the indigenous Malintzin, known popularly as Malinche.[28] The couple sits on a rocky outcrop, a deceased figure at their feet. Cortés has a stony appearance, his white skin tinged with gray to resemble a classical marble sculpture. By contrast, Malinche, rendered in warm, earthy browns, appears much more human, her body fleshy and inviting. Cortes holds her possessively—his right hand takes her right hand, and his left arm crosses over her body diagonally, obstructing her movement. The image visualizes the oppression and subjugation suffered by indigenous peoples and makes of Malinche a victim rather than a temptress and betrayer, as she is often perceived in the popular imagination. Her gaze is downward cast, her expression somber.

On one level, the mural functions as a bleak interpretation of a *casta* painting. Paintings of castes or classifications of racial mixtures were common in Mexican late colonial art.[29] They were typically picturesque curios painted in series portraying the offspring of different races. Beginning with a Spanish father and an Indian mother, the paintings described many different possible combinations generated from the unions of Spaniards, Indians, and Africans. As the bloodlines became more mixed, the families were depicted as increasingly poor, and in some cases greater racial mixing implied moral degeneracy. Typically, though, the mestizo couple began the series, and they tended to be shown as prosperous and content. As opposed to this happy family as well as Rivera's vision of *mestizaje* as a process of spiritual ascendance, Orozco exposes it as a product of violence, predicated on the original act of rape of Malinche by Cortés. Whether one interprets the third character in his scene, the male body lying face down, as the product of their union or else imagines the future mestizo progeny, the family that they engender is decidedly dysfunctional.

The prostate figure was the subject of a debate between the artist and American writer Frances Toor, who featured the mural in her journal *Mexican Folkways* shortly after its production and identified it as representing "the Indian race under their feet."[30] Orozco objected to this interpretation, writing that the person "merely represents the past, the end of a state of things as the Conquest undoubtedly was."[31] "The name, 'The Indian

Figure 8.2 José Clemente Orozco, *Cortés and Malinche*, 1926. Fresco, Antiguo Colegio de San Ildefonso (formerly Escuela Nacional Preparatoria), Universidad Nacional Autónoma de México, Mexico City. Photo by Bob Schalkwijk / Art Resource, NY. © ARS.

Race,'" he continued, "[. . .] in any event would correspond to the figure at the right," referring to Malinche. Orozco was particularly offended by what he interpreted as Toor's implication that he had disrespected indigenous Mexicans. He asserted that, on the contrary, he had "attacked those who exploit, deceive, and weaken the race, as anyone can see in the very patio of the National Preparatory School. I have never flattered nor falsified the true nature of the Indian."[32] Read in conjunction with the mural, his words imply that *mestizaje* "weakens the race" and, extrapolating further, his mural could be read as anti-Vasconcelos and anti-Rivera.[33] Despite his protests, Orozco's own representations of indigenous peoples, along with other statements, were varied and contradictory, ranging from racist caricature—as in the lithograph *Tourists* (ca. 1928)—to images of faceless crowds to creative interpretations of pre-Conquest Mexico in specific murals, such as Dartmouth College's *The Epic of American Civilization* (1932–34). Indeed, the artist was a stringent critic of *indigenismo* considering that it catered to a white U.S. American public: "Neither the Indians here nor those there ever had the slightest idea of the existence of such paintings that exalted their race."[34] In his autobiography, Orozco attacked theories of race and *mestizaje* head on, arguing that both Spanish and Indians were made up of multiple, diverse races themselves and that:

> in order to achieve unity, peace, and progress, it would be perhaps enough to finish with the racial question forever. Never again speak of Indians, Spaniards, and *mestizos* . . . Treat the Indian not as "Indian," but as a man, in the same way as other men.[35]

Orozco's position was untenable for its time and place because it failed to empathize with the plight of the oppressed, victims of injustice for centuries. Discussing the wages of the working class, Carleton Beals described the typical salary as "body- and soul-destroying."[36] In his vivid account of living and working conditions, he observed:

> The Mexican family usually lives in one small, cold, dark, unfloored, windowless room, reeking with moisture and sewer gas. . . . The furniture is very scanty . . . a few broken chairs, a rickety table, some home-made benches, a few home-woven straw mats for beds and blocks of wood for pillows—nothing more. . . . In sleeping the one door is always hermetically sealed, so that in less than half an hour the air is befouled, and, with the humidity and cold, promptly induces tuberculosis, pneumonia, and allied disorders.
>
> Cleanliness under such conditions is no longer even a virtue, it is an impossibility. Food and bones are thrown on the floor to the flea-bitten mangy curs who sleep with the children; the place is infested with lice and rodents till the human body becomes the happy hunting-ground for busy fingers. In the country districts, this one room also becomes the common corral for stray pigs, chickens, and the newest born. Disease reaches out its shriveled hand of death from every corner.[37]

The description is unusual for being its unflinching realism. Latin American intellectuals, more at home with a belle lettrist tradition inherited from France, were unlikely to practice such a style of writing. Visual representation also steered away from depictions of extreme poverty. Similar conditions are addressed in a series of photographs by Tina Modotti of the inhabitants of the Colonia de la Bolsa neighborhood (ca. 1928), but they remain an anomaly in her work and in post-revolutionary Mexican visual culture. On the one hand, traditional aesthetics—the sense that art should be beautiful—still prevailed and, on the other, socially committed artists, seeking to inspire change, likely feared that representing actual experience would confirm negative stereotypes about indigenous people, such as their lack of hygiene, laziness, propensity to vice, etc. In Peru, home to similar economic conditions, intellectuals doubted whether artistic creation of any sort would be possible under such circumstances. In the words of Mariátegui, "If an indigenous literature finally appears, it will be when the Indians themselves are able to produce it."[38] In both countries, then, regardless of political position and intent, most instances of *indigenista* representation—as acknowledged by Mariátegui—were decidedly one-sided, "in which the Indian is depicted from without by an observer who, however well versed in his subject, is not part of the culture."[39]

Writing in 1929 about the indigenous peoples of Mexico, anthropologist Anita Brenner remarked that her subjects were ultimately unknowable:

> [The Indian] is like sculpted volcanic obsidian, of which you see mostly reflections. The Spaniard, the city Mexican, any foreigner, can describe him physically, note his way of living and his possessions and make of these observations a silhouette, an incomprehensible photograph; the live man stays in his own material.[40]

Ulises Juan Zevallos Aguilar argues that such an attitude of reserve was an anticolonial strategy of resistance among indigenous communities of Puno, Peru, which "prevented their dominators from reaching a total understanding of their psychology," and describes how their conduct differed among members of their own community, confounding local *indigenista* intellectuals.[41] In most instances of early twentieth century literary and artistic *indigenista* representation, the creator reveals attitudes ranging from resignation on the voicelessness of the indigenous native to frustration to skepticism as to whether indigenous speech could even be possible.

Writing about the representations of indigenous subjects by the Flemish printmaker and publisher Theodor De Bry in his multi-volume compendium known as *Les Grands Voyages* (1590–1634), Walter Mignolo argues that the concept of the "Indian" is a European invention:

> What we 'see' on the surface of [De Bry's] engravings . . . [is] an assertion of *humanitas*, of Europeans as *subject* of human knowledge imagining their human nature by inventing *anthropos*, the newly encountered indigenous peoples imagined as the *object* of human knowledge.[42]

Marisol de la Cadena and Orin Starn make a similar point when they note that from the time the term arose in the 1590s, "indigenous" referred to "forms of relationality express[ing] European superiority."[43] While De Bry famously never set foot in the Americas and most likely never laid eyes on a Native American, he nonetheless widely disseminated the stereotype of the indigenous "savage." It is interesting to ponder whether similar power relations as those he embodied during the first century of European colonization of the Western Hemisphere were at play in the representation of Indians in the twentieth century. For all their good intentions, to what degree did artists and intellectuals perpetuate stereotypes and contribute to deepening the colonial relationship between themselves and the indigenous communities they depicted? Is the "silence imposed upon the Other" that Mignolo attributes to De Bry reenacted in the numerous examples of *indigenista* representation, pictorial or otherwise in Mexico, Peru, and elsewhere in Latin America?[44] Priscilla Archibald, for one, criticizes Andean *indigenista* literature for narratives featuring "greatly diminished indigenous agency," resulting in "the progressive foreclosure of alternative discourses."[45] She posits that "implicit to the genre is a moral dilemma that will be resolved only when 'authentic' Indians speak in its place."[46]

Among the artists who questioned the conventions of *indigenista* representation from a formal and ethical vantage point was the Mexican Fernando Leal. One of the first to receive a commission from Vasconcelos to participate in the incipient mural movement,

Leal was a product of a revolutionary initiative in art education. He studied under the painter Alfredo Ramos Martínez at the open-air painting school, an institution that had arisen first in 1913 and then again in 1919 to offer new alternatives in artistic training beyond the academic approach of Mexico's traditional art school, the Academia de San Carlos. The school promoted an intuitive approach to art and a direct communion with nature through plein air painting and eventually figuration based on indigenous models. While the earliest work of its students tended towards the picturesque, eventually certain of the artists adopted a more critical approach that challenged the conventional representation of the Indian. With the painter Jean Charlot, a French citizen with maternal Mexican ancestry, Leal was at the forefront of leading this effort. His large multifigural painting *Zapatistas at Rest* (1922) both countered the stereotype of the peasant armies who followed revolutionary leader Emiliano Zapata as violent, dangerous rebels by depicting them peacefully gathered at their camp and also was deliberately artificially composed as a means of questioning the truth value behind seemingly straightforward representation.[47]

In his first mural, *The Feast of the Lord of Chalma* (1922–23), Leal portrayed a religious celebration in the church of Chalma, a destination for pilgrims who worshiped the statue of the Black Christ there, typically through dance (Figure 8.3). The mural revealed the presence of indigenous belief systems four hundred years after the

Figure 8.3 Fernando Leal, *The Feast of the Lord of Chalma*, 1922–23. Encaustic. Antiguo Colegio de San Ildefonso (formerly Escuela Nacional Preparatoria), Universidad Nacional Autónoma de México, Mexico City. Photo by Bob Schalkwijk. © Fernando Leal-Audirac.

Conquest, emphasizing the adaptation of native religions to Catholicism through the staging of an Indian dance set to traditional music inside a church. The Black Christ especially revealed the syncretic nature of popular beliefs; it was believed that he was a surrogate for the indigenous deity, Ozteotl or the Dark Lord of the Cave. Beyond what has often been read as a folkloric subject—Orozco dismissed it as yet another expression of the vogue for indigenous arts and crafts[48]—the mural contains a self-portrait of Leal as one of the dancers, with noticeably exaggerated featured and darkened skin, likely an acknowledgement of his own mestizo heritage. This figure is one of the only two to look out of the mural (the other is a little girl dressed in white). Leal's gaze is confrontational, both berating the viewer for voyeurism but also interrogating his own role as an outsider depicting others, thereby challenging the very basis of *indigenista* representation. Throughout the course of the 20s, the artist became a fervent champion of alternative art education, promoting the establishment of art schools for children and youths from peasant and urban working class communities, advocating for empowering those who for centuries had been the objects of representation by giving them the tools for self-representation. For Leal and his allies, childhood art education was one solution to the predicament of indigenous representation, a practice of great interest to Peruvian intellectuals.[49]

Cuzqueño photographers also offered directions towards indigenous agency, and it is revealing to compare their portrayal of mestizo subjects with the examples discussed previously. Peruvian photography from the 1920s and 1930s is rife with references to mestizos that do not seem to be value-laden. The Cuzco-based photographers Crisanto and Filiberto Cabrera and César Meza identified mestizos in many of their titles, but they do not appear ethnically or socially different from non-identified characters, though their specific naming implies that they are more upwardly mobile than figures labeled *campesinos* [peasants] or *indios*. Florencia Mallón's description, cited previously, of the rift between mestizos and Indians in Peru is not so straightforward as an interpretive framework for visual representation in the case of these artists. Neither does it apply to Martín Chambi's photograph *Mestiza with Chicha, Cuzco* (1931), which pictures an amiable-looking woman seated comfortably in front of a stone dwelling holding an enormous glass of *chicha*, a characteristically Andean drink made of fermented maize (Figure 8.4). Dressed in a thick wool skirt and layers of woven textiles and looking directly at the camera with the hint of a smile, the woman projects an image of comfort and prosperity. The fact that she is posed against a building and not in the studio suggests a sense of belonging, implying her ownership of the space. That she, as a living subject, meets the viewer's gaze is much more convincing than the painting by Sabogal that began this discussion. This photograph, while recalling Mariátegui's acknowledgement that *mestizaje* produces complex variety, also draws attention to the gulf between the discourse of the city and that of the sierra. Marisol de la Cadena's description of the mestizo in Cuzco yields another possible narrative, suggesting a context where both mestizo*s* and indigenous natives possess much greater agency:

> Indigenous mestizo cuzqueños inhabit a cultural space where the indigenous and non-indigenous intepenetrate each other rather than a borderland. The space they inhabit is not interstitial or marginal; instead, it is coterminous with Cuzco as a geographical region and with its hegemonic feeling, cuzqueñismo. Because they inhabit a space where the indigenous and non-indigenous interpenetrate, they are hybrids; but not in the static sense implied by the modern definition of that term, which opposes the rural indigenous individual to the urban mestizo

and assumes an evolutionary terminal process from the former (conceived as an inferior stage of race/culture) to the latter (deemed a superior stage of race/culture). Rather, indigenous mestizos are endlessly processing their hybridity, constantly de-Indianizing and dignifying their practices by using what they consider the best and most *neto* from both rural and urban traditions. The indigenous tradition they produce is not "pure" as modern indigenista intellectual imagined it, but it is "neto," authentic by indigenous intellectuals' definition and fiat.[50]

Figure 8.4 Martín Chambi, *Mestiza with Chicha, Cuzco*, ca. 1931. Modern gelatin silver print. Private Collection. Reprinted with permission of Teo Allain Chambi. Courtesy of ARCHI, Archivo Digital de Arte Peruano.

For all the hand-wringing about authenticity and essence on the part of *indigenista* artists and writers, the example of Chambi and his contemporaries offered new possibilities that very likely went unacknowledged by the Peruvian intellectual elite. Indeed, in his haste to speak for his indigenous countrymen because of his assumption that they could not possibly speak for themselves (or write literature, to be more specific), Mariátegui, to paraphrase Archibald, forecloses alternative discourses.

Much more has been written about *indigenista* literature than art, perhaps because pictorial representation is often taken at face value. Indeed, art history has classified such images as those I discussed here under the rubric of "social realism" while overlooking their nuances. As the examples discussed demonstrate, images exist within a complex web of discourse and express more than meets the eye. In their post-revolutionary context, Mexicans experimented in varying ways with how images and artmaking itself could address issues of injustice and inequality wrought by the colonial legacy. Elite Peruvian artists and thinkers looked to Mexico as a model, aesthetically and sociopolitically, while failing to recognize the complexity of indigenous and mestizo cultural production in their own backyard. Indeed, the representation of indigenous subjects was and continues to be an ethical quandary that resists straightforward resolution.

Notes

1 For a comprehensive history of the Mexican Revolution, see John Hart, *Revolutionary Mexico: The Coming and Process of the Mexican Revolution* (Berkeley, CA and Los Angeles, CA: University of California Press, 1989).

2 Brais D. Outes-León, "'La Barbarie refinada': The Crisis of European Modernity in Gómez Carrillo's Chronicles of the First World War," *Revista Canadiense de Estudios Hispánicos*, Vol 38, No. 3 (Primavera 2014): 503–527. See as well Patricia Funes, *Salvar la nación: intelectuales, cultura y política en los años veinte* (Buenos Aires: Prometeo Libros, 2006), 26–38.

3 Jean Franco, *The Modern Culture of Latin America: Society and the Artist* (New York, NY, Washington, DC and London: Frederick A. Praeger, 1967), 69.

4 T. G. Powell, "Mexican Intellectuals and the Indian Question, 1876–1911," *The Hispanic American Historical Review*, Vol 48, No. 1 (February 1968): 20–22. The same attitude was true of Peru. See Jean Franco, *The Modern Culture of Latin America: Society and the Artist* (New York, NY, Washington, DC and London: Frederick A. Praeger, 1967), 46.

5 José Carlos Mariátegui, *Siete ensayos de interpretación de la realidad peruana* (Mexico City: Ediciones Era, 2005), 306–307. Author's translation.

6 Alexander S. Dawson, "From Models for the Nation to Model Citizens: Indigenismo and the 'Revindication' of the Mexican Indian, 1920–40," *Journal of Latin American Studies*, Vol 30, No. 2 (May 1998): 280–281.

7 Carleton Beals, *Fire in the Andes* (Philadelphia and London: J. B. Lippincott Company, 1934), 433.

8 Ibid.

9 Carleton Beals, *Fire in the Andes* (Philadelphia, PA and London: J. B. Lippincott Company, 1934), 434.

10 Ibid.

11 Estelle Tarica, *The Inner Life of Mestizo Nationalism* (Minneapolis, MN: University of Minnesota Press, 2008), xi.

12 Marisol de la Cadena and Orin Starn, "Introduction," In *Indigenous Experience Today*, edited by Marisol de la Cadena and Orin Starn, 4 (Oxford and New York, NY: Berg, 2007).

13 José Carlos Mariátegui, *Seven Interpretive Essays on Peruvian Reality*, trans. Marjory Urquidi (Austin, TX: University of Texas Press, 1971).

14 Florencia Mallón, "Indian Communities, Political Cultures, and the State in Latin America, 1780–1990," *Journal of Latin American Studies*, Vol 24 (1992): 36–37.

15 Vasconcelos' ideas on *mestizaje* were developed in the 1910s and first published in *Estudios indostánicos* (Mexico City: Editorial México Moderno, 1920) and later in the landmark volume

La raza cósmica: Misión de la raza iberoamericana. Notas de viajes a la América del Sur (Barcelona: Agencia Mundial de Librería, 1925).

16 José Carlos Mariátegui, *Seven Interpretive Essays on Peruvian Reality*, trans. Marjory Urquidi (Austin, TX: University of Texas Press, 1971), 310. For a description of various critical attitudes towards Vasconcelos and a spirited defense of "*la raza cósmica*," see Ignacio Sánchez Prado, "El mestizaje en el corazón de la utopía: La raza cósmica entre Aztlán y América Latina," *Revista Canadiense de Estudios Hispánicos*, Vol 33, No. 2 (2009): 381–404.

17 Alan Knight, "Racism, Revolution, and *Indigenismo*: Mexico, 1910–1940," In *The Idea of Race in Latin America*, edited by Richard Graham, 84 (Austin, TX: The University of Texas Press, 1990).

18 Ibid., 85.

19 Ibid., 86.

20 Fernanda Beigel, *El itinerario y la brújula: El vanguardismo estético-político de José Carlos Mariátegui* (Buenos Aires: Editorial Biblos, 2003), 76.

21 Ibid., 84.

22 Natalia Majluf, "El indigenismo en México y Perú: hacia una visión comparativa," In *Arte, Historia e Identidad en América: Visiones Comparativas*, vol. 2, edited by Gustavo Curiel, Renato González Mello, and Juana Gutierrez Haces, 624 (Mexico City: Universidad Nacional Autónoma de México, 1994).

23 Andrés Molina Enríquez, *Los grandes problemas nacionales* (Mexico City: Imprenta de A. Carranza e Hijos, 1909), 41.

24 See Ibid., 262–63, 271.

25 Ibid., 308.

26 Carleton Beals, *Mexico: An Interpretation* (New York, NY: B.W. Huebsch, Inc., 1923), 200–201.

27 Quoted in Sánchez Prado, 383.

28 Also known as Doña Marina, Malinche now occupies a mythical place in Mexican imaginary. See, among others, Sandra Messinger Cypess, *La Malinche in Mexican Literature From History to Myth* (Austin, TX: University of Texas Press, 1991), Camilla Townsend, *Malintzin's Choices: An Indian Woman in the Conquest of Mexico* (Albuquerque, NM: University of New Mexico Press, 2006), and Octavio Paz, *The Labyrinth of Solitude: Life and Thought in Mexico*, trans. Lysander Kemp (New York, NY: Grove Press, 1961).

29 On casta paintings see Ilona Katzew, *Casta Paintings: Images of Race in Eighteenth-Century Mexico* (New Haven, CT and London: Yale University Press, 2005), and Magali Carrera, *Imagining Identity in New Spain: Race, Lineage, and the Colonial Body in Portraiture and Casta Paintings* (Austin, TX: University of Texas Press, 2004).

30 Frances Toor, "Frescoes of José Clemente Orozco in the National Preparatory School," *Mexican Folkways*, Vol 4, No. 4 (1928): 196.

31 José Clemente Orozco, "A Correction," *Mexican Folkways*, Vol 5, No. 1 (1929): 9.

32 Ibid.

33 Orozco's rivalry with Rivera was well documented. For an early text that criticizes Rivera in the context of Orozco's murals in the Escuela Nacional Preparatoria, see Miguel Bueno, "El arte de Diego Rivera atacado por el genial artista C. Orozco," clipping in the Jean Charlot Collection, University of Hawai'i, Honolulu, HI. The reference for this article, provided in the prologue of Luis Cardoza y Aragón, *Orozco*, 2nd ed (Mexico City: Fondo de Cultura Económica, 2005), 10, is *El Imparcial*, November 23, 1926.

34 José Clemente Orozco, *Autobiografía* (Mexico City: Ediciones Era, 1970), 69.

35 Ibid., 75.

36 Carleton Beals, *Mexico: An Interpretation* (New York, NY: B.W. Huebsch, Inc., 1923), 125.

37 Ibid., 126–27.

38 José Carlos Mariátegui, *Seven Interpretive Essays on Peruvian Reality*, trans. Marjory Urquidi (Austin, TX: University of Texas Press, 1971).

39 Naomi Lindstrom, *Twentieth-Century Spanish American Fiction* (Austin, TX: University of Texas Press, 1994), 51.

40 Anita Brenner, *Idols Behind Altars* (New York, NY: Payson and Clarke, 1929), 105.

41 Ulises Juan Zevallos Aguilar, *Indigenismo y nación: los retos de la representación de la subalternidad aymara y quechua en el Boletín Titikaka (1926–1930)* (Lima: Instituto Francés de Estudios Andinos and BCR, 2002), 127.

42 Walter Mignolo, "Crossing Gazes and the Silence of the 'Indians': Theodor De Bry and Guaman Poma de Ayala," *Journal of Medieval and Early Modern Studies*, Vol 41, No. 1 (Winter 2011): 180.
43 Marisol de la Cadena and Orin Starn, "Introduction," In *Indigenous Experience Today*, edited by Marisol de la Cadena and Orin Starn, 4 (Oxford and New York, NY: Berg, 2007).
44 Walter Mignolo, "Crossing Gazes and the Silence of the 'Indians': Theodor De Bry and Guaman Poma de Ayala," *Journal of Medieval and Early Modern Studies*, Vol 41, No. 1 (Winter 2011): 180.
45 Priscilla Archibald, *Imagining Modernity in the Andes* (Lewisburg, PA: Bucknell University Press, 2011), 63, 67.
46 Ibid., 68.
47 For a more extensive discussion of this painting, see Tatiana Flores, *Mexico's Revolutionary Avant-Gardes: From Estridentismo to ¡30–30!* (New Haven, CT: Yale University Press, 2013).
48 See José Clemente Orozco, *Autobiografía* (Mexico City: Ediciones Era, 1970), 59.
49 On children's art education in Mexico in relation to Leal and his cohorts, see Laura González Matute, *Escuelas de Pintura al Aire Libre y Centros Populares de Pintura* (Mexico City: Instituto Nacional de Bellas Artes, 1987); Chapter 7 in Tatiana Flores, *Mexico's Revolutionary Avant-Gardes*, and Tatiana Flores, "Starting From Mexico: Estridentismo as an Avant-Garde Model," *World Art*, Vol 4, No. 1 (2014): 47–65. On the reception of Mexican children's art in Peru, see Chapter 6 in Harper Montgomery, *The Mobility of Modernism: Art and Criticism in 1920s Latin America* (Austin, TX: University of Texas Press, 2017), 208–215.
50 Marisol de la Cadena, *Indigenous Mestizos: The Politics of Race and Culture in Cuzco, Peru, 1929–1991* (Durham, NC and London: Duke University Press, 2000), 276.

9

CHICANO/A AND LATINO/A STUDIES IN MEXICO (HISTORY AND EVOLUTION)

Academy, Literature, Art, Theater, and Cultural Practices

María del Socorro Gutiérrez Magallanes

The experiences of many Chicana/os and Latino/as from communities in the United States that came to Mexico in the second half of the twentieth century as university-level exchange students or to study for a determined period of time as foreign exchange students were, to say it in a friendly way, disappointing. Many arrived with the illusion and intention of "returning home" and "reconnecting" with their roots, their culture, their history, and their "people." They sought in the universities or research centers where they were enrolled or carrying out research, an academic community interested in their themes and projects, but more than that, they sought interlocutors at the political, intellectual and cultural level with respect to the Chicana/o world in the United States. Unfortunately for those generations, very few people, if anyone, were interested in Chicano studies, or Chicanos in general, with some exceptions that I will address.

In Mexico, much of the intellectual, cultural, artistic, and academic community—to say nothing of the community at large—thought that this cultural studies field was an illegitimate one with no connection to the country despite the fact that at the very least one person in every family had either immigrated and lived in or was temporarily working in the United States. That is to say, that the connections were not only "there" but actually very close to home. Juan Felipe Herrera, the recent poet laureate, mentioned in one of his conferences at the University of California Riverside (2005) that he went to Mexico in 1978 with his friend Francisco Alarcón to "meet with his Mexican poet colleagues," to connect with our people and cross the border toward the south, to reconnect with his "language, knowledge and families, and families of writing" but he found a profound disinterest in the Chicana/o experience of the United States and even less interest of the issues or concerns of those who went south to "reconnect" with their culture and history. It is worth mentioning that Herrera singles out Elías Nandino as a Mexican poet of *los contemporáneos* as one of the few poets interested in Chicano poetry; in general, Mexicans were more interested in the overalls that Herrera and Alarcón wore than in their Chicano poetry.[1] A violent experience, perhaps, that for many Chicanos and Chicanas signifies, in part, a deepening of the wound they have in their memories and on their skin from a history of rejection from both the United States and Mexico.

In the twenty-first century, migration, along with the lived experience of racism for Mexican migrants in the United States, the deportation of many co-nationals, and the round-trip flux of peoples has increased. As a consequence, exchanges, in every sense of the word, have made interests grow in the "Chicano world" and "Latino world" in the United States, legitimizing the field of study, and recognizing that the academic, literary, artistic, and cultural productions of Chicanos and Chicanas have something to contribute to the societies in which they belong and to the world in general.

In consideration of these facts, this essay records and adds to the archive, the forms that Chicana/o and Latina/o studies has taken in Mexico. More specifically, it will record its history and development, as well as what can be called: Chicana and Latina interventions in the academic, artistic, literary, and cultural spheres of Mexico. In other words, the academic, artistic, literary, and cultural practices by and about Chicano/as and Latino/as in Mexico will be recorded as part of a historical archive. The basic questions that will be addressed in this essay are: How has Mexico historically viewed Chicanos? What is the history of Chicano studies in Mexico? What research has been done by and about Chicano/as and Latino/as in Mexico? What influence has Chicano writing had on Mexico? What are the key texts? What works are being read in translation? What influence has Chicana feminism had on Mexico and on Latin America? What have been some of the Chicana and Latina mediations in social movements, in research, in the classroom, in performance art, in graphic, plastic, and visual arts? What are some of the practices and corresponding cultural and academic developments of those who have lived in and visited Mexico? These are some of the questions that motivate the development of this essay.

Chicano/a and Latino/a Studies in the Mexican Academy?

Among Mexican academics, there is negative silence when one enters into a dialogue with the theoretical frames of cultural studies or area studies. Here, in Mexico, as it is in various countries of Latin America, the disciplinary format constitutes—with a few exceptions—the primary frame for teaching and research. Therefore, undergraduate and graduate programs in Latin American studies have not incorporated Chicano/a studies. Nonetheless, there is research done about similar themes of interest, and there are academics using creative and strategic ways to approach the field. Paradoxically, considering the high level of institutional disinterest, the number of people actually reading literature by Chicano and Chicana writers is growing. This growth in readership is surprising because even though there are not many institutional paths, Chicana writing is entering Mexico and Latin America by way of alternative circuits, outside the "norm" or at the margin of institutional circuits.

In this regard, the following three cases are noteworthy. The queer collective *Invasorxs* led a workshop in 2015 on queer theory at the *Centro Cultural Border* in Mexico City; the workshop was mainly about working with feminist writings from around the world, including Chicanas Gloria Anzaldúa and Cherrie Moraga. On the other hand, Chicana/o literary, and theoretical-methodological production entered into formal settings since 2013 through seminars led by young researchers such as Rian Lozano, Nina Hoechtl, and the writer of this essay, through the themes and texts of Chicana literature and visual art. Two of these graduate seminars were offered through the *Museo de Arte Contemporáneo*, MUAC, entitled: "Visual Culture and Gender: Decolonizing Translations, or how to create a third language I & II" inspired by the *nepantlera*-interdisciplinary work of Gloria Anzaldúa, fall 2015 and spring 2016. These graduate seminars were part of the *Orientación Interdisciplina de Estudios de Posgrado* (Interdisciplinary Orientations in Graduate Studies, OIP, UNAM).

In these seminars, readings and conferences were included and led by the writer of this essay, about Chicana literature, especially Gloria Anzaldúa's *Borderlands/La Frontera:*

The New Mestiza[2] as an example of a decolonizing turn in Chicana feminist production. Recently, two lectures were presented within the *Orientación Interdisciplina del Posgrado* (Interdisciplinary Postgraduate Orientation [OIP]) frame about Anzaldúa's work entitled "La Prieta's Pedagogical Calling" and "Gloria Anzaldúa's Decolonial Imagination" in connection to reading the Chicana writer's textual and visual production. In addition, in the spring semester of 2016 an exhibit of Gloria Anzaldúa's visual work took place. This work of Anzaldúa is hardly known to the general U.S. public, much less the Mexican general public. The exhibit was titled *Entre Palabra e Imagen: Galería de pensamiento de Gloria Anzaldúa* or *Between Word and Image: Gallery of thought by Gloria Anzaldúa.*[3] For the first time in Mexico, Anzaldúa's visual works were shown and this was only possible through a collaboration between the Casa de Cultura at the Universidad Autónoma del Estado de México in Tlalpan, UAEM, and the Benson Library Special Collections of the University of Texas at Austin, among others. I was one of the curators of this exhibit along with Director of Special Collections at the Benson Library, UT Austin, Julianne Gilland, independent artist Nina Hoechtl, Universidad Nacional Autónoma de México's Institute of Aesthetics researcher Rian Lozano.

Another effort crucial to mention here is a postdoctoral research project I conducted from spring 2016 to spring 2017 with the collaboration and support of researcher Lorena Carrillo at the Alfonso Vélez Pliego Institute of Social Sciences and Humanities at the Benemérita Universidad Autónoma de Puebla, in Puebla, México. The project is entitled: *Chicana and Latin American Political Autobiography: Conflict, Memory and Subjects in Process.* The main objective of this project is to place in dialogue and exchange the cultural productions and critiques of Chicana/Latina and Latin American authors whose writings revolve around autobiography, violence, memory, and politics. As a result of this project, we are seeking to publish articles in Spanish language on the subject[4] and to include the topics in graduate seminars' curricula.

Even though there was an effort in the 1970s and 1980s to incorporate Chicano and Latino studies departments into the Mexican academic system, today these departments are practically nonexistent. According to Axel Ramirez,[5] in January 1988, the first Department of Chicano Studies was founded within the institutional context of the UNAM (National Autonomous University of Mexico). However, this department existed for only a decade. The only aspect to be reinforced was a Chicano literature course that began in the 1980s within the CEPE, *Centro de Enseñanza Para Extranjeros* [Center for Teaching for Foreign International Students]; the course included texts by Juan Bruce Nova and Sergio Elizondo. Notwithstanding, it can be said that there are solid, sustained efforts to create spaces to read, study, and work with Chicana literature, even if these efforts are not geared toward creating departments. At the same time, we can say that there are new protocols with multiple and more effective strategies to garner the attention of Chicano and Latino academics working in the United States and who are in constant dialogue with their colleagues in Mexico and Latin America. I refer specifically to an initiative launched by Marisa Belausteguigoitia, professor in the School of Philosophy and Letters who, during her tenure as Director of the Programa Universitario de Estudios de Género [Gender Studies Program], promoted a plan to introduce studies of Latinas and Chicanas. This initiative, which continues in various UNAM graduate programs, was articulated as an *Orientación Interdisciplina del Posgrado* (OIP) through which course offerings in numerous graduate programs and departments such as Latin American studies, political and social science, law, and economics, among others, include in their curriculum lectures by and about the literature, art, theory, and methodology of Chicana feminists, historians and artists such as Gloria Anzaldúa, Cherrie Moraga, Alma

López, Chela Sandoval, Alicia Gaspar de Alba, Emma Pérez, Therese Delgadillo, Norma Klhan, and Norma Alarcón, among others.

In this sense, we must concede that if in Mexico there is more recognition than before about Chicano and Latino literature and studies, this recognition manifests in specific and targeted ways. In the particular case of the UNAM, discussions about Chicano literature, theory, and Chicano studies has gradually grown over the last three decades. Thanks to the work by scholars such as Marisa Belausteguigoitia, Claire Joysmith, and Axel Ramírez, this evolution has been made possible.

Additionally, there are others who through various means such as publication, organization of conferences and colloquia, interviews, and translations are actively promoting the reading and study of Chicana literature throughout Mexico: José Manuel Valenzuela Arce from the Departamento de Estudios Culturales from the Colegio de la Frontera Norte in Tijuana, who wrote an essential text about Chicano studies in Mexico;[6] María Socorro Tabuenca from the Colegio de la Frontera Norte in Ciudad Juarez, who has written several books on the subject;[7] Marina Fe of the Faculty of Philosophy and Letters and the Interdisciplinary Seminar on Feminist Studies, who edited a book including Chicana literature topics;[8] and Claire Joysmith, researcher of the Center of North American Studies, who has worked for many years bringing together Chicanas and Mexicanas and translating their work into Spanish and inserting Spanglish texts into the Mexican academy. She has edited a compilation of articles, an anthology of poetry,[9] and she organized the *Coloquio Internacional Nepantla Aesthetics* in 2011, among other events and texts related to Chicana Literature.

Outside of the UNAM and the Colegio de la Frontera, other sites of convergence and dialogue include: the Universidad de Colima, the Universidad de Guadalajara, el Programa Interdisciplinario de Estudios de Mujer (PIEM) of the Colegio de México (COLMEX), several literary publications about Chicana women and gender from the Universidad Autonóma Metropolitana (UAM), as well as anthropological publications about Chicano themes from the Escuela Nacional de la Antropología e Historia (ENAH), in addition to the Seminario Permanente de Estudios Chicanos y de la Frontera. Some examples include the Colegio de la Frontera Norte (COLEF) in Tijuana, Baja California, which hosted two conferences in 1987 and 1988. Both conferences entitled, "Coloquio Fronterizo: 'Mujer y Literatura Mexicana y Chicana: Culturas en Contacto' "; were organized by the Programa Interdisciplinario de Estudios de la Mujer of COLMEX, as well as by COLEF, UCSD, SDSU, and TU.[10] Between 1983 and 1988, the Universidad de Colima and the Universidad de Guadalajara organized several forums around the Chicana question. Even though all of these academic activities have been sporadic, and not necessarily interconnected, they all seek to understand and reflect upon the production of knowledge by and about Chicanos and Chicanas.

Research at the UNAM about Chicano/as and Latino/as

More recently, we can refer the work of young scholars at the UNAM who have written master's and doctoral theses about these topics or that, in one way or another, incorporate Chicano history, art, muralism, and/or feminist literature and theory into their projects across the disciplines. Examples of this graduate work include: Paulina Ramirez Niembro, 2015, in Psychology, who wrote her master's thesis: "El proyecto de vida de una migrante mexicana en Estados Unidos: un análisis interseccional a través de dos ejes: género y descolonialidad" ["A Life Project by a Mexican Migrant Woman in the United States: An intersectional analysis through Gender and Decolonization"], where she documents the life story of a migrant woman and the transformations she lives through in her journey to the Unites States. Selen Arango, 2015, in Education wrote her dissertation on, among other texts, Ana Castillo's *Las Cartas de Mixquiahuala* as a novel of formation, a bildungsroman. Maria Fernanda Bermejo, 2015, in Latin American Studies wrote her master's thesis, "Queer comes the future: los chicanos y la última utopia" ["Queer Comes the Future: Chicanos and the Last Utopia"], about Queer Aztlán and the New Mestiza from a Latin Americanist perspective seeking to build bridges between Latin America and the Chicano world. My 2014 doctoral disseration in Political and Social Sciences, "Autobiografía Pólitica Chicana y Latinoamericana, una producción cultural contrahegemónica: proyectos culturales que revelan proceses sociales que difieren y escrituras que convergen (Palabras, vidas, y utopias de Gloría Anzaldúa y Roque Dalton)" ["Chicana and Latin American Political Autobiography, a Counterhegemonic Cultural Production: Cultural Projects that Reveal Divergent Social Processes and Convergent Writing: Words, Lives, and Utopias by Gloria Anzaldúa and Roque Dalton"], that includes a counterpoint reading of the autobiographical texts written by the authors referred to in the title.[11]

Even though there is no department of Chicano/a studies and that the library catalogue of the most important library in the country, UNAM's La Biblioteca Central [Central Library], registers 321 theses about Chicano and Chicana themes, the previously mentioned theses and dissertations are just a sampling of the research conducted in the UNAM over the last twenty years that account for the topics and interests that exist and grow for Chicanos' and Chicanas' culture, literature, and history.

Key Figures in the Promotion of Chicano/a and Latino/a Studies in Mexico

There is a chasm between Mexican and Chicano educational, academic, pedagogical, and research experiences. However, the gradual interest that has advanced this issue in Mexico has been largely the result of a long effort by the following individuals, each of whom reference Chicano and Latino Studies both in the United States and Mexico: Elena Poniatowska, Marisa Belausteguigoitia, Claire Joysmith, Axel Ramírez, José Manuel Valenzuela, and María Socorro Tabuenca.

On the one hand, the translation of Sandra Cisneros' novel *The House on Mango Street* in 1994 by Elena Poniatowska represented a watershed in the reception and recognition of Chicana literature in Mexico. At the end of the decade of the 1990s and the early 2000s, the reading of Chicano literature grew in Mexico and this difference is noted just after the translation of text by Cisneros, which became a classic also in Spanish. This change was evident because Chicano novels were now available in bookstores, among which, Cisneros's work led the way with *The House on Mango Street*, 1984, and her novel *Caramelo*, 2003, translated by Liliana Valenzuela. This was due in part to the literary influence within the Mexican imagination and within the feminist intellectual circle of cultural icon Elena Poniatowska. Poniatowska's translation of Cisneros' work ended the invisibility of Chicano literature within Mexico's cultural and literary scene in the 1990s. This drew attention to the great diversity of prolific writers and Chicano and Latino academics living in the United States. As Poniatowska eloquently states:

> Chicanas . . . crossed the 3,000 kilometers of border that separates us from the richest country in the world with the Virgin of Guadalupe, la Malinche, la Llorona and Coatlicue in tow and gave these figures a value and a meaning which

> they did not have before. Chicanas cross borders. That is what they do best. That is what they have done all their lives: crossing borders. They return us to our roots, make us go to the source, guide us toward our deepest, most ancient values, and make them essential for us.[12]

On the other hand, the pedagogical practices and cultural feminist critique of Marisa Belausteguigoitia, who, knowing full well the meager or nonexistent acceptance of Chicano literature in Mexico, has resulted in the strategic dissemination of Chicano literature as pedagogical and methodological examples of research. Belausteguigoitia has a long history the task of creating bridges from her strategic position as an academic, and she has built multiple academic and exchange platforms influenced by Chicano and Chicana thought. She has accomplished this by introducing Chicana and Latina literature and theory to Mexican academia through her work as a teacher and scholar at the school of pedagogy and Latin American Studies and the Coordination of Humanities. Currently she promotes these theories in graduate programs in social sciences and humanities at UNAM and through seminars offered through the *Programa de Certificación de Crítica Cultural Feminista.* With respect to the contribution that Chicana and Latina literature offers to Mexican classrooms, and above all to public universities, Belausteguigoitia posits:

> the knowledge produced by Anzaldúa, for example, has to do fundamentally with the act of knowing or transforming crossing 'al otro lado.' From her vision, each act of knowledge signifies building a bridge and crossing, abandoning momentarily the territory that sanctions the meaning and transit of territory where it is only possible and productive to listen, observe, and transform . . . they demonstrate, as if in smoky mirrors, your true dimensions, they oblige you to see.[13]

Second, it is important to mention that during her tenure as Director of the PUEG from 2003–2013 that space became—at the interior of the UNAM and the rest of Mexico—center of teaching, learning, research, and exchange of the themes related to Chicana literature and academic production. For seven consecutive years from 2004–2010, the PUEG organized colloquia entitled, "Las Güeras y las Prietas" which references the classic essays by Gloria Anzaldúa and Cherrie Moraga "La Prieta" and "La Güera."[14]. These colloquia served as a platform and place of dialogue around questions of race, class, and gender in Mexico that echo and make reference to the discussions led by Chicanas and African Americans studies scholars in the United States. In 2006, the third colloquia specifically referenced the theme that gave it its title: "Chicanas, mexicanas y mujeres indígenas: construyendo una sociedad intercultural a partir de la narrativa, la crítica literaria y la cultura" ["Chicanas, Mexicans, and Indigenous Women: Constructing an Intercultural Society Through Narrative"]. In this occasion, one of the key speakers of the event was the well-known Chicana feminist scholar Norma Alarcón, The aim of this colloquium was to address different forms of Mexican national identity: Chicana identity and indigenous identity, and to promote the cultural and literary production of these peoples (communities).

The publication *Güeras and Prietas: Gender and Race in the Construction of New Worlds*[15] contains a selection of some of the reflections which took place in the colloquium. This book incorporates discussions about the epistemological and theoretical concepts proposed by Anzaldúa and other Chicana feminists like Alarcón into Mexican feminist studies and literary and cultural studies.

In these discussions, we can observe the profound and transformative impact that Anzaldúa's *Borderlands/La Frontera: The New Mestiza* has had on the students' learning experience in the classroom: how students take to the text and, who from their own experiences, interpret the theory, the narrative, and the cultural critique to use them as tools that enable them to make sense of their oppressive reality, and acquire a "new mestiza consciousness" to transform it. It is worth mentioning that during Belausteguigoitita's tenure as Director of the PUEG (Programa Universitario de Estudios de Gendero), she promoted the translation into Spanish and publication of Chela Sandoval's *Methodology of the Oppressed*, 2000, done by Julia Constantino[16] and Gloria Anzaldúa's *Borderlands/ La Frontera: The New Mestiza*, 1987, done by Norma Elia Cantú with the aim of making these indispensable texts part of the teaching of cultural studies, pedagogy, literature, social sciences, art, and the humanities in Mexico and throughout Latin America. We can say with much pleasure that the current management of the PUEG finally materialized the labor of these translations and that the texts were released in print in the fall 2015 and spring of 2016, respectively. Experience has shown that not only the UNAM community will benefit from these translations, but that they can also influence other latitudes and sectors of civil society that work with these themes and whose struggles convey these kind of epistemological and political claims: processes of *conscientization*, decolonization, and liberation.

Experience in Mexico shows that, rather than talking about the incorporation of Chicanos/Latinos in the context of "studies," what has been more effective in the Mexican national context and as an actual strategy to reach classrooms and research is the presence of specific authors and their theoretical and conceptual propositions in the curriculum. For example, feminists, theorists, and writers Norma Alarcon, Norma Klhan, Chela Sandoval, Gloria Anzaldúa and Sandra Cisneros are beginning to be read in Mexican classrooms as part of a complex and powerful cultural theory that transcends borders. These authors are read because their theories and narratives focus on questions of race, gender, nation, sexuality, narrative, experience, and oppositional experiences and knowledge. They are read alongside specific class contexts and in combination with Mexican or Latino/a writers who work in art, culture, and literature. The latter strategy is a space that offers a testimony narrated from the experiences and history of racial exclusion in a way that resembles or "speaks" as a model of the experiences of social exclusion and gender. For example, readings of authors such as Rosario Castellanos and Gloria Anzaldúa can be read together as strategies of comparative exercises, or counterpoint, to provide ways of conceptualizing pain and forms of confusion emanating from racist, sexist and misogynistic cultural practices, especially those inflicted on women and indigenous groups, as reflected in their major works *Balún Canán* [17] and *Borderlands/La Frontera*, respectively.

Along these same lines, it is important to include Claire Joysmith's pioneering work in Chicano/a studies. Joysmith specializes in literary Chicana/o and Latina/o studies about transborder culture and identity between the United States and Mexico, and in cultural and linguistic translation. In 1993, Joysmith organized the "*Coloquio de Literatura de Mujeres Chicanas*" ["Colloquium on Chicana Women's Literature"], as well as the "*Encuentro de Escritoras Mexicanas y Chicanas*" ["Mexican and Chicana Writers Conference"]. In 2011, she organized the international colloquium "*Nepantla Aesthetics. La espina de nopal en el corazón. Escritura y representación chicanas*" ["Nepantla Aesthetics: The Nopal's Thorn in the Heart. Chicana Writing and Representation"], with Sandra Cisneros as invited guest speaker. Joysmith has also edited and co-edited numerous books about Chicana writing, testimony, and translation. She has also played a key role in the production, translation into Spanish, and circulation of interviews and Chicana literary texts. In addition, she has interviewed, among others, Gloria Anzaldúa, Norma Cantú, Ana Castillo, Lucha Corpi, and Helena María Viramontes. One of Joysmith's distinctive strategies is her effort to publish bilingual texts, in English and Spanish, by Chicana writers, as well as her effort, since the 1990s, to push for Spanglish within the space of the Mexican university as a legitimate textual and literary form. Joysmith comments on this issue:

> It is language, that passport that allows and legitimizes the crossing of multiple border lines, which allows us to play with, in and also against the borders of meaning. It is the articulated voice that permits us to create and perceive of self-representation.[18]

Another Chicano Studies scholar is Axel Ramirez, who was the first and only director in the 1980s of the now defunct Department of Chicano Studies of the Centro de Enseñanza de Extranjeros (CEPE) in the UNAM. During his association with the CEPE, he organized a series of colloquia, entitled "Chicano-Mexican Colloquiums" and "Chicano Conferences," 1977, 1983, 1987, 1988 and 1993, in Mexico. Ramirez is now a researcher in the Centro de Investigaciones de América Latina y el Caribe (CIALC) [Center for Latin American and Caribbean Research] in the UNAM whose work deals primarily with Chicanos and Latinos. His research interests include: Chicanos and the Mexican Revolution, Hispanics and Latinos in the United States, Latino as a cultural category, and migration from Latin America to the United States. About Chicano literature in Mexico, Ramirez posits that "until Mexican readers accept Chicano literature in all its intensity and content and leave behind their prejudices, only then will this literature form part of their consciousness and help them define themselves as Mexicans in a much more plural way."[19]

Finally, it is essential to recognize the crucial roles that Jose Manuel Valenzuela of COLEF Tijuana and María Socorro Tabuenca of COLEF Ciudad Juárez have played in legitimizing cultural studies where Chicano/a Studies are fundamental to the fields of literature, history, cultural criticism, gender, art, performance, installation art, and other cultural interventions. Both scholars, together with Sayak Valencia, who teaches at COLEF, are situated in the border region of Tijuana, Ensenada, Mexicali and promote the research of Chicano/a and Latino/a studies from a privileged space of historic and continual contact with the protagonists - Chicana writers, theoreticians, historians, and cultural critics. These women are also situated in the geographic and disciplinary border but on the other side of the Rio Grande, and the bridge to California, New Mexico, Arizona, Texas, and beyond.

Chicano/a Interventions in the Cultural, Artistic, and Academic Realms of Mexico

In this final section, I detail the diverse academic and cultural interventions specific to Mexico City and the UNAM. I begin with the UNAM because it is the primary Casa de Estudios de México—the country's most prestigious university—and because it has been an ideal space for many Chicano/a students that have arrived and continue to arrive in Mexico in search of a space of dialogue and research for the academic work they carry out in a variety of graduate programs based in the United States.

The queer, Latina, migrant student Sandibel Borges from the University of California, Santa Barbara researched in the PUEG at UNAM from 2014–2015 about an important topic regarding the intersectionality of indigenous, queer migrants who continually cross the border to make and remake their lives in the United States and Mexico. Borges analyzes the process of subject formation under conditions of vulnerability and resistance: that of queer, indigenous migrants without documents. Through interviews, Borges frames her research as an oral history of these subjects considering the processes of permanent reconfiguration that result from their experiences with forced mobility and the reconstruction of their lives. The interviews she conducts are part of her doctoral dissertation and can be found, in part, in her recent English-language publication "Not Coming Out, but Building Home: An Oral History in Re-Conceptualizing a Queer Migrant Home" published in *Diálogo* in September 2015 and in her Spanish-language essay, "Reflexiones sobre 'el closet', perspectiva de una mujer migrante queer" (Reflections on 'the Closet': a Queer, Migrant, Woman's Perspective) published in October 2015 in the digital journal Morelos 3.0.

Xicana Cristina Serna from Boyle Heights in Los Angeles, California and now a professor at Colgate University in Hamilton, New York, has researched Chicana and Mexican queer art that transcends nation-state borders and transgresses the borders of gender, race, and class. In Mexico, Serna has researched art in the Instituto de Investigaciones Estéticas in the UNAM, 2005, completed an academic residency in the PUEG-UNAM, 2011, and participated in the Third Edition of The Sexual Diversity Day in UNAM, 2011. In the latter, she participated with a lecture entitled, "Memoria, arte y activismo de lesbianas chicanas, mexicanas en California" ["Memory, Art, and Activism of Chicana and Mexican Lesbians in California"]. Since 2005, Serna has participated in dialogues and exchanges with the social organizations that spearhead the Lesbian March in Mexico, the Lesbian Feminist Cultural Week, and the journal *LesVoz*. Since then, Serna has been a bridge between social spaces and Latina and Chicana artists and activists who carry out academic, cultural, and artistic practices and social organizing. These artists and activists include Maya Gonzales, Yan María Yaoyotl Castro, Alma López, Alicia Gaspar de Alba, Adeline Anthony, Celia Herrera, Cherrie Moraga, Sonia Mariscal and Isabel Millán. The contribution and participation of these artists, activists, and academics have been key to the medium- and long-term development of a binational network of Chicana and Mexican lesbian and queer women with shared interests in fighting for a social justice that transcends borders.

Another of the interventions by Chicano artists in the last decade is the production of *Zoot Suit* by director, playwright and founder of *Teatro Campesino*, Luis Valdez. The production was collaboration between the National Theatre Company and the Juan Ruiz Theatre Company of the Centro Cultural Universitario in UNAM, 2010. Translated into Spanish by Edna Ochoa, the play arrived in Mexico for the first time in 2010. The production achieved acceptance and acclaim. The play recreates the political climate of the 1940s, but without a doubt it resonates with the present-day experience of Pachucos, Cholos, Chicanos, and migrants in the United States and the constant persecution and hostility toward these "minority" groups. In 2015, after a successful tour through the interior of Mexico, the Centro Cultural del Bosque of Mexico City announced that it would have another season in Julio Castillo Theatre from April 9 through May 17.

Valdez himself, full of joy about the production of *Zoot Suit* and the validation of the play's themes, remarked:

> It is an honor to present the play here. A dream has been fulfilled; the final point in a journey that began a century ago when my paternal grandparents married in Nogales, where my father was born in 1912 and, because of the

> conditions he would share with peasants, would have to leave the country. So my reality begins at the border, but my family never forgot our identity. My mother would say: we are Yaquis from Sonora. With this production, I now complete a great circle because even though we left the land 100 years ago, we never forgot our identity. Victory is ours [we are victorious] because we have arrived here, which is the heart of America, to represent the connection that was never broken and that points to the future.[20]

After the first production of *Zoot Suit* in the UNAM in 2010, a symposium entitled "Simposio sobre Teatro Chicano" ["Symposium of Chicano Theatre"] organized by Alma Martínez of Pomona College in Claremont, California took up the theme of the "Chicano." The symposium took place in the Sor Juana Inéz de la Cruz Theatre/ Forum in the UNAM in June of 2010, consisting of five panels, and reuniting specialists from Mexico and the United States: intellectuals, academics, artists, writers, cultural critics, and the general public interested in contemporary theater and Chicano art and the experiences and cultural practices of border Chicano/as. One of the symposium's objectives was to generate new languages for mutual and intercultural understanding of the topics and practitioners of Mexican and Mexican American dramatic arts. It is worth mentioning that in one of the main panels, speakers addressed the specific topic of "Bridges between Chicano Theatre and Mexican Border Theatre in light of the Political Conjuncture" of migration north of the Rio Grande, racism, and discrimination. Some of the organizers were Sylvia Núñez, Director of CISAN-UNAM; Aída Hurtado from the Department of Chicano Studies at UC Santa Barbara; Luis de Tavira Director of the Mexican National Theater Company at the time; and Enrique Singer of the Teatro-UNAM. The conference was brought to a close with a masterly talk by Luis Valdez who posited that "the Pachuco struggle of the 1940s was the beginning of a *conscientization* of the Mexican people in the United States, emphasizing who we are and who we were." The event organizer, Alma Martinez, claimed the following about the main character of Valdez's play and the symposium in its entirety:

> The Pachuco character of *Zoot Suit* is the best-known protagonist of Valdez's work, for its emblematic, multi-referential allusion to the image of Tin Tan as the "first Chicano" as well as to Octavio Paz's extreme and derogatory characterizations. The symposium would include participants whose work and research examine, among other themes, Chicano culture, emigration and immigration, the U.S. judicial and penal system, representations of the feminine [of women] and gender, Mexican influence on the aesthetics of Chicano theater, and Chicano and Mexican border theater in light of recent political events. Their far-reaching and complex range of experiences, specialties, and focus offer productive grounds to discuss the significance and impact of the pachuco, Chicano, and pocho to the culture of the United States, Mexico, and the rest of Latin America.[21]

The historian Romeo Guzman participated in one of the panels, and he continues to participate in Mexican cultural and academic spaces. His research topics include migration between Mexico and the United States, family transnationalism as a strategy of social and cultural organization, citizenship, popular culture, and public records. One of the archives he has consulted is *La Casa de Ahuizote* ["The House of Ahuizote"] in Mexico City that houses the Magonista journal *Regeneración*. From this space that seeks to be one of exchange and cultural and intellectual activity, Guzman has worked to construct a transnational network and community of cultural thinkers and workers. He has written a variety of articles about his family and community history of migration and an essay about *Tin Tan*,[22] the icon of popular and Mexican Pachuco cultures *par excellence*. Without a doubt, Guzman is an emergent Chicano/Pocho/Mexican intellectual who is constructing and promoting networks of binational intellectuals and the transnational circuits through which these cross-border ideas, literature, and cultural and intellectual productions circulate.

In this sense, it is important to bring to this archive of instances and cultural practices by and about Chicanos, Chicanas, Latinas, and Latinos in Mexico, an effort by artists and poets on both sides of the border completed in May 2013 in the Museo Universitario del Chopo in Mexico City. This meeting, entitled "The War on Both Sides/La Guerra de los Dos Lados," between at least thirty community members from both sides of the border was organized with the intention to reunite artists from Los Angeles with their counterparts in Mexico City and raise a simple but complex question: "What is the creative community's role in the context of this narco war that has taken a heavy toll on both sides of the U.S.-Mexico border?"[23] The aim of this meeting was to transform distance into proximity, to construct an ethical bridge that crosses the border between the United States and Mexico. In accordance with Rubén Martínez, journalist and Loyola Marymount professor, the idea was to address the theme of violence through the artists and journalists who experience it daily. *II Tertulias* was organized with the support of the Los Angeles Department of Cultural Affairs and the Museo Universitario del Chopo, garnering participation from artists, poets, journalists, academics, and cultural workers from both sides of the Rio Grande such as Raquel Gutiérrez, Rubén Martínez, Javier Sicilia, Mónica Mayer, Víctor Lerma, Cristina Rivera Garza, Rafa Esparza, Raúl Silva, Magali Tercero, Silvia Marcos, Tania Barberá, and Teresa Margolles, among others. Rubén Martínez concluded about the meeting and the talks:

> The omnipresent vocabulary of the Mexican body in crisis is in quotidian conversations: kidnapping, extortion, disappearance, the missing, the mutilated, hitman. We arrive at asking ourselves about the distance that exists between the experience of violence from our point-of-view in Los Angeles and that of our colleagues in Mexico. Our conversations assured us that despite everything we are not as far apart as we think.[24]

In the scope of Chicano art that arrives in Mexican museums, I include the exposition *Asco: Elite de lo oscuro, una retrospective 1972–1987* [*Asco: The Elite of Darkness, a Retrospective, 1972–1987*] which opened on March 21, 2013 in the Museo de Arte Contemporáneo, MUAC, in the UNAM.[25] It was the first exhibition in Mexico that presented a wide spectrum of work by the Chicano art group *Asco*, a collective of conceptual artists from the 1970s and 1980s that included Harry Gamboa Jr., Gronk (Glugio Nicandro), Willie F. Herron III, and Patssi Valdez. This collective of artists from Los Angeles took its name from a word that implies repugnance and nausea. Through performance, public, and multimedia art, the Chicano artists dedicated themselves to responding to the social and political turbulence in Los Angeles and internationally. The collective operated through the mid-1980s and by this point, artists Diane Gamboa, Sean Carrillo, Daniel J. Martínez, and Teddy Sandoval had joined. The exhibition in MUAC consisted of film screenings, sculpture, painting, performance, documentation, collage, mail art, photography and short films. The exhibition's curators were Rita Gonzales and C. Ondine Chavoya, and the associate curator was Alejandra Labastida. It is worth mentioning that this exhibition was first mounted in the Los Angeles County Museum of Art and the Williams College Museum of Art, among others. As part of the exhibition, there was also a roundtable discussion that included the curators, Gonzales and Chavoya, and artist Harry Gamboa Jr. In this talk, the participants discussed *Asco*'s practices and body of work, the implications of political and activist art of the 1970s and 1980s, in addition to the proximity and distance between artists in Mexico City and *Asco* in Los Angeles.

Finally, it is important to mention an event that perhaps synthesizes the ways that Chicano/Latino artists participate in Mexico and some of their most viewed and visited performance art pieces on this side of the border. Between May 26–29, 2015 the *International Meeting of Poetics in Action: Performance, Theatricality, Body and Memory* met at the *Centro Nacional de las Artes* [National Center for the Arts] in Mexico City. In the framework of this conference, performance was understood as "interdisciplinary art, which crosses artistic borders and other art, trying to erase the gap between public and private space, high and low culture."[26] At the conference there were two performative actions by a Latina academic and three Chicano/a artists from California. Dr. Karina Hodoyán of the University of San Francisco gave the keynote address of a meeting entitled "Making Theories: Latino/Chicano Artists in California," leading to three performances: Xandra Ibarra (*La Chica Boom*) held her performance "The Dominatrix del Barrio"; Violeta Luna with her performance "Virgins and Goddesses II: Stones of Memory"; and the well-known Guillermo Gómez-Peña with his performance "Five Texts by/for an Aging Body." This is just a small sample that demonstrates a variety of performance interventions in one of the most popular events of its kind in Mexico.

To conclude this essay, even though we cannot speak of a clearly delimited Chicano/a and Latino/a studies in Mexican academia, we can trace an archive of how the academic work of Chicano/as and Latino/as has strengthened debates and discussions in Mexico about literary criticism, critical theory, epistemology, radical methodologies, and above all, culture. In addition, we can point to specific efforts by people in Mexico within diverse cultural and academic spheres as well as Chicanas, Chicanos, Latinas, and Latinos who "return home" and construct bridges between the United States and Mexico. Despite the dearth of discussions in Mexico about Chicana and Latina intellectual production historically, their place has been growing in creative and strategic ways through pedagogy, translation, literature, cultural studies, gender studies, and feminist cultural criticism. Likewise, Chicanas, Chicanos, Latinas, and Latinos, students, researchers, artists, performers, and cultural workers have taken charge of their own interventions in different academic and cultural circles. We know that Chicano/a and Latino/a bodies, images, imaginations, voices, and words have returned to "speak to" and "introduce themselves" to Mexican students in the classroom, to academic lines of inquiry, and the general public who become more interested in the world and imaginary of Chicano/as in the United States and across borders. The words, images, struggles, causes, arts, and performances have returned to the cubicles and classrooms to transform Chicano/as, *los atravesados, into raised/elevated subjects,* to embolden the volume of their voices, to give them materiality and self-consciousness and to validate their experiences.

We can conclude then that this has been a constant struggle to make relevant in Mexico Chicana/o and Latina/o Studies in general and Chicana and Latina feminist scholarship in particular. One can also say, with certain freedom that comes from experience, that in recent times as Chicanas and Latinas we have sought formal and sometimes forced informal labyrinthine and underground circuits to reach cultural fields and academic spaces in Mexico and UNAM. And so it has been a constant struggle to make ourselves heard and to generate spaces for dialogue and exchange, a constant struggle for mutual recognition, the meeting of the eyes and an attentive and mutual listening. In the twenty first century Chicanas/os, Latina/os and Mexicans and Latin Americans are finally in very culturally rich exchanges and dialogues and Mexico is precisely that bridge and contact zone where we all meet.

Notes

1 "A Natural History of Chicano Literature," Juan Felipe Herrera Lecture as *Tomás Rivera* Endowed Chair in creative writing at University of California, Riverside. (9/2005) Uploaded January 31, 2008. www.youtube.com/watch?v=g7ZLhIjURFw accessed December 2015.

2 Gloria, Anzaldúa, *Borderlands/La Frontera: la nueva mestiza*, trans Norma Elia Cantú (México: PUEG, UNAM, 2015).

3 Jualianne Gilland, Nina Hoechtl, Rian Lozano, and Coco Gutiérrez-Magallanes, *ENTRE PALABRA E IMAGEN: Galeria de pensamiento de Gloria Anzaldúa* (México: UAEM, 2016). See link: http://uaemculturatlalpan.com/entrepalabraeimagen.html accessed November 11, 2015.

4 María del Socorro Gutiérrez Magallanes, "Autobiografía política latinoamericana y autobiografía política chicana: Discusión teórica, formas de abordaje, deslindes y propuestas de categorías para acercamientos y lecturas," In *Revista Digital La Manzana. No. 13, Año X,* Segunda Epoca, Marzo-agosto, edited by Lorena Carrillo y Beatriz Gutiérrez (Puebla: BUAP, ICSyH), "Alfonso Vélez Pliego" (2016): 6–26. www.estudiosmasculinidades.buap.mx/LA_MANZANA_Num_13_FINAL.pdf accessed June 16, 2016.

5 Axel Ramírez, "Espejos y reflejos: los chicanos y su literatura en México," In *Espejos y Reflejos: Literatura Chicana*, edited by Alejandra Sánchez Valencia, 21–36 (México: UAM, 2000).

6 José Manuel Valenzuela, *El color de las sombras: chicanos, identidad y racismo* (México: Plaza y Valdez 1998).

7 María Socorro Tabuenca, *Border Women: Writing From La Frontera* (Minneapolis, MN: University of Minnesota Press, 2003); and *Tendiendo puentes: estudios literarios mexicanos y chicanos* (Juárez: El Colegio de Chihuahua, 2010).

8 Marina Fe, *Mujeres en la hoguera: Representaciones literarias y culturales de la figura de la bruja* (México: PUEG, UNAM, 2009).

9 Claire Joysmith, *Las formas de nuestras voces: Chicana and mexicana writers in México* (México: CISAN, UNAM, Third Woman Press, 1995) and *Cantar de Espejos. Poesía testimonial chicana de mujeres* (México: Claustro de Sor Juana, CISAN, UNAM, 2012).

10 Aralia López-González, Amelia Malagamba, Elena Urrutia, coordinadoras. México, D.F.: Colegio de México, Programa Interdisciplinario de Estudios de la Mujer; Tijuana, B.C., México: Colegio de la Frontera Norte, 1990.

11 Many other students are exploring Chicano Studies, including the following. Itzel Hernández de la Cruz, 2012, in Hispanic Language and Letters wrote her master's thesis: "Canícula: 'Autoetnografía' Ficcional de Norma Elia Cantú" ["Canícula: The Autoethnographic Fiction of Norma Elia Cantú"], conducting a literary analysis and of the deployed strategies in Cantú's work. Elías Ángeles Hernández, 2007, in International Relations wrote his master's thesis on Chicano muralism, entitled: "El despertar de los México-Americanos y el muralismo chicano como expresión de la lucha y afirmación de identidad" ["Mexican-American Awakening and Chicano Muralism as an Expression of Struggle and Affirmation of Identity"], in which he works with the Civil Rights Movement, Chicanismo as an ideology, and Chicano muralism as a politico-aesthetic manifestation. Sara Ugalde Guzmán, 2005, in Hispanic Language and Letters wrote her master's thesis entitled, "La Nueva Mestiza. Obra poética de escritoras chicanas contemporáneas" ["The New Mestiza: Poetry by Contemporary Chicana Writers"], about Gloria Anzaldúa's and Ana Castillo's poetry and the psychological, historical, and literary elements in their work with attention to gender. Victor Hugo Millán Rodríguez, 2005, in Sociology wrote his master's thesis "La identidad cultural chicana desde la mirada del cine estadounidense, mexicano y chicano" ["Chicana/o Cultural Identity from the U.S., Mexican,

and Chicano Filmic Gaze"], about the meaning of pocho, the definition of pachuco, the signification and connotation of Chicano, and the meaning of cholo as categories developed in Chicano film of the struggle for Chicano cultural identity. Ofelia Alfonseca, 2002, in Hispanic Letters wrote her master's thesis "Un acercamiento a la literatura chicana a través de . . . Y No Se Lo Trago La Tierra de Tomás Rivera" ["Approaching Chicana/o Literature Through Y No Se Lo Trago La Tierra by Tomás Rivera"], that situates a reading of the novel (its structure, themes, time, narrators and characters) within its historical context of Chicano literary and cultural production. Mauricio Torres Rico, 2002, in Modern Language and Literatures wrote his master's thesis, "La figura de La Malinche en dos cuentos de autoras chicanas" ["The Figure of Malinche in Two Short Stories by Chicana Authors"], about the authors' use of narrative strategies informed by the literary, feminist model of La Malinche. Mercedes López Martines,1997, in Latin American Studies wrote her master's thesis, "Chicanos y mexicanos: relaciones intersindicales Los Ángeles-Ciudad de México 1970–2994" ["Chicanos and Mexicans: Inter-union Relationships, Los Angeles-Mexico City, 1970–1994"]; and Davíd Ortíz Conseco, 1995, in International Relations with his master's thesis "Los chicanos y la relación México-Estados Unidos: del racismo binacional al enriquecimiento bilateral" ["Chicanos and the Mexico-United States Relationship: From Binational Racism to Bilateral Enrichment"], about the origin of Mexican communities conceptualized as the pioneer generation 1850–1900, the immigrant generation 1900–1940, the cementing (foundational) generation 1940–1960, the Chicana/o generation 1960–1980 and the Aztlán generation 1980–2000, in addition to the themes of racism in Mexico and in the United States and the efforts for recognition and valorization of Chicano culture in both countries.

12 Elena, Poniatowska, "Escritoras chicanas y mexicanas," In *Las formas de nuestras voces: Chicana and Mexicana writers in México,* edited by Claire Joysmith, 48 (Mexico: CISAN, UNAM, Third Woman Press, 1995).

13 Marisa Belausteguigoitia, "*Borderlands/La Frontera*: El feminismo chicano de Gloria Anzaldúa desde las fronteras geoculturales, disciplinarias y pedagógicas," *Debate Feminista,* Vol 40, No. 20 (2009): 199.

14 In *This Bridge Called My Back: Writings by Radical Women of Color,* 2nd edition, edited by Gloria Anzaldúa and Cherrie Moraga (New York, NY: Kitchen Table/Women of Color Press 1983).

15 Marisa Belausteguigoitia, *Güeras y prietas: género y raza en la construcción de mundos nuevos* (México: PUEG, UNAM, 2009).

16 Chela Sandoval, *Metodología de la emancipación,* trans. Julia Constantino (México: PUEG, UNAM, 2015).

17 Rosario Castellanos, *Balún Canán* (México: Fondo de Cultura Económica, 1957).

18 Claire Joysmith, *Las formas de nuestras voces: Chicana and mexicana writers in México* (Mexico: CISAN, UNAM, Third Woman Press, 1995), 13.

19 Axel Ramírez, *Espejos y reflejos Literatura Chicana* (México: UAM, 2000), 36.

20 Mónica Mateos-Vega, "Zoot Suit, repuesta al racismo creciente en EU: Luis Valdez," *La Jornada,* (April 23, 2010): 3.

21 Alma Martínez, *Chicano Theater Symposium at UNAM,* Teatro Juan Ruiz de Alarcón, June 2010.

22 Romeo Guzmán, "Tin Tan," In *Icons of Mexico,* edited by Eric Zolov (Santa Barbara, CA: ABC-CLIO, September 2015).

23 Rubén, Martínez, "La Guerra de los Dos Lados," in *Museo Universitario El Chopo,* May 19, 2013. www.chopo.unam.mx/boletines/mayo2013/guerra.dos.lados.bole.doc accessed November 15, 2015.

24 Ibid.

25 Reed Johnson, "Building Bridges Between Mexican and Mexican American Art," *The Los Angles Times,* April 6, 2013, 7.

26 Program: Encuentro Internacional Poética de la acción. Performance y teatralidad: cuerpo y memoria. May 26-29, 2015, Centro Nacional de las Artes, Mexico City.

10

NEW LATIN AMERICAN REVOLUTIONARY CINEMA

Silvia Alvarez Olarra

Translated by Patricia Berasaluce

The Poetics of Revolutionary Cinema

Combining two concepts such as cinema and revolution in the Latin American scene means going back to the 1960s and revisiting such a problematic term, due to its over-standardization, as "New Latin American Cinema." This term was coined during that decade precisely, and it was used to encompass artistic expressions by very diverse film-makers who had in common, on the one hand, their wish to convey unrepresented national realities onto the big screen, and on the other, their interest in exploring the medium's formal possibilities in order to de-automatize the spectators' gaze and thus turn cinema into an effective tool for social transformation. These two general principles constituted the basis for establishing a pan-American correlation linking the work of directors such as Fernando Birri, Fernando Solanas, Octavio Getino, (*Grupo Liberación*) and Raymundo Gleyzer (*Grupo Cine de la Base*) in Argentina; the work of Glauber Rocha, Nelson Pereira dos Santos, and the *Cinema Novo* in Brazil; the work of Jorge Sanjinés and his *Grupo Ukamau* in Bolivia; the "imperfect cinema" of Julio García Espinosa, the work of Tomás Gutiérrez Alea, and that of Humberto Solás in Cuba; and the work of Miguel Littín, Raúl Ruiz, and Patricio Guzmán in Chile, among others.

From the outset, the New Latin American Cinema was envisaged, in the words of Fernando Birri in 1962, as the cinema of truth; as a cinema that "Shows things the way they are, irrefutably, and not the way we would like them to be (or the way some would have us believe—in good or bad faith—they are)"[1] It is a cinema that reacts against prior (national or international) cinematic models, which are accused of having misrepresented these countries and thus contributed to their economic and cultural subjugation. As opposed to those other models, the new Latin American cinema flies the flag of committed realism, in the belief that the movie camera is capable of capturing, without any intermediation, an ontological truth of a social nature which, with the help of film montage, will lead audiences to develop the necessary critical awareness to be able to understand the world they live in and participate in the process of subverting the oppression mechanisms responsible for underdevelopment. Documentary film and its specific techniques are, therefore, found to be the most appropriate tool for making this type of cinema.[2] "A camera in hand and an idea in mind" became the slogan, not only of Brazil's *Cinema Novo*, but also of all the expressions included under this umbrella label of "New Latin American Cinema." Thus, in Latin America, cinema became an instrument of social and political revolution:

> Always conceived as a challenge to the hegemony of the Hollywood import and foreign control of the cinematic institutions and as an active agent in the process of cultural decolonization, the New Latin American cinema is not just a filmmaking movement; it is a social practice intimately related to other movements struggling for the socio-cultural, political, and economic autonomy of Latin America."[3]

However, is this political and social commitment to the reality of these countries, in turn, linked to realistic aesthetics? If such aesthetics are understood on the basis of André Bazin's theoretical writings, the answer will be no. On first glance, it would seem that Fernando Birri's wish, in the early 1960s, to create new cinema showing "things as they irrefutably are" reproduced the same idea of objectivity held by Bazin in his essay "Ontologie de l'image photographique" (1945) as pertaining to cinema, when he claimed that:

> For the first time, between the originating object and its reproduction there intervenes only the instrumentality of a nonliving agent. For the first time an image of the world is formed automatically, without the creative intervention of man. . . . This production by automatic means has radically affected our psychology of the image. The objective nature of photography confers on it a quality of credibility absent from all other picture-making.[4]

This Bazinean ideal of objectivity could also be considered to be the same as that advocated by Julio García Espinosa in the late 1960s when, in "Por un cine imperfecto" (1969), he argued that the new Latin American cinema should neither analyze nor comment on the reality it showed, because: "To analyze is to preempt any possible analysis by the interlocutor."[5] However, the formal means proposed by the former and by the latter in order to achieve said objective were radically divergent. Whereas the members of the New Latin American Cinema did not hesitate to embrace the semantic possibilities of montage, Bazin advocated an aesthetic consisting in long shots, respecting spatio-temporal continuity to the greatest possible extent.[6]

Despite the important role played by Italian neorealism in the training of several Latin American filmmakers of the time, the formal divergence between Bazin and them—which can initially be explained by the limited popular impact of neorealism[7]—was reinforced by the negative campaign against realistic theories during those years, when certain Marxist-style journals, and even *Cahiers du Cinéma*—a magazine founded by Bazin himself—equated realistic aesthetics with a bourgeois ideology, narrative closure, and an imperialist cinematic model.[8] This tension was revealed in 1969, when in a discussion among Jean Narboni, Sylvie Pierre, and Jacques Rivette about the possibilities of classifying cinema according to its management of montage, these artists included the work of Solanas, together with that of Eisenstein, as an example of cinema based on that technique, and then determined that "montage is the only way to create non-reactionary cinema as opposed to the cinema of beguilement, of representation."[9]

The success of Solanas and Getino with *La hora de los hornos* (1968) would be followed one year later with a prize in Cannes for Glauber Rocha, who was awarded the "Prix de la mise en scène" [Best Director Award] for *O Dragão da Maldade contra o Santo Guerreiro* (1969). In this film, in which he reintroduced the character of Antonio da Morte—who had already appeared in *Deus e o Diablo na Terra do Sol* (1964)—he continued to explore the possibilities that montage had offered him in *Terra em Transe* (1967) for an anti-realistic portrayal of violence.[10] "A baroque allegory" is how Michael Chanan describes *Terra em Transe*, a denomination with which Paul S. Schroeder (2011) agrees when he continues to examine the works of these filmmakers during the following two decades.[11] Films such as *Frida, naturaleza vida* (1983) by Mexican filmmaker Paul Leduc, and even more so *ORG* (1969/1978) by Fernando Birri, are—in this regard—examples of movies in which the rapid cuts and the associations suggested through the montage are extreme. Regarding this latter film, Hermann Herlinghaus explained that:

> The picture, which lasts 2 hours and 57 minutes, constitutes a series of visual stains, an atomized world, a constant sparkling across the screen, accompanied by bits of sound, music and vocals, which, by themselves, are undecipherable. While an average fiction feature film comprises 600 to 800 edited sequences, the number of splices in the negative of ORG amounts to 26,625, the result of 8,340 hours of work."[12]

The experimental radicalism of these films coincided with the theoretical reflections brought up by Glauber Rocha in 1971, in a lecture called "A Eztetyka do Sonho," in which the Brazilian director considered it imperative to embrace poetic and mystical irrationalism in order to liberate film creation from yet another oppressive structure, that of bourgeois reason, and to strengthen the revealing capacity of its metaphors. "*Na medida em que a desrazão planeja as revoluções, a razão planeja a repressão*" ["To the extent that unreason brings about revolutions, reason brings about repression"], he declared in that lecture, thus vindicating a language that is closer to poetry than to Logos as the language both of cinema and of revolutionary historical processes.[13] Fernando Birri, who from the times of *Tire Diré* (1960) evolved from fighting "For a Nationalist, Realist, Critical and Popular Cinema" (1958) to rally "For a Cosmic Cinema, Raving, and Lumpen" (1978) still endorsed—nearly fifteen years later—the poetic and political approach to cinema proposed by Rocha. At the 7th International Festival of New Latin American Cinema (Havana, 1985), he explicitly used the concept of poetry to refer to the film language of New Latin American Cinema, stating that:

> Just as, I confess, I no longer know where the word cinema begins and where the word life ends, neither do I know where the word poetry ends and where the word revolution begins. Art transforms things into something else; the living metaphor is the revolution.[14]

It is impossible to understand what these New Latin American Cinema directors are advocating by equating reality, cinema and poetry without considering these texts and films in the context of broader dialogue. It must be recalled that even though this cinema was self-conceived as an anti-imperialist instrument to restore national identity and propose alternative channels for projection, these directors realized that the cinema being made needed to be economically self-sustainable and to have an international projection.[15] The latter was made possible by circulating New Latin American Cinema films widely in European festivals, where they found an excellent showcase for international projection and cooperation. The Mostra Internazionale del Nuovo Cinema, held in Pesaro, Italy, since 1964, was a crucial platform for circulating and promoting the cinema being made in the American subcontinent at the time, to the extent that, in the words of Judith Burton, "for the most part the lifespan of the militant New Latin American Cinema movement coincides with that of the Mostra."[16] It was precisely in the framework of that festival that, in 1965, Pier Paolo Pasolini compared the semiotic possibilities of cinema with those of literature, and, for the first time, suggested the existence of a *cinema di poesia*, of a cinema that was basically dreamlike and irrational, both for its abundance of archetypes and for the "prevalence of the pre-grammaticality of objects as symbols of visual language."[17] However, in a wonderful example of the transnational fluidity that Kathleen Newman considers a hallmark of cinema,[18] we find that the essence of these ideas had already been expressed twelve years earlier by Luis Buñuel during a presentation made at the National Autonomous University of Mexico and later published under the title "El cine, instrumento de poesía" (1958). In that text, Buñuel contrasted the cinema being made with what he considered could be cinema's real potential. He equated the latter to poetry, the subconscious and the subversive, while identifying the former with novels or drama, with nineteenth century realism, and with the dumbing down of intellectual faculties. In these two pairs in which cinema and literature are identified, Buñuel referred explicitly to neorealism, which he included in the cinematic trend that he associated with what is prosaic and unfitting of genuine cinema.

> Aside from a few exceptions (...) neorealism has done nothing to emphasize in its films what is inherent to cinema; namely, mystery and fantasy. What use are all those visual trappings if the situations, the motives driving the characters, their reactions, the plots themselves are modeled on the most sentimental and conformist literature? (...) Neorealist reality is incomplete, official –reasonable above all else; but poetry, mystery, that which completes and expands immediate reality, is completely absent from its productions.[19]

This criticism of neorealism is hardly surprising, because it is justified, as already mentioned, on the basis of a binary conception of cinema and its possibilities, but what is indeed surprising is the nuance of admiration that he added to his emphatic rejection of this cinematic style. In the same lecture, Buñuel recognized that even though neorealist cinema is subject to nineteenth century narrative principles, it has somewhat of a revolutionary potential in its slowness, in the peculiar suspense arising from the trivial routine of the characters' behavior. And precisely that poetic element of mysterious ambiguity—paradoxically noticeable, Buñuel points out, in the most radically realistic filming—is what some of the most outstanding Latin American filmmakers of the new millennium seem determined to rescue.

Latin American Cinema of Contemplation

The gradual establishment of right-wing dictatorships across Latin America since the early 1970s forced those New Latin American Cinema filmmakers who managed to stay alive into exile. Even though many of these directors continued filming in their host countries, it is unquestionable that this new political scene had an immediate impact on national film production. Censorship and a neoliberal ideology paved the way for "a diet of (national) inoffensive comedies and musicals," while they increased the market access for Hollywood films. 1960s revolutionary films—both in terms of their social relevance as well as of their groundbreaking aesthetic—gave way to "forms that had a proven popular appeal: political thrillers, comedy, melodrama (linking to the tastes formed by television), rediscovering some of the forms that had made Latin American cinema successful in the 1940s"[20] before the arrival of New Latin American Cinema.

Latin American cinema would have to wait until the mid-1990s to return to the notion of poetic film and the use of techniques similar to the ones promoted by the Bazinean realistic cinematography model. The astounding current revitalization of this poetic realism of the ordinary seems to continue suggesting—at least in the case of Latin America—a visionary cinema, with the twofold meaning of this adjective: as a cinema granting pride of place to sight over all other cognitive mechanisms, and as a cinema closely related to poetry, which makes "pure vision an instrument of knowledge and action."[21]

This constitutes de-dramatized cinema, in which the actions that are traditionally the backbone of the story are relegated in favor of purely visual and acoustic situations. The arrival of digital cinema has made it easier for images to break free from the needs of the story, and in this process, the camera has acquired an unprecedented autonomy, which responds to an interest in conveying onto the screen the non-dramatic way in which real-life situations occur; situations whose linear nature is only noticeable or imaginable in hindsight. Carlos Reygadas explained this on the occasion of the premiere of his latest—and to date, most experimental—film, *Post Tenebras Lux* (Mexico-France-Netherlands-Germany, 2012):

> We are used to knowing exactly what's going on when we are watching something, which is very strange because in life it is precisely the opposite. Most of the time in life we are living through things and don't know what they mean at the time, except at a very superficial level. It is only later they become important, or take on a particular relevance.[22]

The autonomy achieved by the camera in breaking free from traditional narrative expectations has led critics such as Stephen Hart to suggest that in many of these cases the tangible presence of the camera enables it to be perceived like just another character in the film.[23] Whether or not the camera is taken into account as an intradiegetic being, there is no doubt that directors such as Carlos Reygadas, Lisandro Alonso, Paz Encina, Kleber Mendoça Filho, Fernando Pérez, Lucrecia Martel, Nicolás Pereda, Federico Veiroj, Fernando Eimbcke, Claudia Llosa, and Gustavo Fontán—just to mention a few internationally renowned names—have made use of said independence to refocus the camera towards targets other than those which would traditionally constitute the storyline. This has entailed, as Reygadas further suggests[24], a leveling of the significance of all the actions and objects represented, in addition to a continued delay in the unfolding of a narration which, as pointed out by Rocío Gordon[25], does not usually evolve towards a conclusion but, rather, is maintained in an infinite state of suspension; a state which, inevitably, implies both conceiving the cinematographic experience differently from that of Hollywood, and discovering and resignifying everyday reality based on its symbolic and poetic potential.

Furthermore, the autonomy achieved by the camera has also led to severing the traditional link between the camera and the character. Whereas it is still possible to identify one or more principal characters, the camera chooses, on many occasions, not to follow the movement of these characters or occupy their space/perspective. This independence is proved in highly diverse and inconsistent ways, but in general it takes the shape of a not always abrupt alternation between the objective and the subjective use of the camera, which makes it difficult (if not impossible) to distinguish between the external and the mental; a distinction visually marked as irrelevant.[26] Such a decision entails, on the one hand, an enlargement of the concept of reality—traditionally confined to the material and factual—and on the other, a reassessment of the entire mise en scène, whose evident banality thus acquires a potential symbolic sense, because any element in this state of absolute leveling may contain a greater significance than what might appear at first sight. Cynthia Tompkins, the author of one of the most exhaustive works about recent Latin American experimental cinema, noted, for example, the effect of this independence between the camera and the character when discussing a scene in *Batalla en el cielo* (Mexico-Belgium-France-Germany, 2005). Even though in this film Carlos Reygadas uses the camera for the most part to depict the viewpoint of the characters, there are a few instances in which it expresses a will of its own. As he did in *Japón* (Mexico-Germany-Netherlands-Spain, 2002), Reygadas recreates in *Batalla en el cielo* an unconventional and very graphic sexual exchange between two atypical lovers; this scene is, however, set aside when the camera decides to divert its focus towards the view of the city through the window, underlining the irrelevance of the action going on, transgressive though it may be, as well as the fact that in this cinema, space may have as much weight as those characters that roam through it.[27] In *Lake Tahoe* (Mexico-Japan-USA, 2008), Fernando Eimbcke's second full-length film, there are several examples of similar effects, albeit achieved by means of the opposite mechanism: In *Batalla en el cielo* it is an unexpected 360-degree pan that creates the severance between the camera and the characters, whereas in *Lake Tahoe*, this split results from the immobility of the lens. The camera flaunts its independence by refusing to accompany the main character through the streets of Puerto Progreso and, instead, choosing to stay still, offering a frontal shot of the empty spaces left by the characters as they move towards the adjacent off-camera areas; empty spaces that, in the case of movies like *Lake Tahoe*, *Año bisiesto* (Mexico; Michael Rowe 2010), or *Hamaca Paraguaya* (Argentina-Netherlands-Paraguay-Austria-France-Germany, 2006)—the central themes of which are waiting and the mourning process—prove to be highly symbolic in that they: "Immediately brings about the identity of the mental and the physical, the real and the imaginary, the subject and the object, the world and the I."[28]

In parallel, these brief severances between the camera and the character, in addition to generating empty spaces, also install in the conscience of the spectator spaces (and events) that are non-visible, i.e., that are located outside the frame. These spaces help to incorporate an element of unsolvable uncertainty into the construction of what is real, by hinting that, despite the slowness and great detail with which events unfold, it is still insufficient to capture all the layers of meaning that are active at any given time.[29] Directors Lisandro Alonso and Martín Rejtman, for example, despite having two very different cinematic styles, resorted in their films to this discrepancy between the camera and the character to the extent of relegating their leading characters to a plane of definitive invisibility far before the end of the film. At minute 62 of *Liverpool* (Argentina-France-Netherlands-Germany-Spain, 2008), Lisandro Alonso, after slowly and painstakingly shooting the movements of sailor Farrel (Juan Fernández) on his return to his family home in Ushuaia, decided to sever the link between the character and the camera, letting the character leave the city and, therefore, the film. From then on, the camera stays and accompanies the leading character's family. The character's absence is, however, only apparent, because he left behind a key ring with the name of Liverpool. This object, albeit random, along with the empty spaces, becomes an element that evokes the absent person, as will be the case a few years later in *Lake Tahoe*, where a sticker with that place name will finally enable the leading character and his brother to verbalize the memory of their deceased father, even when the connection between the character and the place is not underpinned by any emotionally charged memory.[30]

For his part, Martín Rejtman, after eleven years of silence, returned to full-length filmmaking with *Dos disparos* (Argentina-Chile-Germany-Netherlands, 2014), a movie whose title [*Two Shots*] is explained in the first scenes, when Mariano, played by non-actor Rafael Federman, uses the gun he just found to do exactly that: shoot himself twice. The fact that the character survives and returns home could make us believe that from then on, the plot would revolve around revealing the motives behind that suicide attempt. Nothing could be further from the truth; only a few minutes after that event, Mariano becomes just another character among a wide range of people who come together to share a home, holidays, work, travels, etc., before breaking up again and parting their ways. Mariano's suicide attempt not only does not lead to the subsequent unfolding of the storyline, but it even goes unexplained: Mariano, a perfect example of the expressive apathy of this type of character, does not seem to want to commit suicide and declares that he does not know why he shot himself that morning. Pressed by a doctor to give reasons for his decision, he affirms: "It was an impulse; it was very hot." With this answer, Rejtman not only exemplifies the dismantling of any linear narrative and causal rationale, but he also confronts us with another typical device of this new Latin American poetic verism: namely, the inexpressiveness and inscrutability of its characters.

The characters in the films mentioned so far share a marked inexpressiveness which at first sight could be explained in line with the irrelevance of the everyday actions they carry out. However, it serves to underpin the mentioned lack of coordination between the storyline, the camera and the characters, given that the latter remain impassive even in the most dramatic instances, forcing us to recognize a certain degree of absence in characters even when they are at center stage. This quest to achieve an effective dedramatization of actors, an "obscuration of the actor" could explain in part the use of neophyte actors or non-actors, which is commonplace both in films from the 1960s, and in contemporary Latin American cinema.[31] The expressive containment of these actors constitutes a major force for estrangement, which intensifies the narrative discontinuity.[32] Characters not only do not help establish the storyline thread that the camera, with its baffling long shots and unexpected moves, insists on jeopardizing, but in the oddness of their apathy they reveal themselves as another one of the signs of dissolution of meaning facing the spectator. Films like *Octubre* (Peru; Daniel & Diego Vega Vidal, 2010) or *La vida útil* (Uruguay-Spain, Federico Veiroj, 2010), as well as the films previously mentioned, are examples of such inexpressiveness.[33] In these two new cases, the leading role is played by an anti-hero anchored in his obsessions and daily routines, when a particular event (a work-related development in Veiroj's film; recently acknowledged paternity in the case of *Octubre*) offers the possibility of breaking free from his ordinary apathy and refocusing his life. Given the distinct sentimental component involved in the decision to turn around their lives, these characters' rigid inexpressiveness, together with the plot incoherence of a storyline consistently marked both by a slow tempo and by ellipses, prevent us from foreseeing their decisions. But these decisions tend to be incomprehensible even in those cases in which they materialize onscreen, thus thwarting the promise of closure, of unequivocal conflict resolution; and they tend to be incomprehensible precisely because throughout the film spectators have been repeatedly warned of their ignorance regarding the characters' psychological and logical mechanisms, as well as of the fragmented nature of the information provided.

The characters' inexpressiveness is further aided, as already mentioned, by atypical frames that enable the obscuration noted by Flanagan. *La mujer sin cabeza*

(Argentina-France-Italy-Spain, 2008), the third full-length film by Argentinian director Lucrecia Martel, with its use of lighting contrasts, detail shots, back shots, and headless shots, offers good examples of how the camera can contribute to intensifying the impenetrable configuration of characters and, consequently, of the story. In this movie, a woman called Veronica (María Onetto) has an accident due to a distraction with her cellphone while she was driving. However, we do not know whether she has run over a child or a dog, because even though she gets out of the car to check, the camera chooses to stubbornly remain in the passenger seat.[34] As a result of the crash, Veronica suffered a strong concussion. Her subsequent actions appear incongruous to spectators who are aware that they lack the necessary contextual information and a minimal expressive indicator (verbal and/or facial) to make it possible to identify and identify with, over and above her mental confusion, the character's inner emotions.[35]

Despite the differences in style between these filmmakers, these resources that generate spaces void of meaning are what lend unity to the new expressions of Latin American cinema, and in turn connect them to an intercontinental current of filmmakers in Eastern Europe, Asia, and Africa. Mark Bretz, who has chosen to revitalize Boardwell's underused term "parametric film" to encompass the works of these most recent directors, does not hesitate to recognize that the state of conscious uncertainty that this cinema creates in him is intentional and goes beyond what could be considered unavoidable cultural limitations on his part. This marks a turning point in the way in which Latin American cinema is conceived and projected to the world, particularly if we recall that Glauber Rocha did, in fact, explain the European audience's incapacity to appreciate "hunger aesthetics" cinema as more than merely "strange tropical surrealism" based on neocolonialism.[36]

As the New Latin American Cinema directors already foresaw in the early 1980s, poetic cinema is proving to be an effective medium for Latin Americans to explore and reconceive the complexities of their own reality while avoiding the risk of promoting an oversimplified image of the continent due to the dogmatic shortcomings of any ideological agenda.[37] By choosing the *via negativa* to make viewers aware of how subjective and limited their perception/understanding of the image is, contemporary directors are opening up their films to a level of multiple significance powerful enough to resist any attempt at national or regional stereotypification. The rehabilitation of certain distinctive stylistic features of the New Latin American Cinema is allowing twenty-first-century cinematographers to revolutionize the movie scene on a global scale; breaking away from all expectations and preconceptions of Latin America that the public might have. This is a cinema that, in order to achieve its goals, resorts, among other mechanisms, to using non-actors, natural settings and regional languages;[38] a cinema that does not conceive spatial, logical, and temporal linearity as the only way to structure the world; a cinema that recognizes the poetic potential of images and the de-automatizing effect that such images can have on our perception of reality; a cinema that, like the one produced in the 1960s and 1970s, has close ties to the cinematic work being produced in other continents of the Southern Hemisphere, while at the same time thriving in the recognition from European festivals and institutions;[39] and a cinema that, ultimately, liberated from many ideological preconceptions, revives the subversive potential of the neorealist style originally noted and admired by the Latin American directors of the 1960s. In 1985, Fernando Birri reflected on the future of Latin American cinema and noted, in the context of a Cuba that was starting to feel the impact of perestroika, that:

> "Every error in the interpretation of man gives rise to an error in the interpretation of the universe". That is the message handed down by the ancient

> alchemists (...) There is no art without mystery, and without developing acids. Some years ago, my brother Nelson Pereira dos Santos told me, "so far we have used cinema to teach—let's use it now to learn". From clay to gold, from the "aesthetics of hunger" to a hunger for subversive aesthetics, from a still shot to life—this is the Grand Art and we are burning in its furnace. "Let no viewer remain unchanged after watching one of our films", we said more than a quarter of a century ago. "Let no Latin American filmmaker who begins a film remain unchanged after he has finished it", we say today".[40]

The semiotic and philosophical debates involving the New Latin American Cinema in the early 1960s not only led to considering the oppressive effect of the gaze of others on self-perception, but they also paved the way for a reflection on gaze in which sight led to a new way of "being in the world" and even, according to Gonzalo Carbó, to a certain transcendence. "To see is to enter a universe of beings which display themselves," points out Merleau-Ponty; a sentence with which the philosopher shatters the dual conceptualization active-passive/subject-world traditionally associated with the act of seeing[41] and, at the same time, paves the way for a new dimension of visual images, a dimension of renegotiation of meaning in which "cinema is becoming, no longer an undertaking of recognition [or indoctrination], but of knowledge,"[42] a knowledge that can be achieved through poetic visuals capable of suspending, at least temporarily, the order of reason. The new Latin American directors seem to have chosen to listen to these words, replacing the revolutionary message of social commitment with an embroidery of voids and omissions, paradoxically more committed in its ambiguity to the complexities of reality and more revolutionary in its subversion and artistic openness, in that it opens up cinematic text to those who had never been represented in it, as well as to everybody else.[43] Fiercely decried and criticized for the difficulty of his latest film,[44] Carlos Reygadas resorted to a metaphor to explain what could be the poetics of all the directors mentioned here:[45]

> "My films are like earthenware pots: they have been built on something concrete—not postmodern at all—and are definable. Afterwards, people can pour any liquid they want inside them. And this says more about each of these people, about what they see in the film, than about the film itself."[46]

This new poetic verism, with its ellipses, its lapses in focus and its slowness, constitutes, in short, an extraordinary "effort to penetrate the world," according to Gustavo Fontán;[47] not to denounce it, but to be able to discover it in that realistic ambiguity; each with his own gaze; each reading images and voids, sounds and silences in the best possible way.

Notes

1 Fernando Birri, "El manifiesto de Santa Fe (1962)," In *Cine documental en América latina*, edited by Paulo Antonio Paranaguá, 456–457 (Madrid: Cátedra, 2003).

2 Fernando Birri already pointed out in the "Manifiesto de Santa Fe" (1962) the revolutionary function of documentary cinema, wondering how these films could help to contribute to creating a real image of a people, and then answered his own question by saying "How do documentary films present this image? They present it as it is in reality, and they cannot do it any other way." (p. 456). Moreover, Getino and Solanas also included this general opinion in their seminal manifesto "Towards a Third Cinema" (Octavio Getino y Fernando Solanas, *TRI-CONTINENTAL*, No. 14, Octubre [1969]: 107–132), stating that: "The cinema we call documentary—with all the vastness encompassed by this concept today, ranging from educational

films to the reconstruction of an event or a narration—is perhaps the main foundation of revolutionary filmmaking. Every image that documents, bears witness to, refutes, or delves into the truth of a situation, is more than a movie image or a purely artistic event—it becomes indigestible for the system."

3 Ana María López, "An 'Other' History: The New Latin American Cinema," In *New Latin American Cinema vol. 1: Theory, Practices, and Transcontinental Articulations*, edited by Michael T. Martin, 138 (Detroit, MI: Wayne State University Press, 1997).

4 André Bazin, *Qu'est- ce que le cinéma?* (Paris: Editions du Cerf, 1981), 13.

5 Julio García Espinosa, "Por un cine imperfecto," *Una imagen recorre el mundo* (México: Filmoteca de la UNAM, 1982).

6 In an article written in 1958, Glauber Rocha perceived this twofold path, but not only did he not take a stance yet, but, rather, he propounded that the New Latin American Cinema should develop on the basis of a synthesis of both trends, "the dry antiformalism of neorealism and Eisenstein's ultra-expressionism." See Geraldo Sarno, *Glauber Rocha e o cinema Latino-Americano* (Rio de Janeiro: CIEC-UFRJ-Rio Filme, 1994), 13.

7 Enrique García, *Cuban Cinema After the Cold War: A Critical Analysis of Selected Films* (Jefferson, NC: McFarland, 2015), 74.

8 Lúcia Nagib and Cecília Mello, *Realism and the Audiovisual Media* (Basingstike, UK: Palgrave Macmillan, 2009), xvii.

9 Jean Narboni, Sylvie Pierre, and Jacques Rivette. "Montage," In *Cahiers du Cinema Vol 3 (1969-1972): The Politics of Representation*, edited by Nick Browne, 24, 29 (London: Routledge, 1990).

10 Robert Stamm was one of the critics who paid special attention to the fragmented way in which Rocha edits his narrations. With regard to *Terra em transe*, he pointed out:

> Rather than giving us the conventional impression of spatio—temporal coherence, Rocha forces us to reconstruct spatial and temporal relationships. There are no establishing shots to situate us. We are further disoriented by dizzying camera movements and an unorthodox variety of camera angles. Even in sequences characterized by spatial homogeneity, there is discontinuity in the cinematographic treatment of the unified space. We are given fragments which defy organization into a narrative whole.
>
> *See Robert Stamm, "Land in Anguish: Revolutionary Lessons," Jump Cut 10—11 (1976): 49–51. www.ejumpcut.org/archive/onlinessays/JC10—11folder/TerraTranseStam.html accessed August 8, 2015.*

11 Michael Chanan, "Revisiting Rocha's 'Aesthetics of Violence'," *Killer Images: Documentary Film, Memory and the Performance of Violence*, edited by Joram ten Brink and Joshua Oppenheimer, 86 (New York, NY: Columbia University Press, 2012). Schroeder Rodríguez, Paul A. "La fase neobarroca del Nuevo Cine Latinoamericano." *Revista de Crítica Literaria Latinoamericana*, Vol 37, No. 73 (2011): 15–35.

12 Herlinghaus, Hermann, "Exilio-Resistencia-Vanguardia. La película ORG (1969/1978) de Fernando Birri," *Revista de Crítica Literaria Latinoamericana*, Vol 37, No. 73 (2011): 121.

13 Glauber Rocha, "Eztetyka do sonho 71," In *Revolução do Cinema Novo* (São Paulo: Cosac Naify, 2004), 248–251.

14 Fernando Birri, "Para seguir resistiendo." Hojas de cine 1 (1985). www.cinelatinoamericano.org/biblioteca/assets/docs/documento/4 96.pdf accessed August 3, 2015.

15 Even Fernando Solanas and Octavio Getino, who did not hesitate to distinguish between European auteur cinema and the films that both they and other Latin American directors were making, recognized that it was valid and necessary to incorporate these artistic expressions into a transnational context:

> Testimony about a national reality is also an invaluable means of dialogue and knowledge at the global level. No international form of struggle can be successfully executed if there is mutual sharing of the experiences of other peoples, unless the global, continental, and nation balkanization that imperialism seeks to maintain, is vanquished.
>
> *Octavio Getino and Fernando Solanas, "Towards a Third Cinema", TRICONTINENTAL, No. 14 (October 1969): 124.*

16 The Pesaro Festival was not the only festival to pay recognition to this cinema. From the outset, New Latin American Cinema was highly successful at the principal European film festivals of the time, including Karlovy Vary, Moscow, Venice, San Sebastian, Cannes, Berlin, Locarno, and Mannheim. Thus, by 1967—when the movement was granted official recognition—this cinema had already won the interest of the international public, and according to Hennebelle, it had even had a remarkable impact on other nations' film production. Ignacio del Valle, moreover, highlights the impact on the circulation of Latin American cinema of other, less prominent festivals, such as the Leipzig Documentary Film Festival and the Oberhausen Short Film Festival, in addition to the three Rassegna di Cinema Latinoamericano festivals held in 1962 in Santa Margherita Ligure, Sestri Levante and Genoa. (78). See Guy Hennebelle, *Les cinémas nationaux contre Hollywood* (París: Editions du Cerf: 2004), 47.

17 Pier Paolo Pasolini, *"Cine de poesía": Cine de poesía contra cine de prosa* (Barcelona: Anagrama, 1970), 17.

18 I am mentioning Kathleen Newman because I agree with Paul Julian Smith in that our critical approach, both to this New Latin American Cinema and to the film expressions deriving from it, is often restricted for fear that, in a context of globalization and neoliberalism such as today's, the fluidity of the medium could endanger the welfare of local identities. Newman counters this fear by recalling that:

> Current scholarship on the transnational scale of cinematic circulation now takes for granted a geopolitical decentering of the discipline. Areas once considered peripheral (that is, less developed countries, the so-called third world) are now seen as integral to the historical development of cinema. The assumption that the export of European and US cinema to the rest of the world, from the silent period onward, inspired only derivative image cultures has been replaced by a dynamic model of cinematic exchange, where filmmakers around the world are known to have been in dialogue with one another's work.

See Paul Julian Smith, "Transnational Cinemas: The Cases of Mexico, Argentina and Brazil," In *Theorizing World Cinema*, edited by Lucia Nagib, Chris Perriam, and Rajinder Dudrah, 63 (London: I.B. Tauris, 2011).

19 Luis Buñuel, "Cinema, Instrument of Poetry (1953)," *The European Cinema Reader*, edited by Catherine Fowler, 46 (London and New York, NY: Routledge, 2002).

20 John King, *Magical Reels: A History of Cinema in Latin America, New Edition* (London: Verso, 2000), 74.

21 Gilles Deleuze, *La imagen—movimiento: Estudios sobre cine 1* (Barcelona: Paidós, 1987), 33.

22 Andrew Pulver, "Carlos Reygadas: In Defense of Post Tenebras Lux," *The Guardian*, March 14, 2013. www.theguardian.com/film/2013/mar/14/carlos-reygadas-post-tenebras-lux accessed November 10, 2015.

23 Hart explains this change in paradigm stemming from the widespread use of the digital camera, pointing out that "the digital camera took even further the promise of the hand-held camera, which produces an experience of a living, "breathing" camera participating actively in the world around it." See John Hart, *Revolutionary Mexico: The Coming and Process of the Mexican Revolution* (Berkeley, CA and Los Angeles, CA: University of California Press, 1989), 173. It is not my intention to elaborate on this, nor do I intend to engage in the dilemma of the chicken or the egg, but I believe it necessary to recall that such a representative filmmaker as Lisandro Alonso, despite creating cinema marked by the camera's autonomy, did not resort to the digital medium until *Jauja* (2014), his fifth—and, to date, latest—film; all his previous full-length films were made in 35mm. Asked about this, Alonso expressed his preference for celluloid, underlining, precisely, that it provides a closer indexical relationship with reality than the digital medium. See Patricio Fontana, "Lisandro Alonso. La aventura de salir de uno mismo," *Otra Parte: Revista de letras y artes* 19 (2009-2010). http://revistaotraparte.com/n°-19-verano-2009-2010/lisandro-alonso-la-aventura-de-salir-de-uno-mismo accessed October 16, 2015.

24 Carlos Reygadas, "Dos Carlos y un Michel," *Time Out México*, Vol 8 (November 2012): 28–30.

25 Rocío Gordon. "Suspensión: detenimiento y suspenso en la estética de Lucrecia Martel," *A Contra Corriente*, Vol 13, No. 1 (Fall 2015): 239–261.

26 See Gilles Deleuze, La imagen—movimiento: Estudios sobre cine 1 (Barcelona: Paidós, 1987), 7:

> We run in fact into a principle of indeterminability, of indiscernibility; we no longer know what is imaginary or real, physical or mental, in the situation, not because they

are confused, but because we do not have to know and there is no longer even a place from which to ask. It is as if the real and the imaginary were running after each other, as if each was being reflected in the other, around a point of indiscernibility.

27 As stated by Tiago de Luca, the landscape in these movies "is not merely a figurative backdrop, but indeed the main character itself, perpetuating an Italian neorealist tradition while stretching it to contemplative heights" (Tiago de Luca, "Realism of the Senses: A Tendency in Contemporary World Cinema," In *Theorizing World Cinema*, edited by Lucia Nagib, Chris Perriam, and Rajinder Dudrah, 195. [London: I.B. Tauris, 2011]). The importance of these pure contemplative spaces in contemporary Latin American filmmaking has been directly acknowledged by directors such as Alonso, for whom location constitutes the driving force of his films. Reygadas has also addressed the issue, stating that: "Many people asked me whether nature or the city are characters in *Japón and in Batalla en el cielo*. They are not characters, but they are determining factors. I believe that the environment determines the way we feel—context has a constant impact. I remember Herzog saying precisely that he started films on the basis of a landscape. That's what it was like for me in *Japón and in part in Batalla en el cielo*." See Fontana, "Lisandro Alonso" and David López, "Entrevista a Carlos Reygadas," http://septimovicio.com/entrevistas/29112007_entrevista_a_carlos_reygada s/#.V54BBCMrKdY accessed July 13, 2016

28 See Gilles Deleuze, *La imagen—movimiento: Estudios sobre cine 1* (Barcelona: Paidós, 1987), 30.

29 The discrepancy between image and sound also contributes to activating these non-visible spaces in the spectator's conscience and to generating the feeling of uncertainty so magnificently described by David Oubiña when referring to La ciénaga (Argentina-France-Spain-Japan; 2001), Lucrecia Martel's first full-length film: "Neither the framing nor the editing really provide a limit for the image. Rather than a fixed frame, they are ever-fluctuating ends that communicate with others: permeable borders, invaded by what is beyond them and unable to contain any of what they should hold." David Oubiña, *Estudio crítico sobre La ciénaga. Entrevista a Lucrecia Martel* (Buenos Aires: Picnic, 2007).

30 Reygadas, too, in his film *Japón* [Japan] resorted to a place name that has absolutely no objective link to the story it depicts. The director has explained this title thanks to the subjective-evocative power embodied by this place name in his personal—and perhaps in the collective imagination. See Gabriel Anello, "Japón," 23 Abril, 2001. http://leedor.com/2001/04/23/japon/

31 Matthew Flanagan, "Slow Cinema: Temporality and Style in Contemporary Art and Experimental Film," PhD Dissertation, University of Exeter, 2012, 63.

32 Gilles Deleuze, *La imagen—movimiento: Estudios sobre cine 1* (Barcelona: Paidós, 1987), 35.

33 Carlos Reygadas has repeatedly acknowledged his admiration for the films of Robert Bresson, but in referring to the expressive restraint of the actors in Bresson's films, Reygadas considers that such restraint is forced in the case of Bresson, whereas in the case of his own films, it must be seen as a concession to this poetic realism that we are discussing:

> [Bresson] did use a similar method to mine except for one thing. He said to his actors just one thing: 'Be neutral.' And this is not what I want. What I want them to be is whatever they are. And this is different. . . . I try not to kill the individual energy of each of the human beings representing the characters.

See Maximilian Le Cain, "Battle in Heaven: An Interview with Carlos Reygadas," Senses of Cinema 38, February 2006. http://sensesofcinema.com/2006/feature-articles/reygadas/ accessed November 10, 2015.

34 It has been propounded that the omitting of this information, as well as the character's subsequent and unexplainable reactions, could be interpreted as an allegory of the stance taken by the Argentinian nation not to confront the reality of the murders being committed during the military government. This interpretation has not only been proposed by critics such as Daniel Quirós, Stephen Holden, Karen Backstein, Cecilia Sosa, and Stephen Hart, but it has also been endorsed by the director herself, who declared in an interview to Amy Taubin:

> In Argentina, my country, I see people that still carry the weight of the really bad stuff that they did not denounce back when it happened under the dictatorship. A lot of people decided they didn't want to see; they didn't want to know what was happening. And now the same process is occurring, but it's in relation to poverty. A lot of people pretend they do not see that a huge part of the country is becoming poorer and

poorer and is undergoing great suffering. The same mechanism that we used in the past to ignore the suffering of others is still very present today.

See Amy Taubin, "Interview: Lucrecia Martel. Shadow of a Doubt," Film Comment, July–August 2009. www.filmcomment.com/article/shadow-of-a-doubt-lucrecia-martel- interviewed accessed November 17, 2015.

35 In an interview, Martel defended the catatonic and inexpressive state of the character of Veronica on the basis of a traditional belief from the province of Salta and of a personal experience, both of which can be summarized in the idea that a trauma can make the soul leave the body. What is significant about this "realistic" explanation is, as she herself points out, precisely the fact that it makes it possible to conceive trauma in terms of absence, of deprival. See Mariana Enríquez, "La mala memoria," *Página 12*, August 2012. www.pagina12.com.ar/diario/suplementos/radar/9-4766-2008-08-21.html accessed September 27, 2015.

36 Glauber Rocha. "Eztetyka do sonho 71," In *Revolução do Cinema Novo* (São Paulo: Cosac Naify, 2004): 248–251.

37 Mainly due to its experimental and challenging aesthetics, poetic cinema has been repeatedly accused of being elitist, and apolitical; an accusation based on the erroneous notion that aesthetics and politics are two irreconcilable disciplines. Most contemporary Latin American directors have dismissed such a debate on the understanding that all representation is political, not "because they have a clearly defined and didactic goal that is translated into collective action on the part of the spectators"—sustains Tiago de Luca and Nuno Barradas Jorge.

> On the contrary, aesthetics is to be deemed political because it accepts its own insufficiency as a mode of experience, one that does not give lessons and cannot predict results; one that is content with being 'configurations of experience that create new modes of sense perception."

Luca, Tiago de, and Nuno Baradas, Jorge, Slow Cinema. (Edinburgh: Edinburgh University Press, 2016), 13.

38 *Hamaca paraguaya*, for example, was completely shot in Guarani, while the characters in *Luz Silenciosa* [*Stellet Lijcht*] by Carlos Reygadas speak practically all the time in Plautdietsch, the East Low German dialect used by the Mennonite communities in northern Mexico.

39 For a comprehensive list of directors and films on a global scale, see the Appendix included in Orhan Emre Ça-layan, "Screening Boredom: The History and Aesthetics of Slow Cinema," PhD Dissertation, University of Kent, 2014, 243–253.

40 Fernando Birri, "Para seguir resistiendo." Hojas de cine 1 (1985). www.cinelatinoamericano.org/biblioteca/assets/docs/documento/4 96.pdf accessed August 3, 2015.

41 As quoted in Andrews Jorella, *Showing Off! A Philosophy of Image* (New York, NY: Bloomsbury Academic, 2014), 59.

42 Gilles Deleuze, *La imagen—movimiento: Estudios sobre cine 1* (Barcelona: Paidós, 1987), 33.

43 Ben Bollig and David M. J. Wood coordinated, in 2014, a special issue of the journal *Studies in Spanish and Latin American Cinemas* dedicated to the relationship between cinema and poetry, in which they noted the need to study New Latin American Cinema on the basis of its poetic achievements instead of defining it only based on its ideology and political commitment: "The 'cinema of poetry' whose birth the Italian poet, film-maker and theorist Pier Paolo Pasolini identified around the time of the first Pesaro film festival in 1965, is a largely unexplored point of contact between the two continents' cinematic production of the period." This is undoubtedly so. Ben Bollig and David M.J. Wood. "Film-poetry/poetry-film in Latin America. Theories and practices: An introduction," *Studies in Spanish & Latin American Cinemas*, Vol 11, No. 2 (2014): 115–125. See Pier Paolo Pasolini, *"Cine de poesía": Cine de poesía contra cine de prosa* (Barcelona: Anagrama, 1970), 116.

44 Reygadas presented *Post Tenebras Lux* at the 65th annual Cannes Film Festival, where, despite being awarded the prize for best director (*Prix de la Mise en Scène*), it was loudly booed by the specialized press during its screening. The audience's frustration was clearly reflected in Xan Brooks's review for *The Guardian*, in which, addressing the formal difficulty of the film, he wondered: "What is he saying? What does he mean? . . . There is no doubt the director is leading us somewhere . . . If only the route wasn't quite so rocky and circuitous. If only he'd take those damn beer glasses off the camera lens," Carlos Reygadas, "Dos Carlos y un Michel," *Time Out México 8* (November 2012): 28–30.

45 In his most recent film, *Jauja* (Argentina-Denmark-France-Mexico-USA-Germany-Brazil-Netherlands, 2014), Lisandro Alonso sought the help of poet Fabián Casas in writing the screenplay. When asked about this, Casas outlined an answer in order to explain the ultimate meaning of *Jauja*, a historic film in which the fusion of reality–dream shots are taken to the extreme: "It seems to me that in order for a story to work and grow it must always be placed in a state of question, of uncertainty: that way, the reader, the viewer, can imbue it with his own experience." See Javier Diz, "Entrevista a Fabián Casas," *Los Inrockuptibles*, December 2014. www.losinrocks.com/cine/entrevista-a-fabian-casas#.VoBFxMArKCS accessed November 26, 2015.

Gustavo Fontán—whose filmography we have not mentioned here, although it is perfectly in line with the general features we have described—has often quoted the following verses by Argentinian poet Juan L. Ortiz to explain that for him, too, filming means "being open" to the world. "So that men are not ashamed of flowers / so that things are themselves: / sensitive or profound forms of unity / or mirrors of our effort to penetrate the world / [...] we will all go to our ultimate limit." Gustavo Fontán, "Vida literaria: el cine y la forma de la biografía," *CELEHIS: Revista del Centro de Letras Hispanoamericanas*, Vol 21, No. 23 (2012): 277–285.

46 Carlos Reygadas, "Dos Carlos y un Michel," *Time Out México 8* (November 2012), 28.

47 Gustavo Fontán, "Vida literaria: el cine y la forma de la biografía," *CELEHIS: Revista del Centro de Letras Hispanoamericanas*, Vol 21, No. 23 (2012): 277–285.

11

AMERINDIAN FOODWAYS OF THE OTHER BORDERLANDS

Enrique Salmón

My richest family memories are associated with food plants.[1] I frequently remember the seasonings my grandmother, mother, and aunts lovingly added to our meals: *epazote, cilantro, frijoles, salvia, yerba buena*, and *chile pequin*. Comfort foods for me include *frijoles*, guacamole, moles, and of course, maize. These plant-based foods embodied the mural of flavors expressed on the table. These foods were eaten at home but were also central figures at fiestas, weddings, and other gatherings. I recall the many plant-related lessons I learned in my grandma's herb-house. It was a latticed structure filled with hanging dried and living plants. The roof was no longer visible through the layers of vines that draped over the eaves of the roof to the ground. On hot days, the interior would be nearly ten degrees cooler. Inside, grandma ground her herbs for cooking and for medicines on an old *metate*. I would often visit her when she was in her herb-house and enjoy the many scents and aromas. It was during these times that she told me about the lives of plants and their characteristics. She described the relationships the plants had with each other. She taught me that the plants were not only plants but were people, too. Some were Rarámuri, while others were Apaches and non-Indians.

When I was older my grandfather introduced me to the foods that we grew on his small field while we shooed away crows and other critters from his corn, beans, and chiles. We would sit in the shade under his fruit trees, whittle, and enjoy the outside while he retold short bits of traditional knowledge. From many of my immediate relatives I gained scores of plant knowledge. It is difficult now to brew a cup of some medicinal herb or to cook up a batch of *frijoles* without picturing the specific time someone in my family introduced me to that particular remedy or recipe.

Through my family I was introduced to Rarámuri plant foods. I learned the names of plants, their uses, and their place in Rarámuri culture, philosophy, and cosmology. I understood them to be relatives and living beings with emotions and lives of their own. I learned that they were part of my life as well and that I should always care for them. In short, my family led me into the Traditional Ecological Knowledge of the Rarámuri. I recall my grandma's smiling face and her short shuffling gait as she was handing me a steaming mug of *bawena* (Mentha spicata), and I hear her scratchy voice describing the uses of other plants from our yard.

The plant knowledge I learned from my family was one aspect of a trove of culturally accumulated ecological knowledge. When they introduced me to individual plants, they also introduced my kinship to the plants and to the land from where they and we emerged. They were introducing me to my relatives. Through this way of knowing, especially with regard to kinship, I realized a comfort and a sense of security that I was bound to everything around me in a reciprocal relationship.

My upbringing with plant foods was not unique among *indígenas*. Among nearly every remaining tribe from the Americas persists knowledge of foods unique to specific tribes and to specific geographic regions that that tribe occupied when Europeans first arrived. The culinary contributions that *las indígenas* have made to the world have been reported for decades. However, a question that I like to explore is the contributions that those foods have had on the languages, cognition, and land management practices of the people who raised and relied on those foods.

First, however, it must be made clear that we are not Latinos (Latin Americans). Nor are we Hispanos or Hispanics. We are colonized indigenous peoples. Our indigenous identities have remained steadfast despite the myriad of abstract geopolitical demarcations and boundaries denoting us as belonging to or subject to one nation-state or another. For centuries, before the various European *entradas*, there existed geographically specific, sustainable, and culturally recognized and sanctioned indigenous patterns of using and talking about and interacting with local ecosystems. It should not be surprising then, to notice, residing in most of the most biodiverse regions of the world; there are human communities that continue their sustainable cultural land management legacies reflected first in the survival of their language and worldviews. Cultural and tribal boundaries are not noted by lines on a map or by the posting of a sign next to a highway, but rather by ancestral land use, seasonal movements, and natural barriers, all of which are memorized in oral traditions.

My Rarámuri ancestral worldview that has emerged directly from northwest Mexico does not differentiate or separate ontological spaces beyond and between the human and non-human worlds.[2] We feel that we are directly related to everything around us. The trees are us; we are the trees. I am rain; rain is me. The rain is all around me; it aligns inside me. These feelings are reflected in how we classify things such as plants and foods.

La Abundancia

There are several first contact narratives between European explorers and indigenous Americans. There are also many Jesuit and Franciscan reports, governmental documents, and other writings that describe European encounters with indigenous foods. Among these racist and condescending narratives is the feeling that these "savages" and "barbarians" have lots of foods. It's not that there was a lot of the same foods, but that the variety of food was overwhelming to the Europeans who were still getting used to a few spices from Asia to spruce up their boiled and dried meats and root vegetables. In 1534 and 1535 when Cabeza de Vaca and his three lost companions stumbled through what today is the greater Southwest, they met different indigenous peoples who fed them grains of panic grass, chenopods, yucca flowers, piñon nuts, acorn stew, mesquite flour, *papache*, desert hackberry, agave heart, cactus, varieties of squashes which they would call *calabasas*, chiles, mushrooms, different kinds of beans, and of course maize. Cabeza de Vaca did not know exactly where they were in Nueva España, but by analyzing some names and descriptions of the foods being offered as well as the people offering the abundant diversity of foods it becomes clear that the lost party of Spaniards had most likely made contact with Yoeme, Mayo, Jova, Opata, Pima, Guarijio, and Rarámuri.

The bounty served Cabeza de Vaca and his companions in what today is northeast Mexico were the result of a millennia of indigenous stewardship of their landscapes. Foods such as desert hackberry, piñon nuts, and the agave hearts would have been wildcrafted from lands that were managed like huge gardens. Other foods such as the chenopods and cacti were semi-domesticates that were encouraged to grow at the edges of tilled fields of maize, beans, and squashes (see Figure 11.1). As the foods were being offered the Spanish travelers, I can imagine the Pima, Opata, and Yoeme hosts attempting to teach their guests the names of the foods. According to accounts, one of the travelers, Estebanico, was adept at the new indigenous languages. No doubt he managed to learn the names of some of the foods. Unfortunately, without full command of the languages that were being spoken, I imagine true understanding of the significance of the foods that the Europeans were eating was lost to them.

Although they were lost, I have no doubt that from their perspective they were geographically located in Nueva España. This was land claimed by the Spanish Crown and spiritually overseen by the Vatican. Their worldview, their construct of the landscape, did not allow them to perceive the diversity of amazing foods and the landscapes from which they were derived as anything other than additional abundance gifted by God. It was a materialistic, cognitive vantage point vastly alien to the vantage point of the *indígenas* to whom the foods were like direct relatives and with whom they shared life force. To the Spaniards the land was the property of the Crown, with permission from God the Father above. To the native peoples the land and its abundance was perceived as an extension of their very bodies. To the *indígenas*, the notion that an abstract figure now suddenly presided over them was meaningless. This ontological clash has affected indigenous relations with the colonizers up to this day. Fortunately, pre-Columbian indigenous food legacies persist.

Plant foods are one of the many ingredients from nature that constitute rudimentary materials from which human metaphors, stories, mental spaces, cultural models, language, thought, and Traditional Ecological Knowledge (TEK) are created. TEK is perceived by ethnobotanists and applied ecologists to be an integrated body of spiritual and practical knowledge that has evolved over vast stretches of time through the successful

Figure 11.1 Maize dries in a field in Mexico. Courtesy of Robert Cichetti/Shutterstock.

adaptation of a culture to its local environment.[3] TEK includes cultural history that stores generations of accumulated ecological knowledge encoded in the languages of the cultures. TEK is held in common by a community which influences their choices and practices in collecting and processing plants. TEK is also a reserve of knowledge of plants and animals, oral traditions of climatic and environmental shifts, land management techniques, and ceremonial practices that acknowledge the human/nature relationship.[4] TEK encompasses the names and terminology related to plants, the management of plant resources, plant related discourse, and beliefs that determine perspectives on plants.

Humans contemplate their landscape then attempt to express what is seen. The expressions rely on cultural models that embody unique representations of place and relationships. The representations are verbally expressed in metaphors and prototypes, and non-verbally expressed in mental spaces of the local environment. The metaphors and prototypes color the language and discourse and become part of the cultural history that describes how the place was created, how the people arrived, and how the people should sustain their niche in this place. Language and mental operations encode the centuries old ways of conserving the land and the plants, assuring the survival of nature and the survival of the culture.

Ethnobotanists have not been successful in deciphering these linguistic and mental products. But this is not for lack of trying. Current trends in ethnobotany and cognition are focused on ways to understand how people from other cultures think. These researchers hope that from TEK they might be able to decipher cultural narratives and belief systems about plants that reveal cultural perspectives of plants and the natural world. Some suggest that linguists are "most interested in . . . gaining insight into the thoughts of native speakers and therefore improving our understanding of texts, performances, and discourse."[5] The path that cognitive studies currently follows is a search for the "bridge between culture and the functioning of the psyche" which can "provide detailed and reliable descriptions of cultural representations."[6]

The names for the plant foods are markers of our cultural sensitivity to the ecology of the land, and to how the culture has embodied that ecological knowledge into our cognitive workings. In addition, cultural references to plant locations, best sites for agriculture and for plant harvesting, and cultural history add further evidence to how ecological practices have been molded by the bioregion.

TEK provides a basis for understanding indigenous culture and for understanding the influence the bioregion has had upon their history, social organization, and the religious and aesthetic preference. From methods of land management to the application of plant medicines, from understanding the properties of small habitat ecologies to the reflection of ecology in their language, indigenous peoples demonstrate a way of knowing that recognizes that their actions as humans affect the entire ecosystem. Divorced from its bioregion of northwest Mexico, Rarámuri culture loses meaning. The interplay between the people, their minds, and the plants can be revealed only by taking the bioregion into consideration. In this work the elements of plants, landscape, language, and culture merge. They can exist as separate entities but will be coalesced into a kincentric unity. This is a cultural space and worldview where each and every element of the ecosystem is perceived as kin; as a direct relative.

The Rarámuri live on the southeastern flank of the Sierra Madres of Chihuahua, Mexico. For centuries, they have maintained a direct connection and relationship with a rugged mountain range that to them is perceived as the spine of the earth. In many ways, the mountains are also the spine of their culture. The land shapes their lives (Figure 11.2). It is a place where human ecological interactions unfold daily.

Figure 11.2 A Rarámuri residence. Courtesy of Joe McNally/Getty Images.

These interactions are expressed in the language of the place. The Rarámuri speak of the land as the place of nurturing, *Gawi wachi. Gawi* refers to the mountain ridge. *Wa* means to ripen and to help one reach maturity. *Chi* is a derivative of place and a noun ending. Ecological issues dominate their everyday existence. This is because the land is thought of as a kindred relative. The land is an important element in a bioregion filled with interconnecting niches, one of which the Rarámuri occupy.

A bit further north of Rarámuri ancestral lands is the Sonoran Desert of northwest Mexico and southern Arizona. It is home to about sixty species of mammals, 350 different bird species, twenty species of amphibians, a hundred-plus reptile species, thirty native fish, and more than two thousand varieties of native plants. The flora and fauna that thrive in the harsh conditions of the Sonoran Desert have evolved to specialized adaptations to survive arid conditions. Indigenous people co-evolved with this desert as well (see Figure 11.3). At the time of European contact, more than twenty-five distinct indigenous cultures thrived in the Sonoran Desert. The desert is still the homeland for fourteen Native cultures including the Tohono O'odham, Akimel O'odham, Hia Ced O'odham, Seri, Maricopa Apache, Tonto Apache, Yavapai, Mohave, Pima, Cocopah, Quechan, Yaqui, Mayo, and Opata. When most people consider deserts they think of vast, harsh, desolate places devoid of life. Few people realize, therefore, that the Sonoran Desert offers a bounty of diversity stewarded for centuries by seventeen Native cultures including the Yaqui.

One of today's cultural stewards of the Sonoran Desert's bounty is the Yaqui, also known as Yoeme. The Yaqui have tilled the Sonoran Desert for centuries. Today's Yaqui are most likely decedents of the some of the indigenous people who unselfishly fed Cabeza de Vaca when he made his way into the region. Traditional Yaqui perceive of

Figure 11.3 Rarámuri women cook over an outdoor fire. Courtesy of Joe McNally/Getty Images.

their landscape in terms of a historical/mystical space. Deer songs are vehicles for expressing and understanding this space. The songs are performed throughout the year in the various Yaqui villages in Sonora, Mexico and in the newer villages of southern Arizona that were established after the Yaqui Diaspora at the turn of the last century. The songs express notions of a space in an otherworldly time and dimension where everything is perfect and full of flowers. The flower world, the *Sea Ania*, exists beneath the dawn. In this space, all is perfect including Yaqui deer hunters. They stalk the deer and are in communication with this intermediary between one world and another. The Yaqui sacred space is a vivid, spiritually poetic human and natural dimension that is comprised of several components. The night world is called *Tuka Ania*; the dream world is called *Tenku Ania*; the flower world is called *Sea Ania*; and the enchanted world is called *Yo Ania*.

In the East, at the place beneath the dawn, exists the flower world, Sea Ania. This place is an idealistic, prototypical natural world filled with model insects, flowers, animals including the deer, and all the natural components of the Sonoran desert mirrored in its perfected beauty. Deer songs celebrate, describe, and praise the flower world in order to maintain the important relationship with it. The deer dance and songs of *Mayo Maso* [Deer dancers] are poetic expressions of their sacred "little brother" deer, who is closely associated with flowers and the dawn. The accompaniment of the gourd water drum and the Brazilwood rasp form together an integral expression of the flower world and dawn.

Although Deer singers and orators from Native groups are not always the individuals that till the soil, save seeds, and plant crops, their roles are as crucial for the preservation of cultural diversity. Their songs and oratory are expressed in a language that has given voice to their particular landscapes for centuries. Language is an audible expression of symbols. The symbols of language express meanings that are shared by the speakers of that language. Deer singing, it turns out, is more than simply memorizing lyrics to a set of songs; it is an entire way of living, being, and communicating with one's universe. Deer songs are more like conversations between the singer, the deer, and the wilderness world.

Written texts transform nature into silent and static symbols void of being-ness and vitality. When written texts become substitutes for nature, the nature ceases to breathe and loses its color and dynamic un-resting personality. I enjoy Nature writing and recognize its value for those who rarely or never have the opportunity to experience wildness firsthand. My point, however, is that each essay, story, and description is only a snapshot of nature at any given moment. We can pick and choose the moments that we wish to experience. For Native people, however, nature is not momentary nor is it outside ourselves—we breathe with it. When Yaqui deer singers sing Deer songs they are voicing this living and mutual life-giving relationship. The songs renew the life of the Wilderness World each time they are composed and recited.

Many modern Yaqui spend little time in the wilderness. Economic disparities on both sides of the U.S.-Mexico border have created harsh realities where people must work long hours for little compensation. Another reality is that the villages north of the border are in urban settings with little opportunity for wilderness experiences. Therefore, another job of the Deer singers and dancers is to periodically sing the *Huya Ania* and *Sea Ania* to life during ceremonies. For each deer dance a new *ramada* is constructed. A *ramada* is a four-posted structure made from local Sonoran Desert trees and shrubs, usually mesquite and iron woods. It is topped with branches and shrubs to shade the singers and dancers. During that period when the singers and dancers are present, the *ramada* becomes the wilderness world. The space housed within the *ramada* becomes sacred much like an ephemeral portal into another dimension of reality and sacredness. Another way to consider this phenomenon is that the Yaqui people carry with them their sacred space and release their cargo in a sort of shared group consciousness lifting what was at one moment dry soil, mesquite posts, stone, and branches into a reality of sacredness. The deer singers are catalysts for creating a new sacred homeland which each dance and for helping today's Yaqui maintain their kincentric relationships to their homeland.

Further north, up on the Colorado Plateau, there is housed an incredible array of biocultural diversity stewarded today by resilient Navajo farmers, herbalists, medicine people, young Native and non-Native activists, and a host of dedicated individuals that think of this place as a sacred environment. The landscape of the Colorado Plateau includes portions of northern Arizona, the southernmost segment of Utah, the southwest corner of Colorado and the northwest portion of New Mexico. On the surface of things, water is as scarce as is the vegetation, although huge aquifers lie underneath most of the plateau. During normal years the land receives less than 10 inches of precipitation annually and this comes in a bimodal pattern, meaning it comes in torrents during the summer monsoon season when washes temporarily become rivers and once dusty and wash-boarded roads transform into red-brown mud bogs. The other rainy period is during the winter when the female rain comes, as Navajo people refer to it, softly touching the thirsty land. Today, due to climate shifts, the plateau is even drier. Somehow, despite the aridity, peoples have and continue to flourish on this landscape.

Although the current landscape differs from what it was when early Spanish explorers described grasses high enough to tickle the bellies of their horses, Navajo farmers still coax the holy corn, beans, and squash from the red soils of the Colorado Plateau (Figure 11.4). When one reads early accounts written by explorers such as the scouting

Figure 11.4 Oaxacan marketplace. Photo courtesy of Enrique Salmón.

parties of Coronado, or exploring expeditions of John Wesley Powell and James Ohio Pattie, one feels that these men experienced the land much like the ancestors of today's indigenous inhabitants. They felt the land with their noses to the ground and recognized the abundance that can seem to be hidden. In the past, small green fields dotted the landscape throughout the plateau. The people's reverence for the foods that people grow is embedded in the origin stories and in holy plants.

The Navajos maintain a complex series of healing ceremonies often referred to as Chant Ways, Sings, and Beauty Ways. The ceremonies are intended to restore harmony to the patient, or as the Navajos say, "*hózhó*." Some of the ceremonies, such as the Blessing Way, can last as long as nine days and nights during which the entire traditional history of the people is retold. In this way both the Navajo world as well as the patient are revitalized and restored in harmony with their surroundings. An essential ingredient during these ceremonies is the sand painting. A Singer (medicine man) directs the making of a sand painting that illustrates an allegoric tale used in the ceremony after which the painting must be ceremoniously destroyed before dawn, or run the risk of terrible spiritual reprisals that may befall the Singer and/or patient.

In one ceremony, a sand painting called the Whirling Logs, or *Tsil-ol-ne*, is created. In this story, the hero sets out on a journey. During the journey, the hero overcomes several obstacles and barriers and also experiences several events that result in him gaining important ceremonial knowledge. In the sand painting that accompanies this ceremony, two dieties, *B'ganaskiddy* [Talking God], the teacher, and *Hastye-o-gahn* [Calling God] are depicted. They are shown in the painting associated with farming and fertility. To the left and right of the dieties are two humpbacked guardians. The humps on the figures are said to actually be backpacks and the guardians are regarded as seed gatherers and bearers. The two guardians usually carry tobacco pouches. In the story, the hero comes upon a whirling cross where two pairs of male and female *Yeis*, or spirit beings, are seated on the four ends. From them, the hero learned the knowledge of farming and is given seeds. After this, he returns home and shares these gifts with the people. In the sand painting, these plants are shown as corn, beans, squash, and tobacco. The plants are also depicted connected to four sacred colors: white, blue, yellow and black, and to their cardinal positions. These plants are depicted in the Father Sky and Mother Earth Narrative which appear in many of the sand paintings throughout most of the Navajo healing ceremonies. They are invoked not because of a part in a particular story, but because of their strength and all-pervading importance. In the body of Mother Earth are the four sacred plants: corn, bean, squash and tobacco.

As was seen with Yaqui deer songs, Navajo ceremony and associated language play a direct role in how the Navajo perceive their relationship to foods. Food such as corn and beans are more than sources of nutrition. They are also sources of identity and sacred healing. What is seen here is that symbols derived from nature play a role in the development of human language and therefore thought and worldview. A culture's local environment therefore is the source of the linguistic and cultural domains that afford that culture the criteria by which they can categorize, order, and name the elements and facets of their landscape. These actions are fundamental in the developmental dynamic evolution of language. This process begins at childhood. As a result of his linguistic work with Anglo, O'odham, Hispanic, and Yaqui (Yaqui/Mayo) children, Gary Nabhan reflects on the importance of nature in child language development noting:

> The playful exploration of habitat by cohorts of children, as well as the gradual accumulation of an oral tradition about the land, have been essential to child development for over a million years, as the emergence of language allowed the telling of stories and an expression of kinships with the earth.[7]

Sense of Place

Many scholars tend to compare a sense of place to as simple an experience as the human "fondness for certain colors and culinary taste."[8] But anyone who has seriously studied human culinary practices or human color perceptions knows that neither is a simple undertaking. This is because a sense of place is taken for granted until the absence of familiar smells, vistas, and colors are noticed and it is realized that places "are as much a part of us as we are part of them."[9] Santa Clara Pueblo educator and writer Gregory Cajete suggests that:

> There is an interaction between the inner and outer realities of people that comes into play as we live in a place for extended periods of time. Our physical makeup and the nature of our psyche are formed in direct ways by the distinct climate, soil, geography and living things of a place. . . . Ultimately, there is no separation between humans and the environment. Humans affect the environment, and the environment affects humans.[10]

The perceptual processes of indigenous cultures are based on interrelationships with their local environments. One perspective of ecology is that "the basic unit of survival" is not the logically thinking and classifying human animal, "but the form of intelligence immanent in an ecosystem" with which the individual interrelates.[11] From the relationship stems a psyche molded by the bioregion. The psyche influences perceptions that form a language unique to the place. The unique psychological traits lead to metaphors and symbols of place. A cultural system partially evolves from what is afforded it by the region. The foods its members eat, the plants used for medicine and building, the cultural symbols, and the languages are a result of the culture's attempts to organize the regions within which people dwell. The land influences the thought processes of the people and, therefore, the symbols that are eventually used to express their perceptions.

Cultural histories, myths, stories, art, and ceremonial or ritual performance all are expressions of a sense of place. These expressions remind people of where they live, how they arrived there, how to live with this place; their sense of self-identity derives partly from sense of place.

There is a realization of a sense of a connection to the unbroken continuity to Rarámuri origins and their present. Rarámuri TEK influences sustainable land management practices and actions, but functions also as a sociological teaching tool. From their TEK, individuals understand their place in the universe and the manner in which they should participate with it. Rarámuri sense of place in the universe stems from their cultural history that originated in the creation of the world. Participation is ecological where human actions invite reactions from the rest of the natural world. Self-identity traverses Rarámuri cultural history and their ecological role in the natural world. Finally, Keith Basso suggests from his studies of Western Apache linguistic connections to their land that the Apaches maintain a reciprocal relationship with their land. He mentions that they are "inhabitants of their landscape" and that they "are thus inhabited by it as well." Basso adds that this reciprocal relationship, is one "in which individuals invest themselves in the landscape while incorporating its meaning into their own most fundamental experience."[12]

The result of paying more attention to folk-generated categories, metaphors, and ways of talking about the land is that deeper relationships are uncovered, enabling ethnobotany to encompass more information on bio-regional influences on language. This reveals that humans not only impose order on their local environments but are afforded information about their surroundings by the surroundings themselves.

Kinentricity

Leslie Marmon Silko elegantly expresses how indigenous people in North America are aware that life in any environment is viable only when humans view their surroundings as kin; that their mutual roles are essential towards their survival. To many indigenous people, this awareness unfolds after years of listening to and recalling stories about the land. Silko notes that, "I carried with me the feeling I'd acquired from listening to the old stories, that the land all around me was teeming with creatures that were related to human beings and to me."[13] Silko notes that human beings must maintain a complex relationship with "the surrounding natural world if they hope to survive in [it]." To Silko, humans could not have "emerged" into this world without the aid of antelope and badger. The Lagunas sustained living in the arid region of the Southwest could not have been viable without the recognition that humans were "sisters and brothers to the badger, antelope, clay, yucca, and sun." It was not until they reached this recognition that the Laguna people could "emerge."

In simplistic ecological terms, the earth exists as a functioning unit that can be reduced to smaller self-contained entities referred to as ecosystems; functioning and self-sufficient communities of interacting organisms and their biotic and abiotic environments.[14]

Interactions are the commerce of ecosystem functioning. Without the correct mix of essential elements, the ecosystem would collapse. The elements are comprised of the animals, plants, fungi, insects, soil compositions and chemicals, and people, unique to the system. Indigenous cultures of the Northern Hemisphere include human communities in their cultural equations of interacting ecosystems as one aspect of the complexity of life. The cognitive model of nature among the indigenous people of North America is founded on the perception of the natural elements of land, animals, insects, and plants as relatives. To indigenous people, humans are at an equal standing with the rest of the natural world with whom they are kindred. In addition, indigenous people believe that the complex interactions that result from this relationship enhance and preserve the ecosystem. Indigenous kincentricity with the natural world can also be viewed as an indigenous kincentric ecology.

The Rarámuri believe that they live interdependently with all forms of life. Their spiritual, physical, social and mental health depends on the ability to live harmoniously with the natural world. Indigenous identity, language, land base, beliefs, and history are personifications of culture that regulates and manifest the health of the human and natural worlds. It is understood that harming the natural world also harms oneself.

History, identity, language, land base, and beliefs connect, secure and regulate the human/nature relationship. Indigenous cultural history does not remain in a linear past. History is continuous and, more importantly, contextual. Cultural history includes the origins of humans and nature. Like many cultures, our origins are a result of relationships to animals, plants, etc. The Abenaki believe they were created from ash trees. The Lenape tell that humans sprang from a "great tree."[15] The Rarámuri believe we came from corn. The Hopi owe their emergence into this world to a spider, a spruce tree, a pine, and a stalk of reed which functioned as ladders through the sipapu into the Fourth World.[16]

The concepts of identity and language are connected to concepts of self. Words shape thought. Thought is an expression of spirit. The Rarámuri believe that both humans and other life-forms are essentially spirit and matter. Both are manifestations of the interdependency of humans and nature. Self-identity is a result of a developed relationship to the environment as it is perceived by the culture. Cultural perception, language, and thought are related to both the land and cultural histories.

Conclusion

I was on a research trip out in a remote part of the Sierra Tarahumara of Chihuahua, Mexico. An elder I was speaking with reminded me that, although I now live in *el norte*, I should remember that my heart is always in the Sierra Tarahumara. His words remain with me to this day and remind me that although I deeply appreciate and relate to Mariachi music, *conjuntos, corridos, chiles rellenos*, and other iconic Mexican cultural icons, I am first Rarámuri. The plant food knowledge I learned from my family is one volume of a library of culturally accumulated ecological knowledge. This recognition is immanent among other indigenous peoples of Mexico, the Greater Southwest, and throughout Latin America.

The recognition is that one's breath is shared by all surrounding life, that one's cultural emergence was possibly caused by some of the lifeforms around one's environment, and that one is responsible for its mutual survival. It becomes apparent that the local ecosystem is related to you; it shares a kinship with you and with all humans as does a family or tribe. A reciprocal relationship exists with the realization that humans affect nature and nature affects humans. This awareness does not stop or begin at political boundaries, but rather influences indigenous interactions with the environment, solidifying cultural connections to places. It is these interactions, these cultural practices of living within a place, that are manifestations of an indigenous ecology.

An indigenous ecology and deep-seated sense of place fosters a standing base metaphor among *indígenas* that we are as related to our foods as we are to people. This belief helps people recognize their link to the natural world and their responsibility to ensure its survival. We are not truly connected to the natural world nor to our culture if we do not maintain and nurture these physical, social, spiritual, and psychological connections. Together they form the breath of life. Breath is the matter and energy, which many *indígenas* believe moves in all living things. Maintaining a balanced and pure human breath also ensures the purity and health of the breath of the natural world.

Notes

1 It is necessary for me to specify some terminology. This volume is focused on Latin America in which the prevailing language is Spanish. Therefore, when referring to indigenous communities I will use the term *indígenas* or indigenous unless otherwise referring to a specific tribe, language, or culture.
2 The Rarámuri live in the northern part of Mexico in the State of Chihuahua.
3 Dennis Martinez, "Karuk tribal module for the main stem river watershed analysis: Karuk ancestral lands and people as reference ecosystem for eco-cultural restoration in collaborative ecosystem management." (*Prepared by the Karuk Tribe of Northern California Under the Auspices of Cultural Solutions for the US Klamath Nation Forest,* 1994), 41.
4 Ibid.
5 Gary B. Palmer, *Toward a Theory of Cultural Linguistics* (Austin, TX: University of Texas Press, 1996), 19.
6 Felice S. Wyndham, "Environments of Learning: Rarámuri Children's Plant Knowledge and Experience of Schooling, Family, and Landscapes in the Sierra Tarahumara, Mexico," *Human Ecology*, Vol 38, No. 1 (2010): 87–99, 88.
7 Gary Nabhan and Stephen Trimble, *The Geography of Childhood: Why Children Need Wild Places* (Boston, MA: Beacon Press, 1994), 83.
8 Keith Basso, *Wisdom Sits in Places: Landscape and Language Among the Western Apache* (Albuquerque, NM: University of New Mexico Press,1996), xiii.
9 Ibid.
10 Gregory Cajete, "Land and Education," *Winds of Change*, Vol 9, No. 1 (1994): 41–47, 41.
11 Gregory Bateson, *Steps to an Ecology of the Mind* (New York, NY: Ballantine Press, 1972), 467, 490.
12 Keith Basso, *Wisdom Sits in Places: Landscape and Language Among the Western Apache* (Albuquerque, NM: University of New Mexico Press, 1996), 102.
13 Leslie M. Silko, *Yellow Woman and a Beauty of the Spirit* (New York, NY: Simon and Shuster, 1996), 6, 7.
14 Rory J. Putman and Stephen D. Wratten, *Principles of Ecology* (Berkeley, CA: University of California Press, 1984), 15.
15 Michael Caduto and Joseph Bruchac, *Native Plant Stories* (Golden, CO: Fulcrum Publishing, 1995), 11.
16 Harold Courlander, *The Fourth World of the Hopi* (Albuquerque, NM: University of New Mexico Press, 1971), 22–29.

12

POPULAR AND RURAL SCHOOLING IN MODERN LATIN AMERICA

G. Antonio Espinoza and Andrae Marak

The Mexican Revolution (1910–1917) served to mobilize everyday people across Mexico's countryside. Given the high levels of illiteracy, ranging from 55–86 percent depending on the region, the mobilized masses wanted better access to schools and improved educational facilities and opportunities.[1] The political opening that the revolution caused resulted in a wide-ranging mix of actors taking advantage of the situation. For example, cattle rancher José X. Pablo, a member of the indigenous Tohono O'odham Nation whose ancestral lands spanned the U.S.-Mexico border, had spent much of the revolution in the United States working with U.S. government officials and tribal leaders to prevent the different revolutionary factions from sneaking across the border and rustling tribal cattle herds which, when successful, the revolutionaries used to feed their troops or exchange for weapons.[2] When the revolution was over he crossed back across the border and approached Mexican education officials with the idea that "Hopefully someday [the Mexican] government . . . will place schools here in the frontier, very close to us so that we will not have to send our children to schools in Tucson or other American schools that are near the border." In doing so Pablo tapped into longstanding shared language between the Mexican state and everyday people about benefits of the expansion of state schooling. This shared language, which sometimes reflected the real alignment of interests and at others papered over significant differences, was part of an ongoing negotiation that served to create real change to the state, the community, and to produce new forms and practices of local and national culture.[3] In this case, the Tohono O'odham used expanded schooling and their willingness to accommodate themselves to Mexico's modernizing program as a means to negotiate with the state and local elites over retaining and regaining control over the portions of their ancestral homeland located south of the U.S.-Mexico border and weaving in portions of their ancestral culture into the national cultural tapestry.[4] Meanwhile, other Mexicans raised funds so that the new federal schools that they built with their own hands had all the necessary equipment—sewing machines, radios, film projectors, and assorted paraphernalia for an industrial department—for a fully modern education, an education that the federal government could not entirely afford but everyday people really believed was necessary to succeed in a quickly modernizing post-revolutionary economy.[5]

Revolutions in other places also provided newly mobilized citizens with leverage to expand access to schooling. In the Cuban Revolution (1953–1959), it was the middle class that, at first, most strongly supported the revolutionary movement and its cultural project. An "explosion of schools and education"—one contemporary observer noted that "*Everyone* seems to be in school"—aimed at Black and mulatto peasants, women, and uneducated adults, however, quickly garnered broader support and increased mobilization across new working class and rural segments of the population.[6] In fact, even before Cuban rebels succeeded in toppling the Bautista regime in 1959, revolutionary forces collaborated with local peasants to create twenty-five schools in the Sierra Maestra. Some have even argued that the Cuban peasantry's eventual support for the leadership's turn to socialism several years later may very well have been because of its early focus on expanded schooling and literacy (with illiteracy rates dropping an astounding 19 percent in one year). Indeed, responding to popular pressure, expanding access to primary education was one of the first initiatives on which the revolutionary regime focused. Many observers concur that even today as the revolution unwinds, education remains one of the success stories of the Cuban Revolution.[7]

Mexico and Cuba serve as examples of fully mobilized citizenry, but it did not take revolutions for everyday people to support formal education and for state officials to respond by expanding access to schools and schooling. During the first three decades of the twentieth century, indigenous peasant communities in the Puno region (southern Peru) took on the state rhetoric about the value of universal elementary education and began to fund and run elementary schools on their own. As local power holders attacked these schools, viewing them as potentially subversive, Indians sought state protection by sending envoys to the capital city, writing to national authorities and sympathetic intellectuals, and taking antagonistic landowners and politicians to court. Native leaders also established schools in collaboration with Adventist missionaries, who were critical of corrupt landowners and Catholic priests, and who provided Indian communities with education, medical services, and advocacy. Indians and their Adventist allies had relative educational success, contributing to a slow but significant increase in literacy and cultural formation in Puno in comparison to other wealthier Peruvian regions.[8]

As the previous examples have demonstrated, the expansion of educational opportunities and schools has long been popular amongst peasants and the working classes. States and education reformers have often been willing to respond to these popular desires because they have viewed education as a means of creating public goods by properly molding the hearts and minds of their citizens by weaving them into a common national culture,[9] as a means of promoting "social efficiency" by "developing productive workers,"[10] and as a means of making everyday people legible, simplifying the state's "functions of taxation, conscription, and prevention of rebellion."[11] Families, on the other hand, send their children to school for a range of motivations that include engaging more effectively with the state and the market economy, pursuing greater enfranchisement and inclusion, and attaining social mobility. Schools are the venues in which these countervailing forces meet, mingle, clash, and negotiate their differences. In the end, as this chapter will show, schools have been a tool—even if an imperfect one—for molding subjects into citizens who perform nationalism. For this reason, the schools provide a unique and optimal lens through which to understand the history of everyday people in Latin America and their at times effective struggles to attain self-representation and increased influence on both policy and cultural decisions.[12]

In this chapter, we explore the history of popular and rural schooling in modern Latin America as a locus for conflict and negotiation over modernization and as cause and consequence of social and cultural change. We focus on rural and popular education, by which we mean elementary schooling. Elementary education was often all that was available in rural areas; similarly, it was often all that was available to the popular classes in urban settings as well. A focus on rural and popular education, in many places of Latin America, necessarily also means a focus on indigenous education. We begin with a brief overview of the colonial schooling before turning to examine the ways in which Latin Americans have used education and schooling to create cultural shifts.

Colonial Latin American Education

Perhaps it goes without saying, but we will say it anyway: The arrival of Europeans was catastrophic to the already existing peoples in the Americas. After the initial focus on precious metals and other high value primary commodities, the Spanish and the Portuguese adapted already existing European systems—*encomienda, repartimiento, hacienda,* etc.—to local indigenous ones such as the *mita* to extract labor from the highly centralized societies in Mesoamerica and the Andean highlands. Overwork and exposure to diseases against which indigenous peoples did not have genetic defenses resulted in cataclysmic population losses of up to 90 percent. In areas lacking highly centralized indigenous societies (especially the Caribbean and northeastern Brazil), Europeans quickly turned to the importation of African slaves. The decision by Pope Paul III in 1537 that "indigenous people of the Americas had a soul, were human beings, and, consequently, could not be brought under slavery"[13] resulted in the establishment of two separate republics, one of Spaniards and one of indigenous people. And although there would always be a vast separation between the humanistic laws bestowed upon the indigenous peoples of the Americas by the Spanish and Portuguese crowns and their actual implementation in the New World, the fact that people of African descent were thought to be unredeemable in the short and medium terms left them outside of the two republics and with little leverage to improve their social station. From the earliest days of European contact, the schooling available to men, women, whites, and people of color varied greatly. Elite men had the greatest access to schooling, while women and men of color often had no access to schools.

In New Spain (which would eventually become Mexico), education first focused on indigenous elites, but this approach quickly lost favor.[14] As a result, the religious orders shifted their efforts to converting everyday indigenous people, trying to force indigenous people to adopt European work and living habits.[15] Although the orders tried to teach Spanish to indigenous elites, those serving in rural areas tended to learn indigenous languages, especially Nahuatl, Quechua, Aymara, and Tupi.[16] To say that the orders were successful in imposing European culture and mores, however, would be an overstatement. The mission system actually worked as a hybrid system where the missionaries co-produced new cultures. This was true in the fields of art, crafts, farming, animal husbandry, and more.[17] Missionaries needed to accommodate and reciprocate, to adapt European ways to local understandings. In sum, as famed historian Magnus Mörner has argued, Latin America underwent "two parallel processes . . . mestizaje [racial mixing] and acculturation."[18] Neither of these processes was unidirectional.

After the initial focus on evangelizing indigenous people, the religious orders also focused on educating the sons of colonial elites, with a greater initial emphasis in Spanish America than in Portuguese Brazil. Overall, elites used education to both obtain and consolidate their power. In other words, education served to legitimize the already existing unequal social and political order.[19] Non-elites tended to focus their efforts on placing their sons in apprenticeships where they might receive vocational training under the tutelage of guild masters, though not all masters held up their end of the bargain.[20] People of African descent generally had the least options. They were barred from higher education due to "tainted blood," but this "taint" could be negotiated given the proper social status.

For women, convents often served as centers of education for indigenous women, elites, orphans, and abandoned girls. *Beatas*, religiously devoted laywomen of "modest social origin," often served as teachers at orphanages and schools for the poor. Like the poor, even elite women were taught little more than basic literacy and sewing.[21] The eighteenth-century arrival of Enlightenment thinking resulted in the increased popularity of schooling for women, but this training was limited to making elite women better managers of their future households and poor women better prepared for low end wage labor.[22] Not only did educational opportunities expand for women during the second half of the eighteenth century, local *cabildos* [municipalities] began to establish the first public schools aimed at providing basic literacy.[23] In addition, these schools began to promote *criollo* pride, a harbinger of the coming independence struggle and its concomitant negotiation over newly arising national cultures.[24]

Independence: Conservatives, Liberals, Centralists, and Federalists

Immediately after Latin American countries gained their independence, the leaders of the new nations aimed at using schools to create new national cultures and new citizens, but what exactly these were supposed to be like was a point of contention that took much of the nineteenth century to figure out. Nearly all elites agreed that Latin America would now have citizens instead of subjects; this elite consensus was, however, often contested by indigenous people, many of whom preferred their colonial status as indigenous people with a different set of duties and privileges. Regardless, liberals, conservatives, centralists, and federalists often agreed on very little else other than the fact that if Latin America wanted to catch up to the English and the French, then it would require a massive investment in the education of everyday people. The independence struggle and the political turbulence that followed, however, made this aim extremely difficult to accomplish. As new regimes took power in often wild swings of power, they moved quickly (at least on paper) to undo the educational policies of their political enemies and to institute their own agendas. This tended to be easier for conservative regimes than liberal ones because they could rely on the support and financial resources of the Catholic Church. Liberals, on the other hand, often had to resort to the use of the Lancasterian approach to teaching where the most advanced students who already knew how to read and write were tasked with assisting the teacher by spending some of their school time teaching their classmates. Regardless of who was in power, education did not receive the necessary funding to transform early independent societies and cultures in the ways that both elites and everyday people might have hoped.

After the Wars of Independence, *criollo* leaders began the slow process of building new nation-states amidst material destruction and political instability. National governments had restricted institutional and financial capabilities to set up effective systems of public schooling. Local and regional authorities, families, and the Catholic clergy largely assumed the responsibility of opening, funding, and managing elementary schools. These educational establishments tended to be located in areas of denser population settlement, and they had a series of administrative and pedagogical problems. Classes were generally held in improvised locations such as town halls, churches, or rented houses. Official requirements for teaching, usually minimal, included knowledge of the subject matter to be taught as well as "proven morality." Sometimes patronage, rather than proficiency, prevailed in the appointment and dismissal of teachers. In the countryside, geography, poverty, and the demands of agricultural labor negatively affected registration and attendance. After the gradual establishment of *Estados Docentes* or Teachings

States, as historians call the centralized public school systems of the late nineteenth and early twentieth centuries, advocates tried to highlight their advantages by downplaying the extension and achievements of decentralized school networks. Nevertheless, in the decades after independence, communities all over Latin America relied on schools managed by local or regional authorities (which reproduced local and regional cultures), despite their limitations, to educate their children.[25]

Elementary schooling barely reached rural areas with sparse population settlement during most of the nineteenth century. Studies on post-independence Chile and Costa Rica show that schools were located chiefly in cities, towns, and villages, which a had higher concentration of population. In the Costa Rican case, the expansion of the agricultural frontier took the population away from longer-standing communities that could sustain schools. In the countryside outside of the city of Buenos Aires, communities could prioritize education during periods when the threat of indigenous raids was not imminent.[26] All over Latin America, it was difficult for children from hamlets or isolated households to travel long distances to reach schools. Additionally, families in the countryside needed their children's labor for sowing and harvesting crops and herding livestock. Historians of education in Chile argue that literacy was not indispensable to find employment in urban or rural areas. Higher literacy rates in towns and cities were the result of their demographic features and closer contact with the written word.[27]

Early post-independence governments generally did not develop educational policies specific to the indigenous populations of their countries. Nominally, Indians were citizens of new republics, so there was no need to devise special educational conditions for them. In practice, governments did not have the capacity to enforce indigenous attendance to the scarce schools that existed in areas of sparse settlement. In traditional areas of frontier such as southern Chile and the western Rio de la Plata, political authorities continued the colonial practice of relying on Catholic missionaries to provide education to Indians. Missionary schools were to promote Westernization, law abidance, and national allegiance. From the 1840s, national authorities subsidized Franciscan missionary schools in the Chilean south, an effort that was eventually also backed by private philanthropists. By the 1860s, Mapuche families were showing a greater interest in formal education themselves and, over the course of time, the government turned missionary schools into public ones. In contrast, official support to Franciscan missionary schools in the Rio de la Plata was irregular, reducing their actual impact. In Sonora (Northern Mexico), another traditional border area, factional political and military conflicts hindered the effectiveness of isolated municipal initiatives.[28]

Not unlike other areas of Latin America, Colombia's post-independence push (by both political leaders and everyday people) for universal access to primary education remained more rhetorical than reality. In 1827, only about 20,000 children were enrolled in school even though Colombia had a population of over 2 million people.[29] Also like other countries in Latin America, Colombians lived through a seesaw of education policies, depending on who was in power at any given time. Just after independence, primary school was financed locally, leaving it up to locals to determine if they would have a school. This resulted in a mixed response toward the Church and religious education. In some places, priests advocated on behalf of local education while in others, Church properties were seized and turned into public schools as priests were forced out of the classroom to make way for lay teachers. The 1840s are an excellent example of the sudden changes in education policy. The Ospina Plan of 1842 invited the Jesuits to return to Colombia and gave them jurisdiction over higher education (but left primary education untouched); this was countered by the Freedom of Teaching movement in

1848, which kicked the Jesuits back out of the country and "sought to put a definitive end to colonial institutions" by purging Church involvement in education, devolving power to regional governments, and decentralizing schooling.[30] Since primary education had always been locally organized and supported, the Freedom of Teaching movement's most important impact was the separation of church and state, not its impact on local schooling.

The first attempt to nationalize Colombian education did not begin until 1868 as the federal government, in Liberal hands, moved to fund and centralize control over primary education and to make attendance obligatory. Liberals conceived of the school teacher as the ideal citizen, a secular role model of civic culture and virtue, opposed to the backward Catholic priest, the abusive local political boss, and the *tinterillo* or corrupt, unqualified lawyer. The new generation of educators had to be selected carefully according to their academic proficiency and health, and prepared for their careers in *escuelas normales* or special teacher-training schools. At *escuelas normales*, teachers were expected to achieve a deeper knowledge of the subjects they taught, acquire modern pedagogical concepts and practices, and learn their duties as public educators. Once in power, Colombian Liberals sought to implement their educational ideas, but the outcomes were limited.[31] In the Magdalena region, schools faced high absenteeism rates. Regional and local authorities blamed family poverty and labor demands on children, as well as parental neglect. Officers undermined their desire to promote a national secular culture by accommodating local labor needs by adapting the school calendar and hours. Alarcón Meneses argues that families may have also had a "traditional mentality" that led them to resist outside imposition, a claim that requires further investigation.[32] The Church and its supporters did not take the Liberal initiatives lightly, and in less than a decade the Catholic clergy had regained its seat at the educational table. From this point until the 1930s, the Church would maintain its access to public schools, though it would not dominate them. All told, by the end of the nineteenth century, primary school enrollments had quintupled. This was quite an accomplishment, but even so they continued to include less than half of Colombia's school-aged children, and the potential students that they did not reach were, according to elites, the very ones that they needed to encompass most if Colombia were to successfully recast and modernize its national culture.[33]

Argentina also faced a struggle between competing factions, but unlike in Colombia, the conservative centralist Juan Manuel de Rosas managed to consolidate power and dominate the political and cultural scene by 1829. He would hold onto power until 1852, when he was removed by his liberal opponents. Given that Rosas's support, outside of Porteño elites engaged in trade, came largely from Afro-Argentines who made up about 30 percent of the population of Buenos Aires, one might assume that Rosas would direct education funds to meet the needs of this population. However, an ongoing budget crisis during much of his rule, including a French blockade of the port of Buenos Aires, resulted in a lack of funds for primary education. Rosas resorted to the implementation of school fees for primary school attendees. This drove those who could afford the fees out of public schools and into more prestigious private schools and those who could not afford it out of school completely, leaving them mostly untouched by the regime's cultural agenda.[34]

Access to primary education improved after Rosas fell from power. Argentina followed the lead of Domingo Faustino Sarmiento, the author of *Facundo: Civilization and Barbarism*, a fictional critique of the backwardness of the Rosas regime and its embrace of Afro-Argentina. *Facundo* was also a roadmap for the modernization of Argentina and Latin

America, a roadmap based on increased educational opportunities for everyday people and the promotion of European migration. At first, primary schooling was put under the jurisdiction of the provinces, but by 1884 the federal government guaranteed (at least on paper) access to primary school and attendance was declared obligatory for all children. Like in other areas of Latin America, the expansion of schooling in the countryside was aimed at civilizing what elites considered to be culturally backward people not yet ready to be citizens. And while primary school was to be the main tool for assimilating rural folks into a perhaps yet-to-exist mainstream Argentinian culture, immigration was viewed as an even better tool. This is because elites viewed Europeans as already possessing the necessary cultural habits of civilized people. But as Andrea Alliaud correctly notes, immigrants (even if they already were "civilized") created multiple additional cultural and ethnic groups; new people who needed to be taught how to be "Argentinian."[35]

Mexico faced similar struggles between liberals and conservatives, which lasted from 1821–1876 when the dictator and strongman Porfirio Díaz took power. Although the Reform Laws of 1867, passed after the liberals defeated conservatives in a civil war, declared that primary schooling was not only to be free, but also obligatory, it was only during the Porfiriato that the law was enforced, and then only after 1888 and only in and around Mexico City. The *Primer Congreso Nacional de Instrucción Pública*, which met in 1889, provides an excellent case for reviewing the strengths and weaknesses of Porfirian educational policy as a national project. Mirroring similar concerns across Latin America, not only did members of the congress address the important issue of primary schooling, they also spoke to the need for increased access to schools in rural areas and the need for better teacher training and pay.[36] They noted that widespread access to free and obligatory primary schooling in rural areas faced numerous challenges, not the least of which were: (1) the diversity of languages spoken by indigenous people; (2) the large distances and the lack of adequate roads between rural schools; and (3) the need for rural dwellers, parents and children alike, to work long hours in order to maintain even a "miserable subsistence."[37] While the members of this meeting understood from their perspective what the shortcomings of the Mexican educational system were, they did not address them in any systematic way other than the passing of a new series of laws. More importantly, they did not actually take the time to align the rural schooling to the needs of *campesinos*. Instead, they left the actual implementation of centrally-designed policies up to the individual states, which in turn often left them up to the various municipalities. As a result, the majority of budgeted rural schools continued to exist only on paper, resulting in the continuance of a variety of regional Mexican cultures.[38] This may have been just as well from the point of view of locals. In studying schooling in Mexico during the last three decades of the nineteenth century, Acevedo Rodrigo asserts that a literate minority was sufficient to meet the collective administrative and commercial needs of rural settlements. She also finds that rural municipalities with more speakers of indigenous languages had lower literacy rates.[39] By the end of the Porfiriato in 1911, only 16 percent of Mexicans were literate, and they were highly concentrated in urban centers.

Teaching States or *Estados Docentes*: The Mexican Revolution and Beyond

In the early twentieth century, Latin American governments began moving more determinedly toward centralizing the funding and administration of public primary education. Teaching States visibly sought to overcome the flaws of decentralized school networks. Political factions also sought to use these school systems for asserting state authority over local power holders, fostering new national cultures and nationalism, redeeming the lower classes from their perceived deficiencies, and slowing down rural-to-urban migration. Increased investment of national monies, as well as the confiscation of the resources previously controlled by regional and local governments, led to the effective growth of schooling. Reformers also introduced various pedagogical innovations inspired by the progressive "Active" or "New School" (*Escuela Nueva* in Spanish and *Escola Nova* in Portuguese), which included the ideas of Americans William James and John Dewey, Belgian Ovide Decroly, and Italian Maria Montessori, among others. Gradually, governments in countries with large indigenous populations also adopted *indigenismo* as an official ideology. *Indigenismo* criticized traditional abuses against native populations, and exalted certain social and artistic aspects of their culture, while also trying to modernize and assimilate them. *Indigenismo* influenced rural educational policies in Mexico, Peru, and Bolivia, leading to initiatives such as cultural missions, boarding schools, and clustered schools. In Brazil, the authoritarian *Estado Novo* [New State] co-opted educators who supported the New School, and implemented *ruralismo*, an educational policy focused on providing vocational training to rural youth.

Revolutionary Mexico (1910–1940) represented the most dramatic instance of rising political factions, which coalesced in the National Revolutionary Party in 1929, using educational centralization for state- and nation-building in earlytwentieth century Latin America. *Indigenistas* such as Manuel Gamio, José Vasconcelos, and Moisés Sáenz, participants of the post-revolutionary administration, influenced the reorganization of public schooling. Through schooling, *indigenistas* sought to preserve, valorize, and weave into the national culture those indigenous ways of life that they believed were favorable to national cohesion while rooting out those that were disadvantageous.[40] Vasconcelos, in particular, thought that racial and cultural mixing or *mestizaje* ameliorated the capacities of Indians, an assumption inspired by eugenics.[41] "Cultural missions" (1922–1938), created by Vasconcelos as Secretary of Public Education, were groups of educators sent into rural, predominantly indigenous areas. Missions provided instruction and vocational training, both to the general rural population and to local teachers—many of whom had little or no formal training, for a set period of time while also studying community conditions, thus making both the local teachers and communities more legible to state authorities. The *Casa del Estudiante Indígena* (1925–1932), founded by Undersecretary of Public Education Sáenz, was a boarding school for supposedly "pure" Indian young men located in Mexico City. The institution's goals were reducing the mistrust between Westernized and indigenous Mexicans and teaching Spanish and "modern" customs to Indians. The expectation was that these students would later introduce the mainstream Mexican culture that they learned at the Casa back in their home communities. The curriculum included physical education and vocational training, complemented with the study of primary and secondary subjects in local schools. In 1928, the Casa changed its mission and became a teacher-training institution. Due to the high percentage of desertions and the refusal of many graduates to return to their communities to work as teachers, the Casa was closed in 1932.[42]

In northern states such as Sonora, Chihuahua, and Coahuila, the federal government sought to use public schooling to "civilize" indigenous peoples and to ward off U.S. cultural influence. Interestingly, when Mexican schools along the border tried to counter such influence influence by refusing to teach English as a second language, parents threatened to pull their children from school and send them across the border into the United States. Mexican officials relented, allowing the state to advance its modernizing and nation-building mission while parents were better able to prepare their children for the realities of Borderlands living, even if it undercut the state's desire to promote a single national culture. In Chihuahua, government authorities deployed cultural missions to Tarahumara communities until 1927. Thereafter, they established a series of boarding schools in hopes that this would convince the Tarahumara to eschew their transhumance migratory pattern and settle down in one location. Likewise, in Sonora, schools encouraged the Tohono O'odham to settle permanently in Western fashion, ending seasonal migration, and using updated agricultural techniques.[43]

In 1934, President Lázaro Cárdenas' regime launched the program of "socialist education." Some government officers and educators who devised and implemented the program were Marxist, while others were broadly progressive. The program focused on modernizing Mexican society, reducing ecclesiastical influence, assimilating Indians, and increasing rural production. Public schooling sought to impact not only children but also their families and communities. Elementary schools provided children with literacy and training in agricultural work and fostered cooperativism, national cultural cohesion, and nationalism. With varying emphasis according to the region, public teachers also promoted agrarian reform, secularization, temperance and hygiene, more equitable labor relations, and democratized political participation. Locals sometimes disagreed with the curriculum, gender roles, and social practices promoted by schools. The anti-clericalism of the program was especially contentious, leading the government to suspend it in 1935. The redistributive and democratizing purpose of socialist education led to conflicts between educators and local landowners and power holders. In Chiapas, teachers faced slander, physical attacks, high absenteeism in schools, and indifference to civic celebrations.[44] The outcomes of socialist education were ambivalent. The "culture of schooling," or rural demand for education, increased in many areas. Federally-promoted nationalistic narratives and rituals were woven into local practices without fully replacing them. Even though newly educated individuals penetrated local political and social hierarchies, their power was partially sustained on and restrained by clientelistic relations with federal and regional authorities. Temperance campaigns failed,[45] and vocational training did not deter rural-to-urban migration. If socialist education fostered a common political language of inclusiveness, collective rights, and multiculturalism, then the influence of this common language (never fully embraced by either the state or local communities) has been torn asunder in recent times by violence in Mexico.[46]

In the first half of the twentieth century, both the Bolivian and Peruvian governments used similar strategies to provide schooling to their indigenous population. In Bolivia early in this century, nationalistic intellectuals wanted to modernize and assimilate Indians into the national culture through elementary schooling. A grassroots movement for literacy developed within native communities, embracing the nationalistic rhetoric and setting schools. Communities sought to better defend their land and labor through literacy. Some reformist intellectuals, however, experienced tension between their lofty ideals, and fear of both the destabilizing potential of rural-to-urban migration, and of losing the privileges associated with education. The solution to this quandary was implementing a separate system of Indian schooling beginning in the 1920s, aimed at educating Indians in their "natural" rural environment, and fixing them in the countryside. The curriculum emphasized vocational training and basic Spanish, rather than high-level literacy and other subjects considered too "intellectual."[47] Indigenous unrest in the late 1920s and the Bolivian defeat in the Chaco War (1933–1935) prompted authorities to open "clustered schools" [*núcleos escolares*] in rural areas. The purpose of these school clusters was to make the native population more legible to state authorities and to modernize the indigenous communities as a whole within their environments. The communities, however, appropriated the clustered schools and turned them into sites of political activism to defend their interests and their own local cultures. In the 1940s, the Bolivian government, in partnership with U.S. authorities, strove to steer clustered schools back toward their original goals. Although the oppositional character of the schools decreased, they failed to spread vocational education or to prevent the 1952 Revolution.[48] The Peruvian government replicated the clustered-school model from the mid-1940s to the late 1960s, with goals similar to those of Bolivian authorities. Indigenous enrollment and literacy increased, and communities sometimes appropriated schools for their own agendas, but final conclusions about their impact are still tentative.[49]

Before the First World War, schooling in Brazil made limited headway. Under the Brazilian Empire, elites had scarce motivation to effectively extend public schooling to the lower classes. By the end of the monarchical regime in 1889, only 3 percent of the population received any level of formal schooling. With the rise of the oligarchic First Republic (1899–1930), authorities proclaimed the importance of education in addressing the country's social and economic problems. Public schooling, however, was hampered by wavering political will, irregular funding, and clientelistic interference in teacher supervision, problems common to all Latin American countries at the time.[50] The region of Rio Grande do Sul was exceptional in that local elites made a stronger commitment to expanding public schooling. Influenced by Positivism and nationalism, Gaúcho politicians wanted state government to guarantee order, modernize the economy, diversify agriculture, and facilitate industrialization. Assuming a eugenicist standpoint, elites conceived of the poor and non-white masses as racially and culturally degenerate. Schooling could, nevertheless, improve their physical, intellectual, and moral conditions.[51] Physical education, hygienic practices, practical skills, and literacy could effectively integrate the lower class into the national culture and the labor market in an orderly, controlled way. The presence of schools run by immigrant communities, especially German and Italian, in the region made greater state supervision over private schooling a pressing need—at least from the point of view of state officials.

After the Brazilian Revolution of 1930, Gaúcho politicians led by Getúlio Vargas were able to implement their educational ideas at the national level. Vargas remained in power from 1930–1945, with initial support from nationalist military officers who, since the 1920s, had questioned oligarchical rule. For both groups, the state had to have a greater role in shaping society, national culture, and the economy—and public schooling was one of the venues for doing so. The supporters of *Escola Nova*, a new educational movement that emerged in Brazil in these years, shared the view of public schooling as an instrument to modernize society. Although *escolanovistas* initially advocated for educational decentralization, over time they adopted the opposite position. They also promoted the professionalization of teaching. They wanted public primary schooling to be mandatory, lay, free, and coeducational. Influenced by North American pedagogue John Dewey, *escolanovistas* viewed the child as a person with specific capacities to be discovered and nurtured, and with needs and expectations to be channeled and fulfilled. The child, rather than the teacher, had to be center of the educational process. Some *escolanovistas* fully supported Vargas's regime, even as it became increasingly authoritarian. Other ones were critical of the government, but nevertheless collaborated with it in order to advance their modernizing agenda.[52]

Rural education was one of the areas where the interests of *escolanovistas* and those of Vargas's regime coincided. *Escolanovistas* wanted to expand schooling into the largely Afro-Brazilian rural areas, emphasizing its practical aspects. Vargas's regime, for its part, sought to slow down rural-to-urban migration, an elite concern since the 1920s. From the perspective of the upper classes, this population movement drained the countryside of its labor force while creating new social and political challenges in the cities. Vargas and his collaborators developed *ruralismo*, an educational policy that emphasized preparing the rural youth for its future economic activities through vocational training, while discouraging migration. Much like the cluster schools aimed at indigenous people in Bolivia and Peru, Brazilian officers developed the project of *colônias-escolas* or agricultural colonies organized around a public primary school. Government would concentrate rural families in these colonies, providing them with medical services and hygienic instruction, and literacy training and vocational education for their children, all the while making them more legible to state authorities even as they wove them more closely into the tapestry of Brazil's national culture. *Ruralismo* was implemented irregularly across Brazil, in part due to different landholding patterns. It became a priority in the Rio de Janeiro region, where land concentration was higher. Authorities established educational farms, introduced special training for rural teachers, and supervised countryside schools more closely. In Rio Grande, where small landholding was robust, *ruralismo* was implemented later. After the end of *Estado Novo*, state authorities questioned the practicality and effectiveness of *colônias-escolas*. More recently, *escolanovismo* as a whole has been considered elitist, due to its differentiated approach to the education of specific classes which, in Brazil as elsewhere in Latin America, are highly stratified by race.[53]

The Developmentalist State

The end of World War II ushered in the era of the developmentalist state, a centralized anti-communist modernizing project often based on the pillars of Import Substitution Industrialization (ISI), heavy investment in infrastructure, and expanded schooling. The United States and a collection of Western organizations—the World Bank, USAID, UNICEF, and the IMF, among others—sought to use schooling as a means of undermining the lower and working classes' potential support for communism by substituting the possibility of radical reform (or even democracy) with incremental quality of live improvements anchored by economic growth.

Mexico's so called "miracle," the name for its unprecedented average annual growth of six percent from 1940–1970, served as both a model for non-communist Latin America and an alternative to Cuba.[54] The costs of this modernizing project were the capture of labor organizations by the state, rising inequality, and what Mario Vargas Llosa called the "perfect dictatorship," Mexico's authoritarian one-party state.[55] The shift to anti-communist developmentalism in Mexico began in 1943 with the adoption of a newly moderate anti-socialist pedagogy aimed at linking the teachers union with Mexico's dominant one-party state. Along with the consolidation of multiple state and federal teachers unions into one unified federal union answering to the Mexican state, the federal government changed its constitution (in 1946) to make socialist education—the pedagogical basis for federal education in the 1930s—illegal. Along with this ideological moderation, the curriculum for primary schooling aimed at the rural and urban poor was unified to prepare both for Mexico's largely urban modernization program. Rural teachers, who in the past were often the only federal officials to have sustained contact with local communities, had their work restricted to the classroom only—whereas in the past they were expected to undertake cultural and ideological work outside the classroom and beyond school hours. The only ideological work that they were allowed to engage in was to recruit peasants into rural unions tied to the one-party state. The federal government replaced the teachers' old role in local communities with a wide range of government bureaucracies whose job it was to disburse patronage in exchange for loyalty, especially around election time.[56]

The expanded role of the federal government in rural Mexico through schooling and other institutions did not always pacify the most radical sectors of Mexican society; in these cases, federal officials resorted to violence and coercion.[57] The violence, in comparison to that used by other authoritarian regimes in Latin America, tended to be more constrained and targeted. That ended in 1968 when, just prior to hosting the Olympics, the Mexican government murdered hundreds of members of a pro-democracy student movement in Tlatelolco.[58] The labor sector did not broadly support the student movement, but it did create an opening for militant members of labor, including teachers, to contest the state.[59] It was during this period of contestation that the Mexican "miracle" collapsed. The collapse was the beginning of a series of political crises that, in the short term, led to the adoption of neoliberal policies and that, in the long term, led to a democratic transition.[60]

El Salvador provides us with a very different example than that of Mexico; namely, a state that used modernizing developmentalism to forestall radical change that resulted in an all-out civil war rather than low level violence and counterinsurgency.[61] Historians Héctor Lindo-Fuentes and Erik Ching rightly argue that "The modernizing agenda of the Salvadoran military regime is generally acknowledged by scholars, but it gets lost in a metanarrative of civil war that has come to define conventional wisdom." The administrations who ruled El Salvador from 1931–1982, dominated by factions of the military, carried on educational projects that deserve attention. Studying such projects highlights the military's willingness to promote change of certain types. In fact, these very reforms "enflamed the opposition and precipitated societal collapse."[62] Focusing on El Salvador also underscores the fact that because smaller countries lacked the necessary internal population to effectively promote ISI, they had to rely heavily on the Alliance for Progress, the U.S. post-Cuban Revolution anti-communist development program, and international organizations in the design and implementation of their education modernization.

The 1960s in El Salvador witnessed a combination of modernization and anti-communist repression. It was during this time that elites—comprised of the military government and large landowners—began focusing on education reform as a means of modernizing the country without having to undergo meaningful structural change or opening the country up to full democracy. It was also at this time that the Alliance for Progress, USAID, UNICEF, and UNESCO embraced educational television as the perfect means through which to promote modernization and El Salvador as the best place in Latin America to test it out. Here is how educational television (or Televisión Educativa or TVE) was supposed to work:[63] In the face of a shortage of well-trained teachers in rural areas, El Salvador's Education Ministry—in consultation with leading experts in the use of mass communication in education—would develop a television-delivered curriculum. Rural teachers would teach two half-days, repeating the identical television-led instruction to two different sets of students. In theory, this would increase the reach of schooling in rural El Salvador, preparing peasants for entry into the modern workforce. It would also, after some technical training, result in the delivery of a uniform curriculum across the entire country, thus promoting a unifying national culture. El Salvador's elites embraced TVE for three major reasons. First, they believed that it would work. Second, international agencies were willing to provide high levels of funding for it.[64] Third, it would undermine political elites' most organized political opposition: unionized teachers. TVE did have some minor successes. For example, both teachers and students liked the textbooks, the first uniform set of texts ever in El Salvador, created for the program. TVE ultimately failed, however. Because content was broadcast centrally, students were forced to go at the speed of the televised recording, whether they understood the lessons or not. In addition, teachers were unable to alter the content to meet local needs. In the end, it led to increased teacher dissent, ranging from things as simple as refusing to turn on the television, to increased union organizing and teacher strikes in 1968 and 1971. Elites' push for economic modernization was supposed to improve the lives of everyday people, but the "machinery of repression that beat down those same citizens when they voiced their opinions or organized" eventually led to a full-blown civil war.[65]

El Salvador was not alone in either tapping into Alliance for Progress funds through USAID, the World Bank, UNICEF, and UNESCO or in putting in place schooling reforms that aimed at economic modernization without democratic opening. In Brazil, the military government focused on producing "the human resources necessary for economic development" by, for example, eliminating non-vocational training. Colombia did not go as far as Brazil in advancing the interests of the business classes, but it too implemented new educational policies promoted by UNESCO and the World Bank that served economic ends. This is not to say that everything that these international organizations promoted was an unmitigated failure. In Bolivia, for example, USAID, the World Bank, and UNICEF promoted bilingual education as a means of reaching the country's primarily indigenous rural dwellers. The bilingual literacy campaign launched in 1982–1983 lasted ten years and raised literacy rates from 31 percent to 67 percent. Sometimes, education is its own good.[66]

Neoliberalism

The fall of the Berlin Wall, the collapse of the Soviet Union and the rise of the Washington Consensus[67] has ushered in an era of increased democratization and economic openness. Neoliberalism often began as an attack on old patronage systems, but in short order served to weaken the social safety net and undermine the ability of Latin American governments to use the state to respond to the needs of everyday people. Given that neoliberalism called for reduced state expenditures, many governments cut spending on primary schooling even as they decentralized control over the schools, in effect, undoing much of the work that the post-World War II developmentalist state had done. The idea was that state and local governments would better and more efficiently be able to attend to the needs of everyday people. Mexico, for example, officially decentralized control over elementary education (1992) even before it transitioned to democracy (2000). Scholars have argued, however, that what actually occurred was more a de-concentration of federal personnel and resources than a true decentralization. In many cases, the federal government simply shifted resources from the Education Ministry's Mexico City-based offices to state-level ones.[68] This is not unusual; the decentralization of education "has resulted in serious inequities in funding and quality" such that poorer communities often fail to obtain higher levels of academic achievement. In fact, decentralization sometimes leads to worse educational outcomes because local governments are not prepared to handle the new responsibilities handed to them. This is especially true for communities of color.[69] In Mexico, as elsewhere, this has led to the rise of (mostly private) vocational training and a dearth of the humanities.[70] The privatization of education is not unique to Mexico. In Chile, the Pinochet dictatorship—an early implementer of neoliberalism—opened up the education system to private investors in 1981. Schooling was to be based on consumer choice (and the ability to pay). A 1990 law doubled down on the privatization of education my making it illegal for the government to interfere with schooling. The "freedom of teaching" law allowed the state to set a few minimum standards for education, but private schools were allowed to implement them as they saw fit.[71]

The implementation of neoliberal policies during a period of democratic opening, however, resulted in the election of a wave of left-of-center governments. It also led to the rise of new social movements and civil society groups, including feminists, indigenous people, youth groups, and environmental activists. These activists confronted the state (with varying levels of success) in order to mitigate or turn back the austerity policies of neoliberalism.[72] In Venezuela, for example, the election of Hugo Chávez resulted in "a mass mobilization by poor Venezuelans demanding access to the benefits provided by the state." Included among these benefits were a series of "missions that have eradicated illiteracy [and] put high school and college education in reach of most people."[73] In Brazil, Luíz Inácio Lula da Silva, better known as Lula, was elected in 2003. International financial markets pressured him into not undoing the austerity measures implemented by his predecessor. Instead, he designed a targeted cash transfer program for the poor known as *Bolsa Família* [Family Grant]. The process of obtaining *Bolsa Família* was not cumbersome; those interested had to prove poverty as defined by a family income below $42 USD per month. Keeping the subsidy was more difficult. Once someone started receiving *Bolsa Família*, they had to agree:

> that all their children between six and 15 years old attended school at least 85 percent of the time, make sure that any of their children under seven got immunized, and guarantee that both mothers and children got regular medical checkups.[74]

Conditional cash transfer programs are widely popular. The poor who receive them tend to vote to re-elect politicians who implement these programs. Politicians like them. Who doesn't like getting re-elected? International organizations like the World Bank like them as well as they are seen as an efficient tool to alleviate the most damaging aspects of the neoliberal model while investing in future human capital, the health and education of children. As a result, they have been adopted in a number of countries, including Mexico's *Oportunidades* and Nicaragua's *Red de Protección Social*.

In Chile, unequal access to post-secondary education, disproportionate public support for for-profit educational providers, and discriminatory practices against non-elite students led to the "Penguin Revolution" in 2006 and the "Chilean Winter of Discontent" in 2011. In the earlier series of protests, secondary students—called "penguins" for their black and white uniforms—questioned the market-based educational framework, asking for free public education and the elimination of exclusionary practices. A newly-created organization of Mapuche secondary students demanded more equitable treatment from the state. Forced by the protests, the Executive agreed to modify educational legislation, granting increased participation to students in decision-making, and introducing Intercultural Bilingual Education (IBE) as official policy. In 2011, university students demonstrated, asking for increased state involvement and investment in public education, universal and free post-secondary instruction, and exclusion of for-profit institutions from educational provision. The Mapuche university student organization urged the government to create a free public intercultural university and better material support for Mapuche students. While the students' demands have not been fully addressed yet, the government elected in 2013 promised to establish a universal and free system of higher education in Chile.[75]

Conclusion

In this chapter, we have used popular and rural schooling as a lens through which to explore conflict and negotiation over modernization and the state's attempted production of national culture. We traced the struggles that conservatives and liberals waged over the Church's role in education, the rise of eugenics, and the politics of order, then progress, and the ways in which during the nineteenth century federal governments tried, but mostly failed, to extend their reach into rural Latin America. The Mexican Revolution ushered in an era of *indigenismo*, an elite project aimed at weaving indigenous people, or at least certain aspects of their culture, into the newly emerging centralized nation-state. The post-World War II developmentalist state built upon the teaching state of the early twentieth century, resulting, for good or ill, in the further penetration of the state into rural and urban popular spaces. The rise of neoliberalism in the 1980s and 1990s served to hollow out the nation-state, weakening the already limited social safety net for the poor and people of color even as the state, through both action and inaction, adjusted its focus to more closely align is modernization program with the goals of the business classes. The last decade has seen a "pink tide," a series of leftist governments, elected across much of Latin America. These new leaders have pushed back against the neoliberal agenda, sometimes in measured ways such as through limited cash transfer programs like *Bolsa Família* and sometimes in more aggressive ways such as the "missions" in Venezuela. Recent elections in Venezuela, where the conservative opposition just won control of the legislature, and in Argentina, where Mauricio Macri, a conservative businessman and politician, suggest that the pink tide may be reaching its end. Regardless, we are certain that schools and schooling will continue to be loci of conflict and negotiation.

Notes

1 Harold H. Punke, "Extent and Support of Popular Education in Mexico," *Peabody Journal of Education*, Vol 11, No. 3 (November 1933): 122–137 and Mary Kay Vaughan, "Primary Education and Literacy in Nineteenth-Century Mexico: Research Trends, 1968–1988," *Latin American Research Review*, Vol 25, No. 1 (1990): 43.

2 Manuel A. Machado, Jr., "The Mexican Revolution and the Destruction of the Mexican Cattle Industry," *The Southwestern Historical Quarterly*, Vol 79, No. 1 (July 1975): 1–20.

3 Mary Kay Vaughan, *Cultural Politics in Revolution: Teachers, Peasants, and Schools in Mexico, 1930–1940* (Tucson, AZ: University of Arizona Press, 1997), 16.

4 The Tohono O'odham were only partly successful in this. They received an *ejido*—a state-supported piece of land that is used communally among some indigenous and peasant communities in Mexico—in Pozo Verde in 1928, thus regaining control over only a small portion of their ancestral homeland. See Geraldo L. Cadava, "Borderlands of Modernity and Abandonment: The Lines within Ambos Nogales and the Tohono O'odham Nation," *The Journal of American History*, Vol 98, No. 2 (September 2011): 362–383. The Tohono O'odham are still fighting for meaningful transnational educational opportunities. See Adrian Auijada, Edison Cassadore, Gaye Bumstead Perry, Ronald Geronimo, Kimberley Lund, Phillip Miguel, Mario

Montes-Helu, Teresa Newberry, Paul Robertson and Casey Thornbaugh, "For a Sustainable Future: Indigenous Transborder Higher Education," *Tribal College Journal* (February 19, 2015): 32–35.

5 Fernando F. Dworak to Secretaría de Educación Pública (hereafter SEP), May 25, 1928, Sonora, Archivo Historico de la Secretaría de Educación Pública—Escuelas Rurales (hereafter AHSEP-ER), Box 8420, Exp. 6; Ramón Espinosa Villanueva, Inspection Reports, 26 January 1932, 14 November 1932, 16 January 1933, 20 June 1933, and 17 April 1934, Chihuahua, AHSEP-ER, Box 936, Exp. IV/082/1561/7.

6 Cited in Joseph S. Roucek, "Pro-Communist Revolution in Cuban Education," *Journal of Inter-American Studies*, Vol 6, No. 3 (July 1964): 326 (emphasis in original).

7 Harry L. Mtonga, "Comparing the Role of Education in Serving Socioeconomic and Political Development in Tanzania and Cuba," *Journal of Black Studies*, Vol 23, No. 3 (March 1993): 385–386; Eric Selbin, "Conjugating the Cuban Revolution: It Mattered, It Matters, It Will Matter," *Latin American Perspectives*, Vol 36, No. 1 (January 2009): 24–25; and Claes Brundenius, "Revolutionary Cuba at 50: Growth With Equity Revisited," *Latin American Perspectives*, Vol 36, No. 2 (March 2009): 35–37.

8 Annalyda Álvarez Calderón, "Pilgrimages through mountains, deserts and oceans: The quest for indigenous citizenship (Puno, 1900–1930)," PhD Dissertation, Stony Brook University, 2009, chapter 3.

9 Josefina Zoraida Vázquez notes that nearly everyone assumes that education is used to promote nationalism, but very few scholars have actually explored the links between education and nationalism. See Josefina Zoraida Vázquez, *Nacionalismo y educación en México* (Mexico City: El Colegio de México, 2005), 10. See also, John A. Britton, ed., *Molding Their Hearts and Minds: Education, Communications, and Social Change in Latin America* (Lanham, MD: Rowman and Littlefield Publishers, 1997).

10 David F. Labaree, *Someone Has to Fail: The Zero-Sum Game of Public Schooling* (Cambridge, MA: Harvard University Press, 2011), 15–18 (quote on p. 16). See also, Héctor Lindo-Fuentes and Erik Ching, *Modernizing Minds in El Salvador: Education Reform and the Cold War, 1960–1980* (Albuquerque, NM: University of New Mexico Press, 2012), 1–6.

11 James Scott, *Seeing Like a State: How Certain Schemes to Improve the Human Condition Have Failed* (New Haven, CT: Yale University Press, 1998), 2.

12 Aurora Loyo Bramila, "Schooling in Mexico," In *Going to School in Latin America*, edited by Silvina Gvirtz and Jason Beech, 203 (Westport, CT: Greenwood Press, 2008).

13 Silvina Gvirtz and Jason Beech, "Introduction," In *Going to School in Latin America*, edited by Silvina Gvirtz and Jason Beech, 2 (Westport, CT: Greenwood Press, 2008).

14 Mark A. Burkholder and Lyman L. Johnson, *Colonial Latin America* 5th ed (Oxford: Oxford University Press, 2004), 99.

15 Gregorio Weinberg correctly notes, however, that the evangelical missions of the sixteenth century were nothing like the missions of the eighteenth century, whose aim was more about the extraction of resources. See Gregorio Weinberg, *Modelos Educativos en la historia de América Latina* (Buenos Aires: AZ Editors, 1995), 56–57 and Ralph L. Beals, "On the Study of Missionary Policies," *American Anthropologist*, Vol 61, No. 2 (April 1959): 299.

16 It should be noted that many semi-sedentary and non-sedentary indigenous people who lived on the periphery of the areas settled by the Spanish and Portuguese often long escaped contact with Europeans and their descendants for extended periods of time, and when they did, they often did not have their first interactions with missionaries as is often supposed. Rather, their first encounters were often with speculators, colonists, and soldiers looking to make their fortune.

17 Gauvin Alexander Bailey, *Art on the Jesuit Missions in Asia and Latin America, 1542–1773* (Toronto, ON: University of Toronto Press, 2001), 6.

18 Magnus Mörner, *La mezcla de razas en la historia de América Latina* (Buenos Aires: Paidos, 1969), 41. See also, Robert H. Jackson, "Social and Cultural Change on the Jesuit Missions of Paraquay and the Chiquitos Mission Frontier," *The Middle Ground Journal*, Vol 5 (2012). www2.css.edu/app/depts/his/historyjournal/index.cfm?name=Social-and-Cultural-Change-on-the-Jesuit-Missions-of-Paraguay-and-the-Chiquitos-Mission-Frontier&cat=5&art=88 accessed August 30, 2015.

19 Pilar Gonzalbo Aizpuru, "Introducción" and Eduardo Cavieres, "Educación, élites y estategias familiares. La aristocracia mercantil santiaguina a fines del siglo XVIII y sus proyecciones a

comienzos del XIX," In *Familia y educación en Iberoamérica*, edited by Pilar Gonzalbo Aizpuru, 10–11 and 115–138 (México: El Colegio de México, 1999).

20 Francisco García González, "Artesanos, aprendices y sabers en la Zacatecas del siglo XVIII," In *Familia y educación en Iberoamérica*, edited by Pilar Gonzalbo Aizpuru, 83–98 (México: El Colegio de México, 1999).

21 Susan Migden Socolow, *The Women of Colonial Latin America* 2nd ed (New York, NY: Cambridge University Press, 2015), 111, 114, 117, and 179; (quote from 179).

22 Ibid., 178–183.

23 Silvina Gvirtz, Jason Beech and Angela Oria, "Schooling in Argentina," In *Going to School in Latin America*, edited by Silvina Gvirtz and Jason Beech, 6 (Westport, CT: Greenwood Press, 2008).

24 Dorothy Tank de Estrada, "Enseñanza religiosa y patriótica: Historia de la primera historieta en México y su costo de publicación en 1801," In *Familia y educación en Iberoamérica*, edited by Pilar Gonzalbo Aizpuru, 99–114 (México: El Colegio de México, 1999).

25 Ariadna Acevedo Rodrigo, "Muchas escuelas y poco alfabeto: la educación rural en el Porfiriato, México, 1876–1910," In *Campesinos y escolares: La construcción de la escuela en el campo latinoamericano: Siglos XIX y XX*, edited by Alicia Civera Cerecedo, Juan Alfonseca Ginero de los Ríos and Carlos Escalante Fernández, 73–105 (Zinacantepec, Estado de México: Colegio Mexiquense; México: Miguel Ángel Porrúa, 2011); G. Antonio Espinoza, *Education and the State in Modern Peru. Primary Schooling in Lima, 1821—c. 1921* (New York, NY: Palgrave Macmillan, 2013); William Alfredo Chapman Quevedo, "Asociarse para la república: el caso de la Sociedad de Educación Elemental Primaria de Popayán en la década de 1830" *Historia Caribe*, Vol VIII, No. 22 (January–June 2013): 133–166; Steven Palmer and Gladys Rojas Chaves, "Educating Senorita: Teacher Training, Social Mobility, and the Birth of Costa Rican Feminism, 1885–1925," *Hispanic American Historical Review*, Vol 78, No. 1 (February 1998): 45–82.

26 Macarena Ponce de León A., Francisca Rengifo S. and Sol Serrano P., "La escuela de los campos: Chile en siglo XIX," In *Campesinos y escolares*, edited by Alicia Civera Cerecedo, Juan Alfonseca Giner De Los Rios, and Calos Escalante Fernandez, 33–72; Iván Molina Jiménez, "Educación primaria rural en Costa Rica, 1812–1855" In Ibid., 107–138; Lucía Lionetti, "'La revolución moral de la escuela para que el humilde paisano sea un ciudadano útil y laborioso'. Voces y acciones a favor de la educación en la campaña bonaerense (1810–1875)," In *Sujetos, comunidades rurales y culturas escolares en América Latina*, edited by Lucía Lionetti, Alicia Civera, and Flavia Obino Corrêa Werle, 25–44 (Rosario, Argentina: Prohistoria Ediciones—El Colegio Mexiquense A.C.—El Colegio de Michoacán A.C., 2013).

27 Macarena Ponce de León A., Francisca Rengifo Sol Serrano P., "La escuela los campos: Chile en siglo XIX," In *Campesinos y escolares*, edited by Alicia Civera Cerecedo, Juan Alfonseca Giner De Los Rios, and Calos Escalante Fernandez, 33–72.

28 Yoli Angélica Martini de Vatausky, "Los franciscanos del Río IV, indios ranqueles y otros temas de la vida en la frontera (1860–1885)," *Archivo ibero-americano*, Vol 41 (1981): 163–164, 321–388; Lasse Hölck and Mónika Contreras Saiz, "Educating Bárbaros: Educational Policies on the Latin American Frontiers Between Colonies and Independent Republics (Araucania, Southern Chile/Sonora, Mexico)," *Paedagogica Historica*, Vol 46, No. 4 (August 2010): 435–448.

29 David Bushnell, *El regimen de Santander en la Gran Colombia* (Bogotá: Tercer Mundo and Universidad Nacional, 1966), 129.

30 Javier Sáenz Obregón and Oscar Saldarriaga Vélez, "Schooling in Colombia," In *Going to School in Latin America*, edited by Silvina Gvirtz and Jason Beech, 101–102 (Westport, CT: Greenwood Press, 2008).

31 Gilberto Loaiza Cano, "El maestro de escuela o el ideal liberal de ciudadano en la reforma educativa de 1870," *Historia Crítica*, 34 (July–December 2007): 62–91.

32 Luis Alarcón Meneses, "La inasistencia escolar: Un problema secular de la Educación Colombiana del siglo XIX: El caso del Estado Soberano del Magdalena," *Memorias: Revista Digital de Historia y Arqueología del Caribe*, Vol 6, No. 10 (July 2009): 219–230.

33 Ibid., 100–103.

34 Silvina Gvirtz, Jason Beech and Angela Oria, "Schooling in Argentina," In *Going to School in Latin America*, edited by Silvina Gvirtz and Jason Beech, 7–8 (Westport, CT: Greenwood Press, 2008).

35 Andrea Alliaud, *Estudios sobre la educación; Los maestros y su historia* (Buenos Aires: Centro Editor de América Latina, 1993).

36 Luz Elena Galván de Terraza, *Los maestros y la educación pública en México: un estudio histórico* (Hidalgo y Matamoros, Tlalpan: CIESAS, 1985), 27–29.
37 Isidro Castillo, *México: sus revoluciones sociales y la eduación*, vol. 2 (Mexico City: Gobierno del Estado de Michoacán, 1976), 341.
38 John Kenneth Turner, *Barbarous Mexico* (Austin, TX: University of Texas Press, 1984), 269 and 285; Mary Kay Vaughan, "Primary Education and Literacy in Nineteenth-Century Mexico: Research Trends, 1968–1988," *Latin American Research Review*, Vol 25, No. 1 (1990): 42–43.
39 Ariadna Acevedo Rodrigo, "Muchas escuelas y poco alfabeto: la educación rural en el Porfiriato, México, 1876–1910," In *Campesinos y escolares: La construcción de la escuela en el campo latinoamericano: Siglos XIX y XX*, edited by Alicia Civera Cerecedo, Juan Alfonseca Ginero de los Ríos and Carlos Escalante Fernández (Zinacantepec, Estado de México: Colegio Mexiquense; México: Miguel Ángel Porrúa, 2011).
40 Rick López, *Crafting Mexico: Intellectuals, Artisans, and the State After the Revolution* (Durham, NC: Duke University Press, 2010).
41 Mary Kay Vaughan, *Cultural Politics in Revolution: Teachers, Peasants and Schools in Mexico, 1930–1940* (Tucson, AZ: University of Arizona Press, 1997). Stephen Lewis, *The Ambivalent Revolution: Forging State and Nation in Chiapas, 1919–1945* (Albuquerque, NM: University of New Mexico Press, 2005). Andrae M. Marak, *From Many, One: Indian Peasants, Borders, and Education in Callista Mexico, 1924–1935* (Calgary, AB: University of Calgary Press, 2009).
42 For example, Francisco Domínguez, a Tohono O'odham who had graduated from the Casa, refused to teach on behalf of the Education Ministry when he returned to his home community in northwestern Mexico. See Andrae Marak and Laura Tuennerman, *At the Border of Empires: The Tohono O'odham, Gender, and Assimilation, 1880–1934* (Tucson, AZ: University of Arizona Press, 2013), 235–236. On the Casa, see Engracia Loyo, "La empresa redentora. La Casa del Estudiante Indígena," *Historia Mexicana*, Vol 46, No. 1 (July–September 1996): 99–131.
43 Andrae M. Marak, *From Many, One: Indian Peasants, Borders, and Education in Callista Mexico, 1924–1935* (Calgary, AB: University of Calgary Press, 2009).
44 Mary Kay Vaughan, *Cultural Politics in Revolution: Teachers, Peasants and Schools in Mexico, 1930–1940* (Tucson, AZ: University of Arizona Press, 1997); Stephen Lewis, *The Ambivalent Revolution: Forging State and Nation in Chiapas, 1919–1945* (Albuquerque, NM: University of New Mexico Press, 2005); Elsie Rockwell, *Hacer escuela, hacer Estado: La educación posrevolucionaria viste desde Tlaxcala* (Mexico: CIESAS, 2007).
45 Gretchen Pierce, "*Pulqueros, Cerveceros,* and *Mezcaleros*: Small Alcohol Producers and Popular Resistance to Mexico's Anti-Alcohol Campaign, 1910–1940," In *Alcohol in Latin America: A Social and Cultural History*, edited by Gretchen Pierce and Áurea Toxquí (Tucson, AZ: University of Arizona Press, 2014).
46 Mary Kay Vaughan, *Cultural Politics in Revolution: Teachers, Peasants and Schools in Mexico, 1930–1940* (Tucson, AZ: University of Arizona Press, 1997).
47 Brooke Larson, "Forging the Unlettered Indian: The Pedagogy of Race in the Bolivian Andes," In *Histories of Race and Racism. The Andes and Mesoamerica from Colonial Times to the Present*, edited by Laura Gotkowitz, 134–156 (Durham, NC and London: Duke University Press, 2011).
48 Brooke Larson, "Capturing Indian Bodies, Hearths and Minds: The Gendered Politics of Rural School reform in Bolivia, 1920s–1940s," In *Natives Making Nation: Gender, Indigeneity, and the State in the Andes*, edited by Andrew Canessa, 32–59 (Tucson, AZ: University of Arizona Press, 2005).
49 G. Antonio Espinoza, "The Origins of the Núcleos Escolares Campesinos or Clustered Schools for Peasants in Peru, 1945–1952," *Naveg@mérica: Electronic Journal of the Spanish Association of Latin Americanists*, 4 (Winter 2010). http://revistas.um.es/navegamerica/article/view/100051 accessed November 10, 2015.
50 Jens R. Hentschke, *Reconstructing the Brazilian Nation: Public Schooling in the Vargas Era* (Baden-Baden: Nomos, 2007), 57–62, 422–424.
51 Jens R. Hentschke, *Reconstructing the Brazilian Nation: Public Schooling in the Vargas Era* (Baden-Baden: Nomos, 2007); Jerry Dávila, *Diploma of Whiteness: Race and Social Policy in Brazil, 1917–1945* (Durham, NC and London: Duke University Press, 2003).
52 Jens R. Hentschke, *Reconstructing the Brazilian Nation: Public Schooling in the Vargas Era* (Baden-Baden: Nomos, 2007), 68–70, 115–123.
53 Ibid., 153–154, 209–213, and Conclusion.
54 On the Mexican Miracle see Susan Eckstein, *The Poverty of Revolution: The State and Urban Poor in Mexico* (Princeton, NJ: Princeton University Press, 1977).

55 Wayne A. Cornelius, *Mexican Politics in Transition: The Breakdown of the One-Party-Dominant Regime* (San Diego, CA: Center for U.S.-Mexico Studies, 1996).

56 Alberto Arnaut Salgado, *Historia de una profesión: Los maestros de educación primaria en México, 1887–1994* (Mexico: CIDE, 1998), 93–124; Alberto Arnaut Salgado, *La federalización educativa en México: Historia del debate sobre la centralización y la descentralización educativa, 1889–1994* (Mexico: El Colegio de México, 1998), 221–244; and Daniel C. Hellinger, *Comparative Politics of Latin America: Democracy at Last?* 2nd ed (New York, NY: Routledge, 2015), 261.

57 Robert Alegre, *Railroad Radicals in Cold War Mexico: Gender, Class, and Mexico* (Omaha, NE: University of Nebraska Press, 2014).

58 Elaine Carey, *Plaza of Sacrifices: Gender, Power, and Terror in 1968 Mexico* (Albuquerque, NM: University of New Mexico Press, 2005).

59 Maria Lorena Cook, *Organizing Dissent: Unions, the State, and the Democratic Teachers' Movement in Mexico* (University Park, PA: Penn State Press, 1996), 16–18.

60 Miguel Basañez, *La lucha por la hegemonía en México, 1968–1990* (Mexico: Siglo XXI Editores, 1990).

61 In many ways El Salvador's attempts to use education in lieu of structural reform mirrors that of the Callista period in Mexico (1924–1934), except that in many regions of rural Mexico the federal government's presence was ephemeral. Mexico's relative success with this approach from 1940–1970 was probably the result of the fact that deep structural changes preceded it. See Andrae M. Marak, *From Many, One: Indian Peasants, Borders, and Education in Callista Mexico, 1924–1935* (Calgary, AB: University of Calgary Press, 2009).

62 Héctor Lindo-Fuentes and Erik Ching, *Modernizing Minds in El Salvador: Education Reform and the Cold War, 1960–1980* (Albuquerque, NM: University of New Mexico Press, 2012), 6. Some of the works that focus on violence and revolution are: Walter LaFeber, *Inevitable Revolutions: The United States in Central America* 2nd ed (New York, NY: W.W. Norton, 1993); Tina Rosenberg, *Children of Cain: Violence and the Violent in Latin America* (New York, NY: William Morrow, 1991); Bill Stanley, *The Protection Racket State: Elite Politics, Military Extortion and Civil War in El Salvador* (Philadelphia, PA: Temple University Press, 1996); and Mark Danner, *Massacre at El Mozote* (New York, NY: Vintage, 1994).

63 Television education was first used in Japan and would later be used in Italy. See Hector Lindo-Fuentes and Erik Ching, *Modernizing Minds in El Salvador: Education Reform and the Cold War, 1960–1980* (Albuquerque, NM: University of New Mexico Press, 2012), Chapter 3.

64 El Salvador received more than $100 million USD in non-military aid from the United States. This doesn't count the additional millions in aid from the World Bank and the Inter-American Development Bank. See Hector Lindo-Fuentes and Erik Ching, *Modernizing Minds in El Salvador: Education Reform and the Cold War, 1960–1980* (Albuquerque: University of New Mexico Press, 2012), 73.

65 Ibid., 78.

66 Diana Gonçalves Vidal and Luciano Mendes de Faria Filho, "Schooling in Brazil," In *Going to School in Latin America,* edited by Silvina Gvirtz and Jason Beech, 68–69 (Westport, CT: Greenwood Press, 2008); Javier Sáenz Obregón and Oscar Saldarriaga Vélez, "Schooling in Colombia," In *Going to School in Latin America,* edited by Silvina Gvirtz and Jason Beech, 109 (Westport, CT: Greenwood Press, 2008); and Herbert Klein, *Bolivia: The Evolution of a Multi-Ethnic Society* (New York, NY: Oxford University Press, 1982), 264.

67 Early versions of the Washington Consensus focused on fiscal discipline, reduced public expenditures (but with a focus on primary health and educational care), the lowering of taxes and tariffs, privatization, and deregulation. In many places, this early version of the Washington Consensus has been replaced with market fundamentalism, or as, economist John Williamson notes, the (incorrect) belief that markets solve everything. See John Williamson, "What Should the Bank Think about the Washington Consensus," white paper prepared as background for the World Bank's *World Development Report 2000.* http://scienzepolitiche.unipg.it/tutor/uploads/williamson_on_washington_consensus_002.pdf accessed December 22, 2015.

68 Víctor Alejandro Espinoza Valle, *Modernización educativa y cambio institucional en el norte de México* (Tijuana: El Colegio de la Frontera Norte, 1999); Alberto Arnaut Salgado, *Historia de una profesión: Los maestros de educación primaria en México, 1887–1994* (Mexico: CIDE, 1998); and Alberto Arnaut Salgado, *La federalización educative en México: Historia del debate sobre la centralización y la descentralización educativa, 1889–1994* (Mexico: El Colegio de México, 1998).

69 Ben Meade and Alec Ian Gershberg, "Making Education Reform Work for the Poor: Accountability and Decentralization in Latin America," *Journal of Education Policy*, Vol 23, No. 3 (2008): 299–322, citation from p. 317; and Sebastian Galiani, Paul Gertler, and Ernesto Schardgrodsky, "School Decentralization: Helping the Good Get Better, but Leaving the Poor Behind," Working Paper. Buenos Aires: Universidad de San Andres, 2005, cited in Karleen Jones West, "Decentralization, the Inclusion of Ethnic Citizens, and Support for Democracy in Latin America," *Latin American Research Review*, Vol 50, No. 3 (2015): 46–70.

70 Erika Pani, "Soft Science: The Humanities in Mexico," *American Historical Review*, Vol 120, No. 4 (2015): 1327–1342.

71 Rolando Poblete Melis, "Schooling in Chile," In *Going to School in Latin America*, edited by Silvina Gvirtz and Jason Beech, 89 (Westport, CT: Greenwood Press, 2008).

72 Benedicte Bull, "'Pink Tide' Governments in Latin America: Transformation, Inclusion, and Rejection," In *Democratization in the Global South: The Importance of Transformative Politics*, edited by Kristian Stokke and Olle Törnquist, 75–99 (New York, NY: Palgrave MacMillan, 2013).

73 Daniel C. Hellinger, *Comparative Politics of Latin America: Democracy at Last?* 2nd ed (New York, NY: Routledge, 2015), 276.

74 Jonathan Tepperman, "Brazil's Antipoverty Breakthrough: The Surprising Success of Bolsa Família," *Foreign Affairs*. www.foreignaffairs.com/articles/brazil/2015-12-14/brazils-antipoverty-breakthrough accessed December 22, 2015.

75 Cristián Bellei and Cristian Cabalin, "Chilean Student Movements: Sustained Struggle to Transform a Market-Oriented Educational System," *Current Issues in Comparative Education*, Vol 15, No. 2 (2013): 108–123; Andrew Webb and Sarah Radcliffe, "Mapuche Demands during Educational Reform, the Penguin Revolution and the Chilean Winter of Discontent," *Studies in Ethnicity and Nationalism*, Vol 13, No. 3 (2013): 319–341.

13

POLITICAL CULTURES OF SOCIAL MOVEMENTS

Magalí Rabasa

What is most visible from afar are the mass mobilizations in the streets, the protests documented in the mainstream media, the cries of "No!" that echo throughout the Americas: no more police brutality, no more gender violence, no more exploitation of workers, no more dispossession, no more displacement. The "No!" is the expression of the "anti" in popular politics. What is less visible, but far more transformative and enduring, are the movements to generate, create, invent, and construct other ways of being, living, and doing in the world. This is the "Yes!" uttered less audibly by the heterogeneous subject implicitly affirmed not in the "anti" but in the "auto": *autonomía, autogestión, autodeterminación* [autonomy, autogestion, self-determination]. The position of the "auto" is not reactive, but proactive; not passive, but dynamic; not programmatic, but prefigurative. To be sure, this creative "Yes!" is not new—after all it is the call with which Frantz Fanon concluded *The Wretched of the Earth* in 1961: "we must turn over a new leaf, we must work out new concepts, and try to set afoot a new man."[1] Yet, while the ideas are not new,[2] their recent enactment through the articulated practices of *new political cultures* across Latin America is—and that is the focus of this chapter.

Since the late 1980s, Latin America has been the site of a new wave of social movements which challenge the widespread imposition of neoliberal policies across the region.[3] The most recent expression of more than five centuries of popular resistance in the continent, the new movements are collective actors in what has been called the "Fourth World War," a new war waged by neoliberalism, which "as a global system, is a new war to conquer territories."[4] Neoliberalism—popularly understood as the progressive commodification and privatization of all facets of social, cultural, political, and economic life—is one of the most salient expressions of the enduring and far-reaching effects of what Peruvian sociologist Aníbal Quijano names the "coloniality of power": the racial, political, and social hierarchies formed during colonization which persist into the twenty-first century.[5]

In what follows, I describe some of the translocal social movements that have emerged across Latin America since the 1980s, paying particular attention to the material, conceptual, and social forms that articulate these diverse and disperse spaces of resistance. I show how a praxis of autonomy rooted in political engagements with territory, communication, education, and networking is the common axis that grounds these struggles as they reimagine all facets of social life, and in turn, generate *new political cultures*.[6] In presenting a necessarily partial (in the double sense of incomplete and subjective) political cartography of what Raúl Zibechi[7] has called "the continent in movement,"[8] I emphasize the specific cultural practices and tools deployed and developed by current movements across Latin America, while zooming in on specific examples from Mexico, Bolivia, Argentina, and Chile.[9] Because my interest lies in the emergence not of "new movements" so much as new political cultures, this chapter is constructed through ethnographic narratives in combination with references primarily to independently published literature produced in Latin America.

The new wave of Latin American social movements had a two-part inauguration. The first was clandestine, in the Selva Lacandona of Chiapas, Mexico with the foundation of the Zapatista Army of National Liberation (EZLN) in November 1983. The second was public, with the Caracazo, the massive revolt against neoliberal measures which shook the streets of Venezuela beginning in late February 1989.[10] While related movements elsewhere similarly reject the capitalist re-colonization of the world—as is evident in the slogan "We are everywhere"[11]—the movements in Latin America represent the most profound and widespread challenge to capitalism in the late twentieth and early twenty-first century.[12]

From the rural communities of the highlands of Chiapas to the dense urban neighborhoods of Buenos Aires, a praxis of autonomy shapes the new movements as they refuse to be absorbed and exploited by the state and by capital.[13] My understanding of autonomy resonates with the definition proposed by the Argentine militant research group Colectivo Situaciones in their epilogue to Raúl Zibechi's 2006 book *Dispersar el poder:*

> More than being a doctrine, autonomy is alive when it appears as a practical course of action, inscribed in plurality, as the orientation of concrete developments that emerge from particular forces, and the fundamental decision to refuse to be dominated by the mediating-expropriating demands of the state and of capital.[14]

Ana Dinerstein characterizes autonomy in the twenty-first century as intimately linked to prefiguration; that is, the idea that through our day-to-day actions, we build the world we want to see in the future—what she names "a process of learning hope."[15] She asserts that while autonomous practice in itself is not new, the emphasis on prefiguration that brings the politics of resistance into the everyday through all facets of social life represents a turning point. This "quotidianization" of resistance is the foundation of the new political cultures which exceed the usual spaces of politics.[16]

The emphasis on autonomy is apparent not only in the ways that the new movements distance themselves from state institutions and political parties, but also in their emphasis on *autogestión*, a concept that cannot be adequately translated to English, but which can be taken as an expression of prefiguration. The rarely used English cognate "autogestion" is not widely understood. The standard English translation as "worker self-management" is too restrictive, because it does not convey a key aspect of *autogestión* as a *self-sustaining practice* that combines cooperative organization and production with participatory democracy, and extends beyond the formal workplace.[17] For these reasons, I use the Spanish term rather than attempt to translate it. While it has been in circulation in Latin America for over a hundred years, primarily in anarchist circles,[18] today it appears as a common descriptor for the kinds of economic, cultural, and political projects that ground the autonomous movements in Latin America. *Autogestión* appears in practice as the material expression of the more symbolic idea of autonomy through a vast array of collective projects including: workers' cooperatives, alternative schools, independent media projects, community housing, communal farming, food distribution, etc. A combined emphasis within the new movements on autonomy and *autogestión* facilitates the formation of social relations not determined by the hierarchical, exclusionary, and exploitative dynamics of the state and capitalism. And in this way, the new movements develop a transformation of the everyday dynamics of social and political life, and enact a prefigurative politics.

In many ways, the new movements complicate the very category of "social movement" and are perhaps better described as rebellions and resistances. In recent years, some Latin American theorists have proposed a language of "societal movement"[19]—a term that reactivates the dynamism of "movement" by shifting the grammar away from identification of a thing (a social movement) towards description of an action (societal movement). What is most important in this shift is the emphasis on action and *practice* rather than on ossified organizational forms or dogmatic ideology. While recognizing the inadequacy of the concept of "social movements," in this chapter I use this term to refer to a wide array of popular political and social modes of organization, resistance, and rebellion.

Unlike their twentieth century antecedents, the new movements are not defined by any ostensive category, such as identity, party, or class. Rather, they are defined by their practices, which constitute a "new repertoire of action,"[20] and include self-organization, horizontalism, cooperativism, and mutual aid. These practices are the material expressions of a shared repudiation of both neoliberal policies and the post-neoliberal capitalist models of recent "progressive" governments. While the twenty-first century movements undoubtedly draw influence and energy from twentieth century revolutions and social movements, they are distinct from them in at least three significant ways: their objectives, organization, and composition.

First, for the most part, the twenty-first century movements do not seek to seize state power, and in most cases, state reform is not a priority or even a goal. This is not to say that the new movements do not have any engagement with or effect on state politics. In fact, over the past two decades, in some contexts popular movements have directly contributed to the ousting of repressive governments (as in Argentina, Bolivia, and Ecuador), while in others they have directly contributed to constitutional reform processes (Bolivia and Ecuador).[21] And while popular mobilizations have also directly contributed to the election of "progressive" candidates (Bolivia, Argentina, Venezuela, Ecuador, Chile, etc.), in most cases, the movements maintain at best strained, if not outright antagonistic, relationships with these left-leaning governments.[22] The state, which has long been the facilitator if not the purveyor of neoliberal policies, is considered by many to be inextricably linked to capitalist interests, and as such, antithetical to the kinds of alternatives to capitalism that they imagine.[23] And these alternatives are grounded in the formation of social relations that are not driven by the logic of competition, expansion and profitability that capitalism relies on and reproduces. This rejection of the structure and form of state institutions is directly related to the second way that the new movements are distinct from their predecessors: their modes of organization.

"For over a century, anti-systemic movements have developed their organizational structures in parallel to capital, the state, the military, and other institutions of the system they fight."[24] Here, Raúl Zibechi signals what the new movements recognize as a pitfall of earlier modes of rebellion: hierarchical structures of power. The major Latin American movements of the twentieth century included revolutionary organizations, liberation fronts, political parties, unions, and guerrillas—all of which replicate, as Zibechi notes, the hierarchical dynamics of the very institutions they sought to challenge, overthrow, or replace: the military, the state, and capitalism. Furthermore, the structures of power developed by the movements were separate from the collectives they sought to represent, which is to say that they were not reflective of the forms of organization organic to the groups they worked from and for. This distance from, and even opposition to, the social relations of the populations that the movements sought to accompany reproduced not only forms of domination but also of exclusion. This directly limited the liberatory and transformative potential of the movements in their struggles against neocolonialism and capitalism, since the organizational modes reproduced many of the dynamics they sought to challenge. These hierarchies include, most overtly, patriarchal and racist dynamics which maintained the subjugation of the most marginal, though not always minoritarian,[25] sectors of the movements' own communities.

The third, related, way that the new movements are distinct from their predecessors has to do with their composition in terms of the kinds of actors appearing as political protagonists. The shift away from top-down organization and towards a privileging of dialogue and communication has implied greater emphasis on working from the everyday. This praxis has led to the emergence of political subjectivities previously marginalized by leftist movements, including women, youth, LGBTQ populations, indigenous peoples, incarcerated people, migrants, and the urban and rural poor. Significantly, in many movements the foregrounding of gender politics—often in combination with practices associated with forms of anarchism—has had a profound impact, generating less hierarchical modes of organization and greater plurality within the movements. This is perhaps one of the most significant ways that the new movements depart from their antecedents. What makes the inclusion of a radical gender politics so effective and indeed transformative is precisely the fact that it is not separated as a distinct—or additional—realm or area of political action. In this chapter, rather than treat "gender" as a separate arena of political action, I consider its impact in the principle spaces of the new movements: territory, communication, education, and networking.

Territory

Mexico City, 2010. Walking through the black metal gate at the corner of the streets Playa Grande and Playa Encantada, I'm greeted by members of the security commission, an immediate indication that I am crossing into a different kind of territory—one not patrolled by the police or governed by politicians, but rather by the very people who live there. Just inside the gates, I turn to enter an outdoor meeting space where over two dozen people have gathered for an initial organizing session to form a new national network of autonomous and anticapitalist collectives. The participants, who range in age from 15 to 75, have traveled from all over Mexico for the three-day gathering. The facilitators are two teenage members of Jóvenes en Resistencia Alternativa, a collective based in Mexico City, and the host of the gathering is the Frente Popular Francisco Villa Independiente-UNOPII, also known as Los Panchos. Over the past twenty-five years, this organization has grown to include thousands of families across eight autonomous neighborhoods in Mexico City. The neighborhoods, or *predios*, emerged in response to an escalating housing crisis in Mexico City and have evolved into an ongoing experiment in urban autonomy that is unparalleled in scale elsewhere.[26] The site of the 2010 meeting, the *Comunidad Habitacional Acapatzingo*, more commonly called *La Polvorilla*, is the largest of the neighborhoods organized by Los Panchos.

Founded in 1989, Los Panchos (now known as the Organización Popular Francisco Villa de la Izquierda Independiente) fpredate the public appearance of their better known rural counterparts in the southeast: the autonomous Zapatista communities in Chiapas. But what both movements share is a decades-long process of adapting and learning alongside newer movements and younger generations, and the continual integration of less centralized and less hierarchical modes of organization. Los Panchos, like the Zapatistas, are products of an earlier moment of vanguardist, Marxist-Leninist revolutionary politics, though they have both progressively abandoned the kinds of power dynamics that reproduce the forms of racist and patriarchal domination and oppression associated with the very institutions they seek autonomy from: capitalism and the state. And what has emerged in both is a new political culture rooted in the praxis of territorially-based autonomy. While the occupation of large tracts of land and the formation of autonomous communities are more often associated with rural experiences, Los Panchos demonstrate that—while the challenges are distinct—autonomy is also possible in a dense, urban context such as that of Mexico City.[27]

Five years after my first trip to La Polvorilla, I returned on a Saturday—assembly day—to see a friend who had recently visited the United States. In a two-hour walking tour we saw just a small portion of La Polvorilla, but our hosts—members of the exterior relations and politics commissions—led us through a wide range of spaces that give a sense of the integral approach to autonomy that the organization advances. We visited the youth-run radio station, tucked into a second floor apartment; the various recreation and fitness facilities including basketball courts, soccer fields, and exercise spaces for the elderly; two greenhouses where UNAM students were working with residents developing a biodynamic aquaponics system; an outdoor theater; two security stations; the commissions meeting space; an open apartment used to temporarily house people visiting or families in the process of organizing land occupations elsewhere in the city; and an open-air meeting space where the monthly assembly was in process, with hundreds in attendance. As we walked, we learned about the water filtration system that is being developed, the schools that are being built, and the health clinic they hope to open soon. Along the main central road, teams of electricians were installing new LED street lights. Efforts of *autogestión* are being made daily to lessen the reliance of those who form this "community in resistance"[28] on private and state services, be they of education, health care, food, utilities, or information. That Los Panchos count their membership in numbers of families, rather than individuals, is significant for several reasons. First, because it includes all ages as actors in the organization—and indeed, children, teens, adults, and elders all participate. Second, because it reflects the basic units that make up the movement which began as a fight for basic housing rights—households—within which diverse needs and interests converge. And third, because it points to the way that quotidian social relations, like that of the family and the neighborhood, act as the basis for the political relations that propel the movement forward.

Functioning like a small village within a megalopolis, the Comunidad Habitacional de Acapatzingo is a clear expression of urban autonomy, figured broadly to include as many facets of social and political life as the members of the organization can manage. But elsewhere in the city, and indeed across the Americas, the recuperation, occupation, or claiming of territory acts as the material basis from which new political cultures grow. In addition to other autonomous housing communities (like the *Movimiento de Pobladores* in Chile, for example), two of the most common ways that we see territory anchoring autonomous efforts is in the cooperative workplaces that appear most visibly in the recuperated factories and businesses in Argentina since the 1990s,[29] and the collective agricultural projects that can be found in all corners of the Americas. As Gustavo Esteva and others have asserted, the emphasis on land and territory in autonomous practice is an assertion of the right to reclaim that which has been taken away—a rejection of the expropriating violence of capital: "People are increasingly making claim to territories that have been taken away from them, but also demand respect for their own ways of understanding of what is done inside them in terms of land and property."[30] As the following sections will show, the occupation of some physical space—be it private or public, permanently or temporarily—is an ongoing priority and challenge for movements everywhere as they resist the commodification of the basic elements of social life. More broadly, claims to space (through occupation, for example) and the production of autonomous space are also key aspects of the movements' capacity to articulate their efforts with others.

Communication

Buenos Aires, 2011. Just before the ten-year anniversary of Argentina's 2001 popular rebellion,[31] hundreds of people gathered over two days for the nineteenth Feria del Libro Independiente y Alternativa (FLIA) on Calle Bonpland in the upscale Palermo neighborhood of Buenos Aires. On the first day, dozens of bookmakers and booksellers arrived in the morning with their boxes and suitcases of books, lining up along the sidewalk ready to make a loosely coordinated move to occupy the street and block traffic. The street was quickly filled with stands, and dumpsters were used to block one end of the street. Soon after, a local celebrity of sorts—the *Arma de Instrucción Masiva* (an old pickup truck refashioned to look like an army tank made of books)—arrived, serving as the barrier along the other end. The next notable arrival was the police, though their presence was more a symbolic gesture of routine harassment than an actual disruption. The only violation cited was blocking the street; nothing related to unpermitted vending. But when the police demanded to know "who was in charge" to list a name on the citation, the collective response was simultaneously "no one" and "all of us." The FLIA is *not* an organization, but an open assembly with no designated leaders. The fairs are completely run by the participants, and it is difficult to find anyone to step forward as "organizer" or "person in charge."

To most this seemed like an unusual scene for the Palermo Hollywood neighborhood—among the trendiest in the Buenos Aires—known for the upscale restaurants and shops that line its streets. But as some know, the 1600 block of Calle Bonpland is also home to a cluster of political and cultural projects that occupy the space known as the Bonpland Cultural Space. Tucked down a walkway behind the Solidarity Economy Market, out of view of the average passerby, a *comedor popular* [popular cafeteria], a popular library, an independent media group, and a cultural program for formerly incarcerated women—playfully named *Yo no fui* [It wasn't me]—all operate autonomously. In the wake of the 2001 rebellion, Bonpland became the site of the neighborhood assembly, like so many others across the city, and over the past decade the space held by that assembly has changed hands and form multiple times.[32]

In addition to the groups that regularly work out of the space at 1600 Bonpland—and provide a kind of window into the post-2001 movements through their networks of relations that include *Movimientos de Trabajadores Desocupados, piqueteros, bachilleratos populares,* and women's organizations from as far north as Jujuy and as far south as Neuquén—for the days of the FLIA 19, the block was full of books and other print materials. Some of the books for sale directly chronicle the stories of the societies in movement in Buenos Aires and the continent—like those covering the wobbly table of *La Periférica Distribuidora,* a sister project of Tinta Limón and Colectivo Situaciones. While others, like the poetry and fiction being sold by the authors themselves, narrate mundane occurrences, a reflection of the imaginary of the everyday people who make up these societies. The FLIA is much more than a book fair, and this snapshot shows the ways that media production combines with horizontal modes of organization, in initiatives that promote self-representation, network formation, and collective knowledge production by and for the movements. As Marilina Winik, a sociologist and member of the FLIA, has noted, the fair represents "the fusion between the methodology of networks and the territorial necessity of *encuentro.*"[33,34]

Medios libres [independent or free media] is the name given to the diverse and decentralized networks of media producers who participate in and accompany these movements.[35] This phenomenon became most visible, starting in the late 1990s, through the open online platform known as Indymedia, which grew into countless local webpages which anyone could freely access and contribute to with text, video, photography, or audio.[36] The abundance of online media has been crucial for the movements as it enables them to create their own lines of communication with the world, while contesting the silence and misinformation imposed and perpetuated by the "mainstream" or "commercial" media, often described as a *cerco informativo/mediático* [media/information siege or barrier]. Digital and cybernetic technology is what allows communiqués and news to spread rapidly around the planet, as was the case with the EZLN's "*Declaración de la Selva Lacandona*" ["Declaration of the Lacandon Jungle"] on January 1, 1994.[37] But despite the vital place of *medios libres*, there has long been a tension between the efficacy and reach of online media and the importance of face-to-face relations for building grassroots political networks.

The movements' emergence coincides with the appearance of new digital and Internet technologies, and this has been crucial to not only the internal and local formation of webs of activists and supporters, but also to the creation of transnational networks through the unprecedented dialogues and exchanges that the new technologies have, in part, facilitated. In their 2013 book, the *Centro de Medios Libres* in Mexico assert:

> To break with the information siege, the problem is not the machines, but the people who make them work. Communications are made by flesh and bones people, but we live in an era of love of machines that impedes us from communicating with each other. We've forgotten the taste of conversations in the park, in the stairs, or on a walk, and we think that this or that machine will make it so we can have efficient communications. What is important is the human aspect, the new social relations and the street networks of communications, but we don't look there anymore.[38]

The "seduction of machines," they caution, has created too great an emphasis on the *tools* of communication, eclipsing the vitality of the *social relations* that drive and shape them. The FLIA is a demonstration of that vitality, where the networks that travel through "machines" are renewed and reinvented in the face-to-face experiences that happen in the street. The FLIA began in Buenos Aires in 2006, and while it is still organized at least twice a year in the capital city, it has rapidly spread across the Americas, popping up in nearly every province of Argentina, as well as in Chile, Brazil, Colombia, Peru, Ecuador, and most recently Mexico, in Oaxaca, San Cristóbal de Las Casas, and Puebla. The FLIA, in this sense, is a decentralized material expression of the movements—and the lesser defined political cultures—whose voices come through the pages of the books that circulate there. These materials are both tools of communication aimed at expanding networks *and* expressions of the social relations that make and shape the movements. In both senses, they are deeply connected to the educational initiatives that are at the foundation of nearly every movement in the continent, in some form or another, through which we see the vital role of the movements as knowledge producers.[39]

Education

La Paz, 2011. My first interaction with the office of the Vice-presidency of the Plurinational State of Bolivia came through a book, *Pensando el mundo desde Bolivia* [*Thinking the World from Bolivia*], published in 2010.[40] When a friend first shared it with me, I was unaware of its history, knowing only that it was an impressive compilation of essays by Bolivian intellectuals alongside some of the leading critical theorists from around the world—Spivak, Negri, Laclau, Wallerstein, Dussell—the kinds of figures who don't need first names to be recognized. Once I had the book in hand, I realized that it had been edited and published by the Vice-presidency, and was the result of a few years of work, in which they coordinated the visits of the intellectuals to Bolivia, where they participated in workshops with different organizations and movements around the country. My friend later explained that he had received the hefty book for free at a public presentation organized by the Vice-presidency, and that, in fact, this was pretty much the only way to get a copy. This book, and my friend's story about acquiring it, sparked a series of questions in my mind: about state institutions and their relationship with social movements; about the role of intellectuals in both; and about the materials that shape and articulate both state and grassroots politics in Bolivia.

The Plurinational State of Bolivia, which was born in 2009 through the Constituent Assembly that generated a new constitution, is headed up by a self-proclaimed "government of the social movements."[41] This self-identification, which has been—and continues to be—questioned and criticized by non-state actors who work from and with movements across the country, is one of the ways that the Evo Morales administration has sought to (at least symbolically) transform the role of the state through efforts to "decolonize politics."[42] Like other recent progressive governments in the region (Argentina, Ecuador, Venezuela, Chile, Brazil, etc.), Morales owes much of his electoral success to the mass mobilizations of social movements, and he has attempted to harness that energy through efforts to engage the movements through the organizational medium of state institutions. By 2011, it could be said that this process was being heavily questioned, as Evo Morales' MAS Party came to look much like a traditional political party working within the constraints, and adopting the prerogatives, of bureaucratic state institutions. Today, for many reasons and to many sectors, it has lost much of its credibility. But the story of the initiatives in Morales' first two terms reveals an initial creativity to organize beyond—and against—the prerogatives of traditional state bureaucracy, and tells a great deal about the role of education and knowledge production in the process. While the project of radical transformation (in official terms "decolonization") from within the state has been widely criticized, the processes parallel to (and indeed in tension with) Morales' presidency have introduced what Cochabamba Water War organizer (and Morales critic) Oscar Olivera calls a "new discursive structure [that] has transformed the very way of doing politics"[43]—in, against, and beyond state institutions.

That Morales' vice president, Álvaro García Linera, is a prominent intellectual, former *guerrillero,* and professor of sociology is significant, and the initiatives from his office—like the publication of *Pensando el mundo desde Bolivia*—reflect the ways that education has come to play a role in the ongoing articulation of social movements and the state. By 2009, a subsection of the Vice-presidency, the *Dirección de Participación Ciudadana* [Direction of Citizen Participation], had become a de facto publishing house, with the explicit objective of producing *conocimiento propio* [proper knowledge][44] and supporting the emergence of a generation of popular intellectuals tasked with that work. In an interview, an early member of the vice president's team described their work as having three dimensions: political discussion, academic discussion, and the production of *conocimiento propio. Conocimiento propio,* he explains, is not characterized by the common dichotomy of intellectual knowledge production that divides those who "know" from those who do not. Here, *conocimiento propio* is conceived of as *knowledge proper to* a heterogeneous, motley gathering—the *sociedad abigarrada* [motley society] first coined by René Zavaleta and later reconceptualized by Luis Tapia and others.[45] It is knowledge that decenters, and maybe even disorders,[46] the "our" and the "we." The strategies deployed by the team reflect the bifurcated experiences of these radical intellectuals: on the one hand, their training in academic institutions, and on the other hand, their experiences with popular education as militants in grassroots movements. The team's projects combined rigorous theory seminars, political reading groups, popular education workshops, dialogue sessions between intellectuals—international and national—and activists and labor organizers, and collective publications. Their projects, significantly, did not remain limited to the urban center of La Paz/El Alto, but rather extended to various other departments, as their initiatives traveled to engage with rural organizations as well.[47]

The tension—at times productive and at times destructive—between academia and popular politics is a common concern across the continent, and the spaces where it is interrogated are important sites for understanding the fundamental role of education in the development of transformative movements. The example of the Bolivian Vice-presidency is significant because it connects not only social movements and academia, but also the state—an undeniable producer of knowledge in any context. While the Bolivian case is exceptional for obvious reasons, with the autonomous desires implicit in the project of *conocimiento propio,* it is clearly related to the countless sites across the continent where education acts as the bedrock for a wide range of autonomous political processes.

Just as the Bolivian Vice-presidency's publishing project holds as its primary objective the production of *conocimiento propio,* so do the educational initiatives that can be found in virtually every social movement in the continent. These initiatives take many forms: as autonomous revolutionary schools (as in Zapatista communities); *bachilleratos populares* (like those alongside the *piquetero* movements in Argentina); occupied schools and universities (as in Chile since 2006); student and teacher strikes (at the UNAM in 1999, Oaxaca in 2006, and across Mexico in 2013, for example); indigenous schools and universities; and alternative learning communities of all sorts (the Universidad de la Tierra in Oaxaca, Chiapas, and Puebla, hackerspaces, cooperative workplaces, etc.), to name just a few examples. While some closely resemble, or in fact operate within, private or public educational institutions, others completely abandon these models while opting to reinvent the form and meaning of education through the construction of non-hierarchical and collectively organized projects that directly challenge "the division of labor between the knower and the known"[48]and the division between knowing/doing and intellectual/manual labor. As I argued previously, the movements are asserting themselves as knowledge producers—as collective subjects engaged in the theorization of their own experience, the development of conceptual tools for their struggles, and an ongoing critical engagement with their own histories with an aim of better approaching their shared futures. And they do not do so in isolation: Indeed, the educational initiatives of the movements have been one of the most fruitful sites of translocal relations and exchanges. The dialogical connections that form between movements and across territories are continually figured as that which provides strength and creates resonance for the otherwise local, place-based struggles.[49]

Networking: *Encuentro*

Santiago de Chile, 2011. In early 2011, the members of the small, alternative press Editorial Quimantú, along with members of at least a half dozen other collectives and organizations, began organizing the first *Feria del Libro Popular Latinoamericano* [Popular Latin American Book Fair], a three-day book fair that would also function as an *encuentro* (an idea to which I will return) or gathering of social movements from across Chile and Latin America. Here I want to focus on the location of the fair because of its symbolism and significance for thinking about the meaning of *encuentro* as a political concept and cultural practice that characterizes the new movements in Latin America.

Calle República 517: This was the address given for the Feria del Libro Popular Latinoamericano. This and two neighboring street numbers, República 550 and 580, are hugely symbolic in the collective memory of the Chilean people: all three were torture and detention centers. While they have all undergone resignification—one has become a university, another an occupied social center—Pinochet's legacy continues to infect them more than two decades later. The university is tainted by the virus of neoliberal educational reforms, and the occupied social center was the target of ongoing police repression leading to its eviction in 2009. But on the occasion of the fair, the residents of the República neighborhood came out to express their joy at seeing their streets filled with families, young people, music, art, and books. One neighbor explained that this was the first public event on that street since the May Day celebration held there in 1973. In this sense, the fair brought to life the slogan printed on the posters: "*A la calle no hay quien la calle*" [No one can silence the street—*calle* is both street and the verb "to silence"]. Just as the coup d'etat transformed Chile from one moment to the next, Calle República had a silence suddenly imposed on it which lasted for decades. The Feria was embraced by the neighbors and even individuals and family members of those who had passed through 517, 550, or 580 during the dictatorship. This single block of downtown Santiago clearly demonstrated the relational nature of urban space, and the identities and subjects that are forged within it.[50] Over the days of the fair, this urban space acquired new political meaning, as it became a microcosm of the broader translocal networks that the movements work continually to forge and expand.

In conversations with the members of the Editorial Quimantú, they expressed to me that their desire with this fair was not only to create a broader book fair by co-organizing with other presses and organizations, but also, and perhaps most importantly, to connect more deeply with the experiences of other Latin Americans. One collective member described the importance of these connections in terms of combatting—and healing from—the isolation that has afflicted Chile for over three decades:

> among the Chileans, among the people there's a need to learn from about other Latin American experiences, because we are very closed off here. . . . The isolation is very intense. If the fair can happen like this, a multifaceted encounter of Latin American peoples, it will be really beautiful, really strong . . . and really healing for the Chilean people.[51]

To explain the apparent lack of movement and exchange between Chile and Argentina, people often playfully gesture to the mountain range that marks its eastern border, the

Cordillera de los Andes, describing it as a wall. But the way the Quimantús explain this isolation points to something much deeper than just geography. Even the language they use, *encierro*, can mean isolation or seclusion (which can be voluntary), but also confinement or imprisonment, and it is in these kinds of terms that they describe the effects of the dictatorship on Chilean society. In this sense, an important part of the process of healing is breaking that isolation, and in Chile, as in other parts of the Americas, *encuentro* is a key strategy for combatting fragmentation and isolation.

The new movements enact a praxis of *encuentro* [encounter]: a concept-practice that places greater emphasis on face-to-face engagement and dialogue over any program of action. *Encuentro* is contingent and fluid—most of all, it is alive. It is "an ethic of opening oneself to others."[52] A praxis of embodied, non-hierarchical politics, *encuentro* can take many forms: the EZLN's dialogical rhetorical strategies, the assembly organization model of the neighborhood groups in Argentina, or the transnational forums and gatherings where movements converge. But *encuentro* also occurs in ideas, in words, in stories, and in the objects and spaces through which they travel. As Boaventura de Sousa Santos and others have discussed, the twenty-first century ushered in new forms of transnational grassroots political engagement, premised less on programmatic forms of organization and more on facilitating dialogue, exchange, and collaboration, which is to say, *encuentro*.[53]

Conclusion

To speak of new social movements is to speak of the creation of new political cultures. There are myriad ways that the new movements challenge and reinvent the category of the "political," least of which being the assertion of the everyday, quotidian practices of ordinary people as the place of politics, and the related affirmation of subjective experience—collective and individual—as the basis for thinking and acting politically. The new movements, like those described in this chapter, reject the idea that politics is a limited domain of individualist and rationalist activity,[54] offering instead expressions of politics that grow from the collective theorization of embodied experience and a politicization of the everyday. The formation of non-hierarchical, non-exploitative social relations is the horizon towards which the new movements reach, and the logic of prefiguration is the means through which that is achieved. In this way, land, work, housing, education, culture, and communication all become the places of politics. And this happens through the variegated *encuentros* that take place at various scales, propelling societies—and the continent—into movement, through a generative unsettling of concepts, practices, and boundaries. Through ongoing dialogue and exchange, not just within movements but indeed between and across territories, collective imagination and organization of other ways of being and doing give way to new political cultures, with heterogeneous collective subjects constructing new possibilities for affirming "yes."

Notes

1 Frantz Fanon, *The Wretched of the Earth*, trans. Constance Farrington (New York, NY: Grove Press, 1963), 316.

2 Oaxacan writer and self-proclaimed "deprofessionalized intellectual" Gustavo Esteva uses the idea of "one no, many yeses" to describe the Zapatismo and the new movements associated with alterglobalization.

3 Raúl Zibechi, *Autonomías y emancipaciones: América Latina en movimiento* (Mexico: Bajo Tierra Ediciones, 2008).
4 Marcos, Subcomandante Insurgente, "The Fourth World War Has Begun," *Nepantla: Views From South*, Vol 2, No. 3 (2001): 559–572.
5 Aníbal Quijano, "colonialidad del poder, cultura y conocimiento en América Latina," *Dispositio/n*, Vol 24, No. 51 (1999): 137–148.
6 There are two sets of edited volumes which I draw on for my analysis of the new movements. The first set was produced in the north, at the close of the twentieth century: Sonia Alvarez and Arturo Escobar, eds., *The Making of Social Movements in Latin America* (Oxford: Westview Press, 1992); Sonia Alvarez, Evelina Dagnino and Arturo Escobar, eds., *Cultures of Politics, Politics of Culture* (Oxford: Westview Press, 1998). The second set was published from the south one decade into the new century: Raphael Hoetmer, ed., *Repensar la política desde América Latina* (Lima: PDTG, 2009); Mar Daza, Raphael Hoetmer and Virginia Vargas, eds., *Crisis y movimientos sociales en Nuestra América* (Lima: PDTG, 2012). Both are characterized by a recognition of the significance of the emergent political cultures and collective subjectivities of the new movements, though the more recent volumes directly question the geopolitics of knowledge in relation to the new movements: "*planteamos que una mirada desde América Latina . . . traiga a la luz raíces, razones, y dinámicas que no se pueden ver con facilidad desde Europa y Norteamérica, desde donde suelen mirar y realizarse las ciencias sociales hegemónicas.*" Mar Daza, Raphael Hoetmer and Virginia Vargas, eds., *Crisis y movimientos sociales en Nuestra América* (Lima: PDTG, 2012), 23.
7 Raul Zibechi, *Autonomías y emancipaciones: América Latina en movimiento* (Mexico: Bajo Tierra Ediciones, 2008).
8 All translations mine unless otherwise noted.
9 This essay draws on fieldwork conducted between 2009–2015, supported by the International Dissertation Research Fellowship from the SSRC; the Dissertation Grant from UC MEXUS; and the Advanced Graduate Research Fellowship from the Pacific Rim Research Program of the University of California. I would also like to acknowledge the collaboration of *compañerxs*, scholars, and activists in my various research sites, and their important contributions to the formation of the ideas presented here, which are the direct product of collective processes of theorization and imagination.
10 George Ciccariello-Maher, "The Fourth World War Started in Venezuela," *Counterpunch* (2007). Published electronically March 3, 2007. www.counterpunch.org/2007/03/03/the-fourth-world-war-started-in-venezuela/ accessed November 15, 2015.
11 Notes from Nowhere, *We Are Everywhere: The Irresistible Rise of the Global Anticapitalist Movement* (London: Verso, 2003).
12 As Aníbal Quijano (quoted by Escobar) has asserted: "Latin America was the original space of the emergence of modern/colonial capitalism; it marked its founding moment. Today it is, at last, the very center of world resistance against this pattern of power and of the production of alternatives to it." Arturo Escobar, "Latin America at a Crossroads," *Cultural Studies*, Vol 24, No. 1 (2010): 2.
13 Jóvenes en resistencia alternativa, ed., *Pensar las autonomías: Alternativas de emancipación al capital y el estado* (Mexico City: Bajo Tierra Ediciones, 2011).
14 Colectivo Situaciones, "Epílogo," In *Dispersar el poder: los movimientos como poderes antiestatales*, edited by Raúl Zibechi, 227 (La Paz: Textos Rebeldes, 2006).
15 Ana Cecilia Dinerstein, *The Politics of Autonomy: The Art of Organising Hope* (New York, NY: Palgrave MacMillan, 2014), 2.
16 Bolivian philosopher Luis Tapia refers to the "political subsoil" or underground, and calls this the terrain of the "wild politics" of the new movements. Luis Tapia, *Política Salvaje* (La Paz: Muela del Diablo, 2008): 8.
17 Marcelo Vieta, "The Stream of Self-Determination and Autogestión: Prefiguring Alternative Economic Realities," *Ephemera: Theory and Politics in Organization*, Vol 14, No. 4 (2014): 781–809.
18 *Autogestión* has been traced back to nineteenth century anarchist Pierre-Joseph Proudhon. Iain McKay, ed., *Property Is Theft! A Pierre-Joseph Proudhon Anthology* (Oakland, CA: AK Press, 2011); Marcelo Vieta, "The Stream of Self-Determination"; and Autogestión: Prefiguring Alternative Economic Realities," *Ephemera: Theory and Politics in Organization*, Vol 14, No. 4 (2014): 781–809.

19 Luis Tapia, *Política Salvaje* (La Paz: Muela del Diablo, 2008); Raul Zibechi, *Autonomías y emancipaciones: América Latina en movimiento* (Mexico: Bajo Tierra Ediciones, 2008).
20 Harry E. Vanden, "Social Movements, Hegemony, and New Forms of Resistance," In *Latin American Social Movements in the Twenty-First Century,* edited by Richard Stahler-Sholk, Harry Vanden and Glen David Kuecker, 41 (New York, NY: Rowman & Littlefield, 2008).
21 Salvador Schavelzon, *El nacimiento del estado plurinacional de Bolivia* (La Paz: Plural, 2012).
22 For Bolivia, see for example: Alejandro Almaraz, Omar Fernández, Roberto Fernández, Jorge Komadina, Pablo Mamani, Oscar Olivera, Pablo Regalsky, and Gustavo Soto, *La MAScarada Del Poder* (Cochabamba: Textos Rebeldes, 2012).
23 Oscar Olivera, "After the Water War," *ROAR,* Vol 0 (2015): 241–253.
24 Raúl Zibechi, *Dispersar el poder: los movimientos como poderes antiestatales* (La Paz: Textos Rebeldes, 2006), 88.
25 As Julieta Paredes affirms, "women are half of every *pueblo,*" In *Hilando Fino Desde El Feminismo Comunitario* (La Paz: Comunidad Mujeres Creando Comunidad, 2010), 12.
26 Raúl Zibechi, "Challenges and Difficulties of Urban Territories in Resistance," In *Rethinking Latin American Social Movements,* edited by Richard Stahler-Sholk, Harry Vanden and Marc Becker, 49–65 (New York, NY: Rowman & Littlefield, 2014).
27 Enrique Pineda, "Acapatzingo: Construyendo comunidad urbana," *Contrapunto,* Vol 3 (2013): 49–61.
28 Raúl Zibechi, "Challenges and Difficulties of Urban Territories in Resistance," In *Rethinking Latin American Social Movements,* edited by Richard Stahler-Sholk, Harry Vanden and Marc Becker, 49 (New York, NY: Rowman & Littlefield, 2014).
29 Lavaca Editora, *Sin Patrón: Fábricas y empresas recuperadas de la Argentina* (Buenos Aires: Lavaca Editora, 2007); Juan Pablo Hudson, *Acá no, acá no me manda nadie: Empresas recuperadas por obreros 2000–2010* (Buenos Aires: Tinta Limón, 2011).
30 Gustavo Esteva, "The Hour of Autonomy," *Latin American and Caribbean Ethnic Studies,* Vol 10, No. 1 (2015): 137.
31 Colectivo Situaciones, *19 y 20: Apuntes para el nuevo protagonismo social* (Buenos Aires: Ediciones de mano en mano, 2002).
32 Paula Abal Medina, Debora Gordán and Osvaldo Battistini, "Asambleas: cuando el barrio resignifica la política," In *La atmósfera incandescente. Escritos políticos sobre la Argentina movilizada,* edited by en Battistini, Osvaldo (Buenos Aires: Asociación Trabajo y Sociedad, 2002); Hernán Ouviña, "Las asambleas barriales y la construcción de lo 'público no estatal': la experiencia en la Ciudad Autónoma de Buenos Aires," In *La política en movimiento: Identidades y experiencias de organización en América Latina,* edited by Levy and Gainatelli, 65–108 (Buenos Aires: CLACSO, 2008).
33 *Encuentro,* which translates directly as encounter, refers to many forms of conversation, exchange, gathering, or networking, and it is a concept-practice which I identify with the new movements. The praxis of *encuentro* is one which places greater emphasis on face-to-face engagement and dialogue over an program of action.
34 Marilina Winik, "Ediciones Copyleft," In *Argentina Copyleft: La crisis del modelo de derecho de autor y las prácticas para democratizar la cultura,* edited by Beatriz Busaniche, 145 (Buenos Aires: Fundación Vía Libre, 2010).
35 Centro de Medios Libres, *Toma Los Medios, Sé Los Medios, Haz Los Medios* (Oaxaca: El Rebozo, 2013).
36 Guiomar Rovira, *Zapatistas sin fronteras* (Mexico: Ediciones Era, 2009).
37 The now well-rehearsed story of the Zapatistas begins not with their public appearance on January 1, 1994, but on November 17, 1983, when the Ejército Zapatista de Liberación Nacional (EZLN) was founded in the Lacandon Jungle of Chiapas, through a collaboration between members of indigenous communities and a small group of urban mestizos, including the person who would come to be known as Subcomandante Marcos. The basic objectives of the movement have remained constant over the past thirty years; there have, however, been several watershed moments that mark new directions in the movement's orientation, with a progressive shift further away from any engagement with the government, and greater emphasis on the construction of autonomy, in practice, on the ground and the formation of broad non-partisan networks of anticapitalist and autonomous struggles across Mexico and around the world. For a firsthand account of the first two decades of the Zapatismo, see Gloria Muñoz Ramírez, *20 y 10: El fuego y la palabra* (Mexico City: La Jornada Ediciones, 2003).

38 Centro de Medios Libres, *Toma Los Medios, Sé Los Medios, Haz Los Medios* (Oaxaca: El Rebozo, 2013), 9.
39 Casas-Cortés, Maria Isabel, Michal Osterweil and Dana E. Powell, "Blurring Boundaries: Recognizing Knowledge-Practices in the Study of Social Movements," *Anthropological Quarterly*, Vol 81, No. 1 (2008): 17–58; Juan Ricardo Aparicio and Mario Blaser, "The 'Lettered City' and the Insurrection of Subjugated Knowledges in Latin America," *Anthropological Quarterly*, Vol 81 (2008): 59–94.
40 Vicepresidencia del Estado Plurinacional de Bolivia, ed., *Pensando El Mundo Desde Bolivia* (La Paz: Vicepresidencia del Estado Plurinacional de Bolivia, 2010).
41 Dunia Mokrani Chávez, "Algunas reflexiones sobre un 'gobierno de los movimientos sociales' en Bolivia y sus posibles significados y sentidos," In *Crisis y movimientos sociales en Nuestra América*, edited by Mar Daza, Raphael Hoetmer and Virginia Vargas, 351–360 (Lima: PDTG, 2014).
42 Vicepresidencia del Estado Plurinacional de Bolivia, ed., *Debate Sobre El Cambio* (La Paz: Vicepresidencia del Estado Plurinacional de Bolivia, 2010).
43 Oscar Olivera, "After the Water War," *ROAR*, Vol 0 (2015): 245.
44 This is the term used by the Vice-presidency to refer to what the initiative aims to generate: "proper" knowledge, in the double sense of both "one's own" and "appropriate to."
45 Luis Tapia, *La producción del conocimiento local: Historia y política en la obra de René Zavaleta* (La Paz: Muela del Diablo, 2002).
46 See Raquel Gutiérrez Aguilar, *¡A desordenar! Por una historia abierta de la lucha social* (México: Casa Juan Pablos, 2006).
47 Interview, La Paz, 2011.
48 Sara C. Motta, "Reinventing Revolution, an 'Other' Politics in Practice and Theory," In *Rethinking Latin American Social Movements*, edited by Richard Stahler-Sholk, Harry Vanden and Marc Becker, 21–42 (New York, NY: Rowman & Littlefield, 2014).
49 Michal Osterweil, "Place-Based Globalism: Theorizing the Global Justice Movement," *Development*, Vol 48, No. 2 (2005): 23–28.
50 Doreen Massey, "Geographies of Responsibility," *Geografiska Annaler*, Vol 86, No. 1 (2004): 5–18; Doreen Massey, *World City* (Cambridge: Polity Press, 2007).
51 Interview, Santiago de Chile, 2011.
52 El Kilombo Intergaláctico, *Beyond Resistance: Everything: An Interview With Subcomandante Insurgente Marcos* (Durham, NC: PaperBoat Press 2007), 12.
53 Boaventura de Sousa Santos, *The Rise of the Global Left: The World Social Forums and Beyond* (New York, NY: Zed Books, 2006).
54 Sonia Alvarez, Evelina Dagnino and Arturo Escobar, eds., *Cultures of Politics, Politics of Culture* (Oxford: Westview Press, 1998).

14

THE MAPUCHE AND "*EL COMPAÑERO* ALLENDE"

A Legacy of Social Justice, Historical Contradictions, and Cultural Debates

Rosamel Millaman

The purpose of this chapter is to discuss the impact that the government of Salvador Allende had on the Mapuche people in order to distinguish between historical landmarks such as the Agrarian Reform Law, Indian Law 17.729, the relationship between the Mapuche and the political parties, and the so-called old social movements of the period. Secondly, I engage with the complex themes arising from this relationship as expressed in the action and thought of the Chilean left—where the prevalent conception was that the Mapuche were part of the rural poor and because of this were conceived of as "Mapuche *campesinos*" and not as an indigenous society and culture differentiated from the Chilean population. Even though, we must point out, Allende himself maintained the necessity of defining specific policies on the Mapuche beyond the public policies of the Agrarian Reform Law and Indian Law 17.729. In other words, Allende aspired to define specific policies to tackle political and cultural complexity. My goal is to reveal the legacy of the Unidad Popular [Popular Unity] government on the Mapuche in terms of its reach and influence, an unacknowledged legacy in Chile's current neoliberal context.

Preliminary Words

To understand the processes that occurred in the nineteenth century and Chile's political dynamics in the second half of the twentieth century, it is indispensable to consider some of the events and situations that explain the internal colonialism the Mapuche endured in the face of the Chilean state, leading to their population reduction, impoverishment, and oppression.[1]

Historically, Mapuche society was characterized as tribal with high levels of social equality and territorial and political decentralization that enabled the development of autonomous political and cultural practices in this region of the Southern Cone.[2] The anticolonial struggle was a characteristic trace of the Mapuche people who for many centuries were able to resist colonial pressures to submit and dominate them.[3] Conversely, this was not possible during Chile's nation-building period when the Mapuche suffered the loss of their political liberty and territorial autonomy when the military forces burst onto the scene, invading, controlling, and annexing Mapuche territory to the Chilean state. This was achieved by means of the military occupation of Wallmapu territory (Mapuche territory) between 1878–1883 and signified the control of their territory and the removal of Mapuche onto reservations in the case of Chile and of Argentina. It was also achieved by the imposition of a policy of servitude and deterritorialization, which resulted in a Mapuche diaspora in the interior of the Argentinian state.[4] In contrast to other countries in Latin America, here in the Southern Cone, two states came together seeking to eliminate the indigenous. In the case of Chile, the state established a policy of removal and resettlement with the creation of 3,078 reservations or indigenous communities, which corresponds to 475,194 hectares for 77,731 people, and their forced incorporation into the Chilean nation utilizing laws, a system of forced education, and policies of cultural assimilation.[5]

In the postcolonial period, the Mapuche population was settled in ancestral lands in the central-south area of Chile, a vast territory of approximately ten million hectares corresponding to what is called the *Región de la Frontera* (Frontier Region). In this zone, after the long military struggle against colonial Spanish forces, the Mapuche population had concentrated itself, stimulating its political and cultural development. Facing an extensive territory outside of state control, which was also characterized as rich in natural resources, primarily for agriculture and cattle raising, the Chilean state constitued Mapuche territory as its first objective for integration, appropriation, and control.[6]

The founders of the Chilean state established strategies of incursion and intervention into a territory that culturally, economically, and politically did not identify with the national identity promoted by the Chilean *criollos*. As a consequence, it was indispensable for the state to impose its control over the territory and to do so it recruited powerful groups composed of the descendants of the landed elite [*hacendados*], as well as military, political, and religious leaders.[7]

In the search to take *control* of Mapuche territory in the first half of the nineteenth century, proposals were diverse as were the stakeholders proposing them. One such proposal sought to create *pueblos de indios* [Indian towns], a kind of small town with military barracks, schools, and missions, that would aim to make of the Mapuche "people of reason and civilization." Others proposed to divide the land among the *criollos* and colonizers who were ready to exploit the lands in accordance with the emerging state's interest in progress and to remove Indians onto forced settlements under permanent control. Of the various plans to intrude upon Mapuche territory, it was this last one that was finally imposed.

Clearly, this military intrusion and invasion was buttressed by the Terra Nullius doctrine that prevailed in the European colonial projects around the world. In this period, the Chilean *criollos* used the doctrine to civilize and appropriate this supposedly unpopulated territory. This doctrine imposed a project to domesticate the territory and its inhabitants with the colonial model's civilizing project. Chileans were not exempt from this doctrine, but rather reinforced it under the discourse of *criollo* nationalism.

During the process to impose a strategy of domination and control over the territory, the groups in power were taking control of Mapuche lands in a relatively silent but tenable way. The political and economic groups in power considered a military invasion to be the best strategy to take total control and to establish mechanisms to appropriate Mapuche lands that were assumed to belong to no one, lands without use, and without inhabitants. From this perspective, a military strategy was designed that drew from the United States and its campaigns to invade and control indigenous peoples (nations) in North America. As previously mentioned, this plan was subtly articulated between the two nation-states under two campaigns for military occupation: "Desert Conquest" (1878–1884) in Argentina and the "Pacification of the Araucanía" (1880–1883) in Chile. In the Chilean case, military irruption was transformed into a strategy to take control of Mapuche territory and submit the population to a policy of forced removal with the imposition and creation of reservations. This strategy was aligned with a policy to auction Mapuche lands on behalf of the state; the beneficiaries of this policy were farmers, merchants, and military and religious personnel who were called to impose Chilean citizenship into the *Región de la Frontera*. The auction of lands was openly arbitrary and beneficiaries with scarce resources somehow managed to take possession of hundreds of hectares of Mapuche lands. The leaders of the emerging Chilean state, in line with social European thought (predominant for the time), considered that the occupation of Mapuche lands and the settlement of *criollos* in the region was not exploitation according to the principles of progress and agricultural development; for this reason, the government established a foreign policy to promote and recruit settlers from Europe. As a result of this policy, the Chilean government established European colonization in Mapuche territory, as immigrant families benefitted from hundreds of hectares of land, sold at below cost and with state support for its basic, productive activities. As a consequence, in a short period of time, the conditions were set for the rise of a landowning class of European origin that would be the bulwark in the construction and imposition of Chilean citizenship even into the present. The presence of Germans, Basques, Italians, French, and others constitute the economic, political, and ideological representation of this dominant class. Under this policy, foreign settlers received upwards from 400–500 hectares of land; *criollo* settlers, in contrast, received upwards of 40 hectares, and Mapuche received 3–4 hectares per person. The redistribution of Mapuche land was not only arbitrary, but also an example of clear-cut racism and Eurocentrism.

To make this colonization effective, the Chilean state simultaneously implemented an aggressive infrastructural policy, founding new cities, military forces, railway communication networks, roads, and bridges to connect the newly annexed territory and to facilitate productive activities of exchange and distribution.

As a result, the Mapuche population lost its free political status only to be converted into a society dominated, discriminated, exploited, and cut off from its ancestral natural resources to live. This policy of extermination implies that Mapuche families were denied their right to live on ancestral lands, and absurdly, the lands that the state granted them as legal, were now once again objects of theft and usurpation on the part of *criollo* and foreign settlers. In the face of this occupation, the Mapuche population began an imperceptible but continuous process of emigration outward toward the major urban centers of the country, or toward the Republic of Argentina.

Under these circumstances, Mapuche families looked for new survival strategies. The urban world was the only, immediate alternative refuge, and from this the flux of Mapuche migration would be a permanent dynamic and sustained over time. Because of a lack of technical skills and education, Mapuche migrants became wage-earners, incorporating themselves into the urban working class. As a result, the Mapuche population began an irreversible process of proletarianization and incorporation into the capitalist economy of production. In this way, there is a direct relationship between migration and the proletarianization of Mapuche.

Nonetheless, these processes were not only associated with indirect membership into the Chilean working class but also, because of their marginality, reproduced conditions of poverty and internal colonialism as reflected in the strategy to "silence the *indio*." Elsewhere I have labeled this, "a policy of petrifying the living Indian to resuscitate the dead Indian."[8] In this context, the Mapuche population would come to be progressively perceived as poor indigenous peasants and their reality was paradoxically negated and distorted by prejudices and racist notions such as "the lazy, drunk *indio.*" All of these strategies were instrumental in appropriating their lands.[9]

Given the processes of formation and expansion of the Chilean state and the Indian policies it imposed during the nineteenth and part of the twentieth century, processes of change and transformation in the 1970s transcend and constitute points of reflection, analysis, and evaluation. The critical period begins in the 1960s and culminates in Salvador Allende's government (1971–1973). During this period, an important segment of indigenous communities and their leadership experimented with a direct and fervent relationship with the socialist movements and political parties fundamentally aligned with the Chilean left. This experience was a result of a long process of demands and participation on the part of the social movements to enact structural changes in the Chilean state and society.

This alliance was made possible because of earlier historical events that served as a foundation for its development. We need to recognize that Mapuche communities were sympathetic toward Eduardo Frei Montalva's reformist government (1964–1970) and previously sympathetic toward the Unidad Popular (UP), a coalition of progressive groups and traditional leftists that sought to implement structural and political changes, and above all, social justice for marginalized groups such as Chilean workers and peasants.[10] During the right wing government of Jorge Alessandri Rodriguez (1958–1964), the social movement led by workers and peasants challenged the government's order to maintain the privileges of the landowning class and the conservative power of the Chilean society. In this arena, the social movement was able to call attention to workers' demands for social change, thus acquiring public presence and demanding changes in the old, structure of domination prevailing in the country. The peasant movement, considered by the traditional left as the historic ally of the workers movement, demanded agrarian reform in order to distribute land to the peasant farmers, to cultivate the land so as to meet the country's needs, and to modernize the agricultural system.[11] Vast sectors of the Chilean society recognized this need and sympathized with political and economic change in the country. For example, consensus grew between the Catholic church, political parties, and social movements to implement agrarian reform as a way to resolve peasants' needs and the needs of the state. On this level and under the banner of "Alliance for Progress," the United States was distant but locally active in its support for the project of Eduardo Frei Montalva's Christian-Democrat government; in practical terms, U.S. support signified the presence of functionaries, agents, and missionaries who offered nutritional assistance to farmers and Mapuche communities in the form of milk, cheese, oil, grain, and whole wheat flour to make bread. In the scope of demands for change, the Christian-Democrat government promoted "Revolution in Liberty," a campaign seeking reforms in the state's capitalist system and, in political matters, supporting the "chileanization" of copper, agrarian reform, and valorization of workers' and peasants' social movements, among other issues. To this end, the Frei government spurred settlers, peasants, and women's centers to organize under Catholic principles. In this case the Mapuches, who were seen as peasants, were organized by the government as small-scale farmers with the aim of incorporating them into the general system of political participation that the state promoted. Foreseeing the Left's influence on populist sectors, the Christian Democrat Party (PDC) organized workers and peasants to counteract the Left, creating federations such as the *Unión Obrera y Campesina* (UOC) [Union of Workers and Peasants] and designed mechanisms to influence and have political majority in the *Central Única de Trabajadores* (CUT) [Workers' Central Union]. Linked to the Indian question in substance, the government implemented a policy of agrarian reform, creating the Corporation of Agrarian Reform (1962) and the Institute of Agricultural Development (1962), institutions that would attend to the necessities of small-scale agricultural proprietors, of which the Mapuche were identified.

This drive for social mobilization grew even more because the Democratic Christians' Agrarian Reform (Law 16.640 enacted on July 17, 1967) did not fully account for the communities' demands for land and the bureaucratic process of this piece of legislation stopped these demands from materializing in favor of indigenous communities. Nonetheless, the Mapuche movement did not conceive of the project for agrarian reform as its primary objective. Mapuche leadership sought a legislative strategy that was more in line with indigenous reality, and in this sense, their movement sought to reform the prevailing Indian Law 14.511 to make it a legal source to achieve the historic demands of their communities.

A poll from 1966 measuring knowledge of the agrarian reform law in the Mapuche population indicates that an important segment of the Mapuche population perceived the law as:

> a way to acquire free land (45.4%). Another important percentage of the population associated the Agrarian Reform law as restitution (20.1%), and almost a third [of the population] had no knowledge of its contents, and finally, only the remaining 5.4% knew what the law contained.[12]

However, the subsequent processes taking place in Chile opened a field of politicization and ideological reformation, which was at first class-based land reform, eventually transforming into a Mapuche territorial demand.

In this context of political turmoil, many Mapuche leaders were trained to exercise effective leadership but also to access experiences of successes around the world. The government's intention was for the peasant and indigenous leaders to be key agents of social change through imitation and dissemination of ideas. It became evident that the intention was for the leaders, to consciously assume that the incorporation of new technologies would boost the development and progress promoting Frei's regime. The experiences of the capitalist world on agricultural issues, led by the United States, represented the model to follow and imitate.

Under this context, Mapuche communities first began to receive agricultural professionals such as agricultural technicians, agronomists, and veterinarians, among others. With these professionals in the field, the Mapuche world initiated a link with unknown spheres, the Western world and its technology being a factor of progress. Parallel to this, professionals promoted new production technologies such as the use of chemical and organic fertilizers, new seeds, and use of herbicides and insecticides to control pests in the fields.

For the first time, the Mapuche world was living through a revolution in their intercultural relationships and in their relationships to the *winka* world [European]. The level of success that many experienced in agriculture created a high level of expectation to incorporate these technologies, above all, in the imposition (implementation) of a monocrop system such as can be seen in the incentive to cultivate wheat and beets.

By the end of the Frei administration, political activism kept growing. On the one hand, the government's reforms did not offer practical or theoretical responses to the need for economic and social changes that the civil society and social movements demanded. On the other hand, external factors such as the liberation movements around the world, the Vietnam War, and the sympathy that the Cuban Revolution elicited, all coalesced to escalate the ideological debate and the need to stimulate a true social revolution.

Under these circumstances, Mapuche communities, leaders, and organizations redefined their political practices and repositioned their demands. This allowed key indigenous ways of thought to emerge that go beyond the social needs of the small-scale farmer and peasant. One key theme in this demand is the right to recuperate lands that have been stolen or usurped by farmers, as well as tax exemption on lands and state support to educate Mapuche students. As a result, during a decade of political participation, Mapuche communities reclaimed their particular demands as a pueblo, insisting on recognition of their social and cultural distinction from Chilean society. In this context, the Mapuche also initiated a profile of ancestral demands and opened up a space for the design and implementation of public policy in accordance with their cultural, social, and historic particularities.

Unidad Popular and the Pueblo Mapuche

On November 4 1970, Salvador Allende Gossens became president of Chile with the first socialist government supported by a coalition of political parties linked to the Unidad Popular. Allende had three previous attempts at the presidency (1952, 1958, and 1964); these attempts gave him experience in consolidating around his leadership and political through the support of diverse social, intellectual, and political sectors that went beyond the UP coalition.These diverse groups identified themselves as "Allendistas" and were especially important in Allende's nomination and election as the president of Chile.[13]

Nonetheless, despite the triumph of Allende's government, it did not manage to gain complete control of the political power in the Chilean state. For example, to ratify his election in 1970, Allende needed to gain the support of the Christian Democrats solidified in the agreement entitled "statue of guarantee" [Estatuto] in which the new president committed to respect the political constitution during his tenure. Paradoxically, even though Allende counted on support for his election from segments of the Chilean population and groups that were not on the left, he did not have absolute control of the parliament given that the opposition parties maintained their majority; he did not reform the political constitution, nor did he establish reforms for the armed forces or the judicial system. This situation immediately limited proceedings and governance generating spaces for political maneuvering from the opposition, which acquired a defiant role against the government and set up obstacles for the execution of the Unidad Popular's political program. Today, accounts from a variety of sources of the period demonstrate how the opposition and far-right groups took advantage of these conditions to effect various conspiracies, and assassinations of military and political authorities; the opposition and far-right groups looked to create a climate of ungovernability and with it create a climate of political crisis amenable to a military coup.

Despite the internal conflicts that developed in the UP and the external support for the opposition from multinational companies such as Internal Telephone and Telegraphy (ITT) and the international blockade set up by the United States, the Allende government received overwhelming support from the Chilean electorate in the final parliamentary elections of 1973. It gained 43 percent of the parliamentary vote, thus legitimizing the application of the Unidad Popular's Basic Program and the socialist project known as "the Chilean road to socialism."

During the UP's process of change, the Mapuche pueblo initiated a period of active political participation by means of their communities and organizations even though this participation was a part of the peasant movement that sought to transform the landowning system through agrarian reform that would be in line with the interests of the peasants and the Mapuche communities in particular.

In this context, when Allende became president on November 4, 1970, he opened up a space in which Mapuche demands could be integrated and assimilated into the political parties of the traditional left and the social movements of the period. When considering the Allende government from within the frame of capitalist rights and having as a reference the interests of the working class, this assimilation was contradicted by the social situation in the Frontier Region where the working class was not numerically significant and where the sectors most aligned with the workers were reflected by the Mapuche population that lived in conditions of internal colonialism, marginalization, and social and racial discrimination.[14]

As I signaled previously, Allende's arrival into government was influenced by the political experience of the Frei government that promulgated Agrarian Reform Law 16.640 on July 28, 1967, a law that generated a climate of acute Mapuche mobilization that translated into a practice of farm takeovers and demands for the "recuperation of usurped lands." In the provinces of Arauco, Malleco, and Cautín, the burst of indigenous mobilizing accelerated the so-called "class conflict" between the large landowning class and indigenous communities expressed in the emergence of paramilitary groups from the right and armed groups from the left. In the wake of violent encounters between Mapuche communities, defense groups for the landowning class, and police forces, the Allende government saw an obligation to apply repressive means of force against the Mapuche to prevent even larger conflicts between the radicalized groups.

A result of this process is that the Mapuche population assumed a clear identification with the Unidad Popular's program objective to do justice to the most dispossessed, and specifically to do justice to Mapuche communities and organizations. During this period, the Mapuche pueblo is transformed into a political actor that transcends the process of changes compelled by the Unidad Popular's government, but it is also transformed into a political force that defies the power of the landowning class and the capacity of the Allende government to assimilate Mapuche demands.

The symbolism of Mapuche's anticolonial freedom and resistance was taken up by the political parties of the traditional left that supported indigenous demands. In this context, Mapuche political mobilization was incentivized as much by the parties of the Unidad Popular as they were by other political forces outside the government, particularly, the *Movimiento de Izquiera Revolucionario* [Movement of the Revolutionary Left, henceforth MIR], and Maoist groups, among others.

The MIR, founded in the 1960s and led by young university intellectuals, resonated with and influenced Chile's popular sectors with its political abilities and its power to contrast the legacy of the Cuban Revolution, which had hitherto been seen as the most revolutionary model in Latin America. The MIR advanced a strategy under the Cuban Popular Power's slogan that translated into the search for and control of local, political power: "accelerate class conflict" and prepare the popular movement for military insurrection. With this proposition, the MIR created the *Movimiemtno Universitario de Izquierda* (MUI) in the universities; in the high school sector, it created the *Federación of Estudiantes Revolucionarios* (FER); with the people, the *Frente of Trabajadores Revolucionarios* (FTR), and in rural areas, the *Movimiento de Campesino Revolucionario* (MCR). It was this latter political organization that caught on in Mapuche communities because the MCR took up and incorporated the demand for the "recuperation of usurped lands" and the application of agrarian reform to benefit the Mapuche population.

When Allende entered the government in 1970, these parties were active and already maintained control over some sectors with the greatest level of conflict being with the landowning groups. According to Correa, Molina, and Yánez:

> between the years of 1960 and 1966, there were 36 registered cases of farm take-overs; in 1967 there were 9 occupations, and in 1968 there were 27. The number of occupations grew substantially over the next few years producing 148 occupations in 1969 and 192 in the period between September and December 1970.[15]

These Mapuche mobilizations were boosted by the traditional left but also, significantly, by the *Movimiento Campesino Revolucionario* (MCR), an organization controlled by the MIR.

In this context, the contradictions of interests deepened and Mapuche mobilizations for justice and violated rights translated into Allende's act in 1971, a to install a government in the Araucanía region headed by the Minister of Agriculture who would coordinate the administration of the UP government in matters of agricultural policy. In this way, the Mapuche population was transformed into the first focus of the new government's state policy as part of the social transformations Allende promised the Chilean people. This situation was influenced in large part by Mapuche discontent with the Agrarian Reform Law 16.640, introduced by Frei's Democrat-Christian government, as well as by the critical social and economic situation of indigenous peoples summed up by Allende himself when he affirmed: "And I want to say that the living conditions of these people are dramatically tragic. I want to tell you that it is a national obligation, it is an imperative of our conscience, not to forget what Chile owes to the people and the Araucanian race, the origin and base of who we are."[16]

These actions had national political significance. The mobilizations prompted by the political forces outside the UP generated a political crisis in the region between the Allende government that sought legal solutions to indigenous people's demands and the radicalized groups that demanded a more revolutionary and "non-reformist" political action outside the legal framework. These contradictory positions between the left were taken advantage of by the traditional right who contributed to creating a situation of ungovernability that threatened Allende's real political power.

As a result, the government, forced by political circumstances, and not wanting to use unlawful political pressure, sought strategies to persuade the Mapuche social movement through dialogue and negotiation in order to reduce the takeovers and legitimize the legal process of expropriation. Various organizations were faced with this dilemma and ambiguity because the UP government incorporated justice for the Mapuche people into its agenda but also incorporated the notion that these should be achieved through legal and constitutional means. Despite the political disjuncture, in 1971 "they achieved the restitution of 70,103.68 hectares for Mapuche communities."[17]

Between 1972 and 1973, Mapuche mobilization abated for two reasons: First, with the objective of protecting their agricultural interests, the landowning class of the region formed paramilitary groups to counteract the climate of expropriation and farm takeovers; "Homeland and Liberty" was one such group of openly fascist leanings and another "Commander Rolando Matus" was organized by the owners of these farmhouses. These groups were prepared militarily and maintained a stocked arsenal that they used in their terrorist campaigns against local Mapuche leaders and their organization, creating tension and political instability in the region.

This climate of tension was also a result of the divergent political positions in the interior of the UP government. On the other hand, the coalition of political parties that formed the UP began to evidence internal political divisions because some of the parties, such as the *Partido Socialista* (PS), the *Partido Radical* (PR), and the *Movimiento de Acción Popular Unitario* (MAPU), adopted more violent means to counter the right's actions and as means in the struggle against boycotts and sabotage, seeking to prepare a military force of the Chilean left. Under these conditions, the UP's political priorities were reoriented to defend Allende's Basic Program, the internal unity of the coalition, and the institutional respect that Allende had promised. In this context, Mapuche mobilizations were repressed by the government itself and by the groups in power that demanded the full extent of the law be applied to the Mapuche and peasant groups that demanded an acceleration of the agrarian reform process and demanded expropriation that went beyond what was established by the Agrarian Reform Law. Allende had demanded of the Mapuche "do not continue with the appropriation of farms, do not run over fences, because these actions enable the exploitation and intentional campaign being waged to argue that this government has been overtaken."[18] This situation turned critical when the demand for the recuperation of usurped lands, a fundamental indigenous demand, was taken up by the UP and materialized in the government in 1970 when it created the *Corporación de Desarrollo Indígena* (CDI) and the *Comisión de Restitución de Tierras Usurpadas.* These principle demands emanated from the First Indigenous Congress, developed in the locality of Ercilla and the Second Mapuche National Congress in Temuco in 1970, which were convened and organized by Mapuche organizations with Allende in attendance. The resolutions and demands that emerged from these two congresses were constituted as the source and base for the creation of the new Indian Law 17.729 in 1972.

From all this experience, we can identify the implications of Mapuche participation in the UP government. One implication of this political process is that for the first time in their history with the Chilean state, Mapuches participated in the creation of Indian Law 17.729, even though it suffered substantial modification for its approval on September 26 1972. In this respect, Allende recognized the historical demands and the particular nature of their customs, he ventured to say: "we consider that the problems of the Araucanos and Mapuche cannot only be solved through Agrarian Reform; there is a racial and cultural problem . . . that will require years to resolve."[19]

The new Indian legislation, Indian Law 17.729, was characterized by its objective to do social and historical justice to the Mapuche pueblo; above all, to legally restore lands that had been usurped by agrarian, rancher, and latifundia groups.

A second implication is that in this period the Mapuche people come to know closely the aspirations and political projects of the social movements and political parties from the center and the traditional left. This experience is reflected in the fact that the Mapuches began to fight from within these parties of the Chilean center and left; in this sense, their struggle became integrated into the popular government's political process. The primary implication was that the Mapuche pueblo transformed into a relevant political actor and a visible social movement in the social and political struggles of the 1970s. From this point on, the Mapuche pueblo acquired key political relevance in the region's processes of change and transformation. The Mapuche pueblo is no longer conceptualized as a static society anchored to the past, but as a society with political and cultural projects of its own and a perspective distinct from the country. A third implication in the Mapuche pueblo's experience with the UP, is that Allende was the first president of Chile to institutionalize the state's Indian policy through Agrarian Reform Law and Indian Law 17.729, two pieces of legislation that materialized indigenous demands and converted them into public policies underpinned by a moral principle of respect and dignity for the Mapuche pueblo. The fact is that the Agrarian Reform Law was oriented toward Chilean peasants and thus toward the Mapuche pueblo to accelerate is implementation and open spaces so that their direct and indirect ancestral demands were incorporated into the law. It is significant that the Mapuche pueblo was a central actor in the demand for agrarian reform and has as its legacy social justice for the rural poor.

A fourth important implication is the public representation of an indigenous pueblo that maintained its sense of identity. The use of their language, Mapudungun, in public spaces acquired political connotations and a dimension of Mapuche culture as an expression of Mapuche power to bring communities, families, and the Mapuche pueblo together. This experience had been seen prior to the 60s but it was oriented toward political personalities and parties without a sense of radical action. The historical and cultural legacy of the traditional discourse is transformed into the most apt political arena to reclaim rights to resources and rights to culture hitherto negated by the Chilean state. Allende's visit in 1972 alone is transformed into a symbolic space of political practice because the visit was a clear expression of intercultural syncretism. When on the stage, an interaction in Mapuche and Spanish, traditional dress, and the national dance of the Chilean cueca was made visible.

A fifth implication is constituted by the principle that rights (particularly lands and cultural rights) that had been taken away by the Chilean state could be restored. The communities could show how the maintenance and demand for rights can be achieved when communities organize under their own will and even through the influence of the Chilean social movements, as with the union movements and peasant federations. The Mapuche world learned that the law is a result of action and not an absolute mechanism outside their control; the law could be created and reformed through citizens' demands.

Finally, because the struggles were identified in each social and territorial unity, the Indian reservations acquired a new political significance of existence, identity, and cultural resistance. It is during this period that the reservation as a social, economic, and cultural unity is transformed into a supreme referent of the life and cultural space where the practice of Mapuche identity is nurtured. During the period, the Merced Titles, instruments of the colonial juridical system granted by the Chilean state to recognize and guarantee indigenous ownership of the land, are revitalized. The value of these titles would be demonstrated in the Mapuche pueblo's resistance to the neoliberal policy imposed by the Pinochet dictatorship that practically divided the totality of the indigenous reservation system through force and repression.

In conclusion, we can maintain that the Mapuche people's struggle during Allende's government was part of an historic anticolonial struggle by an egalitarian society with pre-capitalist origins, an accumulated history, and a relationship of domination by the Chilean state. The leading role the Mapuche struggle acquired during the decade of the 1970s was that of a declaration of their existence and defiance of the colonial model and its imposition by the Chilean state that did not have the capacity to understand or interpret the Mapuche population in its real magnitude. What continues to resonate is the Mapuche leadership and power to reverse and resist policies and their forms of treatment and their implementation. Just as it was then with the UP, it is today with the Nueva Mayoría government where the Mapuche pueblo resists the neoliberal economic model that is imposed in the country and region.

Notes

1 Wilson Cantoni, "Chile: Relations between the Mapuche and Chilean National Society," In *Race and Class in Postcolonial Society*, edited by Unesco, 220–338 (Paris: Unesco, 1977).

2 Alejandro Lipschutz, "El problema de la tribu minoritaria en el marco de la nación y en el movimiento indigenista Latinoamericano," *América Indígena*, Vol 28 (1968): 45–53.

3 José Manuel Zavala, *Los Mapuches del Siglo XVIII: Dinámica interétnica y estrategias de resistencia* (Pasrral: Editorial Universidad Bolivariana, 2008).

4 Walter Mario Delrio, *Memorias de Expropiación: Sometimiento e incorporación indígena en la Patagonia 1872–1943* (Buenos Aires: Editorial Universidad Nacional de Quilmes, 2005); Enrique Hugo Mases, *El Estado y la Cuestión Indígena. El destino final de los indios sometidos en el sur del territorio (1878–1910)* (Buenos Aires: Editorial Prometeo Libros/Entrepasados, 2002).

5 David Maybury-Lewis, "Becoming Indian in Lowland South America," In *Nation-States and the Indians in Latin America*, edited by Urban Greg and Joel Sherzer, 207–235 (Austin, TX: University of Texas Press, 1991).

6 José Bengoa, *Historia del Pueblo Mapuche. Siglo XIX y XX* (Santiago, Chile: LOM Ediciones, 2000).

7 Ibid.

8 Rosamel Millaman, "¿Racismo Encubierto? El estado chileno y el pueblo mapuche," Website Mapuche International. www.mapuche-nation.org/expanol/html/articulos/art-12.htm accessed October 12, 2002.

9 Stephen E. Lewis, "Myth and the History of Chile's Araucanians," *Radical History Review*, Vol 58 (1994): 112–141; Milan Stuchlik, "Las políticas indígenas en Chile y la imagen de los Mapuches," *Revista Cultura, Hombre, Sociedad*, Vol 2 (1985): 159–194.

10 Luis Corvalán, *El gobierno de Salvador Allende* (Santiago, Chile: LOM Ediciones. 2003).

11 Bernardo Berdichewsky, "Etnicidad y clase social en los Mapuches," *Revista Araucaria*, Vol 9 (1980): 65–86.

12 Martin Correa, Nancy Yañez and Raul Molina, *La Reforma Agraria y las tierras mapuches* (Santiago, Chile: LOM Ediciones, 2005).

13 Alejandro Saavedra, *La Cuestión Mapuche* (Santiago, Chile: ICIRA), 1971.

14 Wilson Cantoni, "Chile: Relations Between the Mapuche and Chilean National Society," In *Race and Class in Postcolonial Society*, edited by Unesco, 220–338 (Paris: Unesco, 1977).

15 Martin Correa, Nancy Yañez and Raul Molina, *La Reforma Agraria y las tierras mapuches* (Santiago, Chile: LOM Ediciones, 2005), 135.

16 Pedro Cayuqueo, "Tiempos de esperanzas: Salvador Allende y el Pueblo Mapuche," Archivo Rebelión Online. www.rebelion.org/noticias accessed November 12, 2015.

17 Martín Correa Cabrera, *La Reforma Agraria y el Golpe Militar en el Territorio Mapuche* (Pacarina del Sur: Revista de Pensmiento Crítico Latinoamericano, September 23, 2013). http://www.pacarinadelsur.com/dossier-9/810-la-reforma-agraria-y-el-golpe-militar-en-el-territorio-mapuche

18 Pedro Cayuqueo. "Tiempos de esperanzas: Salvador Allende y el Pueblo Mapuche" (2008). http://www.rebelion.org/noticias/2008/7/69679.pdf accessed December 11, 2015.

19 Never published Saul Landau interview of Salvador Allende, "Entrevista inédita a Salvador Allende." http://www.sinpermiso.info/textos/entrevista-indita-a-salvador-allende accessed December 11, 2015

15

CATHOLIC SOCIAL MOVEMENTS FACE MODERNITY

Miranda Lida

Introduction

Since the French Revolution, and particularly during and after the Industrial Revolution, it became a commonplace notion to associate the Catholic Church with counterrevolution and traditionalism, through its contacts with reactionary aristocracies. Furthermore, in Latin America, the Church was strongly attached to colonial traditions and social structures, and thus proved in general quite reluctant to accept the changes brought about by independence from France (1804), Spain (1810–1824), and Portugal (1822) as well as the liberal trends originating in Europe. The nineteenth century progressive thinkers, particularly those inclined to liberalism and socialism, had good reasons to mistrust the Catholic Church, and occasionally there was open confrontation with Catholic preachers and authors as if they were irreconcilable enemies. Catholic authors and their teachings tended to remain confined to Church circles and somewhat discredited. The Church was often accused of being a stronghold of the *Ancient Régime*, monarchical and reactionary, as well as an obstinate bulwark against modernization. Moreover, it remained decidedly opposed to the efforts to extend full political rights to the "populace," thus hindering the democratization process and, in particular, rejecting the demands of the nascent working classes for social justice and laws designed to improve the prevailing labor conditions.

Throughout Latin America, the nations that attained political independence during the nineteenth century, national independences soon defied the political and economic privileges generally enjoyed by the Catholic Church as an inheritance from colonial times. In different degrees, new nation-states, most of them young republics, proceeded to change the old rules across the board: Some countries established a separation between religion and the state and proceeded to take over the extensive landed properties owned by religious orders and bishoprics; while other nations chose to secularize education and even marriage, creating civil service offices, abolishing the customary legal and juridical privileges and benefits of clergy, and so on. Those changes transformed the traditional catholic identity of Latin American people; nevertheless, they haven't eroded it substantially, as we shall see.

All along the nineteenth century, Catholicism experienced deep changes in Latin America.[1] The achievement of independence from the European metropolis pushed the Church authorities in the new Latin American nation to seek new horizons by establishing direct relations with the Holy See and no longer through the channels of their respective metropolitan Church hierarchies and crowns. Moreover, with the arrival in the Americas of new missionaries from Europe, particularly in the second half of the nineteenth century, a period of intensive transatlantic mass migrations, a significant renewal of the rank and file of the Church was observed. Considerably less powerful in political and economic terms than in colonial times, the Catholic Churches in Latin America adopted a thoroughly renovated agenda, quite adapted to their new nations and independent societies striving to follow the path of modernization. Thus, a widespread flourishing of Catholic journals could be observed as a means of influencing public opinion, as well as encouraging new social movements most appropriate to deal with changing societies challenged by social and political democratization.[2] Even in strongly stratified societies, such as those in the Pacific Andean nations, the Catholic elites had to face the social question, not without significant unease.

The present chapter, then, focuses on the growth, progress and consequent transformations experienced by social Catholic movements and identities since the appearance of the *Rerum Novarum* encyclical of 1891 until the second half of the twentieth century, marked by the Second Vatican Council and its impact on all aspects of Latin American Catholicism. Since the nineteenth century, the pressures of secularization had not brought about a complete regression of the Catholic faith; on the contrary, they provided an opportunity for its reshaping and resignification in order to assimilate and offer some measure of satisfaction to the increasing requirements of modernization, despite the heavy weight of traditional opposition.[3]

Under the shadow of *Rerum Novarum*

Rerum Novarum was the most mature response of the Church to the social consequences of the Industrial Revolution. With this encyclical, Leon XIII urged Catholics to recognize the claim of social justice and labor legislation, denouncing the abuses of the capitalist system, admitting the need for state intervention in order to mediate between capital and labor, and organizing its own Catholic associations of workers to counteract socialism and anarchism. These new labor-based Catholic organizations were in open contrast to traditional brotherhoods and pious associations, most of them inherited from colonial times, and suddenly spread fear among employers and property owners, especially in the countryside, where paternalism was hard to eradicate. The ultimate goal was to develop a fresh look for Latin American catholic identity, with a flexible approach face to modernity. However, given the moderate outlook of this encyclical, it became difficult to push back nineteenth century Catholic intransigency. In such a way, the innovations on the Catholic identity were half-hearted.

Moreover, the impact of *Rerum Novarum* was quite uneven throughout Latin America. The most traditional rural areas—*e.g.*, Bolivia, Chile, Colombia, Ecuador, El Salvador, Peru—showed strong resistance to accepting the establishment of any kind of labor association, even those with close ties to the Church and therefore extremely moderate. Other countries proved to be more tolerant where even sectors of the upper classes, joined in their consent because they would rather have catholic worker unions than socialist ones as a sort of social safety valve.

Of course, the reception in each country also depended upon the specific conditions of the local clergy. Wherever there were priests who had studied in Europe, it was easier to find more concern with social conditions: When they returned to their native countries, they were more likely to embrace many of the notions of social Catholicism. Since the foundation in Rome of the *Pontifical Pious Latin American College* (1857), Latin American countries had the opportunity to send to Rome their best theology students.[4] As time went by, most of them attained prominent positions in their respective national Churches. We can name, for instance, the Chilean bishop Rafael Edward Salas, the Mexican Jesuit Alfredo Méndez Medina, the Argentine bishop Miguel De Andrea, among many others. Mexico, Brazil, Chile, and Argentina stand out as the Latin American nations with the largest numbers of priests having studied in Europe since the last decades of the nineteenth century. It was a clear reflection of the growingly tight links between Latin American churches, and particularly those of the four countries just mentioned, forged with the Holy See during that period. In 1899, a Latin American Council meeting in Rome contributed to strengthen even more those ties with the papacy.[5] At the same time, the frequent contact of Latin American clergymen with Rome helped to open for them the doors to get in touch with several European Catholic movements and debates, especially in Belgium, cradle of the influential Joseph Cardijn, and in Germany, through the influence of bishop Wilhelm Ketteler, who inspired the Christian *Volksverein*, a leading case in this regard. Both of them had developed different variations and nuances in social Catholicism and proved to be quite influential. Hence, it may be argued that social Catholicism evolved in Latin America not only as the result of a "Romanization" promoted by the Holy See but also, and significantly, as a reflection of the growing pressure towards Europeanization, typical of the years preceding the First World War.

Another vector of this process in Latin American Catholicism was the influx of immigration.[6] Not only should we point out the arrival of many religious congregations, especially those showing an acute social sensibility, derived from the changes brought about in Europe by the Industrial Revolution: such is the case, among others, of the *Salesianos de Don Bosco*, of the *Vicentinos* [Congregation of the Mission], and the *Palotinos*, all of them engaged in missionary expansion, and imbued as well with social Catholicism. These orders and congregations were quite active in Latin America since the last decades of the nineteenth century. They not only attracted a relatively significant number of European clergy (whose impact varied from country to country), but also new devotions, mostly French and Italian—no longer predominantly from Spain and Portugal—as the Sacred Heart of Jesus; there also emerged different types of associations based on mutualism, as well as on renovated notions of piety, social commitment, and action.[7] For example, in Uruguay, Italian Salesians were the first to encourage the creation of Catholic Circles of Workers, and German *Redentoristas* did the same in Argentina.

In the context of a strong movement towards internationalization of Latin American Catholicism, it is not at all surprising that *Rerum Novarum* arrived almost immediately in those countries with closer European ties, such as Argentina, Brazil, Chile, Mexico, and Uruguay. There soon arose heated debates about the strategies for social Catholic action which literally replicated the foreign models from Italy, France, Germany, Belgium, or Spain. Sooner rather than later, each of these new organizations prepared its periodical congresses and conferences: thus, Chile established its first *Asociación Católica de Trabajadores* [Catholic Association of Workers] in 1878; in Argentina, the *Federación de Círculos de Obreros* [Federation of Worker Circles] was founded in 1892; and Mexico created in 1908 its *Unión de Obreros Católicos* [Catholic Workers Union]. Most of them promoted mutual societies and workers' cooperatives dealing with health care, labor security, and job training issues, but they were also vigilantly of labor unions and class-conscious associations, tending instead to advocate social harmony as opposed to class struggle. In fact, Catholic workers' associations were often accused by socialist and anarchists of being strongly conservative, since most of them enjoyed the sponsorship of political and social elites.[8] The Catholic approach was rather to maintain a strong paternalistic tutelage. These traits soon caused Catholic workers' unions to be denounced as so-called "white" organizations, at once confronted by "red" socialists and communists for being just employer-manipulated puppets. When class identity intermingled with religious one, there only aroused conflicts.

The impact of the First World War on the Western Hemisphere accelerated economic and social transformations and contributed to the development of both anti-imperialist and Latin American consciousness. The international markets collapsed during the war years and the Latin American countries increased their trade deficits. Catholicism found itself deeply challenged by social unrest and general strikes, in both cases under the lingering threat of radicalization inspired in the success of the Russian Revolution. Despite the traditional patronage over Catholic workers associations, there was an almost complete replacement of the late nineteenth century leaders of social Catholicism by a new generation of young and mostly middle class Catholics. During the first decades of the twentieth century, these laymen were somewhat less homogeneous—more numerous and variegated in their background, interests, and activities—in pace with the growing massification of society. The Catholic worker associations were soon run by the workers themselves, and the elites had to decline their traditional sponsorship roles. In fact, there emerged new kinds of associations, whose rank and file was mostly made up of young people from both the middle class and the working classes. The *Juventud Obrera Católica* (JOC) [Young Christian Workers], founded by Joseph Cardijn in 1924, were established in many Latin American countries, with strong links both to the *Acción Católica* (AC) [Catholic Action] movements and to the *Círculos Católicos de Obreros* [Catholic Workers Circles], as well as to the intellectuals and leaders active in these organizations. As a direct consequence of these developments, it can be observed that Catholicism became more compact in a way, even ideologically (anti-communism, anti-liberalism and corporatism were its distinctive marks), in order to better counter the increasingly active leftist movements.

Throughout those years, and particularly since the 1930s, the Church did not hesitate to support military dictators across Latin America. Catholic organizations also provided great numbers of participants joining and leading mass demonstrations in the streets of national capitals and other big cities. In the 1930s, Catholic movements felt strengthened throughout most of Latin America. Even in Mexico, the end of the fiercely fought *Cristero* War in 1929 paved the way for a kind of truce (usually called a *modus vivendi*) between Church and state, and also with Rome. Catholic Action was soon established in Mexico and social Catholicism found itself relivened thanks to the spread of social activities inspired by *Rerum Novarum*, which provided quite adequate tools to deal with the problems posed by the emerging and growing working class as well as by the increasingly consolidated middle class. Although often "integrist" and ultra-conservative in nature, the so-called Christian approach to "the social question" soon became a convoking strategy for Catholics in an era of industrialization, urbanization, and modernization, which gained momentum in Mexico with Lázaro Cárdenas as president (1934–1940).[9] The Catholic identity preserved its intransigent and antimodern core, but it remained surrounded by an appealing outer shell, as witnessed by mass demonstrations and street propaganda, accompanied by a inclusive tone, open to different social strata. In Brazil, for instance, Catholic Circles of Workers were established in the 1930s.[10] They shared the notions of corporatism and conservatism, and thus perfectly matched the ideas and policies advanced by Getulio Vargas' *Estado Novo* regime (1935–1944). But as everywhere else, Brazilian Catholic Circles promoted social legislation, cultural and mutual services and offered a complete agenda for workers, attempting to preserve them from communist leanings.

Chile and Uruguay also faced similar changes, but in these two nations Catholicism faced a more hostile context. At the beginning of the twentieth century the Chilean

Church was strongly attached to the higher classes. Nevertheless, in the 1930s, both the working class and the middle class began to play a decisive role in society and politics, thus shifting the balance when the Popular Front was launched in 1936. Catholicism reacted strongly but had to pay the high price of fracture when it gave birth to a branch under the name of *Liga Social*, that admitted the organization of workers in labor unions and called for "social justice" and advances in labor legislation (family wages and protection for women and children workers). The Catholic movement split up, and it was hard to bring back together Catholic workers and Catholic associations of the higher classes.[11] Uruguay was another country where Catholicism coped with harsh conditions because Church and state by constitutional provisions were strictly separate. But even there, a country with established lay tradition, Catholic Action developed strongly during the 1930s, and the Young Christian Workers was founded in 1938.[12]

In the case of Argentina, the course of events proved to be somewhat more complicated: just like in other countries, the Church established Young Christian Workers associations during the 1930s and 1940s. These groups coexisted and even clashed with nineteenth century Circles of Workers, traditionally attached to the higher classes and therefore strongly paternalistic.[13] It was hard for workers emerging from the lower social strata to fill higher leadership positions in such traditional institutions, because Catholic authorities were reluctant to open them to blue-collar workers. Thus, most high positions were held by members of the elites and rarely admitted even white-collar workers. Meanwhile, Catholic Action movements affiliated mostly middle class members, given that the middle strata was already quite numerous in Argentina.

We can thus conclude that throughout Latin America, there were some common trends. In the first place, Latin American Catholicism adopted European answers and attitudes to confront nineteenth and twentieth century social challenges and transformations. From the appearance of *Rerum Novarum* to the teachings of Joseph Cardijn and Pius XI, Latin American countries imported—mostly without significant local adaptations—European ideas and proposals to deal with social unrest. These answers were directly inspired in the European experience after the Industrial Revolution, not always well befitted to the social conditions in the Americas, because many of these nations preserved their traditional, chiefly rural, social structures and also because industrialization delayed its arrival until the early twentieth century—and even later in some countries.

Second, although Catholic thinkers were mostly reluctant to accept the concepts of class society and their alleged consequences, and they conceived society as a mainly harmonic whole, the implications of social class differences became a strong line of cleavage within Latin American Catholicism. Traditionally attached to the upper classes, Latin American Catholic churches did not encourage worker unions, preferring to promote mutual societies and cooperatives in which workers were not openly invited to deliberate and take collective decisions, because deep-rooted paternalism often prevailed. Catholic Workers Circles were mostly hierarchical and could hardly be described as horizontal institutions. There was still a long road ahead before a turn to openness on this feature could be observed. In fact, all during the twentieth century, Catholic identity fractured unavoidably according to social class cleavages.

The Turn of the Postwar and the 1960s

With the end of the Second World War and the outbreak of the Cold War, the papacy felt the pressure to accept Western democracy, as shown by Pope Pius XII in his famous

1944 radio address, and in many other documents from that time onwards. The postwar reconstruction of Europe moved the Catholic Church to be more sensitive to social demands in matters of wealth distribution, housing, education and labor conditions and also paved the way to a broader acceptance of the so-called Welfare State social reforms. However, the new emergent and politically successful Christian Democratic parties in many Western European countries remained staunchly anti-socialist and anti-communist, even when they tried to reconcile social reforms with political democracy and pluralism.

Since the early 1950s, it was not uncommon to hear about priests who enrolled themselves as industrial workers, wearing blue overalls and moving to live in industrial quarters and suburbs while carrying on intense pastoral activities. Echoes of these experiences reached Latin America almost immediately, not without arousing deep discomfort and mistrust, especially among the Catholic hierarchies. This meant a heavy turn: It harmed middle class Catholic and bourgeois identity of Latin American urban societies. And yet bishops were still too conservative, both ideologically and even in their manners, because they were used to behaving as real princes of the Church, in almost baroque surroundings, with showy pomp and ceremony. And yet the incessant progress of industrialization multiplied conflicts and social unrest, since Latin American countries, still mostly rural, were not prepared to satisfy social demands of housing, welfare and services. Moreover, in rural areas there were unattended requests for elementary education and rural promotion, but priests usually turned a blind eye on these issues. In the postwar years, Latin American Christian Democrats endorsed many of these demands, but at the same time they found themselves hampered by notoriously weak democratic institutions that, more often than not, gave way to extremely reactionary military dictatorships. And thus, the social agenda lagged far behind.[14] To a certain extent such developments are illustrated by the first meeting in 1955 of the *Conferencia Episcopal de América Latina* (CELAM) [General Conference of the Latin American Episcopal Council], devoted to discussing several problems of ecclesiastical administration and discipline but only just tepidly mentioning the "social problems" of the continent, for which the convening bishops suggested a "fair solution" between capital and labor.[15] In such a context, Catholic identity couldn't show itself as unitary, homogeneous; meanwhile, Latin American societies became frankly polarized, either because of social inequalities or for political reasons. Latin American Catholic identities, already pluralist, became permeable to Third World values and subjectivities. In such a context, anti-imperialist and anti-bourgeois sensibility became consistent with Latin American Catholic identity.

Moreover, the 1960s brought to most Latin American countries far-reaching social and cultural changes which also left their mark on the Catholic Church and the Catholic populations. In 1959, the call for a new Vatican Council by Pope John XXIII did not take many Catholics by surprise because they were well aware of the variety of complex new relations and new social and political patterns emerging throughout the entire planet, due to the large amount of changes which had occurred since the end of the Second World War. In fact, the Second Vatican Council was perceived as radical and innovative in many aspects—liturgy, discipline, and relations with other religions and, in particular, with different traditions, social values, ethnic identities, and ideologies. Thus, Catholicism was becoming more responsive and adaptive to a new political geography where the Third World was introducing a deep across-the-board transformation in international affairs. Despite the manifold resistances aroused, expressed by the most conservative cardinals and bishops, who were soon described as "pre-conciliar," the Second

Vatican Council was definitely an effort to bring about a measure of *aggiornamento* to a religion usually believed to be adverse to modernity.[16]

In such a context, Latin American Catholicism found an opportunity to play an active role, in accordance to the social transformations of the 1960s. The CELAM conferences thus soon became an obligatory reference not only for Catholicism, but also for other communities subject to inequality, military regimes, and savage repression. This explains why the 1968 Medellin document, drawn up by the second CELAM conference, did not go unnoticed. It not only attracted attention from post-conciliar Catholics imbued in the values of the Second Vatican Council, but it also made a strong impact on Latin American societies as a whole, and particularly on younger generations. Not so long before, Catholic hierarchies in general were seen as almost uniformly conservative and even reactionary, but after the 1960s, some Latin American bishops showed themselves ready to openly engage in all kinds of social and political debates. Catholics, then, became more aware that bishops and clergymen were not uniformly homogeneous nor automatically unanimous. Catholic identities became elusive. The CELAM conferences of the 1960s and 1970s deliberated openly on controversial subjects such as political violence, unattended social justice demands, women's roles in the communities, and even discussed the need for a "change of structures" in the social and political realms. Controversially, the 1968 CELAM document was often read as an invitation for Catholics to enroll in political and revolutionary activism, and sometimes even as inducing them to join in guerrilla activities.

In fact, significant fractions of the clergy and laity in the Americas soon involved themselves in politics and radicalized their position and discourse. Thus, Catholic identities got strongly involved in politics and fractured themselves. The so-called Theology of Liberation was a main nurturing element of revolutionary movements but, meanwhile, Catholic faith became invoked by military power as well, in order legitimate dictatorships. In 1966, the killing of priest Camilo Torres—enrolled in the Colombian National Liberation Army—was the catalyst for the emergence of a "New Catholic Left" (as it was often termed in the media) in many Latin American countries. Seen as a kind of martyr, Torres soon became a powerful icon for politicized Catholic movements throughout the late 1960s and the 1970s. Many Colombian priests joined "Golconda," a group formed in 1968 to strengthen and develop some of the CELAM propositions. Golconda openly predicated social and political involvement for Catholics, commitment to revolution against imperialism, and struggle against all forms of human exploitation. Similarly, in Mexico, Peru, Brazil, and Argentina we can observe the emergence of related or comparable groups and movements. Archbishop Hélder Câmara, in impoverished northeastern Brazil, promoted the signature of a document directly inspired in the encyclical *Populorum Progressio* by Pope Paul VI, focused on social and political conditions prevailing in underdeveloped countries. Thus, the *Message from 18 Bishops of the Third World*, signed by prelates from Latin America, Africa, and Asia, became a kind of manifesto that inspired further movements throughout Third World Catholicism.[17]

We should thus mention, for example, in Argentina, the Movement of Third World Priests, an extended network that soon became close to the *Montoneros* guerrillas in the 1970s and even confronted with ecclesiastical hierarchies; the *ONIS* group in Peru, strongly engaged in agrarian transformations during the 1970s; and the Mexican movement Priests for the People, albeit somewhat more moderate than the others. Many of these groups worked intensely on housing problems in suburban *favelas* (as the Brazilian slum towns are called) and promoted missionary activities in rural areas, where they also encouraged alphabetization. Some of these activities soon reflected even upon the cultural domain because many Catholic priests began to reappraise and value formerly neglected popular devotions, religious expressions and aesthetic forms and styles in liturgical music and imagery, and even idiosyncrasical popular habits. Catholic subjectivities, thus, were suddenly transforming.

However, the political upheavals in the 1970s led to a widespread wave of military dictatorships that imposed harsh social conditions in many Latin American nations, with an almost immediate sequel of human rights violations. This in turn forced moderation on the Catholic renewal in order to avoid repression against its own ranks. The CELAM conference held in Puebla, Mexico in 1979 under the more conservative Pope John Paul II advocated social peace. Even so, the CELAM still tried to preserve its concern for popular culture and its related religious expressions. As a reflection of these developments, from the 1980s onwards, Latin American theology began to call itself *cultural theology* and remained strongly sensitive to the manifold diversity of indigenous cultures.

Epilogue

We can now summarize some keys to the understanding of the most salient historical changes that Catholic identities underwent throughout Latin America during the last two centuries. We expect that they may explain, therefore, the notably resiliency that Catholic identities enjoy nowadays in Latin America.

Once social and political modernization became irreversible, the Catholic Church had little option but to strive to bridge the gap with modernity. In the mid-nineteenth century, Catholicism still had serious difficulties to admit philosophy of individual achievement and universal suffrage in society. However, by the turn of the century it had recognized the "social question" and had begun to accept as legitimate many of the workers' demands. The Church thus made an effort to offer a renovated façade. Social justice demands were endorsed by the *Rerum Novarum* encyclical, a document that soon became a social program in itself, by means of which the Church assigned to the state the role of arbiter between capital and labor, and even recognized the workers' right to join in labor unions as a tool for their social improvement and the right to make themselves heard by their employers.

But this answer from the Church was arriving rather late. In many—mostly European—countries, socialists had already succeeded in organizing strong workers' unions. Thus, social Catholicism, emerging under the shadow of *Rerum Novarum*, engaged in unequal battle against socialism. Catholic trade unions unsteadily began to organize in different European and Latin American countries. Even so, many Catholics expressed their mistrust for these new entities: It was hard for them to accept their working class origin. Catholic workers' unions thus encountered strong prejudice from various sources, which became even more intense at the end of the First World War with the outbreak of the Russian Revolution.

Nevertheless, these developments did not preclude the emergence of certain Catholic social movements strongly rooted in the working classes, quite apart from most conservative Catholic circles. For example, the Young Christian Workers, founded by the Belgian priest Joseph Cardijn, which soon attained considerable scope and international presence in Europe and Latin America. Cardijn was well aware of the usual charges drawn up against Catholic organization and tried not to incur in them. But the interwar years witnessed the rise and spread of fascism over Europe, putting renewed pressure on Catholic organizations to take a clear stand. Since social Catholicism was essentially corporatist and remained quite distant from the left, there was scarce difficulty in associating it to the reactionary values predicated by fascist movements.

By the end of the Second World War, however, there emerged a substantially modified world scenario. In the meantime, Catholic subjectivities acquired plasticity, as if they have rejuvenated. During the Cold War, Catholicism almost at once lined up with the Western powers and openly adopted their liberal and democratic values. In the more developed countries, however, the consolidation of the Welfare State during the second postwar turned those countries less permeable to Catholicism, while Western societies as a whole were enjoying high standards of living, thanks to generous policies aimed at assuring social welfare through increased consumer patterns. All these changes were important steps towards an *aggiornamento* process that would lead to the Second Vatican Council in the 1960s, a Church meeting with enormous impact everywhere, but particularly throughout the so-called Third World, which provided a new scenario for Catholicism. Instead of being an ally of the Western imperialist expansion, as it had been during and after the Spanish and Portuguese Conquest of Latin America, after the Second Vatican Council the Church assumed a missionary nature deeply involved in national liberation struggles throughout the Third World. Thus it recovered a measure of political prestige, even sliding towards the "new (Latin American) left" during the 1960s and 1970s. It even suffered martyrs, such as Monsignor Oscar Arnulfo Romero in El Salvador, recently beatified by Pope Francis.

The Soviet Union's collapse in 1989–1990 posed an even newer scenario. In 1991, John Paul II celebrated the *Rerum Novarum* centennial with great expectations that the social doctrine of the Church would attain great prestige once Western capitalism found itself without its prominent antagonist in Eastern Europe. In 2014, Pope Francis also joyfully celebrated the 25th anniversary of the fall of the Berlin Wall. To complete this picture, we should add the Welfare State crisis since the 1970s, the widespread implementation of neoliberal policies, the recurrent financial crises resulting in serious social, humanitarian and ecological troubles, and an unforeseen byproduct of economic deregulation.

At this time of crisis in the credibility of modernity's great epic stories, Catholicism offers a strong system of values, enhanced by its social doctrine and its commitment to the needs and expectations of the underdeveloped countries, or emergent nations, as they are now called. All these circumstances combined to provide an excellent occasion to rehabilitate and restore the values and principles inherited from Latin American theology, a source for a renovated agenda, a new *aggiornamento* of the Catholic Church, until so recently still quite "Eurocentrical." Thus, it does not appear coincidental that Pope Francis—"the pope from the end of the world"—has become an authoritative voice in contemporary and global debates.

Notes

1 Sol Serrano, *¿Qué hacer con Dios en la República? Política y secularización en Chile, 1845–1885* (Buenos Aires: Fondo de Cultura Económica, 2008); Brian Connaughton, *Entre la voz de Dios y el llamado de la patria: Religión, identidad y ciudadanía en México en el siglo XIX* (México: Fondo de Cultura Económica- UAM, 2010); Roberto di stefano, *El púlpito y la plaza: Clero, sociedad y política de la monarquía católica a la república rosista* (Buenos Aires: Siglo XXI, 2004).

2 Christopher Clark, "The New Catholicism and the European Culture Wars," *Culture Wars: Secular–Catholic Conflicts in Nineteenth Century Europe* (Cambridge: University of Cambridge, 2003), 11–45; Miranda Lida, *Historia del catolicismo en la Argentina: Entre los siglos XIX y XX* (Buenos Aires: Siglo XXI, 2015).

3 José Casanova, *Oltre la secolarizzazione: Le religioni alla riconquista della sfera pubblica* (Bologna: Il Mulino, 2000); David Martin, "The Secularization Issue: Prospect and Retrospect," *The British Journal of Sociology*, Vol 42, No. 3 (1991), 465–474.
4 Luis Medina Ascensio, *Historia del Colegio Pío Latinoamericano 1858–1978* (México: Jus, 1979).
5 Josep-Ignasi Saranyana, *Breve historia de la teología en América Latina* (Madrid: BAC, 2009); Josep-Ignasi Saranyana, *Teología en América Latina: Vol III. El siglo de las teologías latinoamericanas (1899–2001)* (Madrid: Iberoamericana, 2002).
6 Jean Meyer, *Historia de los cristianos en América Latina: siglos XIX y XX* (México: Jus, 1999); John Lynch, *Dios en el Nuevo Mundo: Una historia religiosa de América Latina* (Buenos Aires: Crítica, 2012).
7 Miguel Rodríguez, "El Sagrado Corazón de Jesús: imágenes, mensajes y transferencias culturales," In *Secuencia* (México, 74, mayo-agosto, 2009), 145–168; José Alberto Moreno Chávez, *Devociones políticas: Cultura católica y politización en la arquidiócesis de México, 1880–1920* (México: El Colegio de México, 2013).
8 Manuel Ceballos Ramírez, *El catolicismo social: un tercero en discordia. Rerum Novarum, la cuestión social y la movilización de los católicos mexicanos* (México: El Colegio de México, 1991); Néstor Tomás Auza, *Aciertos y fracasos sociales del catolicismo argentino* (Buenos Aires, Docencia, 1987).
9 Roberto Blancarte, *Historia de la Iglesia Católica en México (1929–1982)* (México: Fondo de Cultura Económica, 1993).
10 Jessie Jane Vieira de Souza, *Círculos Operários: A Igreja Católica e o mundo do trabalho* (Rio de Janeiro: UFRJ, 2002).
11 Andrea Botto, "Algunas tendencias del catolicismo social en Chile: reflexiones desde la historia," *Teología y Vida*, Santiago, Chile, Vol 3 (2008): 499–514.
12 Roger Geymonat and Alejandro Sánchez, "Iglesia Católica, Estado y sociedad en el Uruguay del siglo XX," In *Las religiones en el Uruguay: Algunas aproximaciones*, edited by en Roger Geymonat (Montevideo: La Gotera, 2004).
13 Miranda Lida, *Monseñor Miguel De Andrea. Obispo y hombre de mundo* (Buenos Aires: Edhasa, 2013).
14 Ricardo Arias Trujillo, "La Democracia Cristiana en Colombia," *Historia Crítica* (Bogotá: noviembre de 2009), 188–216; Roberto Blancarte, *Historia de la Iglesia Católica en México (1929–1982)* (México: Fondo de Cultura Económica, 1993).
15 Conferencia Episcopal Latinoamericana (CELAM), "Documento conclusive," Primera Conferencia General del Episcopado Latinoamericano, Río de Janeiro, 1955. http://www.celam.org/conferencias_rio.php accessed July 13, 2015.
16 Gustavo Morello, "El Concilio Vaticano II y su impacto en América Latina: a 40 años de un cambio en los paradigmas en el catolicismo," *Revista Mexicana de Ciencias Políticas y Sociales*, Vol XLIX, No. 199 (2007): 81–104.
17 Young-Hyun Jo, *Sacerdotes y transformación social en Perú 1968–1975* (México: Universidad Nacional Autónoma de México, 2005); Young-Hyun Jo, "Movimiento Sacerdotes para el Pueblo y la transformación socioeclesiástica en México," *Revista Iberoamericana*, Vol 21, No. 10 (2010): 81–104.

16

THE ENERGETIC BODY

Machines, Organisms, and Social Thermodynamics in Colombia's Path to Modernity[1]

Stefan Pohl-Valero

In the early twentieth century in Colombia, as in other parts of Latin America, various discourses ranging from cosmological theories to social and moral discussions about the body, race, and work were approached from a perspective that viewed individual and social functioning as a process of energy transformation. In 1910, the year Colombians celebrated the centenary of independence, journalist Simon Chaux noted that the development of the universe and the organization of all its phenomena was based on the "principle of the conservation of energy, which stresses that no force is created or destroyed in the infinite processes of nature or the action of man-made machines, but rather it is transformed into new manifestations, equivalent to those present before."[2] That same principle of equivalence served to give a new productive dimension to natural resources and their role in the discourses of identity and national progress. As lawyer Juan Quintero mentioned in 1911, the beautiful plunge of Tequendama (a natural waterfall 140 meters high located 30 kilometers southwest of Bogota), besides its poetical meanings, also represented a great source of mechanical energy without precedents in the Andean geography and a huge potential of material progress for the nation: "The average energy of Tequendama is equivalent to 63,000 horsepower, which represents 630,000 working men . . . who are not paid a salary."[3]

Similarly, for the engineer Alberto Borda Tanco, the bodies of those same workers constituted a "true engine; because, in effect [the human body] transformed into work the caloric energy contained in food, and society recognized the analogy between the combustion engine and a man as a motor." For him, if the "brand of the engine" and its "good state" were factors influencing its efficiency, when applied to men, one had to take into account, in the same manner, the "species and race" and the "health, strength, activity and the provisions of the individual" in order to "measure the work produced by men" and increase their productivity.[4] If Borda Tanco's conceptualization of the productive body in terms of energy was related to a racialized view of population (he ensured that normally, "whites produced more work than Blacks"), physician and conservative politician Liborio Zerda related the analogy of the human motor to natural theology. Thus, for this physician, the human body represented a wonderful and efficient machine that transforms energy, which, in turn, showed the existence of an "infinitely powerful and wise author, superior to all the powerful and wise men of the world."[5]

The proper use of energy by the "human motor" was also seen as a moral issue of community welfare and for the differentiation and racial hierarchy between nations. In fact, several articles of the cultural magazine *Cromos* emphasized the idea that the ability to develop "a energy which we could describe as prodigious" by part of the "white races" of Europeans and North Americans was the reason why the Colombians, both the "masses of poor" as well as the elite, adopted among themselves a gesture "of admiration, reverence and fear" and a "position of inferiority" in the presence of a European. Overcoming these issues meant that Colombians had to learn how "to discipline their own bodies" and "tempering their physical and moral strengths."[6] Therefore, local workers had to understand that their bodies were "a machine that suffers damage" and that:

> only with a correct lifestyle and a rigorous work ethic can we conserve the energy needed to obtain favorable success for ourselves and the community. . . . He who forces his machine to save time, and he who wastes it by not putting it to adequate use, are both doing a bad use of energy . . . [The adequate use of energy is] the highest of human interests.[7]

From this perspective on energy optimization, some physicians started to recommend strategies of population intervention in order to "increase the productive power of the country" and improve the health of the working class. As mentioned by the conservative doctor and director of the Central Hygiene Board of Bogota, Pablo García Medina, the activity of the organism was ultimately a process of energy transformation. Consequently, modern public hygiene, informed by experimental physiology and bacteriology, should intervene to achieve the proper energy balance of the workers' activities (in terms of nourishment, clothes, and housing) and therefore ensure the "future of the race."[8] Even within the economic discussions of labor, it was argued that the key to establishing a "scientific method" of setting a salary for workers and peasants was based on the possibility of estimating the amount of calories produced by "any of the foods consumed by the worker" and thus "calculating the fuel necessary to sustain the work of the human machine."[9]

In this chapter I want to argue, focusing on the case of Colombia, that in addition to the analogy of society as an organism in constant transformation, the analogy of the human body as a combustion engine advanced social thought in Latin America in important ways at the end of the nineteenth century and early twentieth century, and added layers of meaning to notions of race, work, and progress. Indeed, once the worker's body entered the confines of the laboratory to analyze their physiological variables in relation to changes in the external environment, and physical labor and food were measured in energy units, common expressions used in the debates about national social problems acquired new meanings. Thus, notions as the "vitality of the people," the "physiological misery [poor diet]" or the "degeneration of the race," were understood as issues likely to be quantified, and to be analyzed through statistical comparison, and therefore amenable to political and scientific intervention. If Social Darwinism (by way of English sociologist Herbert Spencer), Eugenics (informed by Neo-Lamarckism), and bacteriology have been identified by historians as the main specialized knowledge that helped set up a biologized view of society and to shape government strategies on the poor in Latin America, it can be argued that the conception of the body as a thermal engine also played a central role in these processes.[10] It is my argument that "social thermodynamics" represents a new field of historical analysis for what anthropologist Zandra Pedraza recently called "the question of the modern body in Latin America."[11]

In the framework of the projects of construction and consolidation of Latin American nation-states, today suggestive historical analyses relates the production of scientific knowledge on the body (individual and social) with processes of representation of the nation, the territory and the population, as well as with modern strategies for discipline and regulation.[12] However, the roll of the metaphor of the human body as a combustion engine that transforms energy—articulated by notions of thermodynamics, experimental physiology, and political economy—has been seldom explored by scholars analyzing the medicalization of society and the racial discourse of Latin American intellectuals at that time.[13] Additionally, in countries like Colombia—where the processes of industrialization, urbanization, and in general terms, of modernity, have been identified by traditional historiography as late and "deferred"—the study of this metaphor and its relations with the social do not seem to have especially caught the attention of historians.[14] However, from a cultural perspective, where symbolic systems of meaning play an important role in the configuration of reality, besides material structures, one may argue that even with the absence of a true modern production system, an energy-centric conceptualization of the human body and society became one of the conceptual frameworks to understand Colombian reality at the dawn of the twentieth century.[15]

Clearly, this conceptual framework for addressing social dynamics had its own local features and it was articulated with other biological and cultural notions of the body and race. In particular, as I have shown elsewhere, the "physiological regeneration" of the "human engine"—by means of nutritional campaigns, food assistance programs, and the regulation of minimum wage and work schedules—was conceived as an integral part of the local eugenics movement. The energy improvement of the human body was seen as an acquired characteristic that could be inherited, and therefore future generations of workers would be more efficient and have greater job performance.[16] In addition, and as in other countries of the region, the ability to quantify nourishment in caloric and nutritional terms meant a racialization of food. Indeed, different regional and national populations were ranked in terms of their physical and intellectual capacities according to their eating habits and their caloric and nutrient intakes.[17]

Rather than an institutional or disciplinary history of science, technology, and medicine, and their relationships with society and culture, or a study about the medicalization of society in Colombia, what I propose in this text is an outline of the local genealogy of the human body as a thermal engine. I understand this concept of genealogy as a methodological way of trying to ask for the technological, epistemological, and cultural conditions that make it possible for this particular conception of the human body.[18] I argue that these conditions of possibility were the result of the entanglement of particular scientific practices, styles of knowledge production, and social institutions that were being configured since the end of the nineteenth century in Colombia. With this local genealogy of the human engine, I aim to shed additional light on the modern linkages between science, the body and power in the Latin American contexts of the beginning of the twentieth century.

Genealogy of the Energetic Body

Over the last three decades of the nineteenth century, Colombia began to set up a new cultural framework that incorporated notions of technology, thermodynamics, medical physics, political economy, and experimental physiology, converging in an energy-centric conception of the human body. Bogota, capital of Colombia, was a small town in the middle of the mountains of the Andes, and where a very slow process of urbanization and industrialization was beginning to take place. The National University of Colombia was created in 1868, offering, in addition to the traditional careers of law and philosophy, medicine and civil engineering. In this educational space began to be trained the future experts for the modernization of Colombia.[19] Related to a process of professional recognition and political influence, the Society of Medicine and Natural Sciences was established in 1873; and the Colombian Society of Engineering in 1887.[20] The Central Hygiene Board was established a year earlier, representing one of the first steps in a long process of institutionalization and centralization of public health in Colombia.[21] Although the city had very few industries with modern manufacturing processes, and the construction of railway networks was just beginning, the steam engine was becoming a public symbol of the desired modernity and civilization. Revealingly, in 1885 the streets of Bogota exhibited for months, and for the amusement of the public, the first rails built by a local company; and four years later the press announced with pride the first steam engine built entirely in Colombia (designed to operate the laminator that produced those rails). One of the engineers involved in the construction stated that the entire project was overseen by an English engineer and that the engine had, among other specifications, a Watt regulator which controlled the boiler pressure and a capacity for effective work of 68 horsepower.[22]

Thanks to thermodynamics, it was known at that time that the work of a steam engine was the result of a process of energy transformation. The fuel powering the machine has a certain amount of energy that is transformed into mechanical work and heat losses, keeping constant the total amount of energy in the system.[23] But the concept of energy conservation not only caught the attention of engineers in their quest to optimize the working capacity of machines; it also attracted doctors and various social thinkers who sought new tools from the natural sciences to understand the functioning of the human body and society. As happened in other places, this "scientific naturalism" that tried to grasp social and human reality based on natural science, generated a major intellectual dispute. For the Latin American context, this late-nineteenth century dispute has been normally related with Positivism and Social Darwinism, and particularly with the ideas of English social thinker Herbert Spencer. For the Colombian case, the lawyer and liberal politician Salvador Camacho Roldán was one of the main advocates of Spencer's sociology. As he proclaimed at the National University in 1882, sociology was "the branch of philosophy" that should follow the same procedures as the "physical and natural sciences." This idea, according to Camacho Roldán, was based on the fact that "the evolution of human beings" is the "law that prevails equally over individuals and society."[24] His idea to apply evolutionary theories to society were criticized by conservative intellectuals in terms of moral and Catholic arguments. Darwinism and positivism were portrayed as materialistic doctrines that could cause moral degradation and social unrest.[25] Something similar occurred with thermodynamics.

At the same time that Camacho explained social Darwinism to the students of the National University in Bogota, the Colombian government brought Swiss philosopher Ernst Röthlisberger as a professor of the same university. In 1883, in the prologue of a local treatise on "experimental philosophy," Röthlisberger gave a clear account of the central role of thermodynamics in one of the most heated philosophical and social debates of the time about how to understand life. In the light of the new physical law of energy conservation and its applications to all kind of phenomena, Röthlisberger asked himself: "what position will philosophy take? What will be its position on the increasingly popular theory that matter and energy are eternal and maintain the same quantity, although different in manifestations?" For Röthlisberger the "new doctrines about life," based on the law of energy conservation, were crucial for philosophical investigation since they were related to the debate about vitalism, idealism and materialism. As he noted, some scholars at that time argued that life "is the result of an independent vital force, while others attribute it to the soul, and others argue that it is due to the particular structure of our body, the composition and combination of the molecules?"[26]

This debate about how to understand human life and what kind of laws should define its functioning was not new, but thermodynamics helped to give it new prominence. Indeed, at the mid-nineteenth century, the idea to compare the human body with a machine was strongly criticized by local elites as materialist reductionism and as an offense to God, and therefore, as a source of social disorder. As a manual of political economy that circulated in Colombia at that time noted:

> [i]ts hard to believe, and even painful, that it has been necessary to refute the opinion of some writers who have equated man with a machine. . . . To consider the worker as a machine is, in short, an act of wickedness, an insult and a blunder. Man is the son of God, Lord of the Earth, and he is equipped with intelligence: he [the human being] invents machines and puts them at his service.[27]

This quote points out the fear that many intellectuals had of reducing human nature to its purely material characteristics.

As mentioned previously, this concern about materialism gained a new dimension with the emergence of thermodynamics and the new analogy of the human body as a thermal engine that transforms energy. Still in the late nineteenth century, some local doctors indicated their fears about generalizing the laws of nature (and especially the conservation of energy) to the realm of human life due to its materialistic consequences. For example, in 1896 the doctor Carlos Putnam pointed out that:

> The doctrine of the unity of physical, vital, and intellectual forces, so in vogue today, is nothing more than the expression of contemporary materialism, and promotes the denial of any belief. According to this doctrine, everything is reducible to energy; nothing is lost, nothing is created; everything is transformation of matter and movement. . . . To have a complete idea of the constitution of man, it is necessary to admit three orders of phenomena that are different and not reducible into a single one: physical phenomena, vital phenomena and psychic phenomena.[28]

However, since the decade of 1880 medicine and law students started to learn human thermodynamics, where the distinction between these orders of phenomena was not clear. In 1883, a manual was published in Bogota on "experimental philosophy" aimed at the students of the school of philosophy, where future physicians and lawyers did their basic training before entering their respective faculties in the National University. This manual compiled a number of European and American texts trying to account for human nature from branches such as psychology, logic, biology, physiology, chemistry, and physics. The translator, César Guzmán, an intellectual and liberal politician engaged in the business of translations of scientific manuals, did not hesitate to pass on to future intellectual elites in Bogota the idea that the human body should be interpreted primarily as a machine that transformed energy. In fact, the chapter on "The Problem of Life" written by American physiologist and chemist George Barker was a treatise of thermodynamics applied to organic phenomena. Barker not only conceptualized physical activity of living organisms, but also intellectual activity, as processes that obeyed "the universal law of conservation of energy."[29] Thus, feeding, digestion, respiration, blood circulation, muscle action, and the nervous system were presented as processes of energy transformation. As another author of the manual argued, "[t]he comparison between a living animal and a steam engine, as a source of driving force, is today an accurate comparison."[30]

In addition, since the creation of the National University in 1868, Bogota's medical students had to study the subject of "Medical and Mathematical Physics." The professor, who for decades taught this course, was the conservative physician and Minister of Public Instruction Liborio Zerda. He was one of the first professors who taught the laws of thermodynamics at the National University and who instilled on a generation of physicians, aspects such as the "mode of measuring the amount of work done by the human muscles," "the apparent anomaly that results from spent or loss of strength in the human machine," "the equivalent in kilograms of the work produced by men in 8 hours," "the thermodynamic or mechanical theory of heat," and the application of the laws of thermodynamics "to physics, chemistry, mechanics, and physiology."[31] Students who took the physiology course also learned that this modern science "has penetrated and understood the intimate relationship that exists between the movement and heat, and is the origin of thermodynamic theory," and that its practitioners "play with the human body and make it into a machine that converts heat into movement."[32] In the middle of this educational context, it is possible to imagine that when medicine students in Bogota read in the press the technical specs of the first thermal machine built in Colombia in 1889—as it was mentioned at the beginning of this section—they would have thought on the thousands of them that existed in the city: human motors that could be regulated in order to improve their working capacities.

Consequently, despite the intellectual debate about thermodynamics and materialism, the metaphor of the human body as a steam engine began to structure the social thought of the local elites. In the practice, this was reflected in the way lawyers and physicians started to address the "working question." At the end of the nineteenth century, several researchers on working population attempted to quantify in energy units the working conditions of these people. For example, in 1892 the lawyer Ramon Vanegas Mora conducted an investigation on the "political economy" of the life conditions of the "working class" in Bogota. By interviewing different workers, visiting their homes, weighing the food they consumed, finding out the price of their food and clothing in retail stores, and describing their monetary incomes, Vanegas produced statistical tables that accounted for salaries, annual expenditures and consumption of food among three categories of workers (both men and women) who were classified according to their salaries and kinds of work (farmers, masons, and various trades).[33] Its main objective was to put a price on human labor that was not "determined capriciously" and hence overcome tensions between workers and employers.[34] A key element to achieve this purpose, according to Vanegas, was to scientifically determine the quantity and quality of food needed to optimize the workforce, according to the "biological law, which defines the correlation between spending and recuperation."[35]

At the same time, some doctors began to have very similar concerns about how to set the minimum amount of fuel that the human machine required for different types of work. As mentioned by doctor Manuel Cotes in 1893, the aim of his research on the "diets of the laborers of the Sabana de Bogotá" was to increase the "productive power of the country" by studying how the working bodies could "restore the forces annihilated by work."[36] Cotes did a survey on the living conditions of two hundred workers and their daily wages, concluding that, on average, they had poor nutrition. These workers were classified as "road-builders and carriers" (whom everyday consumed on average

600 grams of porridge, 50 grams of meat, 360 grams of bread, 15 grams of chocolate, 100 grams of *aguardiente* and 3575 of *chicha*); "stone masons" (800 grams of porridge, 120 grams of meat, 360 grams of bread, 1300 grams of *chicha*, 15 grams of chocolate and 30 grams of *aguardiente*); and "farmers" (this category included women and children 11 years and older. Men consumed on average 600 grams of porridge, 360 grams of bread, 3575 grams of *chicha* and 40 grams of chocolate; women and children: 400 grams of porridge, 240 grams of bread, 2275 grams of *chicha* and 40 grams of chocolate).

In the search for an adequate diet for the working classes, Cotes stressed the need to combine foods with different nutrients and to know the "absolute amount of different substances necessary to be absorbed by the body so it can sustain life," according to the type of work that "inevitably increases economic costs" in order to avoid "bankruptcy of the living machine."[37] However, he acknowledged that it was "impossible to determine, by direct experiments, the amount of heat produced in the body under the sole influence of diet." Therefore, based on indirect experiments by the Dutch materialist physiologist and social reformer Jacob Moleschott in Germany, Cotes defined the average quantities of proteins, carbohydrates, fats, and minerals that a "robust laborer, of average height and weight" should consume in twenty-four hours.[38]

Although these nutritional studies did not quantify the caloric value of working class rations, tables summarizing their diets broke down the average grams of protein, carbohydrates, and fats consumed daily. In the search for a numerical equivalent to calculate the "relationship between work and the amount of food," several doctors from the late nineteenth century stressed that animal husbandry and its studies on the driving force of the horse had shown that the relationship between work production and the amount of "fuel" consumed could be calculated based on the "mechanical equivalent of protein."[39] Some years later, in 1913, Dr. Calixto Torres Umaña could finally say with certainty that "the principle of energy conservation applies to the living organisms then as accurately as to a steam machine," and that it was now possible to calculate directly both the energy contained in food and that consumed by the body during physical work.[40]

Torres, in a work on the nutritional metabolism of the inhabitants of Bogota and Tunja (a town near Bogota, at a higher elevation), mentioned that thanks to German physiologist Max Rübner and his experiments with an apparatus called calorimeter at the end of the nineteenth century, it was possible to effectively measure the caloric content of food and to demonstrate that the human body transforms these calories into the energy required for the organic activities.[41] It was this perspective of energy equivalence between work and food which finally made it possible to link the amount of energy spent by the body in certain jobs and the energy content of the nutrients absorbed by the body. Although Colombian physicians did not have such scientific instruments as the calorimeter, they were able to calculate the energy content of different local foods thanks to standardized coefficients.

Thus, standardized tables began to appear in local nutritional manuals, which set the minimum diet measured in calories that a worker should take according to the energy expenditure of his trade. Based on various physiological research in Europe, Torres noted, for example, that a man doing normal physical work should have a serving of "maintenance" of 2,876 calories a day, spread over 135 grams of protein, 140 grams of fat and 249 grams of carbohydrates.[42] Torres also indicated that Rübner's isodynamic notion allowed for the calculation of "the energy input of each kind of food" so that individuals ate according to their "social categories."[43] In the early twentieth century, local physicians finally managed to carry out in practice what doctors and lawyers had aspired to do since the 1880s: measure the fuel and the mechanical work of the human machine in order to increase its work capacity. As outlined following, this assembly of knowledge, instruments, and measurements helped to add new meanings to the notion of race, which was beginning to interweave with the notion of social class.

Laboratory Science, Race, and Working Class

In 1913, the same year that Torres published his work on metabolism, the engineer Miguel Triana, in a small article titled "Sociology of the Mountain" assured that

> Having strength should be for men and nations the supreme, primordial aspiration; not because the brute strength of some, and the military of others can by itself, ensure happiness, but because health, intellect, and character have their common origin in the physical energies. Men like the people, take the strength they transform into nutrition, work, comfort, instruction, etc., from the various energy sources offered to them by nature, like natural sunlight, the shelter of the Earth, coal or waterfalls; all manifestations of universal thermal energy. Thus, the degree of civilization and culture could be measured in mechanical units of thermodynamics. Physical life and social developments represent, in the final analysis, pure heat consumption.[44]

As seen in the previous section, Triana's words not only expressed the incipient development of a field of knowledge on labor and food that conceptualized the functioning of human body and of society in terms of energy. His writing also represented a particular style of knowledge production about nature and society based on laboratory techniques and its metrological networks. This style of knowledge production contrasted with the way local scientists at the mid-nineteenth century tried to capture the truth about natural and social phenomena. For them, the proper way to know the relationships between environment, local population, and national progress was related to an attitude toward knowledge production that emphasized direct and personal observation, a holistic approach, and the search of generalizations and ideal archetypes. At the dawn of the twentieth century, some physicians begun to portray their scientific activities as essentially different from the ones performed by an earlier generation. For this new generation of physicians, scientific facts should be obtained at the laboratory, and direct observation was no longer enough for the production of natural and social knowledge. Consequently, some aspects of the relationship between the functioning of the human body and the environment were reduced to quantifiable variables, which could be separated, analyzed, and compared in the laboratory.

A short article about "comparative climatology" published in 1865 illustrates the way scientists produced knowledge about nature and society at the mid-nineteenth century. In this research, Dr. Antonio Vargas Vega assigned innate anatomical and physiological characteristics of Colombia's different races (whites, Indians and Blacks), according to the climate in which they lived. After clinical observations using instruments as the stethoscope, Vargas was assured that the Andean Indians had a wider chest than other races, thus facilitating a greater breathing capacity, and a more dynamic digestion that compensated their frugal nutrition. These anatomical and physiological characteristics, claimed Vargas, made these people "naturally suitable" for manual work, while "whites," with a smaller respiratory capacity and a greater need for plentiful and nutritious food, were predisposed to a sedentary and intellectual life. Vargas also claimed that in the hot lowlands the "blacks" represented the "working race."[45] As discussed elsewhere, this "climatic physiology," responded to a form of knowledge production based on "the personal abilities of the observer, on measurements made *in situ*, and on a holistic approach that sought not the particularity of specific cases but the essential features of regional population idealized in geographic and racialized terms."[46] Besides climatic determinism, this style of science helped to produce a geographical model of civilization and racial hierarchy that was central for the elites' projects of nation building at the mid-nineteenth century: the cool highlands representing civilization and the hot lowlands, barbarism.[47]

In contrast, some aspects of scientific activity in the late nineteenth century began to show a different way to produce knowledge about the relationship betwen the functioning of the body and climate. The place of knowledge production shifted from open spaces and landscapes to the laboratory, where many scientific facts began to be produced according to standardized measurements and statistical indicators.[48] Some of these scientific facts only acquired social meaning (for example, of racial superiority or inferiority) once they were compared with standard values or statistical averages. The aforementioned study on human metabolism done by Calixto Torres in 1913 is a good example of this particular style of knowledge production. In his research, Torres repeatedly noted that the veracity of their conclusions was the result of the search for "physiological facts" after numerous observations and measurements done in the laboratory. In particular Torres measured the mean body temperature, amount of red blood cells and amount of urea in the urine of residents from Bogota and Tunja which were classified as "working class" and "upper classes."[49] After these physiological measurements were compared with average values produced in Europe, Torres concluded that "our race . . . is under attack from a principle of physiological degeneration that renders it incapable of defending themselves against the aggression of the altitude."[50] According to Torres, the local human machine was less efficient in its ability to transform energy from food into physical and intellectual labor than the human bodies located in other latitudes and altitudes.

This national problem, as Torres described it, was part of a series of investigations that were beginning to question the effects of Andean climate in "the physiology and pathology of man."[51] Doing laboratory studies on the physiological conditions of people living in high altitude cities—such as red blood cell counts, body temperature, metabolic processes, and heart function—various Colombian doctors and chemists began to investigate the mechanisms of organic regulation that could compensate for the aggressive effects of altitude, such as the lack of oxygen. These high altitude effects had been identified by some European physiologists as one of the "natural" explanations of the alleged inferiority of the inhabitants of the Andes. In the midst of a Latin American debate on the physical and intellectual "normality" of the "races of high altitudes,"[52] some Colombian researchers noted the existence of some of these mechanisms—such as the organism capacity to increase red blood cells in order to compensate for the lack of oxygen—while others rejected it. But overall, Colombian physicians assured that the working bodies of inhabitants of Bogota and Tunja were in a state of "muscular laziness," "physiological degeneration," or "organic deficit" due to the Andean climate.[53] Faced with this situation, the medical community began to ask the government to take measures for dietary regulation for the "working classes" according to their climate conditions. A rational diet, it was argued, could compensate the physiological problems that caused living in high altitude climates. In contrast with the ideas about climatic determinism that were held at mid-nineteenth century, at the beginning of the twentieth century physicians started to understand the human organism, not only in terms of races, innate abilities, and geographical distribution, but also in terms of social classes, and organic transformations and regulations.

Modern Strategies of Regulation

All of the previously mentioned scientists highlighted in their research that the government should take measures to solve the social/organic problems they had identified. In particular, they insisted that the state should intervene in issues such as the regulation of wages, food cost, conditions of occupational hygiene, and nutritional campaigns. The modern Colombian subject, it was argued, needed to learn how to become an efficient machine and thus it would be possible to improve the "social energy" of the nation.[54] An adequate nutrition was presented as a key element for civilizing local population and for national progress. Physicians also argued that certain food products were essential for social transformation. For example, special attention was paid to nutrients with a high protein content such as meat.[55] As pointed out by Cotes in his already mentioned nutritional study of 1893, Colombia produced the "physiological absurd" that in so far as the altitude increased, meat consumption decreased.[56] Several food hygienists connected the "future of the race" with nutrition and related features such as strength, resistance to work, intelligence, courage, laziness, or weakness to the eating habits of different regions and climates, and in particular, their meat consumption.[57] Based on international statistics of food consumption, a local physician eloquently claimed that "greatness, power, strength and the morale of well managed nations develops in direct proportion to the consumption of meat" and that Bogota was not consuming even a quarter of the beef needed for "a population to be healthy, strong, hardworking and prosperous."[58] One of the measures proposed by Torres to overcome the supposed "physiological degeneration" of the local population was precisely to increase the consumption of meat and reduce the consumption of *chicha*. Thus, regional and national populations were organized in hierarchical terms according to their diet habits and caloric intakes, which in turn defined their physical and intellectual capacities. As occurred in other Latin American countries, this energetic perception of food became a new element in the racialized discourses of the time.[59] For instance, in 1898 the Mexican politician Francisco Bulnes proposed a racial hierarchy based on the nutritional components of different foods and their supposed civilizing effects—rather than on the skin color of people. For him, the "race of wheat" (Europeans) were physical and intellectual superior to the "race of rice" (Asians), and to the "race of maize" (Americans), since the two latter food products were supposedly less nutritious than wheat. This relationship between food and race was eloquently expressed by a Colombian physician a few years later, when he asserted that "the race enters through the mouth." For Dr. Lomabana Barreneche, the racial condition of local populations was profoundly related to their diet habits.[60]

One aspect that all of these investigations discussed was the incredible amount of *chicha* that the poor of Colombia's Andean regions consumed. This traditional drink made from fermented corn was a central element in the local diet and a constant source of concern for physicians and administrators since the colonial era. At that time, the high consumption of *chicha* by the poor was understood primarily as moral weakness and as a source of social disorder.[61] However, since the late nineteenth century, nutritional discourses—and the energy productivism in which these discourses were framed—gave a new shape to these social and moral debates. Although consumption of *chicha* was portrayed as the main source of "racial degeneration" of the poor, which also could be inherited, this alcoholic beverage also began to be understood as the cheapest and most affordable energy source for the demands of manual labor.[62] Therefore, the reason that the poor drank so much *chicha* began to be interpreted, not only as a sign of moral degradation, but as a physiological response to their poor nutritional conditions. As Dr. García Medina assured, given the energy demands of manual labor, the body felt an "instinctive urge to use nervous system stimulants" and in that way sought "alcoholic products to compensate for a lack of energy."[63]

At the end of the nineteenth century, Colombia suffered a political transformation characterized by a conservative, centralized, and interventionist administration. Rafael Núñez, one of Colombia's main political leaders, argued that Colombia should begin a process of "regeneration" to overcome the "catastrophic" social and political situation that radical liberals had supposedly left in place. In an important sense, this regeneration was not only conceived of as political, administrative, and moral, but also racial.[64] Therefore, the first steps to "regenerate" the local population were focused on public health education campaigns. From the beginning of the twentieth century, and after the War of a Thousand Days (1899–1903) and the loss of Panama in 1903, conservative governments began to foster a more pragmatic spirit in the pursuit of economic development for the progress of the nation. Several popular manuals of physiology and school hygiene, childcare and housekeeping, were published and distributed among public schools and Colombian households. One of the main lessons that all these texts tried to instill in mothers and children was the importance of having a rational diet that could maintain health and achieve a balance between energy consumed and then spent at work. The manuals insisted that the working class should understand that their bodies were "precious machines" that needed special care and proper fuel to "produce good work" and that the kitchen of the home was a "laboratory" where raw materials are transformed into nutritional foods.[65]

Some institutions were also created for this purpose of social engineering. For example, one of the main objectives of the Society of Pediatrics of Bogota, founded in 1917, was to improve child nutrition. The Society helped to establish the institution known as "Drops of Milk" ["*Gotas de Leche*"], and the members offered "regular conferences for mothers who wanted to improve the health of their children."[66] Calixto Torres was one of the founding members of this scientific society and played an important role as scientific advisor to *Gotas de Leche*. Many medical students did their internships at this institution, establishing rations of milk and (a chart for) calorie intake that children should consume according to their age and weight.[67] The press portrayed *Gotas de Leche* as a space to produce "beautiful specimens of race and vigor" and to achieve "the renewal of population."[68] It is no wonder then that Torres participated in a public debate that was held in Bogota in 1920 about the "racial problems of Colombia."[69] In this public debate, Torres summarized his 1913 research on local nutritional metabolism and re-emphasized the idea that it is an "experimentally proven fact that biological signs of weakness exist among us [the inhabitants of Bogota and Tunja]." But he also stressed that science and hygiene could "replace what nature had not achieved in its adaptation process."[70] Related with the local eugenics movement of the time, his words reflected the idea shared by many doctors: that the human body could be regulated/regenerated through nutrition in order to optimize productivity, and that this acquired characteristic could be biologically inherited.[71] Later, in the 1930s, other institutions such as school cafeterias and school holiday camps were established. This last institution offered a place where adolescent farmworkers from different regions of the country gathered for periods of three months to be indoctrinated a hygienic way of life that included physical education and a rational diet. These institutions were also created with the intention to achieve the "physiological restoration" of the working population in Colombia.[72]

Similarly, in 1939 Dr. Jose Francisco Socarrás conducted a detailed study on the diet of the working class of Bogota. The daily food consumption of the workers was translated into their caloric content, and these values were compare to international standards that defined the minimum energy intake that a person should have. The prices of local food were also expressed in terms of "cheap calories" and of "expensive calories." In this research, the working class was no longer classified by the type of job they held, but by the neighborhood in which they lived within the city limits. The results of the research on 225 families found that 72 percent of the analyzed population lived in a state of "severe malnutrition."[73] With this caloric language, Socarrás tried to legitimize his aspirations for social reforms and demanded the creation of a national nutrition policy. One of the main objectives of this policy was, in his own terms, to avoid "racial degeneration" of the local population and to overcome the "biological tragedy" of the colonial legacy. The national government did not hesitate to publish his research in order to "make known to the public the basis of the biological policy being developed by the national Government."[74] The optimization of the human machine had become a State policy.

Conclusions

This chapter represents an effort to highlight the importance of analyzing in tandem a series of knowledge, practices, and representations that allow for a more powerful way to explain how social modern thought was configured in Colombia. In some cases, social problems were interpreted and in others intervention strategies were established to mitigate them. Without delving into the different aspects outlined here, it has been argued that the thermodynamic analogy of the human body, once culturally appropriated in the local context, became a fundamental conceptual framework in the discourse of progress, civilization, and modernity. This metaphor was also a condition of possibility for the idea of "physiological regeneration" of the poor population of Colombia at the beginning of the twentieth century. This project of social engineering was only achievable once a particular style of knowledge production based on the laboratory and a metrological network (of "normal" physiological values and nutritional standards) allowed to make possible the view that national progress could be measured in thermodynamic units.

It is important to note that in the context of early twentieth century Latin America, the so called "working-class question," which was connected with the "dietary question," has received growing attention from scholars because it allows us to explore the increasing social role of the state, as well as the rationale and the dynamics of the social projects elaborated by national governments at that time.

As Paulo Drinot recently noted, social policies established in Latin America to face the modern problem of labor have been addressed by historiography either from institutionalist perspectives, which view the state as an autonomous bureaucratic apparatus, or culturalist perspectives, which ponder what Foucault has called "a new art of government or governmentality."[75] Like Colombia, Peru did not experience a real process of industrialization at that time, and the population of industrial workers was very small. Thus, faced with the question of why the Peruvian state devoted such a great effort to the "governmentalization" of industrial work, when in reality the target population was very small, Drinot noted the importance of exploring local social and cultural configurations that gave form to the project of governmentality. One of these particular configurations was a racialized view of labor, in which the indigenous population symbolized, to the Peruvian elite, the main obstacle to industrialization, while industrialization represented the key to material progress and racial advancement of the nation.

Although the indigenous population of Colombia was smaller than in Peru, and the Colombian elites (at least those of Bogota and Medellin) addressed the issue of labor with the idea of a mixed (and also female)[76] population in mind, for both countries it is necessary to ask for "the ways in which certain 'objects' of government [in our case these objects would be the working body and food] became knowable, calculable, and administrative and are rendered amenable to intervention and regulation."[77] By exploring the local genealogy of the human body as a thermal motor, this chapter aims to shed light on how these "rationalities of government" were configured. Not in vain did some Peruvian intellectuals of 1920s defend the creation of state-sanctioned "dining rooms" for workers, stating that:

> It is well known that man as a human engine is subject to physical attrition; it follows that it is in the interest of the state to look after this human capital and of capitalists to maintain the strength and energy of that productive machine[78]

In the process of configuring these rationalities of government regarding work, different racial notions were present, and at the same time, they were redefined. Although the models of civilization based on climatic determinism were different in both countries during the nineteenth century (in Colombia the Andes and its inhabitants represented the model of civilization, whereas in Peru it was the coast),[79] in both cases climate was used by the elites as a central factor for explaining and justifying racial differences. Once the human body was conceptualized as a thermal machine at the beginning of the twentieth century, these racial discourses underwent certain changes. Now the human body was understood as an organism that could be regulated in order to prevent the alleged "physiological degeneration" caused by climate and other external factors. A rational diet became a key factor for improving the working capacities of an impoverished population, which nevertheless kept being perceived by the elites as racially inferior, but susceptible of biological improvement. At least in the case of Colombia, the notions of race held by the local elite at the beginning of the twentieth century proved to be multiple and ambiguous.[80] Race was determined not only by skin color and climate, but also by food and mechanisms of physiological regulation. Furthermore, the notions of race and social class were at that time deeply intertwined.

Notes

1 The results of the research conducted for this article are part of the research project "Estudio comparativo sobre la historia de la fisiología en América Latina," funded by the University of Rosario Research Fund (Fondo de Investigación de la Universidad del Rosario, FIUR DVG-156).

2 Simón Chaux, *Evolución científica o carta abierta* (Bogotá: Imprenta de Sur América, 1910), 25.

3 Juan Quintero, *Necesidad de una revolución legal en Colombia: Conferencia pronunciada el 15 de Julio de 1911 por disposición de la Academia de Jurisprudencia* (Bogotá: Imp. de La Luz, 1912), 4. The Mexican politician, José Vasconcelos, put forth the same arguments. His nationalist rhetoric about the "cosmic race" also alluded to the incredible energy sources in his country:

> What other country in the world can rival Mexico in the abundant, immeasurable amounts of usable energy, that today is wasted on the annual natural rhythms of sea mist converted into clouds, and the wind dragging on the mountain tops to cover

the plateau with a rain that falls, every season, on the narrow passages between the canyons and jumps of thousands of degrees of altitude levels. Each of these changes in level is like an inexhaustible coal mine: a perpetual source of energy, allowing us to build, someday, one of the strongest manufacturing centers of history.

José Vasconcelos, "La otra raza cósmica," In José Vasconcelos: La otra raza cósmica: Prólogo de Leonardo Da Jandra. Traducción y nota de Heriberto Yépez (México: Almadía, 2010 [1926]), 63.

4 Aberto Borda Tanco, "El motor humano," *Anales de Ingeniería*, Vol 21, No. 251–252 (1914): 210–213, 210–211.

5 Liborio Zerda, "Conferencia sobre el calor producido por la vida orgánica en el hombre," *Revista del Colegio Mayor de Nuestra Señora del Rosario*, Vol 13, No. 124 (1917): 214–224, 224.

6 Gonzalo París, "Energía," *Cromos*, Vol 5, No. 132 (1918): 161–162, 161.

7 S.Z., "El ahorro de energía," Cromos, Vol 9, No. 196 (1920): 33–35, 34 and 35.

8 Pablo García Medina, "La alimentación de nuestra clase obrera en relación con el alcoholismo," *Revista de Higiene. Órgano del Consejo Superior de sanidad de Colombia*, Vol 6, No. 88 (1914): 161–176, 171–174.

9 R. G. C., "Modo de obtener la eficiencia del trabajador," *Revista Nacional de Agricultura*, Vol 13, No. 187 (1920): 226–229, 228. In early twentieth century Chile, the metaphor of the mechanized man also helped create discourses against alcoholism, and about the "medicalization of labor" in general. Nicolás Fuster Sánchez, *El cuerpo como máquina. La medicalización de la fuerza de trabajo en Chile* (Santiago de Chile: Ceibo, 2013).

10 Several scholars have pointed out that since the last decades of the nineteenth century, social sciences in Latin America acquired a positivist perspective derived from Comtian and Spencerian ideas, contributing to the "biologization" of social thought. The idea of society as a biological organism has been highlighted as the central metaphor of this medical gaze. Consequently, it was "compared the role of the social scientist to the role of the physician: to examine symptoms of disease and propose therapies." Thus, "[p]hysicians, social scientists, and legal scholars alike filtered social pathology through biological lenses, which led to the rise of medical and anthropometric approaches to social symptoms." Dain Borges, "Puffy, Ugly, Slothful and Inert: Degeneration in Brazilian Social Thought, 1880–1940," *Journal of Latin American Studies*, Vol 25 (1993): 235; and Julia Rodríguez, *Civilizing Argentina: Science, Medicine, and the Modern State* (Chapel Hill, NC: The University of North Carolina Press, 2006), 33. Within these social pathologies, the so-called state of "racial degeneration" of the poor—perceived in terms of race, gender, and class—was interpreted as one of the main obstacles to the civilization and progress of the Latin American nations. A list of the scholarship that has addressed these issues would be very long. Some references that stand out are: Nancy Stepan, *The Hour of Eugenics: Race, Gender, and Nation in Latin America* (Ithaca, NY: Cornell University Press, 1991); Eduardo A Zimmermann, "Racial Ideas and Social Reform: Argentina, 1890–1916," *The Hispanic American Historical Review*, Vol 72, No. 1 (1992): 23–46; Javier Sáenz Obregón, Oscar Saldarriaga and Armando Ospina, *Mirar la infancia: pedagogía, moral y modernidad en Colombia, 1903–1946* (Bogotá: Uniandes, 1997); Julyan Peard, *Race, Place, and Medicine. The Idea of the Tropics in Nineteenth Century Brazilian Medicine* (Durham, NC: Duke University Press, 2000); Carlos Ernesto Noguera, *Medicina y política: Discurso médico y prácticas higiénicas durante la primera mitad del siglo XX en Colombia* (Medellín: Fondo Editorial Universidad EAFIT, 2003); Zandra Pedraza, "El régimen biopolítico en América Latina. Cuerpo y pensamiento social," *Iberoamericana*, Vol 4 (2004): 7–19; Marisa Miranda y Gustavo Vallejo, eds., *Darwinismo social y eugenesia en el mundo latino* (Madrid: Siglo XXI, 2005); Diego Armus, ed., *Avatares de la medicalización en América Latina 1870–1970* (Buenos Aires: Lugar Editorial, 2005); Jorge Márquez Valderrama, *Ciudad, miasmas y microbios: la irrupción de la ciencia pasteriana en Antioquia* (Medellín: Editorial de la Universidad de Antioquia, 2005); Hayley Froysland, "The regeneración de la raza in Colombia," *Nationalism in the New World*, edited by Don H. Doyle and Marco Antonio Pamplona, 162–183 (Athens, GA and London: The University of Georgia Press, 2006); Diego Armus, *La ciudad impura: Salud, tuberculosis y cultura en Buenos Aires, 1870–1950* (Buenos Aires: Editorial Edhasa, 2007); Marisa Miranda y Álvaro Sierra, eds., *Cuerpo, biopolítica y control social: América Latina y Europa en los siglos XIX and XX* (Buenos Aires: Siglo XXI, 2009); Adriana Novoa and Axel Levine, *From Man to Ape: Darwinism in Argentina, 1870–1920* (Chicago, IL: University of Chicago Press, 2010).

11 Zandra Pedraza, "Al otro lado del cuerpo: el dominio de la diferencia en América Latina,"*Al otro lado del cuerpo: Estudios biopolíticos en América Latina*, edited by Hilderman Cardona y Zandra Pedraza, 1–20 (Bogotá: Ediciones Uniandes, 2014).

12 In addition to the previously mentioned references, see, among others, Nancy Appelbaum, ed., *Race and Nation in Modern Latin America* (Chapel Hill, NC: The University of North Carolina Press, 2003); Brooke Larson, *Trials of Nation Making. Liberalism, Race, and Ethnicity in the Andes, 1810–1910* (Cambridge: Cambridge University Press, 2004); Stanley E. Blake, *The Vigorous Core of Our Nationality. Race and Regional Identity in Northeastern Brazil* (Pittsburgh, PA: University of Pittsburgh Press, 2011).

13 A few recent exceptions are, Diego P. Roldán, "Discursos alrededor del cuerpo, la máquina, la energía y la fatiga: hibridaciones culturales en la Argentina fin-de-siècle," *História, Ciências, Saúde—Manguinhos,* Vol 17, No. 3 (2010): 643–661; Stefan Pohl-Valero, "'La raza entra por la boca': Energy, Diet, and Eugenics in Colombia, 1890–1940," *Hispanic American Historical Review,* Vol 94, No. 3 (2014): 455–486; Óscar Gallo, "Trabalho, medicina e legislação na Colômbia, 1910–1946," Tesis doctoral, Universidad Federal de Santa Catarina, Florianapolis, 2015. For the European context see, for example, Georges Vigarello, *Le corps redressé: Histoire d'un pouvoir pédagogique* (Paris: Jean-Pierre Delarge Éditeur, 1978); Donna Haraway, *Simians, Cyborgs, and Women: The Reinvention of Nature* (New York, NY: Routledge, 1991); Anson Rabinbach, *The Human Motor: Energy, Fatigue, and the Origins of Modernity* (Berkeley: University of California Press, 1992); Philipp Sarasin y Jakob Tanner, eds., *Physiologie und industrielle Gesellschaft: Studien zur Verwissenschaftlichung des Körpers im 19. und 20. Jahrhundert* (Frankfurt am Main: Suhrkamp Verlag, 1998).

14 Rubén Jaramillo Vélez, *Colombia: La Modernidad Postergada* (Bogotá: Temis Editorial, 1994).

15 Santiago Castro-Gómez y Eduardo Restrepo, eds., *Genealogías de la colombianidad: Formaciones discursivas y tecnologías de gobierno en los siglos XIX and XX* (Bogotá: Editorial Pontificia Universidad Javeriana, 2008); Santiago Castro-Gómez, *Tejidos Oníricos. Movilidad, capitalismo y biopolítica en Bogotá (1910–1930)* (Bogotá: Editorial Pontificia Universidad Javeriana, 2009).

16 Stefan Pohl-Valero, "'La raza entra por la boca': Energy, Diet, and Eugenics in Colombia, 1890–1940," *Hispanic American Historical Review,* Vol 94, No. 3 (2014): 455–486. On the relationship between nutrition and eugenics in other Latin American countries, see, for example, Francisco de Assis Guedes de Vasconcelos, "Fome, eugenia e constituição do campo da nutrição em Pernambuco: uma análise de Gilberto Freyre, Josué de Castro e Nelson Chaves," *História, Ciências, Saúde—Manguinhos,* Vol 8, No. 2 (2001): 315–339; Alexandra Stern, "Responsible Mothers and Normal Children: Eugenics, Nationalism, and Welfare in Postrevolutionary Mexico 1920–1940," *Journal of Historical Sociology,* Vol 12, No. 4 (1999): 369–397.

17 Paulo Drinot, *The Allure of Labor: Workers, Race, and the Making of the Peruvian State* (Durham, NC: Duke University Press, 2011), chap. 5; Jeffrey Pilcher, *¡Que vivan los tamales! Food and the Making of Mexican Identity* (Albuquerque, NM: University of New Mexico Press, 1998), Chapter 4.

18 For a discussion on this methodological perspective, see Stefan Pohl-Valero, "Perspectivas culturales para hacer historia de la ciencia en Colombia," In *Historia cultural desde Colombia: categorías y debates,* edited by Max S. Hering Torres and Amada Carolina Pérez, 399–430 (Bogotá: Universidad Nacional de Colombia / Pontificia Universidad Javeriana / Universidad de los Andes, 2012).

19 Frank Safford, *El ideal de lo práctico, el desafío de formar una elite técnica y empresarial en Colombia* (Bogotá: Ancora, 1989).

20 Diana Obregón, *Sociedades científicas en Colombia. La invención de una tradición, 1859–1936* (Bogotá: Banco de la República, 1992).

21 Mario Hernández, *La salud fragmentada en Colombia, 1910–1946* (Bogotá: Universidad Nacional de Colombia, 2002); Emilio Quevedo, Catalina Borda, Juan Carlos Eslava, Claudia Mónica García, María Del Pilar Guzmán, Paola Mejía, and Carlos Ernesto Noguera, *Café y Gusano, Mosquitos y petróleo. El tránsito desde la higiene hacia la medicina tropical y la salud pública en Colombia 1873–1953* (Bogotá: Universidad Nacional de Colombia, 2004).

22 Rafael Nieto París, *Riel de hierro y máquina de vapor: fabricados en La Pradera* (Bogotá: Imprenta Echeverría, 1889).

23 It is worth mentioning that the historical development of the law of conservation of energy involved, in the mid-nineteenth century, not just engineers and physicists thinking on the optimization of thermal machines and in the science of mechanics, but also doctors and

physiologists thinking about the functioning of the human and animal organism—as well as the presence of other cultural and cognitive resources such as the German Naturphilosophie, or the language of the political economy of "work and losses." Crosbie Smith and Norton Wise, *Energy and Empire: A biographical study of Lord Kelvin* (Cambridge: Cambridge University Press, 1989); David Cahan, ed., *Hermann von Helmholtz and the Foundations of Ninetennth-Cetury Science* (Berkeley, CA: University of California Press, 1993); Kenneth Caneva, *Robert Mayer and the Conservation of Energy* (Princeton, NJ: Princeton University Press, 1993); Crosbie Smith, *The Science of Energy: A Cultural History of Energy Physics in Victorian Britain* (Chicago, IL: University of Chicago Press, 1998).

24 Salvador Camacho Roldán, "El estudio de la sociología," In *Pensamiento positivista latinoamericano II*, edited by Leopoldo Zea, 210–231, 211–212 (Caracas: Biblioteca Ayacucho, 1980 [1882]).

25 Olga Restrepo Forero, "El darwinismo en Colombia: Visiones de la naturaleza y la sociedad," *Acta Biológica Colombiana*, Vol 14 (2009): 23–40.

26 Ernesto Röthlisberger, "Al lector: Prólogo," In *Curso de Filosofía Experimental* (Bogotá: Imprenta de Medardo Rivas, 1883), iv–v.

27 Gorgonio Petano y Mazariegos, *Manual de economía política* (París: Rosa y Bouret, 1859), 110.

28 Carlos E. Putnam, *Tratado práctico de medicina legal* (Bogotá: Imprenta de Antonio María Silvestre, 1896), 1, 4.

29 George Barker, "El problema de la vida," In *Curso de Filosofía experimental*, edited by César C. Guzmán, 473 (Bogotá: Imprenta de Medardo Rivas, 1883).

30 Théodule Armand Ribot, "Extracto de la psicología de Alexander Bain," In *Curso de Filosofía experimental*, edited by César C. Guzmán, 254 (Bogotá: Imprenta de Medardo Rivas, 1883).

31 Liborio Zerda, "Programa de física matemática i médica," *Anales de la Universidad Nacional de los Estados Unidos de Colombia*, Vol 1, No. 3 (1868): 323–337; Liborio Zerda, "De física médica," *Anales de Instrucción pública*, Vol 13, No. 74/75 (1888): 262–269.

32 Abraham Aparicio, "Sobre fisiolojia," *Anales de la Universidad Nacional de los Estados Unidos de Colombia*, Vol 1, No. 3 (1868): 353–356, 353.

33 Ramón Vanegas Mora, *Estudio sobre nuestra clase obrera* (Bogotá: Imprenta de Torres Amaya, 1892), 19–28. The "various trades" category included the following: armory, blacksmith and tinsmith; carpentry; printing; binding; tailoring; shoemaking and saddlery. All these jobs were performed by men. The work of women was classified as well: seamstresses, maids, washerwomen, fruit loaders, and wage laborers.

34 Ibid., 13.

35 Ibid., 22.

36 Manuel Cotes, *Régimen alimenticio de los jornaleros de la Sabana de Bogotá: estudio presentado al Primer Congreso Médico Nacional de Colombia* (Bogotá: Imp. de La Luz, 1893), 41–42.

37 Ibid., 6, 21.

38 Ibid., 20–21. According to Cotes, an adequate diet for a male worker should include, per day, 430 grams of carbohydrates, 130 grams of proteins, 50 grams of fat, and 30 grams of minerals.

39 Andrés Carrasquilla, *Atrepsia* (Bogotá: Imprenta la Luz, 1889), 12–13; Manuel Cotes, *Régimen alimenticio de los jornaleros de la Sabana de Bogotá: estudio presentado al Primer Congreso Médico Nacional de Colombia* (Bogotá: Imp. de La Luz, 1893), 36.

40 Calixto Torres Umaña, *Sobre metabolismo azoado en Bogotá* (Bogotá: Ed. Arboleda & Valencia, 1913), 14–15.

41 Ibid., 56.

42 Ibid., 26.

43 ibid., 22. For example, it calculated the average in grams of protein, fat, and carbohydrates consumed by different German classes in order to meet their energy demands.

44 Miguel Triana, "Sociología de la montaña," *El Gráfico*, Vol 4, No. 123 (1913): s.p. [First page of the article].

45 Antonio Vargas Vega, "Estudios de climatolojia comparada—Elevación del suelo," *Gaceta Médica*, Vol 1 (1865): 1–2.

46 Mónica García and Stefan Pohl-Valero, "Styles of Knowledge Production in Colombia, 1850–1920," *Science in Context*, Vol 29, No. 3 (2016): 347–377.

47 Julio Arias, *Nación y diferencia en el siglo XIX colombiano: Orden nacional, racialismo y taxonomías poblacionales* (Bogotá: Uniandes, 2005).

48 Monica García and Stefan Pohl-Valero, "Styles of Knowledge Production in Colombia, 1850–1920," *Science in Context*, Vol 29, No. 3 (2016): 347–377.

49 The working class included people with jobs such as laborers, servants, bricklayers, carpenters, car detailers, police officers, tailors, blacksmiths, and cart drivers; meanwhile the "upper classes" included university students, merchants, doctors, and military officers. Calixto Torres Umaña, *Sobre metabolismo azoado en Bogotá* (Bogotá: Ed. Arboleda & Valencia, 1913), 77–89.

50 Calixto Torres Umaña, "La nutrición en la altiplanicie de Bogotá," In *Proceedings of The Second Pan American Scientific Congress: Section VIII Part 2*, edited by Glen Levin Swiggett, 74 (Washington, DC: Government Printing Office, 1917).

51 Juan Corpas, *La atmósfera de la Altiplanicie de Bogotá: en algunas de sus relaciones con la fisiología y la patología del hombre* (Bogotá: Imprenta de Medina e Hijo, 1910).

52 Marcos Cueto, "Andean Biology in Peru: Scientific Styles on the Periphery," *Isis*, Vol 80, No. 4 (1989): 640–658; Laura Cházaro, "La fisiología de la respiración en las alturas, un debate por la patria: mediciones y experimentos," In *México y Francia: Memoria de una sensibilidad común; siglos XIX-XX. Tomo II*, edited by Javier Pérez-Siller and Chantal Cramaussel, 317–339 (México: Centro de Estudios Mexicanos y Centroamericanos, 1993).

53 Stefan Pohl-Valero, "¿Agresiones de la altura y degeneración fisiológica? La biografía del "clima" como objeto de investigación científica en Colombia durante el siglo XIX e inicios del XX," *Revista Ciencias de la Salud*, Vol 13, número especial (2015): 65–83.

54 Stefan Pohl-Valero, "'La raza entra por la boca': Energy, Diet, and Eugenics in Colombia, 1890–1940," *Hispanic American Historical Review*, Vol 94, No. 3 (2014): 455–486.

55 Ingrid Johanna Bolívar, "Discursos estatales y geografía del consumo de carne de res en Colombia," In *El poder de la carne: Historias de ganaderías en la primera mitad del siglo XX en Colombia*, edited by Alberto Flórez-Malagón, 230–289 (Bogotá: Editorial Pontificia Universidad Javeriana, 2008).

56 Manuel Cotes, *Régimen alimenticio de los jornaleros de la Sabana de Bogotá: estudio presentado al Primer Congreso Médico Nacional de Colombia* (Bogotá: Imp. de La Luz, 1893), 39.

57 Ibid; Pablo García Medina, "La alimentación de nuestra clase obrera en relación con el alcoholismo," *Revista de Higiene. Órgano del Consejo Superior de sanidad de Colombia*, Vol 6, No. 88 (1914): 161–176.

58 Carlos Michelsen Uribe, "Carnes. Su consumo en Bogotá," *Revista de Higiene*, Vol 3, No. 29 (1891): 227–229, 228; and Carlos Michelsen Uribe, "Carne," *Revista de Higiene*, Vol 1, No. 4 (1887): 55–59.

59 Jeffrey Pilcher, *¡Que vivan los tamales! Food and the Making of Mexican Identity* (Albuquerque, NM: University of New Mexico Press, 1998), Chapter 4; Paulo Drinot, *The Allure of Labor: Workers, Race, and the Making of the Peruvian State* (Durham, NC: Duke University Press, 2011), Chapter 5; Stefan Pohl-Valero, "'La raza entra por la boca': Energy, Diet, and Eugenics in Colombia, 1890–1940," *Hispanic American Historical Review*, Vol 94, No. 3 (2014): 455–486.

60 Jeffrey Pilcher, *¡Que vivan los tamales! Food and the Making of Mexican Identity* (Albuquerque, NM: University of New Mexico Press, 1998), Chapter 4; José María Lombana Barreneche, "Prevención del alcoholismo," *Revista Médica de Bogotá*, Vol 23, No. 277 (1903): 801–809.

61 Adriana Alzate, *Suciedad y orden: Reformas sanitarias borbónicas en la Nueva Granada 1760–1810* (Bogotá: Editorial de la Universidad del Rosario, 2007).

62 Carlos Ernesto Noguera, *Medicina y política: Discurso médico y prácticas higiénicas durante la primera mitad del siglo XX en Colombia* (Medellín: Fondo Editorial Universidad EAFIT, 2003).

63 Pablo García Medina, "La alimentación de nuestra clase obrera en relación con el alcoholismo," *Revista de Higiene. Órgano del Consejo Superior de sanidad de Colombia*, Vol 6, No. 88 (1914): 170–171.

64 Hayley Froysland, "The regeneración de a raza in Colombia," In *Nationalism in the New World*, edited by Don H. Doyle and Marco Antonio Pamplona (Athens, GA and London: The University of Georgia Press, 2006).

65 Stefan Pohl-Valero, "'Lla raza entra por la boca': Energy, Diet, and Eugenics in Colombia, 1890–1940," *Hispanic American Historical Review*, Vol 94, No. 3 (2014): 455–486.

66 Ministerio de Gobierno. "Estatutos del patronato de 'Gotas del Leche.'" AGN. República, Ministerio de Gobierno, sección 4ta Personerías Jurídicas, tomo 6 ff 131—132 Transcripción (1918).

67 Ibid.

68 Jorge Bejarano, "Las Gotas de Leche. Su significado y valor social," *Cromos*, Vol 8, No. 181 (1919): 189–190, 190.

69 For a historiographical analysis of this 1920 racial debate see, Catalina Muñoz, "Estudio introductorio: Más allá del problema racial: El determinismo geográfico y las 'dolencias sociales,'"

In *Los problemas de la raza en Colombia: Más allá del problema racial: El determinismo geográfico y las 'dolencias sociales'*, edited by Catalina Muñoz, 11–58 (Bogotá: Editorial Universidad del Rosario, 2011).

70 Calixto Torres Umaña, "Cuarta Conferencia," In *Los problemas de la raza en Colombia*, edited by Luis López de Mesa, 151–183 (Bogotá: El Espectador, 1920).

71 Stefan Pohl-Valero, "'La raza entra por la boca': Energy, Diet, and Eugenics in Colombia, 1890–1940," *Hispanic American Historical Review*, Vol 94, No. 3 (2014): 455–486.

72 Norberto Solano Lozano, "Colonia escolar de vacaciones," In *Educación nacional: Informe al congreso 1938. Anexo I*, edited by Joaquín Castro Martínez, 30–95 (Bogotá: Editorial ABC, 1938).

73 José Francisco Socarrás, "La alimentación de la clase obrera en Bogotá según el informe de Londres," *Anales de Economía y Estadística*, Vol 3, No. 7–8 (1940): 32–51.

74 José Francisco Socarrás, *Alimentación de la clase obrera en Bogotá* (Bogotá: Imprenta Nacional, 1939), 3.

75 Cited in Paulo Drinot, *The Allure of Labor: Workers, Race, and the Making of the Peruvian State* (Durham, NC: Duke University Press, 2011), 8.

76 Alberto Mayor Mora, *Etica, trabajo, y productividad en Antioquia* (Bogotá: Ediciones Tercer Mundo, 1984); Ann Farnsworth-Alvear, *Dulcinea in the Factory: Myths, Morals, Men, and Women in the Colombia's Industrial Experiment, 1905–1960* (Durham, NC: Duke University Press, 2000).

77 Paulo Drinot, *The Allure of Labor: Workers, Race, and the Making of the Peruvian State* (Durham, NC: Duke University Press, 2011), 9.

78 Cited in Ibid., 171.

79 Julio Arias, *Nación y diferencia en el siglo XIX colombiano: Orden nacional, racialismo y taxonomías poblacionales* (Bogotá: Uniandes, 2005); Benjamin S. Orlove, "Putting Race in Its Place: Order in Colonial and Postcolonial Peruvian Geography," *Social Research*, Vol 60, No. 2 (1993): 301–336.

80 Regarding the ambiguity of the notion of race held by intellectuals at the beginning of the twentieth century in Colombia see Eduardo Restrepo, "Imágenes del "negro" y nociones de raza en Colombia a principios del siglo XX," *Revista de Estudios Sociales*, Vol 27 (2007): 46–61.

17

FEMINISM IN THE SOUTHERN CONE

The Periodical Press for and by Women

Claudia Montero

In 1905, the Chilean working class typographer Carmela Jeria was the director of the newspaper *La Alborada* (Valparaiso, 1905–1907). Her editorial in the second edition recalls an incident that put her at a crossroads when her employer asked her to choose between her work in the press or to dedicate herself to "her own business."[1] Her "business" was directing a workers' newspaper. Faced with the dilemma, Jeria did not hesitate to resign and devote herself entirely to the newspaper. Although this decision put her livelihood at risk, she remained committed to the defense of her *compañeras* and to fight for a better life. Jeria's determination exemplifies the active response of Southern Cone women who developed new media projects that focused attention on emerging female figures in the public arena.

The aim of this study is to offer a comparative analysis of feminist demands in the political press, ran for and by women of the Southern Cone (Argentina, Uruguay, and Chile). The period between 1900–1950 coincides with the modernization of the region, which brought about the emergence of new female subjectivities. These subjectivities resulted in feminist discourses. Reflected in the women's press, feminist discourse transformed cultural practices associated with the feminine. Feminist journalism analyzed the status of women in society, and expressed their demand for political, social and/or cultural rights, and, in the process, spread the ideology of feminist organizations.[2]

Although the countries of the Southern Cone have a similar cultural matrix, the modernization process was different in each because of the scale of economic development and the characteristics of their political systems.[3] It can be argued that despite these differences, the experience of women in Argentina, Uruguay, and Chile was one of exclusion. The feminist press allowed groups with particular political objectives to articulate and express a variety of feminist discourses. As a cultural object, in each country, the press gave women a means of expressing, gathering, consolidating, and writing about new feminine identities.

I want to begin this chapter by defining what feminism meant in the Southern Cone during the early twentieth century. It is also important to analyze the characteristics that define the press of that time as it related to feminists and laborers. During that time there also existed a press for women associated with traditional political parties and one that was associated with the defense of international causes. However, these topics are beyond the scope of this essay.[4]

As of today, there is no comparative analysis on the women's press in the Southern Cone. This has, however, been studied in Argentina and Chile, and had been characterized as a strategy for women to express subjectivities and political projects associated to their own aesthetics.[5] In this work, investigations on the subject are systemized and advance with an original approach to collecting new records thanks to archival research in all three countries. This study utilizes a broad overview including some media which had been previously overlooked by other analyses. More importantly, it gives comparative visibility to the importance of the press as a cultural object for socially excluded groups such as women.

During the first half of the twentieth century, Latin America was being transformed by the process of modernization initiated in late nineteenth century, which is linked to the development and global triumph of capitalism.[6] This process signaled a change in the life-experience of social subjects, who were both transforming the world and being transformed by it.[7] In the case of women in the Southern Cone, modern sensibility was expressed in the emergence of new subjectivities that questioned the place assigned by patriarchy, disrupting it with new cultural practices and emerging as writers, editors, and feminists.

In the analysis of the feminist press, the concept of the public sphere is an important theoretical element, since it is in that space where publications circulate. Nancy Fraser's ideas[8] are useful when thinking of the press in Latin America, as Mirta Lobato has demonstrated in her writing on the working class press of Rio de La Plata.[9]

Fraser defines the public sphere by considering the characteristics of stratified societies such as those that exist in Latin America. These spaces are characterized, according to Tulio Halperin Dongui,[10] as containing institutional structures with unequal social groups, which foster relationships of domination and subordination. This extends to gender relations, which can be seen in the women's press. Fraser views the public sphere as a place of discursive interaction with a complex dimension because it would be an unrealized utopian ideal, ideologically masculinist and legitimizing the dominance of the privileged class. Faced with the devaluation of the contributions of subordinate groups such as women, Fraser rescues her action as subaltern and counter-public. These generate counter-discourses that allow women to make distinct interpretations about themselves, their interests, and identities.

From these considerations, we can understand why Carmela Jeria's boss gave her an ultimatum with the intent to fire her. A woman who decided to generate opinion in the early twentieth century in Latin America and the Southern Cone spoke about the persistence of control over subordinate groups that Fraser refers to. Moreover, the difficulty of executing a feminist publication speaks of a hierarchical social order set by gender norms. In this sense, according to Joan Scott, these hierarchies are fundamental to understanding the social order in which these publications were developed.[11] For a history of the feminist press in the early twentieth century, it helps to understand how social, political, economic, and cultural conditions played a more complex role than the binary conceptions of feminine/masculine. The existence of Women's Periodical Press in the Southern Cone did not only deny the exclusion of women from formal politics, but brought it to life. It also expresses how women played with established gender roles to reveal how precisely typecast their lives were.

The press is understood as a cultural object, that is to say an expression of the conditions that produce it.[12] This allows us to relate the variety in publications that we define (working class, feminist, etc.) with, for example, the agitation that caused the modernization of society and how these changes affected the daily lives of the subjects, their way of understanding themselves, and their projections of identity. In this case, women used the press as a means of expression, owning the possibilities the medium provided as a material object. Therefore, this work rescues the publication as an object of analysis, as having a unique multidisciplinary delivery, in a determined time and place, acquiring a significance that unfolds in its textual, graphic, and diagrammed discourse.[13]

Feminism in the Southern Cone

Feminism is a phenomenon of modernity and refers to a discourse that questions the subordinate status of women within a patriarchal system, demanding improvements in the daily life of women. The subordination of women is created by sex and gender relationships that encourage the domination of women by predominantly male social institutions.[14] However, feminism should be considered as a diverse phenomenon since it has different manifestations according to historical moments and ideological positions, among other factors.[15] In Latin America, the first feminist demonstrations coincided with the modernization process and from the beginning were a plural phenomenon, although exclusively tied to notions of class. The specificities of Black, indigenous, and peasant women were not part of early twentieth century discourse on feminism in the Southern Cone. Urban women led the initial feminist movement of the Southern Cone at a time when whiteness gave one legitimacy as an urban inhabitant. The silencing of the multiple exclusions of Black, indigenous, or peasant women speaks to the Eurocentric influence found in Latin American nations in the early twentieth century, of which all women were affected.

In Argentina, Uruguay, and Chile, women organized politically by developing a counter-discourse on the basis of gender exclusion, and criticized the tensions caused by economic development and social change. In this way, elite women developed liberal feminism while working class women developed a more socialist or anarchist feminism.[16] Both groups demanded the right to be considered not only "objects of modernization" through public policies, but as "subjects of modernization."[17] The latter meant to extend a certain autonomy that had managed to enter the workforce. These concerns, coupled with the influence of European immigrants (the latter with a greater impact on the countries of the Rio de la Plata), urged the consolidation of women's movements and feminist discourses in the three countries.[18]

Women's Periodical Press of the Southern Cone

Since the nineteenth century, women practiced journalism in the region. In Argentina the first publication was in 1830, in Chile in 1865, and in Uruguay in 1894. In general, these initial publications were produced by elite women with the aim of legitimizing the female voice in the public space. Without seeking to overstep boundaries, although they were aware that they were doing it, they used formats and adaptations of what was expected of a decent woman.[19] These women were concerned about the country's problems and did not seek to critique patriarchy.[20]

The twentieth century marks a new period in the history of the women's periodical press.[21] The heirs of nineteenth century press pioneers assumed the duty of protecting the place for women opened in the public sphere. From 1900, there was an explosion of publications made by women in the three countries. They not only created a political press, but also a cultural and commercial press. This diversity shows the cultural change inspired by the questioning of traditional roles for women. The diversification of women's press also questioned what the new societal relationships would look like and how women understood themselves as writers, publishers, and readers in a new urban space.[22]

Modernization created the possibility for new groups of women to publish. New technologies lowered publication costs, and an increase in literacy allowed editors to spread new ideas through magazines and newspapers.[23] In Chile this was combined with a liberal spirit that allowed for the expression of new social subjects. In Argentina and Uruguay, the arrival of immigrants was fundamental for the consolidation of a literate culture that favored the publication of media as a form of expression.[24]

The feminist press took place in a context of a booming commercial press that established gender patterns in publications. It fought against prejudice found in publications that had serious sections for men and entertainment sections for women.[25] The aim of the feminist press was to position women both as producers and readers who would analyze the political system and its limits, generating a profound cultural change in the consideration of what a woman should be. Through these key features, one should understand their circulation formats, sections and layout. This press was part of a non-commercial circuit of publications produced by certain political groups. It fulfilled the function of bringing awareness to the female collective as a counter-public.

This means that by women assuming the role of social subjects, they were able to form an audience that defied the bourgeois public.[26] These publications generated discussion and controversy, spreading a particular ideology, while at the same time creating a place of socialization and training of militants within the organization.[27] These functions are present in the formats of the publications. They had sections devoted to the dissemination of the activities of the organization, internal documents and minutes of meetings, declarations of principles, etc. However, what characterizes this press was the presence of texts that qualify as gender essays.[28] In all publications, whether magazines or newspapers, liberal feminists, socialists or anarchists, we find such texts, responding to and challenging masculinist narratives about culture and history.[29]

The Working Class Feminist Press in the Southern Cone

Working class media in the countries of the Southern Cone are heterogeneous. They respond to the influence of ideologies like anarchism and socialism, and since the end of the nineteenth century, shed exclusions of class, regardless of race or ethnicity. In Argentina in 1896, *La Voz de la Mujer* was published and defined as an "anarchic Communist newspaper." Fortunately, this publication survived conservation policies as well as gender bias and is accessible today. *La Voz de la Mujer* has been reissued by the Universidad de Quilmes.[30] Unfortunately, the Chilean newspaper *La mujer* (1897) did not have the same fate. *La mujer* was a working class newspaper in Valparaíso, Chile. Today we only know of its existence through a note that was published in an elitist newspaper from the same date.[31] Studies on these publications have categorized them in different ways. For example, Bellucci categorizes them as "oppositional press"[32] or "feminist—anarchist press."[33] However, there is agreement in terms of feminism. Most of these publications circulated during the beginning of the century. This happened during a particular time in the labor movement of the Southern Cone, strengthened by the contradictions of modernization. Similarly, the arrival of Belén de Sárraga greatly influenced women's organizations in these countries. De Sárraga was a Spanish free-thinker who visited Latin America, influencing the formation of the first women's organizations in Chile and the founding of newspapers in the Río de la Plata.

The anarchist working class women's press came about in the countries of the Rio de la Plata (Table 17.1). In fact, the most recognized anarchist activists—Juana Rouco Buela, Maria Abella, and Virginia Bolten—lived between the two countries and are claimed by feminist genealogies in both Uruguay and Argentina. However, considering the principles of anarchism and feminism, it makes sense to think of their actions transnationally, therefore avoiding stereotypical characterizations in national histories.

Table 17.1 Working class women's press in the Southern Cone (1900–1950)

Argentina	*Uruguay*	*Chile*
Nosotras (La Plata 1902–1904) María Abella.	*El Liberal* (Montevideo 1908–1910) Belén de Sárraga.	*La Alborada* (Valparaíso 1905–1907) Carmela Jeria.
La voz del pueblo (Salta 1905) Sarah Bergara.	*La Nueva Senda* (Montevideo 1909–1910) Juana Rouco Buela, Virginia Boltén and María Collazos.	*La Palanca* (Santiago 1908) Ester Díaz.
Tribuna Femenina (s/d 1915–1916).	*La Batalla* (Montevideo 1915–1927) María Collazo.	*El Despertar de la Mujer Obrera* (Santiago 1914).
Nuestra Tribuna (Necochea 1922 and 1924) Juana Rouco Buela and Virginia Boltén.	*Boletín informativo del Sindicato U. de la aguja* (Montevideo 1931–33).	

European activists who arrived on either side of the Rio de la Plata, and who became involved in the labor movement, gave life to these publications. They established the basis for a regional anarcho-feminism associated with the movement in Europe, rather than other Latin American countries. Although they had a relationship with movements in Chile and Brazil, there is a lack of research to deepen the analysis and scope of these relationships. The plausibility of a relationship between this movement and other regions of Latin America has yet to be researched.

The nature of their journalism was that it was not especially professionalized. Their form of journalism was voluntary and discontinuous and its main objective was political education.[34] It is recognized as an expression of conscious women who were subjected to female gender roles as workers and mothers. It contained a critique of the capitalist system that condemned workers because of their gender.[35] However, this criticism was made from an anarchist lens, subordinating themselves to a discourse that considered them only as *compañeras* to the movement. The role of women was to stimulate the militancy of their sons, husbands, and brothers, generating tensions in the anarcha-feminist discourse.[36]

Despite the tensions, the anarcha-feminists were in the forefront of a transgressive action that visualized the situation of women as the result of a unequal social development. In this way, they represented a cultural shift by interjecting new female figures in Latin America's public sphere. This was the result of a new women's subjectivity that questioned the bourgeois norms of female behavior. Thus, a newspaper with a title like *Ni Dios, Ni Patron, Ni Marido* [Neither God, nor Patron, nor husband] represented a phenomenon that even the anarchists themselves would look away from. Likewise, one must understand the rejection of the liberal feminists as consistent with their ideology; the anarcha-feminist refused to support bourgeois order-related causes. Therefore, we can understand the great silence in the anarcha-feminist press on issues of suffragism. This has been described by Barrancos as "counter-feminism by anarchist feminists."[37]

The fundamental anarcha-feminist issues were related to the various areas in which women experienced decline. In the workplace, they proposed equal working conditions to improve the situation of female workers, considering the trinomial women/work/maternity. On the other hand, they questioned the institution of the bourgeois family, proposing free love, so that women could regain their autonomy as subjects and make their own decisions. This also relates to prophylactic campaigns which aimed to protect women from the spread of venereal disease, the right to contraceptives, and abortion.

They fought for women's education, which moved away from gender norms that trained young girls in church-influenced domesticity, and demanded access to scientific education that would allow them to reach their full potential. A summary of these approaches can be seen in the following intervention by Juana Rouco Buela in the first edition of the newspaper *La Nueva Senda* (Montevideo 1909–1910), which she directed along with Virginia Bolten and Maria Collazos, all anarchists and feminists recognized on both sides of Rio de la Plata:

> Oh the law! It unites her forever (according to them) with a man, who like her, is a victim of today's society. When it doesn't work for her, a degenerate, it makes her a double victim, forced by law to obey him blindly since it is stated that he is the patron and owner of the home they created. So in this cursed society women must be continually subjugated: first under the maternal splint that punishes her so society won't criticize her actions, while on the other hand corrupts her. She is then punished under the shameful whip of the infamous and tyrannical patron, and finally under the despotism of a degenerate nobody who acts with pretension and authority, given to him by the law and society; all of this makes her a true martyr.[38]

Aware that women workers experienced more than one form of exploitation (at work and home), the anarcha-feminists proposed and encouraged women's organizing to address specific struggles. In this way, the proposal of Virginia Bolten's organization is celebrated:

> all women who have understood the necessity of establishing a new society, in which humans can live freely and women can be loving mothers and loyal companions of man and not victims and slaves as we are now. . . . The freedom that we obtain depends only on ourselves.[39]

In Chile, the working class political press was part of the Socialist Movement. However, as women became more aware of the nature of their condition, they began taking on a feminist approach.[40] The directors of the emblematic newspapers *La Alborada* and *La Palanca* took on roles for the defense of women's working conditions and denounced violent relationships in the home. For Elizabeth Hutchison, there was a correlation between female problems and the discourse of class struggle. While María Angélica Illanes raised awareness of gender in worker demand,[41] this idea may be seen in views such as the following:

> Wow! Finally the female gender has armed itself with the most effective element against public opinion: the newspaper.[42]

The Chilean female working class accounts for the lack of interest from labor leaders in regards to women's emancipation. Therefore, feminists took a critical stance forging their own position for advancement and autonomy. Certainly, they represent a new female figure, the worker feminist:

> When the daughters of the people are completely free from age old precautions, awkward routines, then they will walk resolved and serene, protected by their own intellectual power to win those rights which until today have been an exclusive monopoly of man.[43]

Like their colleagues in the Rio de la Plata, the demands in Chile were for improvements in working conditions and the consideration of the trinomial women/work/maternity. There is no pronouncement on exclusions of race or ethnicity. They demanded education that would promote women's freedom of thought and to distance women from prejudice. The following quote reveals how they denounced and repudiated physical violence against women committed by men from their own class:

> Abusing the mother of our children; is it not a slap in the face of our descendants to insult future generations? . . . These shameful treatments are spreading widely and make us accomplices with our silence.[44]

In the political press of Chilean workers, there was always tension between proletarian women's identity and the identity of working class women. The first did not challenge the roles of mother and wife, but demanded changes from the intimacy of married life. Meanwhile, the feminist worker denounced the working conditions of women and declared themselves companions of all workers in the struggle against capitalism. Working class feminism in Chile, like the anarcha-feminism of the Rio de la Plata, maintained ambivalent and contradictory notions. However, they rose as new female figures in a patriarchal culture, promoting a change in the forms of relationships. This phenomenon materialized in a cultural process that circulated in the Southern Cone societies, spreading the emergence of new subjectivities representing women in a context of modernization.

The Feminist Press in the Southern Cone

Feminist publications form a heterogeneous group within each country as well as in an international context. They are defined as magazines and newspapers produced by women who discuss "women's problems" or "women's issues." These publications present the question of exclusion, without considering the double or triple exclusions of race and ethnicity. Feminism of early twentieth century in the Southern Cone countries had to be legitimized in a society that wanted to be white and civilized; it did not consider indigenous, Black or peasant communities.

As previously mentioned, by 1900 modernization in the Southern Cone countries caused women to reject labor exclusions. Women became activists and social subjects who were aware of their capabilities in the social life of their countries.[45] This movement allowed them to demand legal, social, and political equality from self-defined feminist organizations, who, nevertheless, had differences in the radicalism of their criticism. For example, *Acción Feminista* in Argentina had a strong impulse from militant socialists who defended the rights of women such as activist Alicia Moreau.[46] There were also other expressions such as the alliance of feminists of different tendencies in the magazine *La nueva mujer* (La Plata 1910–1912). This magazine was directed by Julieta Lanteri, an autonomous feminist, along with Maria Ramirez Abella, who was known as an anarchist.

In Chile and Uruguay, feminism was characterized as an expression of self determined women from various political parties. While they utilized elements of socialism in their speech, both Uruguayan and Chilean feminists formed their own political organizations to defend their rights. One important distinction relates to the power of the discourse. Chilean feminism, especially as it developed before the 1920s, had a cautious tone. There was fear of condemnation and the demonizing of feminists. They draped their claims through discussions of philosophical principles supported by law.[47] Meanwhile,

Argentine and Uruguayan feminists were at the height of radicalism due to the force in which they made their demands.

The feminist political press is very extensive, and can best be understood by dividing it into three periods (Table 17.2): 1900–1920, in which dedicated feminist activism is presented; 1930, which sees the radicalization of feminism given the context of crisis that had particular repercussions in each nation; and 1940–1950, which experienced a decrease in feminist publications as compared to what had been seen to that point.

Between 1900 and 1920 there was an explosion of feminist organizations in each country that were voiced in the feminist publication of magazines and newspapers.[48] Until the 1920s, feminism in Chile was liberal, primarily formed of educated women associated with middle class and some women from the elite. Their relationship with working class women was scarce, and a window for collaboration only opened in the 1930s. A consideration for indigenous women's issues is never visible. The liberal feminism of Chilean women picked up the tradition of European feminism and its claim for equality. An example was the discourse of the journal *Acción Femenina* in its first season (Santiago 1922–1923). It defined the "female problem" as the absence of civil and political rights. They made visible the activism of women in the public sphere and defended women's education, political participation, and the right to vote. They used the format of the magazine to showcase the capabilities of women when contributing to a cultural change in which new female figures took center stage. At the same time, they supplemented this work by setting the goal of mobilizing a large collective of women in Chile around the recognition of inequality, facing the patriarchy:

> Is it not a great pity to see us subject to the condition that mark these words? Should we close our ears to the righteous voice that urges us to rise up against this sad condition singling us out?[49]

These women represented a cultural change that resulted in the circulation of periodicals that could be found under the arms of women using public transportation, in waiting rooms, and on the tables of houses of a growing middle class. However, caution was a characteristic feature of this sort of feminism. This is explained by the autonomy of Chilean feminist action upon disputing their place in the public sphere. They were careful not to appear to be a threat to the patriarchal order in a context where Chilean liberalism had allowed the expression of multiple social subjects within a defined legal framework, without, however, seeing women as plaintiffs. Meanwhile, Chilean feminism was aware that it had inherited a history narrated by men and a political consciousness achieved through ideas, actions and organizations of masculinist power. One of the many examples of this phenomenon is expressed in *Acción Femenina*:

> True feminism does not denature the woman, on the contrary, it makes her a better maiden, nobler wife, more skilled mother and above all a great citizen and a powerful social unit for the true progress of humanity.[50]

Meanwhile, Argentine feminism showed some unity among the various groups, especially among the middle and working classes. The middle class character of Argentine society contributed to the joint action of the different organizations. From 1919, the feminist movement was consolidated through a variety of public actions linked to the

Table 17.2 Feminist press in the Southern Cone (1900–1950)

Argentina 1900–1920	*Uruguay 1900–1920*	*Chile 1900–1920*
Unión y Labor (Buenos Aires 1909–1913) Petrona Eyle, Matilde T. Flaitoro, Sara Justo.	*La Defensa de la Mujer* (Montevideo 1901) Celestina Margain de León.	*La Aurora Feminista* (Santiago 1904) Eulojia Aravena. de Rojas.
La nueva mujer (La Plata 1910–1912) Julieta Lanteri, María Abella Ramírez.	*Acción Femenina* (Montevideo 1915–1924) Paulina Luisi.	*La Voz Femenina* (Santiago 1916) Elisa Valderrama.
Nuestra Causa, Revista Mensual del Movimiento Feminista (Buenos Aires 1919–1921) Petrona Eyle.	*Revista Feminista Uruguaya,* (Montevideo 1921) Elisabeth Delpech de Bertrán.	*Vida Femenina* (Santiago 1919) Inés Allende Aldunate.
		Acción Femenina (Santiago 1922–1923 y 1934–1939) Partido Cívico Femenino.
		Revista Femenina (Santiago 1924) Partido Cívico Femenino.
		Unión Femenina (Valparaíso 1927) Unión Femenina de Chile
1930	*1930*	*1930*
¡Mujer! (Buenos Aires 1931) Revista de los grupos femeninos del Partido Socialista.	*Nueva América* (Montevideo 1932) Zulma Núñez.	*Nosotras* (Valparaíso 1931–1935) Unión Femenina de Chile.
Vida Femenina (Buenos Aires, 1933–1941) Celina L. Lacraux.	*Asociación Estudiantil Femenina* (Montevideo 1933) Lilia E. Pazos, Clelia Dotta Viglietti.	*La Mujer Nueva* (Santiago 1935–1942) MEMCH.
Mujeres de América (Buenos Aires 1944) Nelly Merino Carvallo.	*Ideas y Acción* (Montevideo 1933) Partido Independiente Demócrata Feminista. Sara Rey Álvarez.	*Voz Femenina* (Santiago 1932) Partido Femenino Nacional. Elvira Rogat.
	La Mujer (Montevideo 1938) J. M. Pérez, I. Cl	*Unión Femenina de Chile* (Valparaíso 1934–1935)
1940–1950	*1940–1950*	*1940–1950*
Nuestras Mujeres (Buenos Aires 1948–1963) 1955 UMA Directora: Matilde Alemán.	*Boletín de información de "Unión femenina del Uruguay adherida a la federación demócrata internacional de mujeres"* (Montevideo 1949) María Julia Campistrous.	*Boletín FECHIF* (Santiago 1944–1947) Federación Chilena de Instituciones Femeninas.
Ciudadanas Unión de mujeres socialistas (Buenos Aires 1956) Comité de redacción: Alicia Moreau, Matilde T. de Muñoz, María L. Berrondo, Antonia Díaz y Elena Gil.		*Unión Femenina* (Valparaíso 1950–1951) Unión Femenina de Chile.
Amigas. Boletín Unión de Mujeres de Argentina (Buenos Aires 1957) Unión de mujeres de Argentina.		

struggle for political rights. At least three distinct aspects of feminist discourses emerged: one associated with Alicia Moreau represented by the Socialist Party, another from the radical feminist Julieta Lanteri, and a moderate discourse led by Elvira Rawson of the Radical Party.

The magazine *Nuestra Causa* is a good example to demonstrate the convergence of Argentine feminist groups in their struggle for the political and civil rights of women. Although the magazine was the disseminator of the National Feminist Union, an organization created in 1918 by socialist women, the publication picked up other positions held in Buenos Aires feminism. It was characterized by moving away from the maternalist justification in the demand for equal rights and approached positions of enlightened reason. Their approach was in line with the rise of Argentine feminism in the context of the radical governments. The first issues of *Nuestra Causa* in May 1919 show the consolidation of the organizations led by new groups of women:

> The feminist movement is no longer an isolated manifestation of a few exalted, eccentric women, inspiring repulsion; it is now a global trend that nothing and nobody can suppress. It is necessary to study these manifestations and it is specially important for women to know what feminists intend.[51]

Academic discussion made it possible for Uruguayan feminism to further develop in the 1920s.[52] However, the actions of anarcha-feminists should be considered as precedent to the move for the emancipation of Uruguayan women. Workers and suffragettes found common ground in the demand for better living conditions for workers on the one hand and citizens on the other. In both cases the condition of Black women was not included. They developed different formulas: demand the vote as the cornerstone of all rights and claims for equal pay for equal work.[53] One of the drivers of feminism in Uruguay was the political project of José Batlle y Ordoñez, the country's president between 1903–1907 and then between 1911–1915. His project benefitted urban communities (middle class, the industrial proletariat, and immigrants) with the extension of citizenship as the basis of a "welfare state." For women, this meant direct support from the president in the case of women's suffrage and women's education through the "Universidad de Mujeres"—however, the support did not necessarily translate into specific laws. In fact, this created a myth in relation to equality between men and women in Uruguay.

From early 1910, Uruguayan feminists focused on getting their rights and formed the Consejo Nacional de Mujeres [National Council of Women] in 1916. Under the leadership of Paulina Luisi, they began to sift through the magazine *Acción Femenina* (Montevideo 1915–1925). The Council was composed of women of the elite and educated middle class, close to liberal feminism, though not unknown to the workers there was a complete lack of Black and peasant women. Their goal was to acquire political rights through legal means, associating the struggle for peace, women's education, free access to professions and equal pay for equal performance. They also rose up to the defense of single mothers and against trafficking, regulated prostitution, and the sexual double standard.[54]

The publication *Acción Femenina* was both the expression of new female figures and the means of disseminating their work. The materialization of the magazine strengthened the feminist discourse that confronted authority:

> and we wonder what savage irony or what obtuse unconsciousness inspired the words of those constituents who had no qualms about denying women the right

> to public life in the name of the most sacred of all duties: but that these slaves of hunger, even in the name of humiliated motherhood, are unaware of how to protect us as legislators, and many times they do not know how to show respect as men! So, again, we repeat, woman should be redeemed. So we call to the heart of all women to join us in the work of liberation for our gender; and in the extent of their strength, in developing the skills for the work that their kindness and intelligence may inspire within them, they make common cause with us in this crusade of justice, in this work of redemption that will be the task of this century.[55]

In the 1930s, the Southern Cone experienced the ravages of a global crisis which had economic and political implications in the region. As exporting countries of raw materials, they saw deteriorating living conditions of their inhabitants, which was especially tragic in Chile. In addition, the rise of fascism meant a radicalization of leftist discourse. The feminists of these countries were not oblivious to the crisis and took force to defend not only women's rights but to connect with transnational struggles as a defense of peace and anti-fascism. All this resulted in a radicalized feminist press in these three countries.

In Chile, the radicalization was very evident and one of the most significant examples was the magazine *La Mujer Nueva* (Santiago 1935–1941) published by *Movimiento Pro Emancipación de la Mujer Chilena Memch* (MEMCH). This was the only organization of its kind—and because it was a self-declared radical, feminist organization, it defended its autonomy above all else. However, they established partnerships with other feminist organizations such as *Partido Cívico Femenino*, which also radicalized its discourse. The shift to the left of Chilean feminism in the 1930s led them to establish alliances with political parties like the Communist Party and the Socialist Party, in the fight against fascism. This did not mean they would renounce their perspective of gendered political and social problems. The radicalization of discourse was observed in the use of a newspapers with an urgency that appealed to the action of its readers. These newspapers also used wrenching images and a language that spoke directly to the readers. This phenomenon demonstrates the cultural transformation that created possibilities for women-led actions. These writers were female figures who did not ask permission to comment or draw attention to something. They were demanding change from a safe place, and to permit them to extend national and international feminist networks. In fact, there was a vibrant exchange between *La Mujer Nueva* in Chile and *Vida Femenina* in Argentina.

The radical nature of *La Mujer Nueva* was expressed in the discussion of various social problems, especially those that attacked women. It expressed the relationship between women, maternity, and work, which translated into many problematic issues that lacked legislation such as maternity rights for female workers, sex education regarding contraception and abortion, rights to a family allowance, and decent working conditions. In relation to sexuality, they denounced the double standard for men and women which had repercussions with the spread of venereal diseases. Regarding the situation of women in society, they took a critical look at motherhood, protection of children and the family, and also defended divorce. For the first time in Chile, this group of women called into question the traditional role of being mothers. The following is just a sample of how dramatization was used in feminist mobilization:

> Uncomfortable, head pressed on by an iron ring, physical distress, anguish that squeezes the stomach, nausea, cold sweat. But it is necessary to rise to get to work on time: it is necessary to overcome, because at the end of the week a

> salary means her bread and bread for her children. . . . Stop! Rest! But that is not possible! . . . She must continue. Continue while her aching limbs obey the will of commands. And so it is day after day until her body unfolds in the fierce grimace of birth. And stuck to her chest is a small insatiable being. It's her son! A new child! But instead of feeling the joy of tenderness . . . only one concern overwhelms her. One more mouth![56]

The 1930s began in Argentina with a coup placing General José Félix Uriburu in power. The conservatism that marked his government required feminists to find new ways of organizing. One of these new approaches was to share activism with organizations that were neither feminists or women's organizations, such as the pacifists. Feminism maintained its stability in socialist feminist organizations, but because of the context, adjusted its goals. This weakened the defense for political rights, and favored the defense of democracy and freedom.[57] Also, the defense of the Spanish Republic was an incentive that gave strength to socialist Argentine feminist discourse and is most notably expressed in *Vida Feminina* (Buenos Aires 1933–1941).

Vida Femenina was an established monthly publication released without interruption for eleven years. It dealt with women's issues, although there was a major emphasis on the global advancement of totalitarianism and corruption of local politics. The publication represented a dramatic call by socialists in defense of women's participation against the limitations assigned by nationalist discourse in the 1930s.[58] With the worsening of social problems that painted a picture of social decomposition, they called for intervention with a motivating speech as expressed by Alica Moreau:

> But today! We have the feeling of chaos. The war brutally interrupts slow constructive development, launching at the worker, the artist, the teacher, appallingly at the confused peasant in the battle field, causing us to lose all of our confidence in the future. . . . Everything is dominated by the desire of violence, speed, boldness, strength. . . . They are the expression of a humanity whose exhausted sensibility demands, in order to react, increasingly more powerful catalysts. Only this explains the indifference to the threat of a new war. . . . No, the solution will not arrive by retracing history, returning us to medieval institutions or practices, but by expanding and perfecting democracy. And that's where the woman represents one of the new forces that is to serve the present moment. We must, from this new feminine force, which has not yet become conscious of itself, which continues for the moment the paths marked by man, expect a saving contribution that perhaps requires the experience of more than one generation.[59]

In Uruguay, the economic crisis led to a questioning of the social reformism of *batllismo*.[60] The myth of a modern and egalitarian country cracked, showing the reality of inequality in the worst moment of criticism of Western democracy. The year 1933 began with a coup that repressed social movements, although it had the support of military and political parties that ended up legitimizing it in elections during the same year. In this scenario, Uruguayan feminism concentrated on suffrage, uniting moderate and radical feminists. Activism resulted in the presentation of various projects to reach a common goal, which was achieved in 1932, a decade earlier than in Argentina and Chile. However, this achievement did not necessarily mean greater formal representation of women, or an improvement in living conditions, although a chapter was closed.[61]

From then on efforts were organized to keep women active in Uruguayan politics with their own representation. An example of this is the formation of *Partido Democrático Femenino del Uruguay* (1933). This party had its own source of promotion through the newspaper *Ideas y Acción* (Montevideo 1933), which called for a continued struggle for women's equality:

> [This] new political entity, which is independent of the other parties, will develop the social postulate of equality of the sexes, correcting all inequalities and injustices that still exist in our society as a result of the doctrines and prejudices that grants men a situation of superior privileges and it will make parallel a vast and just program of Social Action with respect to the greatest benefit of the country and the entire community.[62]

The idea of a continued feminist struggle clashed with others who considered it a mistake given the new political landscape. This was expressed in *América Nueva* (Montevideo 1932–1933), a publication that declared itself a defender of women's suffrage but questioned the existence of autonomous women's organizations, since it believed that traditional parties addressed women's demands. In fact, it claimed that the women had been surprised with the right to vote because "it is demonstrating that they still don't know which road to take:"

> In any case, they are placed in the least desirable situation, which would leave their status as it has been until the present day: face to face, man and woman in an absurd battle of the sexes.[63]

Specific research is still needed in order to explain this confrontation within Uruguayan feminism of the 1930s. However, it relates to feminist silence that had been established in other Latin American countries after the recognition of women's suffrage. In particular, the feminist press that developed in Uruguay after this juncture, decreased considerably. An example of this is the publication of the magazine *La Mujer* (Montevideo 1938), which developed some general questions about the status of women, but is mixed with miscellaneous text and notes of national and international reality.

In the 1940s and 1950s, the feminist press in the Southern Cone suffered a considerable decrease and became institutionalized.[64] Most changed their format to become bulletins. This change says a lot, since the publications lost their character to disseminate the objectives of organizations towards the public sphere and focus more on internal news. This reality is most clearly seen in Chile and Uruguay, as Argentina shows a production that continues to give accounts of active, stable organizations that overcame the feminist silence after achieving political rights.[65]

The decline in the production of the women's press in Chile happens despite the fact that in the 1940s, feminism gained strength in the struggle for the vote. They organized by meeting in the *Federación Chilena de Instituciones Femeninas*, FECHIF (1944), which published its newsletter from 1944–1947. In 1949, Chilean women were recognized as citizens with full rights. However, although this empowered them to access positions in office, the two candidates who won elections (María Inés de la Cruz as a senator in 1953 and Inés Enríquez as deputy in 1958) were dismissed in a clear attempt to stop women in politics.[66] In Uruguay, a country with a history of recognizing women as citizens, the 1940s saw the first women elected to office. Many of them militant members of the *Partido Colorado*, who participated in the *Comité Nacional Batllista* (1942). With their action in parliament they succeeded in reforming the Civil Code, a major feminist goal, although it was achieved by women attached to a traditional political party. An example of the institutionalization of the feminist press of this period is the newspaper *Mujer Batllista/ Comité de Organización femenina Batllista Doña Matilde Pacheco de Batlle y Ordóñez* (Montevideo 1946).

In Argentina, the 1940s were marked by the rise of *Peronismo*.[67] In connection with the struggles of women, Peronismo co-opted the demand for women's suffrage through the figure of Evita Peron. Far from being considered feminist, the women's suffrage movement rose like a flag, later being sanctioned in 1947. However, there was opposition to Peronism by women activists. Part of this opposition was expressed in the continuous action of socialist feminist organizations, such as the magazine *Ciudadanas Unión de mujeres socialistas* (Buenos Aires 1956). Recognized feminists Alicia Moreau and Maria L. Berrondo continued their work there. Another organization, but not necessarily feminist, was the *Unión de Mujeres Argentinas* (1947), an arm of the Communist Party which published *Nuestras Mujeres* (Buenos Aires 1948–1963). This publication showed a shift toward the defense of women's rights justified by the concept of maternalism.[68] The amount of political feminist publications in defense of of women's rights in Argentina between the years 1940 and 1950 challenges the feminist silence that occurred in Uruguay and Chile. However, the nature of these organizations argued for public assistance and many of them were not necessarily critical of the system of women's exclusion. This fact exemplifies the dilution of a feminist press.[69]

Conclusion

The panorama of the political press for and by women between 1900 and 1950 in the Southern Cone is so vast and rich that there is not enough space here to delve into detail. However, from the small sample that we have seen, you can draw some conclusions regarding how feminist women (understood in the broad concept as the defense of women and their status in society) used the press in order to harness its potential toward achieving political goals. At the same time the publications put feminist figures into circulation who changed cultural practices and challenged the traditional roles of women. The feminist press was both the expression of new women and the means by which they expressed themselves.

These publications had a major impact on the culture of the Southern Cone as they expanded the possibilities of being a woman, making female agency evident and creating social subjects that could change their living conditions. Even so the reaction to this change resulted in the circulation of cartoons that depicted feminists as ugly, hysterical or spinsters.

While feminism in Southern Cone did not fight for the double or triple exclusions of indigenous, Black, or peasant women, it was heterogeneous in that it gave an account of class differences and ideological views between elite women, working class, socialists, anarchists, and liberals.

The major impact of these publications was that they materialized feminism as a cultural object which no one could deny. For example, both the working class and feminist press were the expressions of groups of women who were aware of the new reality and the role they played in society. Both groups of women analyzed in this paper are examples of a counter-discourse as they expressed subjectivities that questioned the roles assigned by patriarchy. The working class, either anarchists or socialists, saw women as workers and victims of the capitalist system; feminists showed how they suffered exclusion of rights.

In both cases they show another interpretation of women through publications that challenged gender patterns classifying women as readers and producers of light texts, magazines, devoid of opinion.

Gender disparity and the hierarchical social order was also expressed in the difficulty women had in keeping many of its publications alive. There was no space to view the relationship of women's political press over time, but a quick glance of the tables, shows the short life of many publications. Gender disparity can also be seen in the rise and fall of the feminist press in the Southern Cone in the first half of the twentieth century. Early on the women's press concentrated on socialists and anarchists thanks to the explosion of the labor movement in these countries, although not without criticism from their peers; the great presence of feminists in the 1920s was influenced by an international movement that demanded political rights for women. Finally, the women's press transformation in the 30's was a product of the economic crisis and was diluted in the 1940s as a product of institutionalization and cooptation of women by political parties once the right to vote was won.

However, it is important to acknowledge that the women from the Southern Cone took advantage of the possibilities offered by the press and ultimately achieved their political goals. The press itself responded quickly to the contingencies that allowed the transformation of feminist discourse despite the different political contexts, without softening their criticism of the patriarchal system. The women's press knew how to accommodate the circumstances regulating multiple radical positions, finding commonality with the demands of other social movements in order to sustain their ultimate criticism: the subordination of women by patriarchal society.

Notes

1 Jeria, Carmela. "Hoja de Laurel", *La Alborada*, Vol 2 (1905): 1.

2 The production of female press in all three countries went beyond and is of higher quality than the political press associated with the mere claiming of rights. Within it was the Catholic women's press, with broad development in Chile, Uruguay, and to a lesser extent, Argentina. There was also a cultural and commercial women's press.

3 Modernization process was experienced in the Southern Cone countries in similar ways since they entered the world economy as exporters of raw materials. This had an impact on revenue growth, which enabled industrial activity, expanded urbanization, increased investment in public services, the state bureaucracy, and migration. This development generated social inequalities and maintained an exclusionary structure. The difference between the countries was seen in the volume and scope of the changes. For example, European immigration rose in Argentina and Uruguay from 47.1 percent in 1908 to 72.5 percent in 1914. Population growth rose in Buenos Aires from 1,575,814 inhabitants in 1895 to 2,981,043 in 1914. In Montevideo it rose from 309,000 in 1890 to 708,233; and in Santiago from 256,403 in 1895 to 553,458 in 1920. See Leslie Bethell (ed.), *Historia de América Latina. Tomo X, América del Sur 1870-1930*, 21 (Editorial Crítica, Barcelona, 1992).

4 The following are examples of these periodicals: Press for Political Parties and Women in the Southern Cone, (1900–1950)—Argentina, Chile, Uruguay, *Mujeres Argentinas. Vocero Comunista* (Buenos Aires, 1946–1948) Partido Comunista argentino. Directora: Alcira de la Peña, *Mujer Batllista/ Comité de Organización femenina Batllista Doña Matilde Pacheco de Batlle y Ordóñez* (Montevideo: 1946); *Directora: Alba Roballo de Previtali. Política Feminista* (Valparaíso: 1931–1932) Juventud Liberal Democrática, *Humanidad nueva. Revista Socialista Internacional* (Buenos Aires, 1908–1919) Directora: Alicia Moreau, *Lealtad* (Santiago: 1934–1938) Partido (Valdivia: 1939–1940) Juventud Socialista, de la Acción de Mujeres Socialistas, *La mujer en marcha* (Santiago: 1953) Órgano oficial del Partido Nacional Femenino Ibañista. Press for Women in International Organizations in the Southern Cone, (1900–1950)—Argentina, Uruguay, Chile, *Frente Único: Frente único Popular Argentino y Federación Antiguerra de Mujeres Argentinas* (Buenos

Aires: 1935). *Acción Americanista: boletín de la "Liga femenina de Confraternidad Americana"* (Montevideo: 1943) Directora: María Luisa Herrera de Gutiérrez, *Centro Femenino de Asistencia a los Prisioneros Italianos de Guerra* (Buenos Aires: 1944); *Acción Femenina por la Victoria. Periódico de ayuda a las naciones liberadas de los fascismos* (Montevideo: 1946).

5 This analysis is less developed in Uruguay where it has only revealed the production of female press associated with the history of women's organizations.

6 Eric Hobsbawn, *La Era del capital,1848–1875* (Buenos Aires: Crítica, 1998).

7 Marshall Berman, "Brindis por la modernidad," In *El debate modernidad/Posmodernidad*, edited by Nicolás Casullo, 67–91 (Argentina: El cielo por asalto, 1994).

8 Nancy Fraser, "Repensando la esfera pública: una contribución a la crítica de la democracia actualmente existente," In *Habermas and the Public Sphere*, edited by Craig Calhoun, 109–142 (Cambridge, MA: MIT Press, 1992).

9 Mirta Lobato, *La prensa obrera. Buenos Aires y Montevideo 1890–1958* (Buenos Aires: Edhasa, 2010).

10 Tulio Halperin Dongui, "Economy and Society in post-Independence Spanish America," In *The Cambridge History of Latin America Vol III*, edited by Leslie Bethell, 247–252 (Cambridge: Cambridge University Press, 1985).

11 Joan Scott, "El Género: una categoría útil para el análisis histórico," In *El Género: la construcción cultural de la diferencia sexual*, edited by Marta Lamas (México: UNAM, 1996).

12 Roger Chartier, *El mundo como representación: Estudios sobre historia cultural* (Barcelona: Gedisa, 1992).

13 Rafael Osuna, *Tiempo, materia y texto: Una reflexión sobre la revista literaria* (Kassel: Reichenberger, 1998).

14 Ana de Miguel, "Feminismos," In *Diez palabras clave sobre mujer*, edited by Celia Amorós, 217 (Navarra: VD, 1995).

15 Mary Nash, *Mujeres en el mundo: Historia, retos y movimientos* (Madrid: Alianza, 2004).

16 It is important to note that female activism at the beginning of the twentieth century also included conservative women who were organized to keep the traditional order.

17 The concepts of "object" and "subject" of modernization have been developed by Marshall Berman, and have been applied in various academic papers that analyze the status of women in the early twentieth century in Latin America. See Marshall Berman. *Todo lo sólido se desvanece en el aire. La experiencia de la modernidad* (México: Siglo XXI, 1991).

18 Maxine Molyneux, *Movimientos de mujeres en América Latina. Estudio teórico comparado* (Madrid: Cátedra, 2003).

19 Francine Masiello, *La Mujer y el Espacio Público: El periodismo femenino en la Argentina del siglo XIX* (Buenos Aires: Feminaria, 1994).

20 Mabel Bellucci "De la pluma a la imprenta," In *Mujeres y cultura en la Argentina del siglo XIX*, edited by Lea Fletcher, 252–263 (Buenos Aires: Feminaria, 1994).

21 These authors include Mabel Bellucci in Argentina, Claudia Montero in Chile, and Fanny Arango in Peru.

22 Claudia Montero, "Cincuenta años de historia de la prensa de mujeres en Chile," In *Historia de las mujeres en Chile. Tomo II*, edited by Federico Stuven, 319–354 (Santiago: Taurus, 2013).

23 In Argentina illiteracy declined from 77.9 percent in 1869 to 35 percent in 1914, in Uruguay from 40.6 percent in 1900 to 29.5 in 1920, and in Chile from 68.2 percent in 1895 to 50 percent in 1920. See Leslie Bethell (ed.), *Historia de América Latina. Tomo X, América del Sur 1870-1930*, 49 (Barcelona: Editorial Crítica, 1992).

24 Mirta Lobato, *La prensa obrera: Buenos Aires y Montevideo 1890–1958* (Buenos Aires: Edhasa 2009), 34.

25 Juan Poblete, *Literatura Chilena del siglo XIX: entre públicos, lectores y figuras autoriales* (Santiago: Cuarto Propio, 2003).

26 Nancy Fraser, "Repensando la esfera pública: una contribución a la crítica de la democracia actualmente existente," In Habermas and the Public Sphere, edited by Craig Calhoun, 109–142 (Cambridge, MA: MIT Press, 1992).

27 Mirta Lobato, *La prensa obrera. Buenos Aires y Montevideo 1890–1958* (Buenos Aires: Edhasa, 2010), 16.

28 Mary Louise Pratt, "Don't interrupt me: The Gender Essay as Conversation and Countercanon," In *Reinterpreting the Spanish American Essay: Women Writers of the 19th and 20th Century*, edited by Doris Meyer (Austin, TX: University of Texas Press, 1995).

29 Ibid.
30 This facsimile edition was published in 1997 in the collection *La Ideología Argentina*, under the direction of Oscar Terán.
31 Montero, Claudia, "Trocando agujas por la pluma: las pioneras de la prensa de y para mujeres en Chile 1850–1890," *Meridional Revista Chilena de Estudios Latinoamericanos*, Número 7 (Octubre 2016): 55-81.
32 Mabel Bellucci, "De la pluma a la imprenta," In *Mujeres y cultura en la Argentina del siglo XIX*, edited by Lea Fletcher, 252–260 (Buenos Aires: Feminaria, 1994).
33 See Gabriela Fuentes, *Protagonistas y Olvidadas: De la mujer de la Independencia a la Independencia de la Mujer* (Montevideo: Orbe, 2008).
34 Mabel Bellucci, "De la pluma a la imprenta," In *Mujeres y cultura en la Argentina del siglo XIX*, edited by Lea Fletcher, 256–257 (Buenos Aires: Feminaria, 1994).
35 María del Carmen Feijóo and Marcela M.A. Nari, "Imaginando las/los lectores de La Voz de la Mujer," In *Cultura y Mujeres en el siglo XIX*, edited by Lea. Fletcher (Buenos Aires: Feminaria, 1994).
36 Dora Barrancos, *Mujeres en la sociedad argentina: Una historia de cinco siglos* (Buenos Aires: Sudamericana, 2007).
37 Dora Barrancos, *Anarquismo, educación y costumbres en la Argentina de principios de siglo* (Buenos Aires: Contrapunto, 1989).
38 Juana Rouco Buela, "Mujeres," *La Nueva Senda*, Montevideo, 18 de setiembre de 1909.
39 Ibid., n.3.
40 Elizabeth Hutchison, *Labores propias de su sexo: Género, políticas y trabajo en Chile urbano 1900–1930* (Santiago: Lom, 2006), 122.
41 María Angélica Illanes, *Nuestra historia violeta: Feminismo social y vidas de mujeres en el siglo XX: una revolución permanente* (Santiago: Lom, 2012), 15.
42 SAKT, "Charlas," *La Alborada*, no 1 (10 de septiembre de 1905), 4.
43 Jeria, Carmela, "Tras el bienestar," *La Alborada*, No. 17 (Segunda quincena de Julio de 1906), 1.
44 Guerrero O. Ricardo, "Cómo tratamos a la mujer," *La Alborada*, no 20 (18 de noviembre de 1906): 2.
45 For each of the countries there is extensive literature on the women's movement. For example, there is Barrancos from Argentina, Sapriza for Uruguay, the pioneering work of Gaviola et al. for Chile, and the foundational book of Lavrin which compared the actions of women in the Southern Cone. See Asunción Lavrin, *Women, Feminism and Social Change in Argentina, Chile, and Uruguay, 1890–1940* (Lincoln, NE: University of Nebraska Press, 1998).
46 Dora Barrancos, *Mujeres en la sociedad argentina: Una historia de cinco siglos* (Buenos Aires: Sudamericana, 2007).
47 Julieta Kirkwood, *Ser Política en Chile* (Santiago: Cuarto Propio, 1990).
48 From this period, there is *la fundación del Consejo Nacional de Mujeres Argentinas* (1900), e*l Centro Socialista Femenino y la Unión Gremial Femenina* (1902), *el grupo Unión y Labor* (1909), *el Comité Pro Sufragio* (1907), *la Liga Feminista Nacional* (1910), and the creation of the *Primer Congreso Feminista Internacional* (1910), a milestone in the feminism of Argentina. In the 1920s, they formed *el Partido Feminista Nacional* (1919), and *la Unión Feminista Nacional* (1920). At the same time in Uruguay, they formed *Liga Feminista Nacional* (1910), known as the "University of Women" (1912), *el Consejo Nacional de Mujeres (*1916), and *la Alianza Uruguaya de Mujeres para el Sufragio Femenino* (1919); however, the first political party, *el Partido Democrático Femenino del Uruguay*, was founded in 1935. In Chile, during the decade of the 1910s, feminists in Santiago founded *el Círculo de Lectura* (1915), and *El Consejo Nacional de Mujeres* (1919). The first political parties of Chilean women in the 1920s were *el Partido Femenino Nacional* (1921), *Partido Cívico Femenino* (1922) and *el Partido Democrático Femenino* (1924). It is not the objective of this work to detail the action of women through their organizations or review the specific bibliography for each country.
49 "A lo que aspira el feminismo," *Acción Femenina*, Vol 1, No. 3 (Santiago Noviembre 1922): 1–2.
50 "¿Qué clase de feminismo defendemos y por qué?" *Acción Femenina*, año 1, No. 1, (Santiago septiembre 1922): 17–18.
51 Petronila Eyle, "Nuestro anhelo," *Nuestra Causa*, no1 (Buenos Aires: mayo 1919), 2. Gallo, Rosalia, *Nuestra causa: revista mensual feminista: 1919–1921: estudio e indice general*, 29 (Buenos Aires: Instituto de Investigaciones Historicas Cruz del Sur, 2004).

52 Asunción Lavrín, *Women, Feminism, and Social Change in Argentina, Chile, and Uruguay, 1890–1940* (Lincoln, NE: University of Nebraska Press, 1995).
53 Graciela Sapriza, "Experiencias y Perspectivas de Participación Política de las Mujeres en América Latina y Caribe Argentina, Chile, Uruguay." Unpublished.
54 Silvia Rodríguez, "Los papeles de la mujer en una sociedad de cambios (1916–1932)," In *Los Veinte: El proyecto uruguayo. Arte y Diseño de un imaginario 1916–1934*, edited by Museo Nacional de Bellas Artes, 113–120 (Montevideo: Roemers, 2004).
55 La Dirección "Nuestro programa," *Acción Femenina. Revista Mensual: Consejo Nacional de Mujeres del Uruguay*, Año 1, No. 1 (julio 1917): 1–4.
56 Junious. "Maternidad," *La Mujer Nueva*, No. 3, enero 1936, Santiago de Chile, p 1.
57 Dora Barrancos, *Mujeres en la sociedad argentina: Una historia de cinco siglos* (Buenos Aires: Sudamericana, 2007), 175–176.
58 Francine Masiello, *Entre civilización y barbarie: Mujeres, Nación y Cultura Literaria en la Argentina moderna* (Rosario: Beatriz Viterbo, 1997), 228.
59 Alicia Moreau, "¿Cuál será el Porvenir de nuestros hijos?" *Vida femenina* Año I, número 4 (Buenos Aires: noviembre 1933).
60 The reform movement of President José Batlle y Ordoñez.
61 Graciela Sapriza, "Experiencias y Perspectivas de Participación Política de las Mujeres en América Latina y Caribe Argentina, Chile, Uruguay," unpublished.
62 Manifiesto al país, *Ideas y Acción* (Montevideo, No. 1), 1.
63 Zulma Nuñez. "La mujer y sus derechos," In *América Nueva. Revista Quincenal Uruguaya* (Montevideo: Enero 15 de 1933), No. 8.
64 Claudia Montero, "Cincuenta años de Historia de la prensa de mujeres en Chile," In *Historia de las mujeres en Chile. Tomo II*, edited by Federico Stuven, 349 (Santiago: Taurus, 2013).
65 Julieta Kirkwood, *Ser Política en Chile* (Santiago: Cuarto Propio, 1990).
66 Edda Gaviola Artigas, Ximena Jiles Moreno, Lorella Lopresti Martínez, and Claudia Rojas, *Queremos Votar en las Próximas Elecciones* (Santiago: LOM, 2007).
67 Political movement inspired by President Juan Domingo Perón.
68 Dora Barrancos, *Mujeres en la sociedad argentina: Una historia de cinco siglos* (Buenos Aires: Sudamericana 2007).
69 A good overview of organizations of female activists in Argentina at the time can be found in Dora Barrancos, *Mujeres en la sociedad argentina: Una historia de cinco siglos* (Buenos Aires: Sudamericana 2007).

18

FEMINISMS, GENDERS, AND INDIGENOUS WOMEN IN LATIN AMERICA

Astrid Ulloa

Introduction

Currently in Latin America there are approximately forty-five million persons who belong to 826 indigenous groups.[1] In this context and given the cultural and historical diversity in these communities, the idea of feminisms and genders in indigenous contexts is not so common and is difficult to generalize. However, there are crosscutting debates, to which I will refer, that have emerged in my experience of over thirty years of working with indigenous peoples in Colombia. For example, in Colombia there are 1,392,623 people who self-identify as belonging to 102 different indigenous groups.[2] They demand self-determination and sovereignty over their territories, and they are active participants in national electoral politics. In a similar way, in Latin America indigenous peoples are political participants in national and transnational political arenas. In both situations, gender has been a topic of discussion.

I will begin with an analysis of indigenous political processes, through which indigenous peoples have been intricately involved with resistance to conquest and colony, playing a key role in the confrontation of appropriation of their territories. However, historically the differentiated participation of indigenous men and women has not been well documented. Although there is evidence of female figures such as Bartolina Sisa or Gaitana,[3] among others, the demands for civil and political rights of indigenous women is a more recent process. For some authors,[4] understanding these processes means looking at them in a contextualized way. First, a historical overview will situate the cultural practices and account for the colonial dynamics towards indigenous peoples. Secondly, a new perspective is needed that accounts for gender and political participation as a process that occurs in the contemporary context of what is understood by the idea of politics.

In this regard, it is worth clarifying that in colonial contexts, debates over gender did not exist as they do today; not because inequalities were absent between men and women, but because they were responding to other ontological categories and visions of being indigenous and of being men and women. On the other hand, the political dynamics of indigenous peoples began to appear in academic accounts more regularly since the 1970s. Although this history is framed in the context of political participation (in terms of social movements and collective identities), it ignores an analysis of the distinct manifestations of both indigenous men and women, and instead analyzes them under a collective cultural identity as indigenous people.

Since the 1970s the indigenous movements have succeeded in having their demands met with new policies and recognition of rights. They have achieved the recovery of part of their ancestral territory, the recognition of civil and ethnic rights, the creation of their own economic strategies, the conquest of political spaces for indigenous leaders, and the acceptance by non-indigenous sectors, as well as the construction of a pluri-ethnic state, participation in all aspects of society, and the formation of local and international political negotiations.

The processes of the recognition of rights have confronted the modern categories of development and nature, and not so directly, the category of gender in order to strengthen the national and international discussion of indigenous women. Although indigenous movements in Latin America have not had a general position in relationship to gender, the participation of women has been fundamental to them.

Studies on indigenous movements mention, in a very general way, the participation of women. However, there is less information about indigenous women's demands for their rights. This lack of visibility is partly a result of academic analyses that fail to understand their situations. Some authors[5] have argued elsewhere that some of the analysis on indigenous movements tends to focus on actions and political demands when they are of interest to the academy. According to Varese this trend reflects a reductionist or Eurocentric perspective that only views indigenous movements as relevant when the academy recognizes these behaviors as political.[6] Insofar as the presence of indigenous women is concerned, one might think that their active involvement is a recent phenomenon coinciding with the rise of feminist studies. As we entered the twenty-first century, interest rose in the relations of gender and the relationship between women and the environment, which has opened an emphasis on the participation of indigenous women in the areas of socio-environmental conflicts, climate change, and biodiversity.

Currently, participatory processes with and for indigenous women (as a synonym of gender perspective), and their inclusion within the study of gender, are seen favorably and as an imperative to include in projects of grassroots organizations, state policies, global programs, and even within indigenous programs. However, until recently, few programs, plans, actions, or research took this into account, and have failed to question the use of crosscutting gender categories for indigenous peoples. Because of this fact, it is necessary to ask ourselves what are the implications of the rise of this topic and the inclusion of indigenous women under the categories of gender that correspond to other cultural notions. How have the struggles of indigenous women been reimagined as gendered spaces of political participation? What reconsiderations do the various collective proposals of indigenous peoples or female indigenous leaders offer to these categories? How have the ideas and representations of indigenous people and women been viewed both historically and through the lens of feminisms?

Indigenous women's movements have positioned gender issues in local, national, and global contexts, through demands of their rights not only individual but also collective. Their demands are focused on participation and on decision-making in both public and private political arenas. These movements have also positioned and legitimized individual and collective demands related to education, health, and their bodies. All these demands allow them to question exclusions, unequal relations, discrimination, and violence that have been imposed on women by patriarchal domination. These political dynamics also allow them to construct resistances and propose alternatives.[7]

Indigenous women are rapidly constructing spaces of participation for their demands. For example, they created *la Red de Mujeres Indígenas sobre Biodiversidad* (RMIB), *el Foro*

Internacional de Mujeres Indígenas, and more recently l*a Cumbre Continental de Mujeres Indígenas del Abya Yala* (CCMI), among others.[8] In addition, regional indigenous organizations such as *Coordinadora de las Organizaciones Indígenas de la cuenca Amazónica* (COICA), *Centro de culturas indígenas del Perú* (Chirapac), and each community-based organization, have established programs and strategies for the inclusion of women.

However, indigenous women have questioned indigenous movements and organizations for not considering the role they also play in the political demands and struggles. Demands for recognition and the search for a political space are being made by indigenous women within the indigenous groups (as they are also being made in national contexts), which consider the differences between men and women and begin with the relationships that are internal to their cultures, which do no emerge from external requirements or demands.

In addition, indigenous women have questioned academic discussions that seek to understand gender differences and feminist arguments within the local cultural dynamics. In fact, there have been several trends to analyze gender differences in indigenous contexts, which involve differentiating discussions about feminisms, genders, and indigenous women. Also, one must consider the meaning of gender analysis in Latin America in relation to indigenous peoples given that it is central to the current analysis of indigenous political action. Therefore, gender differences are, in fact, central to understanding the political dimensions and inequalities between indigenous men and women, and between indigenous peoples and national societies.[9] According to Segato:

> it is not only about introducing gender as one of the subjects of the decolonial critique or as one of the aspects of domination in the pattern of the coloniality, but it is about offering a real theoretical and epistemic status to examine it as a central category capable of illuminating all the other aspects of the transformation imposed on the life of the communities that are confined by the new modern colonial order.[10]

Therefore, it is important to take note of the historical and colonial relationships of indigenous peoples in order to contextualize how they articulate gender and feminisms. This will clarify the complexity of confrontations, resistances, and the alternatives that emerge in indigenous contexts, especially for indigenous women. Similarly, the dynamics and practices of indigenous women in the context of their own people propose new ways of being women simply through their own perspectives and daily practices.

Under these analytical perspectives, it is necessary to address the historical relations that occurred since the Conquest and colonial times on indigenous peoples. Similarly, the political and territorial demands of indigenous people since the mid-twentieth century, which led to transformations after major political events, gave rise to new themes and alliances that strengthened gender. Since the 1990s these struggles gave indigenous women political space, allowing them to position and reframe issues such as alternatives to development and alternative environmental practices. In these contexts, alternative feminisms revisit elements of the *different feminisms*,[11] but from indigenous perspectives, allowing for a redefinition and re-positioning of other categories of gender and what we know as male and female. In short, a historical recap of the demands and positioning of local or community feminisms in the political scene is necessary. It is important to recapture the feminist voice from its articulation with Latin American indigenous movements, and its ensuing articulation with environmental issues, extractivism, and alternatives to development.

Under these articulations and connections, I argue that discussions of feminisms, genders, and women allowed for the recognition of rights and the visualization of unequal gender relations with and among indigenous peoples. However, at the same time, they have generated other inequalities and exclusions for indigenous women, both in their communities and in relation to national and international dynamics based on external gender categories. These categories led to a rethinking of gender differences in contexts of indigenous peoples. These changes developed through the proposals of indigenous women and by internal discussion, and through the relations between men and women, and with the non-human (all beings such plant, animals, territory), the political, and the territorial. However, these changes have to be understood within historical processes.

Colonial Historical Relations: Indigenous Men and Women

During colonial times and the post-independence period, Western thought used the notion of difference as a power mechanism to mark, assign, and classify otherness as an object of knowledge, control, and colonial assimilation. It promoted separate narratives of progress and order in the religious, scientific, political, economic, aesthetic, and social discourse, among others, in order to explain such cultural differences.[12]

During the Colonial period, it was assumed that people formed an identity based on the connection between nature and those who lived in it. This was based on deterministic environmental notions and it was thought that nature influenced the vices and virtues of the inhabitants of a region. The tropics implied extravagance, extremes, and passions that produced overwhelmed and uncontrolled feelings. On the other hand, moderate climate—similar to that of the European empires—gave inhabitants a balance of emotions.[13] Also, given the Christian assumption that human nature is corrupted, an environment that reduces human control over nature could only produce evil. These initial environmental representations associated with indigenous territories served to organize and name the land.

At the end of the seventeenth century and beginning of the eighteenth century, images of the relationship between indigenous peoples and nature commonly emphasized the affinity between them and animals. Among these images are humans with tails, similar to monkeys, *homos silvestris,* or other characteristics of animals, such as a big-eared human or a *cynocephaly.*[14] These reflect and reproduce the medieval and Renaissance concepts of the animality of indigenous otherness in America.[15] Another common variation of inhumanity or Indians as incomplete humans is found in the expressions of female images.

Amazonian women[16] and mermaids[17] commonly appeared among the representations of the indigenous associating these women as beings without "normal" cultural relations similar to the rest of "humanity." Depictions of Amazonian women arrive with the conquistadors after a long process of Western tradition. The colonial imaginary often personified women and indigenous otherness in the figure of the Amazonian woman: a powerful fighter and "man-eater," whose "natural" behavior violated European standards of feminine nature and threatened to subordinate and neuter European men and their culture.[18] European assumptions about nature and humanity, evident in these personifications, provided the colonizers with important means to justify, not only the Conquest and the destruction of indigenous cultures, but also rape and brutalization of the bodies of women, which fell under the shadow of such personifications. According to Mataix: "to represent the other, the absolute otherness that was America, the European imagination, so Eurocentric and male-centric, maintained the traditional view of the feminization of conquered nature (a recurrent trope of the colonial mentality at least since Hesiod.)"[19]

On the other hand, Amazonian women and mermaids personified the native "other" as a woman characterized by religious ignorance and at the same time as a voluptuous sinner, whose enchantment caused disasters for Christian men who fell under her influence. However, women were no longer viewed as a threat once they were seduced.

During the Enlightenment, some argued that the Native Americans were the children of Mother Nature, who had not yet experienced Western time nor suffered the fall from Paradise (a vision of Rousseau's "noble savage"). The image of indigenous peoples as children was especially common during the nineteenth century.

Descriptions of indigenous peoples also portrayed them as incomplete men (without genitals), which reproduced the ideas of sex during the Renaissance. These ideas labeled women as imperfect men because they didn't have enough heat (fire) in their bodies or they were too cold and humid.[20] Consequently, the Western sexual assumptions regarding indigenous men, such as lack of libido (or heat), places them in a subordinate position, while, as pointed out previously, depictions of indigenous women ranged from an excess of feminine sexuality to the Amazonian, who lacked femininity.

These views of feminization fall under Western categories of gender and involve the dual power relations of domination and protection. This view corresponds to the hegemonic and negative vision of femininity on which the colonial system was built. These circumstances led to the subordination of indigenous peoples to Western values, under the assumption that the Europeans had a paternalistic obligation to save indigenous peoples from themselves, or an obligation, equally paternalistic, to protect them from the corruptive influence of the West. With the advent of modernity, the ideas of superiority and rationality reconfigured representations of indigenous people through a patriarchal display of the secular progressive principles of scientific objectivity, political and economic individualism, private property, and the accumulation of surpluses. These ideas assumed characteristically masculine qualities that were rationally superior to the bodily and emotional characteristics dominant in female life (such as reproduction and breeding). The apparent absence of these qualities, at least within Western representations of indigenous peoples, also suggested they were inferior. As a result, the imposition of these cultural categories classified indigenous peoples as subjects of the state (citizens) with the obligation to comply with the intent and requirements of the laws.

During the nineteenth century and early twentieth century in Latin America, images of indigenous peoples were related to representations from previous centuries. These representations are still reproduced in the discourse of different global media and environments with little or no explanation of its time or place of origin, or of the circumstances of their production or consumption. These images have played an important role in the production and maintenance of the inequalities that still affect the relations of indigenous peoples and equate them with Western notions of the feminine and of nature. Conceptions of the native "other" as a feminized "exotic" have been embodied and reproduced more effectively through *habitus* [body type][21] and everyday contemporary life practices, such as in films, videos, websites, education and academic books, museums and art exhibitions, and—as we shall see—in environmental speeches that emphasize the indigenous as daughters of Mother Nature.

This brief historical account is important for understanding colonial relations that are established for indigenous men and women, crossed by binary and hierarchical notions that maintain historical continuity and permeate relations in national and international contexts with indigenous peoples, and especially indigenous women. According to Segato, modern binary logic generates a process of colonization that includes all indigenous cultural dynamics. These historical processes have effects nowadays in political practices and cultural recognitions.[22]

Yet, this historical process is informed by feminist criticisms of exclusions and absence of indigenous women in national and global policies.[23] Within this context come the different feminisms, which generate as many theories as answers. Feminisms also provide alternatives to rethink these binary categories and call for new representations.

Global Feminisms and Local Effects

Indigenous movements have established networks with other social movements, including feminist movements and processes that are led in defense of the rights of women. These movements can be related to the different feminisms, which, although they respond to Eurocentric and Anglocentric historical perspectives, have generated positions and reactions from indigenous peoples and indigenous women.

The approach and demands from the different feminisms have been articulated in Latin America by the various political processes led by leftist popular student movements, political partisanship, and academics, among others. These processes have varied from assuming the demands of the feminisms to confronting them.[24] I want to highlight the perspectives of indigenous women and their relationship with feminist debates, rather than to make an account of the history of indigenous participation within the different feminisms.

Indigenous feminists have their own perspectives. For example, the Bolivian Aymara Julieta Paredes, a community and decolonial feminist, argues that some of these debates came from outside:

> In Bolivia, Western feminism came from the hand of neoliberalism. In the beginning, these novice Bolivian feminists were confused and used a so-called gender perspective and gender focus, from which it was still possible to use as a revolutionary concept that reveals oppression. But it was in these early years that [ideas of] class and ethnic origin greatly influenced upper and middle class, white feminists and began to eliminate political force from the concept of gender—converting it to gender equality—a postmodern, superficial, and descriptive concept of roles.[25]

Similarly, Aura Cumes, a Maya Kaqchikel scholar from Guatemala[26] argues that multiculturalism and its association with gender and feminism are homogenizing, since indigenous women are left out of the discussion and the power relationships that intersect these relations are ignored. This is similar to the demands of various indigenous women regarding political relations and participation in diverse cultural contexts. Therefore, Cumes considers it necessary to question and contextualize how these categories are constructed, from a diversity of perspectives:

> building from a plurality of positions, experiences and perspectives and proposals, will allow, as it has been done in other contexts, that among diverse women in unequal contexts we can rebuild concepts, and the analytical and political frameworks that control our struggles.[27]

On the other hand, there are debates that present the role of women in new, visible political spaces, which turn to external processes (feminists, women's movements) to incorporate gender and feminist debates.

Georgina Méndez, a Chol Maya from the northern part of Chiapas, Mexico, has analyzed how in Mexico, after the 1994 Zapatista Uprising, indigenous women have become more visible, reclaiming their rights, and making demands. These dynamics have allowed changes to arise in the visions of Zapatista womanhood and advance their participation in new spaces of political power. Also, specific demands for women resulted in the Revolutionary Law of Indigenous Women (1994).[28] Méndez posits that these processes connect with an external gaze that views the political actions of indigenous women as a new awakening: "Recently the eyes of feminists, of men, and society in general, have begun to notice indigenous women."[29]

Alternatively, there are approaches that begin from the understanding of local categories of gender in situated contexts to discuss indigenous women's political participation in relation to cultural practices.

Avelina Pancho, an indigenous Nasa woman of the Cauca, Colombia,[30] analyzes the historic role that Nasa women had in their struggles of resistance and emphasizes her participation in bilingual and intercultural health and education programs. Avelina posits that the struggle of Nasa women cannot be separated from cultural conceptions of complementarity with men with whom they share daily roles and a vision of the world; these relations of reciprocity between man and woman have been established historically. It also highlights how organizational processes have reclaimed the role of women and opened up spaces for political and organizational participation. Women's relationship with the organizational process becomes an important axis in political formation and education.

> In the worldview of the majority of indigenous people, men and women are part of a duality inseparable from harmonious unity with the cosmos, nature, and the territory. The category of gender, a term appropriated from the West, validated in the field of international agencies and applied at the level of government policies or strategies by members of the United Nations, has no equivalent, or at the very least, does not have the same meaning in the indigenous and original languages of the American continent. Laws and ancestral values have historically established the male-female relationships (like the definition of their roles and responsibilities at the level of the household, extended family or community). In many communities these values have been slowly reconfigured by the influence of the broader environment. One could argue that while there is a relationship of complementarity and unity of vision of the male-female relationship, the road toward advancing understanding of this dynamic is long.[31]

These perspectives show how the connections between global feminisms and local dynamics require an understanding of the differences between indigenous political recognition within each country and within different indigenous nations. In fact, various political processes have allowed for indigenous women's participation and for discussions about gender in indigenous contexts both within national and international political arenas.

In this context, it is key to highlight the process of political participation for indigenous peoples and indigenous women.

Political Participation of Indigenous Women: Movements, Indigenous Organizations, and Institutional Programs

Indigenous movements have fostered the recognition of the rights and demands of indigenous peoples. However, there is very little discussion of the role and political participation of women or of the new processes they have generated. The political participation of indigenous women grew because of the following processes: (1) the consolidation of indigenous grassroots organizations; (2) the implementation of policies, programs, and areas of participation for indigenous women; (3) the political and academic training of indigenous women; (4) the formation of grassroots organizations with a focus on indigenous women; (5) the active presence of non-indigenous, non-governmental organizations with a focus on gender; (6) changes in government policies related to gender equity; (7) the rethinking of the role of indigenous women from within the academy; and (8) the relationship between women and nature as part of environmental contexts as new process of recognition of differences.

There are various approaches to address the political participation of indigenous women.[32] On the one hand, there are the feminist analyses in the search for emancipatory processes from unequal living conditions of indigenous women. These approaches are homogenizing and make little differentiations between cultural contexts and particular historical situations. For some indigenous organizations, gender has been associated with feminism, a term indigenous women adopted, resulting in the opening of spaces in programs and indigenous organizations. Similarly, they consider the differences and existing inequalities between men and women. Another perspective is considering the complementarity between indigenous men and women. There are also proposals to analyze the role of international organizations in implementing gender policies and equity, and how this affects indigenous peoples.[33]

Another debate and ongoing analysis occurs within the field of human rights, women's rights and ethnic rights.[34] These debates analyze the political participation of indigenous women and their connection to national and international legal recognition, and their rights of non-exclusion.

Finally, we must consider the local dynamics of indigenous women, their perspectives and visions, and their connection to both feminist perspectives and discussions of gender. It is important to understand the demands of national and international organizations for women's participation in the recognition of equality and gender difference. This will allow us to understand local and global political processes and the new political role of indigenous women.

From these discussions, there are various positions that seek to understand the political dynamics of indigenous women and the processes they have led. Pequeño notes three areas of inquiry in discussions about the political participation of indigenous women, to:

> understand, describe, and document the leadership of contemporary indigenous women, the tensions that arise in women and feminist movements and, finally, the organizational processes of indigenous women themselves, and in this context, policies wielded from ethnic and gender identities.[35]

Apart from understanding the relationship between indigenous movements, indigenous women, feminisms, and gender, it must be understood that indigenous women are reclaiming political participation. These demands are related to national and transnational political processes of recognition about cultural differences and gender as well as environmental awareness that have allowed a space to rethink the relationship between cultural rights and women's rights and the differences among indigenous peoples, which have been seen as homogeneous.

These new organizational positions in general, as well as those of indigenous women in particular, denote aspects such as:

- Demands aimed to claim autonomy and strengthen differentiated political rights that allow them to make decisions about what happens in their territories.
- Critical positions with regard to institutional programs and the results of campaigns or programs for the inclusion of women. These programs affect the social dynamics of indigenous communities in the context of internal decision-making. A specific example has to do with the attempt to reproduce notions of public and private within indigenous contexts.
- Indigenous women's discontent with being the objective of external programs that fail to account for matters relating to their territories and resources.
- Little credibility of external agents, whether institutions, NGOs, or private researchers; this is because in many cases women have not benefitted from processes that such actors lead. Also, in some cases, women, knowledge, and/or practices have been used for commercial purposes without any recognition.

Today organizations and indigenous women—to a greater or lesser extent, and according to their interests and organizational processes—are including topics about women and/or programs for women; they are calling for new relationships with institutions that establish gender or equity processes. These demands respond to the problems indigenous women face in addition to those presented by ethnic differences. One effect of these processes is the consolidation of networks of indigenous women.

On the other hand, since the feminist movements question the exclusions that generate the conceptions of the dual categories of public and private spaces related to men's and women's activities, respectively, there are demands for more participation in public spaces. These demands are extended to indigenous women, who began to participate in public discussions. However, this opening of public participation for indigenous women, doesn't acknowledge other forms of political participation such as the collective dynamics of decision-making, and imposes divisions that were nonexistent among indigenous peoples. Therefore, indigenous peoples confront the political participation of indigenous women, who have to continuously negotiate between the public and private in relation to external and internal political actions.[36]

Nonetheless, a counter-proposal to external categories linked to policies and feminist traditions that do not respond to the cultural contexts are the proposals from the indigenous women and indigenous feminisms that raise alternative processes, practices, and concepts.

Indigenous Feminisms

The links among different ways of feminisms gave rise to diverse trends that analyze and position gender differences in the context of indigenous peoples: a perspective that corresponds to the discussions of hegemonic feminism and identifies universally unequal relations. Other trends analyze how indigenous cultural contexts made no distinction regarding gender differences, and how these differences have been generated in relationship to nation-states.[37] However, this position has been challenged by critical analyses that consider that there are inequalities between men and women within indigenous contexts. Some argue that it is necessary to rethink these unequal relationships under indigenous notions of being male or female.[38] Finally, some authors propose that there are indigenous peoples who are outside these debates and that relationships of male or female dominance can only be understood in specific cultural contexts.[39]

These positions generate frictions and tensions, and are latent issues among indigenous women and their communities. Some argue that men consider gender and the inclusion of women in new spaces of participation pointless because it is seen as their domain. Ortiz and Hernández show how indigenous women in Mexico question the generic notions of indigenous rights because pan-ethnic identities do not consider, for example, the particular concepts and situations of discrimination against women in indigenous communities. Similarly, indigenous women criticize and challenge ethno-cultural revival, because it gives indigenous traditions a status of authenticity that prevents the discussion of inequalities that women face in their daily lives.[40]

In this way, there are many debates between indigenous women, and between non-native researchers, because they question and confront feminisms and their local impacts, and vice versa. These processes are reflected upon at multiple scales (local, regional, national, and international). Nonetheless, they respond to the particularity of each country, e.g. political contexts and the recognition of indigenous and women's rights. Similarly, each indigenous people has responses that articulate a connection to the state or to the different political positions regarding gender in community contexts or organizational bases. Finally, these processes respond locally to the paths of indigenous women and their relationships to feminist debates and/or with the multiple contexts of gender exclusion and oppression. Even if it is difficult to account for all these processes in Latin America, as a methodological strategy, I articulate these general debates about indigenous feminisms and I place them in dialogue with the perspectives of some indigenous women. These proposals respond to my trajectory as a researcher working with indigenous peoples and with indigenous women, and to the historical process that I have experienced with these debates.

There are several paths, diverse positions, and ways of thinking, both individually and collectively, which have created relevant discussions on feminisms, genders, and indigenous women. Among these are autonomous feminisms, communitarian feminisms, decolonial feminism, territorial feminism, and feminisms in daily practice, which are alternatives to rethink the unequal relations between men and women, and what it means to be a women in a specific historical and cultural context.

Autonomous Feminisms

Autonomous feminism in Latin America and the Caribbean was proposed in 1993 in the *Encuentro Feminista Latinoamericano y del Caribe* in El Salvador, as a position that seeks to differentiate itself from the institutionalization of feminism, which was mainstreamed in the 1990s. One group of women distanced themselves from the hegemonic tendencies of feminisms, and since the 1980s, raised a proposal of autonomous feminisms that was expressed first in the book *Feminismos Cómplices*[41] and through different publications, proposals and declarations, their radical perspective became more visible. Among these declarations, two can be highlighted: the *Declaración del feminismo autónomo* (1996)[42] and *Declaración feminista autónoma* (2009).[43] The autonomous feminism,[44] according to Falquet, has three key elements, which pose different approaches to collective actions and positions related to social situations of each woman:

> The importance of the *collective* dimension in the production of theory, its ties with *concrete political practice* in social movements, and the weight of what bell hooks calls "epistemic advantage" (1989), although it is generally about an "unprivileged" situation: *personal-social positions* of nationality, class, 'race', sexual orientation and migratory status, among others.[45]

Falquet summarizes the contributions of this feminism as follows: "In the main, they do criticize the state and the patriarchal, racist and capitalist logics of their countries and the continent. Some reclaim, but they not idealize the 'traditional' indigenous or Black 'cultures.' "[46]

The autonomous feminism has had diverse trajectories that have been linked from proposals of indigenous and Afrodescendent women, to different feminisms.[47] Among these trajectories, the autonomous feminism highlight Latin American indigenous feminist tendencies that pose a critical and epistemological and political estrangement with other feminisms, while drawing on subaltern and dissident feminisms. These contributions create a critique about patriarchal and neoliberal logics of commodification of nature, which fuels economic production processes. In their declaration, they state:

> In the new international context and its expressions and local characteristics . . . we show the resurgence of the effects of neoliberalism on the lives of millions of women and poor people around the world, and the progressive militarization, increased structural violence and vulnerability of whole groups of the population; predation and irresponsible privatization of land, water and natural resources; the primacy of a normalizing and mercantilist science.[48]

However, some indigenous authors see gender as an analytic category that intersects with social inequalities and processes. Paredes states:

> Gender as a concept and category, from our interpretation, has the possibilities of being used to transform the material conditions underlying the oppression of women. The critique of gender, in its conversion to gender equity, produced great theoretical confusion and the political demobilization of women.[49]

In these contexts, the demands of indigenous women are positioned as a process that confronts external visions of gender, and Western—as well as indigenous—forms of patriarchy. The approaches that have had greatest international impact arise in Bolivia with Julieta Paredes and Maria Galindo through the organization *Mujeres Creando*. Their impact was reflected in the preparation of The Fourth World Conference on Women (Beijing, 1995), and through the questioning of Bolivian policy and cooperation programs and how these processes are reclaimed/reworked in other countries. This approach has not only influenced other similar processes, but has also enabled the emergence of local dynamics focused on alternative demands and other proposals of indigenous feminisms.

Communitarian Feminisms

Criticism arising from some indigenous women challenging hegemonic feminisms and unequal relations between men and women in indigenous contexts promotes the idea that forms of indigenous patriarchy exist. These debates consolidate the proposals of communitarian feminisms.[50] Paredes criticized indigenous patriarchy in Bolivia and considers that it is necessary to:

> Recognize that unfair relations between men and women also occurred in our country before the colony and is not only a colonial inheritance. There is also a Bolivian patriarchy and machism, both indigenous and popular. To decolonize gender, in this sense, means recuperating the memory of our great-grandmothers' struggles against a patriarchy that was established before the colonial invasion.[51]

Even though the best-known processes around communitarian feminisms are Bolivian, they also occur in other contexts, such as in the case of Guatemala led by Lorena Cabnal,[52] a Xinca woman, who applies the contributions of community feminisms to the territory-body relationship. Under the indigenous perspectives, the territory is expressed in the body, as the first territory. The body is also a representation a representation of the territory, in which cultural and political dimensions are inscribed:

> What began for us as a political slogan has become a category within communitarian feminism that has to do with the defense and recovery of the body-land territory.[53]

These proposals are connected to criticism of neoliberal capitalism and patriarchy, which are themselves connected to a critique of the economic development model.

Decolonial Feminisms

Drawing on critics of hegemonic feminisms and on debates about decolonization since the 1980s,[54] the Latin American feminists propose other analyses about feminisms and position themselves as decolonial feminists.[55] This perspective calls for decolonization of colonial impositions as a way of producing knowledge, power relations, notions of nature, and self. In the same way, it considers that gender is a colonial introduction that relates to class, ethnicity, race and location, and is critical of their previous articulations with hegemonic feminisms.[56] Most decolonial feminists combine activism in relation to social movements with critical production of knowledge within these movements from a political perspective. According to feminists such as Espinosa, Gómez, and Ochoa:

> Decolonial feminism is a movement in full growth and maturation, that proclaims revision of the theory and feminist political proposal from what it considers its Western, white and bourgeois bias. We understand that decolonial feminism brings together the productions of thinkers, intellectuals, feminist activists, lesbian feminists, Afro-descendants, indigenous, poor-mestizo women, as well as some white academics committed to the task of historical recovery of an own name, and a feminist theory that is antiracist in *Abya Yala*.[57]

Under this analytical and political perspective, there is criticism of the patriarchal and gender conceptions that were introduced to indigenous contexts that implied legal, economic, political, social, and cultural transformations.[58] In the same way, there is a conceptual opening for other epistemologies, spiritualties, practices, experiences, and ways of being.[59]

Feminisms and Indigenous Women's Perspectives in Practice

Indigenous women (academic, activists, and leaders, among others) have been related to different feminisms as well as taking distance from these perspectives to position their own ways of being women according to their historical and cultural contexts. For these reasons, I want to present current processes related to territorial experiences and the dynamics in their territories.

Territorial Feminisms

Processes of inequalities, which have been increased by extractivisms, have generated dynamic political actions by indigenous women, who are territorial advocates based on ancestral knowledge. Their demands have focused on defense of the territory through territorial stewardship, the body and nature, and are critical of the development process. There are several examples, such as the groups of indigenous women in Peru, Guatemala, and Colombia who oppose mining.

Their demands have been associated with the new perspectives of ecofeminisms that revolve around criticism of extractivisms and the search for alternatives to capitalistic development. While not all indigenous women identify as ecofeminists, there is a link to academic and social movements around the defense of the environment. However, here, defense of the territory proceeds from historical and ancestral struggles against the various colonizations engendered by capitalist and patriarchal models, in which nature and territories become commodities that ignore indigenous processes and fragment their territories as well as the bodies of women.

I refer to these political dynamics, not just in Colombia but also across Latin America, as *territorial feminisms*. Under this concept I understand the environmental-territorial struggles led by indigenous, Afrodescendent, and peasant women, and which focus on the protection of territory, body, and nature, as well as on the critique of development processes and extractivisms. The proposals are based on a vision of the *continuity of life* related to their territories. As a central axis, they posit the defense of life, starting from their practices and male/female relationships, and the relationships between human and non-human. Similarly, they propose the defense of their everyday subsistence activities such as food sovereignty and their livelihoods.

Their actions focus on a vision of the *continuity of life*, in which indigenous women are defenders of life that is inextricably linked to the territories. An example is the Kichwa women from Sarayaku, Ecuador,[60] who have led a decades-long resistance to oil exploration and exploitation. In the words of Patricia Gualinga (Kichwa), resistance has come from the women:

> Despite these pressures, Sarayaku was firm and today it is important to emphasize that firmness to reject the oil activity. This struggle came out of women because men, after so many years of harassment, began to think about the economic benefits. At one point, we confronted the men and told them: "well we separate from you, we do not give them the chicha, we do not feed them, we forbid everything."[61] Finally, at the end, they gave a definitive no to oil exploration.[62]

These strategies have resonated with environmental feminist movements.[63] As Aguinaga states in relation to indigenous and peasant women and their care for sustainability of Mother Earth:

> Feminism needs to build bridges with these organizations and processes to achieve a real link with ecology. Sustainability, based on ancestral knowledge, is also what materializes and constructs the sense of political and symbolic resistance of women within indigenous communities.[64]

While these connections between feminisms, ecofeminisms, and indigenous women have been criticized for positing an essentialist relationship between women and "nature," they nonetheless foster new perspectives from demands by indigenous women to care for the non-human, for the continuity of life to confront the processes of appropriation and globalization of natures, and the shock of extractive and environmental degradation.

It should be emphasized that indigenous women's discussions and criticisms about the extraction processes enable a critique of dualities between nature–culture and its relationship to gender inequalities.

Feminisms in Daily Practices

Similarly, there are also indigenous women who work in diverse areas and pose specific demands around rights, recognition of gender equalities, and differences between men and women in political and cultural contexts. These spaces include: political spaces (traditional politics), academic spaces (as researchers and professors), as NGO officers (environmental or development-based), and in governmental institutions.

These indigenous women are immersed in new professional, academic, organizational, and institutional settings and analyze the contexts of participation around and within their communities from critical and meaningful perspectives. In this way, their perspective is a double-take on themselves and on other indigenous women. They are aware of the relationship between their people (as a collective identity) and the external or internal dynamic processes affecting their leadership roles. I call these indigenous perspectives in relation to them as women *feminisms in daily practices*. Since the positionality of indigenous women depends on context, it is necessary to speak in a way that situates their specific trajectories.

Depending on the direction they take, their positions on feminisms, genders, and indigenous women respond to the political strategies of their communities and indigenous organizations, as they do in accordance with their individual interests and positions. Because these processes are culturally situated, in this part I will focus on Colombia.

In the Colombian context and process of formal political participation, for example, Ati Seygundiba Quigua Izquierdo, an Iku woman (Arhuaca) of the Sierra Nevada de Santa Marta, served as an elected councilor of Bogota in 2004–2007. In her role as a representative of a non-indigenous political party (Polo Democrático Alternativo), she issued proposals of general interest, such as the right to water, recycling, and waste management with indigenous perspectives that recognize the rights of Mother Nature. Ati led several discussions on the rights of women and gender equality that echoed debates on women's issues: taxes, employment, and pay equity, political rights of women, with an approach to recognize indigenous women leaders in various communities. She raises the issue of women reclaiming the demands of female indigenous associations on equity and access to education, resources, political space and the process of equality in decision-making.[65] Similarly, she articulates her people's vision of the relationship between men and women:[66]

> The Iku culture assumes men and women are two perfect parts of a necessary equilibrium between, Kaku Serankua, our masculine territory and Businka Distama, our feminine territory. This equilibrium expresses a perfect union between one being and another and from this tradition the woman is a symbol of our universe, a reflection of our Mother Earth; she symbolizes fecundity, fertility, depth, horizontality and calm in the universe's gravitation; she is a producer of life, customs, culture, and peace; she is man's spiritual bastion.[67]

From another political space, that of decision-making within each community, Liliana Pechené Muelas, a Misak woman of Cauca, Colombia, is recognized as an ancestral authority or Mama.[68] Speaking retrospectively about history and her role in it, she suggests that in the 1970s, the struggle was for land. Women organized and "spoke," and their role was very important in the collective process. Prior to this point, women had no power in decision-making or discussion. As a result of their political participation, Misak women have gained new decision-making roles. Among the Misak, the authority of women is recognized; they are called "Mamas" and the men, who have different perspectives and ways of solving collective problems, are called "Tatas.". Currently Mamas, like Liliana, are making decisions as authorities in local processes. In the words of Liliana Pechené:

> That is the new awakening of women; that process is good, as we do not forget the responsibility of women. I cannot only be a political leader, I also need to care for the land, my children, my house; we can do thousands of things, without abandoning any of these. Jeremias leads the men, and I lead the women. Sometimes there are strong conflicts, but this is of much value because right now there is a group of women who for a while now have been talking about women's rights, violence against women; it was very rare to see an elder woman amongst so many men discussing these things, because in old times time there was no support, no backing from a Tata . . . There are women, also in the electorate; right now we have two women councilors who are involved in political life, but their tenure is almost over—Antonia Maria Morales and Cecilia Tope. In Guambía there is a lot of domestic violence, alcoholism and because of this the theme of women's rights "I matter, too," was and is necessary to support and foster women's activity; the Tatas have been giving up. We women are brave, we can do things together, not [as] feminists.[69]

Other processes to make visibile indigenous women and their daily practices in contexts of unequal relationships with their communities and nation-states are seen in the dynamics of academia. This is the position of the geographer Zonia Puenayán Uruá,[70] a Pasto woman of Nariño, Colombia, who has participated in organizational and educational processes. Since her childhood, Zonia has been a part of the process of land reclamation, and she studied outside her community with the commitment to engage organizational processes. Currently she is involved in organizing and recovering knowledge related to territory. Zonia argues the following about Pasto women:

> Pasto indigenous communities, of the department of Nariño, have started processes to strengthen the leadership of indigenous women, processes that

> women themselves have undertaken at the root of the violation of our rights, rights violated since colonial times that cemented ideas about the inferiority of women. But in the struggle for land, the courage and leadership of indigenous women has been shown in the case of the Pasto territory, as in the guardianship of Panan, of Maria Panana, the cacique of the guard, who was allied with John Chiles and the cacique of Cumbe, who defended the territory and indigenous rights, achieving the adjudication of land having been under colonial jurisdiction. This story and many other stories of the Pasto people show indigenous women's leadership, which allows us to reclaim these processes and show that indigenous women are also able to lead important processes within our communities. Women now exercise important roles as authorities within the council's corporations. In this way woman assume participation and decision making within and outside the communities. Therefore, today, we are defending and exercising indigenous women's rights within internal proceedings on the subject of women and gender to recuperate women's rights and generate spaces so that women can participate and appropriate these spaces. These spaces are dedicated to the woman, life-giving, enterprising, fighter, warrior, seeder and weaver of life. This is how women can highlight our work in the family and the community.[71]

There are also other dynamics that have to do with individual choices that are linked to the community and processes among indigenous women, which propose daily practices as the linchpin of the feminine. Kamëntsa Biyá women in Colombia[72] suggest that there is complementarity between men and women; however, they show that they have been transformed because of external and internal processes, which require rethinking the current relations between men and women; they pose strengthening processes based on care. Under this collective process, the women of Kamëntsá Biyá have led processes to recover the Chagra (Jajañ), as the place where:

> the familial, social and cultural fabric begins; where the individual recreates, grows, and learns to relate to nature and others, where the cultivation of their own food and medicinal plants begins, as well as the cultivation of thought and culture of Kamëntsá Biyá men and women.[73]

From this perspective, Lucy Juagibioy (Kamëntsá Biyá) suggests that the relationships between men and women must be formulated from the collective and not only among humans but also in relation to the non-human:

> The Chagra is like a family; some plants will help and protect others; to maintain balance there should be all types of plants and biodiversity; all help each other in the family and so it is with plants; they care for each other, and each plant has its place and has a space next to the other; plants stick and grow in one place and not in others, they have a specific place; in the Chagra one is closest to their children, that's where we learn the main values of respect and care for others.[74]

Finally, the public debate has also been reconfigured from other areas to include indigenous women's struggles: domestic violence, sexual violence, internal inequalities and inequalities in everyday contexts with institutional stakeholders such as inequalities in health and education. These new positions demand the recognition of ethnic differences and the rights of indigenous women in national contexts. As Mercedes Olivera (Mexican anthropologist and feminist forerunner of grassroots work with indigenous women) states:

> In indigenous thought, some people call it circular; I call it collective thinking. For women, the "I" implies a very distant road; one needs to cross the community, the family, the children, and the husband, to reach their feminine identity. This has really led us to building a very different feminism. One can begin working for sexual rights, reproductive rights, abortion, the right to sexual orientation, but we have a job that runs in the opposite direction: we start from systemic violence, economic violence, and gradually we approach individuality.[75]

Perhaps these feminisms in daily practice have less visibility in academic spaces, but they respond to the processes that indigenous women live day to day in relation to their personal choices as students, academics, or officials along with their partners, families, organizations, and community processes. Often these processes are not considered feminism or interpreted as gender relations, but are perceived as everyday experiences in the search for equality in situations where there are ethnic and gender differences.

Trends, Perspectives, and Proposals

Indigenous peoples and indigenous women have led diverse movements around claims for civil and women's rights. There are varied positions and approaches that respond to particular historical contexts, which have led to a diversity of perspectives around feminisms, genders, and indigenous women. In accordance with each community and indigenous organization, distinct internal politics have been generated around gender difference.

These processes have influenced academic debates, which have, in turn, influenced indigenous processes. Similarly, indigenous peoples and indigenous women have expanded national debates on political participation and the inclusion of different proposals on gender and demands about social inequalities. Likewise, personal trajectories of indigenous women have created specific ways to think about differences and gender inequalities in situated cultural contexts.

These debates on indigenous feminisms are vital because they enable criticism of not only modern dual categories but also of development processes and economic extractivisms, and offer alternatives to relationships not only between men and women but also between humans and nonhumans. These alternatives become conceptual references for both public policy and academic settings, in as much as they do for their own proposals.

However, there is a cornerstone of discussion led by organizations and indigenous women alike about the need to recognize the relationships between men and women under different gender categories. Indigenous proposals equally consider the differences between men and women in the processes of access, use, control, and decision-making in territorial, cultural, and environmental matters. Given the existence of cultural processes that are based on other categories of gender and feminisms (associated with the complementarity between men and women), demands emerge for the recognition of and search for political spaces in indigenous communities that consider the cultural differences between men and women that depart from the relationships that are projected onto their cultures.

The globalization of nature fractures social, cultural, and gender relations, both between men and women. These fractures cut across all territorial, environmental, and cultural reconfigurations. In fact, in the environmental sphere, the connections between nature-gender underscore the complex links between science, gender, and politics, which extend to indigenous peoples.[76]

The category of gender has been controversial but important, because although the situations mentioned in this chapter are evident in analyses, there is little discussion about the construction of gender relationships and the effects of the globalization of nature on everyday practices. There are also few studies on the relationships of men and women in extractivist contexts, about their political, environmental, and territorial strategies, but even less about their protests against environmental issues or the relationships, spaces, or gendered subjectivities associated with these practices. To analyze the demands of indigenous men and indigenous women implies an understanding of the culturally and historically situated practices of daily life—the meanings, relationships, and identity construction. All of this production constitutes social experience and builds social relationships from indigenous notions of the similarities and differences between men and women.

In the political realm, demands for political participation of men and women are also being articulated. In particular, for women (independent of approaches to understand the relationship between indigenous movements, indigenous women, feminisms, and genders), it must be clear that indigenous women are leading movements to reclaim political participation and generate actions of confrontation and resistance for the reconfiguration of their territories and identities. These demands are related to national and transnational political processes for the recognition of cultural and gender differences. Likewise, growing environmental awareness has resulted in the creation of spaces to rethink the relationship between cultural rights and women's rights, as well as differences within indigenous peoples, which have traditionally been seen from the outside as homogeneous.

In the same way, the positions of indigenous women reveal the various tensions that arise in the everyday context of indigenous peoples when women demand particular rights. At the same time, they point to the contradictions that are generated within the indigenous movements when women demand greater participation and differentiated rights versus approaches that posit a homogeneous community in their political struggle. In fact, indigenous movements have chosen a discursive strategy of harmony, balance, and complementarity between men and women, over strategies of inequality.[77] These situations are manifested in the following contradictions: general demands versus particular demands, differentiation of public and private, gender versus women, sexualities and identities, national political arenas versus local political spaces, and confrontations with modern processes and capitalism.

These reflections, proposals, and actions allow one to see the diversity of positions held by indigenous women and the processes that they recognize as motivation for the participation of women. Drawing from their perspective, one can assert that indigenous women leaders consider the cultural processes between indigenous men and women as emanating from ancestral values of complementarity and equity. Similarly, they highlight the historical participation of indigenous women in their cultures and in national and international contexts. However, they consider that even though there are ancestral cultural processes working into the present, it is necessary to analyze certain cultural dynamics and internal and external processes that have generated exclusions and inequalities for indigenous women.

Likewise, these reflections, proposals, and actions highlight how the historical processes imposed by nation-states and non-indigenous visions have transformed the economic, political, and social situations of men and women, leading to inequalities and exclusions. These situations compel indigenous women to resort to new strategies of connection within their communities and nation-states, in order to reclaim their rights and consolidate their demands in new spaces of participation such as those offered by resistance movements, political parties, and grassroots organizations.

Finally, it should be noted that the indigenous feminisms raised in this chapter have been accepted at the community level in different ways: Some people do not consider them relevant, while others have modified their programs for the inclusion of gender. In addition, these feminisms (autonomous, communitarian, decolonial, territorial, and in daily practices) have made contributions to discussions of global feminisms and national discussions to such an extent that there is much talk about a "fourth wave" of feminisms. Thus, the demands of women and indigenous peoples for autonomy and self-determination at the community, territorial, and individual political arenas offer new perspectives and reconfigure discussions of indigenous organizations and indigenous feminists and academics, among others. Moreover, the social constructions of the feminine and masculine from within different cultural contexts and under different categories allows us to think in new ways about feminisms, genders and indigenous women.

Notes

1 CEPAL, *Los pueblos indígenas en América Latina. Avances en el último decenio y retos pendientes para la garantía de los derechos* (Santiago de Chile: Naciones Unidas, 2014).

2 Departamento Administrativo Nacional de Estadísticas (DANE), *Colombia una nación multicultural: Su diversidad étnica* (Bogotá: DANE, 2007).

3 Bartolina Sisa was an Aymara indigenous woman who confronted and fought colonial power with her husband Tupac Katari (Julian Apaza), in Bolivia, in the eighteenth century. La Gaitana was an indigenous leader, who confronted colonial power in Colombia in the sixteenth century.

4 Francesa Gargallo, *Ideas Feministas latinoamericanas* (México: UACM, 2006); Rita Segato, "Género y colonialidad: en busca de claves de lectura y de un vocabulario estratégico descolonial," In *Feminismos y poscolonialidad. Descolonizando el feminismo desde y en América Latina*, edited by Karina Bidaseca and Vanesa Vázquez, 17–48 (Buenos Aires: Ed. Godot, 2011).

5 Stefano Varese, *Pueblos indios, soberanía y globalismo* (Quito: Ediciones Abya-Yala 32, 1996).

6 Stefano Varese, "The New Environmentalist Movement of Latin American Indigenous People," In *Valuing Local Knowledge: Indigenous People and Intellectual Property Rights*, edited by Stephen B. Brush and Doreen Stabinsky, 122–142 (Washington, DC: Island Press, 1996).

7 Astrid Ulloa, "Mujeres indígenas: dilemas de género y etnicidad en los escenarios latinoamericanos," In *Mujeres indígenas, territorialidad y biodiversidad, en el contexto latinoamericano*, edited by Luz Marina Donato, Elsa Matilde Escobar, Pía Escobar, Aracely Pazmiño, and Astrid Ulloa, 17–33 (Bogotá: Universidad Nacional de Colombia, Fundación Natura, UICN, UNODC, 2007).

8 Katherine Galeano and Meike Werner, "Mujeres indígenas y aborígenes del Abya Yala. Agendas solidarias y diversas," *Ciencia Política*, Vol 10 (2015): 227–252.

9 Julieta Paredes, *Hilando fino desde el feminismo comunitario* (México: El Rebozo México, 2014).

10 Rita Segato, "Género y colonialidad: en busca de claves de lectura y de un vocabulario estratégico descolonial," In *Feminismos y poscolonialidad: Descolonizando el feminismo desde y en América Latina*, edited by Karina Bidaseca and Vanesa Vázquez, 30–31 (Buenos Aires: Editorial Godot, 2011).

11 In general, the different feminisms are thought of according to different historical processes and in different ways. Some consider that as different waves: The first wave is associated with the suffragette movement of the nineteenth century and the citizenship of women. The second wave is associated with social and political movements and the struggle of women in

the political realm and the demand for equal political spaces. The third wave is associated with liberal, radical feminism and difference. However, there are different interpretations and trajectories. In Latin America, these waves and different feminisms have different historical accounts according to relationships with women's movements and historical and specific contexts. In fact, nowadays there are discussions related to feminisms associate with plurality of feminisms and decolonial, communitarian and autonomous feminisms. See for example, Martha Yanneth Valenzuela Rodríguez, "Los feminismos en América Latina: retos, posibilidades y permanencias," *Esfera*, Vol 1 (2012): 31–40; Florence Thomas, *Conversaciones con Violeta. Historia de una revolución inacabada* (Bogotá: Aguilar, 2006).

12 Catherine Lutz and Jane Collins, *Reading National Geographic* (Chicago, IL and London: University of Chicago Press, 1993). Linda Nochlin, *The Politics of the Vision* (New York, NY: Harper & Row Publishers, 1989). Edward Said, *Orientalism* (New York, NY: Vintage Books, 1978).

13 David Arnold, *La naturaleza como problema histórico. El medio, la cultura y la expansión de Europa* (México: Fondo de Cultura Económica, 2000). Jaime Borja, *Del bárbaro y de la naturaleza agreste: Una historia moral del indio neogranadino* (Bogotá: Manuscript, 2002).

14 Mythical humans with the head of a dog.

15 Miguel Rojas-Mix, *América imaginaria* (Barcelona: Sociedad Estatal Quinto Centenario y Editorial Lumen, 1992). Hernando Cabarcas, *Bestiario del Nuevo Reino de Granada* (Bogotá: Colcultura, 1994).

16 The first descriptions of the Amazons in America were in the fifteenth century in the journal of explorer Christopher Columbus, who described living on the island Matinino or Martinique without men. In 1505, an anonymous author wrote about them "calling them ferinas females" who lived in Brazil and were cannibals (Miguel Rojas-Mix, América *imaginaria* [Barcelona: Sociedad Estatal Quinto Centenario y Editorial Lumen, 1992]) who provided food (human) for his men.

17 In the fifteenth century, Columbus described in his diary three mermaids at sea, but they felt they had male faces and were not as beautiful as those described by Pliny and Marco Polo (Miguel Rojas-Mix, América *imaginaria* [Barcelona: Sociedad Estatal Quinto Centenario y Editorial Lumen, 1992]).

18 Candice Slater, *Entangled Edens: Visions of the Amazon* (Berkeley, CA: University of California Press, 2002).

19 Remedios Mataix, "Androcentrismo, eurocentrismo, retórica colonial: amazonas en América," *América sin nombre*, Vol 15 (2010): 118–136. Hesiod was a Greek poet of the eighth century.

20 Lorna Schiebinger, *¿Tiene sexo la mente?* (Madrid: Ediciones Cátedra, 2004).

21 Pierre Bourdieu, In *The Field of Cultural Production: Essays on Art and Literature*, edited by Randal Johnson, 161–175 (Cambridge: Polity Press, 1993).

22 Rita Segato. "Género y colonialidad: en busca de claves de lectura y de un vocabulario estratégico descolonia" In *Feminismos y poscolonialidad. Descolonizando el feminismo desde y en América Latina*, compilado por Karina Bidaseca and Vanesa Vazquez, 17–48 (Buenos Aires: Ed. Godot, 2011).

23 Astrid Ulloa, "Mujeres indígenas: dilemas de género y etnicidad en los escenarios latinoamericanos," In *Mujeres indígenas, territorialidad y biodiversidad, en el contexto latinoamericano*, edited by Luz Marina Donato, Elsa Matilde Escobar, Pía Escobar, Aracely Pazmiño, and Astrid Ulloa, 17–33 (Bogotá: Universidad Nacional de Colombia, Fundación Natura, UICN, UNODC, 2007).

24 There are various articles and books that describe the emergence of Latin American feminisms. See Yuderkys Espinosa, Diana Gómez and Karina Ochoa, *Tejiendo de otro modo: Feminismos, epistemologías y apuestas decoloniales en Abya Yala* (Popayán: Editorial Universidad del Cauca, 2014a); Yuderkys Espinosa, Diana Gómez and Karina Ochoa, "Introducción," In *Tejiendo de otro modo: Feminismos, epistemologías y apuestas descoloniales en Abya Yala*, edited by Yuderkys Espinosa, Diana Gómez and Karina Ochoa, 13–40 (Popayán: Editorial Universidad del Cauca, 2014b); Francesca Gargallo, "Rutas epistémicas de acercamiento a los feminismos y antifeminismos de las intelectuales indígenas contemporáneas," In *Feminismos desde Abya Yala: Ideas y proposiciones de las mujeres de 607 pueblos en nuestra América*, edited by Francesca Gargallo, 46–109 (México: Editorial Corte y Confección, 2014a); Francesca Gargallo, "Los feminismos de las mujeres indígenas: acciones autónomas y desafío epistémico," In *Tejiendo de otro modo: Feminismos, epistemologías y apuestas descoloniales en Abya Yala*, edited by Yuderkys Espinosa, Diana Gómez and Karina Ochoa, 371–382 (Popayán: Editorial Universidad del Cauca, 2014).

25 Julieta Paredes, *Hilando fino desde el feminismo comunitario* (México: El Rebozo México, 2014), 63.
26 Aura Cumes, "Multiculturalismo, género y feminismos: mujeres diversas, luchas complejas," In *Participación y políticas de mujeres indígenas en contextos latinoamericanos recientes*, edited by Andrea Pequeño, 29–52 (Quito: Flacso Ecuador-Ministerio de Cultura, 2009).
27 Ibid., 48.
28 *"La Ley Revolucionaria de las Mujeres Indígenas Zapatistas de 1994"* recognized the demands of equality and justice for women under ten points.
29 Georgina Méndez, "Nuevos escenarios de participación: experiencias de mujeres indígenas en México y Colombia," In *Mujeres indígenas, territorialidad y Biodiversidad en el Contexto Latinoamericano*, edited by Luz Marina Donato, Elsa Matilde Escobar, Pía Escobar, Aracely Pazmiño, and Astrid Ulloa, 37 (Bogotá: Universidad Nacional de Colombia—Fundación Natura—UICN-UNODC, 2007).
30 Avelina Pancho, "Participación de las mujeres nasa en los procesos de autonomía territorial y educación propia en el Cauca, Colombia," In *Mujeres indígenas, territorialidad y biodiversidad, en el contexto latinoamericano*, edited by Luz Marina Donato, Elsa Matilde Escobar, Pía Escobar, Aracely Pazmiño, and Astrid Ulloa, 53–62 (Bogotá: Universidad Nacional de Colombia, Fundación Natura, UICN, UNODC, 2007).
31 Ibid., 59.
32 Andrea Pequeño, "Introducción," In *Participación y políticas de mujeres indígenas en contextos latinoamericanos recientes*, edited by Andrea Pequeño, 9–25 (Quito: Flacso Ecuador-Ministerio de Cultura, 2009); Georgina Méndez, "Miradas de género de las mujeres indígenas en Ecuador, Colombia y México," In *Participación y políticas de mujeres indígenas en contextos latinoamericanos*, edited by Andrea Pequeño, 51–73 (Quito: Flacso Ecuador-Ministerio de Cultura, 2009).
33 Georgina Méndez, "Participación y demandas de las mujeres indígenas en la ciudad de Bogotá: La pregunta por la inclusión," Master Thesis (Bogotá: Universidad Nacional de Colombia, 2006); Georgina Méndez, "Miradas de género de las mujeres indígenas en Ecuador, Colombia y México," In *Participación y políticas de mujeres indígenas en contextos latinoamericanos*, edited by Andrea Pequeño, 51–73 (Quito: Flacso Ecuador-Ministerio de Cultura, 2009).
34 Juliane Ströbele-Gregor, "Mujeres indígenas, ciudadanía y alcance del derecho: Estado de la investigación tomando como ejemplo Ecuador," (Paper presented at the seminar *"Taller internacional: Derecho, Ciudadanía y Género en América Latina"*, Berlin, December 11, 2006).
35 Andrea Pequeño, "Introducción," In *Participación y políticas de mujeres indígenas en contextos latinoamericanos recientes*, edited by Andrea Pequeño, 10 (Quito: Flacso Ecuador-Ministerio de Cultura, 2009).
36 Aída Hernández and Andrew Canessa, *Complementariedades y exclusiones en Mesoamérica y los Andes* (Lima: IWGIA, 2012).
37 María Lugones, "Hacia un feminismo descolonial," *La manzana de la Discordia*, Vol 6 (2011): 105–119.
38 Rita Segato, "Género y colonialidad: en busca de claves de lectura y de un vocabulario estratégico descolonia," In *Feminismos y poscolonialidad: Descolonizando el feminismo desde y en América Latina*, edited by Karina Bidaseca and Vanesa Vázquez, 17–48 (Buenos Aires: Editorial Godot, 2011).
39 These perspectives resume discussions that have to do with inequalities and/or the complementarity between genders and its connections with local, national, and international proposals, the recognition of the cultural construction of gender categories, and the positioning of indigenous women in political and academic spaces, among others.
40 Hector Ortiz and Aida Hernández, "Constitutional Amendments and New Imaginings of the Nation: Legal Anthropology and Gendered Perspectives on Multicultural México," *Polar*, Vol 19 (1996): 59–66.
41 See Ximena Bedregal, "El feminismo autónomo radical, una propuesta civilizatoria," www.mamametal.com/articulos/en%20pdf/Hitoria_autonomas_mex.pdf accessed January 5, 2015.
42 Declaración del feminismo autónomo, *'VII Encuentro feminista latinoamericano y del Caribe'*, Cartagena–Chile, November 26, 1996.
43 Declaración Feminista Autónoma, "El desafío de hacer comunidad en la casa de las diferencias," *'Encuentro Feminista Autónomo* (México: March 2009).
44 Jules Falquet, "Las 'Feministas autónomas' latinoamericanas y caribeñas: veinte años de disidencias," *Universitas Humanística*, Vol 78 (2014): 39–63.

45 Ibid., 41.
46 Ibid., 60.
47 Declaración Feminista Autónoma, "El desafío de hacer comunidad en la casa de las diferencias," In *'Encuentro Feminista Autónomo'* (México: March 2009).
48 Ibid., 1.
49 Julieta Paredes, *Hilando fino desde el feminismo comunitario* (México: El Rebozo México, 2014), 61.
50 Ibid.
51 Ibid., 72.
52 Lorena Cabnal, "Acercamiento a la construcción del pensamiento epistémico de las mujeres indígenas feministas comunitarias de Abya Yala," In *Feminismos diversos: el feminismo comunitario,* edited by Lorena Cabnal, 11–25 (Madrid: ACSUR—Las Segovias, 2010).
53 Lorena Cabnal, 2013. www.diagonalperiodico.net/global/defender-territorio-la-mineria-sin-defender-cuerpos-mujeres-la-violencia-sexual accessed January 19, 2015.
54 Part of the discussions and debates arise from the Decolonial Feminims Working Group. http://crg.berkeley.edu/content/decolonial-feminisms accessed January 19, 2015; the Programa "*Poscolonialidad, Pensamiento Fronterizo y Transfronterizo en los Estudios Feministas*" del IDAES, directed by Karina Bidaseca; and the *Grupo Latinoamericano de Estudios, Formación y Acción Feminista* (GLEFAS), among others.
55 See Yuderkys Espinosa, Diana Gómez and Karina Ochoa, *Tejiendo de otro modo: Feminismos, epistemologías y apuestas descoloniales en Abya Yala* (Popayán: Editorial Universidad del Cauca, 2014a); Yuderkys Espinosa, Diana Gómez and Karina Ochoa, "Introducción," In *Tejiendo de otro modo: Feminismos, epistemologías y apuestas descoloniales en Abya Yala,* edited by Yuderkys Espinosa, Diana Gómez and Karina Ochoa, 13–40 (Popayán: Editorial Universidad del Cauca, 2014b); Francesca Gargallo ed., *Feminismos desde Abya Yala: Ideas y proposiciones de las mujeres de 607 pueblos en nuestra América* (México: Editorial Corte y Confección, 2014a); Karina Bidaseca and Vanesa Vázquez, eds., *Feminismos y poscolonialidad: Descolonizando el feminismo desde y en América Latina* (Buenos Aires: Editorial Godot, 2011); Ochy Curiel, "Crítica poscolonial desde las prácticas políticas del feminismo antirracista," *Nómadas,* Vol 26 (2007): 92–110.
56 Yuderkys Espinosa, Diana Gómez and Karina Ochoa, "Introducción," In *Tejiendo de otro modo: Feminismos, epistemologías y apuestas desscoloniales en Abya Yala,* edited by Yuderkys Espinosa, Diana Gómez and Karina Ochoa, 13–40 (Popayán: Editorial Universidad del Cauca, 2014b).
57 *Abya Yala* is the name in the language of the Kuna people who inhabit the territory corresponding to Panama and Colombia in the continent that the Spanish colonizers named "America." It means "land in full maturity" or "land of lifeblood." Yuderkys Espinosa, Diana Gómez and Karina Ochoa, *Tejiendo de otro modo: Feminismos, epistemologías y apuestas descoloniales en Abya Yala* (Popayán: Editorial Universidad del Cauca, 2014), 13.
58 Silvia Rivera Cusicanqui, "La noción de 'derecho' o las paradojas de la modernidad poscolonial: indígenas y mujeres en Bolivia," In *Tejiendo de otro modo: Feminismos, epistemologías y apuestas descoloniales en Abya Yala,* edited by Yuderkys Espinosa, Diana Gómez and Karina Ochoa, 121–134 (Popayán: Editorial Universidad del Cauca, 2014); Marisol de la Cadena, "La decencia y el respeto: Raza y etnicidad entre los intelectuales y las mestizas cuzqueñas," In *Tejiendo de otro modo: Feminismos, epistemologías y apuestas descoloniales en Abya Yala,* edited by Yuderkys Espinosa, Diana Gómez and Karina Ochoa, 189–209 (Popayán: Editorial Universidad del Cauca, 2014); Rita Laura Segato, "Colonialidad y patriarcado moderno: expansión del frente estatal, modernización, y la vida de las mujeres," In *Tejiendo de otro modo: Feminismos, epistemologías y apuestas descoloniales en Abya Yala,* edited by Yuderkys Espinosa, Diana Gómez and Karina Ochoa, 75–90 (Popayán: Editorial Universidad del Cauca, 2014).
59 See Brendy Mendoza, "La epistemología del sur, la colonialidad del género y el feminismo latinoamericano," In *Tejiendo de otro modo: Feminismos, epistemologías y apuestas descoloniales en Abya Yala,* edited by Yuderkys Espinosa, Diana Gómez and Karina Ochoa, 135–142 (Popayán: Editorial Universidad del Cauca, 2014); Sylvia Marcos, "La espiritualidad de las mujeres indígenas mesoamericanas," In *Tejiendo de otro modo: Feminismos, epistemologías y apuestas descoloniales en Abya Yala,* edited by Yuderkys Espinosa, Diana Gómez and Karina Ochoa, 143–159 (Popayán: Editorial Universidad del Cauca, 2014). Gargallo, Francesca. "Los feminismos de las mujeres indígenas: acciones autónomas y desafío epistémico." In *Tejiendo de otro modo: Feminismos, epistemologías y apuestas descoloniales en Abya Yala,* edited by Yuderkys Espinosa, Diana Gómez and Karina Ochoa, 371–382. (Popayán: Editorial Universidad del Cauca, 2014).

60 Patricia Gualinga, "Los impactos de las petroleras en el oriente ecuatoriano," In *Mujeres indígenas y cambio climático: Perspectivas latinoamericanas*, edited by Astrid Ulloa, Elsa Matilde Escobar, Luz Marina Donato, and Pía Escobar, 123–127 (Bogotá: Universidad Nacional de Colombia, Fundación Natura, UNODC, 2008).

61 "Bueno nos separamos de ustedes, no les damos la chica, no les damos de comer, les prohibimos todo."

62 Patricia Gualinga, "Los impactos de las petroleras en el oriente ecuatoriano," In *Mujeres indígenas y cambio climático: Perspectivas latinoamericanas*, editee by Astrid Ulloa et al (Bogotá: Universidad Nacional de Colombia, Fundación Natura, UNODC, 2008), 124.

63 Margarita Aguinaga, "Ecofeminismo: mujer y Pachamama, no solo es posible una crítica al capitalismo y al patriarcado," *América Latina en movimiento*. www.alainet.org/es/active/39531#comment-0 accessed March 15, 2015.

64 Ibid., 7.

65 Ati Seygundiba Quigua Izquierdo, "Mujer Vida, Mujer Esperanza, Mujer Libertad," www.todosatierra.com/page/2011/11/mujer-vida-mujer-esperanza-mujer-libertad/#more-5196 accessed May 5, 2012.

66 On her website: todosatierra.com accessed May 5, 2012.

67 Todos Atierra. 2011, "Mujer Vida, Mujer Esperanza, Mujer Libertad," www.todosatierra.com/page/2011/11/mujer-vida-mujer-esperanza-mujer-libertad/#more-5196 accessed May 5, 2012.

68 Liliana Pechené, "Historia de vida," In V*oces de mujeres indígenas: Liderazgo, género e inclusión*, edited by David Cardozo, 22–30 (Bogotá: Universidad Nacional de Colombia, 2011).

69 Ibid., 25.

70 Zonia Puenayán Uruá, "*Mujer indígena*" (Pasto: Manuscript, 2012).

71 Ibid., 1.

72 Luisa Cantor and Lucy Juagibioy, "Mujeres indígenas del pueblo kamëntsá biyá y sus conocimientos en torno al clima y el jajañ (municipiode Sibundoy. Veredas: Llano Grande, San Félix, Sagrado Corazón, La Menta, La Cocha, El Ejido," In *Informe final proyecto Perspectivas Culturales y Locales sobre el Clima en Colombia*, edited by Astrid Ulloa, 155–180 (Bogotá: Universidad Nacional de Colombia-Colciencias 2013).

73 Ibid., 163.

74 Ibid., 163.

75 Reyes, Itandehui, "Mercedes Olivera y la construcción del feminismo indígena,"2014, www.lahaine.org/mundo.php/mercedes-olivera-y-la-construccion-del-f accessed August 28, 2015.

76 Astrid Ulloa, "Mujeres indígenas: dilemas de género y etnicidad en los escenarios latinoamericanos," In *Mujeres indígenas, territorialidad y biodiversidad, en el contexto latinoamericano*, edited by Luz Marina Donato, Elsa Matilde Escobar, Pía Escobar, Aracely Pazmiño, and Astrid Ulloa, 17–33 (Bogotá: Universidad Nacional de Colombia, Fundación Natura, UICN, UNODC, 2007).

77 Georgina Méndez, "Nuevos escenarios de participación: experiencias de mujeres indígenas en México y Colombia," In *Mujeres indígenas, territorialidad y Biodiversidad en el Contexto Latinoamericano*, edited by Luz Marina Donato, Elsa Matilde Escobar, Pía Escobar, Aracely Pazmiño, Astrid Ulloa, 35–46 (Bogotá: Universidad Nacional de Colombia—Fundación Natura—UICN-UNODC, 2007).

19

THE FEMINIST DEBATE IN MEXICO

Gabriela Cano

In 1915, the scholar Manuel Gamio claimed that the presence of feminism was "microscopic" in Mexico.[1] In making this assessment, Gamio appears to have been unaware of the pro-feminist mood that was gaining ground in the country. In the month of September *La mujer moderna*, a weekly publication that defined itself as a feminist magazine in support of women's suffrage, received financial support from the victorious revolutionary government led by Venustiano Carranza, while in the country's southeast preparations were under way for the first of two feminist conferences to be held in Yucatán, sponsored by General Salvador Alvarado, who had been appointed governor of the state by the revolutionary forces. In spite of considering feminism to be of so little importance, Gamio dedicated a whole chapter to the topic of "Our Women" in *Forjando patria*, the influential book in which the anthropologist postulated *mestizaje* (mixed European and indigenous heritage) as the basis of Mexican nationality. For Gamio, feminism was not a worthwhile option for the country because, according to his argument, the traditional Mexican woman, "simple, loyal, and moderate," was dedicated to molding the "strong and virile Mexican race."[2] Gamio's opinion forms part of the great debate over feminism and its repercussions on society that developed over the course of the twentieth century in Mexico, which is the central theme of this chapter.

The different stages of the history of feminism are conventionally characterized as waves, which ebb and flow like the waters of the sea. Although this notion is widespread, it is also problematic because there is no consensus about when the different waves begin and end, or about their characteristic features. Another problem with this metaphor is that it tends to accord greater importance to events occurring on the crest of each wave than at times in between them, when significant events have also occurred. Such limitations can be corrected by keeping in mind that the wave metaphor is merely a means of mapping and characterizing historical stages that are always more complex and nuanced. It is also worth considering the history of feminism not merely in terms of two waves, but as a continuous swell with many smaller waves.[3] In spite of the criticisms, the metaphor is useful for analyzing the feminist debate in Mexico because it facilitates a very general characterization of the main stages of feminism and helps to highlight the relationship between feminism in Mexico and in other parts of the world. It is also important for the purposes of this chapter to remember that the wave metaphor developed in the United States and is adapted to that country's history as a useful periodization model.[4]

In Mexico, the beginning of the first wave can be placed at the start of the twentieth century, when the term "feminism" first appeared in public debate in the context of the educational reform launched by the government of Porfirio Díaz which, expanded female education and opened access of academic and technical education to women, while at the same time promoting school training for motherhood, marriage, and home care as nationalist civic values. The issue of women's suffrage came into the feminist debate during the Mexican Revolution, which, paradoxically, both encouraged and hindered the recognition of voting rights for women. It was for this reason that Mexican women were only given the right to vote in 1953—quite late compared to other Latin American countries. By that time, strictly speaking, the first wave of feminism had already ended, and the feminist movement was in a phase of retreat in many parts of the world.[5] The end of the first wave of Mexican feminism is generally placed around 1940, when there was an effective demobilization of social forces in the period after the government of President Lázaro Cárdenas. During the Second World War, the fight against fascism absorbed all the energies of organizations which consequently turned their focus away from women's suffrage; however, the official mobilization that took place during the election campaign and early days of the presidency of Adolfo Ruiz Cortes represented a small wave of feminism between 1952 and 1953.

Second-wave feminism spanned the last three decades of the twentieth century. It is generally accepted that its immediate origins can be found in the student movements of 1968 and that it came into full force in the early 1970s. There is no consensus about when it ended; however, in the United States, the end of the second wave is associated with the acceptance of the criticism that the feminist perspective imposed by middle class white women was insensitive to the diverse range of identities of other cultures and social classes. In the United States, this criticism was raised by African American, Latina, and Asian women, while internationally a similar reaction was seen in countries that had formerly been under the yoke of British colonialism. In the case of Mexico, the Zapatista Movement's Revolutionary Law for Women (*Ley Revolucionaria de las Mujeres*, 1994) could be considered a breaking point that marked the end of second-wave feminism. In spite of its limited influence, the Zapatista law is significant because it incorporates elements characteristic of second-wave feminism, such as the rejection of physical and sexual violence against women and their right to decide how many children they will have.[6] It also establishes that women are entitled to hold political management and military command positions at a time when traditional indigenous organizations had not considered such matters, which were only considered feasible or even desirable for urban populations, not for rural communities and even less so for indigenous groups. Moreover, the law also recognizes the racism prevalent in Mexican society directed in particular against indigenous men and women.

At another, no less important level of analysis, the end of the second wave of the feminist debate could be located at the time of certain government initiatives that included some feminist issues, like the creation of Mexico's National Institute for Women or the General Law on Women's Access to a Life Free of Violence (*Ley General de Acceso de las Mujeres a una Vida Libre de Violencia*) in 2007. One distinctive aspect of second-wave feminism was its resistance against participation or collaboration in government projects.[7] Therefore, initiatives like these two suggest that by the first decade of the twenty-first century this rejection of involvement in government initiatives was no longer widespread, although it continued to exist among some of the more radical groups.

Contrary to what might be understood, based on the claims of observers like Manuel Gamio, the feminist debate involved not only small groups of activist women or marginalized female writers, but women and men of various ideological persuasions. From their respective spheres of action in politics, the intellectual world, or projects of social revolution or reform, they expressed positions either in their own right or as representatives of different public and private institutions and organizations. Among those engaging in the debate were figures like Justo Sierra, who was the Secretary of Public Education and Fine Arts in Porfirio Díaz's government, and José Vasconcelos, the creator of the

Secretariat of Public Education in the post-revolutionary era, as well as Mexican presidents like Lázaro Cárdenas, Miguel Alemán, and Adolfo Ruiz Cortines, to mention just a few of the more surprising participants in the public discussion about feminism. Other notable contributors included prominent women like Hermila Galindo, María del Refugio García, and Amalia de Castillo Ledón, among many other female politicians active during the first half of the twentieth century.

In the later years of the last century, the debate was given visibility in the mass media in the context of the UN-sponsored International Women's Year Conference, held in Mexico City in 1975. For several years prior to this conference, what was then known as "women's lib" had been attracting the interest of groups of academics and journalists, most of whom were caught up in the anti-establishment mood incited by youth rebellion and opposition movements, which had been exacerbated by the repression of the student movement of 1968. Women began to critique "sexism," a term coined in the mid-1960s to refer to anti-female prejudices, stereotypes, and discrimination. The new feminism was a movement against sexism and brought to the table of public discussion an emphasis on sexual liberation and the immediate transformation of everyday life beyond changes to the legal system and government initiatives.

Exposing and combating sexual violence was a central goal of second-wave feminism, along with reproductive rights, which required the use of contraceptives and, when necessary, even access to abortion; other goals included sexual freedom, ranging from premarital relationships to homosexuality and lesbianism, and criticism of the double standards that were applied to personal and sexual relationships between men and women. These issues were practically ignored in the press and in other public spheres as they were considered to be matters specific to private life which, if discussed explicitly in public, would undermine family values and morals.

As was the case in the first decades of the twentieth century, the public debate over second-wave feminism drew in both men and women. The list of participants in the debate is very long; for the moment I will mention only the writer Rosario Castellanos, the theater director and actor Nancy Cárdenas, and the journalist Esperanza Brito de Martí. Each of these figures contributed in her own way to the winds of sexual liberation and feminism of the 1970s. Of course, the commentary of journalists, politicians, and other figures in Mexican public and cultural life was also abundant.

The feminism debate was waged in the press, in public speeches and even in street demonstrations. Printed materials, from books and brochures to short-lived publications and magazines, were among the preferred discussion platforms. In particular, women's magazines dedicated whole pages to the debate, during both the first and second waves.

It is worth stressing from the outset that intellectuals and journalists were not the only ones who took part in the feminist debate, as members of society at large also contributed through a wide range of social movements and associations. There were also initiatives and pronouncements by agents of the state, who made declarations, passed legislation, or established institutions. As is probably already evident, in this chapter feminism is not viewed as synonymous with a feminist movement, and certainly not with a feminist movement associated with certain political positions like those upheld by the leading figures of the different waves, but more broadly as referring to intellectual and social spaces where gender hierarchies have been challenged with a diverse range of arguments and practices.

Feminism is a historical concept whose meaning is established in specific situations and at specific moments, in the context of certain political, ideological, and cultural conflicts and tensions in accordance with the ideological, political, and cultural profile of the person involved in the exchange. Focusing on the debate makes it possible to understand the volatile and unstable nature of feminism, and at the same time to leave aside the one-dimensional and linear narratives that are all too common, to offer instead a more complex overview that reveals the exchanges between different voices, and the tense and sometimes even repetitive dialogue that characterized the ongoing debate.

Divergences between feminist positions were common, and identifying these nuances enriches the story of feminism and helps to push past the view of the history of feminism as a linear history of inevitable progress that underlies so many studies of the topic. The history of feminism in Mexico has focused on the women who worked in organizations or individually to defend rights and spaces of action for women; the involvement of men has not been taken into account in these studies, as if feminism consisted solely of or was synonymous with contributions made by women.[8] It is undeniably important to give visibility to the feminist positions of women, which continue to be largely unknown and not widely studied. However, it is also important to stress that both men and women have adopted feminist (and anti-feminist) stances, and that feminism does not represent the point of view or the voice of women alone.

The debate developed with contributions in support of feminism, but also with voices that opposed their arguments. Anti-feminism has been a constituent element of the debate whose importance has only just begun to be recognized.[9] In the history of Mexico, anti-feminism has been seen as a background and not as a leading player, yet its reactions of opposition pushed feminists to revise and rework their positions. Moreover, anti-feminism exacerbated fears in society over the modernizing changes that gave rise to feminism, fears that sometimes developed into widespread reactions of moral panic that blocked the effects of feminist initiatives in society.

Although characterized by a diverse range of ideas, feminism has exhibited certain unifying features. Its point of departure has been the recognition of injustice toward women, which has been fought with the language of individual rights and human rights. It is worth highlighting the point that feminism has not been limited to the use of egalitarian arguments that maintain that women's rights should be placed on an equal footing with men's rights, as it has also argued in favor of certain exclusive rights for women. These rights are separate from those of men and have not been defended using egalitarian arguments, as will be shown in this chapter. It also must be stressed that not all pronouncements in favor of the rights of women are feminist, as there may also be arguments that oppose feminism using a language of protection for women. This is the case, for example, of the positions taken in opposition to female suffrage based on the argument that having the vote would lead women to participate in the corruption typical of politics, or positions against reproductive rights that claim to oppose abortion in the interests of protecting women's health. The feminist nature of a position always depends on the historical context, as well as on the cultural and political tensions in which that position is inscribed.[10]

This exploration of the feminist debate in Mexico focuses on certain moments that reveal the different positions in support of feminism (while avoiding a merely one-dimensional view of those positions), as well as the main arguments used to oppose them. It highlights aspects of the debates over women's access to professional careers and the effects thereof on the family in the early twentieth century, over female suffrage and the supposed hazards it posed to the governments of the post-revolutionary era and, finally, over lesbianism in response to the UN World Conference on Women held in Mexico City in 1975. The debates over professional careers and suffrage occurred in the context of first-wave feminism, while the debate over lesbianism took place in the second half of the century. The analysis of each of these moments will touch upon different aspects of the arguments of feminists and their opponents. The anti-feminist position changed over time, adapting itself to each wave and, like feminism itself, the significance of the reactions of its opponents can only be understood in their specific historical contexts.

One of the arguments on which anti-feminism has been anchored is the claim that feminism leads to a masculinization of women, "masculinization" being understood in contexts ranging from the adoption of attitudes of personal autonomy or traits like strength and the capacity to decide on their or their family's affairs, to access to professional or political positions, or even to the use of certain types of clothing or hairstyles. Its meaning has changed from one era to the next, but its disparaging intention remains the same: sometimes the label of masculinity is intended to suggest a subversion of accepted gender roles, while in other cases it may suggest lesbianism. Another anti-feminist argument has involved the dismissal of feminist ideas as being the product of foreign influences that are deemed a threat to Mexican identity. The fear of losing gender and national identity, supposedly leading to the destabilization of the family, of social order, and to the disintegration of the nation has been used as a powerful weapon, which has in some cases been effective in combating feminism. To others, however, it has precipitated a redefinition of feminist arguments to respond to criticism. One anti-feminist position in Mexican history related to the campaign against women's suffrage was the attribution of women as more politically conservative and more prone to being influenced by the dictates of the Catholic Church.

The term "feminism" has itself been controversial, marked by the kind of heated disdain and contempt expressed by Manuel Gamio in *Forjando Patria.* It is worth noting that the feminist conferences in Yucatán and the Pan-American Feminist Conference held in Mexico City in 1923 were the only occasions when a revolutionary government (in the first case) and a post-revolutionary government (in the second) were involved in projects that were described as feminist. The term was effectively abandoned as the post-revolutionary governments began adopting a discourse favorable to the working and rural classes. As in other parts of the world, in Mexico feminism was viewed as bourgeois and irrelevant to the interests of working class women. It was for this reason that the term was not used in two emblematic moments of feminist political mobilization, represented by the Sole Pro-Women's Rights Front [*Frente Único Pro-Derechos de la Mujer*], active from 1935–1940, and the Front for Women's Liberation and Rights [*Frente por la Liberación y los Derechos de la Mujer*], which came to prominence from 1979–1980. Both fronts were strongly supported by communist and socialist organizations, but neither had a revolutionary program; rather, their main activities revolved around legislative demands that could clearly be considered feminist. The *Frente Único Pro-Derechos de la Mujer* had female suffrage as its key issue, while the *Frente Por la Liberación y los Derechos de la Mujer* was initially mobilized to fight for the decriminalization of abortion and also combat sexual violence and harassment among its priorities.

Other organizations, like the International League of Iberian and Hispanic-American Women [*Liga de Mujeres Ibéricas e Hispanoamericanas*], based in New York City, which was defined as an international association with a presence throughout the Americas, and which proposed a form of feminism adapted to Catholic and Spanish-speaking cultures, sought to appeal broadly to all women with its neutral name. However, the League's official publication, directed by Elena Arizmendi, was called *Feminismo internacional.*[11]

With the second wave, the term continued to evoke meanings in which certain defenders of women's rights did not wish to participate. The magazine *Fem,* published by a group of journalists and academics, contributed to the development of a positive connotation for the controversial term.

Women's Intellectual Capacities and Their Access to Professional Careers

What is beyond any doubt is that in the first years of the twentieth century the word "feminism" was a highbrow term and, although it was controversial, it had a positive connotation. Justo Sierra, Secretary of Public Instruction and Fine Arts, and one of the most important intellectuals of his era, used it in a speech to express his support for female education and to take a stand against the idea of the intellectual inferiority of women, which he described as an antiquated legend.[12] In spite of Sierra's declarations, the notion of the inability of females to engage in intellectual and professional activities continued to have its defenders, even in the twentieth century, as suggested by the fact that at the Feminist Conference of Yucatán held in 1916, it was considered necessary to address the question.[13]

For Justo Sierra, the purpose of female education was to prepare young women to become cultured wives and mothers capable of raising their children with civic and nationalist values. He considered the learning of a trade to be an acceptable alternative for women whose families had suffered ill fortune and were thus compelled to go out and earn a living, and that teacher training was ideal for women because teaching was considered to be an activity that was similar in some ways to motherhood.

But for all the advantages that higher education for women might offer, it was not without its risks. One contemporary observer considered that female doctors and lawyers posed a hazard to society because men would end up "rocking cradles" while women would be engaged in "pleading cases in public" and "carrying out dissections in laboratories." This inversion of social roles would lead to "the ruin of the household, the neglect of the family, [and] the extinction of the race."[14] This anxiety was exaggerated, as anti-feminist rhetoric often is. According to census data for Mexico City in those years, there were only two practicing female lawyers and four practicing female doctors, an insignificant proportion of the more than eight hundred lawyers and five hundred doctors in the city.[15]

The fear of the masculinization of female professionals affected Mexico's few female doctors and lawyers, who did what they could to counteract it. The magazine *La mujer mexicana* published articles on Mexico's first female lawyer and one of its first female physicians, which stressed that neither one reflected the fears spread by anti-feminists. With reference to the lawyer María Sandoval de Zarco, the author of the article noted: "you can see that science does not take from the woman any of her poetic beauty, nor does it render her unable to perform the humblest household chores." The home of Mrs. Sandoval de Zarco is "poetic and cheerful," notes Correa Zapata, who goes on to wonder at how "that upright and haughty form that defends the innocent and weak before the jury can also bend over the stove to prepare a succulent soup for her dear father and her beloved husband?"[16]

Another example of the potential compatibility between professional skills and feminine qualities was identified by the same author in the physician Columba Rivera: "Anyone who knows Miss Rivera would have to agree that knowledge neither kills nor poisons, nor does study wither the woman's youth, nor cloud her soul, nor embitter her heart, nor darken nor dry up her spirit."[17] For her part, Professor Rosa Navarro also strove to refute those who believed that "the enlightened woman is harmful to society and incapable of fulfilling her duties as wife and mother." Navarro asserted that:

> many young women, with the same assurance with which they write a parable, can tend to an ill person; they can solve a problem of algebra with the same facility with which they make clothing or learn the art of cooking.[18]

The same magazine proposed extreme femininity as a strategy for intellectual women to gain acceptance:

> They attack us for our cunning? Let us be modest. They insult us because we abandon the cares and obligations of our sex? We must show them that we can fulfill our duty without thereby becoming a mere beast of burden.[19]

The hysteria over female professionals had an impact beyond education and women's magazines, finding its way into the mass media. The satirical magazine *La guacamaya* published a lithograph titled "*El feminismo se impone*" ["Feminism is imposed"].[20] The drawing shows men with mustaches carrying out domestic chores considered feminine: ironing, cooking, or embroidery. The image suggests that effeminacy would not only affect the working world, but also had implications for masculine sexual identity, and that therefore the masculinization of female professionals represented an even greater danger than might be supposed. In the background appears the number 41, an allusion to the number of arrestees during a police raid on transvestite men at a private party held in 1901, which turned into a press scandal with its revelation of effeminate and homosexual male identities in Mexico.[21]

The Late Arrival of Suffrage

With the Mexican Revolution, the debate over feminism led to the issue of female suffrage and took on a political dimension that it had not had previously. The question of the vote was first addressed under the Constitutionalists, the winning faction of the Mexican Revolution, which brought relative stability to the country, established a government and built a new state. The rise of the suffragettes in the United States during the First World War led to the issue being given some importance in revolutionary Mexico, in an era of political volatility and openness to ideas for societal reform. The debate over suffrage was first discussed at the feminist conferences in Yucatán, which brought female school teachers together so that they could engage with the project of secular education and social transformation. The cooperation of female teachers with the revolutionary government was essential for the inculcation of civic and nationalist values in the population and the reduction of the influence of the Catholic Church, considered by the revolutionaries to be one of the biggest obstacles to their project to modernize the country. The two feminist conferences explored a wide range of issues such as women's education, their training for paid work, and women's suffrage, among others.

The question of suffrage sparked intense debate, but the prevailing opinion was that the participation of women would be acceptable in municipal elections but not at state or federal levels. The argument put forward was that the female population lacked the necessary education to take part in broader political affairs. José Domingo Ramírez Garrido, a Constitutionalist from the city of Tabasco, was one of the few voices who spoke out against this point of view, arguing that a lack of education was a problem shared equally by men and women and that therefore there could be no justification for denying voting rights to women alone.[22]

The most forceful argument in support of women's suffrage was made by Hermila Galindo, a close political confidant of President Venustiano Carranza and editor-in-chief of the women's magazine *La mujer moderna*. Galindo appealed both to the principle of equality between men and women and to the specific nature of the perspective of women and the contributions of mothers who could bring their experience to bear in public affairs and thus enrich them. Her position was based on justice as an abstract value of society: The vote for women, she claimed, is a matter "of strict justice because if the woman has social obligations it is reasonable to expect that she should not be without rights." At the same time, this egalitarian argument did not prevent Galindo from advocating the need for the vote for women on the basis of the unique experience and responsibilities of mothers: "women look at humanity in quite a different way than men" and, therefore, they could undertake moralizing civic action with campaigns against alcoholism and pornography, issues which, incidentally, formed part of the activism in support of women's suffrage in the United States.[23]

The suffrage issue was even raised at Mexico's Constitutional Congress of 1916–1917, which drafted a new constitution for the country that included reforms related to land ownership and the relationship between capital and labor. The Constitution established wage equality between men and women, but rejected women's suffrage. The mere mention of the issue incited laughter at the Constitutional Points Committee which, in spite of the mockery, issued a pronouncement on the question because it had received three petitions on the matter (two in favor and one against). Women's suffrage was rejected without considering questions of justice or principles, based on the sole argument that women had not collectively demonstrated an interest in public affairs. One member of the Congress, Félix F. Palavicini, who wanted to go further and prevent any possibility of women participating in future elections, proposed an explicit prohibition against women's suffrage in order to avoid the "danger of women organizing to vote and be voted for."[24]

Although the Constitution of 1917 did not recognize voting rights for women, the states of San Luis Potosí (1923), Tabasco (1925), and Chiapas (1925) legislated on women's suffrage under the governments of Rafael Nieto, Tomás Garrido Canabal, and César Córdoba, respectively. These governors were each very different, but all three had participated in the Constitutionalist movement, all three relied on the support of local parties with socialist and radical political leanings, and all three held anti-clerical views of differing degrees, in addition to being in favor of women's education.

Chiapas was the only state to establish permanent and universal women's suffrage, while the other two states made it subject to certain restrictions: San Luis Potosí established the vote for women who could read and write, were not members of any religious congregation, and had not studied at any religious school, while Tabasco recognized the vote for women of irreproachable sexual conduct and socialist views, in addition to establishing that women could become municipal council members provided they never held more than half of the municipal seats or the position of mayor. Neither of these laws lasted long, and both reflected the prejudices of the revolutionaries with their suggestion that women were more susceptible than men to falling under the influence of the Catholic Church and voting in favor of clerical interests, in spite of the fact that there were many devout Catholics of both sexes.

The argument of political conservatism among women used to deny them the vote gained credence as a result of the notable participation of women in the Cristero movement, on the one hand, and in their support for opposition leader José Vasconcelos in the 1929 presidential elections, on the other. Vasconcelos included women's suffrage in his electoral platform, while the official candidate endorsed by National Revolutionary Party, Pascual Ortiz Rubio, although declaring himself in favor of women's suffrage, advocated a gradual approach. In other words, while recognizing the justice of giving women the vote, Ortiz Rubio claimed that women were not yet ready to receive voting rights and, therefore, the constitutional reform on this point should be postponed until the right moment.[25]

The greatest consequences of the fear stirred up over the possibility of women receiving the vote occurred during the presidency of Lázaro Cárdenas. In the context of the social mobilization of the groups that made up the *Frente Único Pro-Derechos de la Mujer*, which was led by the militant communist suffragette María del Refugio García (who launched an intense campaign in support of women's suffrage and even ran as a candidate in internal elections within the official party), President Cárdenas submitted a constitutional reform to Congress that would have given women the vote in 1939 or 1940, just prior to the presidential elections of the latter year.[26] However, fears that the female vote could jeopardize the future of the revolutionary regime were so great that the reform was blocked at the last stage in the legislative process. Congress passed it but it did not come into effect because it was not formally declared through publication in Mexico's official state journal, *Diario Oficial*.[27] The bill's failure was due to pressures from those who feared that the female vote might tip the electoral balance in favor of the opposition candidate Juan Andreu Almazán, who represented counter-revolutionary interests, rather than Manuel Ávila Camacho, the official candidate for the Mexican Revolutionary Party and the man who would ultimately become Mexico's next president.

President Cárdenas's constitutional reform initiative was founded on a radically egalitarian discourse in support of women's suffrage that was virtually unprecedented in Mexico (its only precursor was the reform in the state of Chiapas). Thus, the historian Salvador Novo would later suggest that:

> for Cárdenas it seemed perfectly natural and fair that women should be given the vote; nevertheless, the President approved the suspension of the women's suffrage reform, which is why he shocked the Congress when he declared that from that time on he would no longer help them pass legislation.[28]

Women's suffrage came back into public debate when women were given the right to vote in municipal elections in 1947. President Miguel Alemán Valdés saw electoral participation as an extension of the home and family, the natural sphere of women. This time the introduction of female voting rights was not based on the individual rights of women, on justice or on equality between the sexes. And precisely because it was limited to the municipal level, there was no talk of the danger that women's suffrage could pose to the stability of the revolutionary regime. By 1953, when universal women's suffrage was finally introduced under President Adolfo Ruiz Cortines, there were still opponents. But in the mid-twentieth century there was less apprehension about women being given the vote and the reform was welcomed as a modernizing measure that reflected the growth of the economy and the Americanization of Mexican society that characterized the beginning of the Cold War.

However, fears persisted that voting rights could result in a masculinization of women. This is reflected in Amalia de Castillo Ledón's persistent, decades-long defense of what she called "*feminine* feminism."[29] With this expression, Castillo Ledón referred to a feminist political stance with equality of rights, wages and opportunities of every kind for women, but maintaining a conventional feminine identity that privileged their responsibilities as mothers and wives above any other aspect of their lives. The adjective *feminine* stressed an attractive appearance, a gentle manner and a readiness to please men. In a certain sense, *feminine* feminism had the same objective as the articles on the lives of the female professionals published in the early twentieth century: to demonstrate that practicing a profession or even having access to political office did not pose a threat to the existing gender order or to the preeminence of the home and family within the female universe. In the personal case of Amalia de Castillo Ledón, *feminine* feminism referred not only to a way of being but to a refined and elegant appearance that was part of the public image she cultivated over the course of her long political career both in and outside Mexico.

By the mid-twentieth century, female doctors and lawyers continued to be a tiny minority, but they enjoyed relative acceptance in their professions regardless of their exceptional nature. In spite of the winds of modernization that were blowing in university education, the fear of masculinization of intellectual women had not dissipated. Luz Vera, the first person, male or female, to receive a doctorate in philosophy from Mexico's National Autonomous University (UNAM) in 1938, was discredited by some who described her as a victim of a "virility complex."[30] The language had been updated, but intellectual women continued to be rejected based on similar arguments to those used to repress the aspirations of female doctors and lawyers at the beginning of the century. The writer Rosario Castellanos became familiar with the academic world in her years as a student and reached the conclusion that female cultural, intellectual, scientific, and artistic creators were viewed rather like Loch Ness Monsters, creatures whom nobody ever saw and whom most believed either did not exist or, if they did, were freaks of nature.[31]

The Second Wave: Reproductive and Sexual Freedom

Second-wave feminism focused on women's reproductive and sexual freedom and on defending their rights to control and enjoy their own bodies and their own lives. Equality under the law was of less importance than exposing and combating the restrictions imposed by stereotypes and practices that excluded women or repressed them in the home and family, as well as in the street, in the workplace, and institutionally.

The term "feminism" was recovered after decades of discredit and oblivion to be gradually and tentatively incorporated into a new language that revealed prejudice against women. The words "sexism" (the term which began to be used in those years to refer to prejudices and stereotypes about women that fostered discrimination in a manner similar to the racism exposed by civil rights movements) and "patriarchy" (a concept covering all forms of power that hindered the personal autonomy of women, used as both a noun and in the adjectival form, as in the patriarchal system or domination) formed part of the vocabulary for exposing and challenging the status quo. New, short-lived publications, like *Fem* in several of its first issues, explained the radical approach of the new feminism and linked it to leftist movements.

The issues of the new feminism were also raised in the halls of power. At a speech in the presence of President Luis Echeverría, Rosario Castellanos declared that "self-denial was an insane virtue." She characterized self-denial as "one of the most praised virtues of Mexican women," the effect of which ran counter to any aspiration of equality or justice for the female sex.[32] The writer rejected self-sacrifice and self-denial as a necessary feature of the maternal identity, opposing the widespread idea that the selfless, long-suffering mother was an immutable and even desirable aspect of the social and family order and emblematic of Mexico's national identity. While first-wave feminism had taken part in the nationalist exaltation of motherhood, the second wave broke with this view and criticized "the myth of motherhood," which concealed the complexities of family dynamics, for being discriminatory against women.

Castellanos was extremely critical of women who willingly submitted to "diets, beautifying treatments," to the "ruthless mold of skirts," or to the use of high heels, which she deemed were "instruments of everyday torture."[33] Similarly, beauty contests were described as a form of tyranny and an expression of the commodification of the female body. Activists protested against the Miss Universe competition held in Mexico City and Acapulco, motivated by the same anti-establishment spirit of the protests held against the Miss America competition in 1968.

That protest and many others followed the model established for similar demonstrations in the United States, while at the same time acknowledging the specific nature of the situation of women in Mexico. In commenting on the question of housework strikes, Rosario Castellanos remarked that the fact that many Mexican women were able to employ domestic helpers to take care of arduous household chores had the effect of mitigating and postponing the feminist protest, acting as a kind of "buffer."[34]

Mexican demographic policy did an about-face in the middle of the decade, abandoning a pro-birth position to adopt policies aimed at reducing the birth rate. The population increase in the years of economic stability began to be seen as an obstacle to the growth and modernization of Mexican society. The new policies facilitated access to contraceptives, but abortion continued to be classified as a criminal offense. A woman's choice to terminate a pregnancy without putting her life at risk was available only to women who could pay for a clandestine private clinic or travel abroad for the operation. Legal abortion became a central pillar in a feminist agenda in which a woman's self-determination over her own body and reproductive freedom were priorities.[35] Beginning in the early 1970s, one of the methods used to call for the decriminalization of abortion was the organization of marches held on May 10 (Mother's Day in Mexico), in remembrance of women who had died in clandestine abortion operations. Participants in the march would dress in mourning attire in honor of the women who had died. Although these demonstrations never attracted huge numbers, they succeeded in communicating their message effectively by ending the march at Mexico City's Monument to the Mother, built in tribute to the nation's many mothers and the social benefits that the state offered or promised to offer them.

Among the aims of the UN-sponsored International Women's Year Conference was to promote the inclusion of women in economic growth and modernization, based on the premise that higher levels of education and paid employment could contribute to slowing down the demographic growth that was emerging as an urgent global problem. The Conference brought together government representatives, and in parallel with the conference a Women's Tribune was organized, also sponsored by the UN, which offered a dynamic space for women from non-governmental organizations and their invited guests to discuss a wide range of issues.

The Conference and the Tribune provoked various anti-feminist reactions. One of these came from Mexican singer Oscar Chávez, a prominent figure in the Latin American folk music movement known as *Nueva Trova*. In a corrido that appeared to applaud the achievements of the women's gathering, Chávez actually distorted the issues related to sexuality that were addressed at the Tribune: "Lesbianism, polygamy, abortion and prostitution/Were discussed calling for no more legalization."[36] With the exception of polygamy, which appears to be an allusion to the sexual debauchery often attributed to feminism, all of the issues mentioned in the song (abortion, prostitution, and lesbianism) were indeed discussed at the Tribune of NGOs, but on none of these issues was there a unanimous pronouncement with respect to their "legalization." Some voices spoke out in support of the criminalization of abortion and prostitution, but there were also some who, like Betty Friedan, the American author of the influential book *The Feminine Mystique*, and the Mexican journalist Esperanza Brito de Martí, one of the organizers of the Mother's Day mourning marches, declared their support for the decriminalization of abortion. One organized group of prostitutes from the United States criticized the hypocrisy and moral double standards that characterized attitudes toward the sex trade and called for recognition of the labor rights of prostitutes, who, they argued, were entitled to social security and retirement benefits, and should have to pay taxes, as should their customers.[37]

One of the panels that received the greatest media attention was the panel on lesbianism, a topic considered taboo and offensive by many. The leading participant was Nancy Cárdenas, who by that time had already gained visibility as a rights activist in the gay liberation movement that had begun to gather force in Mexico. Homophobic reactions came both from conference participants and from media commentators. One of the arguments against the lesbianism panel was that this issue and others related to sexuality were superficial, frivolous matters that distracted attention from the economic issues that many viewed as truly important. This was the view expressed by some of the first-wave feminists who attended the 1975 Conference, and also by certain representatives of female workers' organizations with Marxist and anti-imperialist leanings. One academic who has studied the issue explains that the fierce condemnation of the panel was due to the anxiety provoked by the growing strength of feminism in Mexico, which led some to imagine that the influence of U.S. activists might precipitate the expansion of lesbianism among Mexican women.[38]

As has been shown over the course of this chapter, the ongoing debate in Mexico over feminism has touched some sensitive nerves of Mexican society at different moments in history. In the early days of Mexican feminism, the debate about women's education and access to professional careers was as intense as the controversy over women's suffrage or, some years later, over their reproductive and sexual freedom.

The fact that some women began practicing in the medical or legal professions was a consequence of the educational reform launched by the Porfirio Díaz government. However, it was met with fears of a masculinization of women, which was viewed as a threat to the gender order, to social stability and even to the national identity.

The debate over women's suffrage occurred during the Mexican Revolution and in the post-revolutionary era, when the anti-suffrage movement grew stronger in reaction to fears that the female vote would favor conservative political forces and thus endanger the future of the post-revolutionary governments and their social and economic reforms.

Finally, the debate over women's sexual freedom was marked by a rejection of the idea that an issue like lesbianism was relevant to women in Mexico and other poor nations. There was some discussion of the masculinization implicit in lesbian identity, but toward the end of the twentieth century lesbianism was countered by pathologizing it, a stigmatizing approach that was convincing for many people. It was also argued that lesbian identity was the product of negative foreign influences, and had no relevance for real Mexican women. Anti-feminism once again invoked the social crisis afflicting the family and the nation to refute feminist positions which in the final decades of the century focused on women's freedom and control over their bodies, just as earlier positions had focused on fighting for the intellectual and professional rights of women and their right to vote.

The history of feminism in Mexico has generally been studied without taking into account the long debate of which this chapter has examined certain specific moments. Focusing on the debate reveals the complexity of the relationship between the propositions of feminism and the reactions against them, which have played a role in the definition and redefinition of the meaning of feminism. Feminism itself and its supporters and detractors are defined in specific historical contexts that need to be seen as part of the history of Mexican culture in the twentieth century, as has been done in this chapter, while avoiding one-dimensional and linear perspectives of the evolution of feminism.

Notes

1 Manuel Gamio, *Forjando patria* (Mexico City: Editorial Porrúa, 2006), 128.
2 Ibid.
3 Karen Offen, "Editor's Introduction," In *Globalizing Feminisms, 1789–1945 (Rewriting Histories)*, edited by Karen Offen, xxix–xxxvi (London and New York, NY: Routledge, 2009).
4 Nancy Hewitt, ed., *No Permanent Waves: Recasting Histories of U.S. Feminism* (New Brunswick, NJ: Rutgers, 2010).
5 For example, women's suffrage was granted in Brazil in 1932, in Argentina in 1947, and in Chile in 1949.
6 Rosalva Aída Hernandez Castillo, "Mujeres indígenas: repensando los derechos desde la diversidad," In *Un fantasma recorre el siglo. Luchas feministas en México, 1910–2010*, edited by Ana Lau and Gisela Espinosa Damián, 309–333 (Mexico City: UAM, 2011).
7 Marta Lamas, "De la protesta a la propuesta: el feminismo en México a finales del siglo XX," In *Historia de las mujeres en España y América Latina*, edited by Isabel Morant, 903–921 (Madrid: Ediciones Cátedra, 2006).
8 Gisela Espinosa and Ana Lau, *Un fantasma recorre el siglo: luchas feministas en Mexico, 1910–2010* (Mexico City, UAM, 2011); Marta Lamas, *Miradas feministas al siglo XX mexicano* (Mexico City: Fondo de Cultura Económica, 2000).
9 Christine Bard, ed., *Un siglo de antifeminismo* (Madrid: Biblioteca Nueva, 2000).
10 Christine Bard, "Para una historia de los antifeminismos," In *Un siglo de antifeminismo*, edited by Christine Bard, 25–65 (Madrid: Biblioteca Nueva, 2000).
11 Gabriela Cano, *Se llamaba Elena Arizmendi* (Mexico City: Tusquets Editores, 2010).
12 Justo Sierra, "Improvisación con motivo de la inauguración oficial del Departamento de práctica mercantil en la Escuela 'Miguel Lerdo de Tejada', verificada el día 12 de la Escuela agosto de 1907," In *Obras completas. La educación nacional*, vol. VIII, edited by Agustín Yáñez, 32 (Mexico City: UNAM, 1984).
13 Salvador Alvarado, *El primer Congreso Feminista de Yucatán: Anales de esta memorable asamblea* (Mérida, Yucatán, Mexico: Ateneo Peninsular, 1916), 130–131.
14 Manuel Flores, "La mujer y las profesiones liberales," *El Mundo Ilustrado* 5 de mayo de 1901, In *Debate pedagógico durante el porfiriato México*, edited by Mílada Bazant, 143 (Mexico City: Secretaria de Educación Pública, 1985).
15 *Censo general de la República Mexicana por estados verificado el 28 de octubre de 1900 conforme a las instrucciones de la Dirección General de Estadística a cargo del Dr. Antonio Peñafiel* (Mexico City: Oficina Tipográfica de la Secretaría de Fomento, 1900–1905), 267.
16 Dolores Correa Zapata, "La señora licenciada Victoria Sandoval de Zarco," *La mujer mexicana*, Vol 10 (October 1904): 2.
17 Dolores Correa Zapata, " La señorita Doctora Columba Rivera," *La mujer mexicana*, Vol 8 (August 1904): 1.
18 Rosa Navarro, "La ilustración de la mujer," In *Mujeres notables*, edited by Laureana Wright de Kleinhans, (Mexico City: Tipografía económica, 1910), 453.
19 Guadalupe Gutiérrez de Joseph, "El feminismo en México," *La mujer mexicana*, Vol III (November 11, 1906): 122.

20 José Guadalupe Posada, "El feminismo se impone," *La Guacamaya del pueblo y por el pueblo,* (July 25, 1907).
21 Robert Mckee Irwin, Edward McCaugan and Michelle Rocío Nasser, eds., *The Famous 41: Sexuality and Social Control in Mexico* (Basingstoke: Palgrave Macmillan, 2003).
22 José Domingo Ramírez Garrido, *Al margen del feminismo* (Mérida: Talleres Pluma y Lápiz, 1918).
23 Hermila Galindo, *Estudio de la Señorita Hermila Galindo con motivo de los temas que han de absolverse en el Segundo Congreso Feministas de Yucatán* (Mérida: Imprenta del Gobierno Constitucionalista, 1916).
24 Félix F. Palavicini, *Diario de Debates del Congreso Constituyente de 1916–1917* (Mexico City: Comisión Nacional para la Celebración del Sesquicentenario de la Proclamación de la independencia Nacional y del Cincuentenario de la Revolución Mexicana, 1960), 983.
25 Gabriela Cano, "Debates en torno al sufragio y la ciudadanía de las mujeres en México," In *Historia de las mujeres en España y América Latina,* edited by Isabel Morant, vol. IV, 535–551 (Madrid: Ediciones Cátedra, 2006). Gabriela Cano, "Paradojas del sufragio femenino," *Nexos,* vol. 430 (October 2013), 24–28.
26 Verónica Oikión, *Cuca García, 1889–1973: Una mirada a sus causa revolucionarias* (Zamora: El Colegio de Michoacán, forthcoming).
27 Ward M. Morton, *Woman Suffrage in Mexico* (Gainesville, FL: University Press of Florida, 1962), 17–38.
28 Salvador Novo, "Los hilos y el ovillo," In *La vida en México durante el gobierno de Lázaro Cárdenas* (Mexico City: Consejo Nacional para la Cultura y las Artes, 1992), 165–166.
29 Amalia de Castillo Ledón, "Discurso ante la Columna de la Independencia, 16 de septiembre de 1938," In *Amalia de Castillo Ledón. Mujer de letras, mujer de poder: Antología,* selection and introduction by Gabriela Cano (Mexico City: Consejo Nacional para la Cultura y las Artes, 2011), 86.
30 Luz Vera, "El feminismo en el México independiente," In *Filosofía y Letras* XXX (Mexico City: Universidad Nacional Autónoma de México, 1956): 53, 60–62.
31 Rosario Castellanos, *Sobre cultura femenina* (Mexico City: Fondo de Cultura Económica, 2005).
32 Rosario Castellanos, "La abnegación, una virtud loca," *Debate feminista* (6 September 1992), 287–296.
33 Rosario Castellanos, "Feminismo 1970. Curarnos en salud," In *Mujer de palabras: artículos rescatados de Rosario Castellanos,* edited by Andrea Reyes, 379 (Mexico City, Consejo Nacional para la Cultura y las Artes, 2004).
34 Ibid., 379.
35 Abortion was decriminalized in Mexico City in 2007 and from that time on it was offered as a medical service at public hospitals operated by the municipal government.
36 Oscar Chávez, "Liberación femenina" (1975): "*Lesbianismo, poligamia, aborto y prostitución / Fueron tratados pidiendo no más legalización.*" I would like to thank Bernardo Ibarrola and Pamela J. Fuentes for this reference.
37 Pamela J. Fuentes, "Entre reivindicaciones sexuales y reclamos de justicia económica: divisiones políticas e ideológicas durante la Conferencia Mundial del Año Internacionald de la Mujer. Mexico City, 1975," *Secuencia* 89, (May–August 2014), 165–192; Jocelyn Olcott, "Cold War Conflicts and Cheap Cabaret: Sexual Politics at the 1975 United Nations International Women's Year Conference," *Gender and History,* Vol 22, No. 3 (November 2010), 733–754.
38 Jocelyn Olcott, "Cold War Conflicts and Cheap Cabaret: Sexual Politics at the 1975 United Nations International Women's Year Conference," *Gender and History,* Vol 22, No. 3 (November 2010), 743.

20

CULTURAL IDENTITY IN LATIN AMERICA

Toward a Cooperative Understanding of Our Past

Carlos Manuel Salomon, with Laura Inés Catelli, Jorge Majfud, Paloma Martínez-Cruz, Magalí Rabasa, Enrique Salmón, Umi Vaughan, and Gloria E. Chacón

This essay reflects the intermingling of concepts concerning the idea of culture in the geographic region known as Latin America. Locating a universal meaning of cultural identity, of course, is impossible. Latin Americans and the emerging Latinx population in the United States are so distinct from one another that the goal of finding any such meaning seems strange. Yet the people of Latin American origin have one thing in common that goes beyond the simple markers of religion and language: they traverse borders at an almost unprecedented rate, borrowing new identities, languages, and political concepts along the way, breaking from the confinement of their local worlds and, in the process, becoming transnational actors. We have all heard the anecdote of the migrant who only becomes politicized once he has left the confines of his small town; mingling with other migrants in a foreign land he is able to better understand the globalized forces that caused him to leave in the first place. It is no coincident that migration is a force that unifies the consciousness of distinct people. Latin American migration is rooted in struggle and coercion. The very people who are leaving have ancestors who crossed oceans, were brought over in chains, were stripped of their culture and lands, and forced to relocate. Migration is a continuation of that process and it is in this reality that a new identity emerges.

Jorge Majfud

Many of the authors in this volume have had similar experiences. For example, the Uruguayan scholar Jorge Majfud, who now lives and teaches in Florida at Jacksonville University, explains how he has changed since he left his homeland.

> *First, we should consider an existential detail that we normally omit when answering this type of question: I am no longer exactly the same. I am twelve years older and almost everything looks different from the vantage of forty-seven. Also, what we imprecisely call Latin America has changed, almost as much as the rest of the world. After this we can reflect on cultural dynamics. To see one's culture from within the immersion of another is always revealing. One has to compare and contrast the inner and outer view. The same is true of language: as we learn a second language we become more aware of the nature of the first language.*

Latin America is a vast and extremely diverse region, so talking about "our culture" is the product of another linguistic trap: a Mexican from Chihuahua and another from Arizona or California have more in common with each other than with an Argentine, for example. But Latin American cultures unite us with the language, the awareness of the existence of the other and the way the Great Brother of the North has treated us in the past. It is the gaze and sometimes the intimidation of the US that has been part of our common identity. For example, there is the idea of the other and the denial of Latinidad within the borders of the United States. Ethnic classification, typical of this country, defines hatred and elections even today, like nowhere else in the world.

When I first came to the United States by airplane in 2003 I was given a form where, among other things, I had to mark "race." It seemed very exotic to me and I wrote above: "no race." I never felt Latino or Hispanic until after I lived here for a few years. That classification, in fact, is an American invention, which has now been transformed into a banner of vindication, because we (the others) have entered a game that we did not invent and have learned to play in order not to suffer the consequences of total defeat.

From an academic point of view, it is impossible to delve into the history of U.S.–Latin American relations and not find a long list of crimes presented as salvations, and of dictatorships who served in the name of freedom and democracy. Fortunately, the arrogance and disdain with which Latin America has been viewed from the North (based on ignorance of its own crimes of interventions, plots, imposition of bloody dictatorships throughout the subcontinent) has been limited and mitigated by some of the best Americans. They are people with great intellectual courage who have not allowed themselves to be intimidated by the propaganda or the tribal reactions of their own people.

Today Latin America is not the same region of magical realism populated by guardian dictators of a monoculture system. But its conflict still lives, as does the old tendency of its rulers to perpetuate their power. Latin American corruption served many, although in different ways: it served the world powers to exploit its resources with cheap labor; it served the local oligarchies to enrich themselves with the blood of the rabble and the indigenous; and it served the poorest by allowing them to survive. This continues, especially in large countries like Mexico and Brazil and a few small ones like those in Central America.

Corruption in the United States is different. It is usually legal, like when powerful lobbies pressure their representatives in Congress (more than half are millionaires and come from the wealthiest 1% of the population) to pass laws that benefit them. After this process they are the least interested in violating their own laws, obviously.

CS: It's funny how you began to feel Latin American when you first arrived in the United States. For me, it was the opposite. It was when I traveled and studied in Mexico, and, ironically, when I read the work of your late friend and compatriot Eduardo Galeano. This may have something to do with how Latinos are assimilated into public schools. Studying, living, and learning in Latin America was a revelation. Galeano's work really gave me a sense of the struggle against colonialism that was occurring in Latin America.

In this instance, it is necessary to differentiate the Latin American identity from the Hispanic one. The first was an invention of the French in the nineteenth century that came about during the birth of the new republics; the second is a result of the U.S. government more recently, which ended up classifying "Hispanics" as "the other." This surfaced from an Anglo-American culture that is proud of its "melting pot" (which never melts). The first identity, the Latin American one, was and still is basically regional and cultural, if not regional and political; The second, the idea, the perception and the identity of being "Hispanic" is, as is typical of American history and culture, an ethnic phenomenon, despite the enormous ethnic diversity of what is technically Hispanic or Latino.

Historically the Southern Cone, especially in Argentina and Uruguay, were considered the "southern Europeans" who did not descend from any tribe or pre-Hispanic civilization but from the ships. It was in the middle of the twentieth century that we stopped looking so much at France and began to look at our brothers and sister from the continent. This is exactly what happened to the young Argentine Ernesto Guevara as he travelled across the continent: He discovered Latin America and discovered his Latin American self. The intellectuals had already tried it before, in a somewhat forced way (José Martí, José Rodó, Ruben Darío, José Vasconcelos, etc.). But it was the political consciousness of the twentieth century that made this a reality—in awareness rather than ideas. The Cuban Revolution was a turning point in that direction. The people of the Rio de la Plata region felt they were civilized because we had killed all of the Indians; because we had the best education systems, the best economies; we were the most developed in the continent with a high per capita income and advanced social programs that had balanced the social classes. Suddenly, we experienced our own decline and soon developed a sense of guilt for not having totally belonged to Latin America. It was writers like Neruda, Benedetti, and Galeano who created or consolidated that continental consciousness by which we began to feel Latin American.

However, feeling "Hispanic" or "Latino" is not exactly the same and you have to live in the United States to appreciate the difference, because it is basically a North American identity.

CS: Your experience brings a question to mind: Referring back to your essay, how do you feel connected with the stories of the Aztecs and Incas and to spiritual *mestizaje*? Is there something in them that defines the spirit of Latin America?

I tried to answer that question in my book El eterno retorno de Quetzalcoatl. *For example: the same idea of the Southern Cone as a cultural region built by Europeans and white creoles in the near absence of the indigenous heritage survives today. An extreme example came from the former president of Uruguay, Julio Maria Sanguinetti, who wrote that we did not receive anything from the indigenous Charrúa people, not even a word. Of course, we robbed them and killed them because we thought them to be so savage and because they did not accept our culture in return for their lands and their freedom. But I was always surprised to discover, among thousands of secret clues, that in the Castilian language survived expressions, indigenous ideas, from as far away as the Guarani, the Incas, and even the Maya. The street language of my early teenage friends was full of indigenous expressions that nobody noticed as such. What could you expect from countries with a strong indigenous tradition like Bolivia, Peru, Guatemala, or Mexico? This raises the question of whether it is possible to completely erase a culture in the process of violent colonization. My initial hypothesis is simply no: The repression of a memory does not mean elimination. The repressed element is transmuted, transposed to survive in the shadows, as in one's personal psychology, and is found in an alien format such as writing, documents of the colonizer, the oral tradition collected and expressed in art and literature. The same historical and mythological evolution of an Argentine like Ernesto Che Guevara has much in common with a Mexican god like Quetzalcoatl and retains much of the indigenous, pre-Hispanic and contemporary, way of seeing the world. The Utopias of left-wing intellectuals, like that of Eduardo Galeano, a Uruguayan marked by the indigenous sensibility or, at least, anti-materialist: they were not Marxist at all, nor materialistic, but were influenced by the cosmic/naturalist paradigm of indigenous mentality, of a return to our origins, to a past that was lost, like all that is ahead of us, beyond the future.*

Like Majfud, Laura Ines Catelli studied and lived in the United States for many years. She is now back living and teaching in her native Argentina. Her perspective on the way Latin American culture is written in the English language engages new forms of colonialism, which may or may not be intentionally motivated. This analysis dovetails with the idea that among Latin Americans who have lived in the United States, as Majfud noted, a new analysis has emerged. I asked Catelli about how this exchange has affected her perception of Latin American culture and identity.

Laura Inés Catelli

Your observations pose a truly complex question regarding how Latin America has been imagined and constructed from different loci of enunciation. I personally would not attempt a generalization of how scholars from different countries or regions think of Latin America. One could assert nonetheless that there is often a tension between ideas of nation (national traditions, the nation-state as a problem), and ideas of continental unity that can be traced back to José de San Martín and Simón Bolívar in our region (for former Hispanic colonies), and to twentieth-century dependence theories and the center-periphery model (based on the economist Raúl Prebisch's work). It is almost as if the idea of Latin America coagulates in economic and political terms as a unifying concept that is anticolonial and anti-imperialistic. The underside here is the impossibility of thinking comparatively and to be able to account for the diversity of national projects and internal colonialism (I'm using Pablo González Casanova's and Rodolfo Stavenhagen's term here, more recently theorized by Bolivian Aymara sociologist Silvia Rivera Cusicanqui). This tension is present today in works that are representative of the decolonial turn (Quijano, Mignolo, etc.). At the same time, the decolonial turn has inscribed the problem of race along with that of gender and class into what was understood mostly as a class problem (in Marxist terms). In sum, the idea of Latin America from the Southern Cone seems to be an anticolonial and anti-imperial expression, but only recently and very slowly has race begun to be understood as part of the problem. This is, in part, thanks to Quijano's concept of coloniality of power and Mignolo's insistence on decolonial genealogies, which include Black and indigenous voices that share what Anzaldúa called "una herida abierta," la herida colonial.

From the U.S., I think the idea of Latin America among Latin Americanists is very closely tied up with Area Studies and the resulting Latin American Studies programs, that tend to see the region as a relatively stable object of study. There is a distance in this sense that I find ideologically problematic, insofar as Latin Americanist scholars in the U.S. don't examine their own locus of enunciation (the U.S., U.S. academia, private universities, etc., etc.) when researching, writing, and theorizing about a region that has been affected so deeply by U.S. foreign and economic policies and interests, as if cultural imperialism were not part of the neoliberal agenda. I do find that it would be so important if U.S. Latin Americanists stopped thinking and writing about Latin America as if they were in a non-place, and critically accounted for their own loci of enunciation and the risks of academic colonialism. Even thinkers that identify themselves as part of the decolonial turn seem to write from this sort of "non-place." The impression is that very little if any consideration is given to Latin American research and critical thought, so Latin America is indeed being constructed and imagined through the imperial lens of U.S. academia.

Some of us are constantly trying to filter concepts and critical discourses that are not at all sensitive to local realities. This is part of why I insist in the essay I wrote for your volume and in other recent essays that we all need to be critically aware of the imaginaries we deploy in our analyses, given that we are caught in an oscillating relationship between the institutional and the imaginary.

Did the racial dialogue in the United States have something to do with how you analyze Latin America? To what extent is this dialogue explored in Argentina? How do your students react to it?

Yes, of course. I lived in the U.S. for almost twenty years. I cannot say that institutionally the problem of race was present as something to be discussed. There were, of course, affirmative action policies that did shape the ethnic and sex/gender landscapes of, for example, my college experience (I went to Rutgers for undergrad). I think "race" was more present as relations and as experience for me. Racial diversity was part of my life in the U.S.; this is something that I perceived from an immigrant perspective. Edward Said would call it "a counterpoint experience." Having moved from a mostly white and mestizo region of Argentina (River Plate region), the contrast with central New Jersey and later West Philadelphia was always noticeable for me. The visibility and explicitness of racial relations in the U.S. made me aware of the negation of race and racial difference in Argentina, where racial formations were very different than in the U.S. I try to share with my students this awareness and work against the grain of the negation of race in Argentine imaginaries, by exploring the construction of cultural imaginaries (I concentrate on art and literature, but I work openly with other expressions). I compare race and racial dynamics to those pictures from the nineties called "Magic Eye." When you looked at those pictures, in appearance they were just a bunch of dots, but if you looked long enough the eye would adjust its focus and a three-dimensional image would appear, and then it was almost impossible not to see it. Students react very strongly to discussions on racial dynamics, sometimes from very personal places, and it is incredible how quickly they can adjust their critical mindsets to incorporate race as part of the landscape of sociocultural and economic dynamics. Because university is free and public in Argentina and access is guaranteed universally (so far; we will have to fight to keep it so), I do pose the question in class of why the university population remains mostly white, middle and upper middle class. What are the symbolic walls that keep poor, brown students from imagining themselves as professionals or as part of the community to which they (my students) belong? Many students are involved in political activity and community outreach through university programs, so this is a very relevant question for many of them.

I asked Dr. Catelli about Jorge Majfud's classification of the Latino as a U.S. invention. This process was transformed, in the words of Majfud, "*en una bandera de reivindicación, porque nosotros (los otros) hemos entrado en un juego que no inventamos y hemos aprendido a jugar para no sufrir las consecuencias de la derrota absoluta.*" For Catelli, Majfud's words rang true.

Yes, I think it's common and I agree that those "flags" of identity, reivindicated with pride by the Latinx community, are specific to the U.S. But identity politics are a dangerous game to play when loci of enunciation are not made specific, like I said before. Identity politics can run very close to essentialism and miss the depth of power dynamics and historic contingency. This is why I insisted above that Latin Americanists in the U.S., among which I include Latinx scholars, should not take their identity as ethical guarantees and really begin to examine their privilege, their locus of enunciation, and their part in power relations. Your volume, by focusing on an inclusive dialogue and through this collective epilogue, shows an interesting move and an awareness in that regard.

The cross-pollination of ideas that flow across borders, influence and reshape identities is nothing new. Among Mexicans it has a long history. Some argue that the *Corrido,* which is among the most popular forms of music in Latin America, was created in the Borderlands, an area of conflict over land and culture. While Catelli and Majfud speak of the unique geopolitical matrix of Latinx identity in relation to Argentine and Uruguayan identity, within Latinx communities there exist multiple layers. To the Mexican, the pocho is Mexican only in his physical traits. Pochos are typically second- or third-generation U.S. citizens of Mexican ancestry. But American racism has segregated them and assimilation has made them English-language dominant. Yet the culture emanating from these communities lies in a place between spaces. That vibrant place created an identity not quite *gringo* and not Mexican. Mexican American or Chicanx culture has influenced Latinx communities far and wide. Mexicans represent about 60 percent of the migration to the United States from Latin America. Chicanx culture has entered the mainstream and has heavily influenced Mexican youth both in the United States and in Mexico. Américo Parades, pioneer of Borderlands cultural theory, paved the way toward an understanding of a new borderlands culture, but he also had the idea of "greater Mexico," which connects the new and the old and viewed the evolution of Chicanx culture as part of the flow of Mexican culture across borders. But there still exists the disconnect between Chicanx and Mexican culture. Paloma Martínez-Cruz, who writes about the pocho experience as a site of resistance to linguistic imperialism, has hopes for a more nuanced understand among these related communities.

Paloma Martínez-Cruz

I think that linguistic shame marks migrant experience, and is reflected in subsequent generations and articulated as a "loss" of culture. I am hopeful that an understanding of the history of coloniality, class, race, and gender in literature and other forms of communication will allow people to replace this notion of that which is "lost" with a greater sense of being whole, aligned, and enfranchised participants in a geopolitical process that has claimed them as its denizens.

Latinx culture in the United States is as varied as the nations which make up Latin America. But the influence on U.S. culture is profound. To a large extent, I wanted this book to explore the subjectivities of Latin American/Latinx culture. I saw in Umi Vaughan's writing an opportunity to hear from someone who delved into Latin American music from a very unique place, that of the African American experience. What was it about Black Latin America that attracted him? I wondered if his topic gave him the chance to explore something unique.

Umi Vaughan

As a child, I learned Spanish in school, but I did not have direct exposure to Afro Latin folks. In my house, I heard salsa music and saw Celia Cruz on television from time to time, but I was not fully aware of the African presence in Latin America. My first real experience, the one that opened my eyes and focused my journey, was in Mexico—one of the last places that comes to mind for most when thinking about Black culture. On a Morehouse College summer study abroad trip I traveled to numerous places in the Pacific coast region known La Costa Chica, known for its sizeable population of Black Mexicans. There I met a black Trinidadian priest named Father Glyn Jemmott, an African American scholar Bobby Vaughn, an Afro-Mexican cultural activist, Donají Méndez Tello and had encounters in several black communities that taught me a lot about the African legacy in Mexico. It became clear to me that Africans also richly influenced other Latin American nations, and I determined to learn more.

From then on, I have continually traveled and researched among Black communities in other Latin American countries: Cuba, Brazil, Peru, and Colombia. What attracts me is what Amiri Baraka calls the "changing same." Each nation, each community has its own unique twist on similar rhythms, similar dances, parallel processes. Each evolved from related but distinct historical contexts. As I move, experiencing music/dance styles like pagodão from Bahia, Brazil, Colombian champeta music, Cuban timba, and New Orleans bounce music, it feels like traveling between parallel dimensions.

For me the goal is to document and analyze music/dance styles that hold deep meaning and accomplish important work within and for the communities that practice them. I strive to do so in a scholarly way that swings and vibrates like the performances and performers do. Another aim is to better understand my place in the world as a son of the African Diaspora. This entails tracing the connections between my experiences and circumstances and those of "cousins" in Cuba, Brazil, Peru, Colombia, Mexico, Dominican Republic, and so on.

Culture in Latin America, and Greater Latin America, has influenced political identity in many ways. Umi Vaughan was driven to explore Latin American culture because of his exploration of the many intricacies of the African Diaspora. Similarly, for Magali Rabasa, Latin American culture goes far beyond the traditional focus on "high" art. Culture is embedded within the various forms of protest and social action. I love the fact that she writes about her participation in these events. Her study of Latin American social movements is something that she has witnessed firsthand. I was interested in her thoughts about how social movements are intertwined with culture. Have social movements—activism, protest, etc.—become part of the cultural fabric of the societies she writes about? This may sound like an abstract question, but it seems to me that political struggle against oppression has moved beyond simple political issues. If so, how is this expressed? Has it influenced art, literature, music, lifestyle, etc.?

Magalí Rabasa

I think that the social movements I engage with are very much a part of the cultural fabric of their societies. This is perhaps most clearly explained through a shift in language away from "social movements" as contained, identifiable groups of people, coalitions or organizations towards the notion of "societal movement" (Luis Tapia) as a means of accounting for the way that politics, activism, and protest become more widespread and enmeshed in quotidian patterns and practices, and in social relations that connect people at all levels, be it of the family, the neighborhood, the workplace, the school, the city, the street, etc.

It could be said, then, that "politics" is not understood as being the domain of specific groups or identities (adults, organizers, politicians, academics, bureaucrats, etc.) but rather as the more generalized and dispersed fields of antagonisms and tensions through which the social is reimagined and transformed. This is why I see the kinds of "politics" that propel the movements (anti-capitalism, autonomy, anti-racism, feminism, etc.) in all facets of life: work, education, land, housing, art, media, and communications.

For example, as I explore elsewhere, the books that the movements produce are not simply the vehicle for the transmission of ideas about anticapitalist and autonomous struggle. Through their form (low-cost editions) and their processes of production (spaces of collective theorization, cooperative print shops) and circulation (alternative book fairs, non-commercial distribution networks), they actually materialize the very ethics (horizontality, mutual aid, collectivity, etc.) the texts (grassroots political theory) communicate.

Social movements are growing to include transnational actions. The literature, art, and even the methods used to organize have crossed borders and have contributed to the Bolivarian idea of a unified Latin America. But to indigenous communities, the idea of Latin America itself carries with it a very negative connotation. To Enrique Salmón, his people, the Rarámuri of Chihuahua, Mexico have more in common with the Apache and Navajo of the U.S. Southwest than they do with mainstream Mexico. In his book *Eating the Landscape*, he wrote about how oral traditions of traditional foodways allowed various indigenous groups to combat colonialism. I asked him if the Mexican government was persistent as the U.S. government in trying to eradicate Native traditions. Were there any traditions that were lost? How does migration affect indigenous culture in Mexico?

Enrique Salmón

When we were first discussing my writing something for the volume, I mentioned that indigenas today do not really think of their communities as part of the geopoliticized concept of Latin America. Most do seem to recognize, however, that we are part of a pan-indio community that exist between the U.S.-Mexico borderlands south down to Tierra del Fuego. In addition, there is also the recognition that we are related to and share similar political and social issues that are experienced by indigenous people north of the U.S.-Mexico border. I think that the notion of Latin America has become a politically convenient term that is being used to further separate the oppressed Global South from the North, which also separates indigenous communities from each other.

Remember, prior to the emergence of the Mexican state, the Spanish Crown had had three hundred years of destroying entire cultures, converting and exposing millions to Catholicism, introducing European foods, and creating José Vasconcelos' "la Raza Cosmica" of mestizos. By the time the Mexican government assumed political authority from Spain in 1821, there were only pockets of indigenous communities that had held onto most of their pre-Columbian languages, cultures, and oral traditions. There was really no concerted effort to completely "eradicate" indigenous traditions since the majority of Mexicanos were themselves part indigenous. There were and still are events that have caused the Mexican government to control indigenous populations, i.e. Yaqui communities during the late nineteenth and early twentieth centuries and the Zapatistas beginning in 1994. As a result, many traditions were lost. There are endemic foods such as panic grass that are no longer grown and eaten. The rich oral traditions of the Yaqui, Mayo, and Pima Bajo were deeply compromised and are nearly totally gone, and in the south, entire communities of indigenous peoples are being forcibly removed from ancestral lands which threatens their library of traditions. One of the ways that indigenous peoples have adapted to force removal has been to migrate either to large Mexican cities or to head north to the United States. Removed from their lands oral, food, and linguistics traditions quickly erode with successive generations.

Dr. Salmón is clearly concerned about how colonialism, both historic and modern, affects the maintenance of indigenous culture. In many cases, an adherence to traditional ways is a decolonial tool, in which the strands of colonialist identities are stripped away. Nevertheless, culture is inevitably influenced by the cultural forces of mainstream society. I asked the Mayan scholar Gloria E. Chacon if she sees a major difference between indigenous identity in the United States and in Latin America. Has identity played a role within indigenous literary movements? I was curious because I notice major differences in how U.S. and Latin American society identify indigenous identity or indigenous people in general. These issues recently came up when a student asked me if it is possible to be biracial and indigenous in Latin America, like you can be in the United States.

Gloria E. Chacon

I do see major differences between indigenous identity in the USA and Latin America. For one, because nation-states have predominantly used indigenous languages as the defining marker of identity, and it continues to be an important attribute to indigeneity. Indigenous writers and other intellectuals—who are also bilingual—articulate that language serves as a vehicle to an indigenous way of being and seeing the world. That said, the reality of language loss is not lost to indigenous writers and other intellectuals. I think that is why for many—certainly not all—there is an urgency in establishing readers in indigenous languages. This entails teaching others how to read and write in their native languages since most have been schooled only in Spanish. Yaxnaya Aguilar, a Mixe linguist, points out that the rubric of indigenous languages conflates a diverse group of languages and cultural universes that sometimes can be as different as Chinese and Nigerian. She points out that the only commonalities that indigenous nations and languages share is that they were colonized by the Spaniards and that they are now under a nation-state. This is true. At the same time, these facts alone offer insight into what we may term indigeneity because colonization and the establishment of nation-states initiated a process that has led to cultural, linguistic, and territorial loss. Indeed, that's what we share.

As to your question of biracial identity and indigeneity, the historical separation of indigenous peoples from the rest of the populations through the Republic of Indians and the Republic of Spaniards lent itself to some cultural and linguistic autonomy for many indigenous communities which also meant that outsiders were maintained at a distance. This, of course, does not mean—at least in my experience—that there are less mixed-race people. Again, what seems to matter is language. I know some indigenous peoples whose physical attributes would be considered European (i.e., blue or green eyes, maybe even blonde hair), but who speak Maya and see themselves as Maya. I see something similar with indigenous peoples in the Caribbean coast of Central America who have physical attributes we may see as African, but they speak an indigenous language and consider themselves indigenous.

Recently, I have seen a more open discussion about racial mixture, and it seems to becoming more and more from indigenous women who acknowledge a more culturally diverse background. Adding to this new aperture is the role of immigration. More second and third generation indigenous kids are also returning to their communities even though they may not speak the language. I believe that indigeneity is a political position, but also an affective one.

Language is so important to culture yet we see a major movement in Latin America, and the United States, centered on the idea of a "decolonial" project. I see more mestizos abandoning aspects of Hispanic culture, especially Catholicism, and moving more toward indigenous worldviews. I may be wrong, but it seems that many Latinxs with Mesoamerican origins gravitate toward Azteca or Mayan. How do you see this process and how it has affected literature? Is this an elusive quest? Is this a transitory phase toward decolonial healing? Do you think it adds a new element to indigenous literature/identity?

Yes, I agree. I also want to clarify that just because someone has indigenous origins or speaks an indigenous language does not automatically mean they are decolonial in practice. Indigenous peoples in Latin America struggle with this, too, because colonialism permeates everything. I see that the decolonial process for Latinos with Mesoamerican origins affects this literature, because we are thirsty to engage with this corpus. I have to say that was in some ways my experience. I also see it in my students. After reading, a Maya or Zapotec novel—even if it is in translation—they want more. Getting close to indigenous worldview is not an elusive quest. I think it is part and parcel of trying to imagine a world outside colonialist precepts. This directly affects indigenous authors because they get more exposure, they see their work as moving beyond their own communities and nations. More than anything, I think this process teaches us that indigenous identities are not monolithic or one-dimensional, and that we experience indigeneity differently. Some communities have suffered more language and cultural loss than others. This is real. The fact is that all indigenous languages are in peril of disappearing. I think it is exciting that Latinos take an initiative of learning an indigenous language. I definitively tried to learn a Maya language. We need more dialogues between Latinos and indigenous peoples, both North and South.

Truly Latin America is a complex subject without a definitive set of boundaries, identities, or even languages. The idea of greater Latin America more adequately explains how borders expand while at the same time creating cultural linkages among distinct societies. Culture must be seen not only as pure, aesthetic beauty of forms of art, but also as forms of resistance to multiple forms of colonialism.

21

MIGRANT TRANSNATIONAL ENGAGEMENTS 2000–2015

Xóchitl Bada

Introduction

Transnational immigration refers to a process by which migrants nurture and maintain multi-stranded and multi-sited social relations that link together their communities of origin and settlement through a process of constant ethnic replenishment and revival.[1] Just as the declining cost of postage hastened the flow of letters back and forth over the Atlantic more than a century and a half ago, cheaper airfares, video-equipped cell phones, and the ubiquity of social media in Latin America have allowed the emergence of alternative forms of cross-border identities and belongings. It is no longer the case that Latin American migrants need to choose between being assimilated and uprooted from their culture or transplanted to global cities where cultural pluralism is socially accepted.[2] Migrants from Latin America today do not have to forge their sense of identity and community out of loss or mere replication due to the new possibilities of connectedness between sending and receiving countries.

By the turn of the twenty-first century, the United States underwent dramatic changes in the origin of its foreign-born population, attracting a continuous exodus from Latin American countries (mainly from Mexico), which effectively transformed the character of American cities and traditional melting pot ideologies. In 1960, the foreign-born population represented about 1 in 20 residents, mostly from countries in Europe who had settled in the Northeast and Midwest. By 2010, the foreign-born population reached 13 percent of the total population with forty million, the vast majority (53 percent) coming from Latin America, mostly from Mexico, El Salvador, Cuba, Dominican Republic, and Guatemala.[3]

The expansion of communication technologies creates digital diasporas and Internet-based social networks that unite communities across borders, helping to reduce space-time distances, dis-embed social processes from a limited geographical area, and lift social relations out of their physical contexts. These new technologies of globalization lead to groups and organizations that are more informal, fluid, flexible, and, consequently, less visible.[4] The changes in information and communication technologies have allowed migrants from Latin America to maintain cultural identities and lifestyles, offering their ethnic music, food, and artistic expressions to new audiences. These cultural exchanges are modifying cultural frameworks in many cities with large concentrations of Latino migrants across the United States.

South-North Migration in the Americas

The United States Immigration Act of 1965 increased the possibilities of emigration from Latin American countries to the United States due to the elimination of the blatantly discriminatory national-origins quota system, which since the 1920s had favored migration from Northern and Western Europe and excluded Asians altogether.[5] However, the 1965 legislation also imposed a one-size fits all regulation with all countries limited to no more than 7 percent of the total each year, thus opening the door to a large exodus of migrant workers from Latin America countries.

It is not a coincidence that the largest share of Latin American migrants came mostly from countries that had experienced U.S. military interventions and occupations throughout the twentieth century. The exile produced by the Cuban Revolution, the 1965 U.S. military intervention in Dominican Republic, the U.S. Congress military support to the Salvadoran Army war against the opposition groups in the 1980s, and the agricultural unemployment created by the North American Free Trade Agreement in the mid-1990s are considered some of the push factors leading workers and families to migrate to the United States in the last fifty years.[6]

With few exceptions, the multiple waves of post-Second World War Latin American migrants came to the United States and settled in the West and the South, finding different context of reception when joining previously established immigrant groups. The process of migrant incorporation of diverse groups was largely determined by legal status, racial identification, country of origin, and varied local contexts of reception. Many Latin American migrants, especially Mexican and Central American, came with comparatively low levels of education and fulfilled the demand of jobs in manufacturing and the service sector economy.

In Latin America, the failure of the import-substitution economic model,[7] the debt crisis of the 1980s, and growing income distribution inequality pushed many workers in search of better economic opportunities.[8] While economic liberalization and free trade agreements were taking shape in Latin America, the United States was experiencing a transformation of the manufacturing sector that had provided the working class with the basic means of survival at the end of the Second World War, thanks to a pact between the state, workers, and unions. This pact had established an increase in productivity in exchange for sharing a small fraction of the profits with workers. However, as competitive capitalism transformed to monopoly capitalism and U.S. corporations lost their competitive advantage to Germany and Japan in the early 1970s, low-skill jobs were increasingly exported to countries with surpluses of low-skill workers in peripheral regions of international capitalism, in the corporations' search of low wages and higher profits.

In the 1980s, the agricultural peasant economy in Mexico experienced disinvestment, civil wars in Central America intensified, and growing inequality in the Caribbean and the rest of Latin America created a labor export system that functioned as a form of self-financed private insurance against unemployment, poverty, and civil war conflicts. Meanwhile, in the United States, a growing demand of low-skill workers offered possibilities for thousands of new migrants from Latin America to take jobs in light manufacturing, the agricultural industry, and the service sector economy. In sum, in the last half century, millions of Latin American workers relocated temporarily or permanently to the United States, crossing multiple ethnic, class, cultural, colonial, and state borders.[9] These transborder crossings have reconfigured gender and family roles, community politics, civic engagements, ethnic identities, and survival strategies in the multiple locales these migrants inhabit on both sides of their transnational borders.

According to available official data, the U.S.-Mexico border is the largest migration corridor in the world, accounting for 11.6 million migrants in 2010. In terms of family remittances, Mexico was among the top ten receiving countries with the largest volume, obtaining $22.6 USD billion per year by 2010. As a percentage of national Gross Domestic Product, Honduras and El Salvador are among the top remittance-receiving countries with 19 percent and 16 percent of their GDP being generated from family remittances, respectively.[10] This money has supported the social reproduction of millions of low-income households in Latin America.

Family Remittances, Migration, and Development

Migrants living outside the regions of origin play a crucial role, as evidence by the efforts of international organizations and national governments in wooing diasporas and transnationally active migrant associations to have an active role in development policy. In the views of the World Bank and other international organizations, remittances have become the "new development mantra" as an effective means of reducing poverty and as a form of self-help.[11] Financial remittances increased steadily from the early 1990s until 2008, when they decreased somewhat as a result of the global economic recession. Whether the money harvested by migration yields positive or negative development effects is, however, a question to which research has not provided a conclusive answer yet. Also, as noted in a 2009 report on migration issued by the United Nations Development Program, "remittances alone cannot remove the structural constraints to economic growth."[12]

Mexico comes in third place among the top 10 remittance-receiving countries, following India and China.[13] In an effort to protect the labor rights of its nationals who live in the United States and the vast remittances that they send back to support millions of Mexican households, the Mexican government has created extensive partnerships with regulatory agencies, labor unions, workers' rights groups, and hometown associations (HTAs) to increase the wellbeing of Mexican workers who live abroad.[14] In fact, Mexican federal and state government officials frequently praise migrant remittances, albeit without offering evidence of their actual benefits in poverty reduction or their modest 2 percent contribution to the GDP.

In Mexico, an important missing link in the development and migration nexus is the lack of agricultural policies to stimulate the peasant economy, one of the economic sectors that is most damaged by the North American Free Trade Agreement (NAFTA). Since NAFTA came into effect, the Mexican government has not created successful public policies at the local level to decrease international migration in rural villages above and beyond the Three-for-One program, a Mexican government development initiative which provides federal, state, and municipal matching funds to channel collective remittances for rural development.[15] In fact, rural municipalities with zero or low levels of migration are rapidly disappearing.[16] In 2011, according to estimates calculated by the National Evaluating Council of Social Development Policy (CONEVAL), 67 percent of the population living in municipalities with very high migratory intensity were classified as poor.[17] Therefore, migrant remittances do not significantly reduce income inequalities; rather, they can increase inequalities among those who are excluded from them in rural areas with high expulsion.[18]

Migrant Integration Processes

In the last fifty years, millions of Latin American migrants decided to stay in the United States to settle permanently. However, competition, conflict, accommodation, and assimilation—the four necessary steps that sociologist Robert Park devised to understand migrant adaptation to a new society—were not linearly followed by the transnational migrations of Latin Americans after the Second World War. While many stayed and settled in the United States a few years after their initial arrival, others kept commuting back and forth, which is contrary to the assumption of one-way settlement and assimilation. The classical assimilation process in the United States had been mostly described using examples from European migrant communities that transformed into hyphenated ethnic Americans when their emigration flows to the United States considerably decreased. In the Mexican case, an intermittent flow of new migrant workers to the United States since the early twentieth century would guarantee the replenishment of a fresh ethnic identity.[19] Early observers of migrant integration processes were not able to predict the permanence of the Mexican migratory flows and the fragility of a homogeneous hyphenated identity as they missed the interconnections among migration, development, Latin America-U.S. economic interdependency, the debt crisis, the Washington consensus,[20] neoliberal reforms, and free trade.

In the last fifty years, immigration from Latin America has produced the formation of important ethnic enclaves that have reconfigured urban patterns creating new Latino metropolises across the United States, tropicalizing cold urban spaces and leading towards cultural landscapes that are more autonomous, with hybrid identities, "translated peoples" and imaginaries for "ethnoscapes."[21] The polycentric Latino neighborhoods of Chicago, the primate barrios with small satellites in Los Angeles, and New York City's multicultural mosaic with Dominicans, Puerto Ricans, Mexicans, and Ecuadorians mixed with non-Latino ethnic groups are offering a distinctive Latin American influence to urban planners, pushing for more walking paths, edible gardens, mixed used buildings, communal land use, public transportation, and the repurposing of public spaces. Paradoxically, the historical origins of many barrios are the consequence of uneven development, segregation, repression, discriminatory urban policies, high rents, and low-wage labor concentration. However, Latino migrants have shown resilience and innovation to transform urban cultures and landscapes including music, language, food tastes, and architecture.[22] For example, nowadays guacamole is the most popular dip consumed during Super Bowl Sunday and tortillas are a staple in Latino and non-Latino households. This cultural change in popular culinary tastes has its origins in migration and the activities that accompany it.

Cultural religiosity is an aspect that has also experienced important changes in the United States as a result of Latin American migration. Among Latino migrants, faith and religion provide an important vehicle to affirm ethnic belonging and to organize for improving their quality of life. Although Americans remain far more religious than those in other industrialized countries, net church attendance has fallen, thus bringing a decline in social capital.[23] However, among Latino migrant groups, especially among groups coming from countries with inefficient provision of social welfare, the church represents a vital source of social services in times of economic need and embodies an institution that migrants trust across borders.[24] Among Mexicans, a significant amount of volunteer time and resources is devoted to church-related activities in Mexico and the United States.[25]

Spirituality among migrants from Latin America is rooted in their devotion to cultural religious symbols that represent ethnoreligious communities, helping to create what Elaine Peña calls "devotional capital."[26] Often, devotional capital is the product of a long struggle to find a permanent home for the Virgin of Guadalupe in local churches. In Chicago, New York, Los Angeles, Dallas, and other cities with large Latin American migrant populations, many migrants attend churches offering Spanish Mass to ease the cultural shock. They find a sense of belonging among those sharing the same faith, and pray to find good-paying jobs. They often find both spiritual and practical guidance to access social services.

Religious performances are sometimes different in Catholic congregations across the United States, as they tend to have the flavor of previous migrant groups such as the Irish, Italians, Germans, or Romanians who arrived at a time when the Catholic hierarchy was supportive of ethnic national parishes. For example, for many rural Mexicans, their patron saints and virgins are not always represented in the public space of their new churches, and new arrivals from remote rural towns had to construct their devotional altars to honor particular virgins and saints in the private sphere of their homes until they were able to introduce them to their new parishes. One of the most important religious symbols leading to the formation of devotional capital among Mexicans and Latin American migrants is the Virgin of Guadalupe. In the case of Chicago, Los Angeles, and New York City, Guadalupanismo has spread to dozens of parishes across the metropolitan areas, and the Virgin of Guadalupe now has a shrine in Des Plaines, Illinois, that is a replica of the one in Mexico City's Basilica of Guadalupe.

However, Catholicism is not the only religion among Latin American migrants. According to a 2014 poll of more than five thousand Hispanics conducted by the Pew Research Center:

> most Hispanics in the United States continue to belong to the Roman Catholic Church. But the Catholic share of the Hispanic population is declining, while rising numbers of Hispanics are Protestant or unaffiliated with any religion. Indeed, nearly one-in-four Hispanic adults (24%) are now former Catholics.[27]

Consequently, there has been an increase in Evangelical, Spanish-speaking churches in the states with significant concentrations of Latinos such as California, Illinois, Nevada, and North Carolina. The changes in the ethnic composition of Protestant communities across the United States have altered cultural practices of religiosity both in the United States and in Latin America. Religious communities often provide a place of refuge and encounter for recent immigrants from similar backgrounds, provide tangible services to help them adapt to their life in a new country, and offer a sense of community to those far from their place of origin. Most importantly, religion provides spiritual comfort to those enduring the harsh effects of long-term family separations.

Family Separation and Transnational Parenting

Transnational migrant lives often involve difficult decisions affecting families across borders. Parent-child separation occurs as part of a permanent or semi-permanent movement across borders in which parents—for practical, economic or legal reasons—migrate on their own but hope to send for their children later, after securing employment and stability in the host society. It is also frequent that some families lead transnational lives with irregular sequences of separation and co-residence. Consequently, many parents find new ways of being parents across borders. In some cases, regular migration opportunities exist for individual workers, while it is legally or practically impossible to bring a family. For example, the tightly regulated contract-worker migration among contracted (H-2A visa)[28] agricultural workers in the United States forces many parents to leave their children for seven months of the year. In other cases, migrant parents are unable to bring their children because the parents are undocumented. Each year, thousands of migrants have to accept these restrictive contracts that will provide a higher salary while effectively preventing family reunification or regular travel since those contracts do not lead to legal permanent settlement.

Ties between parents and children are central in transnational families: They are based on a lasting biological relationship and often embedded with asymmetrical expectations and obligations. Securing their children's future is a key motivation for many migrants, even though physical separation might be a challenge for parenting in the short term. The possibility of migration presents families with difficult trade-offs between different aspects of parenting. Besides, the gendering of migration opportunities sometimes creates tensions with traditional gender relations, as when mothers migrate and assume a breadwinner role. When fathers migrate, the parenting role of the mother changes as a consequence of her becoming the head of household. In the light of the increasing focus on the benefits of migration, some have raised questions about the possibility that children left behind are paying the price of economic development through separation from their parents. Others are pointing out that individual children often gain when their parents' migration ensures adequate health care and education.[29]

Among mixed-status migrant families living with and without authorization in the United States, the increases in Mexican migrant deportations during the administration of U.S. President Barack Obama (2009–2017) led to enormous pressures on the Mexican state, which was caught unprepared to receive and reintegrate thousands of forcibly returned migrants who are frequently enduring the trauma of family separation and demanding educational opportunities.[30] In fiscal year 2013, the Obama administration deported a record 438,421 unauthorized migrants, continuing a streak of increased enforcement that resulted in more than 2 million deportations through fiscal year 2013 while Obama was in office, Department of Homeland Security data show.[31] Between 2004–2013, more than 2.4 million Mexican migrants without legal authorization were deported to Mexico.[32] Several grassroots organizations across the United States emerged to halt deportations using tactics of civil disobedience with some modest results.[33]

By and large, the increase in deportations did not produced the desired deterrence effects. According to Marc Rosenblum, Deputy Director of the Migration Policy Institute's U.S. Immigration Policy Program, "between 2011 and 2014, the number of Central American unaccompanied children (UACs) and 'family units'—parents traveling with young children—who arrived at the U.S.–Mexico border increased rapidly, reaching a peak of 137,000 in fiscal year 2014."[34] This massive emigration of UACs from Central America is attributed to a combination of crime and violence affecting youth in the region, economic concerns, poor educational systems, and a desire to reconnect with family members.

Dual and Multiple Nationality

Despite the grim realities faced by undocumented migrants living across borders, the proportion of nations around the world that allow dual citizenship rose from fewer than 5 percent in 1959 to about 50 percent in 2005, and the number is increasing. Dual citizenship arises when persons who acquire citizenship in a new country are allowed to keep their original citizenship, or when children of binational parents are allowed to inherit the (different) citizenships of both.[35] Therefore, more and more countries nowadays are changing their regulations and accepting dual nationality, and consequently more and more migrants are entitled to two passports. For example, since 1998, Mexican citizens have been allowed to acquire a second nationality.

While any foreign citizen seeking U.S. citizenship today needs to take an oath swearing to support the Constitution of the United States and declare that "he does absolutely and entirely renounce and abjure all allegiance and fidelity to any foreign prince, potentate, state or sovereignty whatever whereof he was before a citizen or subject" (as written in the U.S. Naturalization Act of 1795), in practice, migrants are not required to renounce their original nationality and the United States does not actively discourage the practice of having more than one nationality. The substantial population of the United States with origins in Latin American countries has—and will continue to have—access to a second nationality because of the sending country's laws and policies intended to foster enduring ties with citizens abroad to keep loyalties alive and maximize the flow of family remittances.[36]

In 1996 only seven out of seventeen Latin American countries had dual nationality legislations, in 2000 there were fourteen, and today nearly all Latin American countries allow dual nationality. These changes are in response to a new migration context in which so many of these countries' citizens are living abroad, not only in the United States but in Europe and Asia as well. The emigrants' countries of origin are very keen to maintain links with them because the remittances they send often time constitute a massive source of income, and because they are potential voters who could be an important influence in a close election.[37]

The simultaneous citizen engagement with issues of political representation in both Mexico and the United States has been shown to have a positive and highly significant correlation between migrant engagement in the public affairs of Mexico and of the United States. For example, in the 2006 Mexican presidential election, educational and income levels were important predictors of migrant citizens' decisions to register to vote. However, the density of migrant organizations in urban areas also contributed to a higher engagement with Mexico's electoral campaigns.[38] According to an analysis of registration patterns across the United States, two additional variables increased the electoral participation rates among Mexican migrants living abroad: the presence of Spanish-language media, and ethnically oriented civic organizations. In those urban areas where these two variables were significant, the registration rate increased in 30 percent.[39] While these new conceptions to extend political participation beyond geographical boundaries of residence are encouraging to improve participatory democratic governance, it is important to recognize that these dual dimensions can also result in simultaneously empowering and disempowering transnational experiences when differences in socioeconomic power give city residents with higher economic power unequal access and voice in public and private decision-making processes regardless of citizenship. A good case in point is the gentrification processes that U.S. expatriates have created in Sayulita, Nayarit, San Miguel Allende, and Guanajuato, appropriating urban spaces, increasing real estate prices, and rendering property ownership virtually inaccessible to the local native-born population.[40]

Transnational Migrant Organizing

Grassroots migrant organizing covers four arenas of collective action: membership organizations, non-governmental organizations, media, and autonomous public spheres. Decisions to become civically engaged depend on the contexts that are found during departure and upon arrival, and some groups are capable of simultaneous engagements in sending and receiving communities.[41] The collective actions in which these migrants engage in include labor coalitions, faith-based initiatives, and translocal public work committees to build infrastructure in communities of origin. Migrants may organize around their identities as workers, their neighborhoods of residence, their community of origin, their ethnicity, or their faith. Sometimes, these potentially multiple identities overlap, as in the cases of Oaxacan Catholics who reproduce their distinctive public rituals in Los Angeles or religious farmworkers in the Midwest, where union leaders preside over weddings and baptisms. Migrants who participate in these efforts are frequently involved in more than one organization, but not all migrant-led organizing includes binational advocacy activities.[42]

Increasingly, the American public is discovering the exciting and vibrant civic worlds of migrant-led hometown associations (HTAs) in the United States. Southern California alone has hundreds of hometown associations for populations from El Salvador, Guatemala, Mexico, and Nicaragua, but hometown associations also exist in many other parts of the United States. Although Mexican HTAs have the longest history and are the best known across the United States, an increasing number of Dominican, Colombian, Ecuadorian, Honduran, and Haitian hometown associations have appeared since the 1980s and are actively participating in the improvement of their communities of origin and residence. For example, the Salvadoran *Fundación para la Educación Social, Económica y Cultural* (FUPEC) is a good example of collaboration between HTAs and sending communities. Backed by the Inter American Foundation and others, it also draws the support of Salvadoran entrepreneurs in the United States. Trust among members has been built through transparency, which participants attributed to face-to-face engagement among the various actors and technical training in handling incoming funds.

Within Mexico, there is evidence that HTAs from rural communities flourished in Mexican cities since the mid-1940s as a result of internal migration from the provinces to urban centers. Village associations in Mexico City organized by indigenous and mestizo migrants from Oaxaca, Jalisco, and Puebla in the mid-1940s and afterward are well documented.[43] Historically, the persistence or disappearance of these organizations at different points in time is connected to differences in the context of migrant reception that could have encouraged or discouraged the vitality and survival of migrant associations over time.

Also known as *clubes de oriundos*, or migrant clubs, Mexican HTAs are among the best-known migrant-led organizations. HTAs join migrants from the same communities of origin. Mexican HTAs are a paradigm for civic binationality, performing important roles to defend migrant human and social rights. They often begin as informal associations, such as soccer clubs, mutual aid societies, or prayer groups. However, over time, many have not only become formal organizations but have also scaled up to form federations that represent various communities of origin from the same state. Grassroots organizations formed by Mexican migrants have proliferated in the United States since the early 1980s, especially in the metropolitan areas of Los Angeles and Chicago. For example, the *Federación de Clubes Michoacanos en Illinois* and the *Federación de Clubes Zacatecanos del Sur de California* are two examples of federations of hometown associations that have taken leadership positions in the immigrant rights movement since the late 1990s.

In many cases HTAs start as informal groups based on relationships with a town of origin in Mexico. This early organizational model is the first step toward formalization and the emergence of second-level structures: the federations. Some consequences of these activities are a sense of community created by strengthening ties among migrants from the same village, increased recognition of their work by municipal and state authorities, and occasionally, HTAs participation in community development has fostered long-term collaborations with village authorities to participate in decision-making processes for new community development projects at the local level. In rural communities in Mexico, participation in *faenas, cargos,* or *tequios* (voluntary communal work) is widely expected as a mechanism to preserve membership, solve community problems, express solidarity, and be a good citizen. Among those with higher socioeconomic standing in the community, it is acceptable to pay someone else to do their communal work, although people usually assign more value to donated labor than to paid efforts. When systems of voluntary work are no longer possible due to long absences, they are sometimes transplanted to self-help informal groups in the new host societies.

As Jews, Japanese, and Chinese who migrated from the same town or province founded *landmanshaft vereins* [homeland societies], *kai,* and village associations,[44] social cohesion among Mexicans from rural villages aided in the formation of *clubes de oriundos* anchored in common backgrounds that give rise to strong solidarity ties among fellow nationals, family, and friends. These informal associations fill the void immigrant settlement houses left after some of these institutions transformed their mission and devoted their energies to addressing the needs of refugees and other economically disadvantaged minorities.[45] Among the most widely recognized and successful organizations of U.S. migrant communities are the informal rotating savings and credit associations (ROSCAs), commonly known as *tandas.*[46] Among HTA members, social bonding frequently begins in small *tandas* among friends and family. Later the *tandas* transform into funerary associations to provide emergency funds for widows.

The membership of HTAs mirrors the social structure of the Mexican migrant population in the city. A typical organization is composed of ten to fifty families that include dual citizens, legal permanent residents, and undocumented migrants. Those members with higher human capital—that is, those with higher levels of education and socioeconomic standing—tend to take leadership positions and volunteer more hours to organize soccer tournaments, plan monthly get-togethers, and make proposals to finance projects, while those with more unstable jobs and incomes are more likely to contribute with donated labor and volunteering in the preparation of fundraising events. Attending events organized by the clubs unites recent and more established migrants and provides an avenue for socialization, bartering, and networking for new jobs.[47]

When HTAs organize a fundraising event to finance a project in rural Mexico, they usually choose a community member with a good previous track record organizing *tandas* or social events to administer funds. The long-term success of HTAs and their eventual transformation into formal, nonprofit, membership-based organizations depend on sustained mutual reciprocity and trust among members. After small migrant clubs evolve into formally registered federations of HTAs, they maintain the connection to member organizations through shared moral values of civic engagement and transnational moral communities,[48] where constituents are willing to subordinate their private interests for the sake of larger goals to benefit all Mexican and Latino migrant communities across borders, beyond their co-ethnic group.

Despite their invisibility from the mainstream of nonprofit organizations in the United States, the upsurge of these organizations has had important implications. In contrast to the relative informality and political isolation that characterized migrants' groups until the mid-1990s, these new associations have now consolidated their organizational structures and become more outwardly oriented. Notably, the philanthropic activities they carry out for their communities of origin have changed significantly. While these projects have in the past been infrequent and haphazardly organized, investments in home community infrastructure have grown substantially in scale and have become much more formalized and systematic. The number of Mexican HTAs continues to swell nationwide; there may be as many as a thousand registered in forty-six Mexican consulates across thirty-one states in the United States.[49] This "scaling up" has increased the federations' visibility, leading to a growing recognition in both the public and political spheres, which in turn has encouraged extended dialogue between them and all levels of the Mexican government. However, the increased dialogue between the Mexican government and migrant organizations has not yet produced coherent changes in public policies that create the needed infrastructure to prevent further migration. The economic, social, and cultural pressures that trigger migrations still persist in thousands of municipalities across Mexico.

HTA members usually share nationality, faith, and attachment to birthplace, but they have diverse interests and group affiliations. In traditional voluntary organizations engaged in charitable welfare projects, it is common to find a great degree of socioeconomic homogeneity among members. However, a closer look at the members-at-large of HTAs reveals social heterogeneity as participants belong to a wide range of civic and political organizations. In Chicago, HTA members belong to parent-teacher associations (PTAs), block clubs, soccer leagues, Catholic and Protestant church congregations, neighborhood and ethnic chambers of commerce, anti-abortion groups, the National Rifle Association, labor unions, independent worker centers, and the Democratic and Republican parties. In Mexico, members declare affiliations to their parishes, seed cooperatives, and the three main political parties. These binational civic and political ties will likely lead to many more new forms of migrant civic engagement in the future.

Migrant Civic Engagement Looking Forward

Some critics of dual civic engagements argue that bilingualism, multiculturalism, and some transnational practices of Latino migrants pose a threat to the United States' Anglo-Protestant culture, national sovereignty, undivided national loyalty, and electoral system. In fact, until recently, several academics assumed that the question of whether to be involved in the United States or Mexico in the twenty-first century was mutually exclusive, and migrants, especially those who acquire U.S. citizenship, should be forced to choose one national arena for political and civic engagement.[50] There is still a debate over whether civic binationality—based on migrant participation in sustained practices of civic engagement in their countries of origin and their new communities—can or should replace the traditional concept of assimilation. Nonetheless, in practice many Mexican migrants are becoming full members of both U.S. and Mexican civil societies at the same time, engaging in practices of civic binationality that have a great deal to teach us about new forms of Latino migrant integration into the United States and will likely transform the character of this nation when Latinos reach 31 percent of the total U.S. population by 2060.[51]

In the spring of 2006, more than three million migrants—most of them originally from Mexico—marched through the streets of Chicago, Los Angeles, Phoenix, Milwaukee, Detroit, Denver, Dallas, and dozens of other U.S. cities to protest peacefully for a comprehensive immigration reform that would legalize the status of millions of undocumented migrants in the United States. Though few are voters—and even fewer in swing districts—migrants' remarkably disciplined, law-abiding collective actions sent a message—"we are workers and neighbors, not criminals"—that resonated on Capitol Hill. The protests caught almost all observers by surprise—including many in migrant communities. Mexican migrants, who formed a majority of participants in many of the cities, moved from being subjects of policy reform to having a voice in the debate on the reform. Never before had Mexican migrants taken such a visible role in a national policy discussion.[52]

Mexican HTAs have transformed the traditional civic participation that is expected from citizens with full political rights. For example, Mexican migrants living in the United States had been largely disenfranchised in Mexican electoral democracy since they did not have effective access to absentee voting rights until a decade ago. However, political disenfranchisement was never a deterrent for engaging in other types of civic participation, such as improving the wellbeing of their compatriots through infrastructure and beautification projects in their hometowns and villages and, more recently, their civic involvement in the defense of human and labor rights of migrant workers in the United States. Millions of Latino migrants have participated in large marches and demonstrations on behalf of immigrant rights, carrying the important message that civic participation is not only exercised through the voting booths. In these marches, one of the most popular slogans read: "*Hoy marchamos, mañana votamos*" ["Today we march, tomorrow we vote"]. The national migrant demonstrations in the spring of 2006 spurred campaigns to encourage lawful permanent residents (LPRs) to acquire U.S. citizenship and participate in U.S. elections while also making sure that legal status was not an impediment to volunteer for migrant rights advocacy organizations.

Through their actions, Mexican HTAs have shown that there is no contradiction between active transnationalism and successful social and political incorporation of permanent migrants in host nations, even among those who delay the decision to naturalize as U.S. citizens. HTAs' practices of civic binationality show simultaneous loyalty and commitment to two nation-states to address the political, social, and economic rights of all migrants, both in the United States and Mexico.

The future demographic profile of the United States will likely transform multiple cultural landscapes as a direct result of the settlement and integration of millions of Latin American immigrants. Looking ahead, migrant cultures will keep leaking across national boundaries, and their transnational flows will be intimately tied both to the many diasporas that characterize national populations, and to the unstoppable force of media (movies, magazines, cassettes, videotapes, social media, computers, and the like), which will continue closing cultural distances (and accelerate traffic) between Latin American migrants in the United States and their home societies.

Notes

1 A good roadmap to key analytical concepts to understand the transnational perspective across the social sciences is found in Peggy Levitt and Sanjeev Khagram, *The Transnational Studies Reader* (New York, NY: Routledge, 2008); and Thomas Faist, Margit Fauser and Eveline Reinsenauer, *Transnational Migration* (Cambridge: Polity Press, 2013). For an overview including case studies from Latin American and the Caribbean, see Linda Basch, Nina Glick Schiller, and Cristina S. Blanc, *Nations Unbound. Transnational Projects. Postcolonial Predicaments and Deterritorialized Nation-States* (Luxemburg: Gordon and Breach Publishers, 1994); and Michael P. Smith and Luis Eduardo Guarnizo, eds., *Transnationalism From Below* (New Brunswick, NJ: Transaction Publishers, 1998). For a more recent quantitative perspective see Katharine M. Donato, Jonathan Hiskey, Jorge Durand, and Douglas S. Massey, "Continental Divides: International Migration in the Americas," Special issue of *The Annals of the American Academy of Political and Social Science*, Vol 630 (2010): 6–294.

2 To learn more about the concepts of "the uprooted" and "the transplanted" in the context of European immigration to the United States, see Oscar Handlin, *The Uprooted: The Epic Story of the Great Migrations that Made the American People* 2nd ed (Boston, MA: Little, Brown and

Company, 1973) and Joseph Bodnar, *The Transplanted: A History of Migrants in Urban America* (Bloomington, IN: Indiana University Press, 1985).

3 "The Size, Place of Birth, and Geographic Distribution of the Foreign-Born Population in the United States: 1960 to 2010," In *America's Foreign Born in the Last 50 Years*, edited by Elizabeth M. Grieco, Edward Trevelyan, Luke Larsen, Yesenia D. Acosta, Christine Gambino, Patricia de la Cruz, Tom Gryn, and Nathan Walters; Population Division, Working Paper No. 96, U.S. Census Bureau (October 2012).

4 Jennifer M. Brinkerhoff, *Digital Diasporas: Identity and Transnational Engagement* (Cambridge: Cambridge University Press, 2009).

5 For more on the social construction of U.S. immigration policy, see, among others: Mae M. Ngai, *Impossible Subjects: Illegal Aliens and the Making of Modern America* (Princeton, NJ: Princeton University Press, 2004); Aristide R. Zolberg, *A Nation by Design: Immigration Policy in the Fashioning of America* (New York, NY: Russell Sage Foundation, 2006); and Douglas S. Massey, Jorge Durand, and Nolan J. Malone, *Beyond Smoke and Mirrors: Mexican Immigration in an Era of Economic Integration* (New York, NY: Russell Sage Foundation, 2002).

6 For more on the Cuban exile, see Guillermo J. Grenier and Lisandro Pérez, *The Legacy of Exile: Cubans in the United States* (Boston, MA: Allyn and Bacon, 2003); for an overview of Dominican transnational immigration see Peggy Levitt, *The Transnational Villagers* (Berkeley, CA: University of California Press, 2001), and for Salvadoran migrant networks, see Cecilia Menjívar, *Fragmented Ties: Salvadoran Immigrant Networks in America* (Berkeley, CA: University of California Press, 2000).

7 Import-substitution industrialization (ISI) is an economic model implemented by Latin American nations which aims at reducing economic dependency from foreign capitals. Many external and internal factors led to the demise of this model. Among them was its inability to absorb migrant labor in urban areas and the increase in urban poverty. Also, the agricultural sector was stagnant, increasing inflation and making impossible to attain self-sufficiency. After World War II, ISI became a deliberate policy tool for economic development. According to Baer,

> the principal policy instruments used to promote and intensify ISI in Latin America were: protective tariffs and/or exchange controls; special preferences for domestic and foreign firms importing capital goods for new industries; preferential import exchange rates for industrial raw materials, fuels and intermediate goods; cheap loans by government development banks for favored industries; the construction by governments of infrastructure specially designed to complement industries; and the direct participation of government in certain industries, especially the heavier industries, such as steel, where neither domestic nor foreign private capital was willing or able to invest.
>
> *Werner Baer, "Import Substitution and Industrialization in Latin America: Experiences and Interpretations," Latin America Research Review, Vol 7 (1972): 95–122.*

8 For an overview of the economic and labor interdependence between Latin America and the United States, see Frank Bonilla, Edwin Meléndez, Rebecca Morales, and María de los Angeles Torres, eds., *Borderless Borders. U.S. Latinos, Latin Americans, and the Paradox of Interdependence* (Philadelphia, PA: Temple University Press, 1998).

9 For a holistic approach to transnational experiences using a transborder framework to analyze Mexican indigenous migrants, see Lynn Stephen, *Transborder Lives: Indigenous Oaxacans in Mexico, California, and Oregon* (Durham, NC: Duke University Press, 2007); and Adriana Cruz-Manjarrez, *Zapotecs on the Move: Cultural, Social, and Political Processes in Transnational Perspective* (New Brunswick, NJ: Rutgers University Press, 2013).

10 *Migration and Remittances Factbook 2011*, compiled by Dilip Ratha, Sanket Mohapatra, and Ani Silwal (Washington, DC: The World Bank).

11 Devesh Kapur "Remittances: The New Development Mantra?", *G-24 Discussion Paper Series* 29. United Nations Conference on Trade and Development, April, 2004.

12 UNDP, *Human Development Report 2009: Overcoming Barriers: Human Mobility and Development* (New York, NY: Palgrave Macmillan, 2009).

13 *Migration and Remittances Factbook 2011*, compiled by Dilip Ratha, Sanket Mohapatra, and Ani Silwal (Washington, DC: The World Bank, 2011).

14 For more details on these transnational partnerships, see Xóchitl Bada and Shannon Gleeson, "A New Approach to Migrant Labor Rights Enforcement: The Crisis of Undocumented Worker Abuse and Mexican Consular Advocacy in the United States" *Labor Studies Journal*, 40 (2014): 32–53, doi:10.1177/0160449X14565112; and Alexandra Délano, "The diffusion of diaspora engagement policies. A Latin American agenda," *Political Geography*, Vol 41 (2013): 90–100, doi:10.1016/j.polgeo.2013.11.007.

15 See Natasha Iskander, *Creative State: Forty Years of Migration and Development in Morocco and Mexico* (Ithaca, NY: Cornell University Press, 2010).

16 Xóchitl Bada and Jonathan Fox, "Patrones migratorios en contextos de ruralidad y marginación en el campo mexicano, 2000–2010: Cambios y continuidades," *Revista de la Asociación Latinoamericana de Sociología Rural*, Vol 10 (2014): 277–296.

17 Secretaría de Desarrollo Social, *Memoria del Programa 3X1 para Migrantes 2007–2012* (México: Unidad de Microrregiones, 2012).

18 Margit Fauser and Gery Nijenhuis, "Migrants' transnationality, societal transformation and Locality: An Introduction," *Population, Space and Place*, Vol 2, doi:10.1002/psp.1944, 2015.

19 For a revision of the classical assimilation theory applied to the Mexican case in the United States, see Tomas R Jimenez, *Replenished Ethnicity: Mexican Americans, Immigration, and Identity* (Berkeley, CA: University of California Press, 2009).

20 The Washington Consensus is a term coined in 1989 by the economist John Williamson. This concept represents a set of economic policy prescriptions considered as the standard reform package promoted to ameliorate the effects of economic crisis in developing countries including several Latin American nations. The reform packages were determined by Washington, D.C.-based institutions including the International Monetary Fund (IMF), World Bank, and the U.S. Treasury Department. The recommended prescriptions encompassed policies in such areas as macroeconomic stabilization, economic opening with respect to both trade and investment, and the expansion of market forces within the domestic economy. Despite the implementation of many of these prescriptions, most Latin American countries continue to struggle with high poverty and underemployment. See Pedro-Paul Kuczynski and John Williamson, eds., *After the Washington Consensus: Restarting Growth and Reform in Latin America* (Washington, DC: Institute for International Economics, 2003).

21 See Mike Davis. *Magical Urbanism. Latinos Reinvent U.S. Big City* (New York, NY: Verso, 2000). To learn more about the concepts of cultural hybridity, migrant identity, and ethnoscapes, see among others Arjun Appadurai, *Modernity at Large: Cultural Dimensions of Globalization* (Minneapolis, MN: University of Minnesota Press, 1996); Iain Chambers, *Migrancy, Culture, Identity* (New York, NJ: Routledge, 1994); Néstor García Canclini, *Hybrid Cultures: Strategies for Entering and Leaving Modernity* (Minneapolis, MN: University of Minnesota Press, 1995); and Salman Rushdie, *Imaginary Homelands* (New York, NY: Granta Books, 1991).

22 See David R. Diaz and Rodolfo D. Torres, Eds., *Latino Urbanism. The Politics of Planning, Policy, and Redevelopment* (New York, NY: New York University Press, 2012). For a good analysis of language use as a vehicle of identity preservation, see Marcia Farr, *Rancheros in Chicagoacán, Language and Identity in a Transnational Community* (Austin, TX: University of Texas Press, 2006).

23 Robert D. Putnam, "E Pluribus Unum: Diversity and Community in the Twenty-First Century," The 2006 Johan Skytte Prize Lecture. *Scandinavian Political Studies*, Vol 30 (2007): 137–174, doi: 10.1111/j.1467-9477.2007.00176.

24 On the role of religion in the journey of undocumented Mexican and Central Americans, see Daniel Groody, *Border of Death, Valley of Life: An Immigrant Journey of Heart and Spirit*. Lanham: Rowman and Littlefield, 2002; Jacqueline Hagan, *Migration Miracle: Faith, Hope, and Meaning on the Undocumented Journey* (Cambridge, MA: Harvard University Press, 2008). For a comparative study of migrant religious congregations in relation to American identity and belonging, see Peggy Levitt, *God Needs No Passport: Immigrants and the Changing American Religious Landscape* (New York, NY: New Press, 2007). For a cross-national comparison of the role of faith and religious identity among Haitians in France and the United States, see Margarita Mooney, *Faith Makes Us Live: Surviving and Thriving in the Hatian Diaspora* (Berkeley, CA: University of California Press, 2009). For a case study of Chicago immigrant congregations and their moral and social engagement projects, see Fred Kniss and Paul D. Numrich, *Sacred Assemblies and Civic Engagement: How Religion Matters for America's Newest Migrants* (New Brunswick, NJ: Rutgers University Press, 2007).

25 For a detailed analysis, see Edwin I. Hernández, Kenneth G. Davis, Jeffrey Smith, Matthew T. Loveland, Milagros Peña, and Georgian Schiopu "Faith and Values in Action: Religion, Politics, and Social Attitudes among US Latinos/as." Vol 1. Research Reports. A series of papers by the Institute for Latino Studies and research associates. University of Notre Dame, 2007; and Michael D. Layton and Alejandro Moreno, *Filantropía y sociedad civil en México* (Mexico City: Miguel Ángel Porrúa- Instituto Tecnológico Autónomo de México).

26 Elaine Peña, *Performing Piety. Making Space Sacred with the Virgin of Guadalupe* (Berkeley, CA: University of California Press, 2011). For a case study of Guadalupano devotion in New York see Alyshia Gálvez, *Guadalupe in New York: Devotion and Struggle for Citizenship Rights among Mexican Immigrants* (New York, NY: New York University Press, 2010).

27 "The Shifting Religious Identity of Latinos in the United States, Pew Research Center, May 7, 2014. www.pewforum.org/2014/05/07/the-shifting-religious-identity-of-latinos-in-the-united-states/ accessed August 8, 2015.

28 This work visa allows a foreign national entry into the United States for temporary or seasonal agricultural work.

29 For more on this topic, see the special issue on transnational parenthood edited by Jørgen Carlinga, Cecilia Menjívar, and Leah Schmalzbauer, *Journal of Ethnic and Migration Studies*, Vol 38, No. 2, 2012; Joanna Dreby, *Divided by Borders. Mexican Migrants and Their Children* (Berkeley, CA: University of California Press), and Hirokazu Yoshikawa, *Immigrant Raising Citizens: Undocumented Parents and Their Young Children* (New York, NY: Russell Sage Foundation, 2011).

30 To learn more about deported and undocumented migrant youth and their demands, see Jill Anderson and Nin Solís, *Los Otros Dreamers*. Mexico City: Iniciativa Ciudadana para la Cultura del Diálogo and U.S.-Mexico Foundation; and Eileen Truax, *Dreamers. An Immigrant Generation's Fight for Their American Dream* (New York, NY: Beacon Press, 2015).

31 Ana González-Barrera and Jens Manuel Krogstad, "U.S. deportations of migrants reach record high in 2013" *The Pew Hispanic Center Fact Tank: News in the Numbers*. October 2, 2014.

32 Department of Homeland Security, Table 41 "Aliens removed by criminal status and region and country of nationality: fiscal years 2004 to 2013," In *Yearbook of Immigration Statistics: 2013 Enforcement Actions* (Washington, D.C.: U.S. Department of Homeland Security, Office of Immigration Statistics, 2014).

33 To learn more about families organizing against family separation, see Amalia Pallares, *Family Activism. Immigrant Struggles and the Politics of Noncitizenship* (New Brunswick, NJ: Rutgers University Press, 2014).

34 Marc R. Rosenblum, "Unaccompanied Child Migration to the United States: The Tension between Protection and Prevention" Washington, DC, Migration Policy Institute Report, April, 2015.

35 For more on the issue of multiple citizenship in contexts of emigration, see Thomas Faist. "Towards transnational studies: world theories, transnationalization and changing institutions," *Journal of Ethnic and Migration Studies*, Vol 36 (2010):1665–1687, doi:10.1080/13691 83X.2010.489365.

36 To learn more about Mexico's policies to increase ties with its diaspora, see David Fitzgerald, *A Nation of Emigrants: How Mexico Manages its Migration*. Berkeley, CA: University of California Press, 2009 and Alexandra Délano, *Mexico and its Diaspora in the United States: Policies of Emigration since 1848* (Cambridge: Cambridge University Press, 2011).

37 Kirk Bowman and Felipe Arocena. *Lessons from Latin America: Innovations in Politics, Culture, and Development* (Toronto, ON: University of Toronto Press, 2014).

38 Xóchitl Bada. *Mexican Hometown Associations in Chicagoacán. From Local to Transnational Civic Engagement* (New Brunswick, NJ: Rutgers University Press, 2014), 156.

39 David L. Leal, Byung-Jae Lee, and James A. McCann. 2012. "Transnational Absentee Voting in the 2006 Mexican Presidential Election: The Roots of Participation," *Electoral Studies*, Vol 31 (2012): 540–549.

40 Michael Peter Smith and Luis E. Guarnizo, "Global Mobility, Shifting Borders, and Global Citizenship," *Tijdschrift voor Economische en Sociale Geografie*, Vol 100 (2009): 610–622, doi:10.11 11/j.1467–9663.2009.00567.

41 Jonathan Fox and Xóchitl Bada, "Migrant Civic Engagement," In *Rallying for Immigrant Rights*, edited by Irene Bloemraad and Kim Voss, 142–160 (Berkeley, CA: University of California Press, 2011).

42 For an overview on the multiple displays of migrant civil society, see Jonathan Fox and William Gois, "La Sociedad Civil Migrante: Diez Tesis para el Debate," *Migración y Desarrollo*, Vol 7, No. (15): 81–128, 2010.

43 Fitzgerald, *A Nation of Emigrants*; Lane R. Hirabayashi,"The Migrant Village Association in Latin America: A Comparative Analysis," *Latin American Research Review*, Vol 21 (1986): 7–29, www.jstor.org/stable/2503445; and Gustavo López Ángel, "Membresía e identidad en procesos migratorios translocales: La experiencia de la Asociación Micaltepecana," In *Clubes de migrantes oriundos mexicanos en los Estados Unidos: La política transnacional de la nueva sociedad civil migrante*, edited by Guillaume Lanly and M. Basilia Valenzuela V., 287–314 (Guadalajara: Universidad de Guadalajara, 2004).

44 See Francis Fukuyama, *Trust: The Social Virtues and the Creation of Prosperity* (New York, NY: Free Press, 1995).

45 See Michele Wucker, *Lockout: Why America Keeps Getting Immigration Wrong When our Prosperity Depends on Getting It Right* (New York, NY: Public Affairs Press, 2006).

46 The success of nonprofit ROSCAs in Mexico is widely recognized. Despite recent efforts to increase access to traditional banking systems, for-profit ROSCAs are popular credit options for some mortgage and car sales companies that still appeal to this cultural form of wealth accumulation to acquire more customers. For a comprehensive overview of nonprofit ROSCAS in transnational perspective, see Carlos G. Vélez-Ibáñez. *An Impossible Living in a Transborder World. Culture, Confianza, and Economy of Mexican-Origin Populations* (Tucson, AZ: University of Arizona Press, 2010).

47 Xóchitl Bada, *Mexican Hometown Associations in Chicagoacán. From Local to Transnational Civic Engagement* (New Brunswick, NJ: Rutgers University Press, 2014).

48 To learn more about similar examples of shared moral values of civic engagement, bonding social capital, and transnational moral communities among mestizos and indigenous Mexican migrants in Florida's new destinations, see Philip J. Williams, Timothy J. Steigenga, and Manuel A. Vásquez. *A Place to Be: Brazilian, Guatemalan, and Mexican Immigrants in Florida's New Destinations* (New Brunswick, NJ: Rutgers University Press, 2009).

49 "Hometown Associations and Their Present and Future Partnerships: New Development Opportunities?" Manuel Orozco Inter-American Dialogue Report commissioned by the U.S. Agency for International Development Washington, DC September 2003, 17.

50 For a good synthesis, see Roger Waldinger and David Fitzgerald, "Transnationalism in Question," *American Journal of Sociology*, Vol 109(2004): 1177–1195, doi:10.1086/381916.

51 This Hispanic population estimate comes from a U.S. Census Bureau press release projection. "U.S. Census Bureau Projections Show a Slower Growing, Older, More Diverse Nation a Half Century from Now," Press Release CB12–243, December 12, 2012. www.census.gov/newsroom/releases/archives/population/cb12-243.html.

52 To learn more about th marches and the different local contexts that lead to migrant organizing patters see among others Xóchitl Bada, Jonathan Fox, and Andrew Selee, eds., *Invisible No More: Mexican Migrant Civic Participation in the United States* (Washington, DC: Woodrow Wilson International Center for Scholars, 2006); Xóchitl Bada, Jonathan Fox, Robert Donnelly and Andrew Selee, eds., *Context Matters: Latino Migrant Civic Engagement in Nine U.S. Cities* (Woodrow Wilson International Center for Scholars, 2006); Voss and Bloemraad, *Rallying for Immigrant Rights*, and Amalia Pallares and Nilda Flores-González, *¡Marcha! Latino Chicago and the Immigrant Rights Movement* (Urbana, IL: University of Illinois Press, 2010).

22

FOR BREATH TO RETURN TO LOVE

B/ordering Violence and the War on Drugs

Ana Clarissa Rojas Durazo

What we might identify
as residual
within the histories
of settler
or colonial capitalism
does not disappear.
To the contrary,
it persists and endures,
even if less legible
within the obfuscation
of a new dominant.

—*Lisa Lowe*[1]

The narco white van pulled up midstreet, a door opened from the inside, and she ran toward it in an exasperated pursuit of salvation. My brother, holding his 1- year-old son in his arms, ran after her and toward the van, attempting to prevent yet another round of drug-bound disappearances that had nearly claimed her life time and time again. He was taken hostage into the van with a gun held to his head while he still carried Adrian. I ran towards the van and was able to pry my nephew away from the situation before the door shut and the van pulled away. I didn't know if that would be the last time I would see my brother alive.

I ran to my car and chased after the van. Pancho, my other brother, took my nephew and put him in the car seat in his car. As I followed the van, Pancho tailed close behind me for what turned into a high-speed chase through what locals call los meados. Gringos keep trying to name our streets and neighborhoods but we always seem to rename them in a way that makes sense to us. We have no "meadows" in a desert border town, but entre el narco y la migra, we have plenty of meados. We zigged and zagged avoiding cars and curbs, then the van suddenly slowed; I sped around it in an effort to block it from the front and halt yet another drug war tragic encounter.

Unsure if the van would stop or crash into me, I was relieved when the driver attempted to reverse then came to a screeching stop; my other brother, Pancho, had blocked it from behind. I knew at that moment as I faced the van from the driver's seat that I too could be killed. Coming up against the same possible destiny as my brother, Robbie, I jumped out of the car, walked up to the van and stood outside the door calling out his name. I heard nothing and wondered if he was still alive. The van door opened, the driver held the gun, and attempts at negotiating his release ensued. We talked. The gun was dropped at some point yet Robbie willingly remained in the situation vying for Kristina's safety. She sobbed an inextinguishable cry while she shifted glances between narco, my brother, and I.

To better understand this moment, the drug war, how drugs and violence came to Kristina, a young woman growing up in Calexico, and to my family, it is helpful to consider that the surge of violence she faces, we face, exists far before and after "the event." Kristina, my brother's wife and the mother of his children, lost her first love to the drug war. She was 16 and watched him get shot fourteen times right in front of her. Like many young Latinas, she healed the wounds of her loss alongside the wounds of a violent upbringing with one of the most available remedies on the border at the time, crystal meth. Considering the *longue durée* of the life of violence on the border allows us to reframe discursive ramblings of why young Latinas (on the border) "turn" to drugs; instead, we can hone our attentiveness to how it is that violence on the border and the war on drugs (crystal meth, narcos, the cops) finds us.[2]

B/ordering Violence

It was the summer of 2004, and I had returned home to Calexico to work on my dissertation. My brother was living at the house as did Kristina on and off. I grew up on the U.S.-Mexico border. I lived many faces of the border; I lived through the intensification of violence that characterizes the shift from the late twentieth century to the twenty-first century. My ancestors lived many more, including the land's naming/becoming Mexico, the United States and the U.S.-Mexico border. Because colonialism is driven by its chronic characteristic expansionism, the boundaries of empire, las fronteras are in constant re-iteration. Mezzadra and Nielson, in *Border as Method,* argue that *la frontera* is "a mobile front in continuous formation," a space designated by definition as the geopolitical marker of expansion.[3] To reference Aime Cesaire and Frantz Fanon's notions that the imperial center cannot exist without the colonies, the empire cannot exist without its borders.[4] Borders are enlisted to serve as both geopolitical and geo-cultural ends, yet they are poignantly also beginnings, always becoming places where the expression of colonial violence moves with improvisation, testing the limits of the accumulation of land, bodies, and money.

Patterns of violence have histories, are made and remade through time, imagined and reimagined through always changing circumstantial nuance. In legal and medical discourses, violence is conceptually reduced to an imagined singularity; such is the state's frame for understanding violence, a frame that legitimates the prison industrial complex as it obfuscates state violence, yet, violence is born long before and after what might be considered the violent incident. Caribbean historiographer Michel-Rolph Truillot might urge inquiry into what is either muted or obfuscated in the historical narrative.[5] In ascertaining the present life of violence on the border, we might—like sculptors—bring these untold and silenced histories into relief. Considering the historical memory of violence on the border is critical to understanding the contemporary architecture of violence and the war on drugs.

Though we can in no way underestimate the significance, the official rendering of iconographic cartographies reimagined through discursive and material bloodshed that blared the bugle constituting the imperial nation-state's U.S. consumption of indigenous and Mexican territories; nor the tragedies and travesties of border logics and weaponry that this new map and the thirst for it conjured—it was long before the

Mexican–American War and 1848 that the border was imagined and made, long before that colonial violence and the war were imagined and made.[6] For it was the consumptive cannibalism of colonial westward expansion and its technologies of inseparably ideological and material violence that yielded border after border until out of the mid-nineteenth century specific historical conditions materialized the U.S.–Mexico War and the U.S.–Mexico border. In this way, the border has always existed through violence, the severing of land, peoples, life and relations; violence is the indispensible condition through which the border emerges and persists.[7]

The Mexican–American War logics and violence continued to take life and land long after the 1848 border violence—albeit recalibrated for shifting temporalities and corresponding technologies of violence, albeit with shifting nomenclature. In fact, it was not until 1854 that the Gadsden Purchase took effect. Brandishing the name of a slaveholder who believed slavery was a "social blessing," Southwestern territories were consumed into the United States in order to connect the South to the West through a railroad in a move to facilitate the expansion of slavery.[8]

I often think about the late nineteenth century and early twentieth century, the era after the border is drawn and territories and people face consumption, the era after the United States declares the end to the Mexican–American War, and I wonder about the process of incorporation of both people and land. What are the ways that both indigenous and Mexican socialities in the late nineteenth century (and present) are a threat to the very idea of the United States? How does a nation-state create the regulatory mechanisms through which to curtail ongoing resistance that undermines new imperial narratives of national boundaries and governance, citizenship and culture?

Ken Gonzales-Day's book *Lynching in the West* and Natalia Molina's accounts of health institutions as regulatory mechanisms at this time as well as studies on developing educational institutions in the Southwest trigger this recurring inquiry.[9] I think about the rampant violence of the murderous Texas Rangers, the nineteenth century predecessor and genealogical forbear of the Border Patrol, about the widespread lynching and vigilante violence occurring alongside the continuing territorial acquisition deep into the twentieth century as Midwestern settlers go west.[10] I am struck in particular with the notion of the end of war, which is supposed to signal a time of peace—an end to the violence, yet the violence only escalated. And the "war" doesn't seem to end. And wasn't the "end" of slavery supposed to curtail violence and instead lynching gets codified into southern white sociality? This around the time lynching of Mexicans gets codified on Southwestern geographies through among many growing racial topographies: the rendering of Mexican criminality, *el bandido*, the genealogical forbear of *el narco*, and of the migrant criminal.

See, violence does not leave "colonialism's ongoing life"; rather it is requisite, takes new iterations and invented manifestations but lingers—even grows. Violence is a regulating and policing force. We come to see that the border cannot exist without law enforcement because borders are operationalized through containment and law enforcement was born to contain the imagined threat.

In particular, the dual strategy of drug criminalization and migration criminalization, and their corresponding policing regimes, created a new way to regulate indigeneity and *Mexicanidad* and contesting subjects in the twentieth and twenty-first centuries. Since the turn of the nineteenth and into the twentieth century, the U.S. Customs Service and Border Patrol along the U.S.–Mexico border grew—in particular through the assigned charge of surveilling the movement of bodies and drugs into the United States.

Its early formations were charged with the twin racial project of surveilling Chinese laborers returning to the United States after being deported and surveilling the crossing of opium. In *The Intimacies of Four Continents*, Lisa Lowe describes the ways an "emergent Anglo-American settler imaginary" was operationalized through law enforcement and criminal courts that imagined the Chinese as "diseased addicts."[11] In 1914, the Harrison Narcotic Act was an early step in the criminalization of drugs (heroin, opium, and cocaine). But after World War II the intensification of the criminalization of drug use and trade grew into becoming a top strategy of the state, alongside the criminalization of migration.[12]

In *Mohawk Interruptus*, Audra Simpson addresses the historically specific case of the Kahnaw':ke Mohawks, part of the Haudenosaunee or Iroquois Confederacy on the U.S.-Canada border. To better understand their politics to disavow the nation state, Simspon elucidates the contemporary socio-political context of "colonialism's ongoing life."[13] This analytic frame helps to think about the ways colonialism lives in the late twentieth and twenty-first centuries on the U.S.–Mexico border. So the border continues to be remade geographically, politically, and culturally with ongoing attempts at acquisition through the present. In this way, the border did not "cross us" a single isolated time, as Chicanx historical memory suggests, but many times over, and continues to cross us through the continual remaking of the border. So no, the Mexican–American War that gave the border its official demarcation did not end in 1848; it is very, very much alive—in the current era through the militarization of the border leveraged through the War on Drugs, the War on Terror and the policies of brutality not named as such, the war on migrants.

In the twenty-first century, global sociopolitical structures of militarization extend colonial institutions and state power and their attendant neoliberal forms of racial capitalism and heteropatriarchy. The border is still imagined as a threat to national security (especially in the post-9/11 era), a construct that anchors the call for border militarization under the guise of neo-imperial projects of the War on Terror, the War on Drugs, and the war on migrants. As Tony Payan phrases it, the survival of the nation (United States) is discursively framed as threatened by a lawless border where drugs, criminals, and terrorists loom.[14] This is a contemporary iteration of historic settler colonial racial logics of empire that maneuver the representational devices of the frontier as lawless and dangerous, of the indigenous and Mexican peasant *bandido*, of the Apache, a name for indigenous peoples that in French has literally come to mean outlaw, criminal, hooligan, and gang member. These archetypes emerge through and alongside the settler colonial imaginary of indigenous lands and peoples in need of taming, containment and apprehension. Such is the ongoing life of colonialism in the late twentieth century and early twenty-first century.

Enter the collision of neoliberal restructuring in the form of the North American Free Trade Agreement (NAFTA) that produces de-indianization through cultural genocide (Monsanto) and dispossession of land. It produces poverty and slashes social policies aimed at supporting the dispossessed. Thus, NAFTA yields labor migration to the north. Meanwhile, transnational corporate structures move to the south enacting the maquiladorization (American and multinational sweatshop industries) of the south side of the border where sites of unchecked heteropatriarchal, economic, and racial exploitation contribute in part to the structural possibility of feminicide. NAFTA intensifies the War on Drugs: The amplification of militarization becomes indispensible in expanding and controlling the transnational economy so weapons and military funding, training and organization migrate south. NAFTA and the War on Drugs brew nothing less than a neoliberal civil war in Mexico. The loss of life is nothing short of genocidal as the numbers approach a quarter of a million.

Feminicide is another effect; the lives claimed in both Juarez, and even higher per capita murders in Nayarit, reflect an escalation of feminicide as the drug trade intensifies in that region.[15] NAFTA's poverty and the War on Drugs produce indigenous and Mexicana migration to the north. "*O pal narco o pal norte*," are the only ways poor and indigenous women in Oaxaca envision survival.[16] In both *narco* and *norte*, violence awaits *mujeres* not to mention a heightened risk of imprisonment when *mulas* [female drug carriers] are chosen to reach U.S. drug war sentencing quotas in Mexico—yes, in Mexico. The sovereign imaginary looks very different in the age of neoliberalism where funding (aid) is ensured only through structural adjustment policies. Feminicide and the specter of violence against indigenous, poor, and migrant Mexicanas and indigenous women is the condition of the hetropatriarchal colonial order.

When border militarization intensifies in this era, migrants are made to cross through the most dangerous terrain; women and children are the first to die of exposure, and on average two migrants die every day crossing the border while estimates of up to 80 percent of migrant women are sexually assaulted during their journey to the north. Ruthie Wilson Gilmores' assessment of racial violence and mass incarceration in *Golden Gulag* helps us think through the ways the extermination of particular kinds of bodies, ways of being and living, is the modus operandi of racial capitalism and heteropatriarchy.[17] She defines racism and racial violence as the state-sanctioned or extralegal production and exploitation of group-differentiated vulnerability to premature death. The violence that remakes the border through the War on Drugs and war on migrants continues a colonial process tactically bent on the capture, containment, extermination and control of minds, bodies and lands.

I find it impossible to write about the border without voicing the tragic implications, the life of violence on the border, the geopolitics of necropolitics on the border. I am incapable of avoiding—or rather silencing—the magnitude of suffering and death that constitute the border. In the travel of the metaphoric applicability of Borderlands theories, the marker of violence should never be forgotten. Border cities are marked by violence, are made through violence. The texture of our lives on the border, the intimate details of how we live and love, reveal embodied traces of the brutality of the political and economic processes of becoming nation-states and borders over and over again. Yet I am as much concerned with the sociality of love that grows in the trenches of loss and suffering, with the many possibilities the land and its people invoke and make manifest amidst, albeit seemingly, the most powerful of violent forces. We are made through these overlapping memories, the lashing of violence, the utterance of love, the lament of suffering, the tenacity of healing.

On the day of the chase, the fallout from a dispute between my brother and his girlfriend nearly cost many of us our lives. She feared he had cheated on her. She also feared her father's abuse. And both came crashing down on her that day. It is a fallacy that the state is ever outside, beyond intimacy. *La frontera* is a constant reminder of their proximity, reminding us that colonialism is a constant display of abuse that aims at our relations. *La sagrada familia*, constituted as heteropatriarchal by the Church and the transnationalized nation-state's colonial impulse, binds intimacy to violence. The drug war is a contemporary enunciation, a methodology of violence through which the heteropatriarchal *sagrada familia* and the state are imagined and remade on the border.[18] That day, crystal meth may have offered a dose of salvation but it showed up, was delivered through the heteropatriarchal *narco*, confronted by the heteropatriarchal police and prompted and mediated by heteropatriarchal intimate relations/familia. *La frontera* was and is, and again through the war on drugs, made and remade through attacks on indigenous, Mexican and migrant women's bodies.[19]

B/ordering the War on Drugs

> *Drug traffic and the movements of people, capital and ideas that it presupposes have been central to an uneven and hierarchical global modernity.*
>
> Marez[20], p. ix

There is a long history of conjuring the border as the origin of the (drug) problem, the site for the inception of drugs and drug-related violence and crime. Truillot's historiographic intervention in *Silencing the Past* invites critical thinking through "the work of history"; that is, tracing the work that historical accounts do.[21] What histories must be told, unearthed, about the drug war, for us to dig closer to the root of related catastrophic claiming of lives and communities on the border? What accounts might offer insight into how the necropolitics of neoliberalism produce the geopolitical site of the U.S.–Mexico border through the war on drugs in the current/recent era?

It is said that the United States is the largest consumer of drugs in the world (inclusive of those made legal through the medical industrial complex and those made illegal through the punishment industry, or imperial racial politics).[22] Historically, the United States has either directly or indirectly supported drug production and traffic south of the border. For example, during World War II, the United States needed marijuana for the purposes of war materials (hemp rope) and opium for medical supplies (morphine). It appealed to Mexico to produce them.[23] Then in the era after World War II, the United States cut off (drug) trade routes through Europe—and since the demand persisted in the United States and Mexico had already developed the infrastructure for the large-scale production of opium and marijuana as the United States requested, the drugs continued to flow through the border. Because the drugs were destined for export into the United States, the border states of Sinaloa, Sonora, and Durango were chosen as production zones. Once particular drugs are criminalized in the United States, the demand within the United States for those drugs creates a profitable market that economies to the south weakened by neoliberal and other neo-imperial U.S. ventures jump to.

The massive deportation policy known as Operation Wetback in 1954 signaled what Kelly Lytle Hernandez describes as "the Border Patrol's explicit recoding of migration control as a site of policing crime and punishing criminals.[24] It is after 1954 that crossing (from the south) becomes widely culturally legible as criminal through Operation Wetback as the Border Patrol institutes the term "criminal alien," a term that to this day is used by ICE in its "Criminal Alien Program" which oversees the current era's "great expulsion of immigrants," the vast majority of which have no criminal history.[25]

Around the same time, mandatory minimums for drug convictions began with the Boggs Act in 1951. The Narcotics Control Act of 1956 was the first to use steep life sentences and the death penalty for certain drug-related "criminal" activities. In addition to the material and symbolic loss of life and citizenship invoked by this legislation, another attack on citizenship was unleashed as deportation for drug-related activities was scripted into law. While the turn toward criminalization places more and more aspects of daily life under the jurisdiction of state surveillance, it also simultaneously wields paired logics of morality and raciality so that national consciousness grows toward consensus about the "dangers" of drugs and the "evil" drug dealers. Both are racially coded: "Drugs" evokes the site of production and or transmission into the United States from the U.S.–Mexico border/Latin America, while the representational subject of the "drug dealer" grows in racial cofidication as mostly Black and brown, racial classifications also veiled in geopolitical references to the border, Latin America and "the inner city."[26] Criminalization, as another feature of the ongoing life of colonialism, hinges on an imaginary of failed and askew moralities so that we come through the racial criminalization of drugs to imagine Black and brown folks as morally dishonorable and grow to accept their punishment as we grow to accept the expansion of state surveillance.[27]

Interestingly, one of the—if not the—primary racial logics that moves forward anti-immigrant antics, actions, and violence rests on the criminalization of migration which extends a questionable intent and morality onto migrants who "cross illegally" and by doing so conflates migrant with criminal. By the mid-1950s, the Narcotics Control Act increased the size and reach of the border patrol, and so it is through the monitoring of drugs that the monitoring of bodies is intensified on the border. The War on Drugs and the war on migrants are historically co-constitutive of one another.

The border patrol is what it is today because of the criminalizaton of drugs. In *Migra*, Hernandez' assessment of the Border Patrol, she warns, "violence is implicit to the project of controlling humanity."[28] And as their role in the drug trade intensifies, so does their surveillance of migrants and so does their violence. In 1957, during the era of Operation Wetback, an early border closure between San Diego and Baja California was called as a result of the criminalization of marijuana. In 1969, one of Nixon's first moves in his official declaration of a "War on Drugs" was Operation Intercept, deploying radar, dogs, military and other technologies and extending border fences to fight what he was the first to term "the War on Drugs." Thus was instituted a stop of every single car and person crossing the border from Mexico. This maneuver solidified the border as an early ground zero for the War on Drugs. Ideologically and administratively, it also fused the management and surveillance of migrant bodies with the surveillance of criminal (drug) activity, setting the stage for late twentieth century criminalization of migration. Border Patrol militarization, tactics, and violence grew as its task increasingly became defined as fighting "criminals." The racial rhetoric of the War on Drugs anchors the state-sanctioned production and exploitation of migrants crossing the U.S.–Mexico border.[29]

Interestingly, the Nixon era's developments of the War on Drugs and corresponding militarization of the border emerge alongside the Border Industrialization Program (BIP), one of the pilot projects for what would eventually grow in the 1960s into NAFTA, which was the first iteration of the maquiladorization (American and multinational sweatshop industries) of the Mexican side of the U.S.–Mexico border.[30] Soniya Munshi and Craig Willse argue in their joint collection of essays on neoliberalism that "When neoliberalism moves from a set of ideas into practice, it requires an active state to direct . . . the protection of the wealth and assets of transnational corporations and a global elite class."[31] One of Curtis Marez' principal arguments frames the war on drugs as amplifying the logic, power, and practices of the state.[32]

The latter half of the twentieth century signaled a turn toward the carceral era where punishment increasingly comes to be understood as a way to solve social problems.[33] The rise of the carceral era emerges through the war on drugs (the criminalization of drugs). And as the carceral era and the war on drugs deepen border militarization, which is ideologically dependent on the criminalization of migration, the criminalization of migration fuels the carceral strategy. The war on drugs and the war on migrants are two sides of the same coin.

Thus, the borderlands were made into a corridor through which drugs make their way to the United States. The war on drugs turned the drug trade into an increasingly militarized (local) police and federal state battle (increasingly on both sides of the border).[34] This morphed *narco* structures into opposing militia and together they deploy an industry, an economy of violence on the U.S.–Mexico border. What is traded and produced between the two and as a result of the criminalization of drugs, is a deplorable heteropatriarchal and racial project marked by social, ethnic and gender "cleansing," genocide and feminicide. Indeed, the U.S.–Mexico border is the geopolitical site where the necropolitics of neoliberalism come to tragic fruition. This is the drug war. Between narcos, federales and police, terrorism and the threat of violence roams the streets and is magnified, just like the surplus drugs that flow through there. Among its byproducts are the carved-up psyches, minds, and bodies of border inhabitants and our loved ones.

One of the features of Alejandro Lugo's approach to the study of everyday life in a border city that I truly appreciate is his deep concern and inquiry into how it is that the expansion of state surveillance on the border deteriorates the potentiality of collective life among border inhabitants. He extends the commonplace "border inspection station" that signals the cultural and material execution of state power leading to constant determinations on citizenship, belonging, etc. to the way border communities internalize and set up inspection sites routinely to gauge class, access, and belonging. He says these construct a "pervasive pattern of cultural surveillance that dehumanize the Mexican working class in border cities."[35]

This summer I spent some time back home in the border town Calexico, California and I qualitatively assessed the striking differential in my range of experiences with customer service at various stores based on the language I spoke. Speaking in English, I would get a faster response and solution to inquiry. If I spoke in Spanish, I mostly got ignored and/or attitude, or very delayed assistance. Ascertaining belonging through cultural checkpoints translated to the ability to access both social and economic power. In particular, with the War on Drugs, the layer of questionable moral predisposition facilitates greater repudiation and hinders kin relations not to mention deteriorates people's sense of themselves as members of a community and powerful agents of change. This is one of the ways these policies continue the ideological occupation of our communities, of our minds, and one of the ways we are kept marginal, by marginalizing ourselves from one another.

"*La Facultad*": Unraveling the Drug War's Heteropatriarchal Sleight of Mind

The cops arrived and with guns drawn surrounded us. They handcuffed and arrested everyone in the van, took each one to the back of a separate police car and interrogated us all. A neighbor witness to the gridlock in front of his house had called them. I repeated the story again and again. It turns out the van belonged to one of the three top narcos in Calexico. The cop said they'd been trying to get something on him for a while. They were arrested and my brother, after several rounds of police harassment and abuse, was released after he agreed to press charges. Soon after, he dropped all charges. He'd already faced several attempts on his life and pursuing charges might not only land the mother of his children in prison but could be detrimental to us all when the narcos retaliated. My uncle Butch was once mistaken for a narco who had been disloyal and he was beaten to a pulp, face bashed in with his own car jack and left for dead on a highway outside of

> *Tijuana. He lived. And was fortunate to be built like a bull so that he was able to crawl his way to seek help. One of my brother's childhood best friends wrote a news story outing narco and federal judge ties and he was decapitated; his uncle found his head outside his front door one morning. My brother made the right decision, if there is such a thing in the midst of war. And still, nights were harder to sleep through. I lived with the constant fear that they might retaliate. After all, even narco structures ensure chingonas have a price to pay. My brother lived with the fear the cops might retaliate—their structures and logics are mirrored by narcos after all—and they did eventually come for him. A few years later they came to his home, dragged him outside and beat and tasered him to the point where they permanently disabled his leg. He suffered for years until Obamacare made it possible to get a new knee.*

The fear still runs through my veins ten years later as I write this. I can taste the metallic residue that follows the burst of adrenaline when the body faces the threshold of violence. Pupils sharpen and limbs tighten with a keen awareness that survival is a possibility. Heart pounds calling up the strength of ancestor memory coursing through veins. A plenitude of learned lessons gush through the subconscious. Here is where spirit awakens. And the possibilities are endless.

Gloria Anzaldúa describes the spiritual acuity that is capable of emerging when surviving the myriad encounters with violence that constitute the continuum of violence, the context of violence lived and endured by the excluded and exiled, by the feminine, queer, the persecuted racialized others and countless outsiders, the bordered. "When we're up against the wall," she says, "we are forced to develop this faculty."[36] She calls it "a kind of survival tactic that people, caught between the worlds, unknowingly cultivate."[37] The metaphors "caught between the worlds" and "up against the wall" signal her own experiences with innumerable assaults growing up and living on the border. These metaphors offer an epistemological trace to the geography of borders, the ground and seed/seat from where Anzaldúa's intimate knowledge of border violence emerges and from where she sees the spiritual possibility of transcendence and social transformation.

La facultad shifts our way of seeing, understanding, and being in the world and with others. Through our experience we emerge with a keen awareness, a deepened understanding of the modalities of violence. Anzaldúa sees it as a self-protective response for those made different through colonial violence—to help us see from afar and up close when the next attempt on our bodies and psyches might be delivered. In other words, it is a way of altering and interrupting colonialism's ongoing life. While Anzaldúa details the internal and psychic process as it unfolds, *la facultad* also alludes to the ways relations can be deepened and love brewed; *la facultad* is a way of healing and stitching the wounds from the many ways colonialism separates us from each other. *La facultad* is a state of consciousness capable of transforming colonial and border violence.

German psychologists have only recently begun documenting the ways stress responses can yield a greater capacity for love, connectivity, and transformative social relations, countering a century of scientific research that presumed aggression (fight or flight) to be the end result of the psychobiological stress response. The stress response they call the "tend-and-befriend" response signals the way stress responses might trigger our ability to care for, attend to and support ourselves and others.[38]

Colonialism rests on ideological warfare; it aims at our bodies but really seeks to capture our psyches. My deep Chicana feminist convictions were nearly taken by the War on Drugs' sleight of hand. I came to despise my *cuñada*, my sister-in-law; it is still difficult for me to utter her entry into the family. She has put us all through so much, my brother suffered, she stole repeatedly from my mother, even stole my father's car. It seemed every word she spoke was a lie. But the worst was putting my niece and nephew in harm's way again and again. She disappeared with the kids several times. Once she returned with them from a two-day bender in Mexicali. I imagined the worst that could've happened while she got her fix, the danger she placed her children in. My *sobrina* [niece] was 3 or 4 years old. I saw her a few days later; she jumped in my arms, held on so tight, as if her life depended on it, and would not let go. A couple of years later we took the kids to Disneyland and while on the Pirates of the Caribbean ride, I saw the spirit wounds left by this mess as older brother Adey shivered and shook, cried in absolute fear while hovering over and tightly hugging his younger sister repeating to her again and again that it was almost over, that they were going to be all right. It wasn't the ride that terrified him.

I had more than reason to be furious. I didn't speak to Kristina for the longest time. She put my family in harm's way and that was unforgivable to me. Other family members pleaded I show compassion and forgive her. I didn't have it in me. I couldn't stand her for what she had done to my family. And that is where colonialism's sleight of hand took over. The War on Drugs moves, thwarting our understanding of violence by deeply personalizing and individualizing the phenomenon of drug use, drug addiction, and involvement in the drug trade. Drug use and the violence that surrounds the use of drugs in the era of the war on drugs narrows our causal understanding of the events that take place. While the War on Drugs is entirely responsible for the massive influx of drugs moving into and through the U.S.-Mexico border: Through criminalization we grow to desire individual culpability and punishment. The dangers and violence surrounding drug use are catapulted with the war on drugs. Yes, Kristina put the children at risk, but it was the war on drugs that created the violence surrounding drug use. The war on drugs targeted both Kristina and her children by immersing drug use in the violence of war. Yet my anger, my rage at the myriad structural phenomenon wrecking through border towns, through my life and family was diverted away from the capitalist neoliberal project onto a young Chicana. She was at fault. And this too, my reaction, is made of the logics of the drug war and signals one of the most insidious ways the drug war comes to claim Chicanas, our feminism, and our relations. The border is continuously remade after all through the production of colonial difference. Colonial difference becomes a way of knowing that makes sense of what we observe, and I came to think *she* was the problem.

I am not foregoing her agency and the need for accountability for the harm she was complicit in producing. But Kristina is not responsible for the war on drugs. Kristina is not who is responsible for drugs and violence finding young Chicanas on the border. But writing this was the first step in reaching a different consciousness capable of engaging a deeper sense of accountability, of re-building the severed relationship with Kristina, of inviting the best of both Kristina and me to the process. Writing this allowed me to more clearly see what structural forces are culpable and where and how to best direct my rage and where and how to nurture the loss and fear and harm caused to many, including Kristina. And although it is not the focus of this essay, I am also not foregoing my brother's accountability in the ways he might have been and continues to be complicit with colonial heteropatriarchal impulses and the production of harm.

Our lives on the border are ontologically and epistemologically shaped through these projects of war. Quotidian living on the border is intertwined with the rendering of these projects of violence. While crystal meth is made readily available on the border, turning to it can be a self-soothing/healing behavior. It offers healing powers akin to aderall. For young *mujeres* seeking a balm to soothe the pain associated with the violence and loss commonplace in the border during the drug war era, crystal meth offers a jolt to the central nervous system that initially floods it with dopamine, serotonin, and adrenaline, causing initial feelings of pleasure, happiness, and euphoria, and enhancing self-confidence and concentration. Recovering self-confidence—if but for an instant—for survivors of violence whose sense of themselves has been dragged through the mud is not only healing, it is transformative. But it is after all the very criminalization of drugs and the drug war that produce the categorical difference between prescription and "illegal" drugs. Pharmaceutical drugs like Adderall have similar formulations to crystal meth but don't have the stigma, criminality, and violence attached to their use.

But the media did not report on Adderall like it did crystal meth. On the U.S. side of the border, the media is a vital tool in the war on drugs, conjuring the images and representations that legitimate the criminalization of drugs and the militarization of the border. The local newspaper reported on one of Kristina's arrests in a motel where she traded sex for drugs. The report was unnecessarily explicit with pictures and details regarding the sexual encounter. This maneuver was a heteropatriarchal iteration that would conjure the exchange as the ultimate betrayal to the imagined proper (north side of the) border Chicana feminized Christian chaste subject. Such an iteration hinges on the racial trope of the Chicana/indigenous feminine subject as inherently lascivious and second, in need of taming and control for the threat she poses to the colonial heteropatriarchal order. The War on Drugs media representation serves as a medium through which to deliver these colonial epistemologies addressed explicitly in Michele de Cuneo's letter that was the first to document the rape (his rape) of an indigenous woman in the Americas. (CITE Castañeda, Antonia. "History and the Politics of Violence Against Women," In *Living Chicana Theory*, edited by Carla Trujillo (Berkeley: California: Third Woman Press, 1998) It is these logics that hinder the possibility of accountability and transformative justice in the case of feminicide in Juarez, for example, where women who are sexually assaulted and disappeared are more readily imagined as "mujeres de la calle" who brought the violence upon themselves. The War on Drugs media representation of Kristina extends the corporal racial and gendered topography of perversion onto the (imagined as uncontrollable) consumption of drugs. The very definition of vice: "wicked" immoral criminal behavior involving *sex and drugs*. Lastly, this representation also affirms a heteropatriarchal colonial imaginary that positions the masculinized Mexican drug dealer as the lewd culprit demeaning the Chicana subject. Evading scrutiny in this criminalized gaze is the War on Drugs as contemporary colonial structure that makes both incident and the media representation possible.

They eventually left the border and she got clean. It was the only way. They are in the company of the many drug war exiles and refugees from south of the border who flee the violence and drugs that have claimed their lands and their loved ones. My brothers, my parents, and I came to this country around the same time the Reagan intenstification of the drug war catapulted resources and ideological spinning that would call on a full-scale war by depicting the drug threat as a threat to the nation-state. The use and sale of certain non-prescription forms of drugs were reframed from a public health matter and private issue to a criminal one to be solved by law enforcement, prisons and the state, which then legitimated the militarization of the border. Militarization policies, such as Operation Gatekeeper in California, produced an increased morbidity in migrant crossing by deterring migration to the most dangerous climate and geographic conditions for crossing.

But the War on Drugs not only produces the militarization of the borders responsible for the genocide and sexual violence experienced by border crossers; it also produces displacement as refugees of the drug war seek safety and refuge from the devastation that has wrecked their ancestral homes. As young people, we came with our loved ones and families from the south with a generation of migrants fleeing the destruction and slow erosion of Mexican sustainability. The peso was repeatedly devalued against the U.S. dollar, a neoliberal tactic to prepare México for structural adjustment. The predecessor to indebting a nation (through the passage of free trade agreements) is bankrupting it first. Poverty pushed Mexicanxs into both the drug trade and migration to the north. We were displaced from our homes and way of life. Migrants flee to the north in masses mostly as a result of the catastrophic neoliberal political and economic impact on their abilities to survive poverty and the violence of what subcomandante Marcos calls the 4th world war, inclusive of the War on Drugs.

Ancestral Wells of Love and Belonging: For Breath to Return to Love

The intimacy of violence survival.
We are emergent through these histories.

She breathes. She lives. Spirit moves through her. She is made of spirit. Strewed remnants of pasts of long ago, infant futures, would've beens and will bes. She wakes in the middle of the night to stir herself into depths unknown. Remakes herself. Stewing, simmering, resting on time. With finger tongues she licks wounds, sews masks, and tastes the depths of memory. She wanders through nights and deserts and sleeps when day comes blaring flag's orders. She knows and is another way to live. There is always another way living beating inside skin's heart. She listens. Ombligo dreams nascent with possibility. Rhythm. Flow. She. Turns like tides in sand dunes, comforts belly arms. We will make it through. Infinite. Life. Renew. Silhouettes of blossom's spring dancing figures of ancient youth. She is all this. And more. She is before. She is after. Borders. She grace. Weaves tapestries. Of borders. Of the travesties of borders. Of catastrophic crossings. She is mother. She is warm and cold and smiles and suffers. Makes wind sing. To call on us. To speak to us. That we remember. Her. For breath to return to love.

The task of the colonial imperative is a continuous and ongoing dispossession—of a people from their land, from their ways, from their ancestors, and from each other. Yet while the border continues to "cross" us, we never stopped crossing it; for like the land, our spirits and ancestors are far more expansive than the limits of jurisdictional territorial claims, than the lashings of violence. The ancestral memory of the land's people crosses the threshold of the border boundlessly through the potentiality of our being, of our belonging to each other, to the land.

"Borders can be overcome with the revolutionary tenderness of poems," writes U.S. Poet Laureate Juan Felipe Herrera in his call for collective poetry to respond to the violence of policies targeting migrants.[39] Artist Ana Teresa Fernandez also invokes the power of visual poetry, of a tender imagination, when she paints skies on border fences "to emulate the continuation of the sky." Her project sets out to "erase the border" by centering the Mexican sensual/laboring female body in the act of creating altered futurities where border walls fall. As she paints, she says she laments the lives taken from those attempting to cross; she memorializes Mexico's violent subjugation through the war on drugs and NAFTA and she erases the symbol of aggression and violence—the wall.[40]

Long before 1848, my ancestors uttered these words. And long after, these words ensue, we endure. May this slow and intentional telling of memories calibrated with love invoke and honor the connectedness of life and land. May this offering of words from a Yoeme healing song strengthen the dignity of the people and this land:

Anti Nanchi Tutumahawi Matatutanchi Sanamaweh
Anti Nanchi Tutumahawi Matatutanchi Sanamaweh

I am Yoeme I am Warrior I am Strength
I am Yoeme I am Warrior I am Strength

Abuela sings to turn child's fever
Abui sings lulls baby to sleep
Cousin chants to calm sorrow

In my veins runs a profound respect for the dignity of the desert and the integrity of the life it breathes onto landscapes, onto bodies, skies. It humbles. The whiff of deep summer's air singes cilia, the stroke of sun sears bare skin. Ancestors pass on the lessons, how to follow the lead of the land, how to hold her hand and dance, how to live the feverish seasons, how to honor life. The stretch and might of desert runs through, across and in spite of the contemporaneous topographies of colonial carvings. Though the wounds and markings of carnivorous cravings are undeniable, the land and its people carry the genealogy of a will of inherent refutation.

Let us simultaneously narrate, place and displace, war and violence. We must speak of war, of the many faces and traces of war and violence. But the story never begins nor ends there. Ancestral wells of love and belonging forge a prior as well as a spirited survival and defiance driven by other worlds of knowing, feeling, being. While the borderlines cut across our lands, our bodies, our love and families, we persist with bountiful remedios y recetas de amor, songs like healing balms that mend las quebraduras, the breaks; and through the ruptures we find ways to return to the land, to loved ones who live in spirit, to the undying memory of love.

Notes

1 Lisa Lowe, *The Intimacies of Four Continents* (Durham, NC: Duke University Press, 2015), 20.

2 On the long term of the life of violence on the border, see Juanita Díaz-Cotto, *Chicana Lives and Criminal Justice: Voices from El Barrio* (Austin, TX: University of Texas Press, 2006).

3 Brett Neilson and Sandro Mezzadra, *Border as Method, or the Multiplication of Labor* (Durham, NC: Duke University Press, 2013), 15.

4 Frantz Fanon, *The Wretched of the Earth* (New York, NY: Grove Weidenfeld, 1963). Aime Cesaire, *Discourse on Colonialism* (New York, NY: Monthly Review Press, 2000) Walter Mignolo, *The Idea of Latin America* (Oxford: Blackwell Publishing, 2005).

5 Michel-Rolph Truillot. *Silencing the Past: Power and the Production of History* (Boston, MA: Beacon Press, 1995).

6 Mark Rifkin, *Manifesting America: The Imperial Construction of U.S. National Space* (London: Oxford University Press, 2009). Roxanne Dunbar-Ortiz, *An Indigenous Peoples' History of the United States* (Boston, MA: Beacon Press, 2014).

7 Gloria Anzaldúa, *Borderlands, La Frontera* (San Francisco, CA: Aunt Lute, 1987). Rojas, Clarissa, "We Morph War into Magic: The Story of the U.S. Mexico Border Fence Mural, a Community Art Project in Calexico-Mexicali," *Aztlan: A Journal of Chicano Studies*, Vol 38 (2013): 1.

8 Leonard Richards, *The California Gold Rush and the Coming of the Civil War* (New York, NY: Knopf Doubleday Publishing Group, 2007).
9 Ken Gonzales-Day, *Lynching In the West: 1850–1935* (Durham, NC and London: Duke University Press, 2006). Natalia Molina, *Fit To Be Citizens? Public Health and Race in Los Angeles* (Berkeley, CA: University of California Press, 2006).
10 Dustin Craig and Sarah Colt, *We Shall Remain* (Geronimo: PBS, 2008).
11 Lisa Lowe, *The Intimacies of Four Continents* (Durham, NC: Duke University Press, 2015), 8.
12 Michelle Alexander, *The New Jim Crow* (New York, NY: New Press, 2012).
13 Audra Simpson, *Mohawk Interruptus: Political Life Across the Border of Settler States* (Durham, NC: Duke University Press, 2014).
14 Tony Payan, *The Three U.S.–Mexico Border Wars: Drugs, Immigration, and Homeland Security* (New Haven, CT: Praeger, 2006).
15 Rosa Linda Fregoso and Cynthia Bejarano, *Terrorizing Women: Feminicide in the Americas* (Durham, NC: Duke University Press, 2010). Rosa Linda Fregoso, *Mexicana Encounters: The Making of Social Identities on the Borderlands* (Berkeley, CA: University of California Press, 2015).
16 Concepción Núñez Miranda, *Las Caracolas: Deshilando Condenas Bordando Libertades* (Oaxaca: Universidad de Oaxaca, 2005).
17 Ruth Wilson Gilmore, *Golden Gulag: Prisons, Surplus, Crisis and Opposition in Globalizing California* (Berkeley, CA: University of California Press, 2007).
18 Andrea Smith, “Heteropatriarchy and the Three Pillars of White Supremacy,” In *INCITE: Women of Color Against Violence,* edited by INCITE (Durham, NC: Duke University Press, 2016).
19 Rita Laura Segato, “Territory, Soverenighty, and Crimes of the Second State: The Writing on the Body of Murdered Women,” In *Terrorizing Women: Feminicide in the Americas* edited by Rosa Linda Fregoso and Cynthia Bejarano (Durham, NC: Duke University Press, 2010).
20 Curtis Marez. *Drug Wars: The Political Economy of Narcotics* (Minneapolis, MN: University of Minnesota Press, 2004).
21 Michel-Rolph Truillot, *Silencing the Past: Power and the production of History* (Boston, MA: Beacon Press, 1995).
22 See for example United Nations Office on Drugs and Crime, World Drug Report 2016 (United Nations publication) 2016.
23 Kelly Lytle Hernández, *Migra! A History of the U.S. Border Patrol* (Berkeley, CA: University of California Press, 2010).
24 Ibid., 170.
25 Walter Ewing, Daniel Martinez and Ruben Rumbaut, *The Criminalization of Immigration in the United States* (Washington, DC: American Immigration Council, 2015).
26 Curtis Marez, *Drug Wars: The Political Economy of Narcotics* (Minneapolis, MN: University of Minnesota Press, 2004).
27 Fred Moten, speaking at public event “Do Black Lives Matter?: Robin D.G. Kelley and Fred Moten in Conversation” held in Oakland, CA on December 13, 2014.
28 Kelly Lytle Hernández, *Migra! A History of the U.S. Border Patrol* (Berkeley, CA: University of California Press, 2010), 5.
29 Tony Payan, *The Three U.S.-Mexico Border Wars: Drugs, Immigration, and Homeland Security* (New Haven, CT: Praeger, 2006). Kelly Lytle Hernández, *Migra! A History of the U.S. Border Patrol.*
30 Alejandro Lugo, *Fragmented Lives Assembled Parts: Culture, Capitalism, and Conquest at the U.S.–Mexico Border* (Austin, TX: University of Texas Press, 2008).
31 Soniya Munshi and Craig Willse, “Navigating Neoliberalism in the Academy, Nonprofits, and Beyond,” *Scholar and Feminist Online,* Vol 13, No. 2. http://sfonline.barnard.edu/navigating-neoliberalism-in-the-academy-nonprofits-and-beyond/ accessed January 5, 2016.
32 Curtis Marez, *Drug Wars: The Political Economy of Narcotics* (Minneapolis, MN: University of Minnesota Press, 2004).
33 Ruth Wilson, *Golden Gulag: Prisons, Surplus, Crisis and Opposition in Globalizing California* (Berkeley, CA: University of California Press, 2007). Clarissa Rojas, “Fighting the 4th World War and Violence Against Women,” In *The Revolution Will Not Be Funded: The Nonprofit Industrial Complex,* edited by INCITE (Boston, MA: South End Press, 2007).
34 Curtis Marez, *Drug Wars: The Political Economy of Narcotics* (Minneapolis, MN: University of Minnesota Press, 2004).
35 Alejandro Lugo, *Fragmented Lives Assembled Parts: Culture, Capitalism, and Conquest at the U.S.–Mexico Border* (Austin, TX: University of Texas Press, 2008), 116.

36 Gloria Anzaldúa, *Borderlands, La Frontera* (San Francisco, CA: Aunt Lute, 1987), 38.
37 Ibid., 39.
38 Dawson Von, Bernadette, Urs Fischbacjer, Clemens Kirschbaum, Ernst Fehr and Markus Heinrichs, "The Social Dimension of Stress Reactivity: Acute Stress Increases Pro-social Behavior in Humans," *Psychological Science*, Vol 23, No. 6 (2012): 651–660.
39 Juan Felipe Herrera, "Forward," *In Poetry of Resistance: Voices for Social Justice (Camino del Sol)*, edited by Francisco X. Alarcón and Odilia Galván Rodríguez, xi (Tucson, AZ: University of Arizona Press, 2016).
40 Ana Teresa Fernández, web blog "Borrando la Frontera/Erasing the Border," http://anateresafernandez.com/borrando-la-barda-tijuana-mexico/ accessed January 28, 2016.

23

THE INTIMATE LIFE OF THE POCHA

A Genealogy of the Self-Ironic Turn in Chican@ Culture

Paloma Martínez-Cruz

> A word used in California to designate the ungrateful Mexican who denies his Mexican background although he carries it in his blood, and in his acts tries to ape the present masters of the region.[1]
>
> — José Vasconcelos

> I wish to clarify: I don't aspire to find myself. I wholeheartedly accept my constant condition of loss. I embrace my multiple and incomplete identities, and celebrate all of them (or to be more precise, most of them, since there are aspects of my multiple repertoire of performance personae that I truly hate, and that sometimes frighten me).[2]
>
> — Guillermo Gómez-Peña

Hidden Etymology of the Pocho

In 1999, Peter Hong published an article titled "They Were Chicanos but Now Proudly Say They're Pochos," thus signaling the arrival of a new cultural movement that had grown out of the Civil Rights Era's Chicano legacy.[3] The Pocha and Pocho identities (shortened to "Pocho" from here) are characterized by the cultural alienation experienced by Mexican-descended denizens of the United States, with particular emphasis on the experience of linguistic marginalization associated with speaking little Spanish, or Anglicized Spanish (Spanglish). Following the initial contributions of Esteban Zul and Lalo Alcaraz' *Pocho Magazine* in 1990 and the formation of the performance arts collective La Pocha Nostra in 1993 by Guillermo Gómez-Peña, Roberto Sifuentes, and Nola Mariano, the Pocho insult that had begun as a marker of deficiency has become a symbol of resistance for artists who self-identify either specifically as Pochos, or as "Americanized" Mexicans. The 1990s and 2000s witnessed humorists such as George López and Al Madrigal place their cultural in-betweenness at the forefront of their comedic repertoires. Graciela Beltran belts her 1990 Tejano song "La Pochita de Sinaloa" about cultural nostalgia, and the Los Angeles-based group Conjunto Los Pochos was born in 1997 with the idea that their limited Spanish language should not prevent them from celebrating their musical passion for Norteño and accordion. More recently, Sandra de la Loza's oppositional performance interventions are catalogued in her book *The Pocho Research Society Field Guide to L.A.: Monuments and Murals of Erased and Invisible Histories* (2011). The present genealogy serves to historicize Mexican and Mexican American construals of Pocho identity that have culminated in today's burgeoning Pocho phenomenon.

My chapter first considers the etymological roots of the Pocho expression in order to understand the meaning it was assigned by Mexican statesmen and elites in the wake of the Mexican Revolution of 1910. Next, I examine the Pocho consciousness of scholar and poet Américo Paredes, whose poetry in the 1930s prefigured the post-Chicano vindication of the Pocho in the self-ironic works of satirists Esteban Zul and Lalo Alcaraz, and performance artist Guillermo Gómez-Peña. The sum of my sections submits that the Pocho identity may be located in the intimacy of the self-ironic turn. If community is conversation, then the Pochos have long been silenced by the colonially-imposed rhetoric of deficiency. As the following study demonstrates, it was not until the 1990s that satirists claimed the right to enter the conversation and give full rein to the intimacy of their intracultural positionality as a historical and linguistic consequence of the interdependency between the United States and Mexico.

In the literature on Pocho identity, none have left a more encyclopedic legacy than the eminent scholar Luis Leal (1907–2010). My work contributes to Leal's historiography of Chicano literature by turning the focus on the emergence of humorous self-deprecation as a strategy of resistance. This section pursues the etymology of the word Pocho in order to engage the submerged truths of its roots and usage. My next section examines the figure of the Pocho in the period following the Mexican–American War of 1846–1848 that rendered some 100,000 Mexican citizens foreigners on lands that had long been central to their social cohesion. I then analyze Américo Paredes' prose poem "Tres faces del pocho" (1936) that anticipates the self-irony expressed more confidently towards the end of the millennium. Finally, my chapter looks at the full repossession of Pocho subjectivity in the humor of Esteban Zul and Lalo Alcaraz's *Pocho Magazine*, where a shift from "Chicano" to "Pocho" consciousness signals a new capacity to problematize cultural nationalism and promote inclusion across diverse Chicano experiences.

Following the word to its origins, "Pocho" is of Cahita derivation.[4] The Cahita group encompasses eighteen closely related dialects belonging to the Uto-Aztecan family used by native inhabitants of the northern coast of Mexico and the lower courses of the Sinaloa, Fuerte, Mayo, and Yaqui rivers. Numbering in the range of about 115,000 upon the early encounters with the Spanish in 1533, the Cahita had been the largest linguistic group in northern Mexico at the time of contact with Europeans. At the time of Caballero's study of recent developments on Uto-Aztecan languages (2011), Yaqui speakers (locally known as Yoeme or Yoem Noki) in Sonora and Arizona numbered approximately fourteen thousand.[5] References to the Uto-Aztecan language family describe it as the largest in the Americas on several counts. Its geographical extension reaches from the Great Basin to El Salvador and Nicaragua; about sixty varieties are currently spoken; its number of current speakers is close to two million; and its languages have a time-depth between 4,000–5,000 years.[6] Both lexicographer Francisco J. Santamaría and Leal corroborate the term's Yaqui origin, and Rojas's account of the language spoken by Californians in the nineteenth century reports that "pochi" was said to be derived from the Yaqui to denote "lopped off" or "bob-tailed." According to Federico Sánchez, this became the nickname for formerly Mexican Californians when Alta California was severed from Mexico, as the *Californios* now belonged to a part of Mexico that had been "amputated."[7]

First published in 1959, Santamaría's *Diccionario de mejicanismos* 1974 edition includes an entry for "Poche, cha." The Mexican Academy of Language refers to Santamaría's volume as a foundational reference resource on all matters relating to Mexican particularisms.[8] As a post-Mexican Revolution lexicographer, Santamarías scientific compendium of nationalisms had the power not only to curate and sanction regional vernaculars, but also to shape Mexican attitudes about regional identities. As his dictionary entry's implications are central to the modern Pocho subject, the entry is worth quoting in its entirety:

> *1. Nombre con que se designa a los noramericanos descendientes de español, especialmente de mejicano, en el sur de Estados Unidos y particularmente en California; también al residente extranjero del mismo origen.*
>
> *(En Méjico lo más común es decir pocho o pocha, y no es difícil que su origen sea el mismo pochio, sonorismo que procede probablemente del yaqui; a veces también limitado de alcances, más claramente, estúpido.)*
>
> *2. Castellano corrompido, mezcla de inglés y peor español, que hablan los noramericanos y residentes extranjeros de origen español, principalmente mejicano, en California (Estados Unidos), y quien lo habla.*[9]

As the *Diccionario* attests, pocho may denote stupidity in the same measure as it denotes corrupt Castilian. As we will see, Santamaría's contemporaries of the Mexican Revolution laid the groundwork for a centrist ideology in which the Pocho constitutes an official foil to the Mexican nation building project.

Although representations of Mexicans and Mexican Americans who preferred English were common in Borderlands poetry of the nineteenth century, it was in the writings of José Vasconcelos (1882–1959) in the twentieth century that Pocho came to be used as a slur by Mexicans against their "Americanized" counterparts to the north.[10] Along with Octavio Paz and Samuel Ramos, Vasconcelos was a seminal figure in the Mexican arts and letters of the period following the Mexican Revolution of 1910. As minister of education in the 1920s, he helped shape the mural movement headed by Diego Rivera, José Clemente Orozco, and David Alfaro Siqueiros to unify the country and promote the Revolution's ideals of *mestizaje*, indigeneity, and the redistribution of national resources to benefit the disenfranchised. In these circumstances, Vasconcelos was uniquely positioned to be a key arbiter of official nationalism and its cultural coalescence after a bloody civil war. Leal notes that his book *Ulises criollo* (1935) defends Mexican culture from the hostilities of Anglo racism, but he does not discuss the "Americanized" Mexican until the 1920s when Vasconcelos' particular branding of Pocho galvanized national derision. As part of a pan-Latin American mistrust of the United States and its imperialist and expansionist policies, the Latin Americans viewed the U.S. Americans as calculating materialists who lacked spiritual values (Darío, Rodó, Retamar).[11] The linguistic in-betweenness of Pochos garnered suspicion as people who had not only geographically and linguistically abandoned Mexico, but also spiritually transformed into traitors who put Yanqui-style self-interest before country and compatriot.

It must be noted that the literature of Mexicans from the nineteenth century does not universally condemn a *paisano* who speaks a less than Cervantine Spanish, as the Mexican Lieutenant José María Sánchez' remarks about his visit to the region that is now Texas demonstrate. "Accustomed to continued trade with the North Americans, they have adopted their customs and habits, and one may say truly that they are not Mexicans except by birth, for they even speak Spanish with marked incorrectness."[12] Sánchez's observations are delivered in a matter-of-fact tone that conveyed sympathy for their economic and geographic circumstances, but at the same time he suggests that their lack of correct Spanish marks them as the cultural outsider in his centrist assessment of Mexican identity. Sánchez's qualifiably neutral appraisal of language use in Texas notwithstanding, early mentions of Pochos were inclined to subscribe to Vasconcelos-style nationalism, and construe them as corrosive to the national project. In the wake of the Revolution, competing nationalisms made the *poche* into an emblem for that which denigrated the superiority of Mexican cultural values, and embraced the soulless materialism of U.S. life.

An honest and unembarrassed etymology of the Pocho must acknowledge that this word, which took on a negative political valence at the time of the Mexican Revolution, arrives to us originally from the Uto-Aztecan language family. This means that "*pocho*" belonged to the Americas from a time before the segmentation of Uto-Aztecan peoples into Mexican and U.S. territories, and before indigenous peoples were made to speak the Castellano by Spanish and Mexican soldiers and sojourners. From its Yaqui roots, it then became a Mexican insult for speakers of Anglicized Spanish, and finally became an emblem of Chicano pride in the hands of self-ironic satirists and other culture brokers that we will examine. Its hidden etymology reveals that the border crossed the Pocho, rather than the other way around.

Irony and the Border: The Calamities of Code Switching

The self-ironic register is a complex one for communities experiencing the consequences of colonization. Greengross and Miller explain that self-deprecation and other-deprecation involving some form of ridicule are the two most common types of verbal humor, and submit that both seem to be a universal phenomenon, present in both traditional and industrial societies. While self-deprecating humor may be seen as a marker of emotional health, other-deprecating humor, or "dissing," aims derision at perceived—or devised—deficiencies in a rival.[13] One of contemporary humor's major tenets is that comedy "punches up," meaning that the sharpest barbs are aimed at those in power, thus destabilizing normative social orderings. When potentially offending material is directed toward the mirror image of one's own community, it is no longer the abuses of those in power that the speaker is intent on exposing, but the ambiguities located within an intimately held cultural perspective.

While irony has existed in the Americas, both in self- and other-deprecating forms, since pre-Columbian times, the circumstances of U.S. armed incursions into today's Southwest and the very real threat of obliteration for Mexican and indigenous peoples provided the stimulus for other-deprecating humor as a way to maintain dignity and integrity in the face of oppression.[14] According to Padilla, when Mexican statesmen were forced to surrender to the United States, their rhetorical strategies paved the way for the discursive habits found in Chicano self-writing.[15] In particular, the discursive habit with which Padilla is concerned is the expression of narrative irony, in which the Anglo invaders are meant to be welcomed and mollified, while the Spanish-speaking readers are given to understand that measures of surrender were taken under threat, duress, and coercion. This dual consciousness evident after 1848 has long been considered a source of oppositional agency in Chicano expressive cultures (Anzaldúa, Bruce-Novoa).[16]

Oppositional Mexican and Chicano humor in the form of Anglo-deprecation spilled over into the enthusiastic deprecation of Mexicanos who spoke Spanish with English admixture. The author Daniel Venegas's deprecation of the migrant peladito (country bumpkin) figure[17] reveals how this tension between state prescriptions of national loyalty and local linguistic variance can be understood as a mechanism of cultural intimacy. Herzfeld explains cultural intimacy as, "The recognition of those aspects of cultural identity that are considered a source of external embarrassment but that nevertheless provide insiders with their assurance of common sociality."[18] For example, cultural critics and public leaders are eager to show off their modern and classical artistic contributions to outsiders, while deeming "trivial" the decidedly more lowbrow entertainment of the national beauty pageant. If the Spanish of national poetry foundations constituted the nation's finery, then the Mexican legacy of broken Spanish was its embarrassment.

The problem of conflating Castellano with nation building and improper Spanish with treachery is that it denies the fact that Mexico has always been multilingual. This strain between celebrated spectacles and hidden scenes has implications for our understanding of Mexican communication: While the elites in control of publishing houses, journalism, and other forms of state-legitimized media defend the Mexicanness of Castellano, a long trajectory of monolingual speakers of indigenous languages (over one and a half million Nahuatl speakers reside in Mexico today) expose the Mexicanness of languages *other* than Spanish. As the Yoeme word *poche* reminds us, linguistic diversity constituted a historical reality of the Mesoamerican territories at the time of Spanish Conquest, and remains a national attribute to the present day. Owing to colonial prejudice, the fact that many Mexicans are dominant in languages besides Spanish became Mexico's intimate family secret buried in plain view. The elite defenders of Castilian homogeneity reify the façade of what Bonfil Batalla describes as "Imaginary Mexico," or the Mexico in the image of European hegemony.[19] "Deep Mexico," which corresponds to the indigenous Mesoamerican civilizing project, was not less "Mexican" than Mexico City elites, or their mestizo and *indígena* counterparts residing in the regions signed away by Santa Anna. "Bad" Spanish was the language of Deep Mexico, and also the language of Pochos, both of which the proponents of Imaginary Mexico wished to obscure.

While class privilege positions writers within the civilizing project of Imaginary Mexico, gender also played a role in the policing of national loyalty. A frequent trope was to ridicule Mexican-descended women who were accused of becoming *agringadas* and rejecting the Spanish language in order to achieve greater social status and financial security. In New Mexico, an anonymous poet employed code switching in the following poem collected during the first decade of the twentieth century by Aurelio Macedonio Espinosa (1907–2004):

A una niña de este pais [sic]
yo le hablaba una vez;
yo le hablaba en español,
y ella me hablaba en inglés.
Le dije:—¿Será mi amada
mi corazón también?
Y me dijo la agringada:
—Me no like Mexican men.

[To a girl of this country
I was talking once;
I spoke to her in Spanish
and in English she would answer.
I said to her: "Will you be my beloved
and my sweetheart too?"
And the Americanized girl answered:
"Me no like Mexican men."][20]

From as early as 1847, Mexican-authored poetry and *corridos* [moralizing folk ballads], served to remonstrate the behavior of Mexican women who used English to associate with the Anglo oppressors, thereby conflating language pollution with sexual pollution when code switching was engaged by rural and urban women of limited economic means.

Another kind of contempt for Mexicans and Chicanos who "preferred" English appears in the prose of novelist Daniel Venegas, whose *Las aventuras de don Chipote, o cuando los pericos mamen* (*The Adventures of Don Chipote, Or, When Parrots Suckle Their Young*) appeared in *El heraldo de México*, a periodical published in Los Angeles from 1915–1952. Serialized in 1928, the story uses comedy to narrate the tragic plight of a recent Mexican immigrant's economic oppression in the United States. Don Chipote and his companion Policarpo are distressed when they ask a stranger if he knows where they could find work. As the stranger appears to be their countryman and in similar straits, they approach him with confidence. However, he surprises them when he replies, "*Juát du yu sei? Ai du no tok Spanish.*" The man then proceeds to ridicule his companions for not being able to speak English, even though they are all of Mexican descent.[21] Urquijo-Ruíz has pointed out that Venegas' audience was the educated Mexican middle class who enjoyed mocking the working class peladitos on the other side of the border. Venegas' uneducated, English-dominant manual laborer character inspired derision among the paternalistic and elitist readership that enjoyed more secure footing in the Mexican national project, as their economic prospects did not force them to leave their nation of origin, or the comforts of its mother tongue, in order to survive.

Mexico's polyglossia gives rein to the economic uncertainty that rumbles underneath the surface of the national project. That is to say, if Mexico could offer the prospect of living wages, life chances, and employment for its people, there would not be a phenomenon of so many Mexican-descended speakers of Spanglish and English. Indeed, personal remittances from the United States to individuals in Mexico amounted to $23.6 billion USD in 2014, making them rank next to oil exports as one of the two most important sources of foreign income.[22] While the Pochos are historically lambasted for speaking poor Spanish, the health of the Mexican economy has long relied on their value to the U.S. job market, with English constituting a crucial job skill to have. The instability of Mexico's official idiom evokes fears across normalizing institutions and colonial hierarchies that Imaginary Mexico will be unmasked, and Deep Mexico and its descendants will be reconciled as the heart, rather than the periphery, of this modern Mesoamerican state.

The Voice of Américo

Américo Paredes (1915–1999) helped to form the basis of a school of Southwestern cultural studies. Born in Brownsville, Texas to an educated family of Mexico's hacienda society, he sought and celebrated vernaculars of insurgency in his scholarship on machismo, border stereotypes, and folkloric ballads. His first published book of poetry, *Cantos de adolescencia*, was originally issued through Librería Española in 1937 in San Antonio, Texas. His second collection of poetry was not published until 1991 under the editorial supervision of Ramón Saldivar by Arte Público of Houston, Texas. A colossus in the field of ethnomusicology and folklore, Olguín and Barbosa join their generational cohort in lamenting that Paredes's poetry, complex in its recreation of hybrid language and styles, has only recently begun to gain critical attention.[23] In our pursuit of the self-ironic turn in Chicano cultural production, Paredes's Pocho poems provide us with the foundational portrait of cultural intimacy.

Figure 23.1 Américo Paredes. Courtesy of the Nettie Lee Benson Latin American Collection, University of Texas Libraries, UT Austin.

Recent scholarship examining Paredes' transnational subject formation has tended to emphasize the uneasy, even destructive, in-between-ness of Paredes' narrativization of bordered consciousness (Olguín, Herrera, Limón).[24] But whether an observer characterizes Parades as the Mexican nationalist, the self-destructive assimilationist, the proto-Chicano, or any combination of the above, all can agree that his voice contributes one of the earliest stirrings of a Pocho oppositional consciousness. In "Las tres faces del pocho," which appeared in *Between Two Worlds*, the self-ironic turn in the face of Pocho alienation finds its first fluorescence.

Herrera (2010) cogently problematizes the fact that Paredes' following lines—the most frank vindication of the Pocho—did not appear in his volumes of published poetry, but rather continued to languish in a special collections box with other unpublished papers at the University of Texas library.[25]

¡Soy pocho! Dios me haga
orgullo de los pochos
así como los pochos son mi orgullo.
Quisiera llegar a ser
el orgullo de los pochos.[26]

Written around the year 1940, the unadorned stanza declares pride in the Pocho condition, in spite of their lowered status in the eyes of Mexicans and Tejanos who can presumably make more traditional claims to national pride. Rather than the lament of a truncated Mexican, Herrera describes the poem as an "oath of allegiance," that provides us with the clearest message of Paredes's cultural alignment. The long silence obscuring the Pocho verses attests to the absence of English-dominant Mexican and Chicano perspectives from cultural circulation—an occlusion that would color the creative universe of Paredes, as exemplified in the alienation depicted in the works examined below.

"Tres faces del pocho: Comedia in Tres Autos, Modelo T," written about four years before Paredes' "orgullo pocho" lines, provides a stark portrait of cultural intimacy. Appropriately, the first *Auto* begins with the protagonist seated on a toilet seat. The *comedia* is written in three tableaus depicting three areas of Pocho identity. Stage direction is written in English, while the rhymed verses spoken by the monologuists in each tableau are written in Spanish. "The Passionate Spaniard," "The Second-Generation Exiliado," and "El Poeta Pocho" are interpreted sequentially by solitary men who indulge in verses cataloguing their disillusionment. The opening tableau centers on the Spaniard who has spent the day as a tourist in Mexico City, and Paredes' performative imagination might be culled from the pages of Guillermo Gómez-Peña's theatricalization of extreme identities:

> After a weekend of tacos, whores, and mariachis, we find him enthroned on the crapper, spilling out his guts and suffering the torments not of the damend but of the *gademes*. He has been called a pocho, has paid three or four mordidads, and finally had his wallet stolen."[27]

While citing the inventiveness of Paredes' code switching that took place four decades ahead of the Chicano movement's recuperation of the practice, Schmidt Camacho submits that the work falls short of achieving a true border vernacular. "Still, Paredes's poems ultimately choose one language over the other; English and Spanish remained marked off from each other in the poems by stanza breaks."[28] This concern over how Spanish and English are delineated by stanza breaks tragically reasserts the language policing from which Paredes's Pocho imagination seeks refuge.

The Second-Generation Exiliado's monologue touches the theme of nostalgia for a Mexico that he has never visited after being spurned by a *Gringa* that he tried to unsuccessfully bed. Set in a tenement apartment outside Chicago's stockyards, the Exiliado's tableau ends with his jazz selection of "St. Louis Blues" that he selects over "La Zandunga" and "Canción Mixteca." In the final tableau, El Poeta Pocho drinks in a "rundown beer joint." His verses commemorate heroism that subversively belong neither to a Spanish nor to a Mexican past:

> *No le canto a Cuahtémoc, no le canto a Pelayo*
> *Al Cid y a Moctezuma no le canto yo;*
> *El Cortez de quien hablo en Tejas nació.*[29]

Here, epic poetry is dedicated to heroes of border conflict in keeping with the corrido tradition. Aniceto Pizaña, Juan Nepomuceno Cortina, Jacinto Treviño, and Gregorio Cortez were praised in nineteenth and early twentieth century corridos for defending the rights of Mexicans against Anglo brutality, elevating the tequila smugglers and outlaws as heroes to the people.

The isolation of each of the protagonists of "Tres faces del pocho" mirrors the alienation of border identity, which the characters try to escape through the acts of courtship with a *gringa* and inebriation. As the poet for his people, Paredes' Pocho finds himself indelibly alone, reflecting the trajectory of Pocho consciousness that remained unpublished until 1991, when the generative potential of Pocho pride was to find its community.

The Pocho Manifesto

In 1999, Hong's article explained, "Much of the ideology of civil rights-era Mexican American activism—called Chicanismo—was about being taken seriously. Pochismo, the pocho ethos, is about not taking anything too seriously."[30] The team of Esteban Zul and Lalo Alcaraz conceived and created *Pocho Magazine* in 1990, which began as a practical joke. As Zul recalled:

> We didn't do a magazine at first. We'd go around having fake magazine titles and talk a lot of shit. Some guy curating a show on underground zines heard about it and invited us to participate, so the idea was, "We gotta make it." We slapped together that first issue. Everyone loved it. . . . It wasn't like the other shit. It was all fan boy shit. White angst shit. Fetishizing alternative rock bands.[31]

Not all "old school" Chicano culture brokers were prepared for the self-deprecation that filled the pages of the magazine. In my interview with Alcaraz, he cites an example of when an elder believed the Pocho team had taken the joke too far:

> They were another generation and we had our frictions when we would take it to another level. Like one time we put Dr. Loco on the cover of *Pocho* and he got pissed. He didn't get the joke. The title was something like "From Tecate to Tecato." So I guess we implied he was a heroin addict and he didn't like it. But eventually we made peace.[32]

An image of the first *Pocho Magazine* cover was featured in the Los Angeles County Museum of Art's exhibit "Phantom Sightings: Art After the Chicano Movement" focusing on "conceptual and interventionist tendencies," and new directions in cultural identity and social commentary.[33] Along with Hong's article, which proclaims "Now They're Pochos," we can appreciate a clear delineation not only in terms of generational, but also conceptual cohesion. Their first issue in 1990 makes explicit claim to Pocho identity in the avant-garde tradition of the manifesto:

> POCHO MAGAZINE is the first magazine about Pochos, for Pochos and by Pochos. Pocho is a term that has been used by uptight, culturally pompous Mexicanos to describe their "bastard cousins to the north," the Chicano or Mexican-American, (*El Pinche Pocho*), who by their accounts, has lost all of their original culture because of their surrounding US imperialist bullshit environment and Speedy Gonzalez. We at POCHO MAGAZINE accept Pocho as a term of empowerment for tacky, uncultured, fucked-up-Spanish-speaking Pochos everywhere and challenge both the US and the Mexican governments to a foot race down the streets of Oakland while wearing floppy red velvet sombreros and matching Anthony Quinn masks. You didn't know HE was a Pocho, did you? But there's more to Pochismo than free cheese and welfare. It's a deep burning resentment of cultural imperialism from both sides of the imaginary border so let the truth be known! From Taco Bell to Pollo Loco, from El Santo to La Bamba, from Gigante to Kmart, from Tijuana to Bakersfield, Pochos arise and jump start your cars, pull out your bus transfers, wax your huaraches—we must mobilize. POCHO POWER![34]

Juxtaposing the Pocho Manifesto with the earnest and epic notes sounded in poet-philosopher Alurista's 1969 *Plan Espiritual de Aztlán* ("the call of our blood is our power, our responsibility, and our inevitable destiny"),[35] we can plainly discern Pocho pride's incredulity toward the metanarrative of Chicano nationalism. Not "the call of blood," but the call of free cheese and cultural imperialism that galvanizes Pochos into action.

A genealogy of Pocho consciousness demonstrates that the 1990 Pocho Manifesto carries forth the larger legacy of self-irony as a mechanism for negating colonial prescriptions of "authentic" Mexicanness. The Manifesto begins by challenging "uptight, culturally pompous" Mexicanos, but subsequently articulates the Pocho's more menacing opponents, these being U.S. imperialist bullshit, the U.S. and Mexican governments, and, finally, the "imaginary border." Reminding us of Bonfil Batalla's Imaginary Mexico, the Manifesto conceives the border as a fiction that denies the cultural hybridity of Mexican Americans whose lives reflect the ever-shifting meanings of its imprint. Taylor reminds us of the potency of the self-ironic strike:

> The power of the self-irony is in the message of the performance: "in making this joke about myself, or ourselves, I manifestly have more power over myself than you do . . . I can do a better job on myself than you or any so-called sophisticated outsider could do (so don't bother), and I could easily do a job on you."[36]

A genealogy of Pocho consciousness reveals the self-ironic turn to be a powerful technology in the mitigation of paternalistic nationalism such as that espoused by Vasconcelos and Venegas in the aftermath of the Mexican Revolution, and the vindication of language variance that has been Deep Mexico's linguistic landscape since before either English or Spanish arrived to police its frontiers.

Notes

1 Luis Leal and Ilan Stavan, *A Luis Leal Reader* (Evanston, IL: Northwestern University Press, 2007), 16.

2 Guillermo Gómez-Peña, *Dangerous Border Crossers: The Artists Talks Back* (New York, NY: Routledge, 2000), 9.

3 Peter Hong, "They Were Chicanos but Now Proudly Say They're Pochos," *Los Angeles Times*, March 6, 1999. http://articles.latimes.com/1999/mar/06/local/me-14431 accessed September 17, 2015.

4 Mario García, *Luis Leal: An Auto/Biography* (Austin, TX: University of Texas Press, 2000), 105.

5 Gabriela Caballero, "Behind the Mexican Mountains: Recent Developments and New Directions in Research on Uto-Aztecan Languages," *Language and Linguistics Compass*, Vol 5/7 (2011): 486.

6 Ibid., 485.

7 Guillermo E. Hernández, *Chicano Satire: A Study in Literary Culture* (Austin, TX: University of Texas Press), 11–12.

8 Aguilar, Julio. "Mexicanismos: Cómo hablamos en México," *Fondo de Cultura Económica*, September 20, 2009. www.fondodeculturaeconomica.com/Editorial/Prensa/Detalle.aspx?seccion=Detalle&id_desplegado=29331 accessed December 22, 2015.

9 Francisco J. Santamaria, *Diccionario de mejicanismos* (Mexico City: Porrua, 1974), 872. English translation:

> 1. Name that refers to North Americans who are Spanish-speaking descendants, especially Mexican, in the southern United States and particularly in California; also to the foreign resident [of Mexico] of the same origin.
>
> (In Mexico it is more common is to say pocho or pocha, and it is likely that its origin comes from pochio, a Sonoran slang that possibly derives from the Yaqui language; sometimes also meaning of limited ability, or more clearly, stupid.)
>
> 2. North Americans and foreign residents of Hispanic origin, principally Mexican, from California (United States), who speak a corrupted Spanish, a mixture of English and bad Spanish.

10 Mario García, *Luis Leal: An Auto/Biography* (Austin, TX: University of Texas Press, 2000), 105.

11 See Roberto Fernández Retamar, Calibán: Apuntes sobre la cultura de nuestra América (México: Editorial Diógenes, México, 1971); Rubén Darío, *Cantos de vida y esperanza: Los cisnes y otros poemas* (Madrid: Tipografía de Revistas de Archivos y Bibliotecas, 1905); José Enrique Rodó, Ariel (Madrid: Editorial-América, 1919).

12 Guillermo E. Hernández, *Chicano Satire: A Study in Literary Culture* (Austin, TX: University of Texas Press), 11.

13 Gil Greengross and Geoffrey F. Miller, "Dissing Oneself versus Dissing Rivals: Effects of Status, Personality, and Sex on the Short-Term and Long-Term Attractiveness of Self-Deprecating and Other-Deprecating Humor," *Evolutionary Psychology, Vol* 6 (2008): 393–408.

14 Yolanda Broyles-González, *El Teatro Campesino: Theater in the Chicano Movement* (Austin, TX: University of Texas Press, 1994), 34.

15 Genaro Padilla, *My History, Not Yours The Formation of Mexican American Autobiography* (Madison, WI: University of Wisconsin Press, 1993), 44.

16 Gloria Anzaldúa, *Borderlands/La Frontera: The New Mestiza* (1987), 4th ed. (San Francisco, CA: Aunt Lute Books, 2012); Juan Bruce-Novoa, *Chicano Poetry: A Response to Chaos* (Austin, TX: University of Texas Press, 1982).

17 Daniel Venegas, *Wild Tongues: Transnational Mexican Popular Culture* (Austin, TX: University of Texas Press, 2012).

18 Michael Herzfeld, *Cultural Intimacy: Social Poetics in the Nation-State*, 2nd Edition (New York, NY: Routledge, 2004), 3–4.

19 Guillermo Bonfil Batalla, *Mexico Profundo: Reclaiming a Civilization* (Austin, TX: University of Texas Press, 1996).

20 Luis Leal and Ilan Stavan, *A Luis Leal Reader* (Evanston, IL: Northwestern University Press, 2007), 47–48.

21 Daniel Venegas. *Las aventuras de don Chipote, o cuando los pericos mamen.* 1928 (Houston, TX: Arte Público Press, 1999), 43.

22 Associated Press, "Mexican Remittances Jump 7.8 Percent in 2014," *Daily Mail*, February 3, 2015, www.dailymail.co.uk/wires/ap/article-2938233/Mexican-remittances-rise-7-8-percent-2014.html accessed September 24, 2015.
23 Américo Paredes, *Cantos de adolescencia: Songs of Youth (1932–1937)*, translated with an Introduction and Annotations by Ben V. Olguín and Omar Vásquez Barbosa (Houston, TX: Arte Público Press, 2007), xxiv-xxvi.
24 Ben V. Olguín, "Reassessing Pocho Poetics: Américo Paredes's Poetry and the (Trans)National Question," *Aztlán*, Vol 30, No. 1 (2005): 87–121. José Limón. *Américo Paredes: Culture & Critique* (Austin, TX: University of Texas Press, 2012). Spencer R. Herrera, "The Pocho Palimpsest in Early 20th Century Chicano Literature from Daniel Venegas to Américo Paredes," *Confluencia*, Vol 26, No. 1 (2010): 21–33.
25 Spencer R. Herrera, "The Pocho Palimpsest in Early 20th Century Chicano Literature from Daniel Venegas to Américo Paredes," *Confluencia*, Vol 26, No. 1 (2010): 21–33.
26 Ibid., 31. English translation: "I am a Pocho! May God make me pride of the Pochos, just like Pochos are my pride."
27 Américo Paredes, *Between Two Worlds* (Houston, TX: Arte Publico Press, 1990): 38.
28 Alicia Schnmidt Camacho, *Migrant Imaginaries: Latino Cultural Politics in the U.S.–Mexico Borderlands* (New York, NY: NYU Press, 2008), 46.
29 Américo Paredes, *Between Two Worlds* (Houston, TX: Arte Publico Press, 1990): 44. English translation:

I do not sing to Cuauhtémoc, I do not sing to Pelayo

To El Cid and Montezuma I do not sing;

The Cortez of whom I speak was born in Texas

30 Peter Hong. "They Were Chicanos but Now Proudly Say They're Pochos." Los Angeles Times, March 06, 1999. http://articles.latimes.com/1999/mar/06/local/me-14431 accessed September 17, 2015.
31 Esteban Zul, personal interview, August 11, 2015.
32 Lalo Alcaraz, personal interview, August 12, 2015.
33 Rita Gonzalez, Howard N. Fox, and Chon Noriega, *Phantom Sightings: Art after the Chicano Movement* (Los Angeles, CA: University of California Press, 2008), 11–13.
34 Lalo Lopez and Steven Zul, *Pocho Magazine*, Berkeley, CA: 1990, Issue 1, n.p.
35 See Sheila Marie Contreras, *Blood Lines: Myth, Indigenism, and Chicana/o Literature* (Austin, TX: University of Texas Press, 2008), 99.
36 Lawrence J. Taylor, "Paddy's Pig: Irony and Self-Irony in Irish Culture," In *Irony in Action: Anthropology, Practice, and the Moral Imagination*, edited by James W. Fernandez and Mary Taylor Huber, 185 (Chicago, IL: University of Chicago Press, 2001).

24

QUEEN OF *LAS FIESTAS PATRIAS* AND OTHER STORIES

Oral History, Memory, and Latinx Culture

Carlos Manuel Salomon

How do people of Latin American descent remember their history and maintain their culture in the United States? For many this is a challenge. But with the arrival of so many people in the last quarter century, and the natural growth of the community, we are seeing an unprecedented influence of Latinx culture in the United States. Aside from the promotion of our history among academics, one way to remember our traditions and stories is through public history. Family history, oral traditions, and even the land itself can help to promote an understanding of the concept of greater Latin America, which points to the increasing cultural and geopolitical linkages between Latin America and the United States. The key to uncovering this history is to hear the voices of the people who, for centuries, have created these links, erasing borders and forging a new culture along the way. I will use as a backdrop interviews I took of my parents, interviews my students took of Central American immigrants, and pedagogical approaches tied to the community. These voices will help to explain how subjectivity can transform Latin American history from a subject that is often devoid of meaning for the struggling Latinx student, into a transformative experience. The voices of the forgotten often reveal the deepest aspects of culture because they are coming from a subjective retelling of the past. The prospect of oral history is that anyone can contribute to it. Although some historians insist that we write objectively, utilize "primary" documents and the latest methodologies, the truth is that history is made by the people who lived it and can be shared by all who remember the stories of elders. Oral history, memory, performance, oral tradition, and folklore constitute ways of remembering that are counterintuitive to the ways most historians collect information. For the Latinx community, these are essential tools of our collective history. They are not tools indigenous to the Americas, nor are they exclusively Western; they are universal and significantly contribute to the telling of history. In the end, this essay will critique elements of contemporary historical research and will reveal how active self-reflection can help Latinx educators and students to (re)member their history.

Because public history is found in both private and shared spaces, it is often used for cultural preservation. Much has been written about Spanish and Mexican heritage sites in the United States. But these sites are also markers of local memory, which promotes cultural history. Similarly, the oral history interview reveals multiple layers of memories shaped by the learned experiences of life. As one ages and has behind them a lifetime in which an identity was formed, their stories become of repository of culture and history. Even younger folks, once they have had time to reflect on their current situation and have become conscious of the politics and history that contributed to their immediate surroundings, can offer insight. In this way oral history, when used as an archive of memories that recount hardships, discrimination, and perseverance, can be used as a tool not only for cultural preservation, but also for combating racism and creating awareness. This type of history utilizes active self-reflection and is a tool of empowerment.

As a historian trained in the United States, I was presented with a very different view of Mexico and the border than were students studying the same subject in Mexico. I learned these subjects in English, centered within the dominant perspective of "American" universities, which borrowed heavily from European theories. Not that my teachers could not understand Mexican perspectives, but they taught it from their personal subjective experiences. They were no different than any community which sees events based on its own local understandings. My professors gave me a set of tools ideal for studying a particular, highly calculated view of the past. I carried that training like a burden that weighed upon my shoulders and became frustrated at my inability to articulate the experience, vibrancy, and expressions of my community. In essence, there was a conflict between what I had experienced and what I was learning. I wanted to taste and smell history; hold it in my hands and unravel it; I wanted it to reveal my true self. I simply did not have the tools to do so.

History is a gateway to self-empowerment. It enables youth to think differently about their immediate surroundings. In my own community, I learned that by studying the past, young Chicanxs can change from a destructive to a positive path. Perhaps this is why history is much more than a field of inquiry; it is also a tool of change. I have rarely encountered a Chicanx who did not study their own history. Although they exist, I have never met a Chicanx who decided to study Asian, African, or European history. Why is there such a powerful desire to study one's own past? The answer is quite simple. For one, history never seemed relevant. Students become aware early on that the K–12 curriculum omits, distorts, and romanticizes ethnic history, leading to damaging caricatures and stereotypes. This omission takes its toll on the self-image of young Chicanx students; in the popularly accepted version of history, they have made no contributions to society; they were never a part of the building of a country; they see themselves as out of place—immigrants and victims of a violent and corrupt past. Knowledge of the past builds confidence in students of color, who begin to see themselves as offspring of a rich past. The other reason Chicanx tend to study their own history is because they are trying to reclaim that which was taken from them during the process of colonialism. People whose ancestors were once colonized only know that which the colonizer allowed them to know. Although history is not always able to give back all that was stripped away, it puts the student on the road to redemption. I have seen the lives of countless students changed, including my own, due to the exploration of the past.

One major problem I encountered in graduate school was that Latin American history never touched on Chicanx or Latinx history. It was as if the actual border, which attempts to exclude, "protect," and compartmentalize, had somehow taken shape in the classroom. I began to immerse myself in the field and began to attend conferences and read with enthusiasm the latest scholarship. I was lucky to have been at a university with an active center for Latin American studies. I was eager to see how this center and the field of Latin American studies addressed Chicanx and Latinx issues, but the information was not there. I had to go to a small, marginalized, and under-funded Chicano Studies office. It seemed that there was almost no dialogue between the two departments. Although the national Latin American Studies Association has recognized the need to address this dichotomy, most scholars continue to work from either a Latin

American or U.S. perspective. Even within the field of Chicanx Studies we tend to focus on events and issues within the United States.[1]

One of the exceptions to this is the field of Borderlands history, which seeks to view the region and the people who live there from a cross-border perspective. The field itself came about in the early twentieth century but has developed dramatically in the last thirty years. Borderlands history has obvious commonalities with Chicanx Studies in terms of subject matter. However, Borderlands history also looks at Spanish, Anglo, Native American, Asian, and Black history. Borderlands historians have of recent become more engaged in the political issues of the border and have, for the most part, been allies of the immigrant community. Despite its scope, Borderlands history began as an academic pursuit, not as insurgent history. The field has more in common with Western American history and the framework conceived in the nineteenth century by historians such as Frederick Jackson Turner, who argued that United States history was the history of westward expansion. Although Borderlands history attempts to envision the region from a binational lens, Mexicans themselves view it differently. Although the Spanish Conquest and its gradual occupation of Mexico's northern "frontier" was similar to the U.S. movement to the West, Mexicans are not the Spanish. This is where the memory of colonialism comes into play. The ancestral ties that Mexicans have to that time of suffering means that they see it in a totally different way than do most "American" academics. It then becomes quite easy to understand that to the people who are indigenous to the region, the border means little more than an object of oppression. The old saying "history was written by the victors" rings true here.

Despite the differences and the problems associated with Latin American studies and Borderlands history, these fields, along with Chicanx-Latinx studies, are natural allies. Latinx studies and Latin American studies need to speak each other's language and need to work together more seamlessly. Only then can we produce a new history of greater Latin America. Nevertheless, we need new tools to accomplish this. Chicanx history must continue to nurture its roots as an insurgent history and embrace public history. After all, academic institutions have worked to marginalize Chicanx studies and have little respect for our work. It is difficult to not emulate what our professors have written, and what we read in history journals, but there are other ways of healing wounds and creating new beginnings. One of these ways, which I will explore in this chapter, is oral history.

Problems and Pitfalls

If history is, in fact, open to all, why are so many of our experiences written in a way that only an elite, über-educated class can understand them? The problem of complex language and style is often rooted in the process of Western methodology and theory. Postmodern scholars (even Latin American decolonial scholars), have developed important (albeit problematic) theories. Although they take aim at and critique Western power structures, many progressive scholars have internalized aspects of Western aggression in their writing style. The words they choose, the way they put them together along with sentences, paragraphs, and ideas convey the notion of counter-aggression, which is used interchangeably by institutional, conservative, and progressive scholars alike. They are, after all, products of Western ways of understanding and knowing, and so, use the same linguistic tools to combat each other. It is like seeing the eighteenth century armies of France and Great Britain face off; they both line up on the same field, march in unison toward each other, are organized with the same military hierarchy, and both die the same way; it is the only way each knows how to resist. But when we put indigenous warriors into the mix, who use different tactics, it forces the entire scope of war to change and a new meaning emerges. Complex academic language, therefore, is no different from the language of Western aggression because of its power to exclude; it simply has a different conclusion.

This type of language reminds me of a conversation I had in Albuquerque, New Mexico during graduate school. Two Native American elders taught me that a firm handshake, although meant to convey respect, was actually a sign of Western male aggression. That same handshake was used, in years long past, to betray, deceive, and oppress indigenous communities. It pretended peace and honesty when in reality it was a deception. Indigenous people turned it around on them: what is more detested to the self-confident man than a limp, cold handshake? To the Western male, the limp handshake is not to be trusted. It signifies weakness, lack of spirit, and disinterest. In an alarming way, the limp handshake cuts to the core of Western male privilege and patriarchy. Because men with this mentality equate a limp handshake to weakness and femininity, it can in turn reveal aspects of his misogyny. The Native American limp handshake, however, is an affront to the notion of Western dominance; it is a sign of resistance. At the same time, among friends, it is a sign of humility. In Western culture, among men of all beliefs, behaviors and orientations, the firm handshake implies trust and confidence; it implies the opposite in Indian country. A firm handshake is like rigorous academic language; it carries with it a paternalistic and aggressive nature. It is also complex, exclusive, and divisive. It condemns most to a poverty of knowledge and aids in the separation of people, much like the U.S.–Mexico Border.

The Art of Agency

Access to transformative knowledge, therefore, is imperative to the decolonial project.[2] In my own classroom, the merging of oral history, Latin American studies, Ethnic studies, and Borderlands history has given me the tools to make history come alive. This is an important point because the subject does not always seem relevant to youth. Aside from imparting knowledge, I encourage my students to connect history to their own lives and surroundings. The knowledge of what actually happened to the ancestors is an important step toward redemption. Oral history puts the power of that historical narrative into their immediate environment. They begin to take the reins of history utilizing their creative instincts and their passion to create a narrative that defies the official accounts; they become historians armed with knowledge of the past and the subjectivities of their lives.

Oral history smashes the myth of historical objectivity. The very idea of "objectivity" in Western scholarship somehow allows for an unbiased analysis, which is cherished as the only legitimate approach in the social sciences. Within the field of history in particular, the notion of objectivity became the defining principle of what constitutes historical methodology. One notable historian claimed that objectivity "has been the quality which the profession has prized and praised above all others."[3] Many "Western" scholars wear the cloak of objectivity throughout their career, which allows them to write virtually anything about anyone without fear of mainstream critique. Only when the scholar dares to write a polemic or subjective piece is he treading into dangerous territory. Thus, the field of history rarely changes. Theories and perspectives might change; but the rule of objectivity lifts the scholar into "scientific" pursuit, where he can write about marginalized communities, endangered indigenous populations, and non-Western culture, for example, without ever having to be responsive to the communities he studies. Historians can get most of the information needed on a particular group or community from an archive, without really knowing the people. The archive holds letters, government documents, reports, photographs, and any material the historian needs to write a history from an "objective" point of view. Historical objectivity, however, is nothing more than a Western myth that has unraveled as communities begin to question the perspective of the writer. For example, in 2013 Reza Aslan, author of *Zealot: The Life and Times of Jesus of Nazareth*, was routinely questioned about his motives for writing a book about Christ.[4] Fox news commentator Lauren Green even asked why a Muslim would write about Jesus. Shortly after the Islamaphobic controversy subsided, the critiques continued to flow. *The Nation* looked at Aslan's credentials and found that he wrote his dissertation on a Muslim topic and did not work in a history or religious studies department. The critique brought up the idea of who has the legitimate authority of writing a true history, unblemished by the subjective nature of politics. Historians, then, are affected by their questionable objectivity, which is often attached to race or ethnicity and even to one's training and approach. This, in a nutshell, is why Chicanx studies, and particularly the Chicanx decolonial project, is under constant scrutiny; we are biased because we are writing about our own people.

If "objectivity" shields historians from scrutiny and gives them the ability to write about whatever and whoever they please, Latin American studies in general, and to some extent, Borderlands history, has also benefitted from this. Writing about Native American cultures in the United States is no easy matter for non-Indian scholars. In 1969, Lakota scholar Vine Deloria Jr. uprooted anthropologists when he wrote *Custer Died for your Sins: An Indian Manifesto*.[5] As mentioned in the Introduction to this volume, Deloria questioned the practice of anthropological research on the reservation and the publication of findings without any accountability to the community.[6] Bringing this same issue to the field of history, Dakota historian Angela Cavender Wilson (Waziyatawin), gave a scathing critique of the state of American Indian history, arguing that it is a field dominated by non-Indian, male historians who, like Deloria's anthropologists, practice their research without consulting reservation communities.[7] She also critiqued historians for using the topic as a tool to advance their academic careers. She argued that "To truly gain a grasp of American Indian history, the other historians—tribal and family historians—must be consulted about their own interpretations of and perspectives on history."[8] No one, including Cavender, wants a mass of historians to descend upon the reservations, but a slow, painstaking process must be developed so that the non-Indian historian can be taught and reoriented on indigenous perspectives. Even so, there remains the problems of the archive, the audience, and the perspective. The archive is replete with non-Indian accounts of Indians, allowing for a wide range of interpretations that are easily understood, and celebrated, by Western audiences, but are humiliating and regressive to indigenous communities. That is why Native American communities have their own ways of telling history, which is highly useful to them and to the maintenance of their traditions. The audience (and perspective) of non-Indian history remains in the academy, literature, and film. Because there is little or no reciprocity in the research process, the audience remains outside of tribal communities and the perspective is often one-sided. Although there is still a lack of accountability, non-Indian historians who write about American Indians clearly understand that they are being watched and must tread lightly.

What if Latin American studies, and its ever-increasing focus on marginalized, indigenous communities, was put up to the same scrutiny that Deloria and Wilson put on U.S. historians and anthropologists? It would cause an uproar; historians would be running wild in the streets. The indigenous population in Latin America is defined differently than in the United States. First of all, there are many more millions in Latin America. The Maya nation alone, has more members than the entire U.S. Native American population, made up of over 550 tribal nations. In Mexico, there are millions of individuals who primarily speak indigenous languages. There are over a million souls in central Mexico who speak Nahuatl, the language of the Aztec Empire. Yet the indigenous have no (or limited) tribal autonomy as compared to the U.S. Native American populations. So it is difficult to know who is indigenous and who is "Hispanic"—many Mexicans have the same physical traits. Indigenous communities are highly organized. They are both marginalized and have shaped every aspect of Mexican life. Yet for the most part they are absent from institutions of higher education. The historian, therefore, can't simply go to a reservation to conduct research. If he had to follow the Doloria-Wilson protocol, he'd have to hire a translator and his research would be more extensive. He'd have a much harder time because he'd be seen as a double foreigner. But as it stands, the student can access a massive archive on the Native people of Latin America, which can be found not only in Latin America itself but also the United States and parts of Europe. In the United States, a much smaller Native American population has succeeded in entering accountability into the academic dialogue and passing laws like the Native American Graves Protection and Repatriation Act. This has made it nearly impossible for anthropologists to dig up Native American graves, collect all of the booty, and store it in their museums or sell it on the open market. There is simply more access in Latin America. Indigenous communities in Latin America have been too busy with genocide, brutal military dictators, displacement, deforestation, and contamination to deal with research accountability.

Linda Tuhiwai Smith has argued that a growing number of indigenous researchers are calling for such protocols.[9] I for one believe that the dialogue needs to begin in earnest in Latin America. If we are forced to live in an increasingly globalized world, the marginalized communities of the Americas should not be spoken for without a fight. When Western scholars conduct research on communities still suffering the effects of colonialism, accountability is essential because their research contributes to how these communities are seen in mainstream society. Even those who side with the struggles of indigenous communities need to understand the importance of direct contact and accountability, even if they believe their project is contributing to the maintenance of that culture. As Tuhiwai Smith argues, "many researchers simply assume that they as individuals embody this ideal and are natural representatives of it when they work with other communities."[10] For Tuhiwai Smith, Western research is linked to imperialism because these researchers often "claim ownership" of indigenous cultural ways. Like Deloria and Wilson, Tuhiwai Smith believes that indigenous views on history and research are indispensable for the true understanding of these cultures. This is why the use of participant subjectivity is so important, not only to the ethics of researching marginalized communities, but also to the story itself. So where does the mestizo, the Chicanx, the fronterizo fit in this process? Does the Chicanx fit within this equation or is he so fully enmeshed within Western tradition that these types of protocols are unnecessary? This is where oral history and the decolonial project comes into play and why it is so important, in this context, to begin thinking about different approaches to writing and telling our history.

Mexicans have a saying, "*tienes un nopal en la frente*," ["you have a cactus on your forehead"], which sums up the cultural position of the average Mexicano in the context of colonialism. Let me explain. The saying is used when Mexicans living abroad negate their Mexican ancestry. It is used to remind them that they are Mexican. The cactus is used as a symbol referring to a Mexican's indigenous features, his implicit connection to the land. It is a direct result of the Mexican seeing himself, like the nopal, as indigenous. Yet most Mexicans would not see themselves as Native American. Herein lies the great complexity and struggle of Mexican culture. In his famous book *Mexico Profundo*, Guillermo Bonfil Batalla referred to this historical process as "de-Indianizing that which is Indian."[11] While there is a tacit understanding that the two communities are related, they are separate from one another, leading to distrust and inner turmoil within the community. The decolonial project seeks to correct these problems and bring the individual to a positive place based on some of the values and ways of knowing laid out by the ancestors. But this task is not easy to accomplish.

In 1999, I was at the American Historical Association meeting in Manhattan. I was a wide-eyed grad student at a special roundtable meeting of some of the nation's leading Latin Americanists. The discussion moved toward Mexican social movements. At one point a woman, whose work on the post-revolutionary Mexican education system I had ranked among the most influential in my young academic career, stood up and proclaimed that the Chicano Movement was nothing more than a fantasy; a construct promoted by misinformed radicals with no basis in fact. She was particularly troubled by the idea that Chicanxs wished to reclaim their indigenous heritage. Of course, I objected to her position. I told her that the Chicanx community had its own self-determination when it came to the reclaiming of our identity. Most of the panel agreed with me and that professor, whenever I saw her thereafter, gazed at me with seething anger for having embarrassed her in front of her colleagues. But it was at that point I realized, that in the United States at least, Mexicans were not the keepers of their own history. Was she alone in thinking this? Here was a woman at the helm of her field. She studied Mexicans and her interpretations were validated by her position in the field. She was celebrated as a progressive thinker. But she simply could not accept that Chicanxs were ignoring the archive. Instead they were relying on a collective identity. They were relying on the word on the streets, in community halls, in poems like *I am Joaquín*, elders, *curaderas, danzantes*, folk tales, oral history and, of course, Chicanx Studies classes—all of which utilized elements of the oral tradition. Learning an insurgent history, of course, sometimes requires items found in archives. But it is more often a tale, a sacred ritual, *una mirada*, a glance from an elder, from where our history emerges; this is why history is entangled in the everyday performance of life.

While it is important to explore multiple forms of history, Chicanx history should continue to explore its roots as an insurgent history. Although it is often burdened by the demands of academic institutions, Chicanx history has created some of the most dynamic changes in the field. However, a more participatory, community-based agenda must take root if we expect to make the changes the field was envisioned for in the first place.[12] To some extent, these processes have been around since the 1960s with the publication of Pablo Freire's *Pedagogy of the Oppressed*.[13] Freire's work is most known for his teaching pedagogy, which placed the experience of the student at the helm of learning. Experiential learning is participatory in that the professor and the student learn together, and utilize and play off of each other's personal subjectivities. Freire believed in the transformative power of education to give students tools to fight against the powers that oppress them. The student had to first become conscious of the systems of power and of his internal self. This process is not so easy in the traditional field of history, especially when a student is simply trying to tell a story of something that happened in the past. This is why a subjective telling of history is so important. Students of traditional history have to rid themselves of the bias against subjective and experiential material. They need to get over the idea that they should only pursue a "scientific and objective" research agenda that favors the archive over the spoken word and the movements of the community.

The Oral Tradition and the Land

I am fortunate to be able to teach a recurring course on oral traditions at the Peralta Hacienda Historical Park in Oakland's Fruitvale district. The class is part of a California State University East Bay goal to promote "high impact teaching practices," which is an attempt, among other things, to interact with the community as a learning tool. The Peralta Park is the site where Luis Maria Peralta built a small adobe to claim his grant of 44,800 acres of land. Born in Sonora, Mexico, Peralta came to California as a poor soldier with the Anza expedition of 1776. The task of the Spanish expedition was to settle the region, protect it from encroaching rival European empires, and Christianize the indigenous population. In 1820, Peralta applied for the grant after serving forty years in the Spanish military. For his service, he was given the largest grant possible at the time. The land stretched from El Cerrito, north of present-day Berkeley, to San Leandro, including all of Oakland. The small adobe was built in that year, cared for by indigenous *vaqueros*. Luis Peralta divided the land among his four sons and never lived there. After Mexican independence, the new government re-confirmed his grant. With the adobe foundations, the Peralta Creek, and the open space, students enrolled in my class felt the presence of history, despite the presence of urban chaos.

Like most *Californios* of his generation, who were lucky enough to get such grants, Peralta rose in the ranks because of his bravery. As a sergeant, Peralta became known as a formidable warrior against the incursions of raiding Native Americans. Aside from a few meetings with Russian officials, the European conquerors never came. Not until the arrival of the United States in 1845 was there any cause for concern. Most soldiers fought against the resiliency and constant resistance of Native Americans. Such was the nature of Indian-Mexican relations, although they shared a similar ancestry. Once students get the full picture of the history, they begin to realize the true nature of the place. The Peralta Hacienda is the site of multiple conquests. The park is a tiny spot on the map that reveals the truth to the community that surrounds it. The park is located in the historic Fruitvale community, which ironically is also the site of Oakland's Mexican barrio. The community hardly understands the connection between the park and the Mexican/indigenous past. But the tools for an awakening of the senses are in place.

Land and place are so important to one's history. Even for migrants, the land they left and the place they adopt each carries powerful historical ammunition and meaning. Latin American immigrants share stories, culture, and traditions with one another in the new communities. The Peralta Park has become that place. Although is has a colonialist past, it has become a sanctuary for migrants, with the largest Cambodian New Year celebration in the Bay Area, African American programs of exhibits and film screenings, and the site for hundreds of elementary school fieldtrips. In California, all fourth graders receive an introduction to early California history. Usually this means visiting a mission and hearing a romanticized view of Indians and priests living together in harmony. At the Peralta Park, they hear tales from local Ohlone storytellers, make indigenous crafts, and hear about the *vaqueros* who worked on the ranch. Oakland is a city steeped in activism and alternative thought. The birthplace of the Black Panther Party is alive with history. Residents only need a tool to explore it. The community surrounding the Peralta Hacienda has taken this land away from its colonial, elitist roots. That Luis Peralta was revolutionary Che Guevarra's great, great, great grandfather makes the place even more intriguing.[14]

Place has significant meaning to the way we interpret, discuss, and utilize history. In legal terms, land and oral tradition has been at the heart of indigenous land claims. The local Ohlone population, whose land claims were trampled by Spanish and later Mexican claims, were unfortunate enough to have their traditional homeland coveted by the Spanish Empire and later the United States. The massive urbanization of the Bay Area left them scattered, enslaved, and assimilated, if not killed off. As the U.S. government began to catalogue Native American tribes in the twentieth century, many in California were left out. Without federal recognition, they had no official means to protect their culture or to reclaim any of their ancestral homeland. In 1978, the U.S. government established procedures for non-recognized tribes to petition for federal recognition. The Ohlone went through this arduous process and, after multiple setbacks, are still unrecognized. The documented connection to the land was not enough. The oral traditions are still intact and almost everyone except for the federal government understands that the Ohlone are the original caretakers of the land. In court, however, it is difficult for oral traditions to defeat Luis Peralta's official grant from the Spanish government. The subsequent deeds of sale and subdivision of the Mexican ranches in the Bay Area are preserved and well founded. The written word is powerful evidence in Western legal practice. Unfortunately, the U.S. government does not consider oral tradition as legal evidence.[15] The Ohlone will continue to fight and continue to protect their culture despite the decision of the federal government.

But what about the oral traditions and claims of the other displaced victims: the Mexican settlers who came and established farms and villages, many of whom were indigenous, mestizo and Black? Whether we like to acknowledge it or not, the idea that the United States unjustly stole Mexican land and displaced its citizens from the most coveted regions has a historically significant pedigree. The feeling of displacement persists despite the fact that Spain stole the land from indigenous populations, which was later inherited by Mexico. Displacement has been part of the Mexican experience in the United States since the Treaty of Guadalupe Hidalgo was signed in 1848, ending the war between the United States and Mexico. The land from California to Texas still carries with it significant markers of Mexican culture and history, much of which is systematically archived and some has become part of a complex narrative of oral tradition. The *corrido*, a Mexican border ballad, is said to have its origin in the time of conflict after the Mexican-American War. In many ways, they can be seen as songs of rebellion and tradition. Their stories recount episodes of bravery and defiance against oppression. Every Mexican California family, including my own, whose Southwestern roots stretch back to this period, have folk tales and stories connecting them to the land and the struggle to hold on to it. My grandmother used to have on old rusty *sartén* [iron skillet], from which she swore her great grandmother cooked a meal for Joaquín Murrieta, the legendary Mexican bandit who wreaked havoc on *Americanos* who oppressed *Californios.* The long process of displacement devastated Mexican landowners. During the 1960s, there was a solid movement in the Chicano community based in the quest for land reclamation. Some of these claims are still in court and the historical memory of land theft remains. In more recent times, gentrification has displaced Mexican Americans who live in coveted neighborhoods. Across the Bay, San Francisco's Mission District is a prime example. Many Latinos moved to East Bay towns in order to afford a place to live. The Peralta Hacienda may have its roots in Colonial Spanish policy, but it ended in devastating policies that divested Mexican property owners. The park and other sites like it are vital markers and represent the collective memory of the past for local ethnic Mexican populations in California and in the Southwest.

Mexican oral traditions, collective memory, and their association to the land of the Southwest are reminders of centuries of continuous presence. They are what spark a sense of belonging and a rejection of fear. Many Latin American immigrants go through a process of critical self-reflection, brought on by meaningful connections with other immigrants, a shared sense of struggle against oppression, and a growing sense of connection to their new home. Sites like the Peralta Hacienda bring meaning to how they begin to interpret their place in the world. Critical self-reflection happens when we are awoken to the root causes of our biases and insecurities. We begin to reflect on our own assumptions of who we are and perhaps, why we are poor and struggling. We begin to analyze the lens through which we see our own people. This almost always leads immigrants to reflect on why things are the way they are in their own homelands. A political and/or cultural awaking can occur, which in the process of travel, return, and exchange begins a process of change in the immigrant's homeland. This is happening in all communities where a critical mass of immigrants and U.S.-born Latinxs live. The stories, the places, and the traditions all collude to spark collective memory, resulting in an outburst of Latinx culture. The Peralta Hacienda is only one such place that ignites critical self-reflection in the Latinx community. This cultural and political change can happen in Latinx community centers, *mercados*, churches, or schools.

My students organized a program for the park, which is also a community center. The program was an oral history workshop. Our first guest was Olga Talamante, whose incredible story touched the hearts of all who listed and held meaning for many who could relate to her journey. Olga was born in Mexicali, Baja California, Mexico in 1950. Her family migrated to the agricultural community of Gilroy, California. She went to public schools and experienced life as a child of farmworkers, two experiences that heavily influenced her development. By the late 1960s, Olga became involved in the Chicano Movement. Studying Latin American Studies at UC Santa Cruz, Olga went to Chiapas, Mexico for research. There she encountered some Argentinian activists who told her of their situation in their country. With her new friends Olga moved to Argentina and became a community organizer, working for a poverty relief agency. After Isabel Peron declared a state of siege, Olga was arrested as a dissident and tortured. A 1975 NACLA Report wrote the following:

> Olga Talamante, 25-year old daughter of a California farmworker family, a Chicana woman, awakens every morning at 6 AM to the sound of a prison guard's whistle in the town of Azul, 200 miles south of Buenos Aires, Argentina. Olga and 12 young Argentine activists were arrested during a series of predawn raids by Argentine police four days after President Isabel Perón declared a state of siege November 6, 1974. With no explanation for the arrests, the Federal Police had taken Olga and the others to the police station where they were interrogated and tortured for several days and nights. Since that time Olga has remained a prisoner in the provincial jail of Azul. The U.S. State Department, conscious of Olga's support of the farm workers' movement, her role as a Chicana fighter,

and wishing to further encourage the rightward swing of the Argentine government, has dragged its feet in its moves to have her freed.[16]

This brief description reveals the presence of hemispheric solidarity among Spanish-speaking people from different countries. The report also shows how Cold War tactics in the United States had repercussions for Latin America and solidarity activists, and how Cesar Chavez' Farmworkers Movement was a catalyst for many to fight for the rights of the working poor. Luckily, Olga was freed 16 months later largely due to the efforts of the Olga Talamante Support Committee. Once Olga was released, she immediately returned to the Bay Area and went back to organizing. She is currently the executive director of the Chicana-Latina Foundation. The students were emotional about the event and geared up to receive Olga and honor her for her sacrifices. For them, this was history in action and Olga's story encouraged them to take action in their own lives.

The land hides many secrets. Distant as it may seem, California, Arizona, New Mexico, and Texas are still fully connected to the to the life-stream of Mexico, and by extension, Latin America. Many have explored the intersection of place and history; a subject that is hotly debated in the social sciences.[17] The Peralta Park must always be seen as indigenous Ohlone land, stripped from them and doled out as booty to Christian, "Hispanic" settlers; but the layers of loss, settlement, conquest, theft, and finally redemption and reclamation allow this place to hold significant meaning for multiple communities.[18] For the Mexicans who migrates to the Fruitvale neighborhood, the Peralta Park opens a new world of meaning. Not only does it make them more aware of the Mexican past in California, it also insights a sense of belonging, which in turn, alleviates fear, guilt and emboldens them to fight against intolerance. Places like the Peralta Park have the ability to completely rewrite historical "knowledge" as the stories associated with it give ammunition to the displaced. History is literally floating in the air; in this instance, you can smell it, feel it, and use it in multiple ways.

Family History, Genealogy, and the Borderlands

Family history and genealogy are hugely popular today, especially with the advance in online sources. The Church of Jesus Christ of Latter-day Saints and websites like Ancestry.com have gained access to massive volumes of archives from Latin America. While conducting my own family history, and interviewing some of my elders, I realized how interconnected Borderlands communities are. Places like the Peralta Park are tiny spots within urban centers that not only have the power to transform, but also hold specific memories for uprooted communities. Likewise, the Borderlands itself is a terrible reminder of the violent conflict between successive waves of Indian, Mexican, and Anglo conflict. Both sides of my family have ancestry in the Borderlands that predate the arrival of the United States to the U.S. Southwest, that massive stretch of land Mexico was required to forfeit after the loss of the U.S.-Mexico War in 1848. In New Mexico, and to a lesser extent in Texas, these families are quite common. Through the centuries, these *fronterizos* intermarried with indigenous people and formed their own unique cultural traits. This was the case for my parents, whose ancestors both came from towns near Yuma, Arizona. When they met in Stockton, California in 1953, they had no idea that their ancestors lived among one another.

Growing up in French Camp, near Stockton, my mother Maria Luisa Gallego, had a relatively pleasant childhood. She lived in a tight-nit Mexican community where her parents were able to provide a decent life for the family. My grandfather Manuel Gallego was one of the few Mexican American contractors in the area and was able to win large public work projects. My mother remembers that many Mexicans were arriving to the area and that some were extremely political. When the Great Depression hit, my grandfather's business began to slowly decline. But he and my grandmother Frances Ymperial Gallego remained engaged in the community. Eventually my grandmother opened up a restaurant called *El Patio*, which was an important hangout for a young, emerging Mexican community. There were many areas that attracted famous Mexican singers to the area and my grandmother tells me she saw Pedro Infante and Javier Solis perform live. There were also large Mexican clubs like the Palomar in San Jose and Sweets Ballroom in Oakland that my mother used to frequent. The growth of the Mexican community became a cause for alarm during the Great Depression, when Mexicans were scapegoated as a cause for economic decline.

After the Mexican Revolution, the enormous exodus of people to the United States required the Mexican Embassy to pay closer attention to its citizens abroad. Although Mexican consulates had been engaged in the rights of its citizens since the nineteenth century, increased discrimination during the late 1920s made their participation critical. Directly after the 1917 Mexican Constitution became law, new directives required Mexican consuls to perform a number of duties. One of the most important was to "protect the interests and rights of Mexican nationals."[19] During the same time period, Mexican communities across the United States began to form their own voluntary associations, or *mutualistas*. By 1875, Mexican *mutualistas* had been well established in California.[20] These organizations formed not only because of increased discrimination but also the fact that the Mexican community increased 50 percent during the 1920s. Like the consulates, these associations were not new in the 1920s.[21] In fact, many had begun as early as the 1850s. From these organizations alliances formed; members were from different social classes and most came from different parts of Mexico. The *mutualistas* became an important part of community life and from these associations the Mexican community began to organize itself. Spanish language press and radio programs began to flourish. It was a natural fit, therefore, that the Mexican government work directly with the *mutualistas* in order to spread its post-revolutionary program.

Mexico had a long tradition of *las fiestas patrias*, which celebrated Mexican independence. Likewise, the coronation of a queen had a long tradition but in post-revolutionary Mexico took on a special nationalistic purpose. In most of the cases, feminine beauty was a key element for the winner. Equally important was her dedication to the principles of the nation. The connection between gender, patriotism, and pageantry was a device that projected the ideals of a virtuous nation on to the female body, where "aesthetic valuation and performativity" represented the identity of a virtuous nation.[22] As the Mexican government began to call for nationalist pride and promoted Mexico's indigenous past, it even helped to sponsor Mexico's first contest of Indian beauty. The *india bonita* contest of 1921 coincided with Mexico's centennial celebration, and mirrors similar ethnic pageants in the United States that promoted *mexicanidad*, or Mexican cultural pride.

The major difference was that the consulate pageants had to appeal to Mexican citizens and U.S. citizens of Mexican descent alike. How did Mexican consulates maneuver this without offending the nativist sentimentalities of the American public, especially during World War II? My mother's experience, who in 1942 was crowned Queen of *las fiestas patrias* in Stockton, California, helps to explain the delicate interplay between cultural nationalism, the Mexican Consulate, and the American public. It also reveals the burgeoning transnational dialogue between Mexican politics and culture in the United States.

Directly after the Mexican Revolution, in 1921, President Álvaro Obregón ordered Mexican consulates in the United States to establish *Comisiónes Honoríficas Mexicanas* [Mexican Honorary Commissions] in areas with large Mexican populations. The purpose was to maintain Mexican allegiance with its expatriate population, to protect the rights of their citizens in the United States, to maintain their memory and love for Mexico, and to, in some cases, persuade Mexicans to return to Mexico with their savings and newly acquired skills.[23] These organizations, along with *mutualistas* and Mexican consulates, worked together to protect rights and promote Mexican culture. At some point after the revolution, a *mutualista* was formed in Stockton, California. Stockton was a vibrant community in 1940s with an established Mexican community. Although many Mexican immigrants lived in the area, generations of Mexican Americans lived there through the Gold Rush, World War 1, and the Great Depression. The Gallego family, in fact, had moved there from the mining towns of southern Arizona. In 1938, the Gallego family joined the *mutualista* as members. The Gallego family was bicultural, bilingual, and enthusiastic contributors to the community. Manuel Gallego was a contractor who crafted a successful business during this period. Winning numerous contracts for public work projects, Gallego hired many people who were desperate for jobs. Although my mother remembers working in the peach cannery during World War II, she also recalled that her father once came home with a brand new car during the height of the Depression. My grandmother's restaurant *El Patio* became a popular local hangout for the Mexican community in postwar Stockton.[24]

Although the Gallegos were not Mexican citizens, they represented the type of industrious members of *la colonia* the *comisión* wished to attract. *La colonia*, or "the Mexican colony" was a term used, by the Mexican government and the public, to refer the Mexican community, whether citizens or not. The Mexican consulates acted as early civil rights agencies, protecting Mexicans from discrimination and fighting for their legal rights. The consulates often provided legal aid often working with local lawyers. My mother's experience reveals that generational differences and even citizenship was not always a factor in determining *mexicanidad*. Despite the fact that, at that point, she had never been to Mexico, she was required to give a patriotic speech about Mexican independence, in Spanish, with Mexican flags behind her.[25] The goal of the beauty contest was not focused on physical beauty. Rather, the winner of the contest was the female who sold the most tickets to the final dance and dinner. The funds would go to the *mutualista* in order to provide legal aid, economic relief, and cultural events for the local Mexican population. The steadfast organizing on behalf of their constituents proves that the Mexican consulates in the United States had a larger plan in mind that went beyond simple nationalism. At this early point, the government reached out beyond its borders in order to protect a largely marginalized mestizo population, whether citizens or not. Although they typically provided legal representations to individual Mexican citizens, they later broadened their activities to include Mexican American issues.

My father was born in Yuma, Arizona in 1923. Like my mother's family, my father's had their roots in the desert mining towns that spread along the Colorado and Gila rivers. In fact, there is some evidence that the two families knew each other a generation before my parents met. My grandfather was Juan Salomon, a salesman who worked for various companies and stores in order to bring food to the table. As a child of the Depression, money was scarce. When they moved to El Centro, California in the late 1920s, my father got his first taste of discrimination. Although his family had been in Arizona and California for generations, my father spoke only Spanish until he was required to learn in grade school. Teachers routinely smacked his hand for speaking Spanish.

I asked him how it was possible that a third-generation U.S. citizen spoke only Spanish, and he explained that at that time, border communities stretched to both sides of the border. People would shop on either side, date and marry with people on either side, and everyone spoke Spanish.

My father enlisted in the Marines when World War II broke out. He ironically served on the Solomon Islands, and there he learned to build houses, draw up blueprints, and to be an aircraft mechanic. After the war, he became a fisherman and worked in the ocean from Alaska to Central America. He had many incredible adventures and got to visit many ports in Mexico. He distinctly remembers visiting *las Islas Marias*, an archipelago off the coast of Nayarit, Mexico that served as a prison. He was amazed to see that criminals lived on the island with their families.

When the Korean War broke out, my father went again to the front lines. Because my father had experience and was bilingual, he was put in charge of a Spanish-speaking battalion. Some of the guys were from Puerto Rico and others from Mexico. He remembers that there were Mexican soldiers who had enlisted with the promise of gaining U.S. citizenship.[26] Unfortunately, his battalion was captured six months into the war. The capture and long march into a prison camp was met with the realization that his battalion was sacrificed so that the others could escape. In a strategy that allowed all of the surrounded battalions to escape except for one, it was my father's Spanish-speaking group which was captured. After years of starvation, humiliation, and deprivation, my father was lucky to be counted as one of the survivors. Unfortunately, upon his return, the U.S. government interrogated him as a potential communist collaborator, despite the fact that they had no evidence. He was closely watched and placed at the Presidio of San Francisco until they could investigate his case. In the process, the Army interrogated him and made him feel as if he was a traitor. Luckily, the case was dropped.[27]

It was at the Crissy Field in San Francisco, near the Presidio, that an Army officer stopped my father and asked him what was troubling him. The officer could not believe it and offered him a job at a military airport near Stockton, California. My father took the job, transferred to the Army airport, and was given his rank back. Not too long after his move he wandered in to *El Patio*. It was there he first encountered my mother—and the rest is history.

Oral History and Latin American Immigration to the United States

For the past decade, I have led my students on a quest to capture the voices of Latin American immigration to the Bay Area. Oral history is the great equalizer because anyone can conduct the research and because it allows the "unseen" to add to the historical record: In this case, it allows them to tell the story of the greatest diaspora in human history. This is not to say that oral history lacks theoretical underpinnings. Indeed, there are numerous factors that come into play when conducting an oral history and when interpreting it. One of the most important issues in my research is how to deal with trauma; and what impact trauma has on the respondent who offers his or her story. It is argued that for many victims of trauma, the event lives inside of the victim and takes on the essence of an unknown fate. The event is relived over and over again, causing traumatic fear. Oral history and testimony has become a way to re-externalize these events and bring about closure.[28] The researcher must be trained to deal with these situations. Nevertheless, oral history has had a rocky start in academia. It has been accused of being unscientific, based on subjective opinions, and drawn from memories that happened, in some cases, half a century in the past.[29] Latin America's diasporic experience can help us to understand a particular brand of immigrant history embedded within a culture of violence. The telling of these stories signals the release of trauma and a culture of hope. Oral histories can also illuminate how immigrants are uprooted, the scope and process of their journey to the United States, and how they resettle in their new communities. Beyond supplying additional information for researchers who study immigration, oral histories, when collected and archived, can reveal the deep-rooted politics and cultural of an entire group. Subjective experiences can be analyzed to unearth the motives behind people's actions. It is a process of "active self-reflection" that gives oral history the ability to go beyond what is found in the written archive.[30]

The Bay Area received a massive influx of Central American refugees during the latter part of the twentieth century. With the civil wars in El Salvador, Nicaragua, and Guatemala in full force, thousands of Central Americans fled to the United States. Many went to areas that already had Spanish-speaking populations, such as the Bay Area, which also was a center of the Sanctuary Movement. This movement sought to harbor Central American immigrants from deportation. The situation was critical. In 1980, Ronald Reagan became president, winning on an anti-communist platform. This meant getting tough on insurgencies, especially those who had the support of Fidel Castro. U.S. law provided for asylum seekers to seek sanctuary from deportation within U.S. borders. So as thousands arrived, the immigration service was ordered to reject their requests, especially for Salvadorans and Guatemalans. The Nicaraguans were given a bit more leniency because they lived, by this time, under Sandinista control. The United States was friendly toward and sent military aid to the governments of El Salvador and Guatemala, and so were unwilling to admit their friends were violating human rights. Many of the interviews that came from my classes on Latin American immigration, and oral traditions reveal the nature of immigrant culture and the difficult transition from dislocation to resettlement.

The civil wars in Central America grew out of a deep resentment to continued government exploitation of the poor. From the interviews, it is easy to see how this resentment grew in the countryside and spread to the cities, where students became involved. For example, Alejandra L., who was born in Amatitlán, Guatemala in 1941 explains how things went from bad to worse:

> We lived in a ranch outside of town. Our home was made of hay and was supported by eight Y-shaped tree trunks. The hay would be rolled tightly into batches then squeezed together to make the walls; the ceiling was constructed of grass. The house was constructed of corn stalks that served as a fence. Although we had an abundance of animals, like ducks, turkeys, chickens, and dogs, we didn't consider them pets. The dogs were used to guard the house and surrounding area. The town of Amatitlán is located south of Guatemala City. It is a beautiful town surrounded by a lake and lots of trees. There are many chalets at the edge of the lake where rich people live. In the past there were many hotels around the lake. People would come from around the area and stay at the hotels through the weekend. . . . As you enter the plaza, there is a fountain surrounded by four angels. There is also an enormous tree with benches around the base of the trunk and next to it is a gazebo where the band would sit with their trumpets and play marches and marimba while the people strolled around the park that was full of flowers. I would see the couples walking arm in arm. It was very pretty.
>
> My childhood was filled with poverty. I began working with my mother when I was 7 years old. I would pick coffee beans and place them in a basket which was

> on my head. Then I would take the basket to these huge holes in the ground and drop the beans in the hole and the men would cover them all up with soil. I earned enough money to buy fabric to make my own first communion dress. We were very poor; we all worked from a very young age and never attended school or received a formal education. Like my mother, none of the children wore shoes.[31]

Although grinding poverty was a constant, it did not stop people from realizing their goals. Salvadora C. was born in 1954 in the town of Tecunuman, Guatemala. She remembers growing up near a river where the children would look for shell fish. She was fortunate enough to have gone to primary school, which means that she was not among the most exploited. Even so, poverty increased as the years went on and services became more scarce:

> I remember that our schools were so poor that the parents of the students had to provide the desk in order for their children to have one. These social conditions existed because the government would not do much to assist the public schools in rural areas. . . . I attended school until the age of fourteen; then after that age I noticed that it was difficult for our father to support us all, so I decided to leave home in order to provide for myself. So at the age of fourteen, I started to work as a maid in the city of Guatemala.[32]

We know that in some rural areas, political activism escalated as the situation became more serious. Some families had a calling for educating the poor. I find some of the roles local Central American immigrants played in their country's history amazing. We see them every day—and they appear to be humble working class immigrants who live in the Bay Area. But in reality, they have amazing and illuminating stories to tell. Edgar C. came from a political family in the mountains of Nicaragua, near the border of Honduras. They moved frequently to work and to organize but Edgar called the town of Jinotega his home. He eventually moved to Managua with his family where he became even more involved with the political unrest. The deep insurgent roots of his family made his transition into organizing easy:

> My family was all involved with politics. My grandmother is a cousin of Sandino's wife. . . . [Her] brother was a lieutenant for Sandino. I know almost all of the comandantes of the Sandinista Party. I used to play soccer and baseball with Ortega, he was really good.[33]
>
> In Nicaragua I was a union organizer and worked as a CPA, certified public accountant. I worked in a bank as a manager and we organized the first recognized union in a bank in Latin America. It was a huge accomplishment; we had the first strike where seventeen banks and financial institutions stopped for a day. We signed a contract with all the banks, which included health benefits and a 4% salary increase. Keep in mind this occurred in 1978, in the middle of the war. This was just a few weeks after the big legislative takeover. . . . This was also very dangerous, you could get killed. I have at least seven friends that have been killed doing union organizing.[34]

The situation deteriorated so badly that schools, colleges and Catholic churches were seen as breeding grounds for radical thought. All Catholics and students were suspect of collaborating with the rebels. Oscar A. was born in Caserío Valle Nuevo, El Salvador in 1961. Even in this remote pueblo the military harassed the people:

> [In] my third year of high school, in 1976, the military made things difficult. When you were on the bus the soldiers would stop you and make you get out. They would ask us questions, if we were guerillas and if we were friends with anyone on their list. At that time, the military did not like students or teachers. Everyone who studied was an enemy of the government. Almost all of the teachers were guerillas; they were supporting the rebels. The soldiers killed the teachers [and] made them disappear.
>
> I remember that it began in 1976. They began to organize small groups. . . . They would meet in the park, which caused an uproar. All of a sudden the police came and everyone had to run away. En Santa Tecla the guerillas met in a house. The police knew about the meeting but not the location. When they found out they began to surround the house. The soldiers were going to kill them, but it turned out the guerrillas killed the soldiers. With their blood, the guerillas wrote on the walls. Everyone saw this. It was big news that they killed them and wrote with blood the name of their group: 'BPR': BLOQUE POPULAR REVOLUCCIONARIO.[35]

Benjamin F., who was born in Santana, El Salvador in 1960, experienced similar events. By the time the wars began to escalate people from all social classes were affected. Through education as a young student he became radicalized, but eventually became disenchanted with communism.

> My family had a wholesale distributing type of business. We also sold goods to the public, but the bulk of our business was selling wholesale. My father would work at a radio station and would put in many hours in the family business. . . . As for my education, I mostly was sent to private schools. My family was not rich, but did have the means to send me to private Catholic schools.
>
> I can remember being tear-gassed by the police at my junior high. The building was four stories and student protestors from the national university were marching past our school when the police began to suppress the protest. It quickly got violent. There were about six thousand people taking part in it. Some say that the army and police killed about five hundred of them, some of the protestors ran into our school, and that is when we were hit with tear gas. What surprises me is that none of us that were in junior high were killed in all of this. Some of us, myself included, ran to the roof to see what was going on. Soldiers went inside our school after protestors. This was the first protest that the government suppressed. It was when I saw the reality; which was that the government was assassinating innocent people. I can say that this was a life transforming experience. This all took place on July 30 of 1975. It is one thing to kill armed people, but to kill unarmed people is another thing. How many students were killed is not known. In these matters one never knows, but this is when I began to see that the government was killing unarmed citizens, this impacted me a lot. I clearly saw when soldiers were stabbing people with their bayonets. Tanks ran over people. Although I really hadn't developed a political consciousness by this time—I was fifteen; I wasn't a leftist or conservative.

> The government would accuse Jesuit priests of promoting communism in private schools. Many people now say that this wasn't true, but the truth is that they were. I know because in the school I was in, they did teach us communism in sociology class, it was taught by the very Jesuit priest. I received four years of this, and became very indoctrinated in communism. I was already a communist after having been instructed in it for only six months, so when I turned eighteen and enrolled at the university I was already a communist, and an atheist. I don't know how much you want me to get into this subject; it is after all a subject without end. I learned about the theology of liberation; which unites the theories of Marx with Christianity. Marx said that there would be a society of equality, a perfect society. But to achieve this perfect society, we must first defeat the government because it only represents the interests of the rich. After having defeated the government and taking power, we can establish the dictatorship of the proletariat, a socialist society. One thing is communism and another thing is socialism, however, most communist states such as China, Russia and Cuba started off socialist. I now realize that communism does not eliminate poverty, but rather it eliminates the rich. Once the rich are gone, there is equality because everybody is poor. I have come to realize that communism has accomplished very little. Communism is a Marxist dogma that some priests promoted. It is in concept a utopian society that has never been achieved.[36]

Many women took part in the war, some as combatants and some as supporters. Many, however, were caught in the crossfire. Isabel R. was born in Matagalpa, Nicaragua on March 15, 1959. She clearly remembers how the escalation of violence caused chaos for all members of society:

> In 1972, when I was around seventeen years old, the Sandinistas wanted to get rid of the Somoza regime. At the time, the Sandinista regime was getting stronger and more popular. I heard about more conflicts and started seeing a lot more graffiti. If you had any connection with the government or were taking part of any type of government job, you were in essence doing well economically. The government-connected officials did see the conditions that the pueblo of Nicaragua were living in but did nothing to help. The people of Nicaragua started to get tired of the Somoza dictatorship of about forty years. At the time, I did not really understand the Somoza dictatorship regime, but I saw oppression of the Guardia toward the younger generations. The Guardia and government saw the youth and students as the enemy. They saw them as the enemy since most youth had the idea of change. Almost everyone was ready for change and for Somoza to leave. The Sandinistas were right in fighting the Somoza dictatorship. If it was not for the fight, the Somoza regime would have never left. It was another time, unlike today. Now there are international pressures and mass communications. They used to have elections but obviously they where rigged and of course Somoza always won. Some of my brothers took part in the Sandinista movement.
>
> When times became more critical, you had to decide which group to pick sides with. Especially if you were young, you could not be neutral. You were either with The Guardias or the Sandinistas. If you were young and the Guardia found you in your home you either would be sent to prison or be killed. So the way to save yourself was to integrate or join the majority party. At that time, the

> Sandinistas were already the majority. It was safer to be with the Sandinistas, but if you were a well known government official, you would say you are safer with the Guardia. The Somozitas did not know what was happening, but us as a pueblo did know what was happening. So many youth left their houses to a safer place with the Sandinistas.[37]

Olivia G. was from Huehuetenango, Guatemala. She had a peaceful childhood until the violence began to take over their lives. Her story is similar to those of many innocent people who simply could not live under such harsh conditions:

> I still remember the horrible days when I was younger. I would go to the capital with my family on the bus and the military would make the busses stop to check everyone's belongings. Then we had to transfer onto another bus. This was done to make sure that no one on the bus was against the military and/or were carrying any weapons. As we would arrive to the capital, we would see so many dead bodies on the ground. I hated going to the capital for that reason.
>
> All of the boys and men in Guatemala were forced to serve in the military for at least four years. For this reason, my parents would make sure my brothers would hide when they came so they wouldn't take them away to fight. The military came to our ranch several times to ask for all of the boys and men of the house. One day, the military came and found my 15-year-old brother playing outside and took him away. We were so afraid that we would never see him again.
>
> We were so thankful when my brother had finally returned after he had completed his four years in the military. He told us all of the terrible things he was forced to do and all of his bad experiences while being in the military. They had to eat whatever was around; if there was a dog, they had to kill it and eat it. In order for all of the soldiers in the military to be able to kill anything, they were all forced to eat dead animals, like vultures, as well as drink their blood. My brother would throw up after drinking the blood, but was forced to drink the blood again.
>
> All of the soldiers were all threatened in the military that if they didn't obey, they would get beaten or worse things would happen. The sergeants gave all of the soldiers orders and they all had to do what they were told and ordered to do, or else they would kill their families. They had to sleep wherever they could, meaning they had to sleep anywhere on the ground. My brother told us how most of the soldiers were normal; they did not want to kill anyone, but they were forced to do it.
>
> The military my brother was in were given orders to kill the people [who were] "guerillas," or poor people fighting for their own rights. These guerillas were mainly made up of poor, indigenous people, trying to live their own lives without causing any trouble. However, some of the indigenous people were influenced by the fact that the military would tell them they could make a lot of money if they go with them and snitch on all of the people they thought were against the military. The military would kill all the people that were against the military, including the ones they were supposedly going to pay for snitching on them. My brother thought he was living in a nightmare.[38]

It is interesting to note that although most of the oral histories recorded between 2005 and 2015 were anti-military and anti government, some were pro-government. This fact, reflected in my project, is almost exclusively found among Nicaraguan immigrants. The majority of Guatemalan and Salvadoran immigrants who came during the war years blame the government and military for the violence. Two factors that help explain this may be found in the U.S. immigration and foreign policies at the time and perhaps because few members of the Salvadoran and Guatemalan national guards have come forward to give their stories. But at the time, as stated previousy, the United States regarded immigrants from these countries as motivated by their economic situation. However, they regarded Nicaraguans as possible refugees since their country, after 1979, was in the hands of the Sandinista regime opposed by the United States.

Nubia L. was born in Nicaragua in 1949. Her father was the Mayor of Corinto, where Nubia was born. She represents a segment of Nicaragua that enjoyed life under the Somoza regime.

> I never remember being affected by the Somoza dictatorship, if anything I benefited from it. I believe a mixture of this and my young age helped to embrace the new American culture I experienced when my mother brought me here.
>
> After Corinto, my family moved to León, Nicaragua.
>
> León was where I began my schooling and have many childhood memories. León was much bigger than Corinto, although it still had a small-town and colonial feel about it. I began schooling at a private, all-girl Catholic school. My education was very European, as there was still much of the Spanish influence in Nicaragua and in the churches.
>
> Managua was my third home in Nicaragua. Managua was where I lived until I moved to the United States. The big city was a major difference from my first two homes. The pace was much quicker. There was much more traffic, too. My siblings and I never walked or rode city busses. We always had someone to bring us to and from school. I continued in school here, probably to about the American equivalent of fifth grade, in another parochial school. Since I was so young, I do not remember much about the politics in the country at that time. On occasion, we would hear about certain events happening in other cities, but none of them directly affected us. Conditions were bad for many, but if you were under Somoza, life was good. Luckily for me, my family was under Somoza. My father had almost always worked for Somoza. After he was the mayor of Corinto, my father became an accountant for Somoza, which is why we moved to Managua. My father worked in the National Palace as a head accountant. Later on, though, when the Sandinistas moved in, my father became blacklisted and was unable to leave the country.[39]

The eight individuals who recounted their stories in this chapter all left their countries because of escalating violence. They tell the stories of their journeys and the difficulty they had with poverty and discrimination upon resettlement, but are all grateful to have been given a new opportunity in life. Their stories not only illuminate the histories of the Central American civil wars of the 1970s and 1980s, but also reveal a great deal about the motives, the hopes and dreams, and the desire to survive that these individuals had. The stories of Latin American immigrants reveal a different side of immigration and sharply contrast the negative image that the mainstream media upholds. In the end, oral histories like these unleash the voices of millions who would otherwise be forgotten. They also contribute to the story of Greater Latin America. Public history—with its ties to family history, oral traditions, and the land—contribute significantly to the ways in which Latinxs maintain their roots in the United States.

Notes

1 A notable recent exception is Paloma Martínez-Cruz, *Women and Knowledge in Mesoamerica: From East L.A. to Anahuac* (Tucson, AZ: University of Arizona Press, 2011): 2.
2 The decolonial project is a process that encompasses many issues relating to the aftermath and "delinking" colonialism. It was most prominently written about by Peruvian scholar Anibel Quijano, "Coloniality of Power, Eurocentrism, and Latin America" *Nepentla: Views From the South,* 1 (3): 533–580. In the United States, "decolonize" can simply mean the process of shedding Western values, attitudes, and practices.
3 Peter Novick, *That Noble Dream: The 'Objectivity Question' and the American Historical Profession* (Cambridge: Cambridge University Press, 1988), 1.
4 Elizabeth Castelli, "Reza Aslan—Historian?" *The Nation,* August 9, 2013.
5 Vine Deloria Jr., *Custer Died for your Sins: An Indian Manifesto* (New York, NY: Macmillan, 1969).
6 Ibid., 94.
7 Angela Cavender Wilson, "American Indian History or Non-Indian Perceptions of American Indian History," *American Indian Quarterly,* Vol 20, No. 1 (1996): 3–5.
8 Ibid., 3.
9 Linda Tuhiwai Smith, *Decolonizing Methodologies: Research and Indigenous People* (London: Zed Books, 1999), 4.
10 Ibid., 2.
11 Guillermo Bonfil Batalla, *México Profundo: Reclaiming a Civilization* (Austin, TX: University of Texas Press, 1996), 41.
12 For the origins of Chicano/a History see Ernesto Chávez, "Chicano/a History: Its Origins, Purpose, and Future, *Pacific Historical Review,* Vol 82, No. 4 (November 2013): 505–519.
13 Paulo Freire, *Pedagogy of the Oppressed* (New York, NY: Continuum, 2007).
14 María Fermina Peralta married Guillermo Castro. Their daughter Encarnación Castro Peralta married Juan Antonio Guevara, a *Californio,* sometime in the 1840s. Their son Roberto Guevara Castro moved to Argentina and married Ana Isabel Lynch y Ortiz and their son, Ernesto Rafael Guevara Lynch married Celia de la Serna y Llosa, whose son was Ernesto "Che" Guevarra.
15 Hope M. Babcock "'[This] I Know From My Grandfather': The Battle For Admissibility of Indigenous Oral History as Proof of Tribal Land Claims," *American Indian Law Review* Vol 37, No. 1 (2012–2013): 19–61.
16 North American Congress in Latin America. "Free Olga Talamante," NACLA Report (September 1975). https://nacla.org/article/free-olga-talamante accessed December 4, 2016.
17 Charles W. J. Withers, "Place and the "Spatial Turn" in Geography and in History," *Journal of the History of Ideas,* Vol 70, No. 4 (October 2009), 637–658.
18 For example, descendants of African slaves on the Costa Chica of Mexico point to a costal area where a slave ship sank, allowing the human cargo to escape to freedom. Although this land was inhabited by indigenous people, who were later subjugated by Spaniards, it became a significant place in the historical memory of Afro-Mexicans. See Laura A. Lewis, "Of Ships and Saints: History, Memory, and Place in the Making of Moreno Mexican Identity" *Cultural Anthropology,* Vol 16, No. 1 (Feb., 2001), 62.
19 Francisco Balderrama, *In Defense of la Raza: The Los Angeles Mexican Consulate, and the Mexican Community, 1929 to 1936* (Tucson, AZ: University of Arizona Press, 1982): 6.
20 Lawrence Douglas, Taylor Hansen, "Las fiestas patrias y la preservación de la identidad cultural mexicana en California: Una visión histórica," *Frontera Norte,* Vol 9, No. 18 (1997): 38.
21 Nelson A. Pichardo, "The Establishment and Development of Chicano Voluntary Associations in California, 1910–1930, *Aztlan,* Vol 19, No. 2, (1992): 94.
22 Rick A. López, "The India Bonita Contest of 1921 and the Ethnicization of Mexican National Culture," *Hispanic American Historical Review,* Vol 82, No. 2 (2002): 317–318.
23 José Alamillo, "More than a Fiesta: Ethnic Identity, Cultural Politics, and Cinco de Mayo Festivals in Corona, California, 1930–1950," *Aztlán,* Vol 28, No. 2 (2003): 61–62.
24 Interview with Mary Lou Gallego, August 23, 2008, Poway, California. Author's personal collection.
25 Ibid.
26 Interview with Oscar Solomon, Nov. 5, 2005, Poway, California. Author's personal collection.
27 Ibid.

28 Shoshana Felman and Dori Laub, *Testimony: Crisis of Witnessing in Literature* (New York, NY: Routledge, 1992), 69.
29 Lynn Abrams, *Oral History Theory* 2nd ed (New York, NY: Routledge, 2016), 5.
30 Ibid., 23.
31 Testimony of Alejandra L., interviewed by Sylvia Flores Eggert, Oakland, California, May 15, 2006, author's private collection.
32 Testimony of Salvadora Remunda C., interviewed by Richard Audon, San Jose, California, July 23, 2012, author's private collection.
33 Testimony of Edgar C., interviewed by Michelle Ashe, Oakland, California, October 25, 2007, author's private collection. Augusto César Sandino was a rebel leader who defied the U.S. military occupation of Nicaragua. He was assassinated in 1934. Daniel Ortega was the leader of the Sandinistas, a rebel organization inspired by Augusto César Sandino. They overthrew the U.S.-backed Somoza government in 1979.
34 Ibid.
35 Testimony of Oscar A., interviewed by Esperanza Avalos, San Jose, California, March 3, 2015, author's private collection.
36 Testimony of Benjamin F., interviewed by Juan Maciel, Hayward, California, November 8, 2005, author's private collection.
37 Testimony of Isabel R., interviewed by Alvaro Medina, Hayward, California, October 21, 2007, author's private collection.
38 Testimony of Olivia G., interviewed by Christina Rios.
39 Testimony of Nubia L., interviewed by Emily Kreins, Hayward, California, November 8, 2005, author's private collection.

INDEX

Note: Page numbers in bold indicate tables and page numbers in *italics* indicate figures.